Wilbert Q.
Crockett

A BROWNING HANDBOOK

ROBERT BROWNING AT THE AGE OF 47

From a drawing made by Field Talfourd at Rome in 1859. Reproduced
by the courtesy of the National Portrait Gallery.

A BROWNING HANDBOOK

by

William Clyde DeVane

YALE UNIVERSITY

SECOND  EDITION

NEW YORK

Appleton-Century-Crofts, Inc.

❦ PREFACE ❦

When the first edition of this *Browning Handbook* was projected, twenty-five years ago, a smaller and more general book was planned. But a closer view of the scholarship which had been done upon Browning's poetry convinced me that the subject required above all else a complete and detailed treatment. An excellent biography of the poet had been written, a great number of the poet's letters had been collected, and a fair number of special studies, some of excellent quality, had been made of Browning's ideas and of separate poems. But the treatment was uneven; many of the ideas and poems were inadequately dealt with, and others were not accounted for at all. The results, moreover, were scattered in a hundred different places. Browning scholarship, in short, was not mature in the sense that the scholarship upon Chaucer, Spenser, Shakespeare, Milton, or even Wordsworth, was mature. I became convinced that what Browning scholarship needed most of all was the assembling and arrangement of all the pertinent facts concerning each one of the poems; and to accomplish this was the aim of the work. The task was too huge to be done perfectly, but it was done painstakingly. The book would serve, I hoped, as a convenient collection of materials towards the interpretation of Browning and his works, and as a point of departure for further investigations.

Factual and specific as the book aimed to be, however, I was unwilling to ignore the larger aspects of the problem, the development of the mind of Robert Browning. In my treatment of the poems I therefore adopted the chronological order of their publication—which with Browning follows closely the order of writing—in preference to the poet's later and somewhat arbitrary grouping of his poems. Charles Lamb's judgment upon Wordsworth's comparable attempt to build his poems into larger unities still seems to me to have been a good one: "There is only one good order, and that is the order

in which they were written. That is the history of the poet's mind."
The arrangement of the present edition follows the same principle.
Thus while the reader seeking information about a particular poem
will be able to find the facts readily by means of the index, the student
who cares to read the volume consecutively will find, I think, if he
will pardon the repetitions necessary to a handbook arrangement, a
detailed and circumstantial account of the poet's progress in his
thinking, his art, and his reputation.

The hope I expressed in my first edition, that the *Handbook* would
serve as a point of departure for further investigations, has been fully
answered in the intervening years, as the reader may see from the
many additions and corrections which have been made in this new
edition. The great quantity of new material has made the revision a
major task. Browning scholarship has not only increased in bulk and
variety, but has, I believe, proportionately improved in quality. Several new biographies have been published; collections of hitherto unpublished letters have become available, and old letters have been
re-edited; and many excellent special studies of the poet's life and
work have appeared in books and learned journals. These are duly
used and acknowledged, I trust, in the text, footnotes, and bibliography of the present edition of this *Handbook.*

Because my debt still stands and it is pleasant to acknowledge
again, I should like to repeat here the paragraphs of thanks which I
recorded in my Preface to the first edition in 1935:

"My study of Browning's poetry has led me into many pleasant
places, and I cannot forego mentioning here the unfailing kindnesses
which I have encountered abroad in the British Museum, the Bod-
leian, the Balliol College Library, the Victoria and Albert Museum,
and the equal spirit of help which I have found at home, especially in
the library of Yale University where this work was chiefly conducted,
and in the library of Cornell University where it was finished. I have
been graciously permitted to consult the manuscripts and letters in
the Wellesley College Library and in the Pierpont Morgan Library in
New York City, and have had the privilege of access to the private
collections of Professors Chauncey Brewster Tinker and William
Lyon Phelps.

"A full record of my indebtednesses would make this preface grotesque. As much of my debt as I could, I have declared in my list of
acknowledgments below, in my footnotes, and in my bibliography.
But I ought to express here my general reliance upon the admirable

biography of the poet by Messrs. Griffin and Minchin. The student of Browning must be grateful steadily to Sir Frederic Kenyon for his great edition [the *Centenary Edition*] of the poems and for collecting the letters of the poet and his wife; in America, Professor A. J. Armstrong made available in 1923 the illuminating letters which Browning wrote to his friend, Miss Blagden,[1] and in 1933 Dean T. L. Hood earned the gratitude of all students of the poet by making accessible and editing the letters collected by Mr. T. J. Wise, together with a number of his own. To all these I owe much. But there are subtler debts. In spite of my attempts to be independent many of my former students will recognize ideas which are probably and justly their own. The list is long, and will some day be distinguished, and it is not from ingratitude that I do not make a roll-call here. Upon the greatest and subtlest of all my debts, I am forced to bless myself with silence.

"Finally, it is a pleasure to record the generosity of authors and publishers in granting permission to use materials from their works. My thanks are due to Mr. H. C. Minchin for the privilege of quoting from his book, *The Life of Robert Browning;* to the Houghton Mifflin Co. for permission to quote from the revised edition of Mrs. Orr's *Life and Letters of Robert Browning;* to The Macmillan Company for the use of the *Complete Poetical Works of Robert Browning, New Edition, with Additional Poems;* to Dean T. L. Hood and Sir John Murray for permission to quote from *Letters of Robert Browning, Collected by T. J. Wise;* to the Harper and Bros. Co. for *Letters of Robert Browning and Elizabeth Barrett Barrett;* to Professor A. J. Armstrong for the use of *Letters of Robert Browning to Isa Blagden;* to the E. P. Dutton Company for permission to quote from *Elizabeth Barrett Browning; Letters to her Sister,* edited by Leonard Huxley; to the Oxford University Press for Mr. A. K. Cook's *Commentary on Browning's "The Ring and the Book";* to the Yale University Press for permission to use my own book, *Browning's Parleyings;* to Messrs. G. Bell and Sons and Harcourt, Brace and Co. for Mrs. Orr's *Handbook to Browning's Works;* to Messrs. Chapman and Hall for the use of *The Diaries of W. C. Macready,* edited by William Toynbee; to Charles Scribner's Sons for permission to quote from the Blashfield and Hopkins edition

---

[1] These letters have since been edited by Edward C. McAleer in 1951 with the title, *Dearest Isa, Robert Browning's Letters to Isabella Blagden,* and published by the University of Texas Press. With Mr. McAleer's kind permission my references are to his edition throughout.

of Vasari's *Lives of Seventy Most Eminent Painters;* and to the National Portrait Gallery for permission to reproduce the portrait of Browning which serves as frontispiece."

Since the first edition my debt of gratitude has greatly increased. I take great pleasure in expressing my thanks to the John Simon Guggenheim Memorial Foundation and to Yale University for making possible the leisure necessary to complete this work. I must again record my gratitude to the Yale University Library for the use of its rich resources and the help of its efficient staff. The roll-call of my students is longer now, and has grown in distinction, and my debt is constantly increasing. I should like also to thank my colleagues, Professors Richard L. Purdy, Gordon S. Haight, and Alexander M. Witherspoon, for their help with many details.

I should like especially to thank Professor Kenneth L. Knickerbocker whose labors on our *New Letters of Robert Browning* added much to my knowledge. I should also like to record my appreciation of the work of Professor W. O. Raymond, whose steady and luminous judgment has been a beacon to Browning scholars for many years. For that other deeper and subtler debt, greater than all these together, I still have no adequate words.

W. C. DeV.

❧ CONTENTS ❧

		PAGE
	PREFACE	V
I.	The Life of Robert Browning	1
II.	Early Poems	39
III.	Bells and Pomegranates	88
IV.	The Middle Years	194
V.	The Ring and the Book	318
VI.	The Work of the Seventies	349
VII.	The Last Decade	428
VIII.	Uncollected Works	554
	SELECTED BIBLIOGRAPHY	581
	INDEX	589

A BROWNING HANDBOOK

A word about the mechanics of using this *Handbook*. Many books useful for background are listed in the Bibliography, which are not mentioned in the text or notes. On the other hand, a few frequently used books are referred to in the notes by abbreviated titles, the key to which is given in the Bibliography. In some cases, no footnote is given if the reference in the text makes the reference clear; for example, letters that can easily be located by date are given no page citations; these volumes too can be found by recourse to the Bibliography.

The notes are numbered consecutively throughout the discussion of each of Browning's large titles, except for *Men and Women*, which is divided into Volumes I and II for convenience in numbering the notes. Cross references to notes within the same group are by note number; otherwise to separate poems by name.

❦ I ❦

THE
LIFE OF ROBERT BROWNING

I

WHEN Harry Bailly and his company of pilgrims set out from the Tabard Inn at Southwark at sunrise on the morning of April 17, 1386, Geoffrey Chaucer might have peered towards the south in the uncertain morning light and seen the place where, in the course of long time, on May 7, 1812, Robert Browning was born. Camberwell, across the Thames from the main part of London, is today a confused mass of bricks and chimney-pots; there are mean streets and squalid alleys; the desperate poor drive a petty trade in those slums, and the grinding noise of motor-busses seldom ceases. In a short time after leaving the Tabard, Harry Bailly brought his company to the little brook called St. Thomas-a-Watering; he was in the open country and could see the line of road ahead, the trees and the flowers, and even the soft April sun, if indeed the "shoures sote" were not falling at the moment. The Camberwell upon which Browning opened his eyes in 1812 was not the same scene that Chaucer saw, but it had changed less, perhaps, between 1386 and 1812 than it has since that time. When Browning was a boy it was a suburb of the middle classes, with comfortable detached houses here and there, a village green, and a square church-tower that was visible from the Strand, three miles away. Across the meadows from Camberwell a "green half-hour's walk" was Dulwich with its then famous gallery of paintings, and not far away was Dulwich Wood, the haunt of gypsies. Into this pleasant and convenient world Robert Browning was born.

Because of the darkness of Browning's hair and the pallor of his complexion, in both of which he was matched by his sister Sarianna, two years younger than himself, it was the fashion of the older biographers to imagine that he had Jewish or Creole blood in his veins. The first of these suppositions seems founded on nothing more substantial than the facts that two of Browning's uncles were employed in the Rothschild banking houses in London and Paris, and that in later years the poet delighted in rabbinical lore. The legend of Creole blood is hardly more substantial: his grandmother, Margaret Tittle Browning, had been born and bred in the West Indies of an English family. The Brownings came from the substantial yeomanry of Dorset. The poet's grandfather, Robert Browning,[1] was born in 1749 in Pentridge, a small village in northeastern Dorset. He came to London in the last third of the eighteenth century and was a respectable harbinger of that excellent middle class which by the great industrial and economic revolution of the nineteenth century was to own and rule England for nearly a hundred years. The Browning family history reminds one strangely of Galsworthy's family of Forsytes, though the Forsytes would never have thought that they could afford a poet, and a man of genius seems to have been beyond their powers to produce.

This Robert Browning was handsome, vigorous, and capable. He began as a clerk in the Bank of England and rose to be the head of a department with a salary of approximately £500 a year. He was an irascible and strong-willed man, and in time planted his sons by his first and second marriages, their aptitudes hardly considered, in positions in his own business of banking. His oldest son, Robert Browning (1782–1866), the father of the poet, was sent out at the age of twenty to a lucrative position at St. Kitt's, his mother's sugar plantation in the West Indies. But there, as the poet told Miss Barrett many years later,

[he] conceived such a hatred of the slave system . . . that he relinquished every prospect—supported himself, while there, in some other capacity, and came back, while yet a boy, to his father's profound astonishment and rage—one proof of which was, that when he heard that his son was a suitor to *her*, my mother—he benevolently waited on her uncle to assure him that his niece would be thrown away on a man so evidently born to be hanged!— those were his words. My father on his return had the intention of devoting himself to art, for which he had many qualifications and abundant love —but the quarrel with his father,—who married again and continued to

[1] See Sir Vincent Baddeley, "The Ancestry of Robert Browning, the Poet," in the *Genealogists Magazine* 8:1–6 (March, 1938).

hate him till a few years before his death,—induced him to go at once and consume his life after a fashion he always detested.[2]

The young man took a place as clerk in the Bank of England on his return from St. Kitt's and remained there as a superior clerk until his retirement in 1852. He was married to the poet's mother, Sarah Anna Wiedemann, in Camberwell on February 19, 1811, without the sanction of his angry father.

One may well believe that the poet's father merely endured the business of banking. He was at heart an artist, a scholar, and a collector of books and pictures. A considerable number of his drawings for his son, and later for his grandson, remain to us: they are mainly illustrations of stories—grotesque groups gather in a cave around a flickering candle, or sudden fierce expressive faces scowl at us from the fly-leaves of old books. In his collection of pictures his preference ran to the Dutch realists; "Brouwer, Ostade, Teniers—he would turn from the Sistine altar-piece to these," said his son. Naturally, among English artists Hogarth was his special love. The verses which he wrote were of the same kind, anecdotes in jocular verse written for children. His version of the story of the Pied Piper, though inferior, has all the qualities of his son's poem upon the same subject.[3] His taste in serious verse was for the couplets of Pope and the eighteenth century. As a student he had a strong leaning towards curious and out-of-the-way history. He had the scent of the collector for rare books, and the 6000 volumes of his library were made up of many of the substantial and important books of the world.[4] They were in Greek, Hebrew, Latin, French, Italian, and Spanish, and his annotations show that they were read as well as bought. There were also in the library a great number of collections of astonishing anecdotes, culled from all history; the example and archetype of these was Nathaniel Wanley's *Wonders of the Little World*, 1678, from which the poet gleaned much. There were also a considerable number of biographical dictionaries, such as the *Biographie universelle*, 1822, whose fifty volumes seem to have been read *in toto* by the poet.[5] In his hours of leisure from the bank the elder Browning

[2] *Letters of Robert Browning and Elizabeth Barrett Barrett, 1845–6*, II, 477.
[3] It was printed in *The Bookman* (London) for May, 1912.
[4] See the auction catalogue of Sotheby, Wilkinson and Hodge, generally known as *The Browning Collections*, which was published upon the dispersal of the Browning library in 1913.
[5] *The Life of Robert Browning* . . . by W. Hall Griffin, completed and edited by Harry Christopher Minchin, 1938, p. 25.

seems to have read most of these books; his half-brother, Reuben, called him a "living encyclopaedia." He could write out his own notion of the story of Sordello in prose, and in his old age could produce a "regular bookful of notes and extracts" for the use of his son in the historical parts of *The Ring and the Book*.[6] One can see that Browning got many traits from this genial and accomplished man, "who," in the son's words, "might have been a great man had he cared a bit about it." But he did not care enough to assert himself. The good, kindly, unworldly man was content to take his place in the family as a docile child, willing to follow where his wife led, and submitting to the will of his far more aggressive children, Robert and Sarianna.

The poet's mother was more influential in shaping the boy's character. As her name implies, Sarah Anna Wiedemann was of German descent. Her father was a native of Hamburg, connected with shipping; he lived in Dundee and had married a Scotch lady. The poet's father met Miss Wiedemann when she and her sister, Christiana, were living in Camberwell with an uncle. Christiana married John Silverthorne, a wealthy brewer of the neighborhood, and her sons, James, John, and George, became the constant companions of Browning's youth. Mrs. Browning, whom Carlyle called "the true type of a Scottish gentlewoman," seems to have taken charge of the emotional aspects of her son's education. She was an enthusiastic musician, and imparted her delight to her son. She was fond of playing at dusk, and once when she was playing her little son stole downstairs to listen, and when she had ceased flung himself into her arms, sobbing "Play, play."[7] From his mother, too, Browning learned to love flowers and to know the peculiar pleasure of making friends with all the small animals of the garden, as well as the larger ones of the house and stable. He was often bribed to take his medicine by the promise of a toad or a spider which his mother would find for him among her flowers. But above all, Mrs. Browning gave her son her piety. She was a member of the Congregational Church of York Street, Walworth, where her children were christened, and in time she brought to the chapel her husband, who, something of an eighteenth-century rationalist, had not been as devout in his early days as he later became. Her children attended regularly, but not always eagerly. This good, gentle, evangelical Christian inculcated

[6] *Idem,* pp. 17–8, 98–9.
[7] *Idem,* p. 17.

her doctrine in her son, and he became "passionately religious," as he described himself in his later years. From her teachings he never entirely broke free, save in the boyish rebellion which Shelley and Voltaire gave him license for, and the quelling of that revolt is the theme of *Pauline,* his first published book. Browning adored his mother, and when she died in 1849 while he was in Italy, he did not lightly recover from the loss.[8] Such, then, were the parents of the poet, whom Carlyle described as "people of respectable position among the dissenters, but not rich neither."

II

In this world the boy grew, playing in the fields and woods by day, and at night-fall hearing his mother play upon the piano or his father chant the odes of Anacreon. He began early to paint in currant juice, and soon after to make verses of his own. He was reading and writing at five. We get what is probably an authentic piece of biography in the little poem, *Development,* which Browning published when he was seventy-seven:

> My father was a scholar and knew Greek.
> When I was five years old, I asked him once
> "What do you read about?"
> "The siege of Troy."
> "What is a siege and what is Troy?"
> Whereat
> He piled up chairs and tables for a town,
> Set me a-top for Priam, called our cat
> —Helen, enticed away from home (he said)
> By wicked Paris, who couched somewhere close
> Under the footstool, being cowardly,
> But whom—since she was worth the pains, poor puss—
> Towzer and Tray,—our dogs, the Atreidai,—sought
> By taking Troy to get possession of
> —Always when great Achilles ceased to sulk,
> (My pony in the stable)—forth would prance
> And put to flight Hector—our page-boy's self.

When it was time to send the lad to school he was put in a small elementary school in the neighborhood. But there he was so far ahead of the larger boys that he was dismissed to avoid jealousy. He went back to his father's library and buried himself in such books as

---

[8] For the profound sympathy between Browning and his mother, see Betty Miller, *Robert Browning, A Portrait,* 1952, pp. 14–6, 157–62, 165.

Quarles' *Emblems* and, later, in Gerard de Lairesse's *The History of Painting in All Its Branches*. It was not long afterwards that he wrote his first formal poem:

the first *composition* I was guilty of was something in *imitation* of Ossian, whom I had not read, but *conceived* through two or three scraps in other books— I never can recollect *not* writing rhymes, but I knew they were nonsense even then; *this,* however, I thought exceedingly well of, and laid up for posterity under the cushion of a great arm-chair. . . . I could not have been five years old, that's one consolation.[9]

When he was eight or nine the boy was sent to school at Peckham to the establishment of the Misses Ready, and later to the Reverend Mr. Thomas Ready. He was boarded by the week at the school, only a mile from his home, and at the end of the week would return with delight to Camberwell. The school made little impression upon him. His chief recollection in later days seems to have been that the Misses Ready oiled and brushed the children's hair once a week to the tunes of Isaac Watts' hymns. Browning was "unluckily precocious," and the school was too easy for him. John Domett, elder brother to Alfred, Browning's friend in later years, remembered

young Browning in a pinafore of brown Holland, such as small boys used to wear in those days, for he was always neat in his dress; and how they used to pit him against much older and bigger boys in a chaffing match to amuse themselves with the little bright-eyed fellow's readiness and acuteness of repartee.[10]

He remained in the school until he was fourteen, and came forth aggressive, self-confident, and not a little self-centered. Perhaps this unlovely aspect of his boyish nature was in his mind when he described that period of his life in *Pauline,* the biographical poem of his twentieth year:

> . . . long restraint chained down
> My soul, till it was changed. I lost myself,
> And were it not that I so loathe that time,
> I could recall how first I learned to turn
> My mind against itself; and the effects,
> In deeds for which remorse were vain, as for
> The wanderings of delirious dream; yet thence
> Came cunning, envy, falsehood.

But this is to anticipate. In the meantime the young scholar had passed, in his twelfth year, beyond Pope's translation of Homer to the

[9] *Letters of Robert Browning and Elizabeth Barrett Barrett,* II, 469.
[10] Quoted in Griffin and Minchin, *Life,* p. 30.

original and, more important for him at the time, he had made the discovery of Byron at almost precisely the ideal age for appreciating that poet's heroic poems. With a modesty which at that time he did not sincerely possess, he gave to a volume of poems which he produced the title of *Incondita*. His parents were delighted, and sent the manuscript about in search of a publisher. Their search was fruitless, needless to say, but not everywhere did the poems fall on stony ground. In the somewhat narrow limits of the society of Liberal Dissenters in which the Brownings moved there were two sisters, the Misses Eliza and Sarah Flower, daughters of Benjamin Flower who for seven years was editor of the *Cambridge Intelligencer*. This paper was devoted to political and religious liberty, and Flower at one time had suffered imprisonment for his opinions. His daughters grew into beautiful young ladies, intellectual, musical, and devout to a degree. Eliza Flower was twenty-two, nine years older than Browning, when *Incondita* came into her hands from her friends at Camberwell, and she and her sister thought well enough of the poems to copy them out, and Sarah Flower chose two poems to send to her guardian, W. J. Fox. These two poems, *The First-Born of Egypt* and *The Dance of Death*, are the only specimens of the volume which escaped Browning's destructive hand.[11] Fox, brought up on the "sour milk of Calvinism" as he described it, was rapidly moving towards Unitarianism. He was a popular preacher of the day, and on the side an editor and a politician of strong Liberal and reforming tendencies. When Browning's poems came into his hands he praised them, but added, a little ponderously, that they showed "too great splendour of language and too little wealth of thought." It was Fox who first reviewed *Pauline* and found a publisher for *Paracelsus*, and became in Browning's words his "literary father." *Incondita* was destroyed by its author, and the only wrack left behind seems to have been that the lad of fourteen lost his heart to Eliza, and wrote verses and letters to her. It was she, as we know from Mrs. Sutherland Orr, who inspired *Pauline* six years later.[12]

[11] The poems, and the letter in which they were enclosed—dated May 31 (1827?)—were first published by Mr. Bertram Dobell in an article in the *Cornhill Magazine* for January, 1914, called "The Earliest Poems of Robert Browning." They are accessible in the *Macmillan Edition*. For Browning's great anxiety to destroy all copies of his early poems see *Letters of Robert Browning, Collected by Thomas J. Wise*, edited by Thurman L. Hood, 1933, pp. 19–20.

[12] *Life and Letters of Robert Browning* by Mrs. Sutherland Orr, New Edition, Revised and in part rewritten by Frederic G. Kenyon, 1908, p. 35. For a fuller account of Eliza Flower see Miller, *Robert Browning*, pp. 29–34, 36–8, 41–4, 47.

It was probably of the *Incondita* that Browning spoke in the lines of *Pauline,* looking back to an earlier time:

> No fear was mine
> As I gazed on the works of mighty bards,
> In the first joy at finding my own thoughts
> Recorded, and my powers exemplified,
> And feeling their aspirings were my own.

The *Incondita* was indubitably a series of imitations, probably chiefly of Byron, but the poems were surely not so utterly devoid of promise as their adolescent or their aged author imagined. In technical skill and native talent the young poet's lines upon *The First-Born of Egypt* are not unworthy to stand by the youthful Tennyson's lines in *The Devil and the Lady.*

Browning's formal education was practically at an end when he left Mr. Ready's school at the age of fourteen. Henceforth his schoolroom was his father's library. The boy was probably instructed by his father in Latin and Greek; he had a private tutor in French, and Angelo Cerutti was his teacher in Italian. In music he came in time under the tutelage of "great John Relfe," musician-in-ordinary to the king. His singing master was Isaac Nathan, author of the *Hebrew Melodies,* who entertained him with anecdotes of Byron. For the rest, he was "free as a stag" in the woods and fields, and the range of his father's bookshelves was his own. Across the fields was the Dulwich Gallery, and three miles away were the theaters and the excitements of London. Meanwhile he could lie on the grassy tops of Camberwell's little hills and see a good deal of the world. When the new University of London was opened in 1828 young Browning was enrolled to take Greek, Latin, and German, and quarters were engaged for him in Bedford Square. One week of Bloomsbury was enough, and after a little more than half a year the university lost one of its most distinguished pupils, and the elder Browning had lost £100. In their circumstances the Brownings probably expected their son to prepare himself for a profession, and they favored the law for him. He announced his intention to be a poet. Many good battles, as he later said, had to be fought, but his will was stronger than his family's. He was dependent upon his father for all the necessities of life until his marriage in 1846. Well might the poet tell Miss Barrett that he had been " 'spoiled' in this world" by his fond and indulgent parents.

Meanwhile his development into a cocksure and self-centered

youngster had caused his parents and friends no little pain. As a boy he had been publicly rebuked in church for his behavior. When he was fourteen he came upon the works of Voltaire and Shelley, and he rapidly became a vegetarian, a scoffer, an atheist and, as Mrs. Orr tells us, "gratuitously proclaimed himself everything that he was, and some things that he was not." [13] Not finding enough game at home, he sought out Sarah Flower, with what effect we may see from a touching letter which that lady wrote to her guardian, the Reverend Mr. Fox, in November of 1827:

> My mind has been wandering a long time, and now it seems to have lost sight of that only invulnerable hold against the assaults of this warring world, a firm belief in the genuineness of the Scriptures. . . . The cloud has come over me gradually, and I did not discover the darkness in which my soul was shrouded until, in seeking to give light to others, my own gloomy state became too settled to admit of doubt. It was in answering Robert Browning that my mind refused to bring forward argument, turned recreant, and sided with the enemy. . . .[14]

Sarah Flower lived to recover her faith and to write *Nearer, My God, to Thee;* the Griffin and Minchin biography wittily remarks that "Robert Browning may reasonably be said to have contributed to the evolution of this famous hymn."

The true story of Browning's discovery of Shelley's poetry has, after many misguided statements, been told.[15] There is no doubt that in time Browning read "Mr. Shelley's atheistical works," but there is equally no doubt that his first acquaintance with Shelley was through the little pirated edition of the lyrics, published by Benbow in 1826. The volume, called *Miscellaneous Poems,* was given to him by his cousin James Silverthorne soon after its publication, and it is a touch of irony that the poet's mother bought for him the inflammatory *Queen Mab.* Shelley's influence was to last for many years, and was, in all, to be the most potent literary influence which Browning ever experienced. In *Pauline* he represents himself as having escaped from the subversive religious thought of Shelley; but surely not before 1855 was he free from the poetic thought of the Sun-treader, if indeed he ever entirely escaped. The glorious discovery is chronicled in *Pauline,* and it is significant that Browning there at once repudiates and yet follows adoringly his master. It is

[13] Orr, *Life,* p. 43.
[14] Moncure D. Conway, *Centenary of South Place,* 1894, p. 46.
[15] See F. A. Pottle's ingenious study, *Shelley and Browning, A Myth and Some Facts,* Chicago, 1923.

enough to say here that Shelley made Browning the poet he was; he gave him poetical and political ideas, method and technique, and pointed out that the proper subject of poetry is the soul of the poet himself. Thus Browning arrived at his first definition of his art:

> And then thou said'st a perfect bard was one
> Who shadowed out the stages of all life. . . .[16]

In this mood the young man had quit the university, and now began vigorously to prosecute his "plan to look on real life."

Real life included a good deal: riding, dancing, singing, fencing, and boxing were essential parts of it, and attendance upon Dr. Blundell's medical lectures at Guy's Hospital seems not to have been excluded. The best of all places to see real life was in the theater, and many "warm moon-births and long evening ends" saw him walking from London with his cousin James Silverthorne. Coming home from Kean's performance of *Richard III* at Richmond on October 22, 1832, exalted with youth and ambition, he conceived the grandiose plan of writing a poem, an opera, a novel, under fictitious names, and the world was never to guess that all these were from one hand. *Pauline* was to be the work of the poet. In January, 1833, the poem was done, and his aunt, Mrs. Silverthorne, provided the £30 necessary for its publication. It appeared anonymously in March, under the imprint of Saunders and Otley, and the author sent twelve copies to Fox to be distributed for review. He then waited for the world to acknowledge him. Fox welcomed the young poet with a shout, and Allan Cunningham was enthusiastic in the *Athenaeum;* but not a copy of *Pauline* was sold. After a while the bale of unbound sheets was stored in the Browning attic, and it was many years before the world was to know the author of the little poetical biography.

Pauline, however, did not go entirely unmarked, save by Cunningham and Fox. It is not too bold to say that a review of the poem which was not published at the time altered the direction of Browning's poetical aspirations. Fox had given one of his copies for review to John Stuart Mill, a young man then, whose clear and searching mind was to leave its impress upon the age. Mill prepared the notes for his critique, but when the magazine for which he intended it anticipated him with a brief contemptuous notice of *Pauline,* he returned the volume to Fox with marginal comments and a critical

---

[16] I quote from the first edition. Browning's later change of "shadowed out" to "chronicled" gives an entirely different task to the bard.

summary in the end pages.[17] The keen analytical mind of Mill penetrated immediately the thin disguise of the Latin preface and the French note and saw *Pauline* for what it was, the sincere confession of a young writer who seemed "possessed with a more intense and morbid self-consciousness than I ever knew in any sane man." Mill realized also that "Pauline" was not a real woman, or at any rate that the poet was not in love with her, and the best thing he can wish for the author is that he shall find a real "Pauline." Neither was Mill beguiled by the young poet's pretensions to repentance and reform:

The self-seeking and self-worshipping state is well described—beyond that, I should think the writer had made, as yet, only the next step, viz. into despising his own state. I even question whether part even of that self-disdain is not *assumed*. He is evidently *dissatisfied*, and feels part of the badness of his state; he does not write as if it were purged out of him. If he once could muster a hearty hatred of his selfishness it would *go;* as it is, he feels only the *lack* of *good,* not the positive evil. He feels not remorse, but only disappointment. . . . Meanwhile he should not attempt to show how a person may be *recovered* from this morbid state,—for *he* is hardly convalescent, and "what should we speak of but that which we know?"

This was indeed seeing the young Browning plain.

Fox gave the volume back to Browning, who read Mill's criticism on October 30, 1833, as we know from his entry in the same volume. As he read he realized that he had exposed his callow soul to the gaze of a stranger, a thing hateful to him the rest of his days. The thought of *Pauline* became repugnant to him; he hid it from sight. Henceforward, his poetry would be objective and dramatic, the utterances of created characters, not of himself. The perfect bard hereafter was one who "chronicled" the souls of others, preferably historical persons. At the end of his own note in Mill's copy of *Pauline*, Browning wrote, "Only this crab remains of the shapely Tree of Life in this Fool's paradise of mine."

The whole episode of *Pauline* rankled in the heart of the young poet. The poem itself is, perhaps, an admission of defeat, for Shelley had meant to the young Browning rebellion against his parents, the church, and society. *Pauline* is a record of his capitulation, and in some ways his loss of freedom. As his sister, Sarianna, was to say of this period in Browning's life, "The fact was, poor boy, he had out-

[17] This interesting copy of *Pauline* is in the Forster and Dyce Collection in the Victoria and Albert Museum, where I have seen it. See the admirable account of this part of Browning's career in Griffin and Minchin, *Life,* pp. 55–60. See also Miller, *Robert Browning,* pp. 40–2.

grown his social surroundings. They were absolutely good, but they were narrow; it could not be otherwise, he chafed under them." But his first attempt to break into the large world was not only an utter failure; it had left his rebellion tamed and his pride humbled.

III

Happily, the secret of *Pauline* was known to very few, and the world was yet to see the dramatic poet. He could console himself with the fact that he was only twenty-one, and Mill and the other reviewers had seen beauty and promise in *Pauline*. Meanwhile, in the midst of a devoted family he got on with his convalescence. In the spring of 1834 the opportunity came, possibly through the association of his uncle, Reuben Browning, with the Rothschild banking interests, for the poet to accompany the Chevalier George de Benkhausen, the Russian consul general, to St. Petersburg. On March 1, with his mother's gift, a Bible, in his luggage, Browning set out. The packet took his company to the Low Countries, and from there the journey was made by carriage. In later years he chiefly remembered the versts and versts of pine in the flat country of western Russia. *Ivàn Ivànovitch,* written forty-five years later, shows the impression the country made upon him. He recalled, too, years afterward, the Russian songs he had heard and the flowers he had seen. His whole journey took only two months, and he was at home again by the first of May.

For a while Browning was eager to become a diplomat, and his desires were probably whetted by his new friendship with the Comte Amédée de Ripert-Monclar, an agent for the French royalists in London. It was this gentleman who suggested the subject of Paracelsus to the poet, and in the fall of 1834 Browning began his second published poem. He had already begun *Sordello,* that poem of many vicissitudes which was to haunt him for seven years. Late in the spring of 1835, Fox found a publisher for *Paracelsus,* and in August the book was published at the expense of Robert Browning, senior. The new poem was dramatic in form, and was ornamented with elaborate notes. This time the name of the author appeared on the title-page. The soul exposed purported to be that of the German chemist and physician of the Renaissance, but one can see that the desire to "know," which is the chief characteristic of the hero of the poem, was a quality fully developed in Browning himself, and the crying need to couple "love" with "knowledge" was the trait of an historical personage who was not born until May 7, 1812. Some of the reviewers were not far wrong in seeing Shelley behind the scenes, but the young poet was so sure of his historical accuracy that he challenged his readers in a note. "The liberties I have taken with my subject are very trifling; and the reader may slip the foregoing scenes between the leaves of any memoir of Paracelsus he pleases, by way of commentary." This was to do his invention a grave wrong; but the disguise sufficed, and *Paracelsus* and its author were welcomed into the literary world of London. The sales of the poem were not great, and the reviewers, though John Forster in the *Examiner* and Fox in the *Monthly Repository* hailed the new poet, were not extravagant in their praise. *Paracelsus,* however, made its way among the best literary minds of the day. In November Browning met Macready, the great tragic actor, who wrote in his diary that the young man looked and spoke "more like a youthful poet than any man I ever saw." This friendship was to shape the course of Browning's life during the next ten years, and give a permanent cast to his nature. On the last day of the year Browning was at Elstree, Macready's home, and there met John Forster, the dramatic critic, whose first words to him were, "Did you see a little notice of you I wrote in the *Examiner?*" The little notice was three columns in length. The crowning event of Browning's early literary fame came at a supper given by Sergeant Talfourd in honor of the success of his play, *Ion,* on May 26, 1836. Many literary folk were present, not the least of whom was Walter Savage Landor. The host proposed a toast to the "Poets of England," and among others nominated the author of *Paracelsus.* As the health was drunk, William Wordsworth leaned across the table and said, "I am proud to drink to your health, Mr. Browning!"

To make his cup run over on that memorable evening, as the party was breaking up Macready spoke to the young poet and said, "Will you not write me a tragedy, and save me from going to America?" From this casual request the poet, urged on by his dramatic ambitions and by his friend Forster, embarked upon that effort, which dominated him for the next ten years, to write a play that would be successful on the boards. In one sense it is possible to regret the time which Browning expended in writing plays. That form of literature was not suitable to his genius, and the best he could achieve was excellent closet drama in the manner, but without the life, of the Elizabethans. The time was not altogether propitious, and the poet lavished an intellectual subtlety and an amazingly expressive style upon some of the most melodramatic of plots. But deeper than time and circumstance was the internal fact in Browning's personality, that he could never escape from his habit of introspection, and he was never able to project the feelings, motives, thoughts, and words of his characters onto the public stage in the way in which the theater and its audience naturally demanded. But to call the dramas wasted effort is to miss their real import. Through those unhappy plays we see Browning's peculiar genius clearing magnificently; the poet was working his way through modifications of the drama, such as *Pippa Passes,* towards his true province, the short dramatic poem of the *Dramatic Lyrics, Dramatic Romances,* and *Men and Women.*

Since I give the history of the plays in some detail in the body of my book, I propose here merely to cull the biographical effects of his association with the theater. Browning was lured into the writing of his first play, *Strafford,* by his familiarity with the subject. When Forster was sick and could not complete his prose *Life of Strafford,* which he had begun and got well along by February, 1836, the poet completed it for him. Browning's play, drawn mainly from this material, was acted five times in May, 1837, and enjoyed an indifferent success. His position in the esteem of Macready and Forster was somewhat impaired in the course of preparation and in the performance. On several occasions Browning, working upon *Sordello* as well as upon *Strafford,* appeared to Macready to be "jaded and thought-sick." He was knowing that agony of effort which makes poets martyrs for the sake of men. His curious and lonely education had little prepared him to communicate with the world, or indeed to know what the world thought ordinary or strange. At the conclusion of the *Strafford* incident he thought he would never write another play. The experience, however, was valuable to him in more ways than one, for in his effort to master the history of the "grand epoch," as he called that period between 1621 and 1648 when Parliament was wringing its victories from the Stuarts, he came upon a political philosophy which was to last him for many years. In *Pauline,* under the influence of Shelley, he had vowed himself to the cause of liberty. The struggles of Hampden, Pym, Eliot, and the other Parliamentarians against the tyranny of the Royalists suddenly gave body and meaning to his phrase. This feeling was confirmed by his visit to Venice in 1838; and as a result the Italian peasant girl in

Sordello takes the place of the aristocratic Palma as the true heroine. Henceforth he was a Liberal, a champion of the cause of the people in England, France, or Italy, and could deplore what he regarded as the defection of Wordsworth when in 1843 the bard became poet laureate. But the whirligig of time was to bring in his revenges.

The success enjoyed by *Paracelsus* had done little to chasten the pride of the young man. Mrs. Bridell-Fox, the daughter of W. J. Fox, in writing her recollections of Browning in the *Argosy* for February, 1890, opens a window upon the mood of Browning about the years 1836–7:

> I remember . . . when Mr. Browning entered the drawing-room, with a quick light step; and on hearing from me that my father was out, and in fact that nobody was at home but myself, he said: "It's my birthday to-day; I'll wait till they come in," and sitting down to the piano, he added: "If it won't disturb you, I'll play till they do." And as he turned to the instrument, the bells of some neighbouring church suddenly burst out with a frantic merry peal. It seemed, to my childish fancy, as if in response to the remark that it was his birthday. He was then slim and dark, and very handsome; and—may I hint it—just a trifle of a dandy, addicted to lemon-coloured kid-gloves and such things: quite "the glass of fashion and the mould of form." But full of ambition, eager for success, eager for fame, and, what's more, determined to conquer fame and to achieve success.

The hard work and the ill-success of *Strafford* took something of the jauntiness of the young man away, and the fierce struggles to finish *Sordello* and the blank stare of the world upon its appearance in 1840 humbled him even more.

It is possible to see now why *Sordello* was such a chaotic poem. It was written over a period of seven years, and at least four different conceptions are mingled in the final version. Part of the difficulty was that the young poet was attempting to say some things that had never been said in poetry before. But Browning obviously did not know, or in his pride did not care, what the orthodox knowledge of men consisted in, or what co-operation he might expect from readers. He did not realize that *Paracelsus* had been received precisely because of its freedom from real history, and now he packed his new poem with the most remote and tangled history on record. The result is well known. *Sordello* became the jest of English literature, and remained the most incomprehensible poem in the language until some of our own contemporaries got to work. But whoso looks into *Sordello* may find the ruins of once magnificent cities in the lush tropical forests, "by the caper overrooted." The late Sir Edmund Gosse was unusually right in saying of the poem, "It possesses passages of melody and insight, fresh enough, surprising enough to form the whole stock-in-trade of a respectable poet. . . ." [18] *Sordello* was a bold venture in obscurity and subtlety which had the misfortune to be a hundred years ahead of its time.

With the gift of hindsight we can see the necessity which Browning felt to write *Sordello*. Indeed, in his first three long poems, *Pauline, Paracelsus,* and *Sordello,* we see the young man trying to put himself right with God and his world, but most of all seeking to find himself. In *Sordello* especially we see him progressing towards tolerance as he exorcises at last the romantic, impatient utopian that he was, hypnotized by vast visions.[19] He had also to face the problems of communication, methods and means, form and language. In dealing with abstractions he was a "semantic stutterer," [20] and we see him through *Sordello* working, partially and temporarily perhaps, his cure.

The advantages of writing Sordello's story were by-products of the effort. The poem, like a storm, cleared the poet's spirit and led him to *Pippa Passes* and the shorter poems. In search of local color for *Sordello* he took his first journey to Italy in 1838 and saw Venice and Asolo. The country freed his spirit and taught him, somehow, the beauty of simplicity. But in 1840 the disadvantages of having written *Sordello* far outweighed the advantages. The publication of the poem damaged a promising reputation. Browning was in some respects the laughing-stock of the literary clique in London, though men did not laugh in his face. He seems to have lost his hold upon his friends in the sophisticated world, such as Macready and Forster. There were no more healths to the young poet, and instead he was plunged into that semi-obscurity which was to last for nearly twenty-four years.[21] He still had many friends in London, but he was more often to be seen in his mother's garden at Hatcham, and he cultivated more than before his Camberwell friends, "The Colloquials," made up of Alfred Domett, Joseph Arnould, Christopher Dowson, and

[18] *Robert Browning, Personalia,* p. 48.

[19] See Lionel Stevenson, "Tennyson, Browning, and a Romantic Fallacy," in *University of Toronto Quarterly* 13:175–95 (1943–4).

[20] See Stewart W. Holmes, "Browning: Semantic Stutterer," in *PMLA* 60:231–55 (1945).

[21] M. B. Cramer, however, protests this view of Browning's situation in his article, "Browning's Friendships and Fame before Marriage (1833–1846)," in *PMLA* 55:207–30 (1940). There is some justification for his position, but I think he confuses literary with social success.

others less well known. I do not mean to derogate these men. They were as staunch and good in their way as the London set, perhaps better, but they were not in the public eye and their plumage was not so gay. With Domett especially Browning struck up a warm friendship [22] which was to bear delightful fruit in *Waring, Time's Revenges,* and *The Guardian Angel.* When Domett went out of England to New Zealand in May, 1842, on the tide of emigration so indicative of hard times and a smug world, he elicited from Browning some of the best of his letters. On November 8, 1843, Browning wrote Domett, imagining that the far traveller would soon be at home again, "There you walk past our pond-rail (picking up one of the fallen horse-chestnuts), and now our gate-latch clicks, and now— . . . 'Tis worth while running away to be so wished for again."

The early Forties were hard times in England for young men, as one may see from Carlyle's *Past and Present* or Tennyson's *Locksley Hall,* to go no further. In New Zealand one might in time become prime minister, as Domett did, or at least might be free from the cramping social order that had not yet been temporarily rejuvenated by the industrial revolution, on some island of hope in purple seas. Browning decided to stay at home, but his dreams were not so grandiose as they had been ten years earlier. Now he was content, though "vain and ambitious some nights," to pursue the humble way of the poet and publish his plays and poems in the little paper-covered pamphlets, printed in double columns and published by Moxon at a cost to the poet's father of approximately £16 apiece. These are the pamphlets which make up the since famous *Bells and Pomegranates* series which appeared in eight numbers between 1841 and 1846. It began with *Pippa Passes,* that happy blend of his memory of Asolo as he saw it in 1838, his solitary musings in Dulwich Wood, and his experimentation in a freer dramatic technique than the stage at that time allowed. With *Pippa* Browning began to emerge from the shadow of *Sordello,* and he came out into the sunlight, as we can now see, in the shorter poems of the *Dramatic Lyrics* of 1842 and the *Dramatic Romances* of 1845.

In the meantime, the series continued with another desperate attempt at a successful stage play, and in February, 1843, under the most adverse circumstances, *A Blot in the 'Scutcheon* was produced

[22] The whole history of this friendship is recorded in F. G. Kenyon's book, *Robert Browning and Alfred Domett,* London, 1906.

at Macready's theater in Drury Lane without Macready in the cast. The results were the same as those of *Strafford*, save that this time they were magnified. Browning's melodrama, straining too hard to touch the soft hearts of his time in the manner of Bulwer-Lytton, was acted three times to dwindling audiences. In the course of the performances Browning and Macready quarrelled and ceased to speak to each other, and the friendship with Forster was further impaired. Save for one later fling in *Colombe's Birthday* Browning ceased to write for the stage. These were melancholy and somewhat lonely years. Few readers bought his books, and Browning, past his first youth, seemed baffled at every turn. Perhaps he listened for hope to the story of the long struggle towards fame of his new friend of these years, Thomas Carlyle. But Carlyle's encouragement, if hearty at times and tonic, was fitful, and his usual advice to poets was that they should write prose. In the meanwhile, Browning had tried his hand at prose and had written for the *Foreign Quarterly Review* in 1842 a review of a book on Tasso which turned into a passionate defence of Chatterton's good name.[23] His quieter and greater achievement in these years, however, was the slow perfection of the dramatic monologue as a technique for penetrating even to the secret recesses of the heart.

The Brownings moved from Camberwell in December of 1840 to escape from the rapidly filling suburb. They went further out the "interminable Kent road" to New Cross, Hatcham, in Surrey, and it was here that Carlyle came on horseback. He observed from the order in which Browning's room was kept that he was the apple of his mother's eye. There the poet might be seen of a morning in his blue working shirt, with "Polidoro [Caravaggio]'s perfect Andromeda" before him on his desk, the skull and the pet spider who lived therein. Or if the weather were fine, Browning would lie on the grass in his mother's garden while the wind in the horse-chestnut made the flower-castles nod. One may catch the spirit of the place as well as his own mood in the two delightful *Garden Fancies*. In 1844 he was a man of thirty-two, and though he had done some things that the world would remember, he had not fulfilled his promise to himself. The world was a little stale, possibly flat, and undeniably unprofitable. In this mood he remembered Italy. His earlier journeys had been notable for their celerity, but in his second journey to

[23] See Donald Smalley, *Browning's Essay on Chatterton*, edited with Introductory Chapters and Notes, 1948; also my comments below, in Ch. 8.

Italy he was to have more leisure. He was in Naples in September, 1844, whence he had come by ship. He wandered over the Piano di Sorrento and climbed Vico Alvano, and looked down into the clear Mediterranean from a spot near where Shelley had written his *Stanzas in Dejection.* From Naples he went to Rome and saw the monuments of Shelley and Keats, and one day entered the church of S. Prassede. He came home through northern Italy and down the Rhine with his spirit renewed and the subjects of a good many new poems in mind.

During these years he had added new friends. He met "Barry Cornwall," in life Bryan Waller Procter, and was soon welcomed at the brilliant literary salon of Mrs. Procter, "our lady of bitterness." Then too he became the friend of Thomas Hood, and he called upon Leigh Hunt and heard from him of Shelley, Keats, and Byron. He knew Richard Hengist Horne, who had written *Orion,* the "farthing epic," and he was well acquainted with John Kenyon, kinsman to Elizabeth Barrett and an old school-friend of his father.

While Browning was in Italy in the fall of 1844 Miss Barrett had published her *Poems,* and when he read them upon his return he was pleased to find his name linked with those of Wordsworth and the newly great Tennyson in *Lady Geraldine's Courtship:*

Or from Browning some pomegranate which, if cut deep down the middle, Shows a heart within blood-tinctured of a veined humanity.

Much gratified, and persuaded by Kenyon, he wrote to Miss Barrett on January 10, 1845: "I love your verses with all my heart, dear Miss Barrett," he began, and a little further in the letter he said, "I do, as I say, love these books with all my heart—and I love you too . . . ," surely an auspicious beginning. And thus was begun the celebrated romance which one must read in its fullness in the letters of these poets. It may be said that here at last, as John Stuart Mill had wished years ago, Browning attained complete convalescence.

The letters between Robert Browning and Elizabeth Barrett which tell of the courtship of a year and three-quarters are the richest biographical documents in Browning literature, but assuredly they are not the clearest. "Their letters may be published a hundred times over," says Chesterton, "they will still remain private." This is partly because they are genuine letters, written for a single person, and it takes a keen and patient reader to catch the interplay of their noble and subtle spirits. Love here has to do with the head as much as with the heart, and is all the surer for that. When the correspondence began Elizabeth Barrett was thirty-nine, six years older than Browning, and for some years had been shut in her room at 50 Wimpole Street as a hopeless invalid. "I had done with living, I thought, when you came and sought me out," she was later to write. Her illness was real enough; it was possibly caused by a broken blood-vessel in her lungs. But it was the tyranny of her father that kept her an invalid. The peculiar psychology which made Edward Barrett what he was had as its main constituent the religious, patriarchal conception of the family carried to the point of mania—a conception not unique among latter-day Puritans. He had Scripture for it that the Lord was a jealous God, and Barrett was made in His image. The family was not to be broken by marriage, and therefore the children, who at last had to be named Septimus and Octavius from the sheer scarcity of names, never dared mention the subject though they were approaching forty. Later Elizabeth was to write her new friend concerning marriage:

'If a prince of Eldorado should come, with a pedigree of lineal descent from some signory in the moon in one hand, and a ticket of good-behaviour from the nearest Independent chapel, in the other'—?

'Why even *then*,' said my sister Arabel, 'it would not *do*.' And she was right, and we all agreed that she was right.

But even from this tyranny and from her darkened room, with ivy at the window and her books and the busts of Homer and Chaucer inside, she had made herself an important literary figure of the age. She saw few people, but she wrote innumerable letters, and became as she called herself a "regular Richardson heroine." Not foreseeing that she could not keep Robert Browning a whole postman's beat from her door, she began her correspondence with this "king of the mystics."

The love between them, being true, took the proverbial course. One can see Browning in its earlier stages, before he has seen the lady, ready to fall in love with a voice, and yet obviously struggling against the new thing which will upset a well-planned life. He broke through the first barrier which she raised when on May 20, 1845, he was permitted to see her. On that day between three and four-thirty she lay on her couch and talked with him as he sat in her arm-chair opposite. The match was applied to the train. He wrote a decorous little note that evening hoping that he had not tired her, that he had not talked too loud. She reassured him, and then, to her unmitigated astonishment, she received from him a passionate love-letter. She sent it back to him and begged him to destroy it, which he did. She pointed out to him the difficulties of her position, and begged him to come as a friend, but never to refer to the subject of love again. He submitted because it was his only course. But if assault fails to take the fort, there is always the way of siege if one has world enough and time. Browning had, and his love enveloped her in a hundred ways. Flowers from his mother's garden were constantly on her tables. He brought her news from the great world of London which she could not visit. He gave her a vision of what a full life might be. His conduct, however, had not the masterful assurance about it that is popularly ascribed to it. He knew the anguish and the humilities of love, and was frequently indecisive and dependent. Miss Barrett, indeed, often appears as the stronger person. In the crisis, however, it was his will that prevailed, as barrier after barrier was surmounted; but perhaps he never would have won the citadel if her father had not played into his hands. The doctor had ordered her to Italy for her health; Barrett, though it was declared that she could not hope for a cure without a change, would not consent to her going. Browning was enjoined to silence, but his anger and love burst from him, and this time he won the citadel and all but ran up his flag. Elizabeth Barrett now began to write the *Sonnets from the Portuguese,* though he did not know it, and her burden there, as in her letters, was that she loved him too well to fetter his life with hers.

The rest is history. The course of love was deepened by the infinitely tender, and infinitely old-fashioned, exchange of locks of hair: "The soul's Rialto hath its merchandise." The sylphs fluttered but the lock was cut. Miss Barrett's health improved wonderfully in the mild winter. Browning wanted to lay the case before her father, but that, she knew, would be madness. Slowly they came to the conclusion that in September they would be married and go to Italy.

On September 9, 1846, Barrett issued an edict that the family would remove to the country for a month while the house in Wimpole Street was being repaired. On the 11th Browning paid his last visit to the house. All arrangements were made, and on Saturday, the 12th, at eleven o'clock they were married in Marylebone Church, with only two witnesses present. Mrs. Browning returned to her home. The exodus of the Barretts was announced for the 21st, but

Browning would not come to the house again—they felt it would not be right for him to do so. On the 19th the lovers fled; they went to Southampton, to Havre, to Paris, and thence to Marseilles by way of Avignon. They coasted from Marseilles along the Riviera to Leghorn, and came to rest in Pisa.

IV

The life in Italy, which was the golden time of Browning's poetry, was somewhat precariously financed. For their expenses, Browning had borrowed £100 from his father, who wished to make it a gift, and they had besides some £300 a year from Mrs. Browning's funds. These funds were not to continue prosperously for more than three years, and though Mrs. Browning got some returns from her books, Browning's income from his was negligible. In 1850, what with the expenses of Mrs. Browning's illnesses and the birth of a baby, they were sorely put to it to make ends meet.[24] A stout heart makes the road easier and Browning had that. It held out through difficulties until in 1856 Kenyon's munificent bequest of £11,000 relieved them of worry.

In April, 1847, the Brownings had moved from Pisa to Florence and by the end of the summer had settled in an apartment in Casa Guidi which was to be their home for fourteen years. From Florence they made summer excursions to Fano, Bagni di Lucca, and Siena, and three times to Paris and London: besides these sojourns they spent two winters in Rome. It was at Bagni di Lucca in 1849 that Browning first saw the *Sonnets from the Portuguese* which Mrs. Browning had written to him in London in 1846. But at the end of their travels Mrs. Browning, at least, always returned gratefully to their large, cool rooms in Florence. They were visited frequently by English friends, such as Mrs. Anna Jameson and Father Prout, and they came to know such English residents in Florence as the T. A. Trollopes, Isa Blagden, Harriet Hosmer, Frederick Tennyson, and Landor. Many Americans also sought them out, and they became close friends with the family of William Wetmore Story, the sculptor. They knew another sculptor in Hiram Powers; and they became friends with G. W. Curtis, the literary man, and Margaret Fuller (Contessa Ossoli), the

[24] For the financial difficulties of these years, 1847–56, see *New Letters of Robert Browning,* edited by William Clyde DeVane and Kenneth Leslie Knickerbocker, 1950, *passim.*

socialist of Brook Farm. They were visited in 1858 by Hawthorne.[25]
Most of the Americans came to see Mrs. Browning, for Browning in
the Fifties was more renowned as a husband than as an author. Of
an evening their friends would come in to talk, and to share their
chestnuts and wine. By day the Brownings would occasionally visit
the picture-galleries or go for rides in the country. The daily routine
consisted of reading and writing and lessons upon the piano, given
by the poet to his little son, Pen.

In later years Browning was fond of saying that Italy was his university. Italy seemed to give him joy and freedom, and in the long,
quiet days in Florence he settled many matters for himself. With the
encouragement of his wife his interest in religion revived, as we see in
Christmas-Eve and Easter-Day, 1850, and in pondering history he
concluded that the greatest event of history was the incarnation of
Christ with its promise of personal immortality, and the second great
epoch was the Renaissance when personality reached its fullest flowering.[26] In these fruitful years he developed his doctrine of human
and divine love, and the interrelationship between them. He thought
deeply, too, about his own art and about painting. We see him, for
example, significantly enough, indoctrinating young Lytton with the
poetry of John Donne.[27] All this was of immense consequence as a
background for *Men and Women*, the finest flower of his genius.

Soon after their arrival Mrs. Browning became a violent partisan of
the Italian Risorgimento. She watched rather feverishly the vicissitudes in the fortunes of the Piedmontese against Austria, and finally
put all her hopes in Louis Napoleon. Browning was less of a partisan
and more of an observer. Though little appreciated, he must have
seemed to Florentines such a poet, God's spy, as he imagines wandering around Valladolid:

> He stood and watched the cobbler at his trade,
> The man who slices lemons into drink,
> The coffee-roaster's brazier, and the boys
> That volunteer to help him turn its winch.
> He glanced o'er books on stalls with half an eye,
> And fly-leaf ballads on the vendor's string
> And broad-edge bold-print posters by the wall.

[25] For a compact account of the Brownings' life in Florence see Ch. 1 of
Letters from Owen Meredith (*Robert, First Earl of Lytton*) *to Robert and Elizabeth Barrett Browning*, ed. A. B. and J. L. Harlan, Jr.

[26] See H. B. Charlton, "Browning as Poet of Religion," in *Bulletin of the John
Rylands Library* 27:271–307 (1942–3).

[27] *Letters from Owen Meredith*, pp. 144–5, 187.

If you were in Florence,

> You'd come upon his scrutinizing hat,
> Making a peaked shade blacker than itself.

In his walks he bought rococo furniture for the rooms in Casa Guidi, and once picked up some old paintings that seemed to be the work of Cimabue, Ghirlandaio, and Giottino in a grain-shop a mile outside the city. These rambles were memorable to him. Years later when they were long past he said to his friend, Kingsland, "Oh me! To find myself there, some late sunshiny Sunday afternoon, with my face turned to Florence,—ten minutes to the gate, ten minutes *home!* I think I should fairly end it all on the spot." [28]

This was the even mood of Browning's life in Florence; yet the years were filled with accomplishment and event. In 1849 the first collection of Browning's works had appeared in two volumes over the imprint of Chapman and Hall. It included all his works to that date, save *Pauline, Strafford,* and *Sordello.* The same year was full of joy and grief: on March 9 a son, Robert Wiedemann Barrett Browning, already mentioned above, was born, but soon afterwards the poet's mother died suddenly in England, and he was unable to go home. The blow was hard to bear and his health suffered. Perhaps these portents of mortality joined with the public questions of the day and his wife's piety to produce his next volume of verse, *Christmas-Eve and Easter-Day* in 1850, in which the three aspects of Christianity in the western world, Protestantism, Catholicism, and Rationalism, were put in picturesque fashion before the reader. Browning's preference went to the little Independent chapel, for all its ugliness, for there, it seemed to him, love was most abundant. The poem was a harbinger of the matter which was to make up too much of Browning's late verse. *Christmas-Eve and Easter-Day* had a sale of 200 copies in the first fortnight, and then the sales ceased.

This poem owed little to Italy; but under the warm sky Browning's secular genius now burst into bloom. All of western Europe was laid under tribute for *Men and Women* of 1855. Florence, Venice, Fano, Siena, Bagni di Lucca, and Rome contributed essential poems. Paris was laid under fee: its roar after the quiet of Florence possibly helped in making *Childe Roland to the Dark Tower Came,* that astonishingly modern poem; its pictures in the Louvre may have helped memory to create the haunting masterpiece, *Love Among*

[28] W. G. Kingsland, "Robert Browning, Some Personal Reminiscences," in *Baylor University Browning Interests,* Second Series, 1931, p. 37.

the Ruins. London and Florence collaborated in *One Word More.* Married love received such scrutiny as it had not obtained since John Donne died. The British public hardly suspected that it, and not Robert Browning, was on trial when in November, 1855, Chapman and Hall published *Men and Women* in two volumes. Here was the life-blood of a great master: here was truth and beauty, observation, action and reflection, and many varieties of new music. Here were flawless lyrics, and here the poet had perfected his new technique in the dramatic monologue. At last, one may say, Browning deserved the generous praise which Landor (leaving Shakespeare out of the question) had accorded him in 1846:

> Since Chaucer was alive and hale
> No man has walked along our road with step
> So active, so enquiring eye, and tongue
> So varied in discourse.

In *Men and Women* Browning richly endowed English literature, but the British public for ten years took the gift coolly. A few were fervid in their admiration. His old admirer, D. G. Rossetti, was mad with delight; [29] young men here and there began to see his merit, but the applause was far less than full-handed. To an age used to the bardic formality of Wordsworth and Tennyson, Browning's manner was still too new, too familiar and racy, his utterance too broken. It was the manner of the poetry of the future, if they could have but known. Browning knew precisely where he stood and what he was doing, as one may see from the essay which he wrote to serve as a preface to a collection of Shelley's letters in 1851. The letters turned out to be spurious, but the essay stands, and in it the author saw himself as plain as he saw Shelley. One may see the same clear vision in a letter which Browning wrote to Ruskin in defence of his methods in poetry on December 10, 1855, when the great arbiter of taste had objected to certain traits in *Men and Women.*[30] No mere chance led Browning to read *Fra Lippo Lippi,* one of the boldest and freest of his new poems, familiar in manner and racy in diction, to the group gathered in his temporary residence, 13 Dorset Street, London, on September 27, 1855. On this occasion Tennyson read *Maud,* "my little *Hamlet,*" while D. G. Rossetti sketched him. Mrs. Browning and W. M. Rossetti were also present. But though Browning was discour-

[29] See M. B. Cramer, "What Browning's Literary Reputation Owed to the Pre-Raphaelites, 1847–1856," in *Journal of English Literary History* 8:305–21.
[30] See W. G. Collingwood, *Life and Work of John Ruskin,* 1893, pp. 232–5.

aged by the reception of *Men and Women,* it was with no bitterness that he saw his wife's poem, *Aurora Leigh,* go into edition after edition upon its publication in 1856.

Thus it was with mixed feelings towards the British public that the Brownings returned to Florence in 1856. Kenyon's bequest began to make their financial situation easier. They spent some time in Paris and one summer on the sea-coast of France, near Havre. They were enabled to go to Rome for gaiety, and in the summer, when they chose, they took the large and pleasant Villa Alberti, near Siena, as their residence. Here they were near the Storys, and Landor, under Browning's protection now, was a constant vistor at tea. They would sit on the terrace until far into the evening, the fireflies busy in the cypresses, while Landor and Mrs. Browning debated the conduct of Louis Napoleon. She made him "laugh carnivorously" by telling him that he would have to write an ode in honor of the Emperor to humor her. The care which Browning took of the aged Landor shows the younger poet in a most happy light.[31] He always said that he owed more to Landor than to any of his contemporaries, and he took this excellent way of expressing his gratitude. Landor was not easy to care for; he was violent and improvident. Mrs. Browning did not care greatly for him, partly because he was such trouble for her husband, and partly because he was set against the two great passions of her later years, spiritualism and the Emperor of the French.

The years wore on pleasantly and were deeply troubled only by Mrs. Browning's occasional ill health. There were, inevitably, differences in temperament between Browning and Mrs. Browning: he was naturally inclined to seek company and found Florence a little still; she needed the quiet and comfort of home. There were also disagreements of opinion, strongly felt by each, upon such topics as spiritualism, Louis Napoleon, and the bringing up of their son, Pen. But each respected the right of the other to an individual opinion. There were no more "men and women" being written; Browning was discouraged by the reception of his poetry and soothed his restlessness by modelling in clay in Story's studio. In England, however, his fame was slowly but surely growing, and the young men at the universities were beginning to read him.[32] In Florence in June, 1860, he

[31] See H. C. Minchin, *Walter Savage Landor, Last Days, Letters and Conversations,* 1934, *passim.*

[32] See M. B. Cramer, "Browning's Literary Reputation at Oxford, 1855–59," in *PMLA* 57:232–40 (1942). When Browning received an account from Chap-

picked up the "Old Yellow Book" from a book-stall, but the subject
was to lie unused for more than four years still. Then suddenly Mrs.
Browning's health began to decline. All private and public sorrows
seemed to combine against her: her father had recently died without having relented towards her; Cavour had died, and things were
going very badly for Italy. In June, 1861, her health took a turn for
the worse; but yet even her ever watchful husband did not suspect
the danger. On the morning of the 29th she died in his arms. The
happy Italian days were over.

V

In August, 1861, the grief-stricken Browning and his son began to
move towards England where the poet had decided to live henceforth. To stay longer in empty Florence was intolerable; to leave it
was bearable and no more. In this mood he quitted the city and never
returned, save in memory. One of his first acts was to have his son's
curls cut and to dress him in boy's clothes.[33] He arranged with Miss
Blagden, the friend of several years' standing who was with Mrs.
Browning in her last illness, that they should exchange letters
monthly, and it is through Browning's letters to this lady that we may
follow his activities and moods during the next ten years.[34] She, no
doubt, in her letters gave him the news of Florence which his hungry
heart desired. Most of August and September, 1861, Browning spent
at St. Enogat on the coast of France with his father and sister for
company, and there on the lonely wind-swept shore the heart found
some degree of healing. In October he came to London, and after a
few months spent in lodgings he settled into the house at 19 Warwick
Crescent which was to be his home for twenty-six years. He was a
neighbor here to Arabel Barrett, his wife's sister, and in her society
he found much comfort.

Idleness was now the last thing to be thought of, though it had
been pleasant enough in Italy. There was much to be done: Mrs.
Browning's *Last Poems* had to be seen through the press, and her

man in 1863, however, there were still unsold copies of *Men and Women* on
hand; see *New Letters,* ed. DeVane and Knickerbocker, p. 392.

[33] See Gertrude Reese, "Robert Browning and his Son," in *PMLA* 61:784–803
(1946), and also Betty Miller, "The Child of Casa Guidi," in the *Cornhill Magazine* 163:415–28 (Winter, 1948–9).

[34] See *Dearest Isa: Robert Browning's Letters to Isabella Blagden,* edited by
Edward C. McAleer, 1951.

writings collected; their son's education, for Pen was now nearing thirteen, had to be taken seriously in hand; and soon a new collection of his own works was called for. This was to be the collected edition of 1863. These things, especially the training of his son, kept him from morbid thoughts, and summer after summer he found pleasure in ranging the coast of France. The more remote his summer quarters the better he was pleased. After his first grief had passed he was persuaded to go into society, and after 1862 he resumed his old friendships and made many new ones. The friends he sought at first were chiefly literary and artistic people.

Browning was only forty-nine when he returned to London to live. The city was not the same place he had left in 1846. The London of the Sixties had assumed much of its modern aspect: it was richer and huger, with perhaps more human débris than ever in its slums. The industrial revolution had done its first work and the pleasant pastures of Camberwell were no more. The gigantic glass-roofed railway stations were the cathedrals of the new age and the coal-smoke went up like incense. Democracy in its fullest modern sense was now politically in its first decade of existence. Disraeli and Gladstone, and indeed all the characters and furniture of the familiar Victorian scene, were now in place and the curtain was about to rise on England's worldly greatness. The air was full of noises and hoarse disputes. Carlyle and Ruskin were the Jeremiahs of the time, but were already a little out-moded. Arnold viewed the gigantic curves of material prosperity too coldly to please the sanguine draughtsmen of those ascending lines. In 1859 Darwin had published his *Origin of Species,* and the rulers of the universe, aghast, peered into the secret of their lowly origin. At the beginning of the Sixties Huxley and Wilberforce were locked in a none too edifying struggle over the theory of evolution. Further, churchmen of all descriptions, High and Broad, and even the Dissenters, shifted uneasily as they saw the rationalism of Germany and France attack with astonishing success the authenticity of the Scriptures.[35]

The shock of this vigorous new world, together with his musings upon life in his summer retreat on the coast of France, produced Browning's next volume of poetry. *Dramatis Personae* is something of a misnomer for the collection of 1864, for the poet is not primarily

[35] For the major direction of Browning's interest in these years see W. O. Raymond's excellent chapter, "Browning and Higher Criticism," in his book *The Infinite Moment and Other Essays in Robert Browning,* 1950. See also C. R. Tracy, "Browning's Heresies," in *Studies in Philology* 33:610–25 (1936).

interested in the characters he portrays; his book is a running commentary upon the topics of tremendous popular interest in that day. For example, A *Death in the Desert* is an excellent imaginary portrait of St. John, but the poem was written in order to restore the personality of the disciple which the rational criticism of Strauss and Renan had all but obliterated. Again, *Caliban,* as vivid as the character of the brutish half-man is, is a subtle study of primitive religious ideas; Shakespeare, Darwin, and Browning join hands most strangely here. One is not justified in saying that *Dramatis Personae* shows a decline in Browning's power, but the sheer creative faculty is in abeyance. The interest in contemporary questions here displayed was to grow until character and melody were all but stifled in "mere grey argument." But the poet of *Dramatis Personae* is happily still a poet. His manner of expression is surely bleaker and craggier than it had been in *Men and Women.* He courts more frequently the sordid and the grotesque and is happy to get the effects of irony by means of verse which is very near doggerel. His language is both nobler and meaner in *Dramatis Personae* as it strives to depict the poet's aspiration and sorrow on one side and his disenchantment with the world on the other. It is a pleasure to record that the British public saw the merit of *Dramatis Personae*. The volume was taken up by the young men of Oxford and Cambridge, and it soon went into a second edition. Browning's works began to be demanded, and four years later when *The Ring and the Book* was published Browning became, second to Tennyson, the most honored living poet of England.

But in 1864 the great poem was still to be written. How the poet found the "Old Yellow Book" on a book-stall in Florence in the brilliant noon of a June day in 1860, and how he devoured the contents on his way home, have been told by Browning himself in the first book of his poem. He carried the book to Rome with him later that year and made inquiries there and in Arezzo, and in his spare moments after his return to England his mind turned towards the Roman murder-story. From a friend in Florence he obtained in 1862 a supplementary document, but there was little time to spare from other affairs before 1864. The genesis of Browning's poem, the way in which the whole artistic conception flashed upon him when he was at the Pas de Roland late in the summer of 1864, has been told by W. O. Raymond.[36] In the following four years the work gradually grew to the mountainous sum of 21,000 lines. Browning

[36] *The Infinite Moment,* Chs. 4 and 5. For the full growth of the poem one

knew it was the effort of his life, and he knew that the subject was made to his hand. The finished poem is the crown of his work, in thought as well as in technique, and into it he put all his skill, ingenuity, and learning. The poem is the apex of his long development of the dramatic monologue, and it must be accounted one of the boldest and most successful experiments in literary history. Several years of his life were consumed in the work. While the poem was being written he had to look after his son's education; perhaps, since he was worried by the lad's failure to progress, he was unwise in not sending him to a public school. His own father, generous and kindly, died in Paris in 1866, and his sister, Sarianna, came to live with him. But the work upon *The Ring and the Book* went steadily forward. Browning adopted what was for him a new method of composition: he devoted three hours a morning to writing and expected of himself so many lines a day. But he still found time to cultivate his love of music and see his old friends, and add new ones, such as the Victorian blue-stocking, Julia Wedgwood, with whom he had an intellectual flirtation.[37]

On November 21, 1868, the first volume of the poem was published, and the other three volumes followed at intervals of a month each, though a fire in the bindery almost upset the arrangements. When the whole had been published the *Athenaeum* led the literary world in its praise: that review called the poem, forgetting for the moment such works as *Paradise Lost* and *The Prelude*, "the most precious and profound spiritual treasure that England has produced since the days of Shakespeare." The early applause gave way to sharp criticism in the immediate years after publication,[38] but in the public mind Browning was linked with Tennyson, Dickens, and Thackeray as one of the great literary figures of the age.

The fame that the young Browning had aimed at was now achieved and the older man was not slow to enjoy it. Honors were heaped upon

must consult A. K. Cook's *Commentary upon Browning's "The Ring and the Book,"* and read the letters for these years in *Letters of Robert Browning,* ed. T. L. Hood. See also Paul A. Cundiff, "The Dating of Browning's Conception of *The Ring and the Book,"* in *Studies in Philology* 38:543–51 (1941).

[37] See *Robert Browning and Julia Wedgwood, A Broken Friendship as Revealed by Their Letters,* ed. Richard Curle, 1937.

[38] See B. R. McElderry, Jr., "Victorian Evaluation of *The Ring and the Book,"* in *Research Studies of the State College of Washington* 7:75–89 (June, 1939), and also Helen P. Pettigrew, "The Early Vogue of *The Ring and the Book,"* in *Archiv* for April, 1936.

him, chiefly by Oxford, and he became a notable figure in society. His son, after failing to get into Balliol, had been admitted to Christ Church, but in the negotiations Browning had gained the friendship of Benjamin Jowett, the master of Balliol. He was fond of Oxford and was present for great festivities. The undergraduates found him genial and entertaining, and he often kept the table in a roar. In 1871 Alfred Domett came back from New Zealand, but found his old friend too much, for his taste, in the company of lords and bishops, and constantly visiting great country houses. To the friend returning after thirty years' absence the change in Browning's way of living was more apparent than it was to the poet himself, no doubt. He had breathed the atmosphere of that society and loved it, and he strove to make himself a part of it. With very mixed motives, we may suppose, in which social prestige played its part, the new expensive way of living of himself and his son, a young man of sporting and artistic propensities, had a share, and the undeniable fascination of the lady herself was a great factor, Browning in the late summer of 1869 proposed marriage to Louisa Lady Ashburton. She was the brilliant and wealthy widow of Baron Ashburton, at this time at the height of her social career. The poet seems to have been painfully frank in telling the lady his less admirable motives for the match: his "heart was buried in Florence," his fame she might have. He was rejected, of course, but the affair was not finally ended until October, 1871. In the meantime there was recrimination and gossip which left Browning fiercely angry at the lady, but even more hating himself for the rest of his life for his disloyalty to his dead wife. His anger and his scorn of himself were to appear in his future poetry, notably in *Fifine at the Fair* (1873) and the *Parleying With Daniel Bartoli* (1887).[39]

Whether acute discomfort drove him, or whether he was unable to shake off the habits of work which the composition of *The Ring and the Book* had induced, it is not easy to say, but the fact is that the Seventies saw volume after volume come from the poet's pen. The books began brilliantly and pleasantly with *Balaustion's Adventure* in 1871, that "May-month amusement" which combines so happily his homage to his dead wife and to her favorite Greek dramatist, Eurip-

[39] See *Letters*, ed. Hood, *Appendix*, "Browning and Lady Ashburton." The fullest account of this affair and Browning's anguish over it may be seen in Raymond, *The Infinite Moment*, Ch. 7, "Browning's Dark Mood: A Study of *Fifine at the Fair*."

ides, into a modern version of the *Alcestis*. This poem, however, was followed by others not pleasing to any but confirmed and determined Browningites. The studies in intricate and slippery psychology which make up the matter of *Hohenstiel-Schwangau, Fifine at the Fair, Red Cotton Night-Cap Country, The Inn Album,* and even *Aristophanes' Apology,* are forbidding to most readers, and the critics of the day found Browning perverse and wayward. The experiences that he had been through, both publicly and privately, had not sweetened his nature; it seems to have been necessary for him from time to time to work off in his writing the bile which collected in his spirit. Yet there are wonderful things in these volumes, as in the *Sordello* of his youth, for those who have patience to read them. Not only is this so in the exquisite and poignant prologues and epilogues where the poet often addresses himself directly to his dead wife, but in the bulk of the long poems as well. One stumbles suddenly upon a warm appreciation of Browning's friend, Milsand, in *Red Cotton Night-Cap Country,* or an elfish description of his own poetry in *The Inn Album,* put into the mouth of the elderly roué:

> That bard's a Browning; he neglects the form:
> But ah, the sense, ye gods, the weighty sense!

Or, in better fortune, one comes upon a subtle exhibition of the serpentine ways of the human heart in *Fifine at the Fair,* or encounters a memorable portrait in *Aristophanes' Apology.* Browning was never entirely safe from his own genius. But in the main these poems show that his creative faculty had given ground to his critical and argumentative faculties, and it is not without significance that each of these long poems was written for an occasion, to controvert some current opinion which Browning believed mistaken. Even *Balaustion's Adventure* seems to have risen out of his strong desire to vindicate the reputation of Euripides from the aspersions of contemporary scholars.

Pride and impatience, the unlovely qualities of Browning's nature, which were only the reverse sides of his virtues of independence and courage, showed themselves unpleasantly in the volume *Of Pacchiarotto, and How He Worked in Distemper* in 1876. All the stored wrath of many years against the critics fell upon the ingrateful top of Alfred Austin, the five-foot critic and poetaster whom the crude jest of the philistine Salisbury was to make poet laureate after the death of Tennyson.[40] "He has been flea-biting me," said Browning, "for many years past in whatever rag of a newspaper he could hop into. . . ." One need not hold to the unnatural etiquette that a poet may not answer his critic to disapprove of *Pacchiarotto*. Nor is one much inclined to think that Austin got more than he deserved. The difficulty is that Browning is so inept that the reader does not share his anger and scorn. The poet's savage jocularity at Austin's expense is not clever enough to be pleasing, and his attempt to match Byron— Austin's favorite poet—in ingenious rhymes is a miserable failure. Regret may be expressed here too that the controversy led Browning to make some very misleading statements concerning the nature of his own poetry in other poems in the volume, such as *House* and *At the Mermaid*. Browning's spirit, if not his reputation, was better for the outpouring of his wrath. The turn came when in 1877 his friend, Miss Anne Egerton Smith, his companion of many musical evenings in the concert-rooms of London, died suddenly at La Saisiaz, the villa she had taken with the Brownings for the summer. The poetic result of this misfortune was the noble and touching philosophical poem, *La Saisiaz*, which shows the poet chastened and subdued.

VI

In 1879 Browning was sixty-seven years old, but he showed no sign of decreasing vigor; rather the opposite, for in that year he published the first series of his *Dramatic Idyls*, and followed it with a second series in the next year. It was a new and surprising impulse: it took the poet away from philosophical argument temporarily, and the short anecdotes in long rolling verse which made up the volumes were culled from all ages and all climates and the stories were told in dramatic narratives with more subtlety than ever. Occasionally Browning pushed subtlety too far and read more into a simple human story than it would bear. But the music was new and the heart did not always lag behind the brain. Perhaps there is, after all, a hint of old age in these volumes, for several of the poems desert the contemporary and are reminiscences of tales that Browning had heard or read long before.

In the memoirs of these years we catch pleasant glimpses of the

[40] See W. L. Phelps, "Alfred Austin and Robert Browning," in the *Yale Review*, N. S. 7:580–91 (April, 1918). See also *Letters*, ed. Hood, pp. 358–63, for an account of the whole controversy.

florid cheeks and the snowy beard and hair of the poet. Mr. E. F. Benson records in *As We Were* that he once saw Browning surrounded by young ladies, crowned with roses and flushed with laughter. Roses will do excellently until the bays are fitted. To the London of the Eighties Browning seemed more a pattern of fashion than a poet, and Mary Gladstone [Drew] was not alone in her playful suggestion that he had a familiar demon at home to write his verses. It was this double aspect of Browning that Henry James observed in his story *The Private Life*. "One man," he wrote, "is the genius, the other's the bourgeois, and it's only the bourgeois whom we personally know." He was always in London during the winter and for the social season in the late spring and early summer, and he was the lion of many a social event. It was said that he would die in his dinner-jacket. No great musical event and no great gallery could be opened properly without his presence. Old friends were about him among the many new, some great and some humble. Best of all, the young men came to see him and received, if their intentions were honorable and their purpose not to extract biographical information from him, such a welcome as Sir Edmund Gosse describes. As one entered one would hear

the loud trumpet-note from the other end of the passage, the talk already in full flood at a distance of twenty feet. Then, in his own study or drawing-room, what he loved was to capture the visitor in a low armchair's "sofa-lap of leather," and from a most unfair vantage of height to tyrannize, to walk around the victim, in front, behind, on this side, on that, weaving magic circles, now with gesticulating arms thrown high, now grovelling on the floor to find some reference in a folio, talking all the while, a redundant turmoil of thoughts, fancies, and reminiscences flowing from those generous lips.[41]

Thus he was in London; but one might prefer to see him in the Italian Alps, pausing in those delectable mountains on his way to Venice. Here he might be seen walking of a morning with his sister, or standing at the window of the inn to watch a snow-fall in August, his finger marking his place in the *Iliad*. At Venice life was gayer; the American ladies who were his hostesses spoiled him a little, as all ladies were inclined to do. He often held their hands ever so little longer than courtesy demanded, and sometimes raised yearnings in aged bosoms.[42] His gondola was ready to take him to the Lido or

[41] *Robert Browning, Personalia*, pp. 81–2. See also the pleasant picture of Browning in undress in W. L. Phelps, "A Conversation with Browning," in *Journal of English Literary History* 11:154–60 (June, 1944).

[42] See, for example, Miller, *Robert Browning*, pp. 286–7.

some part of the city which interested him. He was lapt in soft adulation all day long. Even the Venetians knew he was a great poet and
felt honored by his presence.[43] But perhaps best of all one likes to see
Browning during his last days at "delicious Asolo," thinking and remembering, watching the sunset, playing at dusk upon the spinet the
almost forgotten songs of his youth. As he climbed the hills of Asolo
again after fifty years, he found that the former magic had fled:

> And now? The lambent flame is—where?
>   Lost from the naked world: earth, sky,
> Hill, vale, tree, flower,—Italia's rare
>   O'er-running beauty crowds the eye—
> But flame? The Bush is bare.

But surely the most persistent mood of the poet's later years was
brought to him by a memory:

> Perhaps but a memory, after all!
>   —Of what came once when a woman leant
> To feel for my brow where her kiss might fall.

But this is to anticipate. In 1882 the reminiscences and musings of
an old man still seemed distant to Browning. He was yet in full vigor,
and work was to be done in the world. The mixture of the grave and
the gay which the poet called *Jocoseria* appeared in 1883. It shows the
dramatic impulse which had rejuvenated his work in the *Dramatic
Idyls* slowly subsiding. The volume is a collection of anecdotes, several of them drawn from rabbinical lore, which serve to point Browning's ideas. In 1884 he published *Ferishtah's Fancies,* and here under
the thin disguise of a Persian sage set himself up as a philosopher—
as he often did in his later years—to defend the tenets of the genuine
Christian faith which he held. Perhaps he was persuaded by the heavy
adulation of the flourishing Browning Society that he could settle the
ills of the world. But his early education was at fault, and like most
self-educated men he had no good notion of the history which lies
behind ideas. *Ferishtah's Fancies* has good poetry in it, mainly in the
lyrics and in the *Epilogue* where a sudden fear assails him that he
may have been grossly mistaken in his reading of life; but "mere grey
argument" prevails, and it is not very good argument. This poem was
followed in 1887 by the *Parleyings With Certain People of Importance in Their Day,* a series of poems surprising in their boldness of

[43] See Mrs. Katherine deKay Bronson, "Browning in Venice," in the *Century
Magazine* for February, 1902.

method and their modernity of diction. Here Browning attempts with considerable skill to chart his own position among his great contemporaries, and to reckon up the major influences which operated upon his mind in his youth.[44] The men with whom he ostensibly parleyed—Mandeville, Bartoli, Lairesse, and others—were an extremely odd lot, and were often misjudged. But they were merely starting points for his comments upon the world as he saw it in 1887. The habit of dealing with contemporary ideas and with living men of his own day in his poetry had been growing upon him since 1855, and is probably the most significant trait of his later poetry. That characteristic finds its apotheosis in the *Parleyings*. And then in December, 1889, his last volume, *Asolando*, was published, a collection of short poems astonishing for their freshness. The ever green heart of the poet at seventy-seven could still write love-lyrics like a lad of twenty, and could give us besides the aged, sweet wine of reminiscence.

While this work was being done life went on as busily as ever. Honors were heaped upon him. In 1881 the Browning Society had been founded in London with Dr. F. J. Furnivall, the Shakespearean and Chaucerian scholar, as its leader. It was at once a pleasure and an embarrassment to the poet; he was flattered, but at the same time he saw the grotesque aspect of the Society. At Oxford he was still a favorite, and when he was granted a D.C.L., a waggish undergraduate lowered a red cotton night-cap on his head, to the consternation of the authorities, but to the amusement of Browning. With great acclaim also he received degrees from Cambridge and Edinburgh. These years were full of social activity, and the poet was to be seen making his courtly bow to duchesses and countesses at the "greenery-yallery Grosvenor Gallery" where his son, now a full-fledged but not very talented painter, exhibited, or sitting beside Gladstone at some fashionable dinner. In his private affairs, he was much pleased to see his son married to Miss Fannie Coddington, a charming American lady. The young couple settled at Venice and nothing could have delighted him more, unless, indeed, they had lived near him in London. His own income, drawn partly from his legacies from Kenyon and his wife, and more from the sale of her books and his, was a very comfortable one in his last years,[45] and he

---

[44] See William Clyde DeVane, *Browning's Parleyings, The Autobiography of a Mind*, New Haven, 1927, *passim*.

[45] See Roma A. King, *Robert Browning's Finances from his own Account Book*, in *Baylor University Browning Interests*, Series Fifteen, 1947.

had no need, he thought, to worry further about Pen's extravagances.

Life was not without its disappointments and sorrows, public and private. When Gladstone announced himself in 1885–6 as in favor of Home Rule for Ireland Browning parted company with him in politics and somewhat in friendship. The poet could still call himself "Liberal," as he did in a sonnet of 1885, *Why I am a Liberal*. But the kind of Liberalism he describes there is the doctrine of *laissez-faire,* the intensely individualistic conception which early Victorian England had learned from Carlyle and the Mills. He was not the Liberal he was in 1840, with a quick and eager sympathy for the masses of men, a champion of the oppressed, an ardent believer in Shelley's doctrines. He had long since regretted his youthful assault on Wordsworth in *The Lost Leader.* He now consorted with the great of the land, and the early sharer in the hope of a liberated Italy had now no sympathy for the aspirations of Ireland. He threatened to write a five-act play against women's suffrage, but luckily that was not perpetrated. He had espoused the orthodox and economic conception of Liberalism of a later time, and it was merely an accident that Liberalism kept its name while its tenets shifted. Political nomenclature had dealt kindly with the poet, and he was still able to call himself a Liberal.

But Gladstone's defection was a small grief. The death of his friends was worse. Carlyle had gone in 1881, leaving a gap not entirely filled, though Browning had come to think less kindly of him. In 1886 his dear friend and companion Joseph Milsand died, and that was a severe blow. Matthew Arnold, with whom Browning had been cordial rather than intimate, died in 1888. In July, 1889, a sharper grief came to him. At the Athenaeum Club he opened a new book, the *Letters of Edward FitzGerald,* edited by Aldis Wright, and unfortunately happened upon a passage which the editor should have deleted. FitzGerald had said, brutally perhaps, but surely for the eyes of none save his correspondent,

Mrs. Browning's death is rather a relief to me, I must say: no more Aurora Leighs, thank God! A woman of real genius, I know; but what is the upshot of it all? She and her sex had better mind the kitchen and the children; and perhaps the poor.

Anger, like that which wrenched the frame of Lear's nature, seized upon Browning. He wrote and sent off to the *Athenaeum* magazine a most violent and vituperative sonnet, without allowing his sister her usual rights of censorship. Though he attempted to withdraw it, it was published on July 13. The sonnet caused an uproar, but its worst effects were upon Browning's heart. The whole incident wounded and pained him beyond expression; he was haunted by the remembrance of it, and I have no doubt it hastened his end.

It has been observed that in his last days Browning seemed to have prepared unconsciously for his death.[46] In 1888–9 he saw the great final collected edition of his works published in sixteen volumes. In the fall of 1889 he journeyed over the Alps again to Italy, and came to Asolo to dwell once more with his memories and to pay his farewells to old friends. On November 1 he went down to Venice, and there with his sister made his home in his son's house, the Palazzo Rezzonico. Late in the month he caught cold from walking in the rain on the Lido.[47] Bronchitis developed and induced heart-failure. In his last illness he was kindness and consideration itself to those about him. On the last day of his life *Asolando,* his final volume of poetry, was published in London; the reviews appeared promptly, and the news of its enthusiastic reception, telegraphed to him by his publishers, deeply gratified him. He died on December 12, at ten o'clock in the evening. On the last day of the year he was buried in the Poets' Corner in Westminster Abbey.

In the course of his long career as a poet he had suffered more than most poets from the excesses of both contumely and laudation. He triumphed over both at last, but not before the laudation had done damage to the quality of his poetic achievement. To his later contemporaries his poetry and his presence had become the very symbols of heartiness, courage, and faith. Some of his spirit has lingered to us who live in a disenchanted world. Yet the critics of our own day are inclined to disregard much of what Browning says, and to fasten intently upon how he says it. He is now seen to have been a pioneer and a revolutionist in the art of the new psychological poetry, a century before his time; and this aspect, at least, of his present fame would have delighted Robert Browning.

[46] See Griffin and Minchin, *Life,* p. 279.

[47] A vivid and authentic account of the last illness and the burial of Browning is given by his daughter-in-law, Mrs. Fannie Barrett Browning, in her little book, *Some Memories of Robert Browning,* Boston, 1928. See also the "Diary of Miss Evelyn Barclay," in *Baylor University Browning Interests,* Fifth Series, 1932, pp. 5–10.

⁂ II ⁂

EARLY POEMS

※━━━━━━━━━━━━━━━━━━━━━━━━━━━━━━━━━━※

PAULINE

PUBLICATION

Pauline, Browning's first published poem, appeared under the imprint of Saunders and Otley, but at the poet's own expense, in March, 1833. Browning's aunt, Mrs. Silverthorne, had given him £30 for the publication, of which £26 5s was spent for the cost of printing, and the remainder for advertising. The little octavo volume, bound in drab paper-covered boards with a white label, was published anonymously—not even the publishers, it is said, being aware of the author's identity. It consisted of a title-page: "Pauline; A Fragment of a Confession. Plus ne suis ce que j'ai été, Et ne le sçaurois jamais être. Marot. London: Saunders and Otley, Conduit Street. 1833."; a prefatory note in Latin from "H. Cor. Agrippa, *De Occult. Phil.*" which was dated "London, January, 1833. V.A. XX."; and the text, pp. 5–71. The poem consisted of 1031 lines of blank verse, and the note in French attached to line 811, purporting to be written by Pauline. The poem was dated at the end, "Richmond, October 22, 1832."

TEXT

Pauline was not republished until thirty-five years later, when Browning included it in the collected edition of 1868, with an explanation in an introductory note:

The first piece in the series [*Pauline*], I acknowledge and retain with extreme repugnance, indeed purely of necessity; for not long ago I inspected one, and am certified of the existence of other transcripts, intended sooner or later to be published abroad: by forestalling these, I can at least correct some misprints (no syllable is changed). . . .

This statement upon the text of the edition of 1868 is not entirely accurate: one or two words have been added, and several have been changed; and the punctuation underwent a thorough revision. The poem was also included in the final collected edition of 1888. Here Browning reprinted the introductory note of 1868 and supplemented it with another, which read in part:

Twenty years' endurance of an eyesore seems more than sufficient: my faults remain duly recorded against me, and I claim permission to somewhat diminish these, so far as style is concerned, in the present and final edition where "Pauline" must needs, first of my performances, confront the reader. I have simply removed solecisms, mended the metre a little, and endeavoured to strengthen the phraseology—experience helping, in some degree, the helplessness of juvenile haste and heat in their untried adventure long ago.

Apparently the revision of *Pauline* was done on an impulse after the proofs of the first volume of the 1888 edition were in Browning's hands.[1] In the edition of 1888 the number of lines remained the same, but the changes in phrase, word, meter and punctuation were very considerable.[2] Perhaps the most significant change was made in line 884, where Browning attempted to define the function of the poet:

> 1833: And then thou said'st a perfect bard was one
> Who shadowed out the stages of all life . . .
> 1888: And then thou said'st a perfect bard was one
> Who chronicled the stages of all life. . . .

The difference implied in the single word is great: the earlier version reveals the autobiographical and confessional poet of 1833; the later shows the "dramatic" poet which he strove to become. In 1886 Mr. T. J. Wise published for the Browning Society of London a type-facsimile of the first edition of *Pauline*.

GENESIS AND COMPOSITION

The date, "October 22, 1832," which Browning appended to *Pauline,* was, curiously, not the date of composition, but of the conception of the poem. That evening Browning had gone to Richmond, ten miles from home, to see Edmund Kean perform in Shakespeare's *Richard III.* A pencilled note in Browning's own copy of *Pauline* explains:

[1] See Orr, *Life*, p. 380.
[2] See N. H. Wallis, *Pauline, by Robert Browning, The Text of 1833, Compared with that of 1867 and 1888.* Edited with an Introduction and Notes, London, 1931.

Kean was acting there; I saw him in *Richard III* that night and conceived the childish scheme. . . . There is an allusion to Kean, page 47 [ll. 669–75]. I don't know whether I had not made up my mind to *act* as well as to make verses, music, and God know what,—*que de châteaux en Espagne!* [3]

In a more famous copy of *Pauline*, once in the possession of John Stuart Mill, Browning explained the childish scheme referred to above. On the fourth page of this copy Browning wrote, sometime before giving the book to John Forster, these words:

The following Poem was written in pursuance of a foolish plan which occupied me mightily for a time, and which had for its object the enabling me to assume & realize I know not how many different characters;—meanwhile the world was never to guess that "Brown, Smith, Jones & Robinson" (as the spelling books have it) the respective authors of this poem, the other novel, such an opera, such a speech, etc. etc. were no other than one and the same individual. The present abortion was the first work of the *Poet* of the batch, who would have been more legitimately *myself* than most of the others; but I surrounded him with all manner of (to my then notion) poetical accessories, and had planned quite a delightful life for him.

Only this crab remains of the shapely Tree of Life in this Fool's paradise of mine.—R. B. [4]

Such was the grandiose conception of which *Pauline* was to be a part.

The poem was written hastily—"on one leg" as Browning wrote W. J. Fox [5]—between October 22, 1832, and January, 1833, the date appended to the Latin quotation from Henricus Cornelius Agrippa. The letters "V.A. XX." which appear under the latter date were explained by Browning as "the Latin abbreviation of Vixi Annos [Viginti]—'I was twenty years old'—that is, the imaginary subject of the poem was of that age." [6] At that time Browning himself was precisely the age of the imaginary subject. I quote part of F. A. Pottle's translation of the Latin passage from Cornelius Agrippa which served as a preface:

I have no doubt that the title of our book may by its unusual character entice very many to read it, and that among them some of biased opinions, with weak minds—many even hostile and churlish—will attack our genius, who in the rashness of their ignorance will cry out, almost before they have read the title, that we are teaching forbidden things, are scattering the seeds

[3] Quoted in Griffin and Minchin, *Life*, p. 45.

[4] This copy of *Pauline* is now in the Forster and Dyce Collection in the Victoria and Albert Museum, where I have seen it. For the fullest list of Mill's notes on *Pauline*, see W. L. Phelps, "Notes on Browning's *Pauline*," in *MLN* 47:292–9 (May, 1932).

[5] Orr, *Life*, p. 52.

[6] *Letters*, ed. Hood, p. 256.

of heresies, that we are an annoyance to righteous ears, to enlightened
minds an object of offense. . . . To these I now give counsel not to read
our book, neither to understand it nor remember it; for it is harmful, poison-
ous; the gate of Hell is in this book. . . . On the other hand, if you find
things which do not please you, pass over them and make no use of them.
FOR I DO NOT RECOMMEND THESE THINGS TO YOU: I MERELY
TELL YOU OF THEM. Yet do not on that account reject the rest. Therefore if anything has been said rather freely, forgive my youth; I wrote this
work when I was less than a youth.

In the edition of 1888 Browning added a note to the Latin. He said,
somewhat shamefacedly, "This introduction would appear less ab-
surdly pretentious did it apply, as was intended, to a completed structure of which the poem was meant for only a beginning and remains
a fragment."

SOURCES AND INFLUENCES

Pauline purports to be an account, from a young man of twenty
to his love, Pauline, of his victory over the forces of doubt, skepticism,
and self-centeredness, and his winning to faith, hope, and love. The
poem is thoroughly autobiographical, and in spite of his later declara-
tions, Browning is the speaker, hardly disguised at all. It was Mrs.
Orr's opinion that the poem was addressed to Eliza Flower, musical
and talented and beautiful, nine years older than Browning. "If, in
spite of his denials," says Mrs. Orr, "any woman inspired *Pauline*, it
can be none other than she." [7] This is probably true, but that Browning was passionately in love with any woman at the time can hardly
be deduced from the poem. John Stuart Mill, in a shrewd analysis of
the poem which he made for a projected review (discussed below),
made a true analysis of the heart of the young author:

I should think it a sincere confession, though of a most unlovable state, if the
'Pauline' were not evidently a mere phantom. All about her is full of inconsistency—he neither loves her nor fancies he loves her, yet insists upon
talking love to her. If she *existed* and loved him, he treats her most un-
generously and unfeelingly. All his aspirings and yearnings and regrets
point to other things, never to her; then he *pays her off* toward the end by
a piece of flummery, amounting to the modest request that she will love
him and live with him and give herself up to him *without* his *loving her*—

[7] Orr, *Life*, p. 35. For the best account of the Flower sisters see M. D. Conway,
Centenary of South Place, London, 1894, *passim.* See also Miller, *Robert Browning,* pp. 29–46, where an excellent account of the Flower sisters is given. The
contention of M. H.-L. Hovelaque in *La Jeunesse de Robert Browning,* Paris,
1932, pp. 117–20, that Sarah Flower, two years younger than Eliza, is Pauline,
does not seem to me well supported.

moyennant quoi he will think her and call her everything that is handsome, and he promises her that she shall find it mighty pleasant.

That is to say, Pauline is a mere lay figure. Browning was making poetic material of a boyish infatuation that was past. Eliza Flower also was soon afterwards to comment on the young poet's arrogance and lack of heart.[8]

The real matter of *Pauline* is Browning's struggle with his religious skepticism between the years 1826 and 1832. In the latter year he thought himself well cured. Before 1826 he seems to have accepted entirely, with only an occasional unruliness, the Non-Conformist principles of his devout and pious mother, and he accompanied her regularly to York Chapel. But in 1826 his growing mind and his wide reading brought him to challenge that faith. He chanced upon Voltaire in his father's library, and soon by his pertinacious questions had upset Sarah Flower's "firm belief in the genuineness of the Scriptures." In November, 1827, she wrote to her guardian, W. J. Fox,

The cloud has come over me gradually, and I did not discover the darkness in which my soul was shrouded until, in seeking to give light to others, my gloomy state became too settled to admit of doubt. It was in answering Robert Browning that my mind refused to bring forward argument, turned recreant, and sided with the enemy. . . .[9]

Sarah Flower, it should be said, lived down her doubts sufficiently to write the hymn, *Nearer, My God, to Thee,* at a later date.

Almost, or quite as soon, as Browning discovered Voltaire, he made the acquaintance of Shelley's poetry through a copy of the lyrics, entitled *Miscellaneous Poems,* published piratically by William Benbow in 1826.[10] This book was given to Browning, probably as soon as published, by his cousin James Silverthorne. The effect of Shelley upon Browning was instantaneous and tremendous. His mother seems to have procured him all of Shelley's works then available, and after Shelley's counsel in *Queen Mab* he became atheist and vegetarian. The older poet's fiery notes to *Queen Mab* and his general practice of writing notes on his poetry may have suggested the Latin and French notes which Browning attached to *Pauline.* How rever-

[8] Miller, *Robert Browning,* p. 47.

[9] M. D. Conway, *Centenary of South Place,* p. 46.

[10] See F. A. Pottle, *Shelley and Browning, A Myth and Some Facts,* Chicago, 1923, pp. 14 ff. Professor Pottle effectively dispels the old myth that Browning was first acquainted with *Queen Mab,* "Mr. Shelley's Atheistical Poem"; and gives as well a succinct analysis of Shelley's influence upon *Pauline,* pp. 34–64. Cp. H.-L. Hovelaque, *La Jeunesse de Browning,* pp. 130–7, 146–57.

ently Browning still regarded Shelley in 1833, even after freeing himself from Shelley's atheism, may be seen in the famous "Sun-treader" lines in *Pauline* (ll. 151–229, 1020–31). Even the casual reader can now see that *Alastor* is the poetic model upon which Browning's poem was formed. The cadences, the fervor, and some of the images owe directly to Shelley. This influence was felt strongly by the younger poet until he was well on in middle life.

Pauline is much more than a song in honor of Shelley: it is in a wider sense Browning's autobiography to his twentieth year, at once his *Sartor Resartus* and his *Prelude*. Most of all he tells of his doubt and despair in adolescence and his return to faith and health. He celebrates the "wisest ancient books" which he read in his father's library. These are mainly Greek—the *Iliad* (l. 325), Plato (l. 435), Aeschylus' *Agamemnon* (l. 567), and Sophocles' *Oedipus* (l. 573). Then there is an astonishing account of what music means to him (l. 365). The delight which he took in Kean's acting (l. 669) has already been mentioned. Caravaggio's *Andromeda,* the "perfect" picture which stood before him as he wrote, represented the art of painting and is described in a passage (l. 656) which was in time to become the perfect symbol of his faith. The star-image in *Pauline,* applying both to Pauline and to poetic aspiration, has a structural function in the poem.[11] Then, too, in *Pauline* Browning's delight in nature is unrestrained, and the imaginary country to which Pauline is to be wafted —a little in the manner of Shelley at the close of *Epipsychidion*—is magnificent. Besides this Browning tells us of his own progress in poetry (ll. 377–404), and shows us that he is musing on the nature and the function of the poet (l. 883). *Pauline* is a comprehensive account of the mind and spirit of the young Browning.[12] It is the story of the revolt of the gifted and proud young man's reason against the narrow religious and social beliefs of his home. It also records his capitulation to his mother's faith. But, as Mill noticed, his restlessness, his desire for freedom, and his youthful self-centeredness have not been entirely subdued.

[11] See C. Willard Smith, *Browning's Star-Imagery,* 1941, pp. 8–9 and 15–6.

[12] M. Hovelaque in his *La Jeunesse de Browning,* pp. 121–5, draws the interesting parallel between *Pauline* and Balzac's *Louis Lambert.* The two are strikingly alike in some details, and the latter was published in 1832. But M. Hovelaque wisely concludes that it cannot be proved that Browning read Balzac at this early age.

When *Pauline* was published, about March 7, 1833, it was noticed by only four or five magazines. Browning sent twelve copies of the poem to his "literary god-father," W. J. Fox, editor of the *Monthly Repository,* and Fox distributed them for review. At Browning's request, Fox himself reviewed *Pauline* in his own magazine [13] and was most enthusiastic. He recognized the poem's "truth and life," in spite of its being "a hasty and imperfect sketch," and said,

In recognizing a poet we cannot stand upon trifles, nor fret ourselves about such matters. Time enough for that afterwards, when larger works come before us. Archimedes in the bath had many particulars to settle about specific gravities and Hiero's crown; but he first gave a glorious leap and shouted *Eureka!*

The young author wrote gratefully to Fox, "I shall never write a line without thinking of the source of my first praise, be assured." On April 6, 1833, a second favorable review appeared; the magazine was the new *Athenaeum* and the critic was Allan Cunningham. After a few strictures upon the want of melody here and there and upon an element of mystery which he did not like, Cunningham said,

. . . all that, however, is as a grain of sand in a cup of pure water, compared to the nature, passion, and fancy of the poem. We open the book at random; but fine things abound: there is no difficulty in finding passages to vindicate our praise. . . .

There seem to have been no more favorable reviews. The *Literary Gazette* of March 23 had a four-line depreciatory notice of *Pauline,* and *Tait's Edinburgh Magazine* for August (No. 17:668) described the poem as "a piece of pure bewilderment." Browning was to say years afterwards that not a single copy of *Pauline* had been sold, and that a bale of unbound sheets was sent home to him and subsequently destroyed.[14] Only twenty-one copies of *Pauline* are now known to exist; and a copy is said to have sold for $16,000 in 1929.[15]

By far the most important copy of *Pauline* is the one now in the Forster and Dyce Collection in the Victoria and Albert Museum in Kensington. This copy was sent by Fox to John Stuart Mill for review. Mill wrote his comments upon the margins, and on the blank pages

[13] *Monthly Repository,* N. S. 7:254–62 (April, 1833). See also Orr, *Life,* pp. 52–4.
[14] *Letters,* ed. Hood, p. 251.
[15] See the census of "First Editions of Browning's *Pauline*," by Mary Dean Reneau, in *Baylor University Browning Interests,* Second Series, 1931, pp. 41–50.

at the end he wrote his general criticism.[16] When Mill's review for the *Examiner* was anticipated, he sent the copy of *Pauline* back to Fox, and Fox returned it to Browning. Mill's strictures were severe. He began with these words:

> With considerable poetic powers, the writer seems to me possessed with a more intense and morbid self-consciousness than I ever knew in any sane human being.

After his comments on the author's imagined love for Pauline (quoted above), Mill finds much in the poem to praise. There are many beautiful passages, he says,

> and the psychological history of himself is powerful and truthful—*truth-like* certainly, all but the last stage. *That,* he evidently has not yet got into. The self-seeking and self-worshipping state is well described—beyond that, I should think the writer had made, as yet, only the next step, viz. into despising his own state. I even question whether part even of that self-disdain is not *assumed.* He is evidently *dissatisfied,* and feels part of the badness of his state; he does not write as if it were purged out of him. If he once could muster a hearty hatred of his selfishness it would *go;* as it is, he feels only the lack of *good,* not the positive evil. He feels not remorse, but only disappointment; a mind in that state can only be regenerated by some new passion, and I know not what to wish for him but that he may meet with a *real* Pauline.
>
> Meanwhile he should not attempt to show how a person may be *recovered* from this morbid state,—for *he* is hardly convalescent, and "what should we speak of but that which we know?" [17]

[16] See above, n. 4. Mill's general critique appears in Griffin and Minchin, *Life,* pp. 59–60. Mill's review seems to have been prepared for the *Examiner,* and when it was declined by that magazine it was sent to *Tait's* where it was anticipated by the review for August referred to above. (See Lewis F. Haines, "Mill and *Pauline:* the 'Review' that 'Retarded Browning's Fame'," in *MLN* 69:410–2 (June, 1944). Browning's comment to F. W. Farrar (*Men I Have Known,* N.Y., 1897, pp. 64–5) that Mill's review would have speeded his fame is hardly borne out by Mill's notes.

[17] The history of this famous copy of *Pauline* is interesting. Some doubts have recently been cast upon the assumption that all the notes are by Mill, and Mrs. Miller advances the idea that some of them are by Harriet Taylor, who later married Mill. (See *Robert Browning,* p. 40.) In any case Mill returned the volume to Fox on October 10, saying that he had done all he could in his marginal annotations and his summary, and adding, "On the whole the observations are not flattering to the author—perhaps too strong in the expression to be shown to him." Browning, however, did get the copy on October 30. Mrs. Miller cites some evidence to indicate that the book might have been still in his possession on December 14, 1838. Sometime later, probably in 1842, he gave the book to John Forster. Browning did not have it in 1868 or 1888 when he prepared *Pauline* for later editions; but after some vicissitudes it was restored in 1899 to the Forster and Dyce Collection.

This critique changed the course of Browning's poetical career. He had exposed his callow soul in his first poem, and the shrewd Mill had seen it. On October 30, 1833, Browning read Mill's criticism with care and attention. He studied Mill's comments in the margins and made long and documented answers beneath them. But his main resolve was that never again would he reveal his own soul so crudely—henceforth his poetry would be "dramatic in principle, and so many utterances of so many imaginary persons, not mine." [18] From this incident dates Browning's "extreme repugnance" to *Pauline*. His next poem, *Paracelsus,* was to be a dramatic poem in five acts. Mrs. Clara Bloomfield-Moore, a friend of Browning's later years, reported:

In the presence of a third person, with one exception, I never heard Mr. Browning speak of himself, nor of his poems. This exception was when Bishop Potter dined with him at my house: to him he spoke unreservedly, for each found in the other a kindred spirit. I remember the poet gave us the history of *Pauline,* and also that he said his early poems were so transparent in their meaning as to draw down upon him the ridicule of the critics, and that, boy as he was, this ridicule and censure stung him into quite another style of writing.[19]

After 1833 Browning did his best to forget *Pauline.* For many years few of his friends were aware of its existence. In January, 1846, he tantalized Miss Barrett with a promise to show her *Pauline,* but the thought of the poem was painful to him. In 1847 Joseph Arnould, a very close friend, heard of the poem somehow, and wrote to their mutual friend Alfred Domett in New Zealand, who had obviously never heard of it, describing it as

a strange, wild (in parts singularly magnificent) poet-biography: his own early life as it presented itself to his own soul viewed poetically: in fact, psychologically speaking, his "Sartor Resartus": it was written and published three [two] years before "Paracelsus," when Shelley was his God.[20]

On October 17, 1847, Dante Gabriel Rossetti, a great admirer of *Sordello,* read *Pauline* in the British Museum, copied it, and wrote to Browning in Florence taxing him with its authorship.[21] After the publication of *Dramatis Personae* in 1864, when Browning's fame had risen, a number of people seem to have been aware that *Pauline* was

[18] See Browning's introductory note to *Pauline* in the edition of 1868. Browning used the same phrases to describe the whole nature of his poetry on several occasions.

[19] *Lippincott's Magazine* 45:691 (May, 1890).

[20] F. G. Kenyon, *Robert Browning and Alfred Domett,* p. 141.

[21] *The Browning Collections* (Sotheby Catalogue, 1913), p. 57.

his. Moncure Conway, in his review of the three-volume edition of 1863, "regrets the omission" of *Pauline,* a poem "in every way worthy" of the poet.[22] In a letter to R. H. Shepherd on February 1, 1867, Browning gave him reluctant permission to publish a few extracts from *Pauline,* but stipulated that Shepherd "preface these with mention of the fact that the poem was purely dramatic and intended to head a series of 'Men & Women' such as I have after- wards introduced to the world under somewhat better aus- pices . . . ," and he forbade Shepherd to make a single remark upon the passages.[23] Such pressure as this caused Browning to include *Pauline,* though "with extreme repugnance," in the collected edition of 1868. We have seen what pains Browning took in his introductory notes to the poem in 1868 and 1888 and in the changes he introduced into the latter version to persuade the world that even *Pauline* was "dramatic in principle." The world has persisted in reading it, how- ever, in the light of its sub-title, "A Fragment of a Confession," and is convinced that the confession is the author's own. It is equally persuaded that the opprobrium which Browning heaped upon it was not deserved.

PARACELSUS

PUBLICATION

Paracelsus was published on Saturday, August 15, 1835. The volume, bound in drab boards with a white paper label, consisted of the half-title; the title-page: "Paracelsus. By Robert Browning. London: Published by Effingham Wilson, Royal Exchange. MDCCC- XXXV."; the dedication: "Inscribed to the Comte A. De Ripert- Monclar, By his Affectionate Friend, Robert Browning."; a preface dated "15th March, 1835"; a list of persons; the text, pp. 1–200; and a note, pp. 203–16. The volume was sold at Six Shillings the copy. Though Browning was helped to a publisher by his old friend, W. J. Fox, to whom he had read the poem in manuscript, the expense of publication was borne by his father. *Paracelsus* did not pass into a

---

[22] This review appeared in the *Victoria Magazine* 2:298–316 (February, 1864). Browning had referred to *Pauline* in a letter to Conway on September 17, 1863; see *New Letters,* ed. DeVane and Knickerbocker, pp. 157–8.

[23] W. L. Phelps, *Browning,* Indianapolis, 1932, p. 382. For a fuller account of Browning's relations with Shepherd, see W. L. Phelps, "Notes on Browning's *Pauline,*" in *MLN* 47:292–9 (May, 1932). Shepherd did not print the extracts.

second edition, but as a result of the suppression of the anonymous *Pauline* it stood as the first work of Browning in the collected editions of 1849 and 1863, and was second in the collected editions of 1868 and 1888.

TEXT

The manuscript of *Paracelsus,* consisting of fifty-six leaves in Browning's hand and three pictures of the Renaissance physician, was given in 1842 to "John Forster, Esq. (my early Understander) with true thanks for his generous & seasonable public confession of faith in me." It is now in the Forster and Dyce Collection of the Victoria and Albert Museum in Kensington. The manuscript does not have the dedication to Ripert-Monclar which appeared in the first edition. The manuscript of *Paracelsus* is made up of 4062 lines, divided as follows: I—824 lines; II—614; III—1061; IV—670; V—893.

The first edition of *Paracelsus* consists of 4152 lines, all in blank verse save the three songs; almost a hundred lines were added to the text while the poem was in the press. Almost fifty of the new lines were given to Part II, and the rest were scattered throughout. Later editions of *Paracelsus* did not alter considerably in bulk—the edition of 1888 had 4151 lines—but within the bulk very considerable changes in the text were made; [1] lines were omitted and new ones put in their places, words were altered and the punctuation revised. Most of the changes were made for the collected edition of 1849, though alterations continued to appear in the successive editions of 1863, 1868, and 1888. A great many of the changes before 1849 attempted to strengthen the speeches of Festus so that his arguments with Paracelsus would seem less one-sided.

GENESIS AND COMPOSITION

In his preface, dated March 15, 1835, Browning asked the indulgence of his readers "towards a poem which had not been imagined six months ago." On March 1, 1834, Browning had set out for Russia

---

[1] See *Browning Society's Papers,* I, 87–9, for "Sample of the End-Changed, Fresh, and Left-Out Lines in *Paracelsus,* Eds. 1835 and 1863." See Cooke, *Guide-Book,* pp. 265–79, for a fuller collation. See especially Bernice Fox, "Revision in Browning's *Paracelsus,*" in *MLN* 55:195–6 (March, 1940). The poem was revised four times and only 1477 lines remain identical with those of the first edition. The great bulk of the changes were made in 1849 for the sake of clarity and smoothness, but the characterization of Aprile was notably strengthened. In the edition of 1863 (after Mrs. Browning's death) 442 lines reverted to their original form and so remained in later editions.

with the Chevalier George de Benkhausen, and was absent from London about two months. Upon his return he was much in the company of the Comte Amédée de Ripert-Monclar, a French Royalist associated, like Browning's uncles, with the Rothschild banking interests, and it was that gentleman who suggested to Browning the Renaissance physician as a subject for poetry.[2] The idea was most congenial to Browning, and early in October, 1834, when he had just recovered from a fever and a bad throat, he began to write the poem.[3] Paracelsus seems to have been already familiar to his father, and several books about him were in the Browning library. Browning himself had attended for a time Dr. Blundell's lectures in medicine at Guy's Hospital. The subject was taken, and the poem was written during the fall of 1834 and the first three months of 1835. That the form of the poem was somewhat dramatic, with persons, acts, places, and times given—though it was still a poem and not a play, as Browning carefully pointed out in his preface—was owing largely to John Stuart Mill's criticism of *Pauline*.

SOURCES AND INFLUENCES

We may read, with caution, a good deal of the character and aspirations of the young Browning in *Paracelsus*.[4] The poem, like *Pauline*, has much autobiography in it; but it is also something of a young man's prospectus of life—he sends Paracelsus and Aprile like spies before him into the strange land. Paracelsus has many of the traits of his creator. In *Pauline* (ll. 620–9) the speaker had aspired "to know," yet he knew that he would perish if he pursued that ambition to the exclusion of all others. Paracelsus makes this mistake, and his character is ambitious, self-sufficient, rebellious, and arrogant, of "wondrous plans and dreams and hopes," early disillusioned, and destined to be triumphant. The influence of Shelley, who had done so much to form the nature of the speaker of *Pauline*, is not far away from *Paracelsus*. As one who desires to save mankind Paracelsus resembles Prometheus; but more particularly from *Alastor* (which had already done service as a model for *Pauline*) Browning

[2] Orr, *Life*, p. 72.

[3] *Robert Browning and Julia Wedgwood*, ed. Curle, p. 86.

[4] Mrs. Miller in *Robert Browning* (Part I. "A Garden in the Environs") reads autobiography extensively into *Paracelsus*: the opening scene is Camberwell, the poet's father and mother are models for Festus and Michal, and of course Browning himself is the aspiring and restless Paracelsus.

derives the character of his hero.[5] In his preface to *Alastor* (1816)
Shelley describes his young man as "one who drinks deep of the fountain of knowledge and is still insatiate"; and there Shelley recognizes
the need of coupling Love with Knowledge ere his hero "descends
into an untimely grave." At the close of his preface Shelley points
the moral that those who

. . . keep aloof from sympathies with their kind, rejoicing neither in human
joy nor mourning with human grief; these, and such as they, have their
apportioned curse. They languish, because none feel with them their common nature. They are morally dead. They are neither friends, nor lovers,
nor fathers, nor citizens of the world, nor benefactors of their country. . . .
Those who love not their fellow-beings, live unfruitful lives, and prepare
for their old age a miserable grave.

Such is the character and fate of Paracelsus. Certain details as well
are borrowed from *Alastor:* the "grey hair, faded hands and furrowed
brow" of the twenty-eight-year-old Paracelsus are taken from the
"scattered hair, sered by the autumn of strange suffering" and the
"listless hands" of Shelley's hero. But the effect of Shelley upon
Browning's poem is even greater, for it is probable that Shelley's own
personality and his career provided the younger poet with a model
for the figure of Aprile, the poet who would *love* as infinitely as
Paracelsus would *know*.[6]

Yet the meaning of *Paracelsus* is by no means completely conveyed in the contrast between Aprile the lover and Paracelsus the
knower. Professor W. O. Raymond has shown that there are two
forces at work in the poem: there is the temper of infinite aspiration
which is born of the Romantic poets and Shelley in particular; there
is also the temper which needs the finite and demands that the idealist "fit to the finite his infinity." To these two tempers correspond the

[5] The effect of Shelley upon *Paracelsus* is excellently described in Griffin and
Minchin, *Life*, pp. 66–8; see also F. A. Pottle, *Shelley and Browning, A Myth and
Some Facts*, pp. 55–64.

[6] See the excellent analysis of *Paracelsus* in E. D. H. Johnson, *The Alien Vision
of Victorian Poetry*, 1952, pp. 73–4. He sees in the poem a study of the struggle
in the poet between the intellectual pride of rationalism, and his "inborn unin-
structed impulses." In this struggle the latter triumphs at last, and pride is
humiliated. Both Aprile and Paracelsus are self-infatuated: Aprile loves un-
realistically and inhabits a Shelleyan world of idealized abstractions; Paracelsus
is equally ineffective in his arrogant desire to help mankind while keeping
himself aloof from them and repudiating their support. In Act V Paracelsus
learns that power must be united to love, and love to power, if an individual is
to be effective in helping mankind, as both Paracelsus and Aprile hoped to be.

two conceptions of Love in *Paracelsus*—the first romantic, scornful of fact and earthly bonds, the other Christian and mundane, asking that Love, as in the incarnation of Christ, shall "stoop to conquer." The first temper is characteristic of both Paracelsus and Aprile in Part II of the poem; they both aspire infinitely in different ways. Aprile does not stand for the Love which Paracelsus rejects for Knowledge, but is a warning to Paracelsus of the imperfections in his methods of loving. In Part V the solution comes when Paracelsus recognizes, just before he dies, that he has failed because he has not understood that Love is not a romantic passion for perfection, but a divine condescension to human frailty. At the end Paracelsus dies "hand in hand with you, Aprile!" as a perfect equal in love and understanding. This analysis shows that Browning, while always retaining much of Shelley's conception of love, had nevertheless pushed beyond Shelley to his own characteristic doctrines of heavenly and earthly love.[7]

Theophrastus Bombast von Hohenstein (*c.* 1490–1541), upon whose career Browning's poem is built, took the name "Paracelsus," as many learned Germans did in the Renaissance, from the Latin; he meant to denote by his name that he was as great a physician as Celsus. The son of a physician, he was born near Einsiedeln. For a while he studied at the University of Basle, and later under Trithemius, Abbot of Sponheim. He soon showed talent in chemistry and prosecuted his studies in the mines in the Tyrol. He returned to Basle in 1526 and became the town physician and the University lecturer on medicine. His revolutionary tactics—burning the books of the older physicians in public and conducting his lectures in German—and his quarrelsome nature raised enemies against him, and because of a dispute with Canon Cornelius von Lichtenfels Paracelsus was forced from his position. He wandered, we know, over most of southern Germany, and legend adds Constantinople, Egypt, and Arabia. In 1541 he was invited to settle at Salzburg under the protection of the Archbishop, and there, after a short time, he died.

[7] See W. O. Raymond, "Browning's Conception of Love as Represented in *Paracelsus*," in *Papers of the Michigan Academy of Science, Arts and Letters* 4:443–63 (1924). The above digest gives a very imperfect conception of the closely reasoned and important paper. This article is now Ch. 9 (pp. 156–74) in Raymond's *The Infinite Moment*, Toronto, 1950. See also the suggestive article by Frederick S. Boas, "Robert Browning's *Paracelsus*," in the *Quarterly Review* 265:285–95. Boas's strictures upon Browning's subjective method are judicious, and so is his analysis of the characters and their ideas.

For the necessary historical material upon the career of Paracelsus, Browning went to three works, all of which were in his father's library.[8] These were, in the probable order of consultation, the *Biographie universelle* (Paris, 1822), Melchior Adam's *Vitae Germanorum Medicorum,* printed at Heidelberg in 1620, and Frederick Bitiskius' edition of the works of Paracelsus in three folio volumes, published at Geneva in 1658.[9] From the *Biographie universelle* Browning got the main features of the career of Paracelsus; the note that he appended to the poem is translated mainly from the *Biographie.* M. Renauldin, who is referred to in the note, was an editor and contributor to the *Biographie.* This account was, in truth, almost all the source that Browning needed for the poem itself; and the passages in the *Biographie* which he did not use in the note supplied him with a brief account of Paracelsus' achievements in medicine, chemistry, philosophy, and theology, and with a good many hints besides for the character. Since Browning's note is appended to all editions of *Paracelsus* it is not necessary to speak further of it here.

From the *Biographie* Browning went to the fuller account of the life of Paracelsus in Melchior Adam's *Vitae Germanorum Medicorum.* Here he read the life in detail, and acquired a great deal of the erudition which he displays in his note. The book recounts Paracelsus' parentage and education, his travels to Arabia and other far places, his achievements and wonderful cures in medicine, his use of laudanum, and tells too of Azoth, his wonderful sword. Here Browning learned the legend of Paracelsus as the great reformer in medicine, the father of chemical medicine in Europe. Melchior Adam thus attempts to summarize the medical system of Paracelsus:

Although he lacked not a few things in the philosophy and medicine of the ancients, he showed a different method in learning and practicing, not only philosophy but medicine also; not taken from the opinions of men, but from experience and from the nature of things, of which sure demonstrations could be given. He determined these three principles of things: sulphur, salt and mercury (or liquid), from which all bodies are composed, and into which they are finally disintegrated. He showed that medicine

---

[8] See the excellent account of Browning's sources for *Paracelsus* and his use of them, in Griffin and Minchin, *Life,* pp. 68–72. Browning certainly knew Samuel Butler's lines in *Hudibras;* "Bombastus kept a devil's bird / Shut in the pommel of his sword, / That taught him all the cunning pranks / Of past and future mountebanks."

[9] *Aur. Philip. Theoph. Paracelsi Bombast ab Hohenheim, Medici et Philosophi Celeberrimi, Chemicorumque Principis, Opera Omnia . . . Edition Novissima et Emendatissima, . . . Genevae, M.DC.LIIX.*

is supported on four columns; the first of these is philosophy, or physics, which is the science of land and water, and of all things which are derived therefrom; the second is astronomy, which is the knowledge of the remaining two elements and of all things pertaining to the heavens; the third is alchemy, which exhibits the composition and decomposition of all substances in working eagerly towards an imitation of nature; the last is virtue, which demands that the physician himself be pious unto God, just towards men, temperate, honest, and fond of all that is good.

From this discussion of the principles of Paracelsus, Adam slips without a pause to the anecdote of the ungrateful canon of Basle, which Browning gives in his sixth note. From this, Adam details the death of Paracelsus in Salzburg and his burial in that same place

in the Hospital of St. Sebastian, where near the wall of the church may be seen an epitaph engraved in stone as follows: "Here lies buried Philippus Theophrastus, a remarkable physician who has removed with miraculous art those dire diseases, leprosy, gout, dropsy and other incurable and contagious diseases of the body, and has paid out his property in distributing and collecting it for the poor. He exchanged life for death on the 24th day of September in the year 1541. Praise be to God. Peace to the living, and eternal rest to the buried."

The third, and possibly the most important, source of Browning's information upon the career of Paracelsus is the preface to Bitiskius' edition of the physician's works, published in 1658. It is the opinion of Griffin [10] that the first five pages and a few marginal comments further on in the works supplied Browning with some of the historical elements of his poem—the defence of the character and works of Paracelsus which he adopted, poetically developed, and idealized. This is, I think, essentially true. Bitiskius' preface is learned, controversial, and judicious. It gave Browning most of the erudite references and quotations for his notes. For example, Bitiskius tells of the treachery of Paracelsus' secretary, Oporinus, and his later remorse; of the enmity of Thomas Erastus, a rival physician; he admits and apologizes for Paracelsus' drunkenness; he comments upon his poverty and his power of creating gold; he mentions and excuses Paracelsus for his wanderings about Europe; finally, he refers to most of the learned contemporaries of the physician who are mentioned by Browning. It is clear that Browning needed to go very little beyond the first five pages, but he did see the preface to the second volume and used for his own notes two marginal notes from page 4:

[10] Griffin and Minchin, *Life*, pp. 69–72.

"Paracels. novit circulationem sanguinis" and "Et sanguification cordis." He also turned to the end of this volume and saw Paracelsus' *Testamentum*, or will, with a preface by Michael Toxites, which comments at length upon the defection and repentance of Oporinus. I think Browning also saw Paracelsus' own preface to his work called *Paragranum*, for there Paracelsus gives a spirited defence of himself and compares himself with Luther.

Browning drew upon these three sources for his note at the end of the poem, where he gave a rather handsome exhibition of erudition. But one is not shaken in the conviction that the chief source of the poem was Robert Browning himself. Hence it is amusing to encounter in the note Browning's statement, "The liberties I have taken with my subject are very trifling; and the reader may slip the foregoing scenes between the leaves of any memoir of Paracelsus he pleases, by way of commentary." In the same way one might slip Shakespeare's *Richard III* as a commentary into the pages of Holinshed! Browning had more truly stated the nature of his poem in the preface to the first edition, which he later discarded:

. . . it is an attempt . . . to reverse the method usually adopted by writers whose aim it is to set forth any phenomenon of the mind or the passions, by the operation of persons and events; and . . . , instead of having recourse to an external machinery of incidents to create and evolve the crisis I desire to produce, I have ventured to display somewhat minutely the mood itself in its rise and progress, and have suffered the agency by which it is influenced and determined to be generally discernible in its effects alone. . . .

That is, he has written a play in which the soul is the stage, and moods and thoughts are the characters. It is all the poet's invention. In no account of Paracelsus, save Browning's, do Festus and Michal appear. The scene which Browning lays in Constantinople (Part II) depends upon the dubious legend of Paracelsus' visit to that city in search of the elixir of life. The fourth scene depends upon the fact that Paracelsus was in Colmar in 1528. The magnificent speech of the fifth part, where Paracelsus, sick to death in his cell at St. Sebastian's, has a pre-vision of the evolutionary ordering of life, owes more to Milton's *Paradise Lost* (V, 403–505) and Pope's *Essay on Man* (VII) than to the Renaissance physician. From these scattered hints Browning built up his poem; the liberties he has taken with his subject are immense.

AFTER-HISTORY

It was the habit of Browning in later years to say that the reviews and newspapers had laughed his *Paracelsus* to scorn when it appeared, and that it had been a "dead failure." As far as the sales went there was some justification for his bitterness, but in almost all other respects one must say that *Paracelsus* had an unqualified success. Professor T. R. Lounsbury [11] has given the fullest account of the reception of the poem, and he dispels many errors which had been fostered by Browning's later remarks. The adverse criticism which appeared in the *Athenaeum* for August 22, 1835, so persisted in Browning's mind that he was able to tell Miss Barrett of it ten years later. The review was brief:

> *Paracelsus,* by Robert Browning. There is talent in this dramatic poem (in which is attempted a picture of the mind of this noted character), but it is dreamy and obscure. Writers would do well to remember (by way of example) that though it is not difficult to imitate the mysticism and vagueness of Shelley, we love him and have taken him to our hearts as a poet, not *because* of these characteristics—but in *spite* of them.

This, said Browning, "was a most flattering sample of what the 'craft' had in store for me."

But in the *Monthly Repository* for November, 1835, W. J. Fox, Browning's "literary god-father," gave eleven pages (pp. 716–27) to an enthusiastic review of *Paracelsus,* and in the *Examiner* for September 6 of the same year John Forster, destined to become a great friend and to play a great part in Browning's life in the next thirty years, spoke most enthusiastically:

> It is some time since we read a work of more unequivocal power than this. We conclude that its author is a young man, as we do not recollect his having published before. If so, we may safely predict for him a brilliant career, if he continues true to the present promise of his genius. He possesses all the elements of a fine poet.

All the effects of *Paracelsus* were not immediate. The poem made its way slowly. In March, 1836, Forster had more to say of *Paracelsus* in the *New Monthly Magazine.* There, in an article of twenty pages

---

[11] See *The Early Literary Career of Robert Browning,* pp. 29–44. But see also Maurice Browning Cramer, "Browning's Friendships and Fame before Marriage (1833–46)," in *PMLA* 55:207–30 (March, 1940). The author is inclined to confuse Browning's social success in London with his very modest literary success. The sales of *Paracelsus* were meagre.

devoted largely to Browning and called "Evidences of a New Genius for Dramatic Poetry—No. I," he wrote of the poem,

> This is the simple and unaffected title of a small volume, which was published some half-dozen months ago, and which opens a deeper vein of thought, of feeling, and of passion, than any poet has attempted for years. Without the slightest hesitation we name Mr. Robert Browning at once with Shelley, Coleridge, and Wordsworth. He has entitled himself to a place among the acknowledged poets of the age. This opinion will probably startle many persons, but it is most sincere. . . . Mr. Browning is a man of genius, he has in himself all the elements of a great poet, philosophical as well as dramatic.

This was praise indeed, and Browning was properly grateful, for he later gave the manuscript of *Paracelsus* to Forster. Leigh Hunt also noticed the poem favorably in his *Journal* for November, 1835. General notices, which were far too removed in time to be reviews, came in, such as that in the *Revue des deux mondes* for April, 1840 (pp. 127–33), where Browning represented the "École Métaphysique" in an article "De l'Art dramatique et du théatre actuel en Angleterre." *Paracelsus* was praised by Milsand with judgment and penetration, again in the *Revue des deux mondes*, in August, 1851 (pp. 661–76), in an article entitled "La Poésie anglaise depuis Byron. II—Robert Browning." On the whole, Browning had little cause to complain of the reception of *Paracelsus*. He was never ashamed of the poem, as he was of *Pauline*, and for a number of years the title-pages of his new works bore the legend "By the Author of *Paracelsus*."

The publication of *Paracelsus* opened a new world to Browning. He soon made the acquaintance of his sympathetic reviewer, John Forster, and of W. C. Macready, the great actor of the time. Macready was greatly taken by *Paracelsus* and thought that "the writer can scarcely fail to be a leading spirit of his time." Forster's praise had been for the "dramatic" element in the poem, and since Macready's whole mind was given to the theater, it is not surprising that Browning was soon launched under the auspices of these two men upon his ten-year attempt to write plays for the stage. One event will serve to illustrate the new world opened to Browning by the publication of *Paracelsus*. On May 26, 1836, a supper was given at Sergeant Talfourd's home in honor of the success of his play *Ion*. Landor was present, and so was Wordsworth. Among others, a health was drunk to the author of *Paracelsus*, and the great bard leaned across the table and said, "I am proud to drink to your health, Mr. Browning." [12] Thus Browning was received among the poets of England.

STRAFFORD

PUBLICATION

Strafford was published on May 1, 1837, the day the play was presented at the Covent Garden Theater. The volume, bound in drab-colored paper with a white label, consisted of the half-title; the title-page: "Strafford: An Historical Tragedy By Robert Browning, Author of 'Paracelsus.' London: Printed for Longman, Rees, Orme, Brown, Green, & Longman, Paternoster Row, 1837"; a dedication: "Dedicated, in all Affectionate Admiration, to William C. Macready, Esq. by His Most Grateful and Devoted Friend, R. B. April 23, 1837."; a preface; and the text, pp. 1–132. The volume was the first of Browning's poems to be published at the expense of the publisher. The advertised price was Four Shillings the copy. Probably because Elizabeth Barrett thought it the poorest of Browning's works, *Strafford* was not included in the collected edition of 1849, but in 1863 it reappeared, and has taken its place in all the collected editions since.

TEXT

Strafford was a play in five acts, made up of twelve scenes, the third and fourth acts having three scenes each, the others two. There were 2200 lines, all in blank verse save the song in the second scene of Act V. When the play was republished in 1863, the number of lines remained the same, but very considerable alterations in lines, words, phrases, and punctuation were introduced. Further minor alterations were made in the editions of 1868 and 1888. [1] In 1882 an acting version of the play was published for the use of the pupils of the North London Collegiate School for Girls, and in 1884 Miss E. H. Hickey published an annotated edition with a notable introduction (of which I shall speak later) by Professor S. R. Gardiner, historian of the Commonwealth period of English history.

[12] Griffin and Minchin, *Life*, p. 77.

[1] In correcting his poems for the 1888 edition, Browning borrowed Miss Hickey's copy of her edition of *Strafford*, 1884, to recall the changes he had made in the text. See *New Letters*, ed. DeVane and Knickerbocker, p. 351.

GENESIS AND COMPOSITION

It was probably Browning's meetings with W. C. Macready, the great actor, at the home of W. J. Fox on November 27, 1835, and soon afterwards with John Forster, that turned his thoughts towards the acted drama. To Macready Browning seemed "more like a youthful poet than any man I ever saw," and he recorded in his diary,[2] "I took Mr. Browning on, and requested to be allowed to improve my acquaintance with him. He expressed himself warmly, as gratified by the proposal. . . ." The acquaintance ripened rapidly into friendship, and in a short time Macready was reading *Paracelsus* with delight. Browning met Forster, who had reviewed *Paracelsus* favorably in the *Examiner,* in Macready's house at Elstree on the last day of the year 1835. Forster was probably busy at the time upon a twenty-page article which appeared in March in Colburn's *New Monthly Magazine* under the title "Evidences of a New Genius for Dramatic Poetry—No. I," in which *Paracelsus* was an important part of the evidence. With two new friends both interested in the dramatic, Browning's thoughts were soon turning towards the stage. On February 16, 1836, Browning and Forster came to Macready to talk over a play that Browning proposed to write upon Narses, Justinian's general. Nothing came of this, but at the famous dinner given by Sergeant Talfourd on May 26, Macready said to Browning as the party was breaking up: "Write a play, Browning, and keep me from going to America!" According to Mrs. Orr [3] Browning immediately proposed Strafford as a subject, but I think this unlikely. In a letter to Macready dated May 28, 1836, Browning promised that after the first of July, when he should have completed *Sordello,* he would give his "whole heart and soul" to the writing of a tragedy to be ready by November first.[4] Strafford was, however, in his mind, for in February and March of that year he had been helping Forster, who was ill, to prepare for the press the prose *Life of Strafford,* which was to be published on May 4. At that time Browning was busy, as we know from his preface to *Strafford,* upon *Sordello.* At any rate, it was not until August 3, 1836, that Macready recorded in his diary the first mention of this play: "Forster told me that Browning had fixed on

---

[2] My references throughout, by date of entry, are to *The Diaries of William Charles Macready, 1833–1851,* ed. William Toynbee, 2 vols., London, 1912.
[3] Orr, *Life,* p. 82.
[4] See *New Letters,* ed. DeVane and Knickerbocker, pp. 11–2.

Strafford for the subject of a tragedy; he could not have hit upon one that I could have more readily concurred in." On October 4 Macready heard the disturbing rumor that Browning had written his play in ten days. Happily this rumor was false, and this was to Macready "a circumstance to rejoice at." On October 31, Browning reported his play as finished, but when he brought it to Macready on November 19, the fourth act was still incomplete. Through the latter part of November Macready read *Strafford* and advised Browning as to the revision of the play. His impressions were not favorable, for on November 23 he recorded, "I find more grounds for exception than I had anticipated. I had been too much carried away by the truth of character to observe the meanness of plot, and occasional obscurity." On December 20 Browning brought the omitted scenes of his play. Macready laid *Strafford* aside for a while for Bulwer's play, the *Duchess de la Vallière*, but by March 19, 1837, was taking it up again: "Read *Strafford* in the evening, which I fear is too historical; it is the policy of the man, and its consequence upon him, not the heart, temper, feelings, that work on this policy, which Browning has portrayed—and how admirably." [5] Through the next few days Macready's admiration fell and his fears rose; but in spite of fears, when *Strafford* was read to Osbaldiston on March 30, the manager of Covent Garden

. . . caught at it with avidity, agreed to produce it without delay on his part, and to give the author £12 per night for twenty-five nights, and £10 per night for ten nights beyond. He also promised to offer Mr. Elton an engagement to strengthen the play. Browning and Forster came in; I had the pleasure of narrating what had passed between Mr. Osbaldiston and myself, and of making Browning very happy; I went over the memoranda I had made of corrigenda in his MS.; the suggestion of the children's voices being heard in the pause following the announcement of Strafford's death he was quite *enraptured* with; he took the book and promised to work hard. Forster is trying to induce the Longmans to publish it; I doubt his success. Browning asked me if I would allow him to dedicate the play to me. I told him, of course, how much I should value such an honour, which I had not anticipated or looked for.

Macready's fears, however, were not allayed. The "dangerous state of the play" troubled him, and on April 5 he and Forster "went over

---

[5] In this comment Macready hit upon the permanent weakness of Browning as a playwright. The poet could reveal internal and psychological action in the mind and spirit of single figures, the heroes of his plays and monologues, but he seldom succeeded in translating these states of mind into the language and form of external conflict.

the play of *Strafford*, altered, omitted, and made up one new scene; we were occupied from eleven till four o'clock. . . ." Browning did not take the changes kindly, and quarrelled with Forster. In early April the play went slowly through the green-room. On the 14th Browning was almost of a mind to withdraw it, but decided to continue. Osbaldiston was parsimonious; Macready was disheartened; and Helen Faucit, later a great friend of Browning's, objected to the poverty of her part as Lady Carlisle. On April 23—Shakespeare's birthday—when Browning was signing his dedication to Macready, the actor wrote in his diary: "Looked at Browning's alterations of the last scene of *Strafford*—found them quite bad—mere feeble rant—neither power, nor nature, nor healthful fancy—very unworthy of Browning. I felt certainly convinced that the play must be utterly condemned."

In the final rehearsals Macready's hopes, for the moment, revived. But he was convinced that "There is no chance . . . for the play but in the acting," and on April 28 he unpacked his heart with words:

In all the historical plays of Shakespeare, the great poet has only introduced such events as act on the individuals concerned, and of which they are themselves a part; the persons are all in direct relation to each other, and the facts are present to the audience. But in Browning's play we have a long scene of passion upon what? A plan destroyed, by whom or for what we know not, and a parliament dissolved, which merely seems to inconvenience *Strafford* in his arrangements. There is a sad want of judgment and tact in the whole composition. Would it were over! It must fail—and it grieves me to think that *I am so placed*. Browning will efface its memory by the production of *Sordello;* but it will strike me hard, I fear.

We learn from the same entry that the printing of *Strafford* has been undertaken by Longman, and that the play will be published the afternoon of the performance.

The last rehearsals went off to Browning's delight and Macready's despair. On May 1, 1837, at a quarter before seven, Browning's first play was performed. It was Macready's benefit night and Covent Garden was crowded to capacity. Macready played Strafford; Helen Faucit, Lady Carlisle; Vandenhoff, Pym; and Dale, King Charles. Browning and a good number of his friends were present at the performance, and after it was over the author took his father behind the scenes to shake hands with the actor. Macready told Browning that "the play was a grand escape, and that he ought to regard it as such. . . ." The play went the course which Macready had predicted. With a lessening attendance *Strafford* ran for four nights—

May 1, 3, 5 and 9—a very short run compared to those enjoyed by Bulwer-Lytton's plays. A performance was announced for May 11, but Vandenhoff deserted and it was not thought worth while to continue. *Strafford* was played again on May 30 for the benefit of Edward Fitzball who chose it because he thought it "uncommonly well received" [6] on its first appearances.

SOURCES AND INFLUENCES

The original preface of *Strafford* is printed here in full because it was discarded later by Browning and is not well known. Part of it was aimed at the spectators of the play, rather than at the readers:

I had for some time been engaged in a Poem of a very different nature, when induced to make the present attempt; and am not without apprehension that my eagerness to freshen a jaded mind by diverting it to the healthy natures of a grand epoch, may have operated unfavorably on the represented play, which is one of Action in Character, rather than Character in Action. To remedy this, in some degree, considerable curtailment will be necessary, and, in a few instances, the supplying details not required, I suppose, by the mere reader. While a trifling success would much gratify, failure will not wholly discourage me from another effort: experience is to come; and earnest endeavor may yet remove many disadvantages.

The portraits are, I think, faithful; and I am exceedingly fortunate in being able, in proof of this, to refer to the subtle and eloquent exposition of the characters of Eliot and Strafford, in the lives of *Eminent British Statesmen*, now in the course of publication in Lardner's *Cyclopaedia*, by a writer whom I am proud to call my friend [John Forster]; and whose biographies of Hampden, Pym, and Vane, will, I am sure, fitly illustrate the present year—the Second Centenary of the Trial concerning Ship-Money. My Carlisle, however, is purely imaginary: I at first sketched her singular likeness roughly in, as suggested by Matthews and the memoir-writers— but it was too artificial, and the substituted outline is exclusively from Voiture and Waller.

The Italian boat-song in the last scene is from Redi's "Bacco," long since naturalized in the joyous and delicate version of Leigh Hunt.

The source for most of Browning's ideas upon the life and character of Thomas Wentworth, Lord Strafford (1593–1641), was the prose life of that general and statesman published under John Forster's name on May 4, 1836. In 1892 the London Browning Society under the auspices of F. J. Furnivall republished this *Life of Strafford* and called it *Robert Browning's Prose Life of Strafford;* it was prefaced by an excellent historical critique upon the biography, by C. H.

[6] Edward Fitzball, *Thirty-five Years of a Dramatic Author's Life,* London, 1859, II, 89.

Firth of Oxford. In February and March, 1836, Forster was ill, and his new friend Browning helped him in some sort to get the *Life of Strafford* ready for the press. In his *Forewords* to the publication of 1892 Furnivall makes a strong, but hardly a convincing, case for the opinion that the *Life of Strafford* is mainly Browning's. On three occasions Browning had spoken to Furnivall on the point and had laid claim to a large share of the work. Very few people, said Furnivall, had any idea how much Browning had helped Forster, and he recounts the story (pp. v–vi):

> Forster had finisht the Life of Eliot—the first in the volume—and had just begun that of Strafford, for which he had made full collections and extracts; but illness had come on, he couldn't work, the book ought to be completed forthwith, as it was due in the serial issue of volumes; what *was* he to do? 'Oh,' said Browning, 'don't trouble about it. I'll take your papers and do it for you.' Forster thankt his young friend heartily, Browning put the Strafford papers under his arm, walkt off, workt hard, finisht the Life, and it came out to time in 1836, to Forster's great relief, and past under his name.

Furnivall then proceeds to list a number of places in the *Life* where he sees Browning's hand.

Browning told his opinion of his share in the *Life* to others, notably to Elizabeth Barrett late in May of 1840, and to Professor Gardiner of Oxford. There is no doubt that he had some share, but I think his partisans have exaggerated his participation. The truth probably is that Forster had collected the materials, had outlined and in part written the *Life* when Browning came to his aid. It is not likely that Browning gathered more materials, but it is probable that the latter part of the biography is colored by Browning's interpretations and by his phraseology. That the poet was very familiar with Forster's materials is amply shown in the play; [7] that he went far beyond Forster's materials for his tragedy there is no reason to believe.

At the outset it should be said that the two great figures of the play, Strafford and Pym, represent the two great forces of the "grand epoch" which Browning refers to in his preface. Strafford is medieval in his belief in the prerogatives of the King; he is the champion of the King's will against the people, and is dangerous because he acts upon the principles of despotism with resolution and intelligence. Pym, on the other hand, is the champion of the people and of the

---

[7] The reader will find the materials used by Forster admirably analyzed by C. H. Firth in his *Introduction* to the Browning Society's edition of the *Life of Strafford,* 1892, pp. xiii–xiv.

new parliamentary principles at the time when the Parliament has begun to gain ground in its great battle against Charles I. The forces of the age are embodied in these men, and to complete the picture the reader needs only to be reminded of the great personal loyalty which the Stuarts were able to command from very worthy men. Browning's tragedy depicts only the twenty months before Strafford's death in 1641, but naturally reference is made to events which had happened years before.

The life of Strafford as given in Forster's biography may be summarized here:

Thomas Wentworth, later to become the Earl of Strafford, was born in 1593 of an aristocratic and wealthy family of Yorkshire. His first public service was to represent Yorkshire in Parliament in 1614, as a supporter of the government. He supported the King (James I) stoutly until 1621, and was rewarded by minor offices, but in that year he could not submit quietly to the King's denial of free speech to Parliament. Under the administration of Buckingham Strafford held to a policy of silence, but in 1626 when he refused to take part in or contribute to a forced loan by the new King, Charles I, he lost his offices in Yorkshire and was imprisoned in the Marshalsea and at Dartford. He looked upon Buckingham as his enemy, and at the first opportunity he represented himself to the King as a loyal and eager servant. But the King and court neglected him, and he appeared as one of the leaders of the Opposition in the first session of the Parliament of 1628. Yet even at this time he was eager to exonerate the King from blame, and directed his attack upon the ministers. It was at this time that Wentworth made friends among the champions of parliamentary rights. He had become so powerful that the King saw fit to give him an audience and request his support. Wentworth yielded to the promises of the King; honors and offices were heaped upon him. To him it seemed that he was following the principles he had always held; to the Parliamentary forces he was an apostate.

The first honors from the King's hand were soon followed by greater ones. In November, 1629 he entered the Privy Council, and in January, 1632 he became Lord Deputy for Ireland. Upon his assumption of the Irish post Wentworth made an excellent review of his theory of government. He was severe with the Irish to the point of savagery. He was the representative of the King, and the King's will must be enforced. Throughout these years, as leader of the Opposition to the Parliamentary forces, as President of the Council of the North, and as Lord Deputy of Ireland, Wentworth regarded himself as defending the constitution against those who sought to assail it. But his conception of the constitution was the will of the King. In Ireland he raised enormous sums for Charles, and for his services there richly deserved the earldom which the King twice refused to grant him. At home, his influence was undermined by enemies in his own party and by the Queen. But when the war against the Scots had gone badly, Charles was forced to call him in as chief counsellor, and to raise him to the earldom. It is at this point in the _Life_ that Browning's play properly begins.

In spite of his bad health Strafford performed prodigious labors in Ireland and England. The new Parliament broke up; the King's troops were routed at Newbourne and on the Tyne; Holland, Hamilton, and the elder Vane intrigued disgracefully with the Queen. Strafford, called too late to the command of the King's shattered forces, fell back upon Durham before the advancing Scots. Suddenly he found that a treaty with the Scots had been conducted without his knowledge. After he had achieved a minor success against the Scots, the King bade him forbear. At the same moment, without previous warning, Strafford was told that the King had summoned a new Parliament. He hurried to London to defend his actions but was hampered and checked by the King.

Strafford was arrested and committed to the Tower; and his impeachment began in Westminster Hall. Scaffolds were erected for the commissioners of Scotland and the lords of Ireland, who had joined with the commoners of England in their accusations against Strafford. In the center sat the peers in their robes, the Lord Keeper and the Judges. Beyond the peers was a chair raised under a cloth of state for the King, but the throne was vacant, for in the presence of the King no judicial act could take place. But the King "brake down the screens with his own hands, so they sat in the eyes of all, but little more regarded than if they had been absent, for the lords sat all covered." Pym presented the twenty-eight articles of accusation, and Strafford's answers were read three weeks later. The 22nd of March was set for the trial. Strafford was accused of subverting the fundamental laws of the country.

The address and resource of Strafford in his trial won him many admirers, so much so that the trial would have broken down had it not been for the indomitable Pym, who in some way secured the notes of the Privy Council when it had debated the Scots affair. The notes were the property of Sir Henry Vane, the elder, and Clarendon says that he gave them to Pym out of hatred for Strafford. Other chroniclers think that the papers were taken by the younger Vane. At any rate, Strafford had there said to the King: "You have an army in Ireland that you may employ to reduce _this_ kingdom to obedience." Strafford urged that the word _this_ referred to Scotland; his enemies knew that it meant England. This evidence was generally considered to be fatal to Strafford. He was eloquent, but he was overmatched by Pym.

The Commons had meanwhile passed a Bill of Attainder, and Charles, in the hope of saving Strafford, had made a very unwise appeal to them. Strafford knew then that he was lost. Pym discovered and crushed a conspiracy of the court to free Strafford. Charles dared not refuse to sign the Bill of Attainder, Strafford's death warrant, but he wrote at once to the House of Lords asking for life imprisonment or at least a reprieve. His request was refused. When Strafford learned that Charles had signed the Bill of Attainder he laid his hand upon his heart, raised his eyes, and said, "Put not your trust in princes, nor in the sons of men, for in them there is no salvation." In the three days left to him Strafford wrote to his wife and to his eldest son, "my dearest Will," a most touching letter, and addressed a petition to the House of Lords asking that body to have compassion upon his innocent children. He desired to have an interview with Archbishop Laud, who was also in prison, but this was denied. On May 12, 1641, Strafford was beheaded on Tower Hill.[8]

From this summary it may be seen that Browning made good use of Forster's biography of Strafford. It ought to be observed, however, that Browning is notably more sympathetic in his treatment of Strafford than is Forster. In some respects the play is more accurate historically than the *Life*. Browning rightfully makes a good deal of the fact that Strafford, when he came to London on November 9, 1640, from his army in the north, came armed with proof that the popular leaders had secretly been in communication with the rebels, and had invited them to bring a Scottish army into England. Strafford was determined to impeach them, and regain for the crown some of the popularity it had lost. Yet when he appeared in the House of Lords he let the opportunity slip. One can only guess that the King made him draw back at the critical moment. The biography makes little of the point, and it is probable that Browning went beyond Forster to Clarendon's *History of the Rebellion* for his facts. Furthermore, Browning in the play has a better appreciation than Forster of the change in tactics in the charges against Strafford in the House of Commons. By substituting a Bill of Attainder for the proceedings of impeachment, the matter of Strafford's death was put in the hands of the King, and Charles did not dare refuse to sign the death-warrant.

Professor S. R. Gardiner, in his critical preface to the edition of *Strafford* which Miss E. H. Hickey published in 1884, had no great respect for the historical accuracy of the play. "So completely," he says, "does the drama proceed irrespectively of historical truth, that the critic may dispense with the thankless task of pointing out discrepancies." And again, "Not merely are there frequent minor inaccuracies, but the very roots of the situation are untrue to fact," and he notes that "the idea of Pym or his friends entering into col-

[8] For a clear and succinct account of "The Trial of Thomas Wentworth (Earl of Strafford)" see The Right Honorable the Earl of Birkenhead, *Famous Trials of History*, 1926, Ch. 2, which stresses the political issues involved. Browning, with his characteristic belief that man's relation to God is infinitely more important than his relation to his fellow-men, makes little of the political and social significance of Strafford's trial; politics never project themselves as motives.

loquies with Strafford, and even bursting in unannounced into Charles's presence, is, from the historical point of view, simply ludicrous." As to the historical truth of the characters, though from "the beginning to the end of the play the personal relations between the actors are exaggerated at the expense of the political," Gardiner's judgment is gentler. "For myself," he says, "I can only say that, every time that I read the play, I feel more certain that Mr. Browning has seized the real Strafford, the man of critical brain, of rapid decision, and tender heart, who strove for the good of his nation without sympathy for the generation in which he lived. Charles, too, with his faults perhaps exaggerated, is nevertheless the real Charles."

For Browning's heroine, too, Gardiner has a good word:

Of Lady Carlisle we know too little to speak with anything like certainty, but, in spite of Mr. Browning's statement that his character of her is purely imaginary, there is a wonderful parallelism between the Lady Carlisle of the play and the less noble Lady Carlisle which history conjectures rather than describes. There is the same tendency to fix the heart upon the truly great man, and to labor for him without the requital of human affection, though in the play no part is played by that vanity which seems to have been the main motive with the real personage.

Strafford's friendship for this lady grew out of his need for an ally near the Queen. A note upon her in Forster's *Life of Strafford* seems to have given Browning the character:

This extraordinary woman, whom Dryden called the "Helen of her country," and from whom Waller borrowed a compliment for Venus, ("the bright Carlile of the court of heaven,") played a conspicuous part in the public affairs of the time. "She was thought to be as deeply concerned in the counsels of the court, and afterwards of the parliament, as any in England." After the death of Strafford she had become the mistress of Pym. Yet her passions were not extreme! Sir Toby Mathews lets us into her character:—"She is of too high a mind and dignity, not only to seek, but almost to wish, the friendship of any creature: *they whom she is pleased to chuse, are such as are of the most eminent condition, both for power and employments;* not with any design towards her own particular, either of advantage or curiosity; *but her nature values fortunate persons as virtuous.*" [9]

In his preface to the play Browning says that his Carlisle was drawn from Waller and Voiture. Waller sings her beauty and aloofness at

[9] *Thomas Wentworth, Earl of Strafford,* by John Forster, in *Eminent British Statesmen* (Lardner's *Cabinet of Biography*), p. 286. The quotation may be found in the Browning Society's *Life of Strafford,* p. 129.

least five times,[10] but the general quality of his flattery may be seen in the following lines from *To Phyllis:*

> Love makes so many hearts the prize
> Of the bright Carlisle's conquering eyes
> Which she regards no more than they
> The tears of lesser beauties weigh.

Voiture gives us the same character in more explicit, though hardly less flattering, terms:

It will not be difficult for you to guess after this that I speak of the Countess of Carlisle. For there is nobody else of whom all this good and evil can be said. No matter how dangerous it is to let the memory dwell upon her, I have not, so far, been able to keep mine from it, and quite honestly, I would not give up the picture of her that lingers in my mind, for all the loveliest things I have seen in my life. I must confess that she is an enchanting person, and there would not be under heaven a woman so worthy of affection, if she knew what it was, and if she had as sensible a nature as she has a reasonable mind. But with the temperament we know she possesses, there is nothing to be said except that she is the most lovable of all things not good, and the most delightful poison that Nature ever concocted . . . all the kindness that ought to reside in the will with her is concentrated in the judgment.[11]

The character of Lady Carlisle and her love for Strafford make a legitimate assault upon the curiosity of the reader, but in the play of great political personages there is little room for her.

The character of Pym in Browning's *Strafford* Gardiner finds to be the least satisfactory from the historical point of view. "It was perhaps necessary for dramatic purposes that he should appear to be larger-hearted than he was, but it imparts an unreality to his character." There is no authenticity in the legend, which becomes a major motif in the play, that Pym and Strafford were once intimate friends—that their friendship had begun in the Middle Temple in 1607 and lasted until Strafford's "apostasy" in 1628. In this, Browning is following Forster, who said that Strafford "had been conversant with the measures, and connected with the men. He had been the associate of Pym, and had spoken and voted in the same ranks with Eliot." And again Forster says of Strafford at the trial:

---

[10] In *The Country to My Lady of Carlisle, The Countess of Carlisle in Mourning, In Answer to One who Writ Against a Fair Lady, Of Her Chamber,* and *To Phyllis.*

[11] *Les Oeuvres de Monsieur de Voiture,* Paris, 1734, I, 119. The passage translated above is from a letter "A Monsieur Gourdon; à Londres," and is dated from Dover, December 4, 1633.

Upwards of twelve years had elapsed since sir Thomas Wentworth stood face to face with Pym. Upon the eve of his elevation to the peerage, they had casually met at Greenwich, when, after a short conversation on public affairs, they separated with these memorable words, addressed by Pym to Wentworth. "You are going to leave us, but I will never leave you, while your head is upon your shoulders!" That prophetic summons to a more fatal meeting was now at last accomplished! [12]

Browning's—and the biography's—striking picture of Pym losing possession of himself on meeting Strafford's gaze is grounded on the fact that at the trial Pym's assurance failed him for a moment.

AFTER-HISTORY

When *Strafford* was produced on May 1, 1837, the dramatic critics varied widely in their comments.[13] The *Morning Herald,* as Macready records in his diary on May 4, called the play the "best that had been produced for many years." Forster in the *Examiner* for May 7 was more temperate: his theme was that Browning as a dramatic writer had possibilities, but that he had not realized them in *Strafford.* The *Literary Gazette* for May 6 admired the vigor of the play, but found the dialogue halting and the interest flagging. The twenty-page commentary upon *Strafford* in the *Edinburgh Review* (July, 1837) dealt severely with the play, but treated it as a literary rather than as a theatrical performance. All the reviews of the acted play were in agreement that the acting of Macready and Miss Faucit was admirable, but that the other actors were intolerably bad. Since the five performances of 1837 the play has seldom been acted, but two revivals are perhaps noteworthy. On December 21, 1886, the play was performed under the auspices of the London Browning Society at the Strand Theater, even though Miss Alma Murray, whose acting in Shelley's *Cenci* had impressed Browning, was unable to play the part of Lady Carlisle. In 1890 the Oxford University Dramatic Society presented the play with Mr. H. B. Irving, of New College, in the part of Strafford.

Strafford was Browning's first attempt to write in the strictly dramatic form. In the next ten years he was to write five plays intended

[12] The Browning Society's *Life of Strafford,* 1892, p. 240. See also p. 143, and C. H. Firth's excellent comment upon the legend in his *Introduction* to this work.
[13] See T. R. Lounsbury, *The Early Literary Career of Robert Browning,* pp. 51–8, for the best account of its reception. For a contrary opinion see M. B. Cramer, "Browning's Friendships and Fame before Marriage (1833–1846)," in *PMLA* 55:207–30 (March, 1940).

for the stage and two closet dramas. The effect of thinking dramatically was to have a profound, and in some respects excellent, influence upon his genius. It was a step in working out his true manner. In 1837, however, the immediate effect of his contact with the stage was disillusioning. Some of the actors, according to the poet, had to be informed that "impeachment" did not mean "poaching," the Scots Commissioners were dressed in kilts, and the acting was very bad. At one moment Browning vowed he would never write another play.[14] Within two years or less he was writing plays again, but it was six years before another of his plays was acted. The exclusion of *Strafford* from the series of *Bells and Pomegranates* (*q. v.*) and from the collected edition of 1849, as well as his apologetic allusion to it in the preface to *Pippa Passes,* indicates that his later opinion of the play was not high.

Browning's studies for the career of Strafford had the effect of developing and making definite his political opinions.[15] His liberalism, fostered by his Non-Conformist breeding and nourished by Shelley's radicalism, from this point on took the definite form of espousing the cause of the people against tyrants. Though he depicts Strafford with real sympathy, and can enter with great zest into the spirit of the Royalists in *Cavalier Tunes,* his deeper sympathies had been aroused by those champions of the people, Pym, Hampden,

[14] See *Letters,* ed. Hood, p. 259, for Browning's recollections in 1886; also see Macready's *Diaries* under May 9, 1837.

[15] See the excellent interpretative paper by D. C. Somervell, "An Early Victorian Tragedy," in the *London Mercury* 16:170–8. Two other significant articles deserve mention here. In 1936 Arthur E. DuBois published "Robert Browning, Dramatist" in *Studies in Philology* 33:626–55. While primarily interested in the several types of drama which Browning wrote, he sees *Strafford,* the historical drama, as the first step toward the irony of *A Soul's Tragedy.* Each play pictures a great figure motivated by an ideal outside himself; Strafford, by his faith in a worthless king's prerogative, is lost between the ideal king and the real. Browning's failure, among others, was that in a play where society was involved, he could not go beyond irony to laughter. He could not laugh at the ideal and the real abstractly. The essay has considerable virtue and some faults.

The second essay, by H. B. Charlton, "Browning as Dramatist," appeared in the *Bulletin of the John Rylands Library* 23:33–67 (1939). Charlton points out Browning's temperamental blindness to the group as an organic unit, and shows that the poet seldom recognizes that a society of men has a reality equal to that of the individual on one side and God on the other. This was fatal since the theater is a corporate thing, needing corporate emotions and language. It is unfortunate that Browning's first two plays were political in theme, for in his hands principles as motives disappear in the presence of single moral giants, or preferences or animosities. Strafford's devotion to the King is a case in point. The essay is an excellent one.

Eliot, and the Parliamentarians. In *Sordello* Browning espoused the cause of the people against the great nobles, and this humanitarianism became the motivating force of the young King Charles in *King Victor and King Charles*. It is the mainspring of the action in *The Return of the Druses;* it shows itself in *Pippa Passes* (Part III); and it is the chief characteristic of Valence in *Colombe's Birthday*. In *A Soul's Tragedy* it shows itself as disillusioned. Its highest expression may be seen in *The Lost Leader*, written in 1843. Its final expression is to be found in the rousing song in honor of Pym which closes the *Parleying With Charles Avison*.

SORDELLO

PUBLICATION

Sordello, a Poem in Six Books, was announced as ready by Moxon, the publisher, on February 29, 1840. It was actually published during the first week of March. The volume was post octavo, bound in drab boards, with a white paper label (later copies of the same issue were bound in dark green cloth), and consisted of a half-title; the title-page: "Sordello. By Robert Browning. London: Edward Moxon, Dover Street, MDCCCXL."; and the text, pp. 1–253. The published price was Six Shillings Sixpence; the expenses of publication were paid by the poet's father. In the six books which made up *Sordello* there were approximately 5800 lines in iambic pentameter, rhyming in couplets. At the end of the volume Moxon advertised as nearly ready *Pippa Passes, King Victor and King Charles,* and *Mansoor the Hierophant,* later published as *The Return of the Druses*.

TEXT

Sordello was not included in the two-volume collected edition of Browning's poems in 1849; but it appeared, considerably altered, in the collected editions of 1863, 1868, and 1888. After the publication of the first edition considerable pressure was put upon Browning for many years, notably by Elizabeth Barrett, Walter Savage Landor, Alfred Domett, and John Kenyon, to clarify and rewrite *Sordello*. In 1845–6 Browning had the matter under contemplation, and in Paris in November, 1855, after the publication of *Men and Women,* he made an attempt to remould *Sordello,* but was not able to achieve it to his satisfaction. The poem appeared, considerably altered, in the collected edition of 1863. It was now dedicated to "J. Milsand, of Dijon," Browning's good friend. Browning's letter to Furnivall on May 25, 1886,[1] is misleading as to the amount of change he had introduced into the edition of 1863:

> I don't understand what Mrs Dall can mean by saying that "Sordello" has been "re-written": I did certainly at one time intend to re-write much of it,—but changed my mind,—and the edition which I reprinted was the same in all respects as its predecessor—only with an elucidatory heading to each page,[2] and some few alterations, presumably for the better, in the text—such as occur in most of my works: I cannot remember a single instance of any importance that is "re-written"—and I only suppose that Mrs Dall has taken project for performance, and set down as "done" what was for a while intended to be done.

The poem was not rewritten, it is true, but the changes and fresh lines in the *Sordello* of 1863, as may be seen from the lists in the *Browning Society's Papers,* are considerable in number.[3] The text of 1863 has 5981 lines, and may be justly characterized as revised. The meaning of passages is clarified, phrases are expanded into sentences, and the punctuation renovated. The helpful elucidatory page-headings of 1863 were dropped in the edition of 1888. In this latter edition there were a few further changes, but they were not as drastic as those for the edition of 1863.

GENESIS AND COMPOSITION; SOURCES AND INFLUENCES

It is probable that *Sordello* cost Browning more time and pains than any other poem or volume of poems, even more, perhaps, than *The Ring and the Book*. He was occupied seven years in its composition,[4] from the publication of *Pauline* in March, 1833, to the appearance of *Sordello* in March, 1840. We may well believe Browning's word in his letter to Miss Barrett on December 22, 1845, that "There were many singular incidents attending my work on that subject." During these seven years there were four distinct periods of composition, and four different *Sordellos* were written. The final

---

[1] *Letters,* ed. Hood, p. 248.

[2] The elucidatory headings were suggested by Alfred Domett, whose copy of *Sordello* Browning borrowed, probably as early as 1840. See Griffin and Minchin, *Life,* p. 301.

[3] I, 80–7, "Changed Rymes and Fresh Lines in *Sordello* . . . ed. 1863, 1868."

[4] See the excellent account of the composition of *Sordello* in Griffin and Minchin, *Life,* Ch. 6; see also my article "*Sordello's* Story Retold," in *Studies in Philology* 27:1–24 (January, 1930).

result may be said to be a conglomeration of all these conceptions.

The first period of composition began soon after the publication of *Pauline* in March, 1833, and lasted, with an interval of two months for Browning's journey to Russia in 1834, until he began work upon *Paracelsus* in mid-September, 1834. In this period he had probably accomplished a good deal, for at the completion of *Paracelsus,* on which he worked steadily once he began, he could, in writing to W. J. Fox on April 16, 1835,[5] speak of *Sordello* as if it were well along: "I have another affair on hand, rather of a more popular nature, I conceive, but not so decisive and explicit on a point or two—so I decide on trying the question with this [*Paracelsus*]." In his dedication of *Sordello* to Milsand in 1863 Browning said, looking back through the many permutations to his original intention in the poem, "The historical decoration was purposely of no more importance than a background requires; and my stress lay on the incidents in the development of a soul: little else is worth study." Many commentators have noticed the likeness between *Pauline* and *Sordello,* and it is the opinion of Griffin[6] that *Sordello* was projected to take the place of *Pauline,* which had been an abject failure. Obviously, Browning had been interested in the development of his own soul in *Pauline,* but he was shamed out of his "intense and morbid self-consciousness" by the excoriating criticism of John Stuart Mill. One may suspect that the famous appeal to Shelley in *Sordello,* that this time he "come not near" (I, 60–73), was originally, before he read Mill's criticism on October 30, 1833, an invocation to the Sun-treader for aid. But though implored to stay away, the spirit of Shelley presides over *Sordello* almost as much as over *Pauline,* and the first Sordello, a poet of the same temper as the speaker in *Pauline,* is a good deal like Shelley himself. *Sordello,* however, was to be the development of a soul against an historical background. In *Paracelsus,* likewise, Browning's aim was again to depict the development of a soul, but the soul of a person he could point to in history, whose life and achievements could be documented by notes.

It is probable that *Paracelsus,* conceived and written within six months, usurped the ideas which Browning had intended to use in

---

[5] See Orr, *Life,* p. 66.

[6] Griffin and Minchin, *Life,* p. 91. For the considerable amount of autobiography in *Sordello* and its relation to the young Browning, see Miller, *Robert Browning,* pp. 23–8, and 47–9. Mrs. Miller stresses the connection between *Pauline* and *Sordello,* and the effect of Kean, the actor, upon Browning's aspirations and his career.

Sordello. For example, when Browning under the sting of Mill's criticism began to think seriously upon the nature and function of the poet, he put Eglamour, a rival poet, into *Sordello* as a foil to Sordello, the poet. In *Paracelsus*, Aprile, a lyrical poet of the same quality as Eglamour, is introduced to do a similar service for Paracelsus—not so aptly, for Paracelsus is not primarily a poet at all. But when Browning turned back to *Sordello* after finishing *Paracelsus*, he realized that he had used the same theme and the same methods of developing it in both poems; he was unwilling to repeat himself in this manner, and temporarily laid *Sordello* aside.

From these bits of evidence we may form a fairly clear conception of the first version of the poem. In that version Browning was chiefly interested in the development of a soul; he wished to explore for his own sake the problem of the individual poet and the society he lives in, his function and responsibility, and his most effective mode of communication, if his voice is to be heard. Browning had no doubt read the thirty-four poems by Sordello, mainly in Provençal, which have remained to us. Sordello is supposed to have begun his career as troubadour at the age of fifteen. In the first version Browning was obviously interested in the long slow adolescence of Sordello at Goito in the court of Adelaide, in the fabulous castle, and in the luxuriant natural scenery of the place. This is the Sordello who remains to us in the first two and a half books; and if we analyze them, we recognize still further the similarity to *Paracelsus*. Like Paracelsus, his soul developed in an historical vacuum; from Goito Sordello aspired, and at Mantua he failed; he met Eglamour and learned another aspect of the truth of life, aspired again, achieved, and died.

Going back to the inception of the poem, it is probable, I think, that Browning's attention was first attracted to the poet Sordello by Angelo Cerutti's edition of Danielo Bartoli's *De' Simboli Trasportati al Morale*, published in London in 1830. Cerutti was Browning's tutor in Italian; Browning subscribed to the edition, and as we know from a study of the *Parleying With Daniel Bartoli*, he read the book and carried it, as a model of Italian style, to Italy in 1838 and 1844. Bartoli had expatiated at length upon Sordello (Book I, Ch. XI), and had directed the reader to the part which Sordello played in Dante's *Purgatorio*. The figure of Sordello in Browning's first version of his poem was essentially the solitary and thoughtful poet, among those who on earth had had great visions and opportunities but had failed, whom Dante had described in his fifth, sixth, and seventh cantos.

Browning's original conception is shown in a letter to Elizabeth Barrett on December 22, 1845:

. . . yesterday I was reading the 'Purgatorio' and the first group of which Sordello makes one struck me with a new significance, as well describing the man and his purpose and fate in my own poem—see; one of the burthened, contorted souls tells Virgil and Dante— . . . Could I 'do' it off hand, I wonder—

> And sinners were we to the extreme hour;
> *Then*, light from heaven fell, making us aware,
> So that, repenting us and pardoned, out
> Of life we passed to God, at peace with Him
> Who fills the heart with yearning Him to see.

Then Browning adds the comment, "Which is just my Sordello's story."

To plump out the lean "development of a soul" it is most likely that Browning looked no further for information about Sordello than the *Biographie universelle* (Paris, 1822), which was in his father's library. This work had already given him material for *Paracelsus,* and was to aid him in *King Victor and King Charles* and other poems of these years. There Browning found an excellent account of the legends which have gathered around the poet: that he was born about 1189, possibly of the Visconti family, in Mantua; that he was associated with Goito, became a troubadour in northern Italy and France, and made his fame as a warrior; that he was beloved of Cunizza, the sister of Ezzelino da Romano and the wife of Count Richard of St. Boniface, and finally met a violent end. It is probable that the love-affair with Cunizza did not play a great part in Browning's first version of *Sordello.* The early Sordello is the figure we now see in the first two and a half books—neither warrior nor lover, but a boy at Goito, cogitating upon poetry and life and moving among such figures as Naddo, Plara, and Eglamour. He aspired, and later died at Mantua under the stress of his emotions—a form of death which Browning had observed in Shelley's poetry and was to use in many of his own plays.

Browning's second period of activity on *Sordello* began after the completion of *Paracelsus* in the early spring of 1835, and lasted for more than two years, but it was a period which was broken into by a number of other interests. The success enjoyed by *Paracelsus,* published on August 15, 1835, had brought Browning many new friends and consequently greater social activity. In February and March of

1836 his work was interrupted while he helped Forster complete his *Life of Strafford*. After the publication of this work on May 4, 1836, Browning turned back to *Sordello*. Three months later [7] he was beginning to busy himself on the play he had agreed to do for Macready on the subject of Strafford—and on this he seems to have been occupied until its production and publication on May 1, 1837. In the eleven months preceding his work on the prose *Life of Strafford,* and the three months between its publication and his work on the play, the second version of *Sordello* was mainly done. This we gather from the advertisement on page vi of the published *Strafford,* where appear the words "Nearly ready. Sordello, in Six Books," and from the preface to *Strafford,* dated April 23, 1837, where Browning says that when he was induced to make this attempt at playwriting he "had for some time been engaged in a Poem of a very different nature," which had left him with "a jaded mind." His friends, including Macready, were aware of his labors on *Sordello. Strafford* finally produced, Browning went back to *Sordello,* this time to be halted by an interruption of a new sort.

On July 15, 1837, Mrs. W. Busk published her two volumes of *Plays and Poems.* The reviewer in the *Athenaeum* for July 22 wrote:

Here we have a first volume, containing two serious dramas and a comedy, which though not, perhaps, colored highly enough for stage representation, is written in lively and polished style; and a second, in which the authoress's fugitive pieces are collected, and headed by a longer poem, "Sordello." Is this founded upon the same subject as that chosen by the author of "Paracelsus" for his announced poem?

It was, indeed! Mrs. Busk's *Sordello,* like his own, was in six cantos, and totalled about 2000 tetrameter lines.[8] As we shall see, her poem was so much upon the same subject as to be in the same manner, and Browning felt it necessary to revise his own poem *in toto.* Thus ended the second attempt to finish *Sordello.*

From certain hints and from remnants in the final form of the poem we may guess with some assurance the nature of this second *Sordello.* The adolescence and aspiration of Sordello at Goito, and the musings upon the nature of life and of poetry which had been the stuff of the first version had been usurped by *Paracelsus,* and Browning found it

---

[7] See Macready, *Diaries,* ed. W. Toynbee, entry under August 3, 1836. See also Browning's letter to Macready dated May 28, 1836, in *New Letters,* ed. DeVane and Knickerbocker, p. 12.

[8] The part played by Mrs. Busk's *Sordello* in the development of Browning's poem was first told in Griffin and Minchin, *Life,* pp. 92–3.

necessary to infuse a new element. It is evident that Browning had seen that the poet's soul could not develop satisfactorily in a vacuum, but had to participate in life to be effective. He naturally turned to developing the later part of the career of Sordello, in which warlike aspiration and romantic passion were inherent. It was probably during the developing of this new theme that the poem took the form of six cantos or books, which Scott had made the traditional form for stories of such a nature, and it is probable that the verse now became rhymed couplets, instead of blank verse. And it was probably at this time that the poet's father projected his plan for the romantic and fantastic tale of Sordello which is printed by Griffin and Minchin; [9] for it was occasionally his habit, after hearing his son's description of plans for or labors on a poem, to try his hand at the same theme. Browning's description of *Sordello* in the preface to *Paracelsus* may, I think, safely be assumed to have been written just before publication in August, 1835, though he dated it March 15, the date of the completion of the poem. Here Browning begged the indulgent reader "that even should he think slightingly of the present (an experiment I am in no case likely to repeat) he will not be prejudiced against other productions which may follow in a more popular, and perhaps less difficult form,"—a strange comment upon the final *Sordello*, but perhaps not so strange for the poem which he had in mind in 1835. It was probably in thinking of the possibilities of the story from this second aspect that James Russell Lowell said of *Sordello*, "It was a fine poem before the author wrote it." [10]

For this second *Sordello* of passion and war Browning pushed further his studies as suggested by Dante and the *Biographie universelle*. Besides being a grave poet and a late repenter who inhabited the *Purgatorio*, Sordello is represented by Dante as a passionate lover. His lady, Cunizza, of the Ezzelino family and five times married, had been placed by Dante in the "swooning-sphere" of the *Paradiso* (IX, 22–61). Probably for the sake of euphony Browning changed the lady's name, and possibly her nature, to that of her more innocent half-sister, Palma. Griffin and Minchin excellently summarize this aspect of *Sordello*:

Yet the love element in the poem of 1840, it must be confessed, is disappointingly vague and subordinate; but had it appeared in the summer of 1837 there seems to be no doubt that *Sordello* might have been fairly de-

[9] *Life,* pp. 98–100.
[10] "Browning's Plays and Poems," in *North American Review* 66:370.

scribed in the words of Tennyson with regard to *Maud* as "the history of a morbid poetic soul . . . raised to sanity by a pure and holy love which elevates his whole nature." [11]

The reason for minimizing the element of love in the final version of the poem is explained, very cloudily, in the last 350 lines of Book III. We shall see the reasons shortly.[12]

For the military achievements of this second Sordello Browning turned once more to the *Biographie universelle*, which made an excellent summary of the many legends. Benvenuto d'Imola, in the fourteenth century, had written a commentary upon the *Divine Comedy*, and had described Sordello as "a citizen of Mantua, an illustrious and able warrior, and a man of the court"; Benvenuto is said, likewise, to have written the life of Sordello in Provençal. Aliprandi, the earliest of Mantuan chroniclers, wrote 3000 lines in *terza rima* to celebrate the exploits of the warrior Sordello, who was proclaimed the greatest soldier of the age. But above all in importance for Browning's second Sordello, the *Biographie* sent him to the chronicler Platina, whose *Historia Urbis Mantuae* was published in Vol. XX of Muratori's great historical work, *Rerum Italicarum Scriptores* (Milan, 1720–30). In Platina Browning read of the tremendous acclaim for Sordello in Mantua when he came home from France in 1229—a square in the city is still named for him—and how he saved Mantua from Ezzelino in 1253, and fought the tyrant again near Milan. It is this legend that Browning refers to in his poem (VI, 822–4):

> The Chroniclers of Mantua tired their pen
> Telling how *Sordello Prince Visconti* saved
> Mantua, and elsewhere notably behaved . . .

This was Browning's second conception of Sordello. But it so happened that it was also Mrs. Busk's conception; and when her poem appeared in mid-July, 1837—a poem in six books emphasizing the elements of war and love—Browning felt it necessary to revise his own poem completely. And thus *Sordello* entered into its third phase.

This third phase began sometime after mid-July, 1837, and is characterized chiefly by a determined effort to infuse the historical element which hitherto had appeared only as a background for the tale of war and love. Browning was determined to finish *Sordello*, but after the appearance of Mrs. Busk's poem he apparently found it dif-

[11] *Life,* p. 97.

[12] See Browning's explanation of this change in a letter to Fanny Haworth, in *New Letters,* ed. DeVane and Knickerbocker, pp. 18–9.

ficult to do much with it. In a letter to Miss Fanny Haworth, about the first of August, 1837,[13] he asks her advice upon subjects which he has chosen for tragedies. These are *King Victor and King Charles* and *Mansoor the Hierophant* (published as *The Return of the Druses*), which may have been written in the fall of 1837 before Browning returned to *Sordello*. But apparently he worked hard at the poem once he went back to it, going out but little during the fall and winter of 1837, and on December 23 Harriet Martineau recorded in her diary: [14] "Browning called. 'Sordello' will soon be done now. Denies himself preface and notes. He must choose between being historian or poet. Cannot split interest. I advised him to let the poem tell its own tale." This glimpse of Browning indicates, I think, that he had made a rather drastic revision of his poem, and that the historical element had begun to assume large proportions. He seems to have struggled desperately to bring *Sordello* to a successful conclusion, but failed. Perhaps feeling the need of a change of scene for himself as well as a need of local color for his poem, he took a rather sudden decision, announced to Miss Martineau on April 11, 1838, to travel to Italy. On Good Friday, the 13th, he sailed, writing a hasty note to his friend John Robertson before he went: "I was not fortunate enough to find you the day before yesterday—and must tell you very hurriedly that I sail this morning for Venice—intending to finish my poem among the scenes it describes." [15] On June 1 he arrived in Venice, where he spent two weeks, and thence northwest to Asolo, Treviso, and Bassano, to Possagno and to Romano. From Romano he could see San Zenone degli Ezzelini. He passed through Vicenza and Padua on his way back to Venice, and from Venice he returned home by way of Verona, the Tyrol, and the Rhine. He was back in London by the end of July, 1838; and thus ended the third phase of *Sordello*. His letter of July 31 to Miss Haworth summarizes the poetic achievements of his journey: "I did not write six lines while absent (except a scene in a play, jotted down as we sailed thro' the Straits of Gibraltar)—but I did hammer out some four, two of which were addressed to you, two to the Queen—the whole to go in Book III—perhaps. I called you 'Eyebright'—meaning a simple and sad sort of translation of 'Euphrasia.' " [16] But the journey was nevertheless productive, in several ways.

[13] Orr, *Life*, pp. 96–7.
[14] Harriet Martineau, *Autobiography*, ed. Chapman, Boston, 1877, II, 325.
[15] Orr, *Life*, p. 88.
[16] *Idem*, p. 91.

The bare outline of his travels hardly tells of the momentous things which had been happening meanwhile to Browning's conception of *Sordello*. We have seen from the comment in Miss Martineau's diary for December 23, 1837, that before the trip to Italy had been thought of the historical element had already assumed great place in the poem. Browning had known, and had used in his second version, the fact that Sordello had fallen in love with Cunizza, a sister of the terrible Ezzelino da Romano. Now looking up the Ezzelini in the *Biographie universelle* to fill out the historical element, Browning was referred to Giambatista Verci's scholarly three-volume work *Storia degli Ecelini,* published at Bassano in 1779. This book was responsible for the historical additions which Browning made in the third version of *Sordello*. Moreover, this book was apparently Browning's guide-book in his travels in northern Italy: all the places he visited were places having to do with the history of the Ecelini family (the name is spelt variously), and only Verona has anything to do directly with Sordello himself. At Romano, the ancestral home of the Ecelini, San Zenone degli Ezzelini could be seen across the valley to the south, and here Browning read from Verci (I, 197) the death of Alberico, the second son of Ecelino Monaco, and later put it into rhyme thus:

> . . . and I think grass grew
> Never so pleasant as in Valley Rù
> By San Zenon where Alberic in turn
> Saw his exasperated captors burn
> Seven children and their mother; then, regaled
> So far, tied on to a wild horse, was trailed
> To death through raunce and bramble bush.
> (*Sordello*, VI, 775–81)

And there a canon told Browning that five years before he had seen Alberic's huge skeleton thrown up from a barrow (VI, 789–93). The travels in Italy were devoted to the Ecelini family of the region near Venice—great Ghibellines and supporters of the Emperor Frederick II in the first half of the thirteenth century.

One other event of great importance for *Sordello*, though not to bear fruit until the fourth version, happened to Browning when he had been six days in Venice. This he described in the last 350 lines of Book III of *Sordello*, representing himself as musing upon his poem in Venice, and being converted to pity for suffering humanity in a moment by the sight of the peasants and townsmen, whose "warped souls and bodies" moved him. It was a conversion which was to have consequences. No more should he write romance. Humanity need not "be dizened out as chiefs and bards" for him to sympathize and champion it. In the second version of *Sordello* the romantic love-element had been a major constituent, and Browning therefore felt it necessary to apologize for diminishing its importance in the final version, though his regret was tempered with joy in finding a greater subject. Palma gave way as the center of Sordello's—and Browning's—interest, in favor of the cause of the people:

> . . . for I regret
> Little that she [Palma], whose early foot was set
> Forth as she'd plant it on a pedestal,
> Now, i' the silent city, seems to fall
> Toward me—no wreath, only a lip's unrest
> To quiet, surcharged eyelids to be pressed
> Dry of their tears upon my bosom. Strange
> Such sad chance should produce in thee such change.
> (III, 773–80)

It is easily seen that the ground for this conversion was prepared by Shelley's liberalism, and more especially by Browning's studies for the *Life of Strafford* in that "grand epoch" of English history of which he had written in his play. This revolt of his spirit from the great princes to the masses, the poor naked wretches of the world, later becomes the whole unhistorical motivating force of the young King Charles in *King Victor and King Charles;* it is the mainspring of the action in *The Return of the Druses;* it shows itself in Browning's sympathy in Part III of *Pippa Passes;* it is the chief characteristic of Valence in *Colombe's Birthday;* and it finally exhibits itself as somewhat disillusioned in *A Soul's Tragedy.* All these pieces were written within five years of Browning's journey to Italy. Perhaps the finest expression of his liberalism may be seen in *The Lost Leader,* written in 1843.

In short, the trip to Italy supplied the local color for which Browning was searching, and provided a new approach to *Sordello* which carried him into the fourth phase of its composition. This fourth and final version of *Sordello* was written between Browning's return from Italy in July, 1838, and the 26th of May, 1839, when he told Macready that *Sordello* was finished. Perhaps this period should be extended to the 7th of March, 1840, when *Sordello* was actually published and Browning presented a copy to his mother. It is likely, however, that after May, 1839, Browning turned to other work, for at the end of *Sordello* several poems—*Pippa Passes, King Victor and King Charles,* and *Mansoor the Hierophant* (*The Return of the Druses*) were advertised as nearly ready.

In the letter to Miss Haworth on July 31, 1838, quoted in part above, and written on Browning's return to London, he promised once again, "You will see *Sordello* in a trice if the fagging fit holds." But much was to be done. The historical matter upon the Ecelini which he had collected and verified in Italy had to be revised at least, and the new sympathy for the masses which he had felt in Venice was stirring in him and crying for expression. Somehow it had to be worked into Sordello's character and made the motivating force of his career. This may not have taken many months, but some time after his return from Italy Browning hit upon the idea of making the magnificent old warrior Salinguerra the central figure of the latter part of his poem. It is possible to say with some precision how this idea came to Browning. He had always taken the phrase which the chroniclers used about Sordello, "*de ipsius familia,*" to mean that Sordello was of the blood of the Ecelini family. Reading in the *Storia degli Ecelini* Verci's account of Cunizza, Sordello's lady, he encountered, five lines above (I, 114), the fact that Sofia, another daughter of Ecelino the Monk, had married Salinguerra, and had borne him one son. Since Sordello's parentage was doubtful, there flashed into Browning's mind the idea of making Salinguerra the father of Sordello.

For the materials out of which Browning built the character of Taurello Salinguerra there was but one source. All roads led to Ludovico Antonio Muratori's *Rerum Italicarum Scriptores,* the celebrated collection of Italian historical manuscripts published at Milan in the third decade of the eighteenth century. In the eighth volume there appears Rolandino's authoritative account of the life and character of Salinguerra in his *De Factis in Marchia Tarvisina.* We have seen above that Browning knew Muratori's work. That he used the eighth volume at this time is further assured by the fact that the *Chronica Parva Ferrariensis,* from which Browning took the gruesome description of Ferrara in a state of siege which begins the fourth book of the final *Sordello,* stands in the same volume directly after Rolandino's account of Salinguerra.[17] That the idea of the siege of Ferrara had

[17] W. M. Rossetti abstracted and translated an account of Salinguerra from Muratori's *Annali d'Italia,* and published it in the London *Browning Society's*

not occurred to Browning before he came back from Italy may be inferred from the fact that he did not visit Ferrara when he was in Italy. Of course, the horror of the slaughter of the citizens of Ferrara in the poem has full effect upon the mind of Sordello, newly quickened to pity for suffering humanity. In *De Factis in Marchia Tarvisina* and the *Chronica Parva Ferrarensis* appear all the color and facts of Browning's later additions to *Sordello*—the landscape of northern Italy and the endless combats between Guelfs and Ghibellines, represented by Azzo d'Este and Count Richard of St. Boniface on one side and the Ecelini family and their great and wily soldier Salinguerra on the other, with the Pope and the Emperor Frederick II as great opposing forces in the background. The struggle continued for years with new reconciliation and new outburst, until at last the Ecelini were broken and Salinguerra went with a heavy heart to treat with his enemies. He was received with all honor and peace was arranged. The Guelf leaders accompanied the old warrior into Ferrara, and in the joyful city he made a feast for them in his palace. But in the midst of the banquet his enemies sprang up and accused him of many crimes. He leapt to his feet and gave them the lie; but when he attempted to speak, the guests drowned his voice with stamping and clapping. He understood that he was a captive. He spent the last years of his life as a prisoner in Venice.

Once Salinguerra was introduced into Browning's story he rapidly assumed a major part. The disclosure of Sordello's identity is the point upon which Browning's whole plot turns. When Adelaide, in whose court at Goito Sordello was bred, confesses to her husband, Ecelino, that Sordello is the son of Salinguerra, Ecelino for no very clear motive goes to the convent of Oliero and becomes a monk. When Salinguerra hears at Naples, as he is about to depart with the Emperor Frederick II on a crusade, that Ecelino has turned monk, he hurries back to Ferrara. There he is attacked by Count Richard of St. Boniface, whose betrothal to Palma has just been announced by Ecelino the Monk in order to secure peace between the Ghibellines and the Guelfs. Count Richard is taken prisoner by Salinguerra. In the meantime, Palma has learned the secret of Sordello's birth. She confesses her love for him and hurries with Sordello to Ferrara to make the revelation to Salinguerra. The scene of recognition between father and son is the greatest scene of the poem. Here Sordello

Papers (1889–90), III, 82–97; but Browning's knowledge of details is too great to have been drawn from Muratori's condensed work.

finds himself, as son of Salinguerra the greatest man of the time, the successor to the rule of northern Italy, and the lover of Palma. His soul is in conflict: ambition and love war on one side; on the other he has sworn himself the champion of the masses of mankind. By blood, he finds himself Ghibelline; but he feels that the Guelf cause is that of the people. Salinguerra, the ruthless practical soldier, has compelled Sordello to see that the poet must incite men to noble actions. The conflict is between altruism and ambition. He sees his plans for his own life thwarted. In this dilemma he dies, the victim of his warring emotions, but not before he has chosen the side of the people and trampled underfoot the badge of Salinguerra.[18]

This, then, was the final *Sordello,* a bewildering potpourri of poetry, psychology, love, romance, humanitarianism, philosophy, fiction, and history. Old and new lie side by side in this effort of seven years. Surely Browning was taking a long view of *Sordello* when in his dedication to the new edition of 1863 he said, "The historical decoration was purposely of no more importance than a background requires; and my stress lay on the incidents in the development of a soul. . . ." In 1839 the wars of the Guelfs and Ghibellines about Ferrara, represented respectively by Richard of St. Boniface and the Este family on one side and Salinguerra and the Ecelini on the other, were of immense interest to Browning and almost bury Sordello from our sight. Yet in the final *Sordello* the careful reader may descry the three stages in the development of Sordello's soul: the poet of Goito, to whom Eglamour and Naddo are foils, against a background of forest and silence; the lover and warrior of Mantua, for whom Palma is invented; the political thinker of Ferrara whose idealistic nature is in sharp contrast with Salinguerra, the fierce man of action. The color of the history of that barbarous time (roughly 1200–50), when the Middle Ages have just begun to give way to the Renaissance in Italy, is in general faithfully painted by Browning. The character of Sordello, of course, is only faintly historical: Browning found him in his own musings and aspirations; in hints from Dante, whence Browning conceived of Sordello as a forerunner of the great Florentine, but one who failed to grasp his world where Dante so brilliantly

---

[18] In "The Sources of Browning's *Sordello,*" published in *Studies in Philology* 34:467–96 (1937), Stewart W. Holmes gives a more detailed account of Browning's sources, especially for the later parts of the poem dealing with Italian history. He sees Browning moving progressively from the *Biographie universelle* to Verci, Rolandino, and Muratori as his main sources, and adds Pigna, Frizzi, and several other historians.

succeeded; and perhaps in hints from the career of his idol Shelley, who was also poet, lover, and political thinker. The Sordello of Browning's poem, like Shelley himself, dies at thirty, and not, as history says, at the ripe age of ninety.[19]

AFTER-HISTORY

Sordello has become so notorious as the least comprehensible poem written in the English language—at least before 1920—that little comment is required here. In its own day it became the jest of literary circles. Mrs. Carlyle said that she had read the book through without being able to make out whether Sordello was a man, a city, or a book. Douglas Jerrold was given the book when he was recovering from a severe illness, and thought he had lost his mind until his wife reassured him by her own failure to comprehend it. Miss Martineau was so unable to understand it that she thought herself ill. Miss Barrett gave *Sordello* more consideration, and thought it "like a noble picture with its face to the wall just now, or at least in the shadow." W. S. Landor wrote what has become the enlightened modern opinion of the poem: "I only wish he would atticise a little. Few of the Athenians had such a quarry on their property, but they constructed better roads for the conveyance of the material." [20] Perhaps the crowning pronouncement upon the poem came in the next century from Lounsbury: "It will remain," he says, "a colossal derelict upon the sea of literature, inflicting damage upon the strongest intellects that graze it even slightly, and hopelessly wrecking the frailer mental craft that come into full collision with it. . . ." [21] *Sordello* became a sore spot in Browning's later life, as the dedication of 1863 testifies. Angry at Macready for the actor's refusal of *The Return of the Druses,* the poet wrote him in August, 1840: "tomorrow will I betimes break new ground with So and So—an epic in so many books . . . let it but do me half the good 'Sordello' has done—be praised by the units, cursed by the tens, and unmeddled with by the

---

[19] Beyond the works already cited, this study of *Sordello* is indebted to several other studies: H.-L. Hovelaque, *La Jeunesse de Robert Browning,* Paris, 1932, Ch. 3 (pp. 279–474), an ambitious and appreciative study, but uneven and sometimes injudicious; H. Brocher, *La Jeunesse de Browning et le poème de Sordello,* Geneva, 1930; R. W. Church, *Dante and Other Essays,* 1888, *Sordello,* pp. 222–60; E. Dowden, *Transcripts and Studies,* 1896, "Mr. Browning's *Sordello.*"

[20] *The Works and Life of W. S. Landor,* ed. Forster, 1876, I, 428.

[21] *The Early Literary Career of Robert Browning,* p. 92. For the reception of *Sordello,* see pp. 74–94.

hundreds!" [22] He was convinced that more than half the difficulty lay with the reading public. Once when he saw a copy on a friend's table, he exclaimed, "Ah, the entirely unintelligible *Sordello!*"

The genuine tragedy of *Sordello* was that its publication ruined a promising reputation which had been carefully nursed. It took Browning twenty-five years to recover fully from the effect of the poem. The contemporary reviewers were few, and their comments show their chagrin and bewilderment. The *Spectator* of March 14, 1840, found whatever beauties there were overlaid "by digression, affectation, obscurity, and all the faults that spring, it would seem, from crudity of plan and self-opinion." The *Atlas* of March 28 found all Browning's faults in concentrated form in the poem, and none of his virtues. The *Athenaeum* for May 3 made a serious study of the poem but found it mannered, obscure, harsh, and full of platitudes. As might have been expected, the poem did not sell well. In 1855 Moxon, the publisher, gave Browning a report of the sale of *Sordello*. Of the edition of 500 copies, 157 had been sold, 86 given away, and the rest were on hand.[23] But *Sordello* found some friends. D. G. Rossetti forced the book as a kind of gospel upon the PreRaphaelite Brotherhood about 1850, reading fifty pages at a sitting to his friends. Swinburne knew *Sordello* from beginning to end when he was nineteen, and got "ploughed for Smalls" at Oxford because he preferred the poem to Euclid.

It is a great pity for Browning's sake that *Sordello* is not better known, for here Browning put forth his strength as well as his weakness. There are magnificent passages which repay much labor, such as the amazing landscapes of northern Italy, the woods near Goito; there are the scenes of Ferrara in siege, and above all the portrait of Salinguerra. There are also Browning's lines to Shelley (I, 60–73), and those to Landor, his "patron friend" (III, 951–68). *Sordello* contains too some of the noblest and boldest of Browning's theories upon the function and method of poetry, ideas which show him well ahead of his time.

To Browning himself the advantages of having written *Sordello* were as considerable as they were painful. On at least two levels his mind and spirit were cleared: on the ethical level he saw the imperfections of the introspective, analytical type of person he was, as was Sordello, and also the imperfections of the man of action, such

[22] *New Letters,* ed. DeVane and Knickerbocker, p. 23.
[23] See *The Browning Collections* (Sotheby Catalogue, 1913), p. 39.

as Salinguerra; and he completed his discovery of his own relation to society. On another level Browning made considerable progress in discovering and curing, at least for a time, his difficulties in conveying his vast abstract impressions and conceptions through his language; and he learned the necessity of dealing with sense objects directly and simply, if he wished to be heard.[24]

[24] See the two remarkable articles by S. W. Holmes: "Browning's *Sordello* and Jung: Browning's *Sordello* in the light of Jung's Theory of Types" in *PMLA* 56:758–96 (September, 1941) and "Browning: Semantic Stutterer" in *PMLA* 60:231–55 (1945). In the first of these articles Mr. Holmes describes Browning's nature as it appears in *Sordello* as the introverted, intuitive type, and records Browning's partial success in becoming one of the "wise men who do not merely talk about the meaning of life and the world, but really possess it." The second article analyzes the reasons for Browning's dilemma: the necessity he had to write as a poet-prophet and his verbal "impotence" on the metaphysical plane. His "semantic blockages" rose from his personality and the idealistic temper of the age, and were not helped by his disastrously irregular education. In *Sordello* Browning almost discovered psychoanalysis, the modern way of stating and healing such troubles.

❧ III ❧

BELLS AND POMEGRANATES

BETWEEN the years years 1841 and 1846—that is, after the publication of *Sordello* and until his marriage and removal to Italy—all of Browning's poetry was published in a series which he called *Bells and Pomegranates*. The eight pamphlets which made up the series, with the date of publication, the number of pages in each, and the price at which each was offered per copy, are listed below:

   I. Pippa Passes, April, 1841; 16 pages; Sixpence.
  II. King Victor and King Charles, March 12, 1842; 20 pages; One Shilling.
 III. Dramatic Lyrics, November 26, 1842; 16 pages; One Shilling.
 IV. The Return of the Druses, January, 1843; 20 pages; One Shilling.
  V. A Blot in the 'Scutcheon, February 11, 1843; 16 pages; One Shilling.
 VI. Colombe's Birthday, April 20, 1844; 20 pages; One Shilling.
VII. Dramatic Romances and Lyrics, November 6, 1845; 24 pages; Two Shillings.
VIII. Luria and A Soul's Tragedy, April 13, 1846; 32 pages; Two Shillings Sixpence.

The mode of publishing his poems in a series of pamphlets was suggested to Browning by Edward Moxon, the publisher of *Sordello*, who also published the poetry of Wordsworth, Tennyson, Samuel Rogers, Coventry Patmore, and Miss Barrett. Moxon had republished Elizabethan plays in this manner, and proposed it to Browning as an economical method. Each pamphlet was to be printed in fine type and double columns, and was to be bound in paper wrappers. The cost of publication was borne by the poet's father, and amounted to approximately £16 a pamphlet. The later pamphlets, being longer, were a little more expensive, and for this reason the price per single copy was increased. When the series was completed in 1846 Moxon bound the remainders of the eight numbers into single volumes, royal octavo bound in dark green cloth, and offered them for sale under the title, *Bells and Pomegranates*. The curiosity of the bound volumes is that most of them have the "Second Edition" of *Bell No. V*. This is a reprint of the first edition, which had been struck off hastily by Moxon at Browning's request to prevent Macready, the actor and producer, from mutilating the play in its first performance on February 11, 1843.

It was Browning's original intention to make the series one entirely of plays, and he thought of re-touching *Strafford* and including it in the series.[1] But Moxon persuaded him to publish his shorter poems, *Dramatic Lyrics* (*Bell* No. III) and *Dramatic Romances* (*Bell* No. VII), for popularity's sake. Though the poet condescended to seek for popularity through his shorter poems, it was only the energetic remonstrances of Miss Barrett which at last made him give the public an explanation of his title, *Bells and Pomegranates*. As a foreword to *A Soul's Tragedy*, and in effect excluding that poem from the series, between the two parts of *Bell* No. VIII, he wrote:

Here ends my first Series of "Bells and Pomegranates": and I take the opportunity of explaining, in reply to inquiries, that I only meant by that title to indicate an endeavour towards something like an alternation, or mixture, of music with discoursing, sound with sense, poetry with thought; which looks too ambitious, thus expressed, so the symbol was preferred. It is little to the purpose, that such is actually one of the most familiar of the many Rabbinical (and Patristic) acceptations of the phrase; because I confess that, letting authority alone, I supposed the bare words, in such juxtaposition, would sufficiently convey the desired meaning. "Faith and good works" is another fancy, for instance, and perhaps no easier to arrive at: yet Giotto placed a pomegranate fruit in the hand of Dante, and Raffaele crowned his Theology (in the *Camera della Segnatura*) with blossoms of the same; as if the Bellari and Vasari would be sure to come after, and explain that it was merely *"simbolo delle buone opere—il qual Pomogranato fu però usato nelle vesti del Pontefice appresso gli Ebrei."* [2]

Neither Miss Barrett nor the general reader was as familiar with rabbinical and patristic lore, or indeed with *Exodus*, whence the symbolism rises (28:33–4), as one should be.

It is significant that all the pamphlets of the series of *Bells and*

---

[1] See F. G. Kenyon, *Robert Browning and Alfred Domett*, London, 1906, p. 38.

[2] For a full discussion of the historical meaning and the great wealth of symbolism connected with Browning's title see Judith Berlin-Lieberman, *Robert Browning and Hebraism*, Jerusalem, 1934, pp. 19–29.

Pomegranates bore the legend "By Robert Browning, Author of *Paracelsus.*" Indeed, the *Bells* show Browning beginning anew in his attempt to rebuild his literary reputation after the havoc which *Sordello* had made of his old one. The *Bells*, especially *Pippa Passes* and the shorter poems, show Browning's genius clearing magnificently, and the poet working towards the perfected dramatic lyrics and dramatic monologues which are to be in time the happiest vehicles of his expression. Through the Forties and Fifties the *Bells* gradually won to Browning not a large but a devoted circle of readers.

PIPPA PASSES

PUBLICATION

Pippa Passes, first of the *Bells and Pomegranates* series, was published in April, 1841. The little pamphlet, bound in yellow paper wrappers, consisted of the title-page (p. 1): "Bells and Pomegranates. No. I.—Pippa Passes. By Robert Browning, Author of "Paracelsus." London:Edward Moxon, Dover Street. MDCCCXLI."; an advertisement (p. 2) quoted below; and the text, pp. 3–16. The pamphlet was published for £16, paid by the senior Robert Browning. It sold for Sixpence a copy. No second edition was necessary at the time, but the poem was, of course, published in all the collected editions of Browning's works.

TEXT

When *Pippa Passes* appeared in 1841 it was made up of a *Proem,* four parts entitled *Morning, Noon, Evening,* and *Night,* and an *Epilogue.* In all there were 1722 lines, mainly in blank verse, but with a great variety of verse-forms, some prose, and seven songs. In the original edition the lines were distributed as follows: *Proem,* 214 lines; I. *Morning,* i—282 lines in verse, ii—161 lines of prose; II. *Noon,* i—327 lines of verse, ii—83 lines of prose; III. *Evening,* i— 229 lines of verse; ii—91 lines of verse and prose; IV. *Night,* prose and song, 221 lines; *Epilogue,* 114 lines. The song, "A king lived long ago," which appears in Part III as a song of sixty lines, was first printed in the *Monthly Repository* for November, 1835, as a poem of fifty-four lines. It is greatly altered in *Pippa Passes.*

The final text of *Pippa Passes* as Browning left it in 1888 differs very considerably from the original text.[3] Most of the changes were made for the first collected edition of 1849. The bulk of the poem remains the same, but there are changes in lines, phrases, words, and punctuation. After 1849 changes were made for successive collected editions, but these were comparatively minor alterations.

GENESIS AND COMPOSITION

It is easy to see that *Pippa Passes* is a happy by-product of the poet's labors on *Sordello*. In his travels in northern Italy in June, 1838, in search of local color for *Sordello*, Browning came upon "delicious Asolo," a town which he was to celebrate in his very last volume of poems. It was his imaginative observation of the life in that small city which gave him most of his materials for *Pippa Passes*. But the poem was certainly not written on the spot in 1838, for we know from the letter which Browning wrote to Miss Haworth upon his return to England late in July of 1838 that he "did not write six lines while absent (except a scene in a play, jotted down as we sailed thro' the Straits of Gibraltar)." [4] It is possible that this "scene in a play" may be the present Part III of *Pippa Passes,* the scene between Luigi and his mother: the matter dealt with there, the questions of tyranny and revolt, of high resolve and noble action, is the matter of *Strafford, Sordello, King Victor and King Charles,* and *The Return of the Druses,* poems which were much in Browning's mind at the time. On his return from Italy he began at once to work upon *Sordello,* which he finished on May 26, 1839. *Pippa Passes,* being in a sense a commentary upon *Sordello,* was probably written in the late spring and early summer of this year.

SOURCES AND INFLUENCES

Camberwell, the home of the Brownings until December, 1840, was not far from Dulwich Wood, and it was here, according to Mrs. Orr, that the conception of *Pippa Passes* took place.

Mr. Browning was walking alone, in a wood near Dulwich, when the image flashed upon him of some one walking thus alone through life; one apparently too obscure to leave a trace of his or her passage, yet exercising

---

[3] The variations in *Pippa* are recorded in Nicoll and Wise, *Literary Anecdotes of the Nineteenth Century,* I, 508–12. We learn from a letter of Mrs. Browning's dated February 4, 1847, that Browning was busy revising *Pippa* for a new edition; see Miller, *Robert Browning,* p. 145.

[4] Orr, *Life,* p. 91.

a lasting though unconscious influence at every step of it; and the image shaped itself into the little silk winder of Asolo, Felippa, or Pippa.[5]

The idea of a series of tenuously connected dramatic scenes was a happy modification of the usual type of stage play which was so much in Browning's mind at the time. When *Sordello* was published on March 7, 1840, *Pippa Passes* was announced as nearly ready, along with *King Victor and King Charles* and *Mansoor the Hierophant* (*The Return of the Druses*). We learn from a letter to Miss Flower that by March 9, 1840, Browning had shown *Pippa* to her, for on this date he wrote suggesting that she compose music for the lyrics.[6]

Probably because of the poor success of *Sordello*, *Pippa Passes* did not appear until more than a year later. In the first edition it was prefaced by an advertisement which in later editions was compressed into the dedication at the end. The advertisement reveals the chastened spirit of the poet in 1841:

Two or three years ago I wrote a Play, about which the chief matter I much care to recollect at present is, that a Pitfull of goodnatured people applauded it:—ever since, I have been desirous of doing something in the same way that should better reward their attention. What follows I mean for the first of a series of Dramatical Pieces, to come out at intervals, and I amuse myself by fancying that the cheap mode in which they appear will for once help me to a sort of Pit-audience again. Of course such a work must go on no longer than it is liked; and to provide against a certain and but too possible contingency, let me hasten to say now—what, if I were sure of success, I would try to say circumstantially enough at the close— that I dedicate my best intentions most admiringly to the Author of "Ion"— most affectionately to Serjeant Talfourd.

As an experiment in dramatic form *Pippa Passes* follows no tradition, and is transitional in Browning's development. The poem shows him attempting to fuse the subjective and objective strains in his writing, and moving towards the dramatic monologue as he learns to project his insights outward and portray imaginary characters under the stress of psychological conflicts.[7] Intensely original as it is, very few sources have been found for the poem as a whole or for the separate

[5] Orr, *Handbook*, p. 55.

[6] Orr, *Life*, pp. 102–3.

[7] See the admirable analysis of *Pippa Passes* in E. D. H. Johnson's *The Alien Vision of Victorian Poetry*, pp. 86–91. In the latter part of his comment Johnson shows how each situation in the poem hinges upon the conflict between an individual and an authority of some sort, and how Browning defies conventional morality, conventional behavior, conventional political ideas, and religious formalism in the course of the poem.

episodes. But first, the relation of the poem to *Sordello* requires some comment. *Pippa Passes* is the better spirit of *Sordello,* and seems to have been written in a mood of revulsion from the longer poem. *Sordello* closes with a poor barefoot boy climbing the dewy hillside of Asolo in the early morning and singing "to beat the lark, God's poet, swooning at his feet." *Pippa* begins where *Sordello* left off. Both Pippa and Sordello were stolen children, who turn out in the end to be the offspring of wealthy parents. Both of them are solitary natures who pass through a series of crises. Pippa is unconscious of the effect she is having upon the world; Sordello is conscious to the point of morbidity. Browning had grown tired of the fruitless life which Sordello lived; he even, towards the end of *Sordello,* called that life a "sorry farce." On the contrary, Pippa is most effective: her songs awaken the hearts of those who hear them, and the awakenings lead to momentous actions. Both poems exhibit to a surprising degree that interest in common humanity which was the great discovery of Sordello, the origin of which we have traced to Browning's study of Strafford's life and policies, and to the journey to Italy in 1838.

But above all else, *Pippa Passes* is the product of Browning's firsthand observation of life in the Italian towns near Venice in June, 1838. He made use of the topography of Asolo and of the conditions in the silk-mills, Asolo's main industry at the time. He made use of the people he saw there—the wealthy mill-owners and the workers, the peasantry, the Austrian police, and the itinerant students from Germany, France, and England. The worldly conditions of the Church and clergy did not escape him; nor did he miss that spirit of latent political rebellion which was rife in Italy at the time. Asolo as it was in 1838 is put before our eyes in *Pippa Passes.*

Perhaps it is worth noticing that the intensity of the emotional crises, as well as the language occasionally, shows that Browning had begun to study Shakespeare as a dramatic model. It is possible that the great passage in *Pippa Passes,* I, telling of the adulterous love of Ottima and Sebald in the forest when the lightning came to find them out, was suggested by Lear's magnificent lines in the storm:

> Let the great gods,
> That keep this dreadful pother o'er our heads,
> Find out their enemies now. . . . (III, ii, 49–51)

In both scenes the lightning is used as the agent of the gods to seek out "undivulged crimes," and Lear's mind is running on adultery and fleshly sins. *King Lear* was perhaps Browning's favorite Shake-spearean play. It has been observed also that the scene between Ottima and Sebald owes something to *Macbeth,* II, ii, and III, ii, 11–12, and that Ottima is like Lady Macbeth "Magnificent in sin." [8] Browning had seen *Macbeth* acted several times in 1840, both by Macready and by Kean.[9] The excellent and vigorous prose of *Pippa Passes* is likewise reminiscent of the Elizabethans.

In his *History of Early Nineteenth Century Drama, 1800–1850,* Allardyce Nicoll noticed in 1930 that Browning used the plot of Lytton's *Lady of Lyons,* with some differences, for the Jules-Phene episode of *Pippa Passes.*[10] As F. E. Faverty has shown, Browning was in the theater on August 21, 1839, when Macready acted Lytton's popular play, and also at other performances of it in the same year.[11] Faverty goes on to show the similarities and the differences. In *The Lady of Lyons; or, Love and Pride,* Pauline Deschappelles scorns the suit of Blauséant, and his friend Glavis, and brings down vengeance upon herself. Pauline, like Jules, is tricked into marrying below her station, but in both cases love eventually conquers pride and forgiveness follows. Professor Faverty shows that this is as far as Browning follows Lytton's plot, but that he goes on to follow Lytton's acknowledged source, *The History of Perourou; or the Bellows-Mender, an Interesting Tale,* translated from the French by Helen Maria Williams, in a number of editions before 1820. Here the plot is the same, but the people who trick the proud Aurora into marrying a poor engraver are six artists or fellow-engravers.[12] The forgiveness and reconciliation follow.

No direct sources for other parts of *Pippa Passes* have been discovered, but Miss Barrett, as we see from an unpublished letter in the Wellesley College Library dated July 15, 1841, saw early the general influence of Walter Savage Landor upon Browning's poem. That was a debt that the younger poet was always eager to acknowledge.

[8] See I. M. Ariail, "Is *Pippa Passes* a Dramatic Failure?" in *Studies in Philology* 37:126–7. This article is summarized below. See also the comment of E. E. Stoll upon Ottima, Lady Macbeth, and Milton's Eve in his volume *From Shakespeare to Joyce,* p. 152.

[9] *New Letters,* ed. DeVane and Knickerbocker, pp. 22–3.

[10] I, 173–5.

[11] See Frederic E. Faverty, "The Source of the Jules-Phene Episode in *Pippa Passes,*" in *Studies in Philology* 38:97–105 (1941).

[12] Professor Faverty is correct in his observation that Browning failed to improve the dramatic situation of his sources and that the revenge is out of proportion to the offence. Browning's scene is feeble in motivation of the preliminary action and weak in dramatic construction.

AFTER-HISTORY

Pippa Passes holds an honorable and significant place in the history of Browning's development as a poet. Here he broke from the rigid form of the acted play and strode towards the free expression of his natural genius. Here he forsook the intellectual analysis of remote historical figures, requiring documentation to be understood, for the close observation of modern life, for the lyrical expression of emotion. In *Pippa Passes* for the first time Browning's voice rings true, and we recognize the poet known to all for his interest in life, his inventive ingenuity in form and manner, and his robust and optimistic spirit.

In 1841, however, and for many years afterwards, very few recognized Browning's achievement. In 1845 Elizabeth Barrett admitted that she could find it in her heart to covet the authorship of *Pippa Passes,* and Browning, whose judgment upon his own work was not always good, declared that he liked it better than anything he had ever done.[13] From the simplicity and beauty of the poem there was every reason to expect its immediate success, but such was the blight left upon Browning's reputation by *Sordello* that, together with the cheap form of publication, *Pippa Passes* received a very cool welcome from the reviewers.[14] Only Browning's friend, John Forster, in the *Examiner* for October 2, 1841, hailed the poem as showing that Browning was upon the right highway. Misapprehensions were numerous. Because *Pippa Passes* was No. I in the series of *Bells and Pomegranates,* the critic in the *Atlas* for May 1, 1841, assumed that the poem was not an independent whole, but was the first part of a larger work, and that Pippa's sinister passing would be explained in a sequel. The moral tone of the scene between Ottima and Sebald was attacked. "In one scene," said the reviewer in the *Spectator* for April 17, 1841, "a young wife and her paramour discuss their loves, and the murder of the 'old husband' needlessly, openly, wantonly, tediously, and without a touch of compunction, sentiment, or true passion." Lounsbury's comment upon this criticism is worthy of quotation: "This was the way in which appeared to this austere literary guide that tremendous scene in which sin, suddenly shown its own grossness, seeks death as the only expiation for guilt." It was such critiques as the *Spectator's* that caused Browning's friend, Al-

[13] *Letters of R.B. and E.B.B.,* I, 22, 28.
[14] See T. R. Lounsbury, *Early Literary Career of Robert Browning,* pp. 106–12.

fred Domett, to boil over into his savage verses, *On a Certain Critique on "Pippa Passes."* [15]

In spite of the adverse opinions of most of the reviewers, *Pippa* was a step in the recovery of Browning's poetic reputation. The sale was poor, but the poem slowly won its way. It has been since recognized as one of the chief stars in Browning's poetic crown. In recent years only Chesterton's criticism has borne much weight against the poem: that the coincidence of Pippa's singing at the critical moments in the lives of the several groups is stretched too far for conviction, and that it was an artistic mistake to involve the fate of Pippa herself in the last scene. This criticism has some force, but Browning's conception will seem to most to be a legitimate poetic extension of the idea that the casual spoken word may have a tremendous effect upon the lives of men.

More recently, a good deal of critical attention has been paid to *Pippa Passes.* In 1936 Arthur E. DuBois in his article, "Robert Browning, Dramatist," [16] found the play potentially great, and the most original and forward-looking since Sheridan. But in his opinion it fails of being even a good play. Browning surrounds the naive Pippa with the irony of real life but dares not laugh at her, and one leaves the play dissatisfied, unreconciled to men by either laughter or tears. But this is to try the poem by dramatic criteria that it never aimed to meet. In 1939 H. B. Charlton published an article entitled "Browning as Dramatist" [17] that was more judicious. In his opinion *Pippa* allows Browning's dramatic gift much more freedom than the formal play, and in the scene between Ottima and Sebald the poet produced the finest single dramatic scene in the nineteenth century. If Browning had written nothing after *Pippa* it would have been said that the world had lost a stupendous dramatist. But in that opinion, says Charlton, the world would have been mistaken, for the poet leaves too much of the world out of his consideration. But he sees in the poem a great advance in dramatic skill.

In 1939, also, two other critics found themselves at odds upon the dramatic merits of *Pippa Passes.* J. M. Purcell in an article entitled "The Dramatic Failure of *Pippa Passes*," [18] based his charges upon three points: (1) that Ottima and Sebald are not saved by Pippa's

[15] First published in *Flotsam and Jetsam*, London, 1877. See also F. G. Kenyon, *Robert Browning and Alfred Domett*, p. 20.
[16] *Studies in Philology* 33:643–51.
[17] *Bulletin of the John Rylands Library* 23:33–67.
[18] *Studies in Philology* 36:77–8.

song and that it is a perversion of Christian doctrine to infer that murder and suicide are compensation for adultery and murder; (2) that Browning has not accomplished his dramatic purpose of making Ottima the most important character in the scene; (3) that the Monsignor of Part IV is not portrayed as a character of evil intentions as it was Browning's purpose he should be. Mr. Purcell's arguments were, in part, theologically slanted, and do not carry conviction. He was effectively answered, especially in his first point, by J. M. Ariail in an article, "Is *Pippa Passes* a Dramatic Failure?" [19] In an excellent analysis of the scene, Mr. Ariail shows that salvation means to Browning the realization of one central truth involving repentance and expiation before death, apprehended in one supreme moment. Moreover, in Part IV the Monsignor is tempted by the opportunity to sacrifice Pippa in order to get her fortune, until Pippa's song saves him. Both commentators agree that there are flaws in dramatic technique in the poem.

KING VICTOR AND KING CHARLES

PUBLICATION

King Victor and King Charles, a pamphlet of twenty pages, bound in yellow paper covers, was published on March 12, 1842. It consisted of the title-page: "Bells and Pomegranates. No. II.—King Victor and King Charles. By Robert Browning, Author of "Paracelsus." London: Edward Moxon, Dover Street. MDCCCXLII."; an advertisement; and the text, pp. 3–20. The pamphlet was printed at the expense of the poet's father, and cost approximately £16. The published price was One Shilling the copy. There was no second edition of the poem, but it has taken its place in all the collected editions of the poet's work.

From a letter written to Macready on April 26, 1842, it is clear that Browning had planned to make *A Blot in the 'Scutcheon* the second issue of *Bells and Pomegranates*. But Macready had delayed in considering the play, and Browning had to publish *King Victor and King Charles* as the second *Bell*. He thought this "a very indifferent substitute, whose success will be problematical enough." [1]

[19] *Studies in Philology* 37:120–9.
[1] *New Letters,* ed. DeVane and Knickerbocker, p. 25.

TEXT

In the original edition, and all other editions thereafter, the play consisted of 1626 lines of blank verse, divided in the following way: *King Victor,* I—313 lines; *King Victor,* II—543 lines; *King Charles,* I—408 lines; *King Charles,* II—362 lines. The text of the play, though not changing in bulk, was subjected to steady revision in phrase, word, and punctuation. Most of the alterations were made for the edition of 1849, but changes continued to appear until the final edition of 1888.

GENESIS AND COMPOSITION

King Victor and King Charles seems to have been conceived, and possibly written, more than four years before it was published. In a letter to Miss Haworth, probably written about August 1, 1837, Browning said:

I am going to begin the finishing *Sordello*—and to begin thinking a Tragedy (an Historical one, so I shall want heaps of criticisms on *Strafford*) and I want to have *another* tragedy in prospect, I write best so provided. . . . I want a subject of the most wild and passionate love, to contrast with the one I mean to have ready in a short time.[2]

The passionate play referred to here can only be the one that came to be *The Return of the Druses,* and the historical one that Browning means to have ready in a short time is *King Victor and King Charles.* Like its immediate predecessor *Strafford,* published on May 1, 1837, the new play was to have a background of statecraft and politics, and to be motivated by Browning's new-found interest in liberal and humanitarian causes. It is possible that Browning wrote *King Victor and King Charles* in August and September of 1837 before he returned to the task of finishing *Sordello.*

For two years we hear nothing of the play, but on September 5, 1839, Macready, the actor and manager, recorded in his *Diaries* that he had "Read Browning's play on Victor, King of Sardinia—it turned out to be a *great mistake.* I called Browning into my room and most explicitly told him so, and gave him my reasons for coming to such a conclusion." [3] From this evidence it seems probable that after Browning had finished *Sordello* in May, 1839, and perhaps written *Pippa Passes,* he turned again in the summer to *King Victor and King*

[2] Orr, *Life,* pp. 96–7.
[3] Macready, *Diaries,* ed. W. Toynbee, II, 23.

Charles and at that time completed or revised it. The play was advertised as nearly ready at the end of the *Sordello* volume, and on March 12, 1842, Moxon announced the "New Dramatic Poem by Mr. Browning."

SOURCES AND INFLUENCES

King Victor and King Charles is a drama "modelled on the simple lines of Alfieri, whose works Browning had been studying very closely." [4] One day is given to each half of the play, and a single scene serves for the whole. Whatever turned his attention to the colorful figure of Victor Amadeus II (1666–1731), Duke of Savoy and King of Sardinia, Browning is at some pains to stress the historical foundations of his play in the advertisement which he prefixed to the first edition and retained in all subsequent editions. Here he mentions as the sources of his conception Voltaire, Condorcet, the Abbé Roman's *Récit,* and the fifth of Lord Orrery's *Letters from Italy.* Of these and other memoirs he says:

From these only may be obtained a knowledge of the fiery and audacious temper, unscrupulous selfishness, profound dissimulation, and singular fertility in resources, of Victor—the extreme and painful sensibility, prolonged immaturity of powers, earnest good purpose and vacillating will of Charles—the noble and right woman's manliness of his wife—and the ill-considered rascality and subsequent better-advised rectitude of D'Ormea.

The course of Browning's researches for the matter of the play was not so formidable as he would make the reader think. He went, as was his custom during these years, to the *Biographie universelle* (Paris, 1822) in his father's library,[5] and from the accounts given there of Victor, Charles Emanuel, and Ormea, he pieced out his plot; he was directed by the *Biographie* to Condorcet's long commentary on Voltaire's brief account, as we shall see, for further details. Browning's main source for the play is the life of Victor Amédée II, twenty-six columns long, in the *Biographie.* Here he read of Victor's youth, spent under the severe tutelage of his mother, of his marriage to the niece of Louis XIV, and his accession to the throne at an early age, of his astonishing astuteness in the political and military conditions of the time as he played France against the league of imperial nations and the league against France, of his becoming king of Sicily in 1713, and

[4] Griffin and Minchin, *Life,* p. 126.
[5] *Idem,* p. 25.

of the forced exchange of Sicily for Sardinia in 1718, and of Victor's achievement in making Savoy a respected country among the powers. But most of the account in the *Biographie* was devoted to a circumstantial account of the last two years of the magnificent old king. After his first wife's death, Victor secretly married the Contessa di San Sebastiano, lady-in-waiting to his son's wife, abdicated his throne and retired to Chambéry in September, 1730. But the Contessa proved to be ambitious and scheming and persuaded him to attempt to take his crown again. His son, Charles Emanuel III, arrested him and confined him in the castle at Rivoli, and later at Moncalieri, where he died on October 31, 1732.

This is essentially the story that Voltaire tells at the end of the third chapter of his *Précis du siécle de Louis XV*, and Voltaire adds, "Neither the abdication of this king, nor his attempt to take again the scepter, neither his imprisonment, nor his death, caused the least motion among the neighboring nations. It was a terrible event without consequences."

Browning's attention was directed to this passage in Voltaire by the account of Ormea in the *Biographie universelle*, which also directed him to the note which Condorcet had appended to Voltaire's words. Condorcet's edition of the *Oeuvres complètes de Voltaire* [6] was probably in the Browning library, and from Condorcet's note, which is long and detailed, the English poet took the features of Charles Emanuel and of Ormea, besides many hints and names for his play. Victor's early neglect of Charles is recounted, as well as his later efforts to educate Charles in statecraft, and the suffering of Charles is ascribed to "his sweetness and his natural timidity," qualities which made his father very impatient with him. But it was in the account of the life of Charles in the *Biographie universelle* that Browning got the hint which he makes, quite unhistorically, the mainspring of Charles's character. There he read that one of the first things the young king did upon his accession was to relieve his nobles from the heavy exactions which his father had put upon them. This act of policy Browning metamorphoses into a strong and determined liberalism. He endows King Charles with that interest in the cause of humanity which he had discovered in himself in his work upon *Strafford* and *Sordello*. From Condorcet's note, also, Browning formed his conception of

---

[6] See the Kehl edition in seventy volumes, printed at Strasbourg in 1785 and edited by several hands, among them Condorcet. His note may be found in XXII, 39–43.

the character of the Ormea whom we see in the first half of the play. Condorcet attempts to make Ormea the villain of the action, plunging both Victor and Charles into misery by his rascality and ingratitude. The Ormea of the last half of Browning's play, however, reformed and honorable, is drawn from the account of Ormea in the *Biographie universelle,* where the biographer is eager to clear the character of his subject. He confutes the view held by Condorcet:

Condorcet, in a long note in which he pretends to set right the narrative of Voltaire, treats as fables the attempts of Victor to regain his throne, and only sees, in all this catastrophe, an odious machination conducted by Ormea. It is in the article upon King Victor that one naturally finds the refutation of the commentator upon Voltaire. . . . If one can suppose that Ormea dared to calumniate his first master, how is it possible that this plot should remain unknown to Charles Emanuel? During the whole course of his reign, he did not cease to see in his minister the person who had discovered the projects of an ambitious woman [Contessa di Sebastiano, Victor's second wife].

The account of the actions of King Victor given by Lord Orrery [7] is a vivid but inaccurate narrative. Its chief interest for us lies in the emphasis which it puts upon the villainy of the Contessa di Sebastiano.

AFTER-HISTORY

The appearance of *King Victor and King Charles* on March 12, 1842, evoked little critical comment. This play is probably the most neglected of all Browning's works. As we have seen, Macready rejected it for the stage. In a review of *Dramatic Lyrics,* the third number of *Bells and Pomegranates,* in the *Examiner* for November 26, 1842, John Forster saw in the play signs of better poetry. The reprinting of the play in all the editions of Browning's works argues that he himself thought well enough of it, but that the play did not affect his life greatly is suggested by the fact that neither he nor Miss Barrett ever referred to it in their correspondence. So far as I know, this play has never been performed.

In recent criticism *King Victor and King Charles* has suffered neglect. In his article "Robert Browning, Dramatist," [8] A. E. DuBois cites Charles as the full-blown idealist who struggles with Victor, the

---

[7] *Letters from Italy in the Years 1754 and 1755 by the Late Right Honourable John, Earl of Corke and Orrery,* London, 1773, pp. 46–52. I have not been able to see Abbé Roman's *Récit.*

[8] *Studies in Philology* 33:646 (1936).

full-blown realist, and points out that this characteristic situation recurs frequently in Browning's plays, to the damage both of dramatic characters and the action. In 1939 H. B. Charlton [9] pointed out as characteristic of the poet's thinking that though the story of *King Victor and King Charles* is a political one, the theme is essentially unpolitical. The kingdom is transferred as if it were a private estate, and Browning does not deal with the issues of kingship or the consequences upon the people. It is a play of individual sentiments. Only Ormea is psychologically real. Charlton concludes that this play is a signal failure. In its history it has had few defenders.

DRAMATIC LYRICS

PUBLICATION

The *Dramatic Lyrics,* a pamphlet of sixteen pages bound in yellow paper wrappers, appeared in the latter part of November, 1842. The booklet, printed in double columns and fine type, consisted of the title-page: "Bells and Pomegranates. No. III.—Dramatic Lyrics. By Robert Browning, Author of 'Paracelsus.' London: Edward Moxon, Dover Street. MDCCCXLII."; an advertisement, quoted below; and the text, pp. 3–16. The cost of printing, approximately £16, was borne by the poet's father. The published price was One Shilling.

TEXT

There was no table of contents in the original *Dramatic Lyrics,* but the pamphlet consisted of the following poems in this order:

Cavalier Tunes	I. Marching Along
	II. Give a Rouse
	III. My Wife Gertrude [later called *Boot and Saddle*]
Italy and France	I. Italy [later called *My Last Duchess*]
	II. France [later called *Count Gismond*]
Camp and Cloister	I. Camp (French) [later called *Incident of the French Camp*]
	II. Cloister (Spanish) [later called *Soliloquy of the Spanish Cloister*]
In a Gondola	
Artemis Prologuizes	
Waring	

[9] "Browning as Dramatist" in *Bulletin of the John Rylands Library* 23:47–8.

| Queen-Worship | I. Rudel and the Lady of Tripoli [later called *Rudel to the Lady of Tripoli*]
II. Cristina |
| Madhouse Cells | I. "There's Heaven above . . ." [later called *Johannes Agricola in Meditation*]
II. "The rain set early in to-night . . ." [later called *Porphyria's Lover*] |

Through the Metidja to Abd-el-Kadr.—1842.
The Pied Piper of Hamelin; A Child's Story.

Of the ten groups listed here only one had been published before 1842. The two parts of *Madhouse Cells* had appeared under the separate titles, *Porphyria* and *Johannes Agricola,* in the *Monthly Repository* in 1836 (N.S. 10:43–6), where they were signed "Z." The title, *Madhouse Cells,* took the place of the separate titles in 1842.

In the collected edition of 1849 Browning reprinted these short poems, together with the *Dramatic Romances* of 1845, under the joint heading of *Dramatic Romances and Lyrics,* the *Dramatic Lyrics* coming first and the *Dramatic Romances* following. In 1849 Browning dropped most of the old groupings of his poems, such as *Camp and Cloister,* and the poems generally appear under their present titles as individual pieces. *Johannes Agricola in Meditation* and *Porphyria's Lover,* however, are still bound together as *Madhouse Cell,* I and II; *Cavalier Tunes* has stood unchanged as a natural unit since its first appearance.

In preparing his collected edition of 1863, Browning took the three groups of the shorter poems which he had published up to that time, *Dramatic Lyrics* (1842), *Dramatic Romances* (1845), and *Men and Women* (1855), and still using the old titles, re-grouped his poems under what seemed to him their logical description. Of the *Dramatic Lyrics* of 1842 only four poems were retained in the new grouping: *Cavalier Tunes, Through the Metidja, Soliloquy of the Spanish Cloister* and *Cristina.* The following poems had become *Dramatic Romances: My Last Duchess, Count Gismond, Incident of the French Camp, In a Gondola, Waring, The Pied Piper,* and *Porphyria's Lover.* Three of the original *Dramatic Lyrics* were put under the heading of *Men and Women: Artemis Prologizes, Rudel to the Lady of Tripoli,* and *Johannes Agricola.* The logic of Browning's re-assignment is not always apparent.

The caption *Dramatic Lyrics,* as it stands in the collected editions of Browning's works after 1863, includes fifty poems, mostly culled from the original *Men and Women*. I shall of course deal with the poems in the original order of publication; but I shall attempt, as I come to each, to trace its history in these subsequent re-groupings.

GENESIS AND COMPOSITION

From Browning's letter to his friend Alfred Domett on May 22, 1842, we learn that Moxon, the publisher of *Bells and Pomegranates,* suggested that he should print a collection of his small poems for popularity's sake.[1] This is the first sign we have of the approaching collection of *Dramatic Lyrics.* In July, Browning has the title, and the new number of the series of *Bells* is taking shape in his mind. On July 13 he writes to Domett:

I shall print nothing till October—the book season has been, says Moxon, no season at all. . . . I then hope to go on with my plays and to get out, what I call, some dramatic Lyrics, which I shall make part of the series. . . .[2]

The poems which appeared in 1842 were written over a period of eight years: *Porphyria* and *Johannes Agricola* are said to have been composed in the spring of 1834 when Browning was in St. Petersburg, Russia; the *Cavalier Tunes* were probably written in the summer of 1842 for the second centenary of the beginning of the Civil Wars.

SOURCES AND INFLUENCES

In the advertisement which appears on the second page of the original *Dramatic Lyrics,* one may observe perhaps Browning's preoccupation at this time with the drama; but one may see more surely his sensitiveness, felt since the publication of *Pauline* and Mill's criticism of it, about being thought to speak personally in his poems. The advertisement read,

Such poems as the following come properly enough, I suppose, under the head of "Dramatic Pieces"; being, though for the most part Lyric in expression, always Dramatic in principle, and so many utterances of so many imaginary persons, not mine.

This warning was perhaps necessary to an age which was steeped in the lyrical poetry of the Romantic poets. Yet new as they are in

[1] F. G. Kenyon, *Robert Browning and Alfred Domett,* p. 36.
[2] *Idem,* p. 42.

method and psychology, it is not likely that the *Dramatic Lyrics* could have been misconstrued as Browning's personal expression. Many of the poems came naturally to him as by-products of his longer works: the *Cavalier Tunes* rose from his studies for his play *Strafford;* *Rudel* and *My Last Duchess* came from two phases of his study for *Sordello.* Several of the poems—and indeed perhaps Browning's delight in attempting to distil the atmosphere of a time and a place into a few lines of verse—are the direct result of his travels: *Porphyria* still has a faint odor of Russia in it; *My Last Duchess* and *In a Gondola* would probably not have been written if Browning had not visited Italy in 1838. The martial music of the *Cavalier Tunes* owes something in manner to Sir Walter Scott. *Through the Metidja to Abd-el-Kadr,* probably written in 1842, is Browning's own, though Macaulay's *Lays of Ancient Rome* appeared almost at the same time as the *Dramatic Lyrics.* Browning had possibly passed through Hamelin in 1834 and again in 1838, but *The Pied Piper,* written in the poet's most natural light manner, came to him from his father's library. One sees in the *Dramatic Lyrics,* in the grouping of the poems under such headings as *Italy and France, Camp and Cloister* (*French* and *Spanish*), Browning's delight in delineating the essential qualities of national types and actions—a trait which was to appear again in *Dramatic Romances.*

AFTER-HISTORY

When the pamphlet of *Dramatic Lyrics* appeared it was scarcely noticed. In the *Examiner* for November 25, 1842, the poet's friend John Forster hailed the volume for what it was, a "continued advance in a right direction"; he admired the versification of Browning, praised admiringly *The Pied Piper* and the *Incident of the French Camp*—though he had nothing to say of *My Last Duchess*—and concluded, "In a word, Mr. Browning is a genuine poet, and only needs to have less misgiving on the subject himself. . . ." [3] This was almost the only recognition Browning won by the volume which, as we now know, was the first in that kind of poem which was to make his name universally honored. In the dramatic lyric and monologue he had at last found his true manner.

[3] Browning asked Moxon to hold up the publication of *Dramatic Lyrics* a week in order that Forster, who was busy, might be its first reviewer. See *New Letters,* ed. DeVane and Knickerbocker, p. 29.

Cavalier Tunes

The three rousing songs which made up this group, *Marching Along, Give a Rouse,* and *My Wife Gertrude* (changed in 1849 to *Boot and Saddle*) stood first in the volume of *Dramatic Lyrics,* published in November, 1842. The manuscript of *Cavalier Tunes* is in the possession of Professor C. B. Tinker, of Yale University, who has kindly permitted me to see it. For the most part it is clearly and straightforwardly written, but two alterations in the manuscript may be of significance. Browning arrived at the word "crop-headed," in the first stanza of *Marching Along,* with some difficulty; and in the third stanza of *My Wife Gertrude* he first wrote "Castle Barham[?]" and cancelled it in favor of "Castle Brancepeth." In the re-grouping of the shorter poems in 1863 the *Cavalier Tunes* remained under the heading of *Dramatic Lyrics.* The texts of the three poems, of twenty-four lines, twenty lines, and sixteen lines, respectively, underwent a few small changes for the collected edition of 1849, and a few changes in punctuation for later editions.

The *Cavalier Tunes* were probably written during the summer of 1842, and were intended to mark the second centenary of the beginning of the Civil Wars in England. The gentleman-soldiers of Charles I had made an early stand against the Parliamentary forces at Nottingham in August, 1642, and it is to this conflict that the Royalist gentleman of *Boot and Saddle* is hurrying from Castle Brancepeth in Durham. The *Tunes* rose naturally from Browning's study of the career of Strafford, King Charles's great champion, which he had made in 1836–7 for Forster's *Life of Strafford* and for his own play *Strafford.* In a brief article entitled, "Scott, Browning, and Kipling," Robert Liddell Lowe has pointed out the numerous similarities in phrase and rhythm between Scott's *Woodstock; or the Cavalier* and Browning's *Cavalier Tunes.*[4] For example, Scott uses the phrase "sound, boot and saddle—to horse and away" (Vol. I, Ch. 1). In his "Glee for King Charles" Scott rhymes the King's name with "base carles"; and again in *Woodstock* he describes Noll Cromwell's soldiers as "crop-eared canting villains" (Vol. I, Ch. 2). There are other likenesses—these are merely samples of Browning's verbal debt; his greater debt is to the manner and spirit of the older novelist and poet. Though Browning has given the Royalist supporters of

[4] *Notes and Queries* 197:103–4 (March 1, 1952).

Charles I voice in these songs, it is evident in *Strafford* and in the song in honor of Pym which concludes his *Parleying With Charles Avison* (1887) that his deeper sympathies were with the Parliamentarians.

My Last Duchess

My Last Duchess. Ferrara was published in *Dramatic Lyrics* in late November, 1842, as *I. Italy* under the general title *Italy and France.* In the collection of 1849 it was made one of the *Dramatic Romances and Lyrics,* and in the re-arrangement of the poems in 1863 it was put under *Dramatic Romances,* where it has remained. It appears in every collected edition. In 1849 the title was changed from *Italy* to *My Last Duchess. Ferrara,* and the present text was then virtually established. The changes in text between 1842 and 1849 are not great; the changes after 1849 are negligible. The poem is composed of fifty-six iambic lines, rhyming in couplets. In 1849 the somewhat meretricious connection between this poem and *Count Gismond (France)* was broken. It is evident, however, that Browning meant in 1842 to catch the tempers of the two countries—national psychologies interested him greatly—as well as to exhibit the nature of the marriage bond—in Italy the wife a chattel, in France an adored mistress.

In his travels in Italy in June and July, 1838, Browning did not go to Ferrara, but, as we have seen, he read deeply in the history of that city for the last phase of *Sordello,* and *My Last Duchess* is in a sense a stone from that great quarry. A more immediate impetus to the idea of the poem occurred in 1842. Between May 27 and July 1 of that year, as Donald Smalley has shown,[5] Browning was occupied in writing his review of R. H. Wilde's *Conjectures and Researches concerning the Love Madness and Imprisonment of Torquato Tasso.* This review turned, after a few pages upon Tasso, into the passionate defence of Chatterton. Browning, of course, knew Tasso's poetry well, but in looking up the facts of Tasso's biography in the *Biographie universelle* or Muratori's *Della Antichita Estensi,* both of which he had used for *Sordello,* the poet would have come upon the figure

---

[5] *Browning's Essay on Chatterton,* 1946, p. 11. Professor Smalley's discovery of this essay is a well-deserved and happy one. The connection with *My Last Duchess* which I here suggest is my addition.

of Alfonso II, fifth Duke of Ferrara, and Tasso's patron who imprisoned him. It is this Duke, Louis S. Friedland has shown,[6] who is the Duke of *My Last Duchess,* as we shall see below. This means that the poem was written in the summer or early fall of 1842.

In an article entitled *"My Last Duchess"* in *Studies in Philology* 29:120–22 in 1932 Professor John D. Rea suggested that the source of Browning's story was the life of Vespasiano Gonzaga, Duke of Sabbioneta (1531–91), by Irenio Affó. This was a plausible suggestion for the time, and the incidents of Gonzaga's life fitted well into the career of Browning's Duke. The weakness of the conjecture lay in the fact that it could not be shown that Browning knew Gonzaga's career or Affó's book, and Gonzaga was not connected with the city of Ferrara. Mr. Friedland has now shown that Alfonso II, last of the great Este family whose early history Browning had encountered in *Sordello,* fits even better as the model for the poet's Duke. Alfonso II was born in 1533. His mother was Renée de France. When he was eighteen years old he went to his mother's country where Nostradamus, the fortune-teller, prophesied that he would be married three times and that his third wife would give him a male heir. In 1558 he married Lucrezia de Medici, daughter of Cosimo I de Medici, Duke of Florence. Alfonso was twenty-five and Lucrezia was fourteen at the time. She is described as "tall, thin, of modest endowment and not very much education, serious, very devout, but taciturn and by no means expansive," and she brought with her a handsome dowry. On the third day following this marriage of policy Alfonso left for France and was away for two years. When his father died Alfonso returned to Ferrara as Duke and in February, 1560, sent for his wife. Seventeen years old at the time, she died on April 21, 1561, and there was grave suspicion that she had been poisoned. This lady, youthful, unspoiled, and possibly a virgin, was the original of Browning's Duchess.

In almost every respect Alfonso II meets the requirements as the model for Browning's Duke. He was a typical Renaissance grandee: he came of the proud Este family, rulers in Italy for hundreds of years, not merchants and upstarts like the Medici; he was cold and egotistical, vengeful and extremely possessive; and a patron of the arts, painting, music, and literature. The incident in the poem of the Duke negotiating for his second wife is also authenticated in Alfonso's career. Soon after the death of Lucrezia he began negotia-

---

[6] "Ferrara and *My Last Duchess,*" in *Studies in Philology* 33:656–84 (1936).

tions through the Spanish court for the hand of Barbara, daughter of Ferdinand I, niece of the Count of Tyrol, whose capital was at Innsbruck. After her father died, this lady was in the Count's charge, and in October, 1564, arrangements were concluded for the marriage. In 1565 Alfonso went to Vienna and stopped on his way at Innsbruck where he saw his future bride. The dowry was a handsome one.

The agent from the Count of Tyrol who concluded the negotiations with Alfonso for the marriage was Nikolaus Madruz, a native of Innsbruck, and he may be the person to whom the Browning's Duke speaks in the poem. If so, the Duke may be flattering him by mentioning Claus of Innsbruck, a fellow townsman. But so far as we know Claus is imaginary. So also is Frà Pandolf. Pandolfi was a common name, and Browning possibly made him a friar to remove all implications of an affair between the painter and the Duchess. No paintings of the Duchess are known to exist in Ferrara. Mr. Friedland's article is entirely convincing.

It has been suggested that *My Last Duchess* owes its origin to Shakespeare's *A Winter's Tale* with Leontes as the model for the Duke and Hermione for the Duchess.[7] But that is to see Browning's Duke as the jealous husband rather than the fiercely possessive one of the poem who reduces his Duchess to an object of art.

When Browning was questioned by Professor Hiram Corson on the meaning of the lines, "I gave commands; Then all smiles stopped together," the poet said that "the commands were that she should be put to death, . . . or he might have had her shut up in a convent." [8] The poem far surpasses its source in subtlety and suggestiveness. In the character of the Duke, Browning makes his first brilliant study of the culture and morality of the Italian Renaissance, a study which reached its apex in *The Bishop Orders his Tomb*, and continued into his portraits of the Italian painters in *Men and Women*. The Duchess of the poem appears again with altered features and a very different fate in *The Flight of the Duchess* in 1845. *My Last Duchess*, though one of the earliest of Browning's dramatic monologues, has always been considered one of his greatest.

[7] Lionel Stevenson, "The Pertinacious Victorian Poets," in *Studies in Philology* 21:232–45 (1952).

[8] H. Corson, *An Introduction to the Study of Robert Browning*, note to 3rd ed., p. viii.

Count Gismond

In *Dramatic Lyrics,* published in November, 1842, the poem which has become generally known as *Count Gismond. Aix in Provence* appeared under the title *Italy and France* as *II. France.* In 1849 this union with *Italy* (*i.e., My Last Duchess*) was broken, and the poem assumed its permanent name. In 1849, also, *Count Gismond* was grouped under the general title *Dramatic Romances and Lyrics,* and in the arrangement of the poems in 1863 it naturally became one of the *Dramatic Romances,* being really a romantic anecdote. It has remained in this category, and has been reprinted in all the collected editions.

The poem is composed of 126 tetrameter lines; *i.e.,* twenty-one stanzas of six lines each. The text after 1849 became fairly stabilized, only slight changes, mainly in punctuation, being made after that year. But between 1842 and 1849 Browning mended the meter and wording of the poem in several places, though not adding to its length or at all altering its meaning.

The incident in *Count Gismond* is imaginary, and the hero is characteristically a Browningesque hero of the chivalric tradition. He is equipped to see virtue through evil appearances, and leaps to its defence. It is an illustration of the medieval belief, in which Gismond's wife who is the speaker fully shares, that "God will have a stroke in every battle." It should be observed that virtue is instantaneously recognized, as it so often is in Browning's poetry. This is especially true when love is involved, as it is here. In this sense *Count Gismond* is related to *The Glove,* to *Caponsacchi* in *The Ring and the Book,* and more intimately to the lines upon Andromeda in *Pauline* (ll. 656–67), which become perfect symbols of Browning's chivalry and of his religious faith.

The scene of *Gismond* is laid in Aix in Provence and the time is obviously in the days of chivalry. Time and place suggest that this poem may be distantly related to *Sordello,* for Sordello was a troubadour who passed a great part of his life in Provence. The poem was a great favorite with Elizabeth Barrett, and later with the PreRaphaelite poets.

Incident of the French Camp

The poem known as *Incident of the French Camp* appeared first under the general title *Camp and Cloister* as *I. Camp (French)* in the *Dramatic Lyrics* in November, 1842. In the collected edition of 1849 the general title was dropped, the artificial connection with *Cloister* (*Spanish*) was broken, and the poem attained its permanent title. Except for one or two changes in punctuation the text has remained the same since its first printing. In the edition of 1863 *Incident of the French Camp* came under the head of *Dramatic Romances*. The poem is composed of five stanzas of eight lines each, in iambic measure.

Nothing is known of the composition of this poem, but it probably dates from 1842. In December of 1841 a second funeral was held for the burial of Napoleon's body in Paris, and this naturally roused great interest in the history of the Emperor. This interest hardly needed quickening, for biographies of Napoleon and memoirs by his various marshals had been pouring from the press during the two decades since his death. Among the English biographies those by Sir Walter Scott and Hazlitt are notable. Browning certainly knew *The History of Napoleon* written by his friend Richard Hengist Horne, and published in two volumes in 1840. Browning's father was a great reader of memoir and history, and his son inherited that taste, with a delight in founding his poems upon historical characters and events.[9] The precise event related in the *Incident of the French Camp* I have not been able to find after an exhaustive search through Napoleonic literature. Browning told Mrs. Orr [10] that the story was true, except that the hero was a man, not a boy. It was probably one of the countless legends of heroism which sprang up to illustrate the devotion of the Emperor's soldiers to him. The background is genuinely authentic. On April 23, 1809, Napoleon attacked Ratisbon (the German Regensburg) in Bavaria on the south bank of the Danube, as the critical blow of his brilliant battle of three days against the Austrians under the Archduke Charles. Ratisbon was stormed with great gallantry, Marshal Lannes, Duc de Montebello,

---

[9] It was probably early in 1842 that Colburn, the publisher, told Browning confidentially that "he wanted more than his dinner 'a novel on the subject of Napoleon.'" Browning mentioned it in a letter to Miss Barrett on September 13, 1845, when he was casting about for means of supporting her if they eloped to Italy.

[10] *Handbook,* p. 300.

leading the attackers in person. At the critical juncture of the battle the Marshal seized a ladder and began to mount the walls, exclaiming, "I will show you that your general is still a grenadier." The town was taken and the Austrians driven over the river. Towards the end of the battle Napoleon, who was observing the affair at some distance and speaking at the time to Duroc, was wounded in the foot by a spent musket-ball. "That must have been a Tyrolese who has hit me from such a distance," said the Emperor; "those fellows fire with wonderful precision." On May 22, 1809, after the battle of Aspern-Essling, Marshal Lannes was wounded fatally and died in Vienna on May 31. He was one of Napoleon's most resourceful, vigorous, and self-sacrificing marshals.

There is an anecdote related by Cardinal Fesch, the uncle of Napoleon, which may have a common source with the legend Browning relates. The scene is at the taking of Ratisbon. Exhausted by the battle of three days, Napoleon

retired to a short distance in order to enjoy a few minutes' repose, when, making his steed lay down, he stretched himself upon the turf, and reclined upon the belly of the animal. While in that situation one of his aide-de-camps arrived, to make known a position taken by the enemy, and, while in the act of explaining his errand, he pointed with the right hand, when on the instant a shot severed the limb from his body, the ball passing close to the Emperor's head. Napoleon manifested his sincere regret, and proceeded to assist his unfortunate aide-du-camp, without displaying the least personal fear, or quitting his dangerous position.[11]

In the *Incident of the French Camp* the reader will observe, besides Browning's delight in heroic action, the essential similarity in the heroism of *How They brought the Good News, Childe Roland to the Dark Tower Came,* and *Pheidippides.* The poem has been a general favorite, and has appeared not only in all the collected editions, but in many volumes of selections from Browning.

Soliloquy of the Spanish Cloister

The *Soliloquy of the Spanish Cloister* was *II. Cloister (Spanish)* in the group called *Camp and Cloister* in *Dramatic Lyrics,* published in November, 1842. In the collected edition of 1849 it took its permanent title, *Soliloquy of the Spanish Cloister,* and was separated from

[11] Baron Karlo Excellmanns, *The Eventful Life of Napoleon Bonaparte,* London, 1823, III, 196.

the *Incident of the French Camp*. In 1863 Browning grouped it with *The Flower's Name* and *Sibrandus Schafnaburgensis,* making it No. III of a group called *Garden Fancies*. This arrangement did not last, for in 1868 the poem regained its independence, and became permanently one of the *Dramatic Lyrics*. It is made up of nine stanzas of eight tetrameter lines each, in trochaic meter. The text of the poem has remained the same since 1842, except for the usual small changes in punctuation.

The *Soliloquy* probably owes something to Browning's travels in Italy in the early summer of 1838, when he had ample opportunity to observe the monasteries. It shows as well his interest in the tempers of various nations. The portrait of the speaker is as intimate and unflattering as that of the Bishop of St. Praxed's. It is obvious from Browning's mention of scrofulous French novels that he intends the poem to be a modern incident, but it has Renaissance elements. It was then that revenge became a fine art, and men were no longer content to kill merely the bodies of their enemies, but insisted upon the destruction of the soul as well. Browning refers to the same belief in *Count Gismond*. As an analogy to the soliloquizing monk's desire for the damnation of Brother Lawrence's soul, observe the following from the *Brief Discourse of the Spanish State, with a Dialogue annexed, entitled Philobasilis* (1590), p. 24:

One of these monsters meeting his enemie unarmed, threatened to kill him if he denied not God, his power, and essential properties, viz. his mercy, suffrance, etc., the which when the other, desiring life, pronounced with great horror, kneeling upon his knees; the hero cried out, *nowe will I kill thy body and soule,* and at that instant thrust him through with his rapier.

Hamlet's decision not to kill the King at his devotions, and thus send his soul to heaven, but to wait and trip him unawares, is perhaps the best-known example in English literature of this Renaissance psychology.

The speaker of the soliloquy in his desperate hate of Brother Lawrence thinks in a disorderly fashion of several ways to trap the soul of the man he hates, even to the point of being willing to risk his own soul (stanza 9). In stanza 8, which deals with the French novel, his attack is upon Lawrence's morals. In stanza 7, which deals with the text in *Galatians,* the imagined assault is to be upon Lawrence's dogma in the hope of catching him in a heresy just as he is dying.[12] Chapters 2 and 3 of *Galatians* are full of difficult texts, con-

[12] See the admirable analysis of these points in Arnold Williams' article,

cerning which theological treatises point out the many errors which might arise in interpreting the status of the old Judaic law in the light of Christian doctrine. The great text is probably *Galatians* 3:21. In *Galatians* 5:19–21 St. Paul mentions the seventeen devices of the flesh for entrapping the soul. Browning probably uses "twenty-nine" largely, as the French use *trente-six*, to indicate a good number. There have been many ingenious but no satisfactory explanations of *"Hy, Zy, Hine."* The words may be the beginning of an imprecation or incantation; or perhaps they echo the ringing of the vesper bell, which causes the monk to cross himself and begin his "Hail, Mary, full of Grace." An Arian is one who adheres to the heresies of Arius (fourth century), who held Christ to be created inferior to God, though first among created beings. The Manicheans were followers of Mani, the Syrian (fourth century), who tried to combine Oriental doctrines with Christianity. The *Soliloquy*, like Tennyson's *St. Simeon Stylites*, exhibits a Protestant's dislike and distrust of asceticism. The poem was probably written after the completion of *Sordello* in May, 1839, when Browning was studying Elizabethan plays. In *Notes and Queries* for June 9, 1951, James U. Rundle observed the many likenesses between the speaker in Browning's poem and Willie in Robert Burns's *Holy Willie's Prayer*.

In a Gondola

In a Gondola first appeared in *Dramatic Lyrics* in November, 1842. In 1863 it was put under the head of *Dramatic Romances* and has remained there. The poem consisted of fifteen sections, made up of 233 lines. Between 1842 and the collected edition of 1849 there were material changes: not only are lines mended, but passages are altered. The sense is much the same, but the poem is improved in rhythm and clarity.[13] Since 1849 the changes have been very few, mainly in punctuation. In the final text there are 231 lines.

We hear first of the poem *In a Gondola* in a letter of Browning's to Miss Fanny Haworth. The letter is undated but probably belongs to the end of 1841:

I chanced to call on Forster the other day—and he pressed me into committing verse on the instant, not the minute, in Maclise's behalf—who

"Browning's 'Great Text in Galatians'," in *Modern Language Quarterly* 10:89–90 (1949).

[13] See Nicoll and Wise, *Literary Anecdotes of the Nineteenth Century*, I, 482.

has wrought a divine Venetian work, it seems, for the British Institution—Forster described it well—but I could do nothing better than this wooden ware (All the "properties," as we say, were given—and the problem was how to cataloguize them in rhyme and unreason)—

I send my heart up to thee—all my heart. . . . Singing and stars and night and Venice streets in depths of shade and space are "properties," do you please to see. And now tell me, is this below the average of Catalogue original poetry? [14]

Forty years later, on September 15, 1881, the poet told Furnivall the same story and added a detail:

I wrote the Venice stanza to illustrate Maclise's picture [*The Serenade*],—for which he was anxious to get some line or two: I had not seen it, but, from Forster's description, gave it to him, in his room, *impromptu*. . . . When I did see it, I thought the Serenader too jolly somewhat for the notion I got from Forster—and I took up the subject in my own way.[15]

Maclise's picture was exhibited at the British Institution in 1842, and upon seeing it Browning was stimulated to add 226 lines to the original few lines, telling a tale and presenting a situation entirely his own. The poem obviously owes much to his visit to Venice in June, 1838, though Mrs. Orr asserts that Browning later thought that he had seen Venice imperfectly on that occasion. A contrast between the Venice of the romantic imagination and the reality is implied in *A Toccata of Galuppi's*, which was published thirteen years later. Perhaps, too, Venice quickened Browning's interest in painting, especially in the Venetians, Titian, Bartolommeo Schedone, and Giorgione, who are mentioned in the poem. But he had become acquainted with these painters at the Dulwich Gallery much earlier in his life. "Haste-thee-Luke," or Luca-Fa-Presto, was Luca Giordano, several of whose pictures were in Venice and may have been viewed with pleasure there by Browning. The melodramatic ending of the poem probably owes something to Browning's interest in the contemporary stage, possibly to Bulwer-Lytton's plays.

It is almost impossible now to see even a copy of Maclise's picture, but it made a great impression in 1842. Writing from Albaro, a suburb of Genoa, in 1844, Charles Dickens refers to the collaboration of Maclise and Browning:

In a certain picture called the Serenade for which Browning wrote that verse in Lincoln's-inn-fields you, O Mac, painted a sky. If you ever have

---

[14] *Letters*, ed. Hood, p. 7.
[15] *Idem*, p. 196.

occasion to paint the Mediterranean, let it be exactly of that colour. It lies before me now, as deeply and intensely blue.[16]

The device of sending the illicit but happy lovers past scenes of unhappiness for the sake of contrast is a device used a number of times by Browning, notably in the poem *Respectability* (1855); in *Pippa Passes* he uses the device with a difference. The artifice of sending the imagination upon far quests in order to accentuate the supreme excellence of actuality is also a favored one with Browning. *In a Gondola* has always been reckoned one of his greatest metrical triumphs, but the melodramatic situation and action remind the reader too much of the early Victorian theater.

Artemis Prologizes

Artemis Prologuizes was published in *Dramatic Lyrics* in November, 1842. In 1849 it appeared in the collected edition under the general title of *Dramatic Romances and Lyrics,* but in the re-distribution of 1863 it became, for no clear reason, one of *Men and Women,* where it has remained. At that time the spelling of the second word in the title was changed to *Prologizes.* In 1842 the poem was made up of 121 lines of blank verse, as is the final text. But between the years 1842 and 1849 Browning made several verbal changes, of which the last line may serve as an example:

> 1842:   In fitting silence the event await.
> 1849:   Await, in fitting silence, the event.

Since 1849 the changes in the poem have been in punctuation only.

According to Mrs. Orr, Browning attached to the first proof of *Artemis Prologuizes* the following note:

I had better say perhaps that the above is nearly all retained of a tragedy I composed, much against my endeavour, while in bed with a fever two years ago—it went further into the story of Hippolytus and Aricia; but when I got well, putting only thus much down at once, I soon forgot the remainder.[17]

In a letter to Alfred Domett, dated in March, 1840, Browning quotes lines 732-7 of Euripides' *Hippolytus,*[18] but the illness during which Browning wrote the poem occurred in December, 1840, and January, 1841.

---

[16] J. Forster, *Life of Charles Dickens,* ed. Ley, London, 1928, p. 331.
[17] Orr, *Life,* p. 121.
[18] F. G. Kenyon, *Robert Browning and Alfred Domett,* p. 31.

According to Euripides, Hippolytus, son of Theseus and Hippolyta the Queen of the Amazons, was beloved by his step-mother Phaedra. When he repelled her advances she hanged herself, but left written word to her husband accusing Hippolytus of an unnatural love for her. Theseus banished Hippolytus, and persuaded Poseidon to raise a monster from the sea to frighten the horses of Hippolytus. The young man is dragged over the rocks by the wild horses, and is mortally wounded. Theseus is delighted at his revenge until Artemis appears and tells him the truth. The play closes as Hippolytus is brought into the presence of Theseus. There is a scene of reconciliation, and the young man dies as he is told by Artemis, goddess of chastity and the moon, that this was the decree of fate.

Artemis Prologuizes was intended by Browning to be the prologue to a tragedy in imitation of Euripides, which was to concern itself with the further adventures of Hippolytus after he had been healed by Aesculapius, great physician and son to Apollo. According to Virgil (*Aeneid,* VII, 765–77) and Ovid (*Metamorphoses,* XV, 530–46) Hippolytus, after being brought back to life by Aesculapius, was carried by Artemis to Italy. There the faithless Hippolytus fell in love with Aricia, from whom the place Aricia takes its name. It was for this legend that *Artemis Prologuizes* was to serve as prologue. But the fragment as we have it makes the goddess, as speaker, summarize the story of Euripides' *Hippolytus* from the moment his destruction was thought of by his step-mother Phaedra, to the present moment when Aesculapius is gradually bringing Hippolytus back to life.

It is probable that when Browning recovered from his illness he set about completing *Pippa Passes, King Victor,* and other plays, and forgot his imitation of Euripides. The poem, however, shows his life-long affection for the Greek dramatist—a trait which is evident notably in the Pope's monologue in *The Ring and the Book,* in *Balaustion's Adventure* (1871) and in *Aristophanes' Apology* (1875), as well as in a superb description of Artemis in the *Parleying With Gerard de Lairesse* (ll. 226–31), where Browning is reckoning up the influences on his own life. In the preface to his *Agamemnon* in 1877 Browning defended his practice of transliterating Greek names —a practice which accounts for the strange spelling in *Artemis Prologuizes.* For after lasting as a fashion for a time, especially among German scholars, the project failed of acceptance, and scholars have gone back to the traditional English spelling.

Artemis Prologizes has never been a popular poem, but the reason probably lies in its very excellence. Matthew Arnold greatly admired the flawless fragment. Writing of his own *Merope* to Madame du Quaire in 1858 he says, "Make Browning look at it, if he is at Florence; one of the very best antique fragments I know is a fragment of a Hippolytus by him." [19]

Waring

Waring was published in *Dramatic Lyrics* in November, 1842. In the collected edition of 1849 it was put under the general head of *Dramatic Romances and Lyrics* and in 1863 it was permanently assigned to the *Dramatic Romances*. The poem was in two parts, Part I having six sections, 210 lines; Part II, three sections, 54 lines. There were in all 264 lines. In the final text Part I has 208 lines; Part II, 53. A moderate number of verbal changes have been made in the poem, most of them before 1849. After that date the changes were mainly matters of punctuation.

Since the poem is "a fancy portrait of a very dear friend," Alfred Domett, it is certain that the poem was not begun before Domett's departure for New Zealand—not in "the snowiest of all December," but about the first of May, 1842. The letters written to Domett and dated May 22, July 13, and September 31 (*sic*), 1842, contain phrases and ideas which are coincident with those in the poem, and it is therefore most probable that *Waring* was written in the early summer of 1842.[20] In the first letter Browning states strongly his belief in Domett's great abilities. "You can do anything," he writes. On July 13 he shows his disgust with England's drowsiness and her "distinguished names." "Here everything goes flatly on," he writes, "except the fierce political reality (as it begins to be). Our poems, etc., are poor child's play." In September he tells Domett that in speaking with Sir John Hanmer concerning books and bookmakers, "I said there would be a rare Godsend by some New Zealand packet soon!" Browning's affection for his friend appears all through his letters.

Caution must be exercised in reading biography too precisely into *Waring*. The hero was, by Browning's admission, Domett, but it is

[19] *Letters of Matthew Arnold, 1848–1888*, ed. Russell, London, 1895, I, 61.
[20] For a full account of the friendship between Browning and Domett see F. G. Kenyon, *Robert Browning and Alfred Domett*, London, 1906. See also Griffin and Minchin, *Life*, Ch. 5; and W. Hall Griffin, "Robert Browning and Alfred Domett," in *Living Age* 244:393–410 (February, 1905).

a "fancy portrait." The name "Waring" Browning took from a king's messenger whom he had met in Russia in 1834, and his imagination sends Domett to Moscow in the poem. Alfred Domett, the son of a naval officer and ship-owner, was born in Camberwell in 1811. He had attended Cambridge, but left in 1834 without a degree. Before he met Browning he had published two books of poetry, one in 1834 and the other in 1839, and had travelled in Canada and in Italy and the Tyrol. His journey to Italy made poetic capital for him, for the volume of 1839 was called *Venice*. Browning is probably referring to an experience common to them both, which they must have talked much about, when he imagines Waring at the ship's side with "great grass hat and kerchief black" in the harbor of Trieste.

It is probable that Domett and Browning were not acquainted before 1840, but after that they quickly became intimate. They were both members of a club called "The Colloquials," all young men of Camberwell, which included Joseph Arnould, Newdigate prize poet at Oxford in 1834 and afterwards Judge of the Supreme Court in Bombay and a baronet; Christopher Dowson, Joseph Dowson, William Young, and Captain Pritchard, who mysteriously would not tell his friends where he lived—a fancy which may have suggested to Browning that Waring really had not gone away, but was hiding in London. In 1841 both Arnould and Domett were called to the bar, but Domett, probably impatient at slow progress, and moved by the tide of emigration which swept over England in 1842—and which is an essential part of the background of *Waring*—left suddenly in May for New Zealand, but not so suddenly as Browning playfully imagines. There he distinguished himself in the government and became Prime Minister in 1862. In 1872 he returned to England with his poem *Ranolf and Amohia,* which contains lines of tribute to Browning (p. 342), and which Browning used his influence to have published by his own publishers. In 1877 Domett dedicated a collection called *Flotsam and Jetsam* to Browning, calling him a "mighty poet and a subtle-souled psychologist." In this volume there was a diatribe written in 1841 against the critics of *Pippa Passes*. After his return Domett renewed acquaintance, though hardly the old intimacy, with Browning, and kept a diary which supplied Griffin and Minchin with material on Browning's later years. Domett became a member of the Browning Society. He died in 1887. His character is certainly referred to in Browning's poem *Time's Revenges* (1845) and he is mentioned by name, "Alfred, dear friend," in *The Guardian*

Angel, written in 1848. If any further evidence of Browning's affection is needed, one may see it in Browning's letter to Domett of November 8, 1843, in which he imagines Domett coming home. "There you walk past our pond-rail (picking up one of the fallen horse-chestnuts), and now our gate-latch clicks, and now— . . . 'Tis worth while running away to be so wished for again."

The poem, besides showing the poet's affection for a friend, exhibits many personal interests of Browning. His concern with the stage, music, painting, politics, is shown in his ambitions for Waring. His weariness with England, and the impulse to escape, the interest in far places and in many nations appear clearly. The playful torrents of words and fancies show permanent characteristics of the poet. The *Dramatic Lyrics,* containing *Waring,* were sent to Domett in New Zealand on December 13, 1842. To him they became a constant delight.

Rudel to the Lady of Tripoli

Rudel to the Lady of Tripoli was published in *Dramatic Lyrics* in November, 1842. There called *Rudel and the Lady of Tripoli,* it was linked with *Cristina* under the title *Queen-Worship.* In 1849 it appeared under the general title of *Dramatic Romances and Lyrics,* and the connection with *Cristina* was ended. In the re-arrangement of 1863 *Rudel* was put under *Men and Women.* In 1849 the title was changed to its permanent one, *Rudel to the Lady of Tripoli.* In its first appearance the poem consisted of thirty-six irregular lines; the changes for the edition of 1849 were extensive. The sense was not changed, but the meter was greatly mended. The lines are now regular iambic pentameter.

The poem probably had its inception in Browning's studies of the troubadour literature when he was writing *Sordello,* and it is probable that the poem was written in 1838 or 1839. It is not possible to say where Browning learned of Rudel, a troubadour of the twelfth century. Mrs. Jameson, later to be his friend, had told the story in her *Loves of the Poets* (1829), pp. 27–32; but the legend had been dealt with by Petrarch, Carducci, Uhland, and Heine. It appears in all histories of troubadour literature, of which Browning probably knew well Nostradamus, Tiraboschi, and Sismondi.[21] The legend

[21] See J. C. L. Simonde de Sismondi, *Historical View of the Literature of the South of Europe,* translated by Thomas Roscoe, New York, 1827, pp. 57–8.

upon which Browning builds his poem may be given briefly. Geoffrey Rudel, Prince of Blaye or Blieux, in Provence, became enamoured of the Princess of Tripoli, a small duchy in Syria on the Mediterranean. He had never seen her, but he had heard reports of her beauty and graciousness from returning crusaders; and he sang her praises and his love for her in high verse. She became the distant lady of his adoration, and at last in 1162 he embarked for Syria, singing

> Angry and sad shall be my way,
> If I behold not her afar,
> And yet I know not when that day
> Shall rise, for still she dwells afar.

But once at sea he developed a serious malady, and his companions thought him dead. His vessel at last touched Tripoli and Rudel, seemingly dead, was brought to an inn. The Princess, hearing the sad story, came to the inn and took the hand of Rudel, whereupon he recovered to see, to hear, and to adore her. He thanked heaven that he had been permitted to live until that moment. Then he died in the arms of his lady, who had him buried in a magnificent sepulcher in the house of the Templars.

Such is the legend. Browning takes, as the speaker, Rudel sending a message before he sets forth to his lady, and uses the characteristic troubadour device of portraying the love of Rudel by the symbolic use of flowers. Rudel is the sun-flower, turning to the sun which represents love. But the sun has little effect upon the Mount, which represents his lady, cold and lofty as the convention of courtly love demanded. Browning seems to catch the tone and quality of Rudel's poetry, especially of the poem *On Distant Love,* a stanza of which is quoted above.

It is interesting that Gaston Paris was of the opinion that the legend has no foundation beyond vague allusions in Rudel's verse to a "distant love," the fact that he went to Palestine on the second crusade, and the fact that he died there.[22] It was a common thing for troubadours, if they had any pretensions to nobility at all, to take the title of prince or count.

[22] See the reprint of Gaston Paris, *Jaufré Rudel,* Paris, 1904, with an essay *Sur l'Oeuvre de Gaston Paris* by Joseph Bédier, pp. 45 ff. Paris's article first appeared in the *Revue historique,* 1893, tome 53.

Cristina

Cristina was first published in *Dramatic Lyrics* in November, 1842. It was there linked with *Rudel and the Lady of Tripoli,* and was Part II under the general title of *Queen-Worship.* In 1849 it was dissociated from *Rudel* and appeared under the general head of *Dramatic Romances and Lyrics.* In 1863 it came again under the head of *Dramatic Lyrics* and has so remained. It is made up of eight stanzas of eight lines each. Some clarification of sense and meter took place for the collected edition of 1849, to the improvement of the poem. Since that date changes have been mainly matters of punctuation.

The poem was addressed in fancy to Maria Cristina (1806–78), Queen of Spain between 1829 and 1841, and fourth wife to Ferdinand VII. This fact gives light and meaning to the poem. Cristina was daughter of Francis I, King of the Two Sicilies. She was young, beautiful, passionately devoted to pleasure, and she transformed by her presence the gloomy court of the old and sinister Ferdinand. Before his death in 1833, Cristina had persuaded the King to name her daughter, Isabella, as next in succession, and Cristina ruled as regent until 1840. In the latter year Cristina's secret marriage to an officer named Muñoz was discovered, and she was forced to abdicate. After her abdication Cristina resided in Rome, Naples, and Paris. In 1843 when Queen Isabella came of age, Cristina returned to Madrid and took an active part in politics; her husband, Muñoz, was created Duke of Rianzares in 1845. It was probably Cristina's abdication which drew Browning's attention to her, and his poem was probably written soon afterwards. It is founded upon the great reputation for coquetry enjoyed by the Queen. The likeness of the love of the speaker of the poem for Cristina, and the love of Rudel for the Lady of Tripoli is at once apparent; the contrast in the reception of that love is equally noticeable.

Cristina has usually been interpreted as an example of Browning's interest in elective affinities,[23] a doctrine advanced by Goethe in 1809 in his novel *Wahlverwandschaften,* to the effect that as certain chemical substances are attracted to each other, so certain men and women are inevitably and immediately drawn to each other by love. This interpretation of the poem has been challenged by Clyde S. Kilby,[24] who does not think there is a mutual understanding between

[23] See W. L. Phelps, *Robert Browning,* pp. 116–24.
[24] See "Browning's *Cristina*" in the *Explicator* II, Item 16 (November, 1943).

the speaker and the Queen. Rather, he sees the speaker as a rationalizing egoist who is arguing with a skeptical friend, and he thinks Browning wishes to emphasize the mental oddity of the speaker. Poems like *Evelyn Hope* remind us, however, that Browning had a good deal of sympathy for doctrines similar to Goethe's elective affinities.

Johannes Agricola in Meditation

Johannes Agricola in Meditation first appeared in January, 1836, in the *Monthly Repository*,[25] a magazine edited by W. J. Fox, old friend and mentor of Browning. It was there called *Johannes Agricola*, and followed *Porphyria*, but was quite dissociated from it. Both poems were signed "Z." In the *Dramatic Lyrics*, the two poems were grouped under the general title *Madhouse Cells*, of which *Johannes Agricola*, now untitled, was No. I. Line 42, which originally read "With unexhausted blessedness," was altered in 1842 to its present reading. Except for one or two verbal changes and the usual correction of punctuation and spelling, the text has remained the same. In the collected edition of 1849 the title was altered to *Johannes Agricola in Meditation*, but as *I.—Madhouse Cell* it was still linked to *Porphyria's Lover*. In 1863 *Johannes Agricola in Meditation* was classed under *Dramatic Romances*, and completely dissociated from its old companion. In 1868 it became one of *Men and Women* and has so remained. The poem consists of sixty iambic tetrameter lines. In the *Monthly Repository* this note prefaced the poem:

Antinomians, so denominated for rejecting the Law as a thing of no use under the Gospel dispensation: they say, that good works do not further, nor evil works hinder salvation; that the child of God cannot sin, that God never chastiseth him, that murder, drunkenness, etc. are sins in the wicked but not in him, that the child of grace being once assured of salvation, afterwards never doubteth . . . that God doth not love any man for his holiness, that sanctification is no evidence of justification, etc. Potanus, in his Catalogue of Heresies, says John Agricola was the author of this sect, A. D. 1535.—*Dictionary of all Religions*, 1704.

Browning has slightly garbled the text of the *Dictionary*, which is now attributed to Daniel Defoe. The date actually ascribed by Potanus in his *Catalogus praecipuorum . . . haereticorum* is 1538.

Since *Johannes Agricola* was published in January, 1836, one would suppose that the poem was an offshoot of Browning's studies for *Paracelsus*. But Griffin and Minchin assert, upon what authority I do not know, that *Johannes Agricola* and *Porphyria* were written during Browning's stay in St. Petersburg in April and May of 1834.[26] In reading Melchior Adam's *Vitae Germanorum Medicorum,* published at Heidelberg in 1720, for his account of Paracelsus, chemist, doctor, philosopher, heretic, Browning encountered the name of John Schnitter or Schneider who had, in the German custom in the Renaissance, chosen the classical name Agricola. Added to the *Vitae . . . Medicorum* were two sections dealing with the *Vitae Germanorum Philosophorum* and *Vitae Germanorum Jureconsultorum;* among the latter was a generous account of Johannes Schneider [Agricola] (pp. 179 ff.). Agricola (1494–1566) was coadjutor with Martin Luther in the Reformation, and was the founder of Antinomianism, a heresy which held that while the unregenerate were still under the Mosaic law, Christians were entirely free from it, being under the dispensation of the Gospels. After some years of propagating his beliefs he asserted at Wittenberg in 1536 that works are indifferent, and that man is saved by faith alone, without any regard to moral character. "Art thou steeped in sin," he asked, "an adulterer or a thief? If thou believest, thou art in salvation. All who follow Moses must go to the devil. To the gallows with Moses." Upon this occasion he debated with Luther, and Luther gave him the title of Antinomian. The doctrine was directed against the law of Moses, and was a species of moral anarchy. John Wesley later defined Antinomianism as a doctrine which "makes void the Law through faith." The contention of Agricola was that Christ had freed Christians from the Old Testament. Agricola subsequently retracted, and was partially reconciled to Luther, but fanatical followers carried on the doctrine. Antinomianism, indeed, had appeared in the day of the Apostles, and has had a long history. It was espoused by some high Calvinists in England during the Commonwealth, and found supporters among the followers of Wesley, though he fought it earnestly. The belief in predestination is, of course, akin to Antinomianism. The fact that Browning kept the poem under the title *Madhouse Cells* from 1842 to 1863 perhaps indicates his opinion of the doctrine.

In a well-reasoned article, entitled "Browning's Heresies," [27] C. R. Tracy suggests that from the place of the poem's publication—that

---

[26] *Life*, p. 73.
[27] See *Studies in Philology* 33:610–25 (1936), esp. pp. 618–9.

is, the *Monthly Repository*, a magazine edited by W. J. Fox, the Unitarian minister—"the conclusion is unavoidable that in it Browning intended to satirize the Calvinistic doctrines of election and reprobation." Professor Tracy also sees the poem as an example of Browning's habit of referring covertly to a contemporary subject by means of an ancient prototype of it, and so slightly concealing the point of his weapon. The poem shows the influence of Unitarian thought upon Browning in these years when W. J. Fox exerted a powerful influence upon him.

Porphyria's Lover

In the *Monthly Repository* for January, 1836,[28] the poem called *Porphyria* preceded *Johannes Agricola,* and like the latter was signed "Z." In the *Dramatic Lyrics* the poem was linked with *Johannes Agricola* under the title of *Madhouse Cells,* and *Porphyria* was No. II. In 1849 the poem was still *Madhouse Cell,* No. II, but the subtitle *Porphyria's Lover* was added. In 1863 the tie was broken, and *Porphyria's Lover* appeared as an independent poem, one of the *Dramatic Romances;* the title *Madhouse Cells* was of course dropped. The poem has remained one of the *Dramatic Romances* since 1868. It is composed of sixty four-measure iambic lines, and except for changes in punctuation has remained as it was first printed.

According to Griffin and Minchin,[29] *Porphyria* was written during Browning's stay in St. Petersburg in April and May of 1834, and it is possible that some of the atmosphere of Russia still lingers in the poem. If it were not for this statement of the biographers, one would have supposed that this poem, like *Johannes Agricola,* rose naturally from Browning's work for *Paracelsus.* In *Paracelsus* (I, 770–4) Browning had written,

> One man shall crawl
> Through life surrounded with all stirring things,
> Unmoved; and he goes mad: and from the wreck
> Of what he was, by his wild talk alone,
> You first collect how great a spirit he hid.

These lines, by Browning's admission, refer to the mad poet, Christopher Smart, who according to legend had indented his *Song to David* upon the walls of his cell in Bedlam with a key. It is possible that his

28 N. S. 10:43–4.
29 *Life,* p. 73.

musing upon Smart's condition and the nature of madness gave Browning the title *Madhouse Cells* and the idea for *Porphyria*. This poem has the distinction of being the first of Browning's studies in abnormal psychology, and one of the earliest of his dramatic monologues; though in *Porphyria* he is possibly more interested in the strange story than in the character of the speaker.

It is the opinion of Professor Tracy that the lover in the poem is no more mad than many others of Browning's heroes; [30] he remarks that in calling this poem and *Johannes Agricola* "Madhouse Cells" the poet, lacking the full courage of his convictions, adopted a convenient means of fobbing off these two poems as objective studies of mental aberration. In his essay, "Browning as Dramatist," [31] H. B. Charlton brilliantly exhibits the theatrical possibilities of *Porphyria's Lover* as a one-act play.

Through the Metidja to Abd-el-Kadr

Through the Metidja to Abd-el-Kadr.—1842 first appeared in *Dramatic Lyrics* in November, 1842. In 1849 it was reprinted under the head of *Dramatic Romances and Lyrics,* and in 1863 it was put under *Dramatic Lyrics.* It consists of five stanzas of eight lines each, and the text, save for changes in punctuation, has remained unchanged.

The date attached to the title indicates that the poem was written in the year 1842. In June of that year news came to England of the fierce fighting and the disasters suffered by the Algerian chieftain Abd-el-Kadr at the hands of the French under Marshal Bugeaud. Browning's voyage to Italy in 1838 had taken him near the scene of the action, and the news probably made him recollect these coasts. The poem was composed in the summer of 1842 when Browning had been ordered to ride horseback every day for his health.[32]

Abd-el-Kadr (1808–1883) was a popular hero in the Thirties and Forties. Descended from Mahomet, he championed Islam against the infidels, and was proclaimed amir of Mascara in 1832. He waged fifteen years of intermittent war against the French for the independence of Algeria. Until the year 1842 the contest went in his favor, but through Marshal Bugeaud he suffered great reverses in that year;

[30] *"Porphyria's Lover,"* in *MLN* 52:579–80 (December, 1937).
[31] *Bulletin of the John Rylands Library* 23:37–43 (1939).
[32] W. Hall Griffin, "Robert Browning and Alfred Domett," in *Living Age* 244:400 (February 18, 1905).

Mascara was occupied, and Abd-el-Kadr barely escaped. This news in June, and the subsequent rallying of the tribesmen to Abd-el-Kadr probably brought recollections of the coast of Africa to the poet's mind; and he probably composed the verses as he rode on his good horse York, whose gallop seems to me as much the real inspiration of this poem as it was of *How They brought the Good News*. Browning dramatically imagines himself one of the Arabs riding through the Metidja, the great plain southwest of Algiers, to the rallying of the tribes to Abd-el-Kadr. In 1847 the chieftain was forced to surrender to the French. He was held prisoner in France until 1852, when Napoleon III released him upon his oath not to disturb Algeria. He died in Damascus on May 26, 1883. Browning might well be expected to sympathize with the indefatigable, chivalrous, and resourceful chieftain, fighting for the independence of his country, and the poem has been accounted one of Browning's metrical triumphs.

The Pied Piper of Hamelin

The Pied Piper of Hamelin; A Child's Story. (Written for, and inscribed to, W. M. the Younger.) was the last poem in the *Dramatic Lyrics* pamphlet, published in late November, 1842. It was included under the general head of *Dramatic Romances and Lyrics* in 1849, and in 1863 it became one of the *Dramatic Romances,* which it has since remained. It was made up of fifteen sections, or 305 irregular lines. Two lines disappeared between 1842 and 1849. Since 1849 the text has remained the same except for minor changes in word and punctuation. The inclusion of the poem in *Dramatic Lyrics* was somewhat accidental. Browning seems not to have thought highly of it, and sent it to the printer late—probably in October—when Moxon reported that the poems on hand were insufficient to fill the sixteen-page pamphlet.[33]

"W. M. the Younger" is William Macready, "Willie," the eldest son of the great tragedian. In May, 1842, the boy was confined to his room with a bad cough, and Browning, knowing his talent at drawing, composed two poems as subjects for illustration. The first of these was *The Cardinal and the Dog* (*q.v.*), and the second was *The Pied Piper.* Mr. C. Elkin Mathews published two letters from Willie Macready to Browning, in the *Times Literary Supplement* for September 15, 1921. In the first of these, which is undated, Willie thanks

[33] Orr, *Life,* p. 122.

Browning for *The Cardinal and the Dog,* which he has illustrated, and hopes Browning will like his drawings. The second letter, dated May 18, 1842, reads in part as follows: "I have finished the rest of the illustration of the Pied Piper which I hope you will like as well as the others but I am sorry to say I do not think them so good as the Council Chamber, or the other one that I did." The manuscripts and illustrations of these two poems are now in the Browning Collection at Baylor University. It may be conjectured that *The Pied Piper* was written in the first few days of May, 1842, though the legend that the poem was admired by Alfred Domett seems to indicate that it may have been written towards the end of April, for Domett left England about the first of May.[34]

The question as to which version of the ancient legend of the Pied Piper Browning followed has been much debated.[35] It is fairly certain that Nathaniel Wanley's *Wonders of the Little World* (1678),[36] which supplied Browning with *The Cardinal and the Dog,* and a great many other poems besides, was the poet's starting-point. Indeed, Browning seems to have authorized Furnivall's statement in the *Bibliography of Robert Browning*[37] that Wanley and the authorities there cited were the entire sources of the poem, and that the poet had not seen, until his poem was written, Richard Verstegen's *Restitution of Decayed Intelligence in Antiquities* (1605), an account of the legend much nearer to Browning than any other. The authorities quoted by Wanley are Johann Wier, *De Presdigiis Daemonum* (1564); G. Schott, *Physica Curiosa* (1622); Howell, *Epistolae Ho-Elianae* (1645). These books do not account for many details of the story, however, and Mr. Dickson is probably justified in his contention that the account given by Verstegen got to Browning in some way, possibly through the verbal account by the poet's father. Then, since Browning told Furnivall forty years after the event, and his memory was notoriously inaccurate in his later years, it is possible that he may have forgotten. It is possible, again, that Browning en-

---

[34] See the *Times Literary Supplement* for September 8, 1921; letter by Stephen Wheeler, headed "Browning's *Pied Piper.*" The legend that Domett persuaded Browning to publish the poem in 1842 is untenable, for Domett left England about May 1, 1842. It is hardly possible that he saw *The Pied Piper* before his departure for New Zealand.

[35] An excellent treatment of the problem may be found in Arthur Dickson, "Browning's Source for *The Pied Piper of Hamelin,*" in *Studies in Philology* 23:327–32 (July, 1926).

[36] Book VI, Ch. XIX, p. 28.

[37] *Browning Society's Papers,* I, 159.

countered the story in Mérimée's *Chronique du temps de Charles IX,* 1829 (pp. 39 ff.), or some author who repeated Verstegen, and refreshed his mind with Wanley's account when he came to write the poem in 1842. Because it has found such general currency, and because it is nearest in its details to the story as Browning tells it, I have thought it best to append the account from Verstegen's *Restitution of Decayed Intelligence in Antiquities:*

And now hath one digression drawne on another, for being by reason of speaking of these Saxons of *Transilvania,* put in mind of a most true and marvelous strange accident that hapned in *Saxonie* not manie ages past, I cannot omit for the strangenesse thereof briefely here by the way to set it downe. There came into the town of *Hamel* in the countrie of *Brunswicke* an old kind of companion, who for the fantasticall coate which he wore being wrought with sundrie colours, was called the pide Piper; for a Piper he was, besides his other qualities. This fellow forsooth offered the townsemen for a certaine somme of money to rid the towne of all the rats that were in it (for at that time the Burgers were with that vermine greatly annoyed). The accord in fine being made; the pide Piper with a shrill pipe went piping through the streets, and forthwith the rats came all running out of the houses in great numbers after him; all which hee led into the river of *Weaser* and therein drowned them. This done, and no one rat more perceived to bee left in the towne; he afterward came to demand his reward according to his bargaine, but being told that the bargain was not made with him in good earnest, to wit, with an opinion that ever he could bee able to doe such a feat; they cared not what they accorded unto, when they imagined it could never bee deserved, and so never to be demanded: but nevertheless seeing he had done such an unlikely thing indeed, they were content to give him a good reward; and so offered him far lesse then he lookt for: but hee therewith discontented, said he would have his full recompense according to his bargain, but they utterly denying to give it him, he threatened them with revenge; they bade him doe his worst, whereupon he betakes him againe to his pipe, and going through the streets as before, was followed of a number of boyes out at one of the gates of the Citie, and comming to a little hill, there opened in the side thereof a wid hole, into the which himselfe & all the children being in number one hundreth and thirtie, did enter; and being entred, the hill closed up againe, and became as before. A boy that being lame and came somewhat lagging behind the rest, seeing this that hapned, returned presently backe and told what he had seene, foorthwith began great lamentation among the Parents for their children, and men were sent out with all diligence, both by land and by water to inquire if ought could be heard of them, but with all the enquirie they could possibly use, nothing more then is foresaid could of them be understood. In memorie whereof it was ordained, that from thenceforth no Drumme, Pipe or other instrument, should be sounded in the street leading to the gate through which they passed; nor no Osterie to be there holden. And it was also established, that from that time forward in all publike writings that should bee made in that towne, after the date therein set downe of the yeare of our Lord, the date of the yeare of the going foorth of their children should bee added, the which they have accordingly ever since continued. And this great wonder hapned on the 22. day of July in the yeare of our Lord, 1376.

The occasion now why this matter came into my remembrance in speaking of *Transilvania*, was, that some do report that there are divers found among the Saxons in *Transilvania* that have like surnames unto divers of the Burgers of *Hamel*, and will thereby seeme to inferre, that this Jugler or pide Piper, might by negromancy have transported them thither, but this carrieth litle appearance of truth; because it would have beene almost as great a wonder unto the Saxons of *Transilvania* to have had so many strange children brought among them, they knew not how, as it was to those of *Hamel* to lose them: and they could not but have kept memorie of so strange a thing; if indeed any such thing had there hapned.[38]

It is only fair to say that some of Browning's details, such as the mention of Koppelberg Hill and the story on column and church-window, are not in Verstegen. It is possible that in 1834 on his way to Russia, and again in 1838 on his return from Italy, he may have passed through Hamelin, and noted these details. It is interesting to conjecture whether, at the time of his earlier journey, the city might not have been preparing for some commemoration of the legend; for July 22, 1834, was the five hundred and fiftieth anniversary of the visit of the Pied Piper; and the city celebrated the anniversary duly in 1934. But to return to the written sources of the poem; with the exception of these details possibly supplied by observation, the likeness of the poem to Verstegen's account is striking. Moreover, Browning uses Verstegen's date, 1376, for the event, rather than the accepted date, 1284.

Robert Browning the elder began in 1842 a version of his own, for the children of a friend and fellow-banker named Earles. After about sixty lines, the elder Browning wrote, "I began this not knowing that Robert had written on this subject; having heard him mention it, I stopped short. I never saw his manuscript till some weeks afterward." This note was written after the publication of the poem in November, 1842, for it is signed "R.B. 2nd March, 1843." Later Mr. Browning did complete his poem, and it may be seen in the *Bookman* for May, 1912. His version is very much like his son's in manner and

---

[38] London, 1628, pp. 85–7. The account given by Verstegen was reprinted in Chambers' *Book of Days* under July 22, with the last paragraph, about Transylvania, omitted; and there must almost certainly have been a copy of this book in the Browning library.

event, but it is not nearly so thoroughly imagined, and has some significant differences. Its existence helps to make it evident that the tale was one well known to the family, and that Browning's story is a composite of a number of sources, chief of which was the account ultimately traceable to Verstegen.

The poem has always been a favorite, and is probably more widely known than any other of Browning's poems. It has appeared in many illustrated editions, notably the one by Kate Greenaway. It has been translated into almost all the European tongues. The assertion that Browning is making a sly hit at Macready in the "keeping promises" moral of the poem, is hardly credible; they were on good terms in May, 1842.

To go back of Browning's sources, it should be added that the legend of the rats may possibly have risen from the migrations of the lemmings in Scandinavia. At irregular intervals these rodents migrate in prodigious numbers, devouring all before them, and instinctively rushing towards the sea they plunge to their ultimate death without hesitation. They have been seen swimming seven miles at sea. The legend of the children may be an echo of the Children's Crusade of 1212, or of some wholesale abduction of children in the Middle Ages. The legend is also, of course, an attempt to account for the widely scattered habitations of the Saxons.

THE RETURN OF THE DRUSES

PUBLICATION

The Return of the Druses, a pamphlet of twenty pages bound in yellow paper wrappers, was published in January, 1843. The pamphlet consisted of the title-page (p. 1): "Bells and Pomegranates. No. IV.—The Return of the Druses. A Tragedy. In Five Acts. By Robert Browning. Author of "Paracelsus." London: Edward Moxon, Dover Street MDCCCXLIII"; a list of persons, the time (14—), the place, and the scene (p. 2); and the text, printed in double columns, pp. 3–19. The play was printed at the expense of the poet's father for approximately £16. The price was One Shilling the copy. There was no separate second edition, but the play took its place in all the collected editions.

TEXT

In the original edition the text of this play was made up of a total of 1780 lines of blank verse, divided as follows: Act I—367 lines; Act II—374; Act III—327; Act IV—319; Act V—393. Like Browning's other works, the play underwent steady minor revision in word and in punctuation in the successive collected editions. The total number of lines remained the same.

GENESIS AND COMPOSITION

Browning's letter of August 1, 1837, to Miss Haworth, quoted in part in my discussions of *Sordello* and *King Victor and King Charles,* mentions for the first time the theme of *The Return of the Druses.* He says to her:

I want a subject of the most wild and passionate love, to contrast with the one I mean to have ready in a short time [*King Victor*]. I have many half-conceptions, floating fancies: give me your notion of a thorough self-devotement, self-forgetting; should it be a woman who loves thus, or a man? What circumstances will best draw out, set forth this feeling? [1]

Miss Haworth's reply is not preserved, but we may judge from Browning's letter that the *The Return of the Druses,* or *Mansoor the Hierophant* as he first planned to call the play, was not sufficiently matured in his mind to have been written immediately, though the drama is one of those which is said to have been written in five days.[2] It is possible that the play was written in the fall of 1837 just after Browning finished *King Victor and King Charles* and before he returned to work upon *Sordello,* but I think it probable that he merely jotted the idea down at this time and wrote the play after he had finished *Sordello* on May 26, 1839, or after he had published that poem in March, 1840. At the back of *Sordello, Mansoor the Hierophant* was announced as one of the plays nearly ready. In a letter to Domett in March, 1840, Browning says that he is busy with his plays. In a letter of June, 1840, we learn that Browning has considerably altered his play, making the three acts into five as Macready had advised.[3] The play, with its title changed to *The Return of the Druses,* was submitted to Macready, the actor-manager, who on August 3

---

[1] Orr, *Life,* p. 97. Mrs. Orr does not date the letter, but the allusion in the letter to R. H. Horne's *The Death of Marlowe* which appeared in the *Monthly Repository* for August, 1837, supplies the date.

[2] Griffin and Minchin, *Life,* p. 108.

[3] *New Letters,* ed. DeVane and Knickerbocker, p. 20.

recorded his opinion as follows: "Read Browning's play, and with the deepest concern, I yield to the belief that he will *never write again*— to any purpose. I fear his intellect is not quite clear. I do not know how to write to Browning." [4] On August 23, Browning wrote a vigorous defence of his play to Macready, saying that he had the actor in mind all the time he was creating the part of Djabal, and justifying his dealing with such a recondite subject as the Druses.[5] At the same time he rejected Macready's offer to send the play on to Webster, the manager of the Haymarket Theater. But the poet continued to argue his case. On August 27 Macready recorded, "Browning came before I had finished my bath, and really *wearied* me with his obstinate faith in his poem of *Sordello,* and of his eventual celebrity, and also with his self-opinionated persuasions upon his *Return of the Druses.* I fear he is for ever gone." On September 17, 1840, Browning retrieved his manuscript. He had it in hand as he published *Pippa Passes* and *King Victor and King Charles,* but evidently did not wish to use it at that time. The play was not published until January, 1843.

SOURCES AND INFLUENCES

It is the opinion of Griffin and Minchin that the *Biographie universelle* suggested the idea of *The Return of the Druses* to Browning.[6] This may well be so, for it seems to have been his constant book of reference and was easily available in his father's library. But it could hardly have supplied much more than the framework of the play, the action of which is obviously imaginary. For instance, no account of the Druses which I have seen mentions any tribe or group which went from Lebanon to an island of the Sporades; nor in the genealogy of the magnificent crusading family, Dreux, descended from Louis (VI) le Gros, King of France, one branch of which bore the title "Duc de Bretagne," is there any Loÿs de Dreux—one of the chief characters of Browning's play—or a member of the Dreux family who might have been at Rhodes in the fifteenth century. In the *Biographie* Browning probably found that Robert de France, Comte de Dreux, was at Jerusalem in 1147, that his son, Philippe de Dreux, made two crusades to the Holy Land, and was captured in the siege of St. Jean d'Acre in 1191 and was carried to Babylon. Robert, second Comte de Dreux, was also present at St. Jean d'Acre, and Pierre de

---

[4] Macready, *Diaries,* ed. W. Toynbee, II, 72.
[5] *New Letters,* ed. DeVane and Knickerbocker, pp. 20–3.
[6] *Life,* p. 25.

Dreux, Duc de Bretagne, followed the King, St. Louis, to the Holy Land, was wounded, taken prisoner, and regaining his freedom died in his ship before he could reach home again. The curious legend which Browning mentions and rejects in his play, that the Druses may be descended from the crusading family of Dreux, he may have read in Daniel Defoe's *A Dictionary of All Religions,* London, 1704, a book which he had quoted in connection with his poem *Johannes Agricola in Meditation* in 1836. There he would have found these words, under *Druzes:*

It's said they expect a Wise Man out of *Egypt,* who is to give them a Law; it's not probable (as some would have it) that they are descended from the *Franks,* who followed *Godfrey* of Bouillon; and after the loss of *Jerusalem* in 1187, retired into the Mountains, for there were some of that Religion in 1170; but 'tis more likely that these *Druzes* are not different from the *Darares* or *Durazes,* mentioned by *Elmatimi,* who lived in Syria. . . .

From the *Biographie* Browning probably learned about Hakem (Biamr-Allah), Abou Aly Mansour, the Third Fatemite Caliph of Egypt, who was the founder of the Druse religion. Browning mentions Hakem in a letter to Edmund Gosse in 1879 [7] when he is speaking of *The Return of the Druses,* and uses the form of Hakem's name which appears in the *Biographie.* In 1016 Hakem announced himself as the tenth incarnation of God, and with his associates Hamza and Darazi, he undertook to disseminate the new religion. Darazi was sent by Hakem to the region of Lebanon, and he established the faith there. At home in Cairo, Hakem was bitterly opposed by those who would not accept his divinity, and he was probably assassinated. At any rate, he vanished, and his mysterious disappearance became a part of the Druse conception of his incarnation. After his death Lebanon became the center of the religion. At the close of the account of the various atrocities of Hakem-Biamr-Allah, the *Biographie universelle* says,

Who would have believed that such a monster as Hakem would have become the object of a religious cult? Hamza-ben-Aly pretended that this Caliph had been elevated to the skies and that he would return one day to reign over all the earth: he made from this dogma the fundamental belief of the sect of the Druses, of which there still exist to-day some remnants in Syria.

The *Biographie* directed the reader to the work of Silvestre de Sacy, the *Chrestomathie arabe,* published at Paris in 1806. The last book

[7] *Letters,* ed. Hood, p. 187.

of this great scholar, published in two volumes in 1838, was the *Exposé de la religion des Druzes,* and it seems likely that Browning's attention was called to this work, perhaps through his friend Ripert-Monclar, or through his own association with the Institut Historique and the Societé Française de Statistique Universelle.

At any rate, from de Sacy Browning probably acquired the several important principles of the Druse religion, which are as follows: 1) There is only one God, indefinable and incomprehensible, ineffable; but He has made himself known to men by successive incarnations, the last of which was Hakem-Biamr-Allah the Third Fatemite Caliph. 2) Hakem will one day reappear to conquer the world and make his religion supreme. 3) The Druses scattered in the world will then return to Lebanon. 4) Druses are allowed to make outward profession of whatever religion is dominant around them. 5) Only a special class is permitted to be initiated into the secret and deeper mysteries of the religion. 6) Rigid secrecy is maintained against the alien world.

It needs only to be added that when Browning changed the name of the play from *Mansoor the Hierophant* to *The Return of the Druses,* as he did in the spring of 1840, he changed the name of the leading character from "Mansoor" to "Djabal." [8]

AFTER-HISTORY

The Return of the Druses encountered the same indifference at the hands of the critics which had greeted *King Victor and King Charles.* The *Gentleman's Magazine* for August, 1843, reviewed the first four pieces of the *Bells and Pomegranates* series, but paid little attention to the play. That Browning himself thought well of the *Druses* we may judge from his expostulations to Macready and from its appearance in every collected edition. There was a plan afoot in January, 1888, for Miss Alma Murray to act in several of Browning's plays; the performance of *The Return of the Druses* was set for 1889; so far as I am aware it never took place. But if the play was never acted, it never lacked for readers after Browning's fame came upon him, and a number of critics now judge the play to be the most suitable of Browning's dramas for acting.

Yet later critics have not commented at great length upon this play. Arthur E. DuBois finds it the most romantic of Browning's plays and sees irony in the mixed motives of the characters, who

[8] *Ibid.*

with good intentions are defeated on every hand as Djabal and Anael are caught between realities and their ideals. The motives are too complex and the action obscure.[9] H. B. Charlton finds the play full of spectacular scenes, but finds the personal tragedy of the characters poorly integrated with the political fate of the Druses as a people.[10] Donald A. Smalley sees in Djabal the prototype of Browning's long gallery of impostors, as the hero is torn between his Frankish brain and his Arab impulses.[11]

If the death of Anael, who dies in Act V under the stress of her emotions, still shows the lingering influence of Shelley upon Browning, the violent action and the melodramatic nature of the play show, perhaps, the effect of the plays of Bulwer-Lytton, whose *Lady of Lyons, Richelieu,* and *Money* swept the boards between 1838 and 1840. The action of the hero Djabal, who is willing to damn his soul utterly by pretending that he is Hakem in order to rescue his people from the European political yoke, ties *The Return of the Druses* up to *Strafford, Sordello, King Victor, Colombe's Birthday,* and *A Soul's Tragedy* as a point in the development of Browning's political thinking.

A BLOT IN THE 'SCUTCHEON

A Blot in the 'Scutcheon was published on February 11, 1843, the day of its presentation at the Drury Lane Theater. A pamphlet of sixteen pages bound in yellow paper covers, it consisted of the title-page (p. 1): "Bells and Pomegranates. No. V—A Blot in the 'Scutcheon. A Tragedy, In Three Acts. By Robert Browning, Author of "Paracelsus." London: Edward Moxon, Dover Street. MDCCCXLIII.";on the reverse the words, "Theatre Royal, Drury Lane, February 11, 1843," the persons of the play and the time (17—); and the text, pp. 3–16. The text was printed in double columns, conforming with the other volumes of the *Bells and Pomegranates* series. The pamphlet, printed at an expense of approximately £16, was paid for by the poet's father. The price per copy was One Shilling. There was no genuine second edition of the play in 1843. The poem was struck off in twenty-four hours by Moxon, to prevent Macready from mutilat-

---

[9] "Robert Browning, Dramatist," in *Studies in Philology* 33:626–55 (1936).
[10] "Browning as Dramatist," in *Bulletin of the John Rylands Library* 23:48–9 (1939).
[11] *Browning's Essay on Chatterton,* pp. 51–65.

ing the play, and copies were ready to be sold at the theater. When Moxon in 1846 bound together all the numbers of the *Bells and Pomegranates* into one volume for sale he was evidently forced to print more copies of *A Blot in the 'Scutcheon.* This reprint he called "Second Edition"; it is identical in all respects with the first. Collected volumes of *Bells and Pomegranates* with a first edition of *A Blot* are rare. The play was included by Browning in all the collected editions of his works.

TEXT

The text of *A Blot in the 'Scutcheon* was made up of three acts in seven scenes. There were in the first edition 1324 lines—all blank verse save the song, "There's a woman like a dew-drop"—divided as follows: I, i—101; ii—169; iii—241; II—433; III, i—226; ii—154. This play, in common with all of Browning's works, suffered constant though minor revision by the author. The total number of lines remained the same, but a considerable number of changes of phrase, word, and punctuation were introduced in the successive editions.

GENESIS AND COMPOSITION

A Blot in the 'Scutcheon was written expressly for the stage. On September 5, 1839, Macready, the tragedian and manager of Drury Lane, had refused *King Victor and King Charles,* and on September 17, 1840, he had given back to Browning *The Return of the Druses.* With these rejections in mind, therefore, Browning seems to have written, some time during the fall of 1840, *A Blot in the 'Scutcheon.* Before the end of the year the new tragedy was ready to send to Macready, and Browning wrote a note to prepare the way:

"The luck of the third adventure" is proverbial. I have written a spick and span new Tragedy (a sort of compromise between my own notion and yours—as I understand it, at least) and will send it to you if you care to be bothered so far. There is action in it, drabbing, stabbing, et autres gentillesses,—who knows but the Gods may make me good even yet? [1]

The phrase in Browning's letter, "a sort of compromise between my own notion and yours," refers to the good advice which Macready had given Browning when he was reading *The Return of the Druses.* In all probability the poet sent the manuscript of *A Blot* to Macready, to be read at his leisure, either very late in the year 1840, or early in 1841. From Browning's account of his quarrel with Macready over

[1] *Letters,* ed. Hood, p. 5.

the production of the play—written in 1884, forty years after the event—we learn that the actor kept the manuscript for more than a year.[2] We may see from Macready's diary that during 1841 he was overwhelmed by domestic and business troubles. He had, moreover, lost faith completely in Browning's ability to write a play suitable for the stage. At any rate, we hear nothing of *A Blot* until September 26, 1841, when Macready records that "Forster importuned me after dinner to read Browning's tragedy, which I did." Macready and Forster were doubtful, and finally sent the manuscript to Charles Dickens for an opinion. It was not until another year had elapsed that Dickens sent his verdict, on November 25, 1842:

Browning's play has thrown me into a perfect passion of sorrow. To say that there is anything in its subject save what is lovely, true, deeply affecting, full of the best emotion, the most earnest feeling, and the most true and tender source of interest, is to say that there is no light in the sun, and no heat in blood. It is full of genius, natural and great thoughts, profound and yet simple and beautiful in its vigour. I know nothing that is so affecting, nothing in any book I have ever read, as Mildred's recurrence to that "I was so young—I had no mother." I know no love like it, no passion like it, no moulding of a splendid thing after its conception, like it. And I swear it is a tragedy that *must* be played: and must be played, moreover, by Macready. . . . And if you tell Browning that I have seen it, tell him that I believe from my soul there is no man living (and not many dead) who could produce such a work.[3]

Dickens' praise was probably the deciding factor. On December 13, 1842, Browning wrote Domett that Macready had promised "to keep his Theatre open till he has played my Tragedy." Macready turned, rather reluctantly, to preparing *A Blot* for production on January 25, 1843.

Browning's version of the production of the play and the consequent quarrel with Macready has been current for many years, and I shall speak of it below. In 1912 Mr. William Toynbee published Macready's *Diaries* in full, and it is from this account, written as the events happened, that I shall first quote:

[1843]
    January 26th. . . . Finished *Blot*, etc. Went over *Athelwold*—will not do at present. Wrote to Serle for *Honest Man's Fortune*. Received

----

    [2] See Orr, *Life*, pp. 110–4. Mrs. Orr prints two of Browning's letters of 1884 to the editor of the *Daily News* explaining his side of the quarrel. The poet is confused and inaccurate in many details. See Macready's account, given below.
    [3] John Forster, *Life of Dickens*, 1873, II, 25.

and read it—*not do*. Searched, hunted, ruminated; could find nothing.

January 28th.—Went to Drury Lane theatre, finishing by the way the *Blot on,* etc. . . . Willmott [Browning's "grotesque person with a red nose and wooden leg ill at ease in the love scenes"], to whom, on Anderson's declining, I had entrusted the reading *Blot on,* etc., came and reported to me that they laughed at it, and that Anderson passed his jokes on it—not very decorous for an official! I fear—I fear this young man's head is gone.

January 29th.—Browning called, told him of the reading on Saturday and the conduct of the actors. Advised him as to the alteration of second act. . . .

January 31st.—Went to Drury Lane theatre. Found Browning waiting for me in a state of great excitement. He abused the doorkeeper and was in a very great passion. I calmly apologized for having detained him, observing that I had made a great effort to meet him at all. He had not given his *name* to the doorkeeper, who had told him he might walk into the green-room; but his dignity was mortally wounded. I fear he is a very conceited man. Went over his play with him, then looked over part of it. Read it in the room with great difficulty, being *very unwell*.

February 1st. . . . Read Browning's play. Rose, and read and cut it again. Serle called, and I told him of my inability to meet my work— that I *could not* play this part of Browning's unless the whole work of the theatre stopped, that I thought it best to reduce it to its proper form—three acts, and let Phelps do it on all accounts. He concurred with me. . . . I wrote a note to Browning. . . .

February 4th.—Rehearsed Browning's play, the *Blot on the 'Scutcheon*.

February 6th.—Mr. Phelps was too ill to play to-night. I decided on under-studying his part in Browning's play.

February 7th.—Went to Drury Lane theatre. Rehearsed Browning's play, with the idea of acting the part of Lord Tresham, if Mr. Phelps should continue ill. Browning came and in better humour than I have lately seen him. . . .

February 8th.—Went to Drury Lane theatre. Rehearsed three acts of *Much Ado About Nothing* and the *Blot on the 'Scutcheon,* of which I began to despair. . . .

February 9th. . . . Resolved to do the part of Tresham for Mr. Phelps.

February 10th.—Began the consideration and study of the part of Tresham, which was to occupy my single thoughts till accomplished. About a quarter past one a note came from Willmott, informing me that Mr. Phelps would do the part, if he "died for it," so that my time had been lost. Arrived I applied to business; offered to give to Browning and Mr. Phelps the benefit of my consideration and study in the cuts, etc. I had made one I thought particularly valuable, not letting Tresham die, but consigning him to a convent. Browning, however, in the worst taste, manner, and spirit, declined any further alterations, expressing himself perfectly satisfied with the manner in which

Mr. Phelps executed Lord Tresham. I had no more to say. I could only think Mr. Browning a very disagreeable and offensively mannered person. *Voilà tout!*

February 11th.—Directed the rehearsal of *Blot on the 'Scutcheon,* and made many valuable improvements. Browning seemed desirous to explain or qualify the strange carriage and temper of yesterday, and laid much blame on Forster for irritating him. Saw the play of *Blot on the 'Scutcheon,* which was badly acted in Phelps's and Mrs. Stirling's parts—pretty well in Anderson's, very well in Helen Faucit's. I was *angry* after the play about the call being directed without me. . . .

Such is Macready's account of the production of the play. Browning's version of the quarrel as he saw it at the time and as he recalled it years later is recorded in all the biographies. Perhaps the best summary of it is to be had in the letter which Joseph Arnould, a friend, sent to Alfred Domett in May, 1843. After telling of Macready's difficulties and vacillations Arnould relates:

Meanwhile judicious friends, as judicious friends will, had a habit of asking Browning when the play was coming out—you can fancy how sensitively Browning would chafe at this. At length the paramount object with him became to have the play acted, no matter how, so that it was at once. With these feelings he forced Macready to name an early day for playing it. The day was named, Macready was to take the part of [Thorold, Lord] Tresham, which was made for him, and everything was going on swimmingly, when lo! a week or so before the day of representation, Macready declines altogether his part unless the play can be postponed till after Easter. Browning, naturally in "a sulky chafe" at this, declines postponement with haughty coolness; indicates that if Mr. Phelps will take the part he shall be perfectly satisfied; and under this new arrangement, Mr. Phelps having zealously laboured at his part, comes the last rehearsal day. Macready then again appears, hints that he has studied the character, will act the first night. Upon this our Robert does not fall prone at his feet and worship him for his condescending goodness—not that at all does our Robert do, but quite other than that—with laconic brevity he positively declines taking the part from Phelps, dispenses with Macready's aid, etc., and all this in face of a whole green-room. You imagine the fury and whirlwind of our managerial wrath—silent fury, a compressed whirlwind, volcano fires burning white in our pent heart. We say nothing, of course, but we do our spiteful uttermost; we give no orders—we provide paltry machinery—we issue mandates to all our dependent pen-wielders—to all tribes of men who rejoice in suppers and distinguished society. Under penalty of our managerial frown they are to be up and doing in their dirty work.[4]

[4] F. G. Kenyon, *Robert Browning and Alfred Domett,* pp. 63–4. It is quite clear from the style that Arnould had been reading Carlyle.

Browning himself told Mrs. Orr how Macready, on hearing that Browning wished Phelps to have the part of Tresham, had crushed up the manuscript and thrown it to the ground. But it is not necessary here for us to judge between the overwrought, desperate, almost bankrupt and entirely temperamental actor, and the exasperated playwright. The play was performed on February 11, 1843, with Phelps as Lord Tresham. Browning's refusal to let Macready take the leading part from Phelps, who had appealed to the author's sense of justice, was, in Macready's own theater, fatal to the play, as Browning later realized.

SOURCES AND INFLUENCES

A *Blot in the 'Scutcheon* does not, of course, deal with historical personages as do *Strafford* and *King Victor and King Charles*. Both of these are political dramas; *A Blot* is a tragedy of the passions, and falls in the class of domestic drama. Browning sets the time of the play as the eighteenth century and attempts to make the properties, the manners and customs conform to aristocratic life in rural England in that epoch. But the eighteenth century failed to catch the poet's imagination here. His play turns upon the theme of honor, the conventions of a limited aristocratic group. The code of honor, dramatically dangerous at any time, leads him into a medley of confused moral gestures, and the values of his characters are fictitious. Tresham's castle is as unreal as Walpole's Castle of Otranto, and so are the manners and the language of the characters. Only Guendolen and Austin were modern in their speech and reasonably sensible in their actions.[5] But, as one can see from *Strafford, The Flight of the Duchess, My Last Duchess*, and several other poems of these years, Browning was keenly interested in life as it was lived in great houses —both in the relations between the members of a family under an autocratic head, and the relations between the head of an ancient family and his retainers.

The action of *A Blot* is imaginary, but one easily sees that Shakespeare's *Romeo and Juliet* is Browning's model. The extreme youth of Mildred—she is fourteen—is owing to the romantic convention which made Juliet fourteen. The passionate and tragic love between the representatives of great houses, the clandestine visitations, the duelling, the suicide by poison, all go back, I think, to Shakespeare's

[5] See the excellent comment upon *A Blot* by H. B. Charlton, "Browning as Dramatist," in *Bulletin of the John Rylands Library* 23:50–3 (1939).

play. But the houses of Tresham and Mertoun are not at bitter war, as are those of Capulet and Montague, and in discarding the enmity of the great houses Browning has thrown away the motive for the secrecy of the lovers. Romeo and Juliet suffer their tragedy because their joyous and passionate love is thwarted by a fate which works through the bloody feud of their families. Mertoun and Mildred undergo their tragedy because of embarrassment, lack of control, and gnawing consciences. Browning's tragedy is not as well grounded in reason as Shakespeare's, and is therefore not as convincing. From *Romeo and Juliet* we get the tragic catharsis. The Romeo of Act V excites our admiration as well as our pity; he is worth his suffering. The calamity in *A Blot in the 'Scutcheon* seems by comparison a misfortune that a little good sense would have averted; it is pitiful indeed, as Dickens testified, but our admiration is not aroused; without a struggle Mertoun gives up life and love when both are in his hand.

Macready, the actor-manager, is responsible for the present form of the play in more ways than one. It is evident from Macready's entry in his diary for February 1, 1843, that Browning gave him the play in five acts. Macready's suggestion that it be cut to three is probably a mere juggling of scenes, though we know that he cut Browning's play considerably. But his influence was more far-reaching. It has been noticed that the pairs of lovers, Guendolen and Austin on one side and Mildred and Mertoun on the other, afford a comparison to the pairs of lovers in *Much Ado About Nothing*, Benedick and Beatrice and Claudio and Hero. The most striking resemblance appears in Guendolen's loyalty to Mildred when she has admitted her guilt and fainted. This reminds one of Beatrice's loyalty to Hero when that lady is slandered in the famous church scene (IV, i), and seems to admit her guilt by fainting. Austin, won over belatedly to Mildred's cause by his wife, Guendolen, finds his prototype in this respect in Benedick. The resemblances between *A Blot* and *Much Ado* become suddenly significant when we realize that Macready was rehearsing Shakespeare's play at the same time that he was preparing Browning's for presentation, and that he produced *Much Ado* immediately after *A Blot* had failed. For example, Macready recorded on January 29, 1843,

Browning called, told him of the reading on Saturday and the conduct of the actors. Advised him as to the alteration of the second act [the likenesses to *Much Ado* occur particularly in this act]. Note from Mr. Compton declining the part of Verges. . . .

It is likely that Browning, upon Macready's advice, strengthened some scenes of his play by adapting portions of *Much Ado About Nothing*.

Not all of Macready's suggestions were equally acceptable to Browning. At the sale of the Browning Collections in 1913, there was offered a manuscript copy, forty pages folio in Sarianna Browning's hand,[6] of *A Blot* with Macready's proposed excisions and alterations, which affect over 290 lines. Macready wished to change the ending of the play: he would send Thorold, Lord Tresham, into a convent instead of allowing him to swallow poison:

> Within a convent's shade in stranger lands
> Penance and prayer shall wear my life away.

Then again, Macready wished to change Browning's pathetic lines (II, i) which had so moved Dickens,

> I was so young—I loved him so—I had
> No mother. God forgot me—and I fell . . . ,

to

> His foot is on the yew tree bough—the turf
> Receives him;—now the moonlight, as he runs,
> Embraces him;—but he must go:—is gone!
> Ah! once again he turns!—thanks, thanks, my love!
> He's gone!—Oh! I'll believe him every word.[7]

As we have seen, Browning thwarted these changes by publishing his play on the day of the performance.

The strange trait that Browning exhibits in all his dramas, the "evaporation" and death of his characters under the heat of their emotions, is nowhere more surprisingly illustrated than in the death of Mildred. It is, perhaps, a remnant of the influence of Shelley, though it is equally a feature of the melodramatic play of the period.

AFTER-HISTORY

A Blot in the 'Scutcheon, performed at Macready's theater without Macready and under his displeasure, did not enjoy much success. It was performed three times in February, 1843, the 11th, 13th, and 15th. It ceased because of a lack of patronage. One of Bulwer's plays

---

[6] Miss Sarianna Browning was his amanuensis for most of the *Bells and Pomegranates* series; see *Letters*, ed. Hood, p. 180.

[7] *The Browning Collections* (Sotheby Catalogue, 1913), p. 42.

of the same time ran for eighty performances.[8] The *Literary Gazette* for February 18, 1843, printed a typical review of the play. The writer found many scenes touching, and the acting of Helen Faucit in the part of Mildred exquisitely done, but the inherent faults of the plot seemed to him to be fatal to the chances of the play. Of all the reviews that in the *Athenaeum* for February 18, 1843, was the most severe. It said, in part:

> If to pain and perplex were the end and aim of tragedy, Mr. Browning's poetic melodrama called *A Blot in the 'Scutcheon* would be worthy of admiration, for it is a very puzzling and unpleasant piece of business. The plot is plain enough, but the acts and feelings of the characters are inscrutable and abhorrent, and the language is as strange as their proceedings. . . . A few of the audience laughed, others were shocked, and many applauded; but it is impossible that such a drama should live even if it were artfully constructed, which this is not. . . .

This review still rankled in Browning's mind forty years later. Perhaps the most vivid account of what took place in the theater is that of Joseph Arnould in a letter to his friend Domett. Arnould was present at all the performances in 1843.[9]

On November 27, 28, and 29 and December 7, 8, and 9, 1848, *A Blot* was acted at the Sadler's Wells Theater in Islington by Phelps, who had acted the part of Tresham in the first performance. In February, 1849, the play was acted twice by Phelps's company. In 1884 it was performed by Lawrence Barrett in Washington, D. C., and on March 15, 1888, it was acted under the auspices of the Browning Society of London with Miss Alma Murray taking the part of Mildred. In all these later representations the play was much better received than in 1843.

Perhaps the most unhappy part of the history of *A Blot in the 'Scutcheon* was the estrangement which the play caused between Browning and his friends, Macready and Forster. The break with Forster did not come at once, but the breach which had threatened during the presentation of *Strafford* was now much wider. Browning had some cause for complaint against Forster, though he did not know it at the time, because the critic had never shown him Dickens' letter in praise of *A Blot,* and Browning only saw it when it appeared in Forster's *Life of Dickens* in 1873. Then he commented that Dick-

---

[8] For the best account of the reception of *A Blot* see T. R. Lounsbury, *The Early Literary Career of Robert Browning,* pp. 113–31.

[9] See F. G. Kenyon, *Robert Browning and Alfred Domett,* pp. 65–7.

ens' praise would have made a considerable difference to his reputation. This was, however, a mistaken assumption. As early as 1848 Dickens' words had been quoted in English and American publications.[10] Browning probably did not hear of them because of his absence in Italy. This play was the last which Browning wrote for Macready, and the two men did not speak to each other for many years.

A *Blot* sold better than most of the other numbers of *Bells and Pomegranates,* and there is evidence that it reached the hearts of many eminent readers in its generation. It has steadily held its place in collections of the drama as a representative play of the nineteenth century.[11]

COLOMBE'S BIRTHDAY

PUBLICATION

Colombe's Birthday was sent to the printer on March 9, 1844, and was published as a pamphlet of twenty pages, bound in yellow paper wrappers, about April 20. The pamphlet consisted of a title-page: "Bells and Pomegranates. No. VI.—Colombe's Birthday. A Play, In Five Acts. By Robert Browning, Author of "Paracelsus." "Ivy and violet, what do ye here, "With blossom and shoot in the warm springweather, "Hiding the arms of Monchenci and Vere?" Hanmer. London: Edward Moxon, Dover Street. MDCCCXLIV"; the dedication to Barry Cornwall, dated March, 1844, a list of persons, the place and the time (16—), on the reverse of the title-page; and the text, pp. 3–20. The cost of publication was probably a little more than £16, and was borne by the poet's father. The price was One Shilling the copy.

TEXT

In a letter dated July 2, 1877, to Buxton Forman who had bought the manuscript of *Colombe's Birthday,* Browning wrote a full account of its history:

[10] See Gertrude Reese, "Robert Browning and *A Blot in the 'Scutcheon*," in *MLN* 63:237–40 (1948).
[11] For a spirited defence of the play from its detractors, see Mr. G. H. Clarke "Browning's *A Blot in the 'Scutcheon: A Defence*," in *Sewanee Review* 28:213–27 (1920).

I made it for the use of Charles Kean and his wife, to whom I read it. They would have acted· the play—but in perhaps two or three years to come, and in the meantime I was to keep it unprinted—an arrangement which did not suit me—whereupon I withdrew it, and included it in my *Bells and Pomegranates*. It was never in the prompter's hands, I think. The excisions were my own, also the pencil-marks, which emphasize any word in a passage. When it came back from the printer, my father caused the MS. to be bound, and I have no notion how it passed out of his or my possession. It is the single poem in the series that I copied with my own hand, my sister being my amanuensis in those days.[1]

In the first edition of *Colombe's Birthday* there were 1909 lines of blank verse, divided as follows: I—372; II—350; III—379; IV—419; V—389. In the final text there were 1910 lines, but in spite of the close approximation in size the play underwent considerable change in line, word, and punctuation. Most of the changes are in Act IV, and were introduced into the collected edition of 1849. In 1853 when Helen Faucit was eager to present the play upon the stage, Browning gave his consent, but added, "only, pray follow the corrections in the last [1849] edition (Chapman and Hall will give you a copy), as they are important to the sense." [2] There was no separate second edition of the play, but it appeared in all the collected editions of the poet's works. Sir Edmund Gosse possessed a first edition of *Colombe,* marked for stage presentation and embellished with marginal advice, but in 1881 Browning could not remember for what occasion he had made the stage directions—he supposed for Helen Faucit. A letter of Mrs. Browning's dated April 12, 1853, however, declared specifically that her husband did nothing to prepare *Colombe* for the stage in that year.

GENESIS AND COMPOSITION

Colombe's Birthday was probably begun shortly after the publication of *A Blot in the 'Scutcheon* on February 11, 1843. On May 15, Browning wrote to Domett, "I have a desk full of scrawls at which I look, and work a little. I want to publish a few more numbers of my 'Bells'—and must also make up my mind to finish a play I wrote

---

[1] *Letters,* ed. Hood, pp. 179–80. This "beautifully neat folio manuscript written upon 30 sheets of blue foolscap paper, on one side only," is said to be in America.

[2] Orr, *Life* pp. 185–6. See also *New Letters,* ed. DeVane and Knickerbocker, pp. 58–9, 61; and "Helena Faucit Martin's Unpublished Letters to Robert Browning," in *Baylor University Browning Interests,* Second Series, 1931, p. 9.

lately for Charles Kean, if he will have it." [3] After Browning's quarrel with Macready over the *Blot* he was offered a handsome sum to write a play for Kean, a rival actor-manager. Writing to Miss Barrett on September 13, 1845, the poet remembered the sum as £500, but it had probably grown in his memory. The money was not sufficient to speed the completion of *Colombe,* for it was not until March 9, 1844, that the play was read to Kean, though it was certainly finished some time before that date. Browning reported the results to his friend Dowson in a letter dated March 10:

Yesterday I read my play to him and his charming wife (who is to take the principal part) and all went off *au mieux*—but—he wants to keep it till "Easter next year"—and unpublished all the time! . . . my play will take him two months at least to study, he being a 'special slow-head, and after the Haymarket engagement nothing is to be done till this time next year.—Of all which notable pieces of information I was apprised for the first time *after* the play was read and approved of . . . for, it certainly never entered into my mind that anybody, even an actor, could need a couple of months to study a part, only, in a piece, which I could match with another in less time by a good deal.

But, though I *could* do such a thing, I have a head,—that aches oftener now than of old,—to take care of; and, therefore, *will* do no such thing as let this new work lie stifled for a year and odd,—and work double-tides to bring out something as likely to be popular this present season—for something I *must* print, or risk the hold, such as it is, I have at present on *my* public: and, on consideration of the two other productions I have by me in a state of forwardness, neither seems nearly so proper for the requirements of the moment, as this play—and two or three hundred pounds will pay me but indifferently for hasarding the good fortune which appears slowly but not mistakeably setting in upon me, just now. You will not wonder, therefore, that—tho' I was so far taken by surprise as to promise Kean a copy for Scotland and a fortnight's grace, to come to terms in, before I either published the play or accepted any other party's offer—I say, you will not wonder if I have determined to print it directly (acting on the best advice, I sent it to press yesterday) and merely put the right of *the acting* at his disposal. . . .[4]

In this letter one encounters many interesting things, such as Browning's speed in his work—he could write another *Colombe* in less than two months—his disgust at actors, his desire to keep before his public—he had not published for thirteen months—and the slow but sure growth of his reputation in a small circle of readers. Kean

[3] F. G. Kenyon, *Robert Browning and Alfred Domett,* p. 55.
[4] *Letters,* ed. Hood, pp. 9–10.

never acted the play, and on April 20, 1844, Moxon announced it as just published.

SOURCES AND INFLUENCES

There is no historical source for the events which happen in *Colombe's Birthday,* though the background is, characteristically of Browning in these years, political-historical, and he dates it 16—. In spite of the political eminence of the main characters, however, the play is essentially domestic in its nature. Colombe, nominally ruling her state, is unaware of her public obligation and the impending crisis in Cleves. Her subjects are near revolt and her throne is claimed by a great prince. But in Colombe there is no real conflict between love and duty; the choice is rather between a castle and love in a cottage. No moral or political issues are involved. Valence pleads for the people, and Colombe falls in love with him rather than with the prince.[5]

The duchies of Juliers and Cleves, on the Rhine in southwestern Germany, had been united by a marriage of the ruling families in 1543, and continued to be precariously independent until they were given to Prussia after the battle of Waterloo. Browning had twice been through this region, in 1834 on his way to and from Russia, and again in 1838 on his return from Italy. He shows his knowledge of the locality in *How They brought the Good News from Ghent to Aix.* The situation, in which the heroine chooses the less distinguished suitor, Browning seems to have adapted from the *Memoires* of the Marquis de Lassay,[6] which he knew as early as 1840 and used for *The Glove, The Flight of the Duchess* and later for the *Parleying With Daniel Bartoli,* among other poems. In the *Memoires* Marianne Pajot, at the point of marriage with the Duke of Lorraine, gives up the opportunity of becoming Duchess and wins the more genuine love of the obscure de Lassay. In essence, this is what Colombe does in *Colombe's Birthday.* Browning has modified the story somewhat, transferred it a little to the west, to the lesser-known duchy of Juliers, but has kept approximately the time and the manners, and even the main theme of the preference of love to worldly station, as he found it in de Lassay. It ought to be said, however, that Browning's

[5] See the excellent discussion of *Colombe* in H. B. Charlton, "Browning as Dramatist," in *Bulletin of the John Rylands Library* 23:54–5 (1939).

[6] See *Recueil de differentes choses,* par M. de Lassay, Lausanne, 1756, I, 5–19 (The Book of Marianne). See also DeVane, *Browning's Parleyings,* pp. 50–91.

interest in chivalric love is peculiarly his own, and that that interest, especially directed to the presence of love in the courts of the great, had recently found expression in *Sordello, King Victor, Rudel to the Lady of Tripoli,* and *My Last Duchess.* It was to show itself soon again in *The Flight of the Duchess* and *The Glove.* In another minor way *Colombe* is related to *The Flight of the Duchess;* for *Colombe* is prefaced by a motto from Sir John Hanmer's volume, *Fra Cipollo and other Poems,* and it was at Bettisfield Park in Flintshire, Hanmer's estate, that Browning was staying in September, 1842, when he conceived a new idea for *The Flight.*

Another motif of the play, quite as important as that of chivalric love, is the motif of political liberalism which is embodied in Valence. His passionate interest in the welfare of the common people of Cleves is Browning's interest, which had shown itself in *Strafford, Sordello, Pippa Passes, King Victor,* and *The Druses,* and was to inform *A Lost Leader* and *A Soul's Tragedy.*

AFTER-HISTORY

The reviews of *Colombe* were not numerous. The article upon the play by Forster in the *Examiner* for June 22, 1844, caused a complete but temporary rupture between himself and Browning. After some dubious praise, Forster had concluded, "As far as he has gone, we abominate his tastes as much as we respect his genius."

But of all Browning's plays, *Colombe* had perhaps the happiest stage-history. It was produced seven times by Helen Faucit in April, 1853, at the Haymarket Theater, to the general approval of the critics.[7] The reviewer in the *Athenaeum* for April 30, 1853, remarked upon the delicacy of the play: "The involuntary tear was often felt upon the cheek. . . . Whether the taste of the public for so refined a creation on the stage is yet formed, remains to be seen." Mrs. Browning wrote anxiously for news of the performances on April 12, and in May gave a very fair judgment upon it: "Yes, Robert's play succeeded, but there could be no 'run' for a play of that kind. It was a succès d'estime, and something more, which is surprising, perhaps, considering the miserable acting of the men. Miss Faucit was alone in doing us justice. . . ."[8] The play was also performed by Miss Faucit in Manchester, and was certainly presented once at the Athenaeum in Boston, on February 16, 1854. Under the auspices of

[7] For these criticisms see *Browning Society's Papers* I, 122-5.
[8] *Letters of E.B.B.,* ed. Kenyon, II, 112-6.

the Browning Society of London on November 19, 1885, the play was revived at St. George's Hall, Miss Alma Murray, "most poetical of actresses," taking the part of Colombe.[9] Browning wrote appreciatively from Venice of the event.

The general view of the later critics, as of the earlier, was that *Colombe's Birthday* was tender and delicate as literature, but was not well adapted to the stage. Literary commentators have generally found it one of the most satisfactory of Browning's plays for reading. It was the last that he wrote specifically for the stage. On July 31, 1844, Browning sent the play to his friend Domett in New Zealand with the words, "here you shall have it—but I feel myself so much stronger, if flattery not deceive, that I shall stop some things that were meant to follow, and begin again. I really seem to have something fresh to say." This feeling probably forecasts the *Dramatic Romances* of 1845, the next of the *Bells and Pomegranates* to be published.

DRAMATIC ROMANCES AND LYRICS

PUBLICATION

The *Dramatic Romances and Lyrics,* a pamphlet of twenty-four pages bound in yellow paper wrappers, appeared on November 6, 1845. The volume consisted of a title-page: "Bells and Pomegranates. No. VII. Dramatic Romances and Lyrics. By Robert Browning, Author of "Paracelsus." London: Edward Moxon, Dover Street. MDCCCXLV."; a dedication to John Kenyon, Esq., dated November, 1845, and a list of the contents on the reverse of the title-page; and the text, pp. 3–24. The text, as in all the other numbers in the series, was printed in double columns of fine type. The cost of publication, something more than £16, was borne by the poet's father. The published price was Two Shillings the copy.

TEXT

The table of contents in the pamphlet listed the poems in this order:

How They brought the Good News from Ghent to Aix (16—)
Pictor Ignotus. Florence, 15—.
Italy in England [called in 1849 *The Italian in England*]
England in Italy [called in 1849 *The Englishman in Italy*]

[9] *Browning Society's Papers* II, 93*–7*.

The Lost Leader
The Lost Mistress
Home Thoughts from Abroad
The Tomb at St. Praxed's [called in 1849 *The Bishop Orders his Tomb at St. Praxed's Church*]
Garden Fancies
   I. The Flower's Name
   II. Sibrandus Schafnaburgensis
France and Spain
   I. The Laboratory
   II. The Confessional
The Flight of the Duchess
Earth's Immortalities
Song ["Nay, but you, who do not love her"]
The Boy and the Angel
Night and Morning [called in 1849 *Meeting at Night* and *Parting at Morning*]
Claret and Tokay [called in 1863 *Nationality in Drinks*]
Saul [the first nine sections only]
Time's Revenges
The Glove

In the collected edition of 1849 these poems—all save *Claret and Tokay* and the section of *Home-Thoughts, from Abroad* beginning, "Here's to Nelson's memory," which were dropped temporarily—followed the *Dramatic Lyrics* under the general title of *Dramatic Romances and Lyrics*. In the edition of 1863 Browning distributed all the short poems in a new arrangement, descriptive rather than chronological, and placed them under the titles which he had earlier used for the various volumes as they were published. In this reorganization six of the *Dramatic Romances and Lyrics* of 1845 came under the head of *Dramatic Romances,* thirteen became *Dramatic Lyrics,* and two were assigned to *Men and Women.* I attempt to give the history of these shufflings for each poem under its own name. The title *Dramatic Romances,* used by Browning in 1863 and thereafter, covers twenty-five poems culled from *Dramatic Lyrics, Dramatic Romances and Lyrics,* and *Men and Women.*

Of the poems in the pamphlet of 1845, *The Laboratory, Claret and Tokay, Garden Fancies, The Boy and the Angel, The Tomb at St. Praxed's,* and the first nine sections of *The Flight of the Duchess* had been published in *Hood's Magazine* between June, 1844, and April, 1845. These, in spite of the poet's prejudice against publication in periodicals, were given to F. A. Ward, sub-editor of the magazine, to help Thomas Hood in his illness. Hood died on May 3, 1845.

GENESIS AND COMPOSITION; SOURCES AND INFLUENCES

Like the *Dramatic Lyrics* of 1842, the new pamphlet of small poems was urged upon Browning by his publisher, Moxon, as a bid for popularity. The poems which make up the *Dramatic Romances* were the gleanings since November, 1842. The range is wider than in the volume of 1842, and the hand is surer. One sees in this new collection old traits; such as, for example, Browning's delight in catching the quality of a nation at a particular time, in *France and Spain* and *Claret and Tokay*, which is later called *Nationality in Drinks*, and above all in *The Tomb at St. Praxed's*. But a good many of the new poems rise less from Browning's study than from his observation and his personal experience. Had it not been for Browning's second Italian journey, taken between August and December, 1844, the *Dramatic Romances* would have been very different, and very much poorer, as one can see by a glance at the contents. One of the old elements in Browning's poetry, his interest in the passion of love, is now given a new emphasis, for several of the poems were written as he courted Miss Barrett. The *Dramatic Romances* in their vigor and freshness of subject, as well as in their perfection of a highly individualized style, show us that Browning has finally found his natural voice, and that the even greater triumphs of *Men and Women* are now inevitable.

AFTER-HISTORY

Writing to Browning on October 22, 1845, after she had seen the proofs of *Dramatic Romances*, Miss Barrett said, "Now if people do not cry out about these poems, what are we to think of the world?" There was no outcry; even the reviews were few in number. The notices in the *Athenaeum* on January 17, 1846, and the *Examiner* on November 15, 1845, were mildly favorable, but with reservations. The *Examiner*, however, concluded graciously. In commenting upon the appearance of *Bells and Pomegranates*, it said, "They look as though already packed up and on their way to posterity; nor are we without a confident expectation that some of them will arrive at that journey's end." Elizabeth Barrett was perhaps the most enthusiastic reader, though the praise which Landor sent from Italy, fourteen lines in blank verse, is easily the most notable. It read, in part:

> Since Chaucer was alive and hale,
> No man has walked along our road with step

> So active, so inquiring eye, or tongue
> So varied in discourse.[1]

Browning's father was so proud of this tribute that he had the poem printed and distributed it among his friends. Though the reception of *Dramatic Romances* was indifferent, the little volume gradually won its way. It delighted the Rossettis, and through them the Pre-Raphaelite Brotherhood in 1848. The judgment of time has come to be that there are few individual books of such sustained excellence by any author in English.

"How They brought the Good News from Ghent to Aix" [16—.]

This poem was first published in *Dramatic Romances* on November 6, 1845; it was the first poem in the pamphlet. In the collected edition of 1849 it came under the head of *Dramatic Romances and Lyrics,* and in the distribution of 1863 it became one of the *Dramatic Lyrics.* The poem was composed of ten stanzas of six four-measure anapaestic lines each. Browning told Joachim Miller that he got the meter for the poem from Virgil—probably the eighth book.[2] Save in punctuation, the text has suffered no change since 1845.

Concerning the composition of *"How They brought the Good News,"* Browning wrote on January 23, 1881,

There is no sort of historical foundation about "Good News [from] Ghent." I wrote it under the bulwark of a vessel, off the African Coast, after I had been at sea long enough to appreciate even the fancy of a gallop on a certain good horse "York," then in my stable at home. It was written in pencil on the fly-leaf of Bartoli's *Simboli,* I remember.[3]

Browning repeated this account several times, and in 1884 added the detail that the gallop was "in relief of an invested town whereto access, by a certain road hitherto impracticable, was discovered to be

---

[1] The manuscript of Landor's lines, formerly in the possession of William Lyon Phelps, is now in the Yale University Library. The lines were first published in the *Morning Chronicle* for November 22, 1845. For Browning's excitement over Landor's praise see his letter of November 19 to Moxon, his publisher and friend, in *New Letters,* ed. DeVane and Knickerbocker, pp. 37–8. See also W. L. Phelps, "Landor and Browning," in *Journal of English Literary History* 1: 231–4 (December, 1943).

[2] See E. D. Cressman, "The Classical Poems of Robert Browning," in the *Classical Journal* 23:198–207.

[3] *Browning Society's Papers, Chronological List of Browning's Works,* I, 49.

open for once." [4] And in another statement he inaugurates the legend which has been repeated with the addition of circumstantial detail by all the biographers, that the poem was written on his first journey to Italy in 1838. Sir Frederic Kenyon was the first commentator to question the accuracy of Browning's memory on this point.[5] The fact that the poem was not included in *Dramatic Lyrics* in 1842, when Browning had to put in *The Pied Piper* to fill up the pamphlet, and the fact that he took Bartoli's *Simboli* with him on his second Italian journey of 1844, make it seem probable that Browning's recollection, forty years later, was at fault. His own earlier evidence seems to settle the matter.[6] Since he left England on his second Italian journey early in August, 1844, I think *"How They brought the Good News"* was written in the latter part of that month.

In another statement concerning the poem Browning asserts, "there is *no* historical incident whatever commemorated by the Poem you mention, which I wrote at sea, off the African coast, with a merely general impression of the characteristic warfare and besieging which abound in the Annals of Flanders. This accounts for some difficulties in the time and space occupied by the ride in one night." [7] Browning had passed through Flanders twice when he wrote the poem, once on his journey to Russia in 1834, and again on his return from Italy in 1838. The country was therefore generally familiar, though he did not have a strictly accurate conception of towns and mileage. This accounts for the indirect route taken by the riders, and the 120 miles which Roland is supposed to have covered. Browning came through the Low Countries again on his return to England on the voyage of 1844.

The copy of Bartoli's *Simboli* in which Browning wrote this poem (see also *Home-Thoughts, from the Sea*) is in the Balliol College Library, Oxford; the writing on the fly-leaf is nearly obliterated. *"How They brought the Good News"* is akin to *Through the Metidja to Abd-el-Kadr* in meter, and to *Childe Roland* and *Pheidippides* in meaning. It is possible that seeing the coasts which had inspired *Through the Metidja*, with its galloping measures, led Browning to write *"How They brought the Good News."* The poem has always been held in great popular esteem.

<hr>

[4] *New Letters*, ed. DeVane and Knickerbocker, pp. 300 and 203.
[5] See *Centenary Edition* III, xiii.
[6] See above, my discussion of the third phase of *Sordello*, and n. 16.
[7] *Letters*, ed. Hood, pp. 215–6.

In recent years a considerable difference of opinion has risen concerning the meaning of the word "pique" in line 10 of the poem, which the context seems to make some part of the saddle or gear. Francis V. Lloyd suggested that the word should be the English word "peak," meaning the crownpiece of the bridle. Adrian Van Sinderen pointed out that an English saddle has no pommel, the usual gloss for the word "pique." Charles D. Smith thinks that Browning was making a noun from the French word *piquer*, meaning to spur, and that the rider adjusted his spur, an action which logically follows tightening the girth and shortening the stirrups.[8]

Pictor Ignotus

Pictor Ignotus, Florence, 15—. was published in *Dramatic Romances* on November 6, 1845. In 1849 it was one of the *Dramatic Romances and Lyrics* and in 1863 it assumed its permanent place as one of *Men and Women*. The text was altered in several places, notably lines 45–8, for the edition of 1849. The purpose of the alterations was to delete an unpoetic expression; the sense is not changed. Since 1849 there have been a few verbal changes and the usual revision of punctuation. There are in the poem seventy-two iambic lines, rhyming alternately.

Pictor Ignotus was certainly conceived, and possibly written, during Browning's visit to Florence, which may have been early in November, 1844. But we hear nothing of the poem until it is in proof and the poet sends it to Miss Barrett on October 18, 1845. It is certainly the fruit of his observation of pictures in Florence, and embodies his conception of how the early, and now unknown, painters of those pale, formal, monastic series—Virgin, Babe, and Saint—might defend themselves in the face of the great vogue for the newer, more vulgar, painters who depict the expressions of contemporary human beings. Here we get the first notion of Browning's theory of the development of Italian painting in the fifteenth and sixteenth centuries, the theory which is to inform such later pieces as *Andrea del Sarto, Fra Lippo Lippi, Old Pictures in Florence,* and the *Parleying With Francis Furini.* Fra Lippo is the worldling whose theory and practice, according to Browning, are the direct opposites of the "painter unknown" signified by the title.

[8] For this debate see the *Explicator* VI, Q. 10; VI, Item 35; VII, Item 10; XI, Item 42.

The above interpretation of the poem has been strongly challenged. Paul F. Jamieson is of the opinion that such an interpretation reads into *Pictor Ignotus* ideas that were not in Browning's mind until several years later. The painter of the poem, he contends, was not early, but belongs to the high Renaissance, the century of Raphael and Michael Angelo. The youth the painter praises may be Raphael, thirty-seven years old in 1520. Mr. Jamieson thinks Pictor's conventionality is not a protest against naturalism, but is a gesture of personal timidity. Pictor shrinks from original creation, but is piqued by the fame of a contemporary. He is deceiving himself, and is motivated by envy. His sensitivity is only half-truth.[9] Mr. Jamieson's argument is persuasive, but I think that Browning had already at least in part worked out his theory of the development of Italian painting by 1845. If I am correct in this, the speaker in *Pictor Ignotus* is a belated traditionalist who has been left stranded by the change.

Line 32 of *Pictor Ignotus* possibly refers to the Borgo Allegri in Florence; the street was so named when a Madonna painted by Cimabue was borne along it.

The Italian in England

Italy in England, called in 1849 and thereafter *The Italian in England,* first appeared in *Dramatic Romances* on November 6, 1845. In 1849 it was under the general heading *Dramatic Romances and Lyrics;* in the distribution of 1863 it was grouped permanently as one of the *Dramatic Romances.* The poem was composed of 162 four-measure lines in rhyming couplets. Since its first publication it has suffered only a very few verbal changes and the usual changes in punctuation.

The poem was conceived, I think, in the early part of October, 1844, when Browning was in the region of Naples on his second Italian voyage. Sir Frederic Kenyon has suggested with considerable plausibility that the poem rose from Browning's interest in the uprising of the Bandiera brothers on the Neapolitan coast in June and July of 1844. Ottilia and Emilio, sons of Baron Bandiera, an admiral in the Austrian navy, and themselves in the service, espoused the cause of Young Italy and fled in the early part of 1844 to Corfu. They set sail on June 12 with nineteen men to raid the Neapolitan coast for

[9] Paul F. Jamieson, "Browning's *Pictor Ignotus, Florence, 15—,*" in the *Explicator* XI, Item 8.

the purpose of liberating political prisoners. After fighting and hiding they were betrayed by one of their own company, captured, and executed with seven of their companions on July 23. As they died each of them shouted *"Viva l'Italia!"* [10] The effect was enormous, and the country was still ringing with the event when Browning was there in late September and early October. It must not be forgotten that the poet's Italian master in England was Angelo Cerutti, a refugee from Italy. The scene of the poem is, of course, Padua, but the poem aims to be a vivid picture of all Italy under Austrian rule. Perhaps the scene was shifted to avoid referring directly to the Bandiera affair. The poet probably had the Neapolitan event in his mind, but wrote as if he were thinking of the uprising of 1823 in the north. The Italian refugee, the speaker, tells his story as if it had happened some years since.

The poem was probably not written in 1844; though the idea was conceived at Naples, the poem was recollected in tranquillity. On August 13, 1845, Miss Barrett had the manuscript of this poem and its companion-piece, *England in Italy*, in fairly rough condition in her hands. We know that she suggested that Browning change the lines,

> I would grasp Metternich until
> I felt his throat and had my will,

to the present much stronger reading, and that she called the piece a "serene, noble poem." [11] The poem is one of the few expressions of Browning's intense sympathy with the cause of Italian freedom. Mazzini, then an exile in England, later informed Browning that he had read the poem to his fellow exiles to show them how an Englishman could sympathize with them.[12]

The Englishman in Italy

England in Italy [*Piano di Sorrento*], renamed in 1849 *The Englishman in Italy*, first appeared in *Dramatic Romances* on November 6, 1845. In 1849 it was grouped under *Dramatic Romances and Lyrics;* in 1863 it became one of the *Dramatic Romances*, and has so remained. It is composed of five sections, 292 lines rhyming *abcb*. About August 11, 1845, Browning sent the poem in an unfinished

---

[10] *Centenary Edition*, III, xxxiv.
[11] See *Macmillan Edition*, p. 1344.
[12] Orr, *Handbook*, p. 306.

state to Miss Barrett, and she mended the meter in a number of instances; [13] most of her suggestions the poet adopted. The text was further slightly changed for the 1849 edition, and in one or two cases after that; these changes were mainly for meter and in punctuation.

Browning was in the region of Naples about the first of October, 1844, on his second journey to Italy, and probably witnessed then the rich pageantry of the Neapolitan autumn. We know he wandered over the Piano di Sorrento and climbed Vico Alvano, and that he visited the Isles of the Sirens on October 4, experiences which are related in the poem. The poem was not written, I think, at this time, but was, like its companion-piece *The Italian in England*, recollected in tranquillity—possibly, in May, 1845, for Browning's letter to Miss Barrett on May 3 is a prose account of the matter of the poem. At any rate, we first hear of the poem when Miss Barrett criticizes it on August 13, when it is in an unfinished condition.

When Browning sent the poem to her it was not in its present state; the title then seems to have been *England in Italy. Autumn at Sorrento,* and notably the last section of the poem as it now stands was lacking. This section, embodying his feelings against the Corn Laws, is one of the few places where Browning spoke frankly in his poetry his own opinions on politics. Browning sent the poems to press on October 13, 1845, and therefore it was between August 13 and October 13 that he added the last section to the poem. On October 22 Miss Barrett read the first printer's proofs and said, "The end you have put to 'England in Italy' gives unity to the whole . . . just what the poem wanted. Also you have given some nobler lines to the middle than met me there before." [14]

The debates upon the Corn Laws had been at fever-pitch in March, 1845, when Disraeli was nightly delivering his philippics against Peel in Parliament. Then the ruin of the crops after a rainy July, and the potato blight in August in Ireland and the south of England, made action imperative. On October 31 Peel proposed to his cabinet to open the ports to free grain and food. In the next year the Corn Laws were repealed. It was probably in September, 1845, when the situation was darkest, that Browning wrote his lines. He is expressing in them the natural belief of a young Whig-Liberal

[13] See *Macmillan Edition*, pp. 1343–4.

[14] It is possible that among the new lines were ll. 22–4, about "Pomegranates . . . splitting," a reference which Miss Barrett would have appreciated. See Hoxie N. Fairchild, "Browning's Pomegranate Heart," in *MLN* 66:265–6 (1951).

of the early Forties. He was later to follow Gladstone to the Liberal party; see his sonnet of 1885, *Why I am a Liberal,* and also *The Lost Leader,* 1845.

One or two further comments ought to be made. It is possible that Browning meant to speak of the condition of Italy in the line "How fair! but a slave." This poem takes its place naturally beside the poet's other pictures of Italian life, such as its companion-piece *The Italian in England, Up at a Villa—Down in the City,* and *De Gustibus.* Further, one cannot imagine Browning looking down into the crystalline depths of the Mediterranean without remembering Shelley's *Stanzas written in Dejection, near Naples,* written in such a different mood, and his *Ode to the West Wind.*

The Lost Leader

The Lost Leader was published in *Dramatic Romances* on November 6, 1845. In the collected edition of 1849 it was placed under the *Dramatic Romances and Lyrics,* and in the distribution of 1863 it was classed permanently with the *Dramatic Lyrics.* Between 1845 and 1849 the text suffered a very few verbal changes; since 1863 a few changes in punctuation and in words have been made for the sake of euphony. The poem is composed of two sections, each of sixteen dactylic four-measure lines.

The occasion, and perhaps the composition, of the poem seems to have risen upon Wordsworth's acceptance of the laureateship on April 4, 1843. On October 15, 1842, Wordsworth had accepted a civil list pension amounting to £300. Possibly the pension is Browning's "handful of silver," as the "riband to stick in his coat" may represent the laureateship. Wordsworth's acceptance of the office was probably not in itself such a blow to Browning: it was merely the culmination of the "apostasy" of which Browning had learned from Shelley, Byron, Hazlitt, and possibly by word of mouth from Leigh Hunt. It had seemed to Browning since he had read Shelley, and especially since he had worked upon *Strafford* and *Sordello,* that humanity needed a defender. He had himself espoused the cause of the people, and in the struggles towards reform between 1837 and 1845, and especially in the anti-Corn Law agitation (1842–6), Browning felt the need of a liberal spokesman from among the poets. Through Wordsworth's acceptance of the laureateship Browning saw bitterly the whole course of Wordsworth's life since, let us say, 1813 when he accepted the office of distributor of stamps for Westmorland. Turning his back utterly upon his own fiery youth, Wordsworth had become by 1821 an ardent Tory. That Browning had Wordsworth in mind as the lost leader we know from letters he wrote in 1875 to Grosart and to Miss Lee, when he was older and not quite so eager to condemn Wordsworth for his action. On February 24, 1875, he wrote to Grosart:

I have been asked the question you now address me with, and as duly answered it, I can't remember how many times: there is no sort of objection to one more assurance, or rather confession, on my part that I *did* in my hasty youth presume to use the great and venerable personality of Wordsworth as a sort of painter's model; one from which this or the other particular feature may be selected and turned to account: had I intended more, above all, such a boldness as portraying the entire man, I should not have talked about "handfuls of silver and bits of ribbon." These never influenced the change of politics in the great poet; whose defection, nevertheless, accompanied as it was by a regular face-about of his special party, was to my juvenile apprehension, and even mature consideration, an event to deplore. But just as in the tapestry on my wall I can recognise figures which have *struck out* a fancy, on occasion, that though truly enough thus derived, yet would be preposterous as a copy, so, though I dare not deny the original of my little poem, I altogether refuse to have it considered as the "very effigies" of such a moral and intellectual superiority.[15]

But this letter was written thirty-two years after the event, and by the Browning who was in 1880 to become a member of the Wordsworth Society, even to serve as temporary chairman on one occasion. The letter to Miss Lee on September 7, 1875, was to the same effect: the poet "with shame and contrition" acknowledged that he had had Wordsworth in mind for *The Lost Leader,* and he added, "I thought of the great Poet's abandonment of liberalism, at an unlucky juncture, and no repaying consequence that I could ever see." [16]

But there is unmistakable evidence that Browning meant in dead earnest his portrait of 1843–5. We see from his letters to Miss Barrett in 1845–6 that he got a good deal of malicious pleasure in picturing Wordsworth as laureate attending at court dressed in the court clothes of Samuel Rogers, a much shorter man. Browning's earlier attitude towards Wordsworth is summed up in his words to Miss Barrett on August 22, 1846,

I would at any time have gone to Finchley to see a curl of his [Byron's] hair or one of his gloves, I am sure—while Heaven knows that I could

---

[15] *Letters,* ed. Hood, pp. 166–7.
[16] Orr, *Life,* p. 123.

not get up enthusiasm enough to cross the room if at the other end of it all Wordsworth, Coleridge, and Southey were condensed into the little China bottle yonder. . . .

It is no accident, therefore, that in arranging the poems for *Dramatic Romances* he should make the lost leader of English liberalism follow directly upon the heroism of the Italian patriots and his own comment upon England's Corn Laws. Wordsworth's defection did indeed come at "an unlucky juncture." The phrase which Browning uses concerning Wordsworth, "Pardoned in Heaven, the first by the throne," and indeed his whole attitude of lofty charity towards a political apostate, seems to be an echo of the great speech of forgiveness to Strafford, another apostate, which Browning had put into Pym's mouth in his drama, *Strafford* (V, ii, 268–303).[17] Strafford's apostasy is as unhistorical as Wordsworth's; and in history Pym's love for Strafford was no greater than Browning's for Wordsworth, which means that it was non-existent. It is to be wondered if the likeness of Strafford's name, Wentworth, to the poet's name, Wordsworth, suggested *The Lost Leader* to Browning.

The poem seems not to have been submitted with others to Miss Barrett for corrections in August, 1845. She saw it for the first time on October 22, 1845, in printer's proof, and delighted in "that 'Lost Leader' which strikes so broadly and deep . . . which nobody can ever forget—and which is worth all the journalising and pamphleteering in the world!"

Wordsworth's opinion of Browning was not high, but at the supper given by Talfourd, author of *Ion*, in May, 1836, when the company was toasting the author of *Paracelsus* as one of the "Poets of England," Wordsworth had leaned across the table and said, "I am proud to drink to your health, Mr. Browning!"

Browning had also probably met Wordsworth at the house of John Kenyon, where the elder poet often stayed on his visits to London. It is an odd coincidence that *Dramatic Romances*, in which *The Lost Leader* appeared, should have been dedicated to John Kenyon, their mutual friend. The attack seems never to have been noticed by Wordsworth, but after his death it was to have a considerable effect upon his fame—an effect which Browning later regretted.[18] *The Lost*

[17] See D. C. Somervell, "An Early Victorian Tragedy," in the *London Mercury* 16:170–8.
[18] See H. C. Minchin, "Browning and Wordsworth," in the *Fortnightly Review* 97:813–24.

Leader is an excellent instance of a poem written on a special occasion and about a particular person, achieving in time a universal application.

The Lost Mistress

The Lost Mistress first appeared in *Dramatic Romances* on November 6, 1845. In the collected edition of 1849 it was under the heading of *Dramatic Romances and Lyrics,* and in the distribution of 1863 it became permanently one of the *Dramatic Lyrics.* It was composed of five stanzas of four lines each, rhyming alternately, and in four and three measures. The text, except for changes in punctuation, remains the same as it was in 1845. Miss Barrett first saw the poem on October 22, 1845, and asserted that the fourth stanza was obscure. After the publication she still felt that though Browning had changed a word, the stanza was difficult.

The poem was probably written in May of 1845. If Browning had finished the poem before his travels to Italy (August–December, 1844), he would probably have published it in *Hood's Magazine* in 1844 or early in the spring of 1845. The poem may well be from apprehended experience. Browning's too sudden declaration of his feelings for Miss Barrett, after their first meeting on May 20, startled her almost into breaking off relations with him altogether. The poem was a transmutation of experience into poetry such as he was to practise extensively in *Men and Women* in 1855.

Home-Thoughts, from Abroad

The poem "Oh, to be in England . . ." was Part I in the group entitled *Home-Thoughts, from Abroad* in *Dramatic Romances,* published on November 6, 1845. In the collected edition of 1849 the lines "Oh, to be in England . . ." were dissociated from "Here's to Nelson's memory" and "Nobly, nobly Cape St. Vincent . . ." and assumed the whole title *Home-Thoughts, from Abroad.* As a separate poem it appeared in 1849 under the *Dramatic Romances and Lyrics;* in 1863 it was assigned to the *Dramatic Lyrics,* where it has since remained. The poem, consisting of two stanzas, one of eight and the other of twelve lines, has undergone one or two slight verbal changes since its first printing, and the usual changes in punctuation. Browning was apparently going to publish as mere fragments the three poems which comprise this group, but the protest of Miss Barrett when she saw them in manuscript on October 6, 1845, made him devise a title for them, that they might be presented as they deserved. It may be of interest that Newman, later Cardinal, had written a pamphlet in 1836 which he called *Home Thoughts Abroad:* this may have suggested Browning's title.

Mrs. Orr's contention and Griffin and Minchin's elaboration upon the story, that "Oh, to be in England" was written during Browning's first visit to Italy in the late spring of 1838, seems hardly tenable. Sir Frederic Kenyon [19] justly rejects it. It is likely that Browning, who probably gave Mrs. Orr her information, either confused in his memory the journeys to Italy, one in 1838 and one in 1844, both by sea, or he confused this poem with the lines, "Nobly, nobly Cape St. Vincent," which made up the third part of *Home-Thoughts* in 1845. It is my opinion that "Oh, to be in England" was probably written in England during April, 1845, when Browning was recollecting and poetizing the experiences of his second Italian tour, as we have seen him do in the case of *The Englishman in Italy.* In the first place, if Browning had had the poem in 1842 he would have used it in the *Dramatic Lyrics* when he was in need of material to fill up the pamphlet. Better evidence, perhaps, for dating the writing of the poem in the spring of 1845 is that we know that when Browning returned to England in December, 1844, he renewed his acquaintance with Christopher Smart's *Song to David,* which suggested the subject of *Saul* to him at that time; [20] and from Smart's *Song* he got a hint for his own lines. One stanza of Smart's poem reads,

> For *Adoration,* beyond match,
> The scholar bulfinch aims to catch
>   The soft flute's iv'ry touch;
> And careless on the hazel spray,
> The daring redbreast keeps at bay
>   The damsel's greedy clutch.

Browning's poem is indeed a contrast between Italian summer and English spring, but from the point of view of England in April. Italy fares better in *De Gustibus* (1855). When Miss Barrett praised *Home-Thoughts* delightedly on October 6, 1845—probably her first

[19] *Centenary Edition,* III, xxi. See also Orr, *Life,* p. 94; and Griffin and Minchin, *Life,* p. 128; also my discussions of "Nobly, nobly Cape St. Vincent" (*Home-Thoughts, from the Sea*) and *How They brought the Good News.*
[20] See DeVane, *Browning's Parleyings,* pp. 116–9.

view of it—she anticipated the judgment of the English-speaking world.

"Here's to Nelson's Memory"

The poem "Here's to Nelson's memory . . ." was first published as the second of three under the title *Home-Thoughts, from Abroad* in *Dramatic Romances* on November 6, 1845. It was dropped altogether in 1849 when the general title was given to "Oh, to be in England," but was restored to the *Dramatic Lyrics* in 1863 as the third poem in the group called *Nationality in Drinks;* it was there called *Beer (Nelson).* The poem is composed of fifteen lines—six couplets and a triplet—in four-measure verse. The text has remained the same since its first publication.

Browning's own statement in the first four lines of the poem indicates that it was conceived and probably written off Cape Trafalgar on his second Italian journey; that is, probably late in August, 1844.

Neither Southey's *Life of Nelson,* nor any other that I know of, relates the facts which Browning sets down, and Browning's ascription of the anecdote to the captain of his ship is probably sober fact. After Nelson had died—just as the battle of Trafalgar was won, about half past four on the afternoon of October 21, 1805—his body was brought home and laid in state in the Painted Hall at Greenwich Hospital until it was buried, as Nelson wished, in St. Paul's. Nelson had lost his right arm in his rash assault upon Santa Cruz de Tenerife on July 24, 1797. It is likely that Browning had seen the relics of Nelson many times at the Greenwich Hospital. The tar is upon the right shoulder of his coat, for he kept his left arm free when he leaned against the mizen-rigging. It is an interesting connection that Browning's friend, Alfred Domett, had a kinsman, Admiral Sir William Domett, K.C.B., who was "one of Nelson's captains, and the friend and familiar of that famous man."

Home-Thoughts, from the Sea

The lines "Nobly, nobly Cape St. Vincent . . ." were first published in *Dramatic Romances* on November 6, 1845, as Part III of *Home-Thoughts, from Abroad.* In 1849 "Nobly, nobly Cape St. Vincent" was given an independent status and a new title, *Home-Thoughts, from the Sea,* and the poem appeared under *Dramatic*

Romances and Lyrics. In the distribution of 1863 it kept its distinctive title and was classed permanently as one of the *Dramatic Lyrics.* The text, composed of seven eight-measure trochaic lines, has remained as it was first printed.

Griffin and Minchin, following Mrs. Orr, set the precise date of the writing of this poem as April 27, 1838, when Browning, aboard the Norham Castle, was off Cape St. Vincent on his first voyage to Italy. Sir Frederic Kenyon rightly rejects this date in spite of circumstantial evidence.[21] Had Browning possessed these poems he would have included them in his volume of *Dramatic Lyrics* of 1842, when he needed material to fill up the pamphlet. The middle poem of *Home-Thoughts,* "Here's to Nelson's memory," definitely refers to his second voyage to Italy. Browning, after his return from his first Italian tour, wrote specifically to a friend, "I did not write six lines while absent. . . ." [22] The further point made by Mrs. Orr that the lines were written in Bartoli's *Simboli* [23] does not greatly aid, for Browning seems to have carried the *Simboli* to Italy with him on both of his tours. The probability is that these lines were conceived and written just after the lines to Nelson, on Browning's second Italian voyage, towards the end of August or the first of September, 1844. A few days later in the cover of the *Simboli* he wrote *How They brought the Good News.*

Browning, in the poem, is still in the historic waters which inspired "Here's to Nelson's memory," and the words "Here and here did England help me" refer to the two great battles which Nelson fought in this vicinity, Cape St. Vincent (February 14, 1797), where Nelson received the swords of the Spanish officers on the deck of the San Josef, and Trafalgar (October 21, 1805), where Nelson met his death in battle.

When Miss Barrett saw "those grand sea-sights in the long lines" in printer's proof on October 22, 1845, she deplored placing so good a poem among the fragments. Browning's early opinion of these three pieces was not high; this probably accounts for their failure to appear in *Hood's Magazine* in the spring of 1845. Yet *Home-Thoughts, from the Sea* has taken its place as one of the noblest expressions of patriotism in the English language. The poem is

[21] *Centenary Edition,* III, xxi. See also my discussions of *How They brought the Good News* and *Home-Thoughts, from Abroad* and "Here's to Nelson's memory. . . ."

[22] Orr, *Life,* p. 139.

[23] *Idem,* p. 145.

elaborately and skilfully analyzed by Frederick L. Gwynn in the *Explicator* XII, Item 12 (November, 1953).

The Bishop Orders his Tomb at St. Praxed's Church

The Bishop Orders his Tomb at St. Praxed's Church, at first called *The Tomb at St. Praxed's,* Browning sent to F. A. Ward, sub-editor of *Hood's Magazine,* on February 18, 1845, and Browning added to Ward ". . . I pick it out as being a pet of mine, and just the thing for the time—what with the Oxford business. . . ."[24] It appeared in that magazine for March, 1845 (3:237–9), over Browning's name, and was reprinted in the *Dramatic Romances* on November 6, 1845, under the same title. In the collected edition of 1849 the poem appeared under the *Dramatic Romances and Lyrics* with its permanent title, *The Bishop Orders his Tomb at St. Praxed's Church* [*Rome, 15—*]. In 1863 the poem was assigned to *Men and Women.* In *Hood's Magazine* and in the *Dramatic Romances* the poem consisted of 122 lines of blank verse. At Miss Barrett's suggestion line 17 was changed when it appeared in *Dramatic Romances,* and a few other changes for meter and for clarity were made.[25] In the collected edition of 1849 three new lines (106–8) were added. Since that time the text has remained the same, save for the usual changes in punctuation.

The poem has generally been regarded as the product of Browning's second Italian tour, taken between August and December, 1844. If he had written it before his journey he would probably have published it in *Hood's Magazine* during the summer of 1844. It is the first of his contributions after his return. The poem was probably conceived in Rome late in October, 1844, when Browning visited the church of S. Prassede, named for the virgin daughter of Pudens, a Roman senator under Antoninus Pius in the second century A.D. It has been suggested by Mr. John D. Rea that Irenio Affó's life of Vespasiano Gonzaga[26] gave Browning the idea for *The Bishop Orders*

---

[24] *New Letters,* ed. DeVane and Knickerbocker, pp. 35–6. The Oxford business is, of course, a reference to the Tractarian Movement. In 1843 John Henry Newman issued a retraction of all he had said against the Roman Catholic Church, and was received into the Catholic Church on October 9, 1845. The matter was of national interest in 1845.

[25] See *Macmillan Edition,* p. 1343.

[26] See *"My Last Duchess,"* in *Studies in Philology* 29:120–2. See Irenio Affó's *Vita di Vespasiano,* Parma, 1780, pp. 111–28.

his Tomb as well as *My Last Duchess*. But since that theory has been discredited,[27] a more possible notion has been advanced that the model for the bishop may have been Cardinal Ippolito d'Este the Younger, brother of Ercole II, Duke of Ferrara.[28] At least we know that Browning was intensely interested in the Este family and read their history extensively. (See above, my discussions of *Sordello* and *My Last Duchess*.) This cardinal was notoriously stingy and worldly, fond of splendor and show, and has some of the qualities of Browning's bishop, but the case has by no means been proved. Certainly Browning had much Renaissance history, both ecclesiastical and secular, in his mind when he entered the church of S. Prassede, which was called the "Garden of Paradise" because of its ornateness and richness, and saw the tomb of Cardinal Cetive there; and it was probably then that the idea of the bishop ordering his tomb occurred to him. The worldly Renaissance was suddenly wedded to the ecclesiastical Renaissance. The poem embodies all of Browning's wide knowledge of the Italy of that time—the opulent villas at Frascati, twelve miles southeast of Rome, the degenerate Latin of Domitius Ulpianus, the extravagant love of color, of jewels, horses, manuscripts, and beautiful women. The poem was probably not put into anything like its final form until Browning was at home again in December of 1844. It is possible that Tennyson's *St. Simeon Stylites*, which Browning told Domett, soon after its publication in 1842, that he considered perfect,[29] had some effect upon the verse-form and the matter of *The Bishop Orders his Tomb*. Both are perfect dramatic monologues in blank verse, and St. Simeon bargaining with God for his saintship and the bishop bargaining with his sons for his own future state, have something in common.

The poem has been accounted one of Browning's most notable poems. In her letter of November 15, 1845, Miss Barrett gave first place among Browning's *Dramatic Romances* to *The Tomb at St. Praxed's*. In his *Modern Painters* (IV, 380) Ruskin in 1856 gave the poem generous praise:

I know of no other piece of modern English, prose or poetry, in which there is so much told, as in these lines, of the Renaissance spirit,—its

[27] See Louis S. Friedland, "Ferrara and *My Last Duchess*," in *Studies in Philology* 33:656–84 (1936), esp. pp. 659–60.

[28] See Lionel Stevenson, "The Pertinacious Victorian Poets," *University of Toronto Quarterly* 21:241 (1952). Friedland, however, denies any association between the poems.

[29] See F. G. Kenyon, *Robert Browning and Alfred Domett*, p. 41.

worldliness, inconsistency, pride, hypocrisy, ignorance of itself, love of art, of luxury, and of good Latin. It is nearly all that I have said of the central Renaissance in thirty pages of the *Stones of Venice,* put into as many lines, Browning's also being the antecedent work.

Garden Fancies

I. The Flower's Name

The two poems called *Garden Fancies* were first published in *Hood's Magazine* for July, 1844 (2:45–8). They are some of the small poems secured by F. A. Ward, sub-editor of the magazine. The *Garden Fancies* were republished in *Dramatic Romances* on November 6, 1845. In 1849, still together, they were put under *Dramatic Romances and Lyrics;* in 1863 they were assigned to *Dramatic Lyrics,* and the *Soliloquy of the Spanish Cloister* was put with them as *Garden Fancies III.* In 1868 the *Soliloquy* was dissociated from them and made a separate poem.

Garden Fancies I. The Flower's Name, was composed of six stanzas of eight four-measure lines each. On July 21, 1845, Miss Barrett reported to Browning her criticisms of *The Flower's Name,*[30] all of which he received gratefully. The greatest alteration was the complete change of line 16, which in *Hood's* read, "But this—so surely this met her eye!" Most of the changes in the text of this poem were made for the republication of 1845. Since then the changes have been matters of punctuation.

Because of the reference in the poem to June, and its publication in *Hood's* for July, 1844, I conjecture that June, 1844, was the time of its composition. The poem celebrates, I think, Browning's mother's garden at Hatcham, New Cross, Surrey. She was very fond of flowers and animals, a fondness inherited by her son. The poem shows Browning in the proper mood to fall in love with Miss Barrett early in the next year, and this garden was to supply roses for her room. The poem is rather in the temper of the poems of *Dramatic Lyrics* (1842) than of those poems written after Browning's second Italian tour between August and December, 1844. He here exhibits that interest in the qualities of nations which he had shown in the earlier volume. In 1838 he wrote to Miss Haworth, his "English Eyebright" in *Sordello,* "How I remember the flowers—even grasses—of places

---

[30] See *Macmillan Edition,* p. 1342.

I have seen! . . . Snowdrops and Tilsit in Prussia go together; cow-slips and Windsor Park, for instance; flowering palm and some place or other in Holland." [31] One sees this trait throughout Browning's poetry; notably, *e.g.*, in *Home-Thoughts, from Abroad. The Flower's Name* delighted Miss Barrett, especially the new use of the word "meandering" to express the sound of the Spanish name. What the name for the Spanish flower is, I do not know. It has been suggested that the poem has a certain affinity with Part II of Shelley's *The Sensitive Plant*.[32]

II. Sibrandus Schafnaburgensis

Sibrandus Schafnaburgensis first appeared as the second of *Garden Fancies* (see *The Flower's Name*, above) in *Hood's Magazine* for July, 1844 (2:46–8), signed by Robert Browning. It was republished in *Dramatic Romances* on November 6, 1845. It was included in the collected edition of 1849 under *Dramatic Romances and Lyrics,* and in 1863 it was allocated to the *Dramatic Lyrics,* still under the general title of *Garden Fancies*. Miss Barrett on July 21, 1845, approved and corrected the poem,[33] and with her emendations and some of Brown-ing's own it appeared in 1845, considerably improved in smoothness. After 1845 the text suffered a few verbal changes, and the usual ones in punctuation.

Like *The Flower's Name*, its companion-piece, *Sibrandus Schafna-burgensis* bears the marks of Browning's home at Hatcham, New Cross, Surrey. The incident of the poem happened in his mother's garden, probably in the month of May, 1844. The spiders, worms, slugs, efts, and water-beetles were always of considerable amuse-ment to Browning. The name of the author whose book suffered such indignity occurred in a favorite book in Browning's father's library, Nathaniel Wanley's *Wonders of the Little World;* there Sibrandus, a native of Aschafenburg (*i.e.*, Schafnaburgensis), is mentioned. Browning has taken the name as a type of all pedantry. The antidote to Sibrandus, Rabelais, was also a favorite with Browning, who is akin to him in his delight in grotesque humor. With her corrections of the poem Miss Barrett wrote, "Do you know that this poem is a great favorite with me—it is so new, and full of a creeping, crawling,

---

[31] Orr, *Life,* p. 91.
[32] Miller, *Robert Browning,* p. 165.
[33] *Macmillan Edition,* p. 1342.

grotesque life. Ah, but . . . do you know besides, it is almost reproachable in you to hold up John Knox to derision in this way!" [34]

The Laboratory

The Laboratory (*Ancien Régime*) was one of the poems contributed to *Hood's Magazine*. It appeared in June, 1844 (1:513–4), signed by Robert Browning. It was republished in *Dramatic Romances* on November 6, 1845, where it was coupled with *The Confessional* under the general title *France and Spain*. In 1849 this misalliance was ended, and the poem stood as a separate piece under *Dramatic Romances and Lyrics*. In 1863 it became one of the *Dramatic Lyrics*. The poem consists of twelve stanzas of four lines each, rhyming *aabb*. The text as it appeared in *Hood's* was criticized by Miss Barrett on July 21, 1845,[35] and as a result a considerable number of changes were made to improve the meter and clarify the sense before the poem reappeared in 1845. Since then there have been only changes of punctuation.

The Laboratory was probably written between March, 1844, when *Colombe's Birthday* was published, and early May, 1844, when it was sent to *Hood's*, though of course it may date from 1843. The attempt to catch the atmosphere of a country and a time is typical of Browning in 1842–4. No precise source has been found for *The Laboratory*. In designating the poem as typical of France in the *ancien régime* Browning meant to characterize the temper of a time and place. He may have had in mind such a person of the court of Louis XIV as the notorious poisoner, Marie Madeleine Marguerite D'Aubray Brinvilliers (c. 1630–1676), who among other atrocities poisoned her father and her two brothers, and planned to poison her husband. Her motive, however, was greed rather than jealousy. Her fellow-conspirator and lover, Godin de Sainte-Croix, died in 1672 when his glass mask fell off as he was preparing poison.[36] Browning, we know, was much interested in chemistry and medicine, and for a while, about the time he was writing *Paracelsus*, attended with enthusiasm and with profit Dr. Blundell's lectures at Guy's Hospital.

The Laboratory has been frequently praised for its economical

[34] *Ibid.*
[35] *Idem*, p. 1343.
[36] That some such figure was in Browning's mind as characteristic of the court of Louis XIV was suggested by Arthur Symons, *An Introduction to the Study of Browning*, 1887, p. 75.

statement of an intricate and tense situation. It was the subject of Dante Gabriel Rossetti's first water-color.

The Confessional

The Confessional did not appear in *Hood's Magazine* as did its companion-piece *The Laboratory*, but was first published in *Dramatic Romances* on November 6, 1845, as the second poem under the title *France and Spain*. In 1849 it achieved its independence and appeared as a separate poem under *Dramatic Romances and Lyrics*. In 1863 it became one of the *Dramatic Lyrics*. The poem consisted of thirteen stanzas of six four-measure lines each, and each composed of three rhymed couplets. The text was criticized by Miss Barrett,[37] possibly on October 22, 1845, and her suggestions, having mainly to do with the clarification of the last stanza, were adopted. The text, except in punctuation, was not changed after 1845.

The poem seems to be a product of Browning's second voyage to Italy (August–December, 1844), and probably was not written until June or July, 1845. Though the scene is laid in Spain, and the poem may arise from Browning's interest in the revolutions there under Cristina, upon whom he had written a poem for the *Dramatic Lyrics* of 1842, yet the poem seems much more akin to *The Italian in England*, which was a product of his tour of 1844. *The Confessional* is such a story as he might have heard in Italy in her troubled state. It has been suggested that Browning meant the time of his poem to be set during the Inquisition, but I see no indication of this purpose. Rather, his failure to indicate a time seems to me to make the poem a contemporary utterance. When he wanted the reader to think of a past age he invariably indicated that fact, as he did in *The Laboratory*, the companion-piece to *The Confessional*.

The Flight of the Duchess

The Flight of the Duchess was published in two parts; the first appeared in *Hood's Magazine* for April, 1845 (3:313–8) and consisted of the first nine sections of the poem as we now know it, approximately a fourth of the final poem. Upon Hood's death on May 3, the magazine was discontinued. Browning completed the poem, sections 10–16, and published the whole in *Dramatic Romances* on

[37] *Macmillan Edition*, pp. 1344–5.

November 6, 1845. The finished poem consisted of 926 irregular iambic lines, rhyming irregularly and occasionally internally. It was placed among *Dramatic Romances and Lyrics* in the collected edition of 1849, and became one of the *Dramatic Romances* in 1863.

The whole of *The Flight* was subjected to the criticism of Miss Barrett in July, 1845, and therefore the first nine sections of the poem are slightly altered for clarity and smoothness when they reappear in *Dramatic Romances* in November. The last seven sections also profited greatly through her criticism. Browning sent her the poem in small lots as he composed it between May 6 and July 18, 1845. Miss Barrett's criticism of the new material was detached from her other comments on *Bells and Pomegranates* No. VII, and has only recently been found and brought to the attention of scholars.[38] Miss Barrett suggested seventy-three changes, all but four of which were adopted, and was occasionally severe in her criticisms of Browning's carelessness, obscurity, and perversity. So extensive were the changes that Professors Snyder and Palmer were almost at the point of calling *The Flight* "a poem by the Brownings." But that, I think, would be an extravagant judgment. The text was not greatly changed thereafter; a few verbal changes appeared in 1849, and the usual changes in punctuation followed in later years. The poem has lost eleven lines during the course of its history.

The poem was conceived and written over a period of three years. Writing on April 15, 1883, to Dr. Furnivall, Browning asserted that the idea of the poem "originally all grew out of this one intelligible line of a song that I heard a woman singing at a bon-fire Guy Faux night when I was a boy—*Following the Queen of the Gypsies, O!*" [39] This song was probably one of the many variations of the Scotch ballad, *The Gypsy Laddie*, the story of Johnny Faa and the Countess of Cassilis, which is, in effect, the whole of Browning's first conception of his plot. I quote the song in a version probably much like the one Browning heard:

> There were three gipsies a-come to my door,
> And down-stairs ran this a-lady, O!
> One sang high and another sang low
> And the other sang bonny, bonny Biscay, O!

---

[38] See Edward Snyder and Frederick Palmer, Jr., "New Light on the Brownings," in *Quarterly Review* 269:48–63 (July, 1937).

[39] *Letters*, ed. Hood, p. 217. For a vivid account of the gypsies on Camberwell Green in the poet's youth, see Miller, *Robert Browning*, pp. 270–1.

Then she pull'd off her silk finish'd gown
And put on hose of leather, O!
The ragged, ragged rags about our door,
She's gone with the wraggle taggle gipsies, O!

It was late last night, when my lord came home,
Enquiring for his a-lady, O!
The servants said, on ev'ry hand:
She's gone with the wraggle taggle gipsies, O!

O, saddle to me my milk-white steed,
Go and fetch me my pony, O!
That I may ride and seek my bride,
Who is gone with the wraggle taggle gipsies, O!

O, he rode high and he rode low,
He rode through woods and copses too,
Until he came to an open field,
And there he espied his a-lady, O!

What makes you leave your house and land?
What makes you leave your money, O?
What makes you leave your new-wedded lord,
To go with the wraggle taggle gipsies, O?

What care I for my house and my land?
What care I for my money, O?
What care I for my new-wedded lord?
I'm off with the wraggle taggle gipsies, O!

Last night you slept on a goose-feather bed,
With the sheet turn'd down so bravely, O!
And to-night you'll sleep in a cold open field,
Along with the wraggle taggle gipsies, O!

What care I for a goose-feather bed,
With the sheet turn'd down so bravely, O?
For to-night I shall sleep in a cold open field,
Along with the wraggle taggle gipsies, O! [40]

Perhaps a further sight of the gypsies in Dulwich Wood, a favorite haunt of theirs near his home, made the poem begin to take shape in his mind. At any rate, the poem was begun probably in the spring of 1842. In the letter to Furnivall quoted above Browning says

There was an odd circumstance that either mended or marred the poem in the writing, I fancied the latter at the time. As I finished the line (which ends what was printed in *Hood's Magazine*) "and the old one—you shall

[40] *The Wraggle Taggle Gipsies, O!* as given in *One Hundred English Folk-songs,* ed. Cecil J. Sharp, Boston, 1916, pp. 13–6.

hear!" I saw from the window where I sat a friend opening the gate to our house, one Captain Lloyd, whom I jumped up to meet, judging from the time of day that something especially interesting had brought him—as proved to be the case, for he was in a strange difficulty. This took a deal of discussing. Next day other interruptions occurred, and the end was I lost altogether the thing as it was in my head at the beginning, and, subsequently, gave it to Hood as a fragment. Some time afterwards I was staying at Bettisfield Park, in Wales, and a guest, speaking of early winter, said, "the deer had already to break the ice in the pond." A fancy struck me, which, on returning home, I worked up into what concludes the story. . . .

We know from a letter to Domett dated September 31 (*sic*), 1842, that Browning visited Sir John Hanmer at Bettisfield Park in September. On his return home, he probably had in hand the text of the first nine sections in a form very much like the fragment published in *Hood's*, and some suggestions to himself concerning the finishing of the poem. Lloyd's interruption, together with Browning's visit to Bettisfield Park, had changed the direction of his thinking. Concerning this change Browning wrote to Miss Barrett on July 25, 1845,

It is an odd fact, yet characteristic of my accomplishings one and all in this kind, that of *the poem,* the real conception of an evening (two years ago, fully)—of *that,* not a line is written,—though perhaps after all, what I am going to call the accessories in the story are real though indirect reflexes of the original idea, and so supersede properly enough the necessity of its personal appearance, so to speak. But, as I conceived the poem, it consisted entirely of the Gipsy's description of the life the Lady was to lead with her future Gipsy lover—a *real* life, not an unreal one like that with the Duke. And as I meant to write it, all their wild adventures would have come out and the insignificance of the former vegetation have been deducible only—as the main subject has become now; of course it comes to the same thing, for one would never show half by half like a cut Orange.

The poem, then, was in a brief and rough form when, pressed by F. A. Ward for something to aid Hood in his illness, Browning transcribed "at a day's notice" the first part—nine sections—and sent it off. The second part—sections 10–16—was written slowly during the late spring and early summer, and delivered to Miss Barrett during July, 1845. Browning went over the poem once more for last improvements before it went to press on October 13.

To summarize briefly the progress of the poem, I would mark three phases: (1) Browning's original conception rose from the line in the ballad of the gypsies, probably in 1842; the poem as he imagined it then was to deal with gypsy life as it was described to tempt the duchess. But that poem was never written. (2) The second phase consists of the nine sections approximately as we have them in *Hood's Magazine* for April, 1845; but this was merely preliminary matter setting the scene. This fragment probably lay in the poet's portfolio from October, 1842, to March, 1845, then was transcribed in a day and sent off. (3) The third phase of the poem took place between May and July, 1845, when sections 10–16 were written with Miss Barrett very much in mind, as we shall see, and the whole poem put in final condition.

The *Flight of the Duchess* shows kinship to several other of Browning's poems, notably to *My Last Duchess* (1842), where the situation, except for the outcome, is roughly the same, and to *The Glove* (1845), where the versification and manner of the narrative are similar to those in *The Flight of the Duchess*. The poem began, I think, with Browning imagining an innocent young lady, imprisoned like the duchess of *My Last Duchess*, but in a northern and more contemporary situation, who was to escape to real life among the gypsies. Besides the sources which he had drawn upon for *My Last Duchess*, Browning possibly used the *Memoires* [41] of the Marquis de Lassay which had helped him with *Colombe's Birthday* and *The Glove*. But in the part of the poem written in the spring and summer of 1845, it is quite clear that in Browning's mind Miss Barrett took the place of the duchess, and that he used the poem as a part of his courtship.[42] In depicting the imprisonment of the modern duchess in a medieval situation and in showing her flight, Browning, forbidden at this time to speak his love to Miss Barrett, had in mind Miss Barrett's plight in Wimpole Street, and was urging her by means of the poem to flight to Italy. The day after *The Flight* went to press (October 13) Miss Barrett told Browning that her hoped-for journey to Italy for her health had had to be cancelled. On November 6 she withdrew her prohibition, and Browning could speak his love. Life and literature are indistinguishably mingled here. The poet's awkward and inhibited relation to Miss Barrett may have affected the

[41] See the *Recueil de differentes choses* par M. de Lassay, Lausanne, 1756, I, 5–19.

[42] The case has been presented independently, and I think conclusively, twice: first by Snyder and Palmer (see footnote 38 above), and also by Fred Manning Smith in two articles, "Elizabeth Barrett and Browning's *The Flight of the Duchess*," in *Studies in Philology* 39:102–17 (1942), and "More Light on 'Elizabeth Barrett and Browning's *The Flight of the Duchess*'," in *Studies in Philology* 39:693–5 (1942).

broken and embarrassed utterance of the huntsman, the spokesman in the poem.

The poem shows, in addition, certain currents of thought in England between 1840 and 1845. There is that romantic tendency towards escape from over-civilized and over-crowded England—a tendency to be seen in *Waring* and in *Pippa Passes,* and best seen in Tennyson's *Locksley Hall* (1842); there is also, as a corollary, that interest in gypsies, who lived a simpler and freer life, which George Borrow had begun to stimulate by his books *The Bible in Spain* and *Lavengro.* There is also in *The Flight of the Duchess* a record of the curious fashion that swept English country-life afresh in the early Forties—the desire to re-create antiquity, to follow the sports and the manners of the Middle Ages. The mining district which is in the duke's domain may have been that region in southwest Germany through which Browning had passed in 1834 and again in 1838; or the picture may have been suggested to him by the mines in Wales, near Sir John Hanmer's place in Flintshire. The vividness, novelty, and ingenuity which Miss Barrett found in the poem have since delighted many other readers. The poem is peculiarly characteristic of Browning, and is hence a favorite.

Earth's Immortalities: (1) Fame—(2) Love

The two parts of *Earth's Immortalities,* originally untitled, were first published in *Dramatic Romances* on November 6, 1845. In 1849 they appeared in the collected edition in the group of *Dramatic Romances and Lyrics,* but there, still under the title of *Earth's Immortalities,* they bore the sub-titles which they have since retained, *Fame* and *Love.* In 1863 *Earth's Immortalities* was put under *Dramatic Lyrics.* The text has not been altered since first publication.

Earth's Immortalities is, I think, a product of Browning's second Italian tour. We know that when he was in Rome—probably in late October, 1844—he visited Shelley's grave, and possibly it was that which inspired his comment upon fame. His equally mournful comment upon love was probably written as a companion-piece. It is hardly possible to say upon existing evidence when these poems were written. If Browning had written them by March, 1845, would he not have published them in *Hood's Magazine?* Yet he may have considered them fragments, as he did "Oh, to be in England . . ." and "Nobly, nobly Cape St. Vincent. . . ." The lines "So the year's done with" possibly suggest December, 1844, as the date of their composition. Miss Barrett in praising *Earth's Immortalities* on October 27, 1845 speaks of it as one of the "new poems." She means, I think, that she has not seen it before—in contradistinction to *Saul* and *The Flight of the Duchess,* which she has been reading for him. In a letter dated February 22, 1889, Browning asserts that he meant the refrain "(*Love me forever!*)" to be "a mournful comment on the short duration of the conventional 'For Ever!'" [43]

Song

The *Song,* "Nay but you, who do not love her," appeared first in *Dramatic Romances* on November 6, 1845. In the collection of 1849 it came under the general head of *Dramatic Romances and Lyrics,* and in the distribution of 1863 it was made one of the *Dramatic Lyrics.* The text has remained the same, save for punctuation, since its publication. It is impossible to say when the poem was written. Miss Barrett praised it when she saw it in printer's proof on October 27, 1845, among the "new poems" that she had not seen before. Possibly it owes its being to Browning's own feelings in the spring of 1845. Certainly the poet's praise of his mistress's hair came to have a personal meaning to Miss Barrett; she sent him a lock of her hair in a ring on December 1, 1845, and wrote one of her sonnets for the *Sonnets from the Portuguese,* "The Soul's Rialto hath its merchandise."

The Boy and the Angel

The Boy and the Angel, signed by Robert Browning, appeared first in *Hood's Magazine* for August, 1844 (2:140–2). It was submitted to Miss Barrett for criticism,[44] and when it appeared in *Dramatic Romances* on November 6, 1845, it had five new couplets, bringing the total to thirty-eight, and one was substituted for an old one (37). The couplets added were 28, 29, 32, 34, and 36. The poem was put under *Dramatic Romances and Lyrics* in the collected edition of 1849. In the distribution of 1863 the poem remained one of the *Dramatic Romances,* and one new couplet (19) was added. Besides the addition of these six couplets, making thirty-nine in all, many minor

[43] *Macmillan Edition,* p. 1350.
[44] *Idem,* pp. 1342–3.

improvements were made for the sake of smoothness and clarity before the text became stable in 1863. After that date the only changes were in punctuation.

The Boy and the Angel was the last poem to be published in *Hood's Magazine* before Browning's second Italian tour (August to December, 1844); it appeared in the August number. It was probably written in the spring, possibly at Easter, in 1844. The poem is imaginary; no Theocrite was ever pope. The poem is the artistic expression of a favorite idea with Browning, which had found notable expression in *Pippa Passes*—God's need for the humblest human praise. On July 21, 1845, when Miss Barrett first saw the poem, she praised it for "all its beauty and significance," and as the poem was improved during the summer it became more and more a favorite of hers.

Meeting at Night—Parting at Morning

The two parts of *Night and Morning, I. Night* and *II. Morning,* were first published in *Dramatic Romances* on November 6, 1845. In the collected edition of 1849 the poems were made two separate poems, though placed next to each other, and were called *Meeting at Night* and *Parting at Morning*. They were in the general group called *Dramatic Romances and Lyrics*. In 1863 they were assigned to *Dramatic Lyrics*. Since first publication the text of the two poems has remained the same.

It is not possible to say when these two small poems were written. The landscape reminds one of Italy, and it is possible that a view of night and morning in Italy inspired them. Elizabeth Barrett seems not to have seen them until October 27, 1845, when they were in printer's proof. She says, "For the new poems—they are full of beauty. You throw largesses out on all sides without counting the coins: how beautiful that 'Night and Morning' . . ." In answer to a question put to him concerning the interpretation of *Parting at Morning*, on February 22, 1889, Browning declared in effect that the man was the speaker in both halves of the poem: "it is *his* confession of how fleeting is the belief (implied in the first part) that such raptures are self-sufficient and enduring—as for the time they appear." [45] The reference to "him," then, in the third line of *Parting at Morning*, is to the sun.

[45] *Idem,* pp. 1350–1.

Nationality in Drinks

The illness of Hood and the requests of Monckton Milnes prevailed upon Browning to give F. A. Ward, sub-editor of *Hood's Magazine,* his *Claret and Tokay* for the June number of 1844. The poems were reprinted with hardly any changes in *Dramatic Romances* on November 6, 1845. They were omitted, probably because of Miss Barrett's disapproval of them, from the collected edition of 1849. In 1863 *Claret and Tokay* were joined by "Here's to Nelson's memory" (printed in 1845 as No. II of *Home-Thoughts from Abroad,* but dropped in 1849); the new addition to the group was called *Beer* (*Nelson*), and the group was given the title *Nationality in Drinks.* In the assignment of 1863 *Nationality in Drinks* became one of the *Dramatic Lyrics.* The text, save for one or two matters of spelling, and the substitution of "Sir Ausbruch" for "from Ausbruch," has not been changed.

Since *Claret and Tokay* were printed in June, 1844, in the same issue as *The Laboratory,* I conjecture that these poems were written during the late spring of 1844. Like *The Laboratory, Claret* is an attempt to catch the spirit of France in a small incident; *The Laboratory* represents the *ancien régime, Claret* the modern. Browning had not, so far as is known, been in France before the poem was written. He had been in Austria (Innsbruck) upon his tour of 1838, and again in 1844.

Miss Barrett in a letter to Browning on July 21, 1845, admitted that she thought *Tokay* and, by inference, *Claret* inferior to the other poems Browning was producing during 1844–5. Her judgment has been confirmed by posterity, though *Claret* finds some admirers. For "Here's to Nelson's memory," see *Home-Thoughts, from Abroad.*

Time's Revenges

Time's Revenges was first published in *Dramatic Romances* on November 6, 1845. In 1849 it came under the general head of *Dramatic Romances and Lyrics,* and in the arrangement of 1863 it was given to *Dramatic Romances.* The poem consists of sixty-six lines of four-measure verse, rhyming in couplets. It was probably late in the summer that the poem was submitted to Miss Barrett. She criticized it severely; most of her suggestions were adopted when the poem appeared in print. Between 1845 and 1849 two new lines were substituted for lines 54–5, which in the first edition read,

> As all my genius, all my learning
> Leave me, where there's no returning.

Since 1849 a few verbal changes and the usual changes in punctuation have been made.

From the unfinished condition of this poem when it was shown to Miss Barrett,[46] I judge that the poem was probably composed during the spring or summer of 1845, and that Miss Barrett saw the first draft. The situation delineated in the poem is wholly imaginary and fanciful. Griffin and Minchin found something of Waring (Alfred Domett) in *Time's Revenges*, but Sir Frederic Kenyon denies that there is any biographical intention in the poem.[47] I confess that it is quite impossible for me to read the poem without seeing in it a highly fanciful and imaginary picture of the situation Browning found himself in during 1845. He had already painted in *Waring* (see *Waring* and *The Guardian Angel*) a "fancy portrait" of his friend Domett, who had gone to New Zealand; and now, I think, he is continuing it. The heavy boots, the devotion to the poet, the fierce slaughtering of the critics who could not appreciate his friend—these qualities are obviously qualities of Alfred Domett, and one cannot read Sir Frederic Kenyon's admirable *Robert Browning and Alfred Domett* without thinking so. We know that Domett knew about Browning's headaches and brain-fever in 1841.[48] The lady of the poem, on the other hand, is certainly not Elizabeth Barrett; but perhaps in musing upon the manner in which the first place in his affections had been taken from Alfred Domett and given to her, Browning hit upon the ironical situation which is embodied in the poem. At any rate, one sees in *Time's Revenges* the humiliation of love, a theme which is seldom found in Browning's poetry. The title of the poem is drawn from Shakespeare's line in *Twelfth Night*, V, i, 384: "And thus the whirligig of time brings in his revenges."

[46] *Idem*, p. 1345.
[47] See Griffin and Minchin, *Life*, p. 88; and the *Centenary Edition*, III, xxxiii.
[48] See W. Hall Griffin, "Robert Browning and Alfred Domett," in *Living Age* 244:399–400 (February 18, 1905). See also pp. 408–9 for Domett's fierce defence of *Pippa Passes*.

Saul

(The discussion of *Saul*, the first nine sections of which were first printed in *Dramatic Romances*, may be found below, under *Men and Women*, where the poem appeared complete.)

The Glove

The Glove (Peter Ronsard *loquitur*) was first published on November 6, 1845, in *Dramatic Romances*, where it concluded the pamphlet. It was reprinted in 1849 under *Dramatic Romances and Lyrics*, and in the distribution of 1863 it remained one of the *Dramatic Romances*. The text of the poem, for reasons given below, was not submitted to Miss Barrett for criticism, and she saw it first in printer's proofs on October 27, 1845. Since 1845 the text has been altered a little in word and punctuation; and two lines were added between 1845 and 1849. In the first edition the text consisted of 188 three-measure lines rhyming in couplets.

Leigh Hunt's poem, *The Glove and the Lions,* which spurred Browning into writing his own version of *The Glove,* was first published in the *New Monthly Magazine* for May, 1836. Browning's poem was probably not written before the summer of 1845, however, for it is similar in tone to other pieces written during this time, such as the latter half of *The Flight of the Duchess.* Then too, I think the situation in *The Glove* bears some resemblance to the situation of Browning's affairs in 1845.

Leigh Hunt's story, from which Browning took his start, has a long history. As it stands it is obviously a transposition of the story told by Schiller in his poem *Der Handschuh.* But in the *New Monthly Magazine* Hunt refers the reader to Saint Foix' *Essais historique sur Paris,*[49] and both Hunt and Saint Foix send the reader to Brantôme [50] as the original source of the story. Because it is certain that Browning knew it, and because it is the most circumstantial of the accounts, I append Hunt's version:

[49] See the fourth edition, printed in Paris in 1766, I, 226–7. Saint Foix is explaining the *Rue des Lions, près Saint Paul.*
[50] See *Oeuvres complètes . . . de Brantôme . . .* ed. Prosper Mérimée, Paris, 1858, XII, 354–5. *Recueil des dames (seconde partie).*

The Glove and the Lions
A Ballad
By Leigh Hunt

King Francis was a hearty king, and loved a royal sport,
And one day, as his lions fought, sat looking on the court;
The nobles fill'd the benches round, the ladies by their side,
And 'mongst them sat the Count de Lorge, with one for whom he sigh'd:
And truly 'twas a gallant thing to see that crowning show,
Valour and love, and a king above, and the royal beasts below.

Ramp'd and roar'd the lions, with horrid laughing jaws;
They bit, they glared, gave blows like bears, a wind went with their paws;
With wallowing might and stifled roar they roll'd on one another,
Till all the pit, with sand and mane, was in a thunderous smother;
The bloody foam above the bars came whizzing through the air;
Said Francis, then, "Faith, gentlemen, we're better here than there."

De Lorge's love o'erheard the King, a beauteous, lively dame,
With smiling lips and sharp bright eyes, which always seem'd the same;
She thought, The Count my lover is brave as brave can be;
He surely would do wond'rous things to show his love of me;
King, ladies, lovers, all look on; the occasion is divine;
I'll drop my glove, to prove his love; great glory will be mine.—

She dropp'd her glove to prove his love, then look'd at him and smiled;
He bow'd, and in a moment leap'd among the lions wild:
The leap was quick, return was quick, he has regain'd the place,
Then threw the glove, but not with love, right in the lady's face.
"By God!" cried Francis, "rightly done!" and he rose from where he sat;
"No love," quoth he, "but vanity, sets love a task like that."

The wide divergence of Browning's story from Hunt's is immediately apparent, but Hunt's was the foundation upon which Browning built. It has always been believed that Browning's re-interpretation of the facts of the story is peculiarly his own. So it is, but he was guided to that re-interpretation by two factors, his reading and his personal experience. The *Memoires* of the Marquis de Lassay—to which, indeed, I think *Colombe's Birthday* (1844) owes its plot—supplied Browning with the new elements for *The Glove*. In the *Memoires*, a story which Browning was to retell in the *Parleying With Daniel Bartoli*,[51] the Marquis de Lassay told of the courageous action of Marianne Pajot who, betrothed to the Duke of Lorraine, chose

---

[51] *Recueil de differentes choses,* par M. de Lassay, Lausanne, 1756, 4 vols. I, 5–19. For a detailed treatment of the relation of the *Memoires, The Glove,* and Browning's own experience see my chapter on the *Parleying With Daniel Bartoli,* in *Browning's Parleyings,* esp. pp. 81–9.

disgrace rather than betray the interests and the honor of the duke. The Marquis de Lassay read aright the motives of the lady, followed her from court into obscurity, and married her, though he was several years her junior. And the addition of the youthful, understanding lover, who was willing to earn in silence rather than force by wordy protestations the love of his lady, is not the only change in Leigh Hunt's version suggested to Browning by the *Memoires*. There he found too a prime minister who wishes to understand human motives and inquires out the reasons for the lady's action. In *The Glove* that part is played by Peter Ronsard, the supposed relater of the tale: he is made to exemplify Browning's ideal of a poet, but he was not, as was Browning, particularly interested in the psychology of character.

Beyond this, many of the details of *The Glove* were taken by Browning from books and things around him. The lion Bluebeard was drawn from life. The great beast with the black mane, stiffening tail, and glowing eyes was seen by Browning in Surrey Gardens, not far from his home. The device of subtly undermining the value of the feat of De Lorge, by showing how the poor savages who first caught the animal must have done it, he learned from Bartoli's *Simboli*. The Latin moral is a proverb—"go to meet approaching ills," and possibly came from Persius Flaccus.[52] The theorbo is a light, stringed instrument, with a double neck and two sets of tuning pegs, the lower holding the melody strings and the upper the bass strings. From this construction of the instrument Louise Schutz Boas argues that Browning meant to refer to De Lorge's two actions in fetching gloves for the two different ladies.[53] But this is possibly too subtle an interpretation. Miss Boas is undoubtedly correct in thinking that Browning got the name and the idea of the theorbo from the *Invocation* to Quarles' *Emblems,* a book of which he was fond. At the same time, the theorbo was an appropriate instrument for the court of King Francis, and served equally well for the ballad-like story Browning was telling. Lines 171–88 are obscure in their precise meaning, and have caused some argument.[54] The probable explanation of Browning's meaning is given by Mr. Whidden: ". . . the mortification of De Lorge is not to approach the King but to withdraw from

[52] See Louis S. Friedland, in the *Explicator* II, Item 30 (February, 1944).
[53] The *Explicator* II, Item 13 (November, 1943).
[54] See Louis S. Friedland in the *Explicator* I, Item 54 (May, 1943) and II, Item 30 (February, 1944); also R. W. Whidden in the *Explicator* II, Item 23 (December, 1943).

the King, who remains with his mistress while De Lorge looks for her gloves."

In addition to the literary influences, a great deal of Browning's own experience went into *The Glove*. Written at that time and on such a subject, the poem could hardly fail to be, in part, autobiographical.[55] Elizabeth Barrett, whom Browning was courting, was six years older than he; and again like the lady of the poem after her disgrace, she was, as an invalid, withdrawn from the world. She "had done with living" when Browning sought her out and with the eyes that love lent him saw in her what the world could not see. Her appreciation of his insight may be seen in all the *Sonnets from the Portuguese*, but especially in the thirty-ninth and fortieth, where she pours out gratitude for his power of understanding and his patience in waiting. It was probably because *The Glove* expressed so directly Browning's love for her, that he was unwilling to show her the poem in the spring of 1845, but waited until October when they had reached an understanding.

The poem has always been accounted one of Browning's most successful attempts at case-making, a trait which grew upon him in later years. *The Glove* was a favorite with Elizabeth Barrett, who on October 27, 1845, wrote her appreciation of his interpretation of the story:

And for your 'Glove,' all women should be grateful,—and Ronsard, honored, in this fresh shower of music on his old grave . . . though the chivalry of the interpretation, as well as much beside, is so plainly yours, . . . could only be yours perhaps. And even *you* are forced to let in a third person . . . close to the doorway . . . before you can do any good. What a noble lion you give us too, with the 'flash on his forehead,' and 'leagues in the desert already' as we look on him! And then, with what a 'curious felicity' you turn the subject 'glove' to another use and strike De Lorge's blow back on him with it, in the last paragraph of your story! And the versification! And the lady's speech—(to return!) so calm, and proud—yet a little bitter.

LURIA AND A SOUL'S TRAGEDY

PUBLICATION

On April 13, 1846, *Luria* and *A Soul's Tragedy* were published together in a paper-covered pamphlet of thirty-two pages. This consisted of a title-page: "Bells and Pomegranates. No. VIII. and Last.

---

[55] The case is given at length in DeVane, *Browning's Parleyings*, pp. 83–91.

Luria; and A Soul's Tragedy. By Robert Browning, Author of "Paracelsus." London: Edward Moxon, Dover Street. MDCCCXLVI"; the printer's name on the reverse of the title-page; a separate page for the dedication to Walter Savage Landor, dated March 29, 1846; on the reverse of the dedication the title: "Luria, A Tragedy in Five Acts," a list of persons, the time and the scene; and the text, pp. 5–32. *Luria* occupied pp. 5–20. The cost of the pamphlet, which must have been a good deal more than the originally planned £16, was borne by the poet's father. The price of a single copy was Two Shillings Sixpence.

Luria, a Tragedy

TEXT

The play, *Luria,* is divided into five acts, and the action takes place at Luria's camp between Florence and Pisa in the course of one day; the respective acts are entitled, Morning, Noon, Afternoon, Evening, Night. There are 1812 lines of blank verse, divided as follows: I— 392; II—354; III—399; IV—329; V—338. The text of the play underwent the usual revision to which almost all of Browning's poems were subjected; the changes were almost entirely matters of punctuation here, but the final text is four lines shorter than the first edition. *Luria* has been included in all the collected editions of the poet's works.

GENESIS AND COMPOSITION

The first intimation we have of *Luria* is also an interesting commentary upon Browning's methods of work. On February 11, 1845, in writing to Miss Barrett, he mentions " 'Luria'—so safe in my head, and a tiny slip of paper I cover with my thumb!" When Miss Barrett complained to him against the drama as a proper vehicle for the poet's work, Browning asserted on February 26 that *Luria* was to be his last play. In this letter we are given a complete plan of the piece; Luria, he writes,

. . . is a Moor, of Othello's country, and devotes himself to something he thinks Florence, and the old fortune follows—all in my brain yet, but the bright weather helps and I will soon loosen my Braccio and Puccio (a pale discontented man), and Tiburzio (the Pisan, good true fellow, this one), and Domizia the Lady—loosen all these on dear foolish (ravishing must his folly be), golden-hearted Luria, all these with their worldly-wisdom and Tuscan shrewd ways; and, for me, the misfortune is, I sympathise

just as much with these as with him,—so there can no good come of keeping this wild company any longer. . . .

His increased interest in Miss Barrett, and painful headaches,
stopped the immediate composition of *Luria*, but by May 24 Browning had hit upon the style of his play, which he called "high fantasti-
cal." It then lay dormant while the *Dramatic Romances* were being
prepared for the press, but on October 27 he wrote Miss Barrett:
"Yesterday I took out 'Luria' and read it through—the skeleton—I
shall hope to finish it soon now. It is for a purely imaginary stage,—
very simple and straightforward." Between this date and January 22,
1846, *Luria* was written, at least through the fourth act. On the latter
date Miss Barrett praised the play in a strain of high enthusiasm, but
objected to the unheroical suicide of Luria. Browning's letter of the
same date defended the dramatic appropriateness of Luria's death:

> If you have gone so far with 'Luria,' I fancy myself nearly or altogether
> safe. I must not tell you, but I wished just these feelings to be in your
> mind about Domizia, and the death of Luria: the last act throws light back
> on all, I hope. Observe only, that Luria *would* stand, if I have plied him
> effectually with adverse influences, in such a position as to render any
> other end impossible without the hurt to Florence which his religion is,
> to avoid inflicting—passively awaiting, for instance, the sentence and
> punishment to come at night, would as surely inflict it as taking part with
> her foes. His aim is to prevent the harm she will do herself by striking
> him, so he moves aside from the blow.

But all was not yet well with *Luria*. On February 11, 1846, Browning
wrote to Miss Barrett:

> And now, 'Luria,' so long as the parts cohere and the whole is discernible,
> all will be well yet. I shall not look at it, nor think of it, for a week or two,
> and then see what I have forgotten. Domizia is all wrong; I told you that
> I knew that her special colour had faded,—it was but a bright line, and
> the more distinctly deep that it was so narrow. One of my half dozen
> words on my scrap of paper 'pro memoria' was, under the 'Act V.' 'she
> loves'—to which I could not bring it, you see! Yet the play requires it
> still,—something may yet be effected, though . . . I meant that she should
> propose to go to Pisa with him, and begin a new life. But there is no
> hurry—I suppose it is no use publishing much before Easter—I will try
> and remember what my whole character *did* mean—it was, in two words,
> understood at the time by 'panther's-beauty'—on which hint I ought to
> have spoken! But the work grew cold, and you came between, and the
> sun put out the fire on the hearth *nec vult panthera domari!*

In her answer to this letter Miss Barrett admitted "that your hand
has vacillated in your Domizia."

On February 13, Browning doubted the wisdom of publishing *A Soul's Tragedy* with *Luria,* fearing that the first would discourage readers from the second. His letter of this date makes an interesting admission: "I have lost, of late, interest in dramatic writing, as you know, and, perhaps, occasion." On March 25, when Browning has been reworking *A Soul's Tragedy,* he expresses again his dissatisfaction: "I repeat, both these things, 'Luria' and the other, are *manqué,* failures—the life-incidents ought to have been acted over again, experienced afresh; and I had no inclination nor ability." Five days later it is clear that Elizabeth Barrett admired *A Soul's Tragedy* more than she did *Luria.* On April 1, Browning wrote that at the last minute he had

corrected everything,—altered, improved. . . . Well, and then there is Domizia—I *could not* bring her to my purpose. I left the stiff neck that was to have bowed of its own accord—for nothing graceful could be accomplished by pressing with both hands on the head above! I meant to make her leave off her own projects through love of Luria. As it is, they in a manner fulfil themselves, so far as she has any power over them, and then, she being left unemployed, sees Luria, begins to see him, having hitherto seen only her own ends which he was to further.

A few minor alterations were made in the text in the proofs on April 7. The play was published on April 13, 1846.

SOURCES AND INFLUENCES

It is asserted by Mr. G. W. Cooke in his *Guide-Book* that Browning found the historical background for *Luria* in Sapio Amminato's *Florentine History,*[1] where the siege of Pisa by the Florentines in the fall of 1405 and the spring of 1406 is described in some detail. Mr. Cooke finds special significance in the remarks of the three commissaries who are sent out to their own camp by the Florentine government to report upon the conduct of the commander of their army, who was not, in history, a Moor, but one of their own nobles:

For although we have every confidence in the honor and fidelity of our general, you see it is always well to be on the safe side. And in the matter of receiving possession of a city . . . these nobles with the old feudal names! We know the ways of them!

But this worldly wisdom of the Florentine government and its agents, as well as the secret visit of the Pisan leader, Gambacorta, to the

---

[1] P. 199. Cooke's account is taken from one by H. S. Pancoast in *Poet Lore* 1: 553, and 2:19.

Florentine camp, appears in all the histories which deal with this war. It is more probable, I think, that Browning went to the sources which he had found useful for *Sordello,* and that he got his background for *Luria* from Muratori's reprint of Matheus Palmeri's *De Captivitate Pisarum Liber.*[2]

But the background is of no great consequence, and we must turn our attention to the chief character of the play. When Browning was asked if he had any historical basis for the character of Luria, he replied, "None whatever; it is pure invention." It is, rather, unconscious imitation, for Luria, the general, owes his existence to the greater Moor, Othello, and the careers of the two are rather closely paralleled.[3] Luria is a younger Othello, who has not yet met his Desdemona; his passion is all for the city he serves.[4] Each is large-minded, simple and "golden-hearted," and each is unfitted to cope with the sophisticated world in which he moves; each loses faith in the thing he loves, and ends in suicide. Othello, in his death, does justice upon himself, as he had earlier thought he was doing justice upon Desdemona. Luria restrains his hand from destroying Florence when the city deserves it, perhaps, and leaves his own suicide, it may be, insufficiently motivated. The emotional natures of the two find expression in parallel outbursts. The characters which Browning "loosens" upon Luria have the function in Browning's play that Iago has in *Othello.* The relenting of these characters in Act V finds no parallel in Iago. The unities of time, place, and action observed in *Luria* may have been suggested by the speed of the action in *Othello,* once the Venetians have reached Cyprus, though it should be said that Browning uses the unities in several other plays.

In a letter to F. J. Furnivall on October 11, 1881, Browning points out a modern element in *Luria,* certain anticipations of the Darwinian theory.[5] But in the main the play is one in the long line of Elizabethan imitations, as the style and manner amply show. The style,

---

[2] In *Rerum Italicarum Scriptores,* Milan, 1730–40, XIX, Parte II. See also Muratori's *Annali d'Italia,* XIII, 59–61, 72–3.

[3] See Mr. G. R. Elliot's excellent study, "Shakespeare's Significance for Browning," in *Anglia* 32:90–162; esp. pp. 127–34, for the likenesses between the plays. For the differences see T. R. Lounsbury, *Early Literary Career of Robert Browning,* pp. 68–71.

[4] See the paper by Ernest Radford on *Luria* in the *Browning Society's Papers,* I, 251–2, where the connection between Browning's thought and the unfinished Duomo in Florence is drawn. Luria draws the Duomo with a Moorish front, objectifying himself as the leader of the Florentines.

[5] *Letters,* ed. Hood, p. 200.

though exhibiting many similarities to *Othello,* is perhaps nearer to
that of Webster and Shirley, as the following speech of Luria's (II,
269–76) illustrates:

> Oh world, where all things pass and nought abides,
> Oh life, the long mutation—is it so?
> Is it with life as with the body's change?
> —Where, e'en tho' better follow, good must pass,
> Nor manhood's strength can mate with boyhood's grace,
> Nor age's wisdom, in its turn, find strength,
> But silently the first gift dies away,
> And though the new stays, never both at once.

AFTER-HISTORY

Luria was not accorded much attention from the official reviewers
in 1846, but two of these notices should be singled out. In the *Examiner* for April 25, Forster praised it, as did J. R. Lowell in the
North American Review for April, 1848. But in the main, the critics
then and now have found that the length of the speeches and the
paucity of the action make the play oppressive, and only a few have
praised it for its "grave Elizabethanism." Arthur E. DuBois in his
study, "Robert Browning, Dramatist," [6] in 1936, observed the similarity in theme in *Strafford* and *Luria.* The hero of each play gives
disinterested service to an empty cause. Each of them earns high
appreciation and suffers disillusion which is more tragic than his
death. Miss Barrett's misgivings, that Luria's suicide would seem to
be insufficiently motivated, have been shared by the critics, and
upon the validity of the motives for suicide the whole tragedy hangs.
Luria has never been performed.

A Soul's Tragedy

PUBLICATION

A Soul's Tragedy was published with *Luria* (*q.v.*) in the eighth
and last pamphlet of the *Bells and Pomegranates* series on April 13,
1846. It occupied pages 21–32, consisting of a half-title, "A Soul's
Tragedy"; on the reverse an explanation of the meaning of the title
of the whole series, *Bells and Pomegranates* (quoted above in my
general discussion of *Bells and Pomegranates*); and the text, pp.
23–32. By placing the explanation where he does, Browning in effect

[6] In *Studies in Philology* 33:639–40.

excludes *A Soul's Tragedy,* or half desires to exclude it, from the series.

TEXT

A Soul's Tragedy was made up of two parts, "Part First, being what was called the Poetry of Chiappino's Life: and Part Second, its Prose." Part I was made up of 401 lines of blank verse; Part II of 648 lines of prose. The text of the work was subject to numerous minute changes in the interest of meter, clarity and systematic punctuation in successive editions. One line has been added to Part I. In 1868 Browning called the parts "acts," added a list of persons, transferred the place (Faenza) from the stage directions to a position under the list of persons, and added the information, "Time 15—." In the edition of 1868, also, *A Soul's Tragedy* was given a place of some prominence. It began the fifth volume, and preceded *Luria.*

GENESIS AND COMPOSITION

It is probable that *A Soul's Tragedy* was conceived four years before it was published. Browning's letter to his friend Domett on May 22, 1842, can hardly refer to any other poem: "I shall go to the end of this year," he writes, "as I now go on—shall print the Eastern play [*Druses*] you may remember hearing about—finish a wise metaphysical play (about a great mind and soul turning to ill), and print a few songs and small poems. . . ." [7] *A Soul's Tragedy,* a "great mind and soul turning to ill," was probably written in 1843, and put away in Browning's portfolio to await revision. At any rate, we learn from a letter to Miss Barrett on February 26, 1845, that the poem is in existence: "I have one [play] done here, 'A Soul's Tragedy,' as it is properly enough called. . . ." We may see from Browning's first words to Miss Barrett about the poem, as well as from the fact that he kept it by him unpublished while several numbers of *Bells and Pomegranates* went to press, that he did not think highly of it. Miss Barrett, however, was encouraging: "the 'Soul's Tragedy' . . . sounds to me like the step of a ghost of an old Drama!" Browning was not eager to show it to her, and a year elapsed before he considered it again. On February 11, 1846, he wrote:

For the 'Soul's Tragedy'—*that* will surprise you, I think. There is no trace of you there,—you have not put out the black face of *it*—it is all

[7] F. G. Kenyon, *Robert Browning and Alfred Domett,* p. 36.

sneering and *disillusion*—and shall not be printed but burned if you say the word—now wait and see and then say! I will bring the first of the two parts next Saturday.

Two days later, he again gave his opinion:

Two nights ago I read the 'Soul's Tragedy' once more, and though there were not a few points which still struck me as successful in design and execution, yet on the whole I came to a decided opinion, that it will be better to postpone the publication of it for the present. It is not a good ending, an auspicious wind-up of this series; subject-matter and style are alike unpopular even for the literary *grex* that stands aloof from the purer *plebs*, . . . so that, if 'Luria' is *clearish*, the 'Tragedy' would be an unnecessary troubling the waters. Whereas, if I printed it first in order, my readers, according to custom, would make the (comparatively) little they did not see into, a full excuse for shutting their eyes at the rest.

He then proposed to reserve *A Soul's Tragedy* for a possible second edition of *Bells and Pomegranates,* when it could be inserted unobtrusively, "in its place, too, for it was written two or three years ago."

It was almost a month before Elizabeth Barrett saw the poem, and during this time it was probably revised. On March 10, 1846, she wrote, astonished and delighted, rebuking Browning for his lack of appreciation of *A Soul's Tragedy.* She was "quite possessed with it" and could not see how he could have any doubt about publishing it:

It is very vivid, I think, and vital, and impressed me more than the first act of 'Luria' did. . . . But this 'Tragedy' shows more heat from the first, and then, the words beat down more closely. . . . Yes, and the worst is (because it was stupid in me) the worst is that I half believed you and took the manuscript to be something inferior.

At this time she has seen only the first part of the poem, but when she had read the second part, by the end of March, she was more convinced than ever of its excellence. She gave advice on minor points. Ogniben seemed almost too wise to her. Her praise did not restore Browning's confidence in the poem; both it and *Luria* seemed to him "*manqué*, failures"; but it is probable that it was Miss Barrett's insistence that caused him to publish it. On April 5, 1846, the printer's proofs were in Miss Barrett's hands. "For my part," she wrote, "it delights me—and must raise your reputation as a poet and a thinker. . . ." The poems Browning referred to as "'Luria' and the other" were published on April 13, 1846.

A *Soul's Tragedy* has no literary source, I think. It is as pure invention as any of Browning's dramas. Yet it has the air of reality, and probably rose from his studies of Italian history; but its main source appears to be his observation of men and conditions in Italy during his tour of 1838. He had not been to Faenza, which lies between Bologna and Ravenna, when the play was written. The poem is obviously related to *Pippa Passes*, though entirely different in temper, in its swift dialogue in prose, its observation of Italian life, and in its variety. The title, and perhaps the manner of the prose, may be traced back to Elizabethan origins. But the substance of *A Soul's Tragedy*—the deterioration of a gifted soul who once acted upon the most generous and liberal of motives, but who then comes to value most highly the mere place and office which his good intentions have obtained—is a point in the development of Browning's political thinking. The liberal spirit which his reading of Shelley had implanted in Browning had borne fruit in *Strafford*, had been the generating force in *Sordello, Pippa Passes* (Part III), *King Victor and King Charles*, and *The Return of the Druses*. This flaming spirit had led Browning to accuse Wordsworth of apostasy in *The Lost Leader*. In *A Soul's Tragedy*, Chiappino is a lost leader, in truth, and Browning's faith in liberalism—at least in the virtue of its leaders—shows itself disillusioned almost to the point of cynicism. The taste one gets of politics and politicians in *Luria*, published with *A Soul's Tragedy*, is likewise unsavory. Indeed, as Miss Barrett remarked, the two plays of this *Bell* chimed together most harmoniously.

AFTER-HISTORY

A *Soul's Tragedy* attained even less notice from the reviewers upon its publication than did *Luria*. Neither the *Examiner* nor the *Athenaeum* for April 25, 1846, does more than mention it. The most appreciative words came from *Douglas Jerrold's Shilling Magazine* for June, 1846: "Mr. Browning has fulfilled the mission of the poet and the dramatist by giving new and valuable illustrations of our human nature." Lowell, in the *North American Review* for April, 1848, was appreciative of the humor of the poem. Perhaps the praise which Browning enjoyed most, after that of Miss Barrett, was the hearty expression of delight which Landor, to whom the two plays were dedicated, sent from Italy.[8] There is no sign, however, that Browning ever changed his low opinion of the work. In later years *A Soul's Tragedy* has won the praise of almost all discerning critics, but has never been a popular poem. It was not written for the stage, and met with but little success when it was produced by the London Stage Society on March 13 and 14, 1904.

In our present century two critics have good words to say of *A Soul's Tragedy*, which both recognize as Browning's only comedy. In "Robert Browning, Dramatist" [9] Arthur E. DuBois praises the excellent irony of the piece, and sees in Ogniben a comic humorist. He is of the opinion that the play is a conscious rebellion on Browning's part against tragedy as a type of drama. H. B. Charlton, in his article "Browning as Dramatist," [10] likewise praises Ogniben as a character in the play, recognizing that his flow of common sense is really an extended dramatic monologue. Alone in this play of Browning does Charlton find much social awareness of the benevolent pressure of a world order, something that is not ourselves, nor God, but society. These critics are inclined to ascribe Browning's surprising failure to produce practical drama, first, to the romantic temper of the age, and second, to Browning's own inadequate appreciation of the nature of society as a distinct entity apart from the individual and from God.

A Soul's Tragedy concluded the series of *Bells and Pomegranates*. In a rather remarkable letter to Alfred Domett on July 13, 1846,[11] Browning recognized that he had come to a breathing-space in his labors. He had cleared his mind and his spirit by the *Bells and Pomegranates*, and though a little dispirited at the small effect which he had had upon the world, he believed that he had now served his apprenticeship, and that he was ready for better things. On September 12, 1846, he married Miss Barrett, and a week later set out for Italy. He thus concluded one period of his literary career, and began another.

[8] Sidney Colvin, *Landor*, 1881, p. 188.
[9] *Studies in Philology* 33:642 (1936).
[10] *Bulletin of the John Rylands Library* 23:55–6 (1939).
[11] F. G. Kenyon, *Robert Browning and Alfred Domett*, pp. 126–30.

☙ IV ☙

THE MIDDLE YEARS

CHRISTMAS-EVE AND EASTER-DAY

PUBLICATION

Christmas-Eve and Easter-Day, companion poems which have always been linked together, and indeed utter Browning's mind upon two aspects of one subject, were published in a small octavo volume of 142 pages, bound in dark green cloth, on April 1, 1850. The book consisted of a half-title, with advertisements of the works of Mr. and Mrs. Browning on the reverse; the title-page: "Christmas-Eve and Easter-Day. A Poem. By Robert Browning. London: Chapman & Hall, 186 Strand. 1850."; and the text, pp. 1–142. This was the first of Browning's books, except for *Strafford,* to be printed at the expense of the publisher. The book was offered for sale, probably as a timely book for Easter, for Six Shillings.

TEXT

The manuscript of *Christmas-Eve and Easter-Day,* a small book of seventy-one leaves, bound in green cloth, and written partly in the hand of Robert Browning and partly in the hand of his wife, is in the Forster and Dyce Collection in the Victoria and Albert Museum at Kensington. The poem was printed from this manuscript. In the edition of 1850 *Christmas-Eve* consisted of 1359 octosyllabic lines, divided into 22 sections; *Easter-Day* was made up of 1040 octosyllabic lines, divided into 33 sections. In each the rhyme-scheme was irregular, but with couplets chiefly predominating. *Christmas-Eve and Easter-Day* was reprinted in the collected editions of 1863, 1868 and 1888, but never had a second separate edition. The number of lines in the poems has remained the same throughout their history, but between 1850 and 1863 a considerable number of changes in word, meter, and punctuation were introduced.[1]

GENESIS AND COMPOSITION

The origins of *Christmas-Eve and Easter-Day* are to be found in Browning's deepest nature, the intensely religious spirit which he inherited from his mother, his upbringing in his Non-Conformist home, and the distinctly Dissenting atmosphere of Camberwell. Through Browning's biography and his works one may trace the warring of this earnest and narrowing spirit and the more genial, worldly, and intellectual spirit which he inherited from his father. In his youth Browning attended faithfully with his mother the Independent Congregation which met in York Street, Walworth. He was, as he described himself, "passionately religious," but at the same time he was not without an occasional burst of rebellion. When he was fourteen he encountered Voltaire and Shelley, and rapidly outgrew the orthodox thought of his home. He revolted with violence, as we may see in *Pauline,* and was only slowly won back from atheism and vegetarianism by his mother's kindness and patience. The success of *Paracelsus* in the literary world, and the young poet's consequent interest in the stage, did a great deal to lure him towards worldly society and worldly activities, as Mrs. Browning may have termed the company and the theaters which her son frequented between 1837 and 1843. But the failure of his plays upon the stage, and the unfortunate effect of *Sordello* upon his reputation, drove Browning back to some degree upon Non-Conformist society, and in 1845 his acquaintance with Elizabeth Barrett, herself a Dissenter and as religious as Browning's mother, brought the poet back almost to his first position, though, of course, with an enriched and broadened nature. It was Miss Barrett, in truth, who brought out Browning's innate religiosity, and it was she who led him to write such a poem as *Christmas-Eve and Easter-Day,* a poem in which he attempted to review in a personal and direct fashion—as opposed to the "dramatic" and objective method which he had attempted to develop in his dramas and his short poems—the three aspects of Christian thinking as he saw them in 1850, and finally to pitch upon the Dissenting position as the one most acceptable to him. Miss Barrett cared little for the theater, though she paid lip-service to it, and the correspond-

[1] For some of the changes see Nicoll and Wise, *Literary Anecdotes of the Nineteenth Century,* I, 456–7.

ence between herself and Browning had barely begun, when on January 15, 1845, she spoke her mind:

A great dramatic power may develop itself otherwise than in the formal drama; and I have been guilty of wishing, before this hour . . . that you would give the public a poem unassociated directly or indirectly with the stage, for a trial on the popular heart.

In effect, as Browning himself recognized, Miss Barrett made him lose interest in the drama; and hers was good advice, for Browning had tried the stage for almost ten years without success. But what Miss Barrett wanted Browning to write was a long moral and religious poem addressing himself to the reader without the shield of a speaker between. She wished him to write "R. B. a poem." He must have received this with something of a grimace when he remembered *Pauline,* but he was drawn to Miss Barrett, and he wrote on February 11, 1845: "But I never have begun, even, what I hope I was born to begin and end—'R. B. a poem.' . . ." But Browning did not speak in his own voice in the poems of 1845 and 1846, and on May 26, 1846, Miss Barrett gave some characteristic advice:

But *you* . . . you have the superabundant mental life and individuality which admits of shifting a personality and speaking the truth still. *That* is the highest faculty, the strongest and rarest, which exercises itself in Art, —we are all agreed there is none so great faculty as the dramatic. Several times you have hinted to me that I made you careless for the drama, and it has puzzled me to fancy how it could be, when I understand myself so clearly both the difficulty and the glory of dramatic art. Yet I am conscious of wishing you to take the other crown besides—and after having made your own creatures speak in clear human voices, to speak yourself out of that personality which God made, and with the voice which He tuned into such power and sweetness of speech. I do not think that, with all that music in you, only your own personality should be dumb, nor that having thought so much and deeply on life and its ends, you should not teach what you have learnt, in the directest and most impressive way, the mask thrown off. . . . Therefore I do want you to do this with your surpassing power—it will be so easy to you to speak, and so noble, when spoken. . . . *Now* let us have your own voice speaking of yourself.

It was in this temper, I think, and with this encouragement that Browning, feeling deeply the pressure of religious controversies in 1850, wrote *Christmas-Eve and Easter-Day.* It was not, however, easy, and the result could hardly be called "R. B. a poem." It is Browning's attempt to use the "white light" of his own personality, rather than the "broken lights" of the characters through whom he had spoken hitherto.[2] The first results of Elizabeth Barrett's influence upon her husband's poetry may be seen, perhaps, in *The Guardian Angel*, a confessional and personal poem, written at Ancona in 1848. Italy gave him the leisure to think, and his wife gave direction to his thinking, but it was probably the birth of his son, and the death of his much-beloved mother in England when he could not leave his wife to go to her in March, 1849, that made Browning ponder in his heart the problems of life and death, the power of love, the ways of worship and the hope of resurrection—themes which make up *Christmas-Eve and Easter-Day*. In a dangerous physical and mental condition, caused by his extreme grief at the loss of his mother, Browning spent the summer at Bagni Caldi, above Bagni di Lucca, and the autumn in Florence. Earlier in 1849, Arthur Hugh Clough had been in Florence, and may have met the Brownings. He had written that year in Italy his *Epi-Straussium* and his *Easter-Day, Naples, 1849*, and his talk may have been the final touch which put Browning's poem in motion.[3] Very late in 1849 or early in 1850 Browning began to write *Christmas-Eve and Easter-Day*. We first hear of it on January 9, when Mrs. Browning wrote, "Robert is engaged on a new poem." [4] At that time the poem must have been well started, for it was sent to England and published on April 1, 1850.

SOURCES AND INFLUENCES

The substance of *Christmas-Eve* is Browning's review of the three distinctively Christian points of view upon religious matters in 1850: first, the Dissenting, or Non-Conformist, reception of Christ's birth in the Christmas-Eve service in the Independent Chapel; second, the Catholic reception of the birth in the Christmas-Eve service at St. Peter's in Rome; third, the reception of the birth in the Christmas-Eve lecture by the professor in the university of Göttingen. Those are the simple, the ritualistic, and the rational ways of looking at the central fact of Christianity. When the review is concluded, Browning casts his choice upon the first. It is an interesting fact that Miss Bar-

[2] See the excellent chapter, "The White Light," in Mr. F. R. G. Duckworth's *Browning: Background and Conflict*, London, 1931; esp. pp. 187–93. In spite of Mr. Duckworth's remarks, I feel that Browning meant the poem to be "white light."

[3] *Letters of E.B.B.*, ed. Kenyon, I, 429.

[4] *Idem*, I, 432.

rett in a letter of August 15, 1846, had anticipated the matter of her husband's poem. Referring to their conversation of the day before, she says,

I meant that I felt unwilling, for my own part, to put on any of the liveries of the sects. The truth, as God sees it, must be something so different from these opinions about truth—these systems which fit different classes of men like their coats, and wear brown at the elbows always! I believe in what is divine and floats at highest, in all these different theologies—and because the really Divine draws together souls, and tends so to a unity, I could pray anywhere and with all sorts of worshippers, from the Sistine Chapel to Mr. Fox's, those kneeling and those standing. Wherever you go, in all religious societies, there is a little to revolt, and a good deal to bear with—but it is not otherwise in the world without; and, *within,* you are especially reminded that God has to be more patient than yourself after all. Still you go quickest there, where your sympathies are least ruffled and disturbed—and I like, beyond comparison best, the simplicity of the dissenters . . . the unwritten prayer, . . . the sacraments administered quietly and without charlatanism! and the principle of a church, as they hold it, *I* hold it too. . . . Well—there is enough to dissent from among the dissenters . . . you feel moreover bigotry and ignorance pressing on you on all sides, till you gasp for breath like one strangled. But better this, even, than what is elsewhere. . . . The Unitarians seem to me to throw over what is most beautiful in the Christian Doctrine; but the Formulists, on the other side, stir up a dust, in which it appears excusable not to see. When the veil of the body falls, how we shall look into each other's faces, astonished, . . . after one glance at God's!

Here, in compact prose, the substance of *Christmas-Eve* is hinted, and even the magnificent scene of the Day of Judgment in *Easter-Day* is suggested. In his letter of August 17, Browning agrees with her entirely, and also feels unwilling to constrain his religion to any sect, but if a choice must be made, he too chooses the Dissenting position. His desire for freedom from the sects was of old standing, and he had probably been encouraged in his feeling by W. J. Fox, the Unitarian minister and political reformer, who was never happy for long in any position, and by Thomas Carlyle, who valued his independence above all.

In reviewing the position of the Dissenters, Browning was, as we have seen, on familiar ground. Camberwell was the headquarters of Non-Conformity and Browning grew up in the midst of it. His wife was later to complain that though he was a poet, he was "descended from the blood of all the Puritans." It is not to be supposed that the York Street Chapel which Browning attended, and where he was baptized, was the model for the cheap, squalid, and ugly Independent Chapel which is described in *Christmas-Eve,* nor were the middle-class people who attended at York Street the congregation which Browning depicts with startling realism in the poem. In a conversation with W. G. Kingsland Browning asserted, concerning Zion Chapel, that "all the incidents are imaginary—save the lunar rainbow: I saw that." [5] In the poem Dissent is purposely shown in its most unlovely aspect. The parson may well, however, be drawn in part from the life, for some of his characteristics may be discerned in the Reverend Mr. George Clayton of the York Street Chapel whose long prayers made the young Browning gnaw the mahogany pew-top.[6] The Reverend Mr. Irons of Camberwell Grove was no better, and he expressed the opinion that "Roman Catholic and midnight assassin are synonymous terms." It is the smug satisfaction of the congregation under the parson's preaching that finally drives Browning out of Zion Chapel, but though out of the church, in his poem as in his life, his leanings in religion were nearer to the Dissenters than to any others. Perhaps in 1849 his wife's strong feelings and the sudden and affecting death of his mother flung Browning for the time back into the ranks. His lasting choice may be seen in the *Epilogue* to *Dramatis Personae,* a poem akin to *Christmas-Eve,* where he prefers to worship outside formal churches altogether. After his wife's death, Browning attended Bedford Chapel in London with Miss Arabella Barrett, his wife's sister, for several years. In his later years, though he was never a regular church-goer, he seems to have drifted somewhat towards the Anglican or Established Church.[7]

In delineating the Catholic position in *Christmas-Eve,* Browning fell, perhaps, into the prejudice of his class and nation against Rome. Writing to Mrs. Jameson on April 2, 1850, concerning the new book, his wife said: "There is nothing *Italian* in the book; poets are apt to be most present with the distant." [8] This statement is only partially true. Rome and all the splendor of a Christmas ceremonial, the "raree-show" as Browning calls it, certainly leave their mark upon the poem. The poet had not at that time witnessed the Christmas

---

[5] Nicoll and Wise, *Literary Anecdotes of the Nineteenth Century,* I, 456.

[6] See the *Browning Society's Papers,* III, 43*. See also Griffin and Minchin, *Life,* p. 50.

[7] The commentary upon Browning's religious opinions by Mrs. Orr, "The Religious Opinions of Robert Browning," in the *Contemporary Review* for December, 1891, though able and interesting, is not free from her own bias. But see A. C. Pigou's *The Religious Opinions of Robert Browning,* 1900, and Henry Jones, *Browning as a Philosophical and Religious Teacher,* 1891.

[8] *Letters of E.B.B.,* ed. Kenyon, I, 441–2.

service in Rome, but he had seen the festivals of the churches in Florence, and he had undoubtedly heard his friend, William Wetmore Story, describe the spectacle he had just seen at Christmas in Rome, "with a pennyworth of religion to a ton of form." [9] There is little doubt that Browning's disgust at the Pope's "posturings and petticoatings" was increased by the disappointment which he and his wife keenly felt in the proved incompetence of the new and liberal Pope, Pius IX, from whom they expected so much. But through the ritual Browning had tolerance enough to see the embers of love and faith.[10]

What Mrs. Browning meant by her remark that there was nothing Italian in *Christmas-Eve* was, I believe, this: the book was written for English readers, and Browning had his eye upon the Tractarian, or the Oxford, Movement in England rather than on Rome, and saw in the Roman Church the ultimate goal of the Tractarians. Bred as he was in Dissenting Camberwell, the poet seems not to have been affected at all by the Oxford Movement. In the famous *Tracts for the Times*, published between 1833 and 1841, the Oxford Movement, led by Keble, Pusey, and Newman, was making its courageous attempt to re-vivify and re-create the Church of England. Of this Browning, immersed in his literary and dramatic affairs, took little notice.[11] Even the famous *Tract XC* of 1841 did not rouse him, and he was probably neither surprised nor much interested when in 1845 Newman found the goal of his long journey in the Church of Rome. Yet he knew what was going on, for he makes a number of references to "Puseyitism"—that is, the Oxford Movement—in his letters to Miss Barrett, but most of them are not friendly. On January 13, 1845, he wrote, "I don't think I shall let *you* hear, after all, the savage things about Popes and imaginative religions that I must say." This attitude continued, and in 1850 when Mrs. Browning was alarmed at her little son's religious fervor, "kneeling on his knees to the first sound of music, and folding his hands and turning up his eyes in a sort of ecstatical state," Browning remarked that "it is as well to have the eyeteeth and the Puseyistical crisis over together." [12] Yet much as he disliked to surrender himself to authority, Browning could ap-

[9] See Henry James, *William Wetmore Story and his Friends,* I, 100–2.

[10] For Browning's attitude towards Catholicism, see E. M. Naish, *Browning and Dogma*, London, 1906; esp. pp. 95–177.

[11] But see above, my discussion of *The Bishop Orders his Tomb.*

[12] *Letters of E.B.B.*, ed. Kenyon, I, 466.

preciate the beauty of the ritual and the goodness of many of the priests in the Roman Church and in the High Church in England, and in *The Ring and the Book* he was to deal more generously with the Catholics.

The third great aspect of Christian thought in 1850 which Browning dealt with in *Christmas-Eve* was Rationalism, and this point of view was represented by the lecture of the "hawk-nosed, high-cheekboned Professor" in the university at Göttingen on Christmas-Eve. The person and the doctrine are composites of rationalistic criticism—Auguste Comte and his philosophy of Positivism may be seen there faintly—but the figure and the discourse mainly represent the German critic of the Scriptures, David Friedrich Strauss and his book, *Das Leben Jesu,* published in Germany in 1835. Browning's German was not adequate for reading the book in the original, and it seems likely that he did not see Strauss's work in the English translation of 1841 or the American reprint of 1843, but read it first in the translation by Marian Evans (George Eliot) which appeared in the late spring of 1846. Browning had shared the atheism of Shelley in his youth, and possibly the Unitarianism of W. J. Fox in his young manhood,[13] so that the tenor of Strauss's book, attacking the Gospels as "Gospel Myths" and referring steadily to the "myth of Christ" which the earliest Christian partisans had created, probably did not shock him. It was the purpose of Strauss to clear the supernatural away in favor of a rational view of Jesus, but the effect of the German critic's work was to reduce Christ from a divine being, the Son of God sent for the salvation of mankind, to a man—the greatest of men, but a man. Towards the end of his *Leben Jesu,* Strauss anticipates what was probably the feeling of Browning concerning his book:

The results of the inquiry which we have now brought to a close, have apparently annihilated the greatest and most valuable part of that which the Christian has been wont to believe concerning his Savior Jesus, have uprooted all the animating motives which he has gathered from his faith, and withered all his consolations. The boundless store of truth and life which for eighteen centuries has been the aliment of humanity, seems ir-

---

[13] See the able account of the influence of Fox's preaching at South Place Chapel upon Browning in C. R. Tracy, "Browning's Heresies," in *Studies in Philology* 33:610–25 (1936). In 1845 the Rev. Philip Harwood gave a series of lectures in the Chapel upon Strauss, and advanced the "myth" theory of the Gospels (p. 616). Browning often attended during Fox's ministry.

retrievably dissipated; the most sublime levelled with the dust, God divested of his grace, man of his dignity, and the tie between heaven and earth broken.[14]

It was the purpose of Strauss to establish Christianity upon different grounds, but Browning felt that if the disputes of the Dissenters and the Catholics had poisoned the air, the effect of the professor was to pump all of the air out of the bell-jar and leave humanity gasping in vacuity. Browning quits the discourse at Göttingen less pleased with Rationalism than with Dissent or Catholicism, because among the Rationalists he did not find love, but only the "ghost of love."

When the three great aspects of the Christian doctrine have been canvassed, Browning, as we have seen, makes his decision in favor of the Dissenting Chapel, for the Chapel seems in the poet's opinion to have received most fittingly the gift of God's Son to the world.

The ground cleared by *Christmas-Eve*, the poet undertakes in *Easter-Day* to build his conception of the belief of a modern Christian, discussing this time not man's relation to the various creeds, but his direct relation to Christ, who lived and died on earth for him and rose from the dead on Easter-Day. In spite of the protestations of Browning himself in later years, and of all the early biographers and critics, the consensus of modern opinion is that *Easter-Day* is not "dramatic," but is "his fullest though not his final confession of faith," [15] and no one who has read the correspondence between Browning and Miss Barrett can believe otherwise. The difficulty lies in the fact that there are two speakers in *Easter-Day*, one an easy believer and another who feels "how hard it is to be a Christian," and neither of them is represented as being the speaker of *Christmas-Eve*. But this is not difficult of resolution. As we have seen, Brown-

---

[14] *The Life of Jesus, Critically Examined by Dr. David Friedrich Strauss.* Translated from the Fourth German Edition by Marian Evans . . . N. Y. 1860, p. 867. See also the article by Fräulein Käthe Göritz, "Robert Brownings *Christmas-Eve and Easter-Day* und *Das Leben Jesu* von D. F. Strauss," in *Archiv für das Studium der Neueren Sprachen* 147:197–211 (1924). Fräulein Göritz compares the poem and the *Leben* well, but does not have a keen appreciation of the conditions in England at the time. See the excellent comprehensive study by W. O. Raymond, "Browning and Higher Criticism," Ch. 2 in *The Infinite Moment.*

[15] See for example Oliver Elton, *A Survey of English Literature, 1780–1880,* III, 373; J. W. Cunliffe, "Elizabeth Barrett's Influence on Browning's Poetry" in *PMLA* 23:176; and A. W. Crawford, "Browning's *Christmas-Eve*" in *Methodist Review* 110:379. See also H. B. Charlton's illuminating essay, "Browning as Poet of Religion," in *Bulletin of the John Rylands Library* 27:271–307 (1942–3).

ing was broken by the death of his mother in March, 1849, and recovered very slowly. The debate between the easy believer and the austere believer is a debate, carried on in Browning's mind, between his old confident belief and the new and harder one, very much like the debate in Tennyson's poem, *The Two Voices,* when he had lost his friend Hallam in 1833, or indeed like the debate in Browning's own *La Saisiaz* in 1878 when his friend, Miss Anne Egerton Smith, had died.

In *Easter-Day* Browning is searching for tenable grounds upon which one might be a Christian. In this search Nature is rejected as offering no final evidence for the existence of a plan by which life is directed. The problem of how to view the good things of the earth, which troubled Browning in the composition of *Saul,* is debated. Neither too great delight in them for their own sakes, nor too great an asceticism, is possible in reason. Will Art, then, giving the impress of the human spirit to the works of Nature, allow any reason for faith? Art, says Browning, developing a doctrine which is to inform all his later poems upon painting and music, is an earnest of heaven, the broken arc of earth, but it mainly tells of man's aspirations and limitations. The searcher then turns to Intellect for the assurance of faith. But Browning believes that the Intellect—and this is a doctrine that was first expounded at length in *Paracelsus* and was to be reiterated again and again in later years—is earth-bound and dependent upon the physical senses, and therefore unreliable. And thus the speaker comes to the conclusion that the only worthy evidence for faith is Love—not human love, which like Art is only a reflection, though of a most valuable sort, of a greater light—but Divine Love, such as God showed in sending His Son to live and die among men. This revelation of Divine Love links *Easter-Day* to *Christmas-Eve.* Browning has here, for the first time, reasoned out his characteristic religious ideas, the ideas which inform all of his religious and philosophical poems, such as *Saul, Cleon, Karshish, A Death in the Desert,* and *The Pope* in *The Ring and the Book.* The senses and the intellect of man admit the strength and intelligence of God, and the problem, as it always seemed to Browning, was to prove that God's love was the equal of His other attributes. This led Browning naturally to the divine revelation of Christ. The magnificent vision of the Day of Judgment, appropriate to Easter as the time when Christ's love is most in evidence, is fittingly the apex of the poem. The ascetic and austere tone of *Easter-Day,* which bewildered later critics as being most uncharacteristic of Browning's eager and earth-loving nature, first troubled his wife. On May 4, 1850, she wrote, "I have complained of the *asceticism* in the second part, but he said it was 'one side of the question.' Don't think that he has taken to the cilix—indeed he has not—but it is his way to *see* things as passionately as other people *feel* them." [16] The truer explanation lies, as we have seen, in the effect of his mother's death.

AFTER-HISTORY

We learn from a letter of Mrs. Browning's [17] that two hundred copies of *Christmas-Eve and Easter-Day* were sold in the first fortnight. But with the passing of Easter the sale flagged, and the publishers could not call the book a commercial success. Browning was vexed at the lack of interest in the poem. Chapman's account of the sales on July 29, 1864, shows that the publisher still had a number of copies on hand.[18] The reviewers, perhaps naturally enough in a religious poem, seem to have been swayed in their comments by their religious views; but whether they praised or blamed, they generally misunderstood. The reviewer in the *Athenaeum* for April 6, 1850, which possibly represented the Anglican position, misread Browning's theology, praised the poem for some magnificent passages, but condemned the flippancy and doggerel with which the poet had treated high subjects, saying, "he has recklessly impaired the dignity of his purpose by the vehicle chosen for its development." The reviewer in the *Examiner* for April 6, probably John Forster and representing the Dissenting position, was extremely enthusiastic, finding the poem "a most remarkable production," and was inclined to see in the mixed style "an effluence of irrepressible thought, in harmony with each varying shade, of the sentiment conveyed by it. . . ." As might be expected of those more interested in art than in religion, W. M. Rossetti in his review of the poem in the PreRaphaelite *Germ* for April, 1850, confined himself to a commentary upon the style. In America the ablest review was that by John Weiss in the *Massachusetts Quarterly Review* for June, 1850 (III, 347–85). He expressed, perhaps, the Dissenting opinion of Massachusetts. But by far the most competent review of the poem was written by Joseph Milsand,

[16] *Letters of E.B.B.*, ed. Kenyon, I, 449.
[17] *Idem*, I, 447.
[18] See *New Letters*, ed. DeVane and Knickerbocker, pp. 392, 400; also 52, 58, 61.

a French Protestant destined to become one of Browning's closest friends, in his article, "La Poésie anglaise depuis Byron, II—Robert Browning," in the *Revue des deux mondes* for August, 1851. Milsand really grasped the significance of the poem in relation to Browning's other works, and saw the philosophical position at which the poet had arrived.

In the last two decades of the nineteenth century when Browning was accepted with the utmost seriousness as a religious teacher, *Christmas-Eve and Easter-Day* was the subject of quotation, debate, and panegyric. Today, we are interested rather in the magnificent descriptions scattered through the poem—Zion Chapel, the lunar rainbow, St. Peter's at Rome, and the Last Judgment—and in the position which the poem holds in the development of Browning's ideas. As we have seen, it was in this poem that Browning first formulated his peculiar and independent interpretation of Christianity, and after 1850 it was hardly possible for him to write without referring in some way to the background of his religious thought. The conclusions which Browning came to in *Christmas-Eve and Easter-Day* inform his thinking to the day of his death.

MEN AND WOMEN

The two octavo volumes of *Men and Women,* bound in green cloth boards, containing fifty poems and an epilogue, were published on November 17, 1855. Volume I consisted of the title-page: "Men and Women. By Robert Browning. In Two Volumes. Vol. I. London: Chapman and Hall, 193 Piccadilly. 1855."; a list of the contents; and the text, pp. 1–260. Volume II consisted of a title-page, as above, save that "Vol. II" was substituted for "Vol. I"; a list of contents; and the text, pp. 1–241. The two volumes were offered for sale at Twelve Shillings.

TEXT

The first volume of *Men and Women* was made up of twenty-seven poems, printed in the following order:

Love Among the Ruins	A Woman's Last Word
A Lovers' Quarrel	Fra Lippo Lippi
Evelyn Hope	A Toccata of Galuppi's
Up at a Villa—Down in the City	By the Fire-Side
(As Distinguished by an Italian	Any Wife to Any Husband
Person of Quality)	An Epistle containing the Strange

Medical Experience of Karshish, the Arab Physician
Mesmerism
A Serenade at the Villa
My Star
Instans Tyrannus
A Pretty Woman
"Childe Roland to the Dark Tower Came"
Respectability

A Light Woman
The Statue and the Bust
Love in a Life
Life in a Love
How it Strikes a Contemporary
The Last Ride Together
The Patriot—An Old Story
Master Hugues of Saxe-Gotha
Bishop Blougram's Apology
Memorabilia

The second volume of *Men and Women* was made up of twenty-four poems, printed in the following order:

Andrea del Sarto. (Called "The Faultless Painter")
Before
After
In Three Days
In a Year
Old Pictures in Florence
In a Balcony—First Part
       "   Second Part
       "   Third Part
Saul
"De Gustibus—"
Women and Roses
Protus
Holy-Cross Day. (On which the Jews were Forced to Attend an Annual Christian Sermon in Rome)

The Guardian-Angel: A Picture at Fano
Cleon
The Twins
Popularity
The Heretic's Tragedy. A Middle-Age Interlude
Two in the Campagna
A Grammarian's Funeral
One Way of Love
Another Way of Love
"Transcendentalism:" A Poem in Twelve Books
Misconceptions
One Word More. To E. B. B.

This was the rich offering of the original *Men and Women*. In the general distribution of his shorter poems in the collected edition of 1863, Browning kept the title *Men and Women* for a group of thirteen poems culled from the three collections of shorter poems which he had published to that date, but the poems originally printed under the heading of *Men and Women* were scattered among the *Dramatic Lyrics, Dramatic Romances,* and *Men and Women*. Thirty of the poems of *Men and Women* (1855) became *Dramatic Lyrics,* twelve became *Dramatic Romances,* and eight remained *Men and Women*. *In a Balcony* was made independent of all these categories. The history of the peregrinations of each poem will be given under the treatment of that particular piece. Of the fifty-one poems of the original

Men and Women only *The Twins* and the first nine sections of *Saul* had appeared in print before. The pamphlets containing *The Statue and the Bust* and *Cleon* which purported to be printed before *Men and Women* have now been branded as forgeries, as will appear in the discussion. No second edition of *Men and Women* as a separate unit was called for.

GENESIS AND COMPOSITION

The poems that make up *Men and Women* were the gleanings of the best ten years of Browning's life. His last volume of shorter poems had been published as *Dramatic Romances* in November, 1845. The next decade saw his marriage and removal to Italy, and towards the end of this period most of the poems of *Men and Women* seem to have been written. It is quite likely that some of these poems were written or conceived before Browning left London in September of 1846, but the earliest poem of which we can speak with assurance is *The Guardian Angel,* written early in July, 1848, at Ancona. The latest is *One Word More,* written in London as a dedication of the work to his wife, in September, 1855. The title of the volume was unconsciously in Browning's mind as early as February 26, 1845, when he spoke of his *Dramatic Lyrics and Romances* as "this dancing ring of men and women hand in hand"; but *Christmas-Eve and Easter-Day* intervened in 1850, and it is probable that *Men and Women* as we know it did not form itself in Browning's mind until later. We know that he wrote at least three poems, *Women and Roses, Childe Roland,* and *Love Among the Ruins,* in Paris in the first days of 1852.[1] On February 24, 1853, he wrote to his friend Milsand from Florence, "We live wholly alone here. I have not left the house one evening since our return. I am writing—a first step towards popularity for me—lyrics with more music and painting than before, so as to get people to hear and see. . . . Something to follow, if I can compass it." From a letter of Mrs. Browning's dated August 24, 1853, and written from Bagni di Lucca, we learn that the poet was at work, and Browning tells his friend Forster, in a letter on June 5, 1854, that he has written "a number of poems of all sorts and sizes and styles and subjects . . . the fruits of the years since I last turned the winch of the wine press. The manner will be newer than the matter. I hope to be listened to, this time, and I am glad I have been made to wait

[1] See below, my discussion of *Childe Roland* and *Love Among the Ruins.*

this not very long while." [2] A visitor to the Brownings in Florence in September, 1854, recorded that Mrs. Browning "told me that Browning was also ready with a volume of miscellaneous poems," and that the poet had proposed going to England in the summer of that year to publish them, but Mrs. Browning was not ready.[3] But Browning still added to his store. The spring of 1855 saw him "swallowed up in work," as we learn from a letter of Mrs. Browning to her sister. Mrs. Browning reports that the poems are "magnificent." On July 12, 1855, Mr. and Mrs. Browning arrived in London with the manuscript of *Men and Women*, and it was soon in the hands of the publishers. In August the printing had begun, and in September *One Word More* was added. Renewing old acquaintances in London, Browning read the proofs to W. J. Fox, his first critic and old friend. On September 27, Browning read *Fra Lippo Lippi*, one of his most characteristic poems, to a group which had assembled at his house in Dorset Street. Tennyson, D. G. and W. M. Rossetti, and Mrs. Browning were of the group, and D. G. Rossetti drew a sketch of the Laureate while he read *Maud*.[4] In October the Brownings went to Paris and awaited, a little impatiently, the publication of the work, which finally appeared on November 17, 1855.

SOURCES AND INFLUENCES

It has been well said of *Men and Women* that "The new poems, both in subjects and treatment, are closely akin to the old. It is a case rather of development than difference; the range has widened and the depth of thought is more consistent," [5] but the degree of development is very great. Naturally, most of the poems have an Italian flavor, and some, like *De Gustibus* and *Up at a Villa*, are mainly devoted to Italian landscape. Some, such as those concerned with painting, rose from advantages that only Italy could give. Browning was fond of saying in after years, "Italy was my university." In a large and profound way Italy had freed and clarified his poetic spirit. He saw himself and his art in a generous perspective and no longer felt

---

[2] The letter to Milsand is quoted in Th. Bentzon (Mme. Blanc), "A French Friend of Browning—Joseph Milsand," in *Scribner's Magazine* 20:115; see also Griffin and Minchin, *Life*, p. 189. Mrs. Browning's letter was printed by E. C. McAleer in *PMLA* 66:607 (1951). For the letter to Forster see *New Letters*, ed. DeVane and Knickerbocker, p. 77.

[3] See letters edited by Leonard Huxley, "A Visitor to the Brownings," in the *Yale Review*, N.S. 13:243.

[4] See *The Browning Collections* (Sotheby Catalogue, 1913), p. 6.

[5] Griffin and Minchin, *Life*, p. 198.

it necessary to justify himself, save through the quality and unique-ness of his poetry. London produced one poem, and Paris several, but most of the poems of *Men and Women* owe their existence to Florence and the other cities of Italy. Most of the poems are dra-matic in Browning's characteristic manner, only more perfectly so, and he has here created some of his most famous characters. His in-stinct to see the individual rather than the mass of men is here al-lowed full play, even to the extreme of eccentricity and the grotesque. This led him, as H. B. Charlton observes,[6] to the Renaissance, the second crisis in history, when a new and overwhelming interest in personality developed. It was in this period that the first modern biographies were written and, significantly, were written about artists whose medium was color.

But the personal element is not lacking, as one may see from *The Guardian Angel, By the Fire-Side, One Word More,* and perhaps several other poems. As in the earlier volumes of short poems, the passions are again anatomized in *Men and Women,* but here Brown-ing's attention is mainly taken up by the passion of love. The subtle relationships of married love are portrayed again and again, and one may say that all the wisdom which Browning has gained from his own happy marriage here finds expression in lyrical verse. The central problem in his love poetry is communication between the sexes. Love exists in and through intuition, and is perfect when the lovers tran-scend the barriers of their separate individualities; it is destroyed by too much ratiocination and the temptation in the man to establish his intellectual superiority.[7]

Browning's thinking upon his own art of poetry, too, bears noble fruit in *How it Strikes a Contemporary, Saul,* and *"Transcendental-ism."* The results of his religious thinking may be seen in the deeper tones of the completed *Saul, Cleon, Karshish,* and *Bishop Blougram's Apology.* Religion is no longer a mere back-drop for his poems, as it was in his *Dramatic Lyrics* and *Dramatic Romances,* but the central issue it is to remain in *Dramatis Personae* and *The Ring and the Book. In a Balcony* is an echo of the drama, with which Browning had now ceased to concern himself. But this enumeration is merely to peer into the entrance of "that Aladdin's treasure-cave of verse."

[6] "Browning as Poet of Religion," in *Bulletin of the John Rylands Library* 27:300–2 (1942–3).
[7] See E. D. H. Johnson, *The Alien Vision of Victorian Poetry,* pp. 101–8.

AFTER-HISTORY

There can be little doubt that Browning expended the utmost of his strength in the making of *Men and Women,* and that from the interest and quality of his work he had every right to expect the applause of the intelligent world. But several things militated against the proper appreciation of his work. In his long absence in Italy Browning had not kept his name before the British public, and when *Men and Women* appeared the Crimean War was at its height. Browning felt, also, that his publishers were not sufficiently active in his interests, and this led him in 1866 to transfer his works to Smith, Elder and Co. The early brisk sale of *Men and Women* was probably caused by the little circle of the poet's faithful admirers, such for example as the PreRaphaelite group, but the sale soon flagged. There were a considerable number of reviews of *Men and Women* and almost all of them were appreciative, though hardly anyone realized the surpassing excellence of the work. William Morris, still at Oxford, reviewed the book with an immense and naïve enthusiasm in the *Oxford and Cambridge Magazine* for March, 1856, and he was a harbinger of the acclaim which Browning was to receive in the next ten years from the youth of the universities.[8] Perhaps *Fraser's Magazine* for January, 1856, not a little condescending to Browning, may be taken as the normal feeling of the time.[9] *Blackwood's* comment (79:135) was that "there is no getting through the confused crowd of Mr. Browning's Men and Women." The most curious review of the work was that which appeared in the Catholic magazine, *The Rambler,* for January, 1856 (pp. 54–71), which Browning learned from his friend Father Prout was written by Cardinal Wiseman, who had unconsciously served as a model for the "fancy portrait" of Bishop Blougram.

[8] See M. B. Cramer, "What Browning's Literary Reputation Owed to the Pre-Raphaelites, 1847–1856," in *Journal of English Literary History* 8:305–27; and "Browning's Literary Reputation at Oxford, 1855–1859," in *PMLA* 57:232–40 (1942). Mr. Cramer's enthusiasm for finding admirers and friends for Browning in these years needs to be tempered by a consideration of the sale of his books. There is no doubt, however, that these groups helped Browning's fame immensely.

[9] See also *Bentley's Miscellany* 39:64–70; *British Quarterly Review* 23:151–80; *Dublin University Magazine* 47:673–5; *Irish Quarterly Review* 6:21–8; *The Westminster Review,* N.S. 9:290–6; *The Athenaeum* for November 17, 1855; and *The Examiner* for December 1, 1855. *The Athenaeum* perpetrated this judgment on *Men and Women:* "Who will not grieve over energy wasted and power misspent,—over fancies chaste and noble, so overhung by the 'seven veils' of obscurity, that we can oftentimes be only sure that fancies exist?"

Though the Cardinal found much that was offensive to Catholics in the work, he felt confident of Browning's early conversion. The most penetrating understanding of *Men and Women* was that contributed by Milsand, Browning's friend, to the *Revue contemporaire* on September 15, 1856. In speaking of the subjective and the objective in the new work, Milsand wrote,

Mr. Browning sympathizes equally with both sources of inspiration, and I am inclined to think that his constant endeavor has been to reconcile and combine them, so as to be, not in turn, but simultaneously, lyrical and dramatic, subjective and objective. . . . His poetry would have us conceive of the inner significance of things by making us see the exteriors.[10]

To say that Browning was disappointed at the reception of *Men and Women* is to put it mildly. He knew the worth of his work, and saw infinitely weaker poets receiving great acclaim. Moreover, he was in financial straits. He justly concluded that his poetry was too new and original to appeal to the public, but he could not see why intelligent people should not appreciate it. When Ruskin undertook to tutor him in the art of poetry, Browning wrote to him from Paris on December 10, 1855, a defence of his poetry which deserves to be printed in full. He there defends himself in his right to be suggestive rather than complete; he defends his meter; he denies that he puts himself in the characters he has created; he even has to insist that his poetry does teach, in the best sense of the word. He concludes with these words:

I look on my own shortcomings too sorrowfully, try to remedy them too earnestly: but I shall never change my point of sight, or feel other than disconcerted and apprehensive when the public, critics and all, begin to understand and approve me. But what right have *you* to disconcert me in the other way?[11]

It is safe to say that Ruskin gave Browning up for lost, but the world has gradually come to see that in *Men and Women* Browning made a great and lasting contribution to the form, range, and spirit of English literature. Since 1855 the fifty-one poems of *Men and Women* have steadily grown in popularity, and are now recognized as representing the highest level of Browning's poetic achievement.

[10] *Revue contemporaire*, 107e livraison, art. III, 546.
[11] See W. G. Collingwood, *Life and Work of John Ruskin*, 1893, pp. 232–5. For Browning's bitter disappointment in the reception of *Men and Women* see *New Letters*, ed. DeVane and Knickerbocker, pp. 85–97. After eight years Chapman still had copies of *Men and Women* on hand: see *New Letters*, p. 400.

MEN AND WOMEN—VOL. I

Love Among the Ruins

Love Among the Ruins was justly given the place of honor in Volume I of *Men and Women,* where it was first published. There the poem was composed of fourteen stanzas of six lines each, the long six-measure line followed by the two-measure rhyming line. In 1863 Browning reduced the number of stanzas to seven, by making each stanza twelve lines long. This rearrangement was easy and natural, for each of the new stanzas breaks in the middle, six lines describing the landscape as it now is and six lines describing it as it was in ancient times. In the distribution of the poems in 1863 *Love Among the Ruins* was put among the *Dramatic Lyrics,* where it has remained. Except for a few minor changes in punctuation, the text has remained the same since 1855. A manuscript draft of the poem, entitled "Sicilian Pastoral," is in the Lowell Collection at Harvard University.

Love Among the Ruins was written in an apartment in the Champs Elysées in Paris, on January 3, 1852, when Browning had resolved to write a poem each day.[12] Under the same resolution *Women and Roses* and *Childe Roland* had been written on the two preceding days. The incidents and the landscapes of *Love Among the Ruins* and *Childe Roland* are reminiscent and imaginary, and *Women and Roses* is the recollection of a vivid dream. This indicates, perhaps, that Browning was drawing upon his deepest resources for his subjects at this time.

It has generally been assumed that Browning had an Italian city in mind as the scene of the ruins upon which the lovers stand, but Bernhard Fehr has shown how closely Browning's ancient city resembles Herodotus' description of Babylon,[13] and how the Apocalypse of St. John seems to supply some of the details of the scene.

[12] Mrs. Orr is authority for this statement; see *Life,* p. 362, and Griffin and Minchin, *Life,* p. 189. But Mr. Johnstone Parr, relying upon a phrase which Browning used in a letter to Forster on June 5, 1854 (*New Letters,* ed. DeVane and Knickerbocker, p. 77), that the poems of *Men and Women* were "not written before last year"—a statement demonstrably lacking in precision—believes that the poem was written in Italy in 1853. See "The Date of Composition of Browning's *Love Among the Ruins,*" in *Philological Quarterly* 32:443–6 (October, 1953). See also below, my comment on *Childe Roland.*

[13] See his article "Über Robert Brownings *Love Among the Ruins,*" in *Archiv für das Studium der Neueren Sprachen und Literaturen* 142:260–2 (1921). See Herodotus, I, 178–80, 191–2.

It is the opinion of Robert Adger Law that the phraseology and ideas of the poem were suggested by *I Chronicles*, 18 and 21, and that the ruins are not Italianate, but "a composite picture of Babylon and Jerusalem, fused by the poet's imagination." [14] In a recent article, however, Johnstone Parr [15] has demonstrated the tremendous interest in western Europe in archaeology between 1839 and 1852. Such ancient capital cities were excavated as Tarquinia and Veii on the Roman Campagna, Thebes in Egypt, and Babylon and Nineveh in the Near East. The details of Browning's poem—the tombs, ruins, aqueducts, now overwhelmed by mounds of grassland upon which the sheep graze—appear in most of the literature on the excavations. These accounts were very popular, and one of the most popular was A. H. Layard's *Nineveh and its Remains*, published in 1849; his description of Nineveh perhaps is nearest of all to that of the ancient city in Browning's poem. Nineveh, Babylon, and Thebes were said to have had the hundred-gated walls, and were capable of sending forth an army of a million men. The poet and Layard were friends in 1867, and it possible that they met in Paris as early as 1851. At any rate, Browning's poem appeared at a time when there was great interest in ancient cities. Whatever ancient city Browning had in mind, the idea of the necessary subjection of antiquity to the uses of the modern world engrossed him more and more as he grew older. His fullest expression of this opinion may be seen in the *Parleying With Gerard de Lairesse*. *Love Among the Ruins* is now accounted one of Browning's surest triumphs in poetry, and by its subject and its doctrine was an appropriate choice as the first poem in the collection of *Men and Women*. The meter, his own invention, has been especially praised.

A Lovers' Quarrel

A Lovers' Quarrel was published in *Men and Women* and was composed of twenty-two stanzas of seven lines each, in anapaestic meter.

[14] See "The Background of Browning's *Love Among the Ruins*," in *MLN* 37:312 (1922).

[15] "The Site and Ancient City of Browning's *Love Among the Ruins*," in *PMLA* 68: 128–37 (1953). See also the suggestion of C. R. Tracy that *Love Among the Ruins* may have been suggested by Letter CXVII of Goldsmith's *Citizen of the World*, a book in the Browning library, where the Chinese philosopher imagines London, the victim of luxury and vice, as a desert of ruins overgrown with weeds. See *PMLA* 61:600–1 (1946).

Since 1855 the text has been amended a very little in word and punctuation; the changes are negligible. In the distribution of 1863 it became one of the *Dramatic Lyrics.*

In November, 1852, the Brownings returned from Paris to Florence, and settled there for the winter. They found there Edward Robert Bulwer-Lytton, the son of the novelist, himself to become a writer under the name of Owen Meredith, and later Earl of Lytton and Viceroy of India. Florence, during the winter of 1852–3, had gone mad on the subject of spiritualism, rapping and table-tipping. Lytton gave much comfort to Mrs. Browning, who was an ardent believer. Browning himself was skeptical and usually, in Mrs. Browning's phrase, "was playing Mephistopheles."

The Emperor referred to in the poem was certainly Napoleon III of France. On January 30, 1853, he married. The Brownings were both immensely interested in the Emperor, partly for his own character and their own political ideals, and partly for the effect his government would have upon the fate of Italy. Mrs. Browning was an admirer and expected much from him; Browning, again, was a skeptic and a scoffer. Though the poem is imaginary and there never was, as far as we know, even a lovers' quarrel in the Browning household, it is interesting that the two main subjects of disagreement in their married lives should have been used for material in this poem.

The poem was probably written soon after January 30, 1853. March is mentioned in the poem as the month in which the speaker is repining, and this may be a true indication of the date of composition.

Evelyn Hope

Evelyn Hope was first published in *Men and Women* and was composed of seven stanzas of eight four-measure lines each. In the distribution of 1863 it was classed with the *Dramatic Lyrics.* Except for the changes in punctuation consistent with Browning's practice, the text has not been altered since 1855.

It is not known when *Evelyn Hope* was written, and I know of no event that might have suggested the poem. Because of the likeness in thought to *Cristina,* I should be inclined to put it among the earliest of the poems written for *Men and Women.* Like the earlier poem it touches upon the doctrine of elective affinities. Possibly it may have been written in London in 1846. The poem is upon the theme that Edgar Allan Poe thought the most poetic in the world, the death of a young and beautiful woman. The ideas concerning the immortality and invincibility of love are peculiarly Browning's, as is also the conception of life after death as a series of worlds through which we progress. Its philosophy of love is perhaps the reason for its place in the popular estimation among the most admired of Browning's poems.

Up at a Villa—Down in the City

Up at a Villa—Down in the City (As Distinguished by an Italian Person of Quality) was first published in *Men and Women*. It was composed of ten sections—64 lines in all—of six-measure dactylic and anapaestic lines. In 1863 the poem was classed under *Dramatic Lyrics*. Since 1855 the text has remained the same, except for a few changes in punctuation.

It is not known precisely when *Up at a Villa* was written. Griffin and Minchin conjecture that it was done at and about Bagni di Lucca in 1853.[16] To me, however, the poem suggests much more definitely the Brownings' residence two miles above Siena in the hills, during September and part of October of 1850. In a letter to her sisters, on September 7 and 8, 1850, Mrs. Browning describes their new residence, which cost little more than eleven shillings a week:

From one window you have a view of Siena, with its Duomo and its campanile, and its Italian colouring over all! From another, you look over the vast sweep of the maremma to the mountains of Rome. From another, the whole country leaps under the sun, alive with verdure and vineyards —very beautiful it is indeed. All we want is water. Then our villa stands in the midst of its own extensive grounds—its own vineyard and olive-ground.[17]

From the villa Browning went down to Siena for newspapers and supplies, and possibly for diversion; for he took as much delight in the city streets as his Italian person of quality. In any case, the scene described in the poem is as thoroughly Tuscan in character as *The Englishman in Italy* is Neapolitan. The substance of the poem is Browning's acute and humorous observation of Italian life.

[16] *Life*, p. 199.
[17] E.B.B., *Letters to her Sister*, p. 128.

A Woman's Last Word

This poem was first published in *Men and Women,* and was composed of ten stanzas of four trochaic lines each. In 1863 it became one of the *Dramatic Lyrics.* The text has suffered changes only in punctuation.

While *A Woman's Last Word* obviously belongs to the Brownings' life in Italy, it is impossible beyond this to say when it was written. It shows a keen perception of the many delicate adjustments which must be made in married life. The poem is dramatic. The speaker is the wife who has been exhausted by argument with her husband, and is ready to make an abject surrender of body and soul, subverting all moral and theological values, in order to protect their intimacy from the hostile world. The poem stresses the idea that love is endangered through man's determination to establish his intellectual superiority.

Fra Lippo Lippi

Fra Lippo Lippi was first published in *Men and Women.* It was composed of 392 lines, all blank verse save the six and one-half *stornelli,* or flower-songs. In the distribution of 1863 the poem retained its place in *Men and Women.* The changes in text since 1855, consisting of a very few verbal changes and the usual changes in punctuation, are negligible.

The poem owes its inception to Florence, where at the Accademia delle belle Arti Browning saw the *Coronation of the Virgin,* the picture described by Lippi in the poem as the one he will have finished in six months. The Pitti and Uffizi Galleries at Florence also had pictures by Lippi. It is most probable that *Fra Lippo Lippi* was one of the "lyrics with more music and painting," which Browning was writing in February, 1853.[18] In a letter of April 13, Mrs. Browning reports her husband as "digging at Vasari." [19] The subject was possibly suggested by Landor's use of Lippi in one of his *Imaginary Conversations, Fra Filippo Lippi and Pope Eugenius the Fourth.*

While visiting the galleries and collecting old pictures in Florence, the Brownings were assiduously reading Vasari's *Le Vite de' Pittori;* the edition they used was published in Florence, 1846–57.

[18] Griffin and Minchin, *Life,* p. 189.
[19] Miller, *Robert Browning,* p. 187.

It was from this account of Lippi, inaccurate and rather highly colored, that Browning drew most of the facts for his poem.[20]

Beyond the bare outline of Lippi's life, Browning got many hints for his poem from Vasari's account, such as the names of Lippi's pictures—St. Jerome doing penance, "which is now in the *guardaroba* of Duke Cosimo," and the many pictures based on the story of John the Baptist, concerning which Vasari speaks in praise of "the address of Herodias, the astonishment of the guests, and the inexpressible sorrow when the head is presented on a charger." Vasari calls attention, too, to Lippi's *Coronation of the Virgin*, with the self-portrait of the painter in the lower corner; but see the comment upon the picture, below. Vasari also supplied the character of Lippi, not only through his actions, but in a few downright comments: "Fra Filippo was very partial to men of cheerful character, and lived for his own part in a very joyous fashion. . . . He lived creditably by his labours, and expended very large sums on the pleasures to which he continued to addict himself, even to the end of his life."

Yet many of Browning's ideas in the poem—particularly Lippi's place in the history of art as the harbinger of the new manner of painters, warm, naturalistic, and full of expression, as contrasted with the old formal religious artists, and his delight in painting the portraits of contemporaries in his work—are barely hinted at in Vasari. Browning was justly suspicious of much of the data which Vasari had given concerning the painter; *e.g.*, the dates of Lippi's birth, which Vasari gave in the first edition as 1402 and changed in the second edition to 1412. To verify his account Browning went to Filippo Baldinucci's *Delle Notizie de' Professori del Disegno da Cimabue.* . . .[21] Writing to Edward Dowden in 1866 about some details of *Fra Lippo Lippi*, Browning says,

I was wide awake when I made Fra Lippo the elder practitioner of Art [than Masaccio; *i.e.*, Hulking Tom], if not, as I believe, the earlier born. I looked into the matter carefully long ago, and long before I thought of my own poem, from my interest in the Brancacci frescoes, indeed in all early Florentine Art. I believe the strange confusions and mistakes of Vasari are set tolerably right now: you may know, he took Lippino the son for Lippo the father. I suppose Lippo to have been born, as Baldinucci says, about 1400.[22]

[20] See *Lives of Seventy of the Most Eminent Painters, Sculptors and Architects,* by Giorgio Vasari, ed. and tr. by Blashfield and Hopkins, N. Y., 1896, II, 62–70.

[21] Published at Florence, 1767–74, in 20 vols. For the account of Lippi see III, 212–20.

[22] *Letters,* ed. Hood, p. 104.

Thus Browning added to Vasari's account Baldinucci's notion that Masaccio was Lippi's pupil; but it is now generally accepted that Masaccio, the painter of the great frescoes in the Brancacci Chapel of the Carmine at Florence, was senior to Lippi and probably his master. Baldinucci comments in his account upon the *Coronation of the Virgin* and Lippi's self-portrait there, and emphasizes much more strongly than does Vasari the notion that Lippi was one of the first painters to break with the formal traditions of ecclesiastical painting which Fra Angelico (1387–1455) and Lorenzo Monaco followed. Browning was quick to catch Baldinucci's hint that Lippi was the first naturalist and realist in painting, selecting by preference contemporary scenes and figures. This was of course Browning's view of his own position in poetry in the nineteenth century.[23] Certainly the artistic creed which Browning ascribes to Fra Lippo Lippi is much more his own than Lippi's, and finds expression in the poet's own person in *Old Pictures in Florence*.

The portrait which has traditionally been thought to be Lippi's self-portrait has been proved to be the portrait of the benefactor, the Very Rev. Francesco Maringhi.[24] The figure is not dressed in Carmelite robes as Lippi would have been, but in the cassock of a secular priest. The Latin phrase, *Iste perfecit opus* (which in the scroll in the picture reads *Is perfecit opus*), is properly translated as "This is the man who caused the structure and whole foundation to be made," and is applicable to the Canon Maringhi who ordered the picture in 1441 for the altar of the church attached to the Benedictine nunnery of Sant' Ambrogio.

Fra Lippo Lippi is one of the happiest expressions of Browning's belief in art and in the joy of living, and therefore it was a most appropriate choice for the poet to make for reading aloud at a memorable literary evening. Tennyson, Dante Gabriel and William Michael Rossetti, and Mr. and Mrs. Browning were all assembled at the Browning residence at 13 Dorset Street, on September 27, 1855.

[23] For a full account of this connection, see DeVane, *Browning's Parleyings,* pp. 170–3, 228–9.

[24] See Montgomery Carmichael, "Fra Lippo Lippi's Portrait," in the *Burlington Magazine* 21:194–200. Katherine B. Nelson in her *Filippino Lippi,* 1930, agrees with Carmichael that the figure is Maringhi (p. 17) and thinks that if the portrait of the painter occurs in the picture it is "the rather disdainful young Carmelite leaning his chin on one hand, in the left foreground of the picture." I am grateful to Mr. Bernard Kottler for drawing this matter to my attention.

Tennyson read *Maud,* while Dante Gabriel Rossetti, unobserved, made a pen-and-ink sketch of the Laureate.[25] Browning then read *Fra Lippo Lippi.* He could not have chosen a better poem with which to challenge the orthodox conception of poetry in mid-nineteenth century, or one that better expresses the new elements in poetry which he was to introduce. Browning found in the Renaissance painter a very sympathetic character; like himself highly individualistic, suffering from the tyranny of artistic convention, and like himself energetic and instinct with seemingly well thought out aesthetic and religious opinions which chimed with Browning's own. The poem has always been accounted one of his most characteristic and successful dramatic monologues.

A Toccata of Galuppi's

A Toccata of Galuppi's was published in *Men and Women.* The poem consisted of fifteen eight-measure triplets, forty-five lines in all. In the distribution of the poems in 1863 it became one of the *Dramatic Lyrics.* Since 1855 the poem has been improved in phraseology in one or two places, and has undergone the usual changes in punctuation.

It is possible that the poem may have been written as early as July, 1847. G. W. Cooke quotes from an account by an American, who may have been G. W. Curtis, which purports to describe the Brownings in 1847:

Mrs. Browning was still too much of an invalid to walk, but she sat under the great trees upon the lawn-like hillsides near the convent, or in the seats of the dusky convent chapel, while Browning at the organ chased a fugue, or dreamed out upon the twilight keys a faint throbbing toccata of Galuppi.[26]

I have not been able to find the source of this description, but it bears signs of having been written after Browning had published *A Toccata of Galuppi's* and *Master Hugues of Saxe-Gotha.* It is possible that it may be an authentic account of the five-day sojourn which the Brownings made in Vallombrosa in July, 1847, accompanied by G. W. Curtis, the American literary man, when Browning sat at the convent organ upon which Milton had played two cen-

[25] See *The Browning Collections* (Sotheby Catalogue, 1913), p. 6.
[26] Cooke, *Guide-Book,* p. 416.

turies earlier, and played "some Gregorian chant, perhaps, or hymn of Pergolesi's." [27] The fact that Curtis was going on to Venice after leaving the Brownings, and pressed Browning for information concerning that city, may well have put in the poet's mind the idea of catching in a poem the spirit of Venice as he felt it in Galuppi's music. In any case, it is certain that *A Toccata of Galuppi's* is one of the "lyrics with more music and painting than before," which Browning referred to in his letter to Milsand on February 24, 1853.[28] This was probably the first poem which Browning devoted entirely to music, though he had frequently written of the effect of music in his early long poems.

The reference in the poem is to no specific piece of music by Baldassare Galuppi (1706–85), the Venetian who made his great fame chiefly as a composer of light operas, of which he is said to have written fifty-four. Some of these were for libretti by Goldoni, whom Browning was to praise in a sonnet in 1883. Galuppi was also a composer of church music and sonatas. Browning had heard Galuppi's music in Venice in 1838,[29] and had in his possession two large manuscript volumes mainly made up of Galuppi's music.[30] The toccata is a "touch-piece," a preliminary flourish or overture, illustrating technique, and was first made an important kind of composition by Bach. Browning uses the music of Galuppi to catch the character of Venice in her decadence and gaiety.

The poem marks an interesting point in the development of Browning's characteristic conceptions of the ephemeral quality, the function and the effect of music. As in *Pauline,* the effect of music upon the poet is to people melody with the figures of ancient men, now dead; its function is to re-create the moods of history in this very manner; but however poignant it is, its life is brief. The motto Browning had learned from the memoir of Claude le Jeune—"In Music, the Beau Ideal changes every thirty years"—remained a major tenet in his belief. These ideas constantly appear in different guises in all Browning's poems upon music, *Master Hugues of Saxe-*

[27] See G. W. Curtis, "Robert Browning in Florence," in *From the Easy Chair,* N. Y., 1892, p. 203.

[28] Griffin and Minchin, *Life,* p. 189.

[29] See Miller, *Robert Browning,* p. 71.

[30] See the letter of Browning's quoted in Herbert E. Greene, "Browning's Knowledge of Music," in *PMLA* 62:1099 (1947). In this article see also a professional musician's (Charles Villiers Stanford's) comment on the poet's superficial knowledge of music, as well as Browning's own account of his musical training.

Gotha, Abt Vogler, Flute-Music With an Accompaniment, and above all in the *Parleying With Charles Avison.*[31]

In recent years a considerable amount of discussion has taken place [32] concerning Browning's intentions in the poem. Does he mean to condemn Galuppi's music? Or is Galuppi ironical or mocking in what his music says to the untravelled and unsophisticated speaker of the poem? It seems clear to me that Browning intends the speaker to be the kind of person who expects Venice to be the very symbol of romance, made up of canals, doges, gaiety, and love—in short, just such a place as Browning had pictured in *In a Gondola.* Instead, Galuppi's music is disconcerting to the speaker. It is cold, intellectual, and even taunting, and almost persuades him that he with all his learning will die just as surely as the light people of the Venetian past have died. Browning is not the speaker any more than he is Galuppi's music, but his sympathies incline toward the unsophisticated Englishman.

By the Fire-Side

By the Fire-Side was published in *Men and Women.* It was composed of fifty-three stanzas of five lines each. In 1863 the poem became one of the *Dramatic Lyrics.* Since 1855 a few changes in wording have been made, chiefly for the sake of smoothness, and the usual changes in punctuation. In stanza 51, line 1, "hour's feat" has now become "moment's feat."

It is obvious that *By the Fire-Side* is a personal poem and not dramatic in the sense in which Browning's poems usually are. It is not literally autobiographical, for the event which Browning describes in the poem had taken place at 50 Wimpole Street in London in 1845. The scene of the poem has been identified as the ruined chapel which stands beside the mountain path to Prato Fiorito, to which the Brownings had made an expedition in the company of

[31] An extended discussion of Browning and music is given in DeVane, *Browning's Parleyings,* Ch. 7. See also the two articles by Friedrich Bitzkat in *Englische Studien,* "Robert Browning's A Toccata of Galuppi's" 57:196–212 (1923), an analysis and interpretation of the poem; and "Zur Psychologie von Robert Brownings A Toccata of Galuppi's" 59:316–9 (1925). An excellent small study is to be found in Paul de Reul, *L'Art et la pensée de Robert Browning,* Brussels, 1929, pp. 214–24.

[32] See in the *Explicator:* W. D. Templeman, II, Item 25 (February, 1944); F. A. Pottle, *ibid.;* R. P. Basler, II, Item 60 (June, 1944); Arthur Dickson, III, Item 15 (November, 1944); E. H. Duncan, V, Item 5 (October, 1946).

the American artist, W. W. Story, in September, 1853. On October 5 Mrs. Browning wrote from the house which they had taken that summer near Bagni di Lucca, "I have been donkey-riding, and so has Wiedeman [her son]. I even went (to prove to you how well I am) the great excursion to Prato Fiorito, six miles there and six miles back, perpendicularly up and down." [33] Story gives a colorful account of this expedition and identifies the chapel for us: "After climbing an hour we arrived at a little old church near which the view was magnificent." [34] Possibly soon after this event, while the Brownings were still near Bagni di Lucca, but more likely in November when they were by their own fireside in Florence, the poem was written.

The view expressed above concerning the place of the event recounted in the poem and the date of its writing has recently been challenged. In an article entitled "The Central Episode of Browning's *By the Fire-Side*," [35] Jean Stirling Lindsay contends that the poem was written in 1847 when the Brownings were planning a summer tour to the region of the Lake of Orta in Piedmont. Browning's use of the name of Pella, a village near that lake, seems to confirm her, as does the use of the word "Alp." The Brownings never went to the region, but Murray's *Handbook for Travellers in Switzerland, Savoy and Piedmont* described the Lake of Orta, and we know that the Brownings used the book. The author of the article also argues, less cogently I think, that the union of the Brownings was not confirmed until their days of perfect intimacy in Florence. But in spite of Browning's confusing employment of "Pella" and the "Alpine gorge," W. W. Story's identification of the scene and the little chapel and the circumstantial accounts of the expedition persuade me that the scene was Prato Fiorito and the year 1853.

By the Fire-Side has always been precious to enthusiastic lovers of the Brownings, for here and in *One Word More* the poet speaks more intimately than anywhere else of himself and his wife. The portrait of "My perfect wife, my Leonor," a name taken from the devoted wife in Beethoven's opera *Fidelio*, is of course of Mrs. Browning, and the fire-side is that of Casa Guidi in Florence. The poem, a perfect illustration of Browning's belief in the "good minute," should be

[33] *Letters of E.B.B.*, ed. Kenyon, II, 142.
[34] Henry James, *William Wetmore Story and his Friends*, I, 273.
[35] *Studies in Philology* 39:571–9 (1942). See also the account of the expedition in *Letters from Owen Meredith*, ed. A. B. and G. L. Harlan, Jr., 1936, p. 46.

read with *Two in the Campagna,* where the good minute goes and the lovers fail to attain the perfect understanding which is the achievement in *By the Fire-Side.*

Any Wife to Any Husband

Any Wife to Any Husband was published in *Men and Women.* It consisted of twenty-one stanzas of six pentameter lines each. In 1863 it became one of the *Dramatic Lyrics.* Perhaps for contrast, or to point the irony of the poem, it has always just followed *By the Fire-Side.* Since 1855 the text has undergone little change.

The poem, again in contrast to *By the Fire-Side,* is entirely dramatic. It is, however, assuredly of the Italian period of Browning's life, and shows him musing, as he does very frequently in *Men and Women,* upon the nature of love in the two sexes. Beyond this, it is impossible to say exactly when the poem was written. The poem is in part, in its analysis of the man's attitude, an unconscious prophecy of Browning's state of mind during his affair with Lady Ashburton.[36] It may also reflect Browning's dismay at the unaccountable conduct of his father, who three years after his wife's death got himself involved in a breach of promise suit; he went into exile in Paris in 1852 rather than pay the large damages.[37]

An Epistle . . . of Karshish

An Epistle containing the Strange Medical Experience of Karshish, the Arab Physician, was first published in *Men and Women.* It contained 312 lines of blank verse. It has always remained in the group of *Men and Women.* Since 1855 the text has been altered in a few places verbally for the sake of smoothness and clarity, and the usual revision of punctuation has taken place.

Karshish grew naturally out of Browning's cogitations and studies for *Christmas-Eve and Easter-Day* of 1850. In that work Browning had made his confession of faith and had shown that though the intelligence and strength of God were abundantly illustrated in the world, the love of God for mankind was only properly exhibited by the coming of Christ. *Karshish* is an imaginative attempt, like *Cleon,*

[36] See DeVane, *Browning's Parleyings,* pp. 90–1; and *Letters,* ed. Hood, *Appendix I.*
[37] See Miller, *Robert Browning,* pp. 180–1.

Saul, A Death in the Desert, and *Imperante Augusto Natus Est*—to name only a few poems—to show to men the significance of that most important event in history. In *Easter-Day,* also, Browning had concluded that doubt was a condition of spiritual health: this is the informing idea of *Karshish,* for the poem is mainly concerned with the case of Lazarus who has been dead and is now alive, and who has therefore experienced the hereafter and is not subject to doubt. These two ideas are the cardinal tenets in Browning's religious and moral thinking.

It is probable, I think, that *Karshish* was begun in Rome late in 1853 or early in 1854, and completed in Florence during the following summer. Possibly a view of some of the relics of the Emperor Vespasian who invaded Palestine in 66 A. D., the year of Karshish's supposed letter to Abib, may have suggested the subject to Browning. Possibly, also, the epidemic of gastric fever which the Brownings encountered at Rome upon their arrival in December, 1853, and which had caused the death of the small son of their friends the Storys, suggested the medical aspects of the poem. It is likely that *Karshish* was completed by June 11, 1854, when Browning wrote to Story that he was trying to make up for time wasted in Rome by setting his poetical house in order.

Both Karshish and Abib are imaginary characters. The word "Karshish" in Arabic means "the picker-up of learning's crumbs." [38] The source of Browning's subject-matter in the poem is the *Gospel of St. John,* 11:1–44, the gospel of which Browning was especially fond, and which he defended from the findings of the higher criticism in *A Death in the Desert.*[39] Browning used poetic license in making Lazarus a man of fifty years in 66 A. D., for it must have been at least thirty-three years earlier that he had been raised from the dead, and that would have made him a boy of sixteen or seventeen at the time. To Karshish Lazarus seems a man of fifty, though of course he may have seemed a younger man than he actually was because he had been preserved from the petty worries of our world.

Karshish has always been held in great esteem, both for its art and its matter. Part of the beauty of the poem lies in the fact that it

[38] Maureen Wright in the *Times Literary Supplement* for May 1, 1953.

[39] The interesting suggestion is made by R. D. Havens in his article, "Blake and Browning," in *MLN* 41:464–6, that Browning's Lazarus, after he had risen from the dead, is a good deal like the description of the poet William Blake in Crabb Robinson's *Diaries,* under the date of February 23, 1852. Robinson met the Brownings, with whom he had much pleasant talk, in October of 1852.

contains no argument. Rather, the poet is here presenting the mind and feeling of a character in a particular time and circumstance; and he increases our awareness of life by transmitting the awe of Karshish in his stupendous speculation about man's destiny.[40] The figure of the physician as well as that of Lazarus has been well conceived. The open-mindedness of the scientist contrasts well with the arrogant and closed mind of Cleon, the Greek philosopher and poet, in Browning's poem *Cleon*, where the subject is again the impression made on a contemporary by Christ's coming to earth. Browning rated *Karshish* highly among his poems, and it is therefore strange that in *One Word More*, in naming some of the characters he had created in the volume, he should have substituted the name "Karshook" for "Karshish" in the first edition. This error was subsequently corrected. The lines called *Ben Karshook's Wisdom*, dated from Rome on April 27, 1854, were not in *Men and Women*, but first appeared in *The Keepsake*, an annual, for 1856; the poem was never collected by Browning, but has been included in a number of editions since his death.

Mesmerism

Mesmerism was published in *Men and Women* and consisted of twenty-seven stanzas of five lines each. In 1863 it was classed under *Dramatic Romances*. Since 1855 the text has suffered a few verbal revisions, and the usual changes in punctuation.

There is nothing to indicate the date of composition of this poem. Mesmerism was in its hey-day in 1844–5, and Elizabeth Barrett was, and continued to be, a believer. Towards 1852 mesmerism, which had steadily held the interest of people, was displaced by spiritualism. Browning became gradually a more and more violent disbeliever in supernatural manifestations. In November, 1852, the Brownings made a new friend in young Lytton, son of Bulwer-Lytton, who was "inclined to various sorts of spiritualism, and given to the magic arts." Because of the kinship of *Mesmerism* to *A Lovers' Quarrel* (*q.v.*) in meter and in matter, I am inclined to date the composition of *Mesmerism* in March, 1853. Lytton visited the Brownings at Bagni di Lucca late in September, 1853, and it is possible that the poem

[40] See H. B. Charlton's excellent comment upon *Karshish* in his essay "Browning as Poet of Religion," in *Bulletin of the John Rylands Library* 27:271–306 (1942–3). But see also Hoxie N. Fairchild's objection to the "give-away" at the end of the poem in "Browning, the Simple-hearted Casuist," in *University of Toronto Quarterly* 18:234–40 (1949), especially p. 237.

was written then. It bears some relation to *By the Fire-Side* (stanzas 24, 28, etc.), where Browning is willing to believe, if not in mesmerism, at least in the intuitive knowledge of each other's minds which is given to lovers. *Mesmerism* expresses Browning's belief in the sacredness of the individual soul; he feels that it must not be invaded.

A Serenade at the Villa

A Serenade at the Villa was first published in *Men and Women*. In the distribution of 1863 it became one of the *Dramatic Lyrics*. It consisted of twelve stanzas of five lines each. Since 1855 the changes in the text have been negligible—one or two verbal changes and the usual ones in punctuation.

The poem obviously describes the garden of an Italian villa, on a hot, close, southern night before a storm. The landscape suggests that the country is that of Bagni di Lucca, where the Brownings spent the summers of 1849 and 1853. Beyond this, there is no evidence to indicate the date of composition. The poem is a favorite with some because of its perfect blending of scenery and mood. Like *The Last Ride Together* and *One Way of Love*, the poem exhibits Browning's rejected lover in a characteristic mood.

In spite of recent attempts to interpret Browning's meaning in the poem,[41] the statement above seems to me essentially correct. In the light of this discussion I should modify the word "characteristic" somewhat to add that the lover in the *Serenade* is treated more humorously and less sympathetically by the poet than is usually the case. This lover perhaps more consciously blinds himself with hope than most of Browning's rejected lovers. Arthur Dickson points out that Browning uses a favorite device in the poem; that is, a pair of imagined speeches by the lover and the lady contrasting with each other.

My Star

My Star was first published in *Men and Women*. It consisted of thirteen anapaestic lines, eight of two-measure, and five of five-measure. The text has remained unchanged. In 1863 it was grouped

[41] In the *Explicator* see the following: T. O. Mabbott, VIII, Q. 6 (December, 1949); Walter Gierasch, VIII, Item 37 (March, 1940); Arthur Dickson, IX, Item 57 (June, 1951).

with the *Dramatic Lyrics.* The date of its composition is unknown, but it probably belongs to Italy and Browning's married life. The tradition is that the poem was written to Elizabeth Barrett Browning; and Browning's use of the figure of the star is comparable to his use of the moon in many places in his poetry, notably in *One Word More,* in *Men and Women.* It has been suggested, however—I believe mistakenly—that Browning is referring in *My Star* to his own peculiar poetic genius, and his gift for seeing in events and things a significance hidden from other men.[42]

Browning placed this poem at the beginning of the volume of selections he made from his own work in 1872; and it was his custom, when admirers asked for his autograph, to write out this poem.

Instans Tyrannus

Instans Tyrannus was published in *Men and Women.* It consisted of seven sections of anapaestic verse rhyming in couplets, seventy-two lines in all. In 1863 it became one of the *Dramatic Romances.* The text has undergone one or two verbal changes and the usual changes in punctuation.

Sir Frederic Kenyon suggests that the poem may have been composed earlier than the Italian period, for the reason that in the final distribution it is put, with *Mesmerism,* in the midst of poems dating from 1845. It is possible, however, that the poem may have been composed at Rome in the winter of 1853–4. The title was suggested by the first three lines of Horace's third *Ode* of the third book of *Odes.* Horace's poem is in honor of Romulus, and Browning may have seen it as an inscription in Rome; this is, however, mere conjecture. The *Ode* reads:

> Justem et Tenacem proposti virum,
> Non civium ardor prava jubentium,
>   Non vultus instantis tyranni . . .

[Not the heat of the people pressing to harmful measures, not the aspect of a threatening tyrant, can shake from his settled purpose the man who is just . . .]

The idea of Browning's poem is a variation on the chivalric theme that "God will have a stroke in every battle."

[42] But see C. Willard Smith's *Browning's Star-Imagery,* pp. 151–2. See also for a different implication. Miller, *Robert Browning,* p. 92.

A Pretty Woman

A Pretty Woman was first published in *Men and Women*. It was composed of eighteen stanzas of four lines each. In 1863 the poem was grouped with *Dramatic Lyrics*. The changes in text since 1855 have been very few, chiefly in punctuation.

The poem has been called a mere metrical experiment; it seems to me something more than that. The model for the poem, I think, may have been Gerardine Bate, niece of Mrs. Anna Jameson; the two ladies visited the Brownings in Florence late in April, 1847. Mrs. Browning writes an account of Browning's impatience with the beautiful but shallow young lady:

> Mrs. Jameson was like a fond mother—(Geddie at least ought to love her) and Robert took the liberty so often of telling her what he took to be the truth in a very blunt fashion, and also what "he should do if he had the misfortune of having a wife like Gerardine" (which was not by any means an agreeable form of sympathy to Mrs. Jameson, though it gave Robert an occasion of showing a wonderful quantity of ferocity and savage determination) that I was half nervous with the discussion. Poor Mrs. Jameson used, then, to turn round into abrupt comments on her charming qualities, and observe how *three men out of every five would be in love with her forthwith.*
>
> "Oh, not *you*, Browning, of course! I am aware that under no possible circumstances, she could have been calculated to please *you*—I only speak of ordinary men . . ."
>
> And it *was* rather absurd to be sure, seeing that Gerardine is just pretty and no more at most. . . .[43]

If the poem was, as I think, inspired by this lady, it was probably written in 1847. It should be added that the young lady had her revenge for, inspired by the domestic happiness of the Brownings, she fell in love with a poor artist in Rome, married him in 1849, and lived contentedly thereafter.

"Childe Roland to the Dark Tower Came"

"Childe Roland to the Dark Tower Came" (*See Edgar's Song in "Lear"*) first appeared in *Men and Women*. It was composed of thirty-four stanzas of six iambic pentameter lines each. In 1863 the poem was put among the *Dramatic Romances*. Since 1855 several

[43] *E.B.B., Letters to her Sister,* pp. 62–3.

words in the text have been changed, and there have been a few changes in punctuation.

Childe Roland, according to Browning himself, was written on January 2, 1852, in Paris. *Women and Roses* was written the day before, and *Love Among the Ruins* the day after, in fulfilment of a New Year's resolution to write a poem a day. Under these conditions, it is evident, Browning called upon his deepest resources, for the three poems thus written represent a vivid dream, a fantasy that might almost be called a nightmare, and possibly reminiscence. When Browning was asked by a stranger in 1887 if he agreed with an allegorical analysis which had been made of *Childe Roland,* he said,

Oh, no, not at all. Understand, I don't repudiate it, either. I only mean I was conscious of no allegorical intention in writing it. 'T was like this: one year in Florence, I had been very lazy; I resolved that I would write something every day. Well, the first day I wrote about some roses, suggested by a magnificent basket that some one had sent my wife. The next day Childe Roland came upon me as a kind of dream. I had to write it, then and there, and I finished it the same day, I believe. But it was simply that I had to do it. I did not know then what I meant beyond that, and I'm sure I don't know now. But I am very fond of it.[44]

Except that Browning was in Paris at the time of writing *Childe Roland,* and that probably more poems were written at that time than Browning mentions, this statement does not need further elaboration.

Many times in his later days Browning denied that *Childe Roland* had any source other than the line in *King Lear,* uttered by Edgar, which gives the poem its title; and Browning had recently been reading Shakespeare afresh for the essay upon Shelley. In a letter to A. W. Hunt, a painter who had done a watercolor of the scene in *Childe Roland* in 1866, Browning wrote: "My own 'marsh' was only made out of my head,—with some recollection of a strange solitary little tower I have come upon more than once in Massa-Carrara, in the midst of low hills . . . ," and he told Mrs. Orr that the blind old horse of the poem had been suggested by a figure in a tapestry of his own.[45] Scholars have justly been dissatisfied with Browning's as-

[44] See Lilian Whiting, *The Brownings,* Boston, 1917, p. 261. See also Orr, *Life,* p. 362, and Griffin and Minchin, *Life,* p. 189. But see also Mr. Johnstone Parr's objections to the accepted dating for these three poems, in "The Date of Composition of Browning's *Love Among the Ruins,*" in *Philological Quarterly* 32:443–6 (October, 1953).

[45] *New Letters,* ed. DeVane and Knickerbocker, pp. 172–3, and Orr, *Handbook,* p. 274.

sertion, and have ransacked literature for parallels to the poet's thought and imagery—anything which Browning might have used, unconsciously, as a source.[46] By far the best of these searches is the article by Mr. Harold Golder in 1924,[47] which surveys the literature of fairyland, such as *Jack and the Beanstalk, Jack the Giant-Killer, Hop-o'-my-Thumb* and *The Seven Champions of Christendom,* in order to see what Browning might have unconsciously drawn upon. In an article in 1925 I described the book which I think provided Browning at an early age with his conception of the beautiful and the horrible in landscape, and became so much a part of his intellectual equipment that he forgot what it had done for him. This was Gerard de Lairesse's *The Art of Painting in All its Branches,* translated from the Dutch by J. F. Fritsch in 1778. Browning wrote in his copy of this work,

I read this book more often and with greater delight, when I was a child, than any other; and still remember the main of it most gratefully for the good I seem to have got from the prints and wonderful text. Robert Browning, Feb. 13, '74.[48]

And again when he was summing up the major influences upon his life in the *Parleyings,* Browning included Lairesse,

. . . moved
To pay due homage to the man I loved
Because of that prodigious book he wrote
On Artistry's Ideal.

[46] See, for example, Irene Hardy, "Browning's *Childe Roland*—A Literary Parallel," in *Poet Lore* 24:53–8; M. Sears Brooks, "*Childe Roland* and its Danish Source," in *Poet Lore* 4:425–8; T. W. Higginson, "*Childe Roland* and Heine's *Die Schwabenspiegel,*" in *Poet Lore* 13:262–8; and T. P. Savin, "*Childe Roland* and Tennyson's *Vision of Sin,*" in *Poet Lore* 9:256–65. The latest of these is Lionel Stevenson's suggestion that Browning had in mind Malory's *Tale of Gareth of Orkney,* in which the knight reaches the castle of the Red Knight of the Red Laundes. But this carries conviction only so far as the notion that Browning had the generic idea of the quest in mind. See "The Pertinacious Victorian Poets," in *University of Toronto Quarterly* 21:239–40.

[47] "Browning's *Childe Roland,*" in *PMLA* 39:963–78. Mr. Robert Liddell Lowe has shown that in stanzas 5 and 6 of *Childe Roland* Browning has borrowed the idea and imagery of the dying man from John Donne's *A Valediction Forbidding Mourning.* Browning knew much of Donne's poetry by heart. See *Notes and Queries* 198:491 (November, 1953).

[48] See *The Browning Collections* (Sotheby Catalogue, 1913), p. 107. See also my article, "The Landscape of Browning's *Childe Roland,*" in *PMLA* 40:426–32 (1925). Griffin and Minchin first commented upon the general influence of Lairesse on Browning; see *Life,* pp. 9–10.

Lairesse's Chapter 17, *Of Things Deformed and Broken, Falsely called Painter-like,* consists of a walk which Lairesse imagines himself to have taken in order to instruct his pupils in what the pseudo-classical school of painters, of which he is a member, would find to be horrible in painting. Here the old cripple, the pathless field, the desperate vegetation, the spiteful little river, the killing of the water-rat, the enclosing mountains, the leering sunset, and many other details of *Childe Roland* are to be found. The "walk" is remarkably like the poem, though of course Lairesse's prosaic manner fails to arouse the sense of fear and horror which Browning's imagination achieves in the poem. Probably Lairesse's material had become so familiar to Browning that he did not think of Lairesse as a source for *Childe Roland;* Lairesse had, however, shaped his imagination and stocked his mind with certain conceptions of what was horrible in landscape. It is an interesting fact that Mr. Thornton Wilder, purposely relying only on his memory of Browning's poem and not aware of the source of Browning's landscape, should have written as a stage direction for his own play, *Childe Roland to the Dark Tower Came* (in *The Angel That Troubled the Waters, and Other Plays*): *"The sun has set over the great marsh, leaving a yellow-brown Flemish light upon the scene."* It may be interjected here that there is no such instrument as a slug-horn. Browning adopted the word from Chatterton, who misunderstood the word "slogan," a battle-cry.

Because of the nature of the poem it became a favorite exercise of the Browning Societies to attempt its explanation. That Browning's conscious intention was not allegorical, we know: the poem came upon him "as a kind of dream." He told Mrs. Bloomfield-Moore that the poem was "only a fantasy," and when a friend, J. W. Chadwick, asked the poet if the meaning could be expressed in the phrase, "He that endureth to the end shall be saved," Browning replied, "Yes, just about that." [49] But poets often write better than they know, and many people have attempted to fasten an allegorical meaning to *Childe Roland.* The usual interpretations of the ending of the poem may be seen, admirably summarized, in Professor W. L. Phelps's *Browning.*[50] Writing in a dream Browning expressed the innermost

[49] See *The Christian Register* for January 19, 1888; see also *Lippincott's Magazine* 45:683–91.

[50] Ed. 1932, pp. 232–7. For some of the elaborate allegories worked out of *Childe Roland* see the essay upon the poem in T. J. Nettleship's *Essays and Thoughts,* 1908; *The Critic* 5:201, 231, 246; and *Browning Society's Papers,* I, 21*–7*.

pattern of his mind, and Childe Roland pushing resolutely and courageously toward an unknown goal resembles many of Browning's poems in different degrees—*The Lost Leader, How They brought the Good News, Prospice,* and the *Epilogue* to *Asolando,* to name the most notable. Two recent commentators have seen in the nightmare which produced *Childe Roland* a profound sense of guilt in Browning,[51] but they differ concerning what he is guilty of: one sees "the macabre and brutal imagery" of the poem as the obverse side of the poet's humanity; the other sees the guilt as rising from Browning's failure "to deliver to mankind the full burden of the message with which he has been entrusted." *Childe Roland* is one of the most imaginative and noble of Browning's poems, and has taken its place among the great expressions of courage in English literature.

Respectability

Respectability was first published in *Men and Women.* It was composed of three stanzas of eight iambic lines each. In 1863 the poem became one of the *Dramatic Lyrics.* Since 1855 the text has undergone only a few changes in punctuation.

The poem probably owes its composition to the Brownings' presence in Paris in February, 1852, when on February 5, François Guizot (1787–1874), the statesman and historian, delivered the *discours de reception* to Charles Montalembert (1810–1870) upon the latter's election to the Academie Française, a branch of the Institut de France. Convention compelled Guizot to receive Montalembert, though there was a bitter enmity between the men, for Guizot was a constitutional royalist and Montalembert a liberal. The matter of the poem is the contrast between hate, conventionalized into pretty speeches inside the Academy, and unconventional love outside. The device had been used before in *In a Gondola.* As in *The Statue and the Bust* Browning here flouts the usual social conventions.

Professor Hiram Corson suggested that the unconventional lovers in *Respectability* were George Sand, the French novelist and playwright, and Jules Sandeau, with whom she lived after leaving her husband, M. Dudevant.[52] In support of this suggestion, one can say that George Sand was in Paris in 1852 when the Brownings were

---

[51] See J. M. Cohen, "The Young Robert Browning," in *Cornhill Magazine* 163:245–7; and Miller, *Robert Browning,* p. 180.
[52] H. Corson, *An Introduction to Browning,* p. 110.

there, and that they called upon her on several occasions.[53] Mrs. Browning was George Sand's enthusiastic admirer, but Browning did not care for her. Mrs. Browning described the society around George Sand as a "society of ragged Red diluted with the lower theatrical." In any case, Browning's poem has a more universal application than is implicit in the local situation.

A Light Woman

A Light Woman was published first in Men and Women. It consisted of fourteen stanzas of four lines each. In 1863 it became one of the Dramatic Romances. Since 1855 a very few verbal changes have been made in the text of the poem.

There is no evidence to fix the date of composition. The chief point of interest in the poem is the idea which concludes it,

> And, Robert Browning, you writer of plays,
> Here's a subject made to your hand.

Browning's last plays (Luria and A Soul's Tragedy) had been published in 1846; but he had written In a Balcony in 1853, and it is possible that this poem may have given him leave to think himself still a writer of plays. A Light Woman exhibits Browning's delight in a hard, bitter, intricate situation.

The Statue and the Bust

The Statute and the Bust was first published in Men and Women on November 17, 1855.[54] The poem consisted of 250 lines in terza rima, arranged in stanzas of three lines each, except the last, which has four. In 1863 the poem was put among the Dramatic Romances. Since 1855 a few changes in word and punctuation have been made in the text.

It is not possible to say precisely when the poem was written, but the places described in the poem and the legend therein recounted were known to Browning soon after his arrival in Florence in April, 1847. The poet deals in his own manner with the tale that "the towns-

---

[53] Letters of E.B.B., ed. Kenyon, II, 50, 51, 55–7, 59, 60, 63, 66.

[54] The pamphlet form of the poem which purported to have been published by Moxon in the summer of 1855 as a trial publication is now condemned by John Carter and Graham Pollard, in their Enquiry into the Nature of Certain Nineteenth Century Pamphlets, London, 1934, pp. 179–80, as a forgery.

men tell." Giovanni da Bologna (John of Douay, 1525–1608) did make the equestrian statue of Ferdinand di Medici (1549–1608), the third of the Medici to assume the title of Grand-Duke, and set it up in the Annunziata Piazza in Florence so that it looked towards the eastern window of the palace of the Riccardi. The legend does not give Browning warrant for the bust of the lady, though there is an empty shrine under the window, and artistic balance demanded the bust. The last of the great della Robbias who might have been commissioned to make the bust had died in 1566, some years before the events of the story happened, though della Robbia ware continued to be made.

Caution should be taken not to confuse the two palaces mentioned in *The Statute and the Bust.* The palace of line 1 was originally built by the Medici family, but was owned by the Riccardi at the time of the story, and it was here that the lady was imprisoned. This palace is now known as the Palazzo Antinori. The palace of the Grand-Duke (ll. 33–4), which casts a shadow over the Via Larga (now Via Cavour), was built by Cosimo di Medici in 1430. In 1659 it came into the hands of the Riccardi and is now generally known as the Palazzo Riccardi. It does not figure in the poem save as the scene of the feast which the Grand-Duke gave for the bride and groom. Browning makes the shadow which this huge palace casts, the symbol of the crime which Cosimo and his "cursed son," Piero the Gouty, committed in beguiling Florence of her freedom. The house of the Medici dominated Florence for three centuries after Cosimo's recall in 1434. His son Piero only kept authority for five years, and it is possible that Browning was thinking of Lorenzo the Magnificent, the next of the Medici to rule. Ferdinand, the Medici of the poem, assumed the title of Grand-Duke in 1587.

The moral of *The Statute and the Bust,* as one can see at a glance, is Browning's own; the doctrine of individualism there pronounced is peculiarly his. The poem should be contrasted with Tennyson's *Locksley Hall* (1842), a poem which Browning admired greatly; Tennyson's moral is that "the individual withers and the world is more and more"; that is, the social ideal is set up against the individual.

Concerning the interpretation of the line, "When your table's a hat, and your prize, a dram," a lively discussion was conducted in June, 1945, in the *Explicator* (III, Item 62) by R. P. Basler, Dudley Fitts, and DeLancey Ferguson. Browning means by the imagery to suggest a cheap, improvised game, played for a trifle. Such a game is as good an indication of character as a high action and Browning advises that if one enters such a questionable game one should play it just as earnestly as if great stakes were involved. The Duke and the Lady show that they lacked the qualities needed to win any sort of game. The poem is one of Browning's most provocative analyses of failure.

The poem, as might be expected, became the subject of controversy, and the obtuseness of some readers drew from Browning the following letter to Mr. T. J. Wise on January 8, 1877:

> I have seldom met with such a strange inability to understand what seems the plainest matter possible: "ball-goers" are probably not history-readers, but any Guide-book would confirm what is sufficiently stated in the poem. I will append a note or two, however. . . . 1. "This story the townsmen tell:" "when, how, and where," constitutes the subject of the poem. 2. The lady was the wife of the Riccardi, and the Duke—Ferdinand —just as the poem says. 3. As it was built by, and inhabited by the Medici till sold, long after, to the Riccardi,—it was not from the Duke's Palace, but a window in that of the Riccardi, that the lady gazed at her lover riding by. The statue is still in its place, looking at the window under which "now is the empty shrine." Can anything be clearer? My "vagueness" leaves *what* to be "gathered" when all these things are put down in black and white? Oh, "ball-goers"! [55]

It is interesting to recall, as a commentary on the ethics promulgated in the poem, that Browning was fond of saying to his wife that it would have been wrong if they—the Brownings—had not married. Mrs. Miller suggests that Browning may have had in mind the love affair of John Stuart Mill and Mrs. Harriet Taylor—which Browning certainly knew about—which lingered for twenty years before they were married. [56]

Love in a Life

Love in a Life first appeared in *Men and Women*. It consisted of two stanzas of eight lines each. In 1863 it was placed with the *Dramatic Lyrics*. Since 1855 the text has not been changed. There is no evidence to indicate the date of composition; it may have been written at any time in the years 1846–55. The poem and its com-

---

[55] *Letters*, ed. Hood, p. 260.
[56] *Robert Browning*, p. 52. See also p. 132, where it is suggested that Browning and Elizabeth Barrett narrowly escaped such a fate.

panion-piece are products, I think, of Browning's married life in Italy. They are imaginative rather than strictly biographical, and depict love frustrated, as do *A Serenade at the Villa* and *Two in the Campagna.* The figure of "room after room" is a favorite of Browning's; see the *Parleying With Christopher Smart.*

Life in a Love

Life in a Love is the companion-piece of *Love in a Life,* and the statements made for the one hold true for this, except that here we have twenty-two lines, without stanzas, and that since 1855 one or two small changes in punctuation have been made.

How it Strikes a Contemporary

How it Strikes a Contemporary was first published in *Men and Women.* It consisted of 115 lines of blank verse, divided into five unequal sections. In the distribution of 1863 it remained one of *Men and Women.* Since 1855 the text has been changed verbally a very little, and the usual changes in punctuation have taken place. One change may be significant. In the first edition all the pronouns referring to "Our Lord the King," for whom the poet labors, are capitalized, as if the poet meant the reference to be to the Deity. In the later editions of his works it was Browning's habit not to use capitals unless they were necessary, and I think that in this case he decided to make the allegorical meaning less obvious. The title of the poem was suggested to Browning, I think, by a story of Jane Taylor's (1783–1824), *How it Strikes a Stranger,* which he had read as a boy. This story was published as Chapter XVI in her volume, *The Contributions of Q.Q. to a Periodical Work.* Browning used the substance of Miss Taylor's story for his poem, *Rephan,* in the *Asolando* volume. Recently Mrs. Miller has shown that the French book which Browning "did" in 1835 for his French master, M. Loradoux, "Professeur de Langues, Walworth," was Lesage's *Le Gil Blas de la Jeunesse;* and in the chapter called "Histoire de dona Mencia de Mesquera" there is the "corrégidor de Valladolid" whose housekeeper is named Jacinte. This echoed in Browning's mind when he was writing *How it Strikes a Contemporary.*[57]

In my opinion *How it Strikes a Contemporary* grew out of Brown-

[57] Miller, *Robert Browning,* p. 22.

ing's cogitations upon the nature of the poet—a subject he had been concerned with in his *Introductory Essay* to twenty-five. *Letters of Percy Bysshe Shelley* for Moxon, the printer, in the later part of 1851. Browning had finished his essay by December 1, 1851, and sent it to Moxon soon after. The volume was published in 1852, but was soon withdrawn because the letters proved to be spurious. In his essay Browning had debated at length the nature of the poet—putting Shelley on one side as representative of the lyric poets, and Shakespeare on the other as representative of the dramatic. There Browning had said, "The whole poet's function [is that] of beholding with an understanding keenness the universe, nature, and man, in their actual state of perfection in imperfection. . . ." Browning must have remembered too Shelley's own comment upon the position of the poet in his *Defence of Poetry,* that "poets are the unacknowledged legislators of mankind."

But I think that Browning's favorite play, Shakespeare's *Lear,* supplied the suggestion for the poem. It was in Browning's mind, we know, on January 2, when he wrote *Childe Roland.* These lines from Act V, Scene iii, when Lear, captured with Cordelia and not realizing his great danger, looks forward to a life in prison with her, are the real germ of *How it Strikes a Contemporary:*

> So we'll live,
> And pray, and sing, and tell old tales, and laugh
> At gilded butterflies, and hear poor rogues
> Talk of court news; and we'll talk with them too,
> Who loses and who wins; who's in, who's out;
> And take upon 's the mystery of things
> As if we were God's spies. . . .

This idea of observing men and women as if one were in the service of God is expressed clearly in a letter from Browning to John Ruskin, written from Paris on December 10, 1855, in defence of his own poetry,

It [poetry] is all teaching, on the contrary, and the people hate to be taught. They say otherwise,—make foolish fables about Orpheus enchanting stocks and stones, poets standing up and being worshiped,—all nonsense and impossible dreaming. A poet's affair is with God, to whom he is accountable, and of whom is his reward. . . .[58]

This conception of his art was held steadily by Browning, and so offers little clue to the date of the writing of the poem. It was written,

[58] W. G. Collingwood, *Life and Work of John Ruskin,* 1893, p. 234.

I think, late in December, 1851, or very early in 1852, when the Brownings were in Paris.

How it Strikes a Contemporary is interesting as well for its own sake as for its commentary on Browning's idea of the function of the poet. It should be read with three related poems in *Men and Women* —"*Transcendentalism*," *Memorabilia*, and *Popularity*.[59] The poem has been taken to be an excellent description of the tremendous interest in human affairs, with perhaps a similar conscientious purpose, that Browning himself possessed. The poet's conception of the method and the responsibilities of his art are not unlike those of Fra Lippo Lippi upon the art of painting: the artist is not only the lover and observer of life, but God's "recording chief-inquisitor." As one reads the poem one can hardly escape the mental image of Browning himself wandering about Florence, "An old dog, bald and blindish, at his heels." The dog, of course, would be Mrs. Browning's Flush.

The Last Ride Together

The Last Ride Together was published in *Men and Women*. It consisted of ten stanzas, of eleven four-measure lines each. In 1863 the poem was grouped with the *Dramatic Romances*. Since 1855 the poem has suffered only a few changes in punctuation.

It is impossible to say at what time between the years 1846 and 1855 the poem was written. The theme of the poem—that as makers of happiness, life and love, even when love is rejected, are superior to all the arts—is a perennial one with Browning. It is more prevalent in his poetry after 1850. The poem is perhaps the earliest of Browning's attempts to analyze the functions and effects of the various arts—poetry, sculpture, and music—a problem which he was to deal with more boldly in *Abt Vogler* and the *Parleying With Charles Avison*. The speaker of the poem is one of Browning's incredibly noble rejected lovers, and should be compared to the speaker of Tennyson's *Locksley Hall*.

The Patriot

The Patriot.—An Old Story was published in *Men and Women* on November 17, 1855. It consisted of six stanzas of five four-measure

---

[59] For its place in Browning's theory of poetry in general, see Edward Dowden's two essays upon Browning in his *Literary Studies;* see also my own book, *Browning's Parleyings*, Ch. 3, and also pp. 226–40.

lines each. In 1863 it was classed with the *Dramatic Romances,* and a number of changes were made in the sixth stanza of the poem; the most notable was the dropping of the name Brescia, the Lombard town.

The story is "An Old Story" because it is often repeated, and the poem is a satire upon the fickleness of the public. It grew, it is thought, from Browning's sympathetic observation of the cause of the Risorgimento, Italy's attempt to attain unity and to free herself from Austria in 1848–9. Browning denied that he had Arnold of Brescia in mind and probably to avoid that specific association thereafter, removed the name of Brescia from the text in 1863. Probably the poet had in mind no actual incident; but the wild delight of the Florentines in March, 1849, when they planted the tree of liberty in the square just in front of the Brownings' door, and the contrasting scene a short time after, when with some bloodshed they received the Grand-Duke home again in an Austrian uniform, we know made a strong impression upon Browning, and could not have been without an effect on this poem. The collapse of the Italian cause after Novara in 1849 greatly disheartened the Brownings.[60] The poem was probably written late in the spring of 1849. Browning undoubtedly meant the irony in the poem to have a broad universal rather than a particular application.

Master Hugues of Saxe-Gotha

Master Hugues of Saxe-Gotha was first published in *Men and Women.* It consisted of twenty-nine stanzas, twenty-eight of five lines each, and the twenty-ninth of nine lines—144 lines in all. In 1863 the poem became one of the *Dramatic Lyrics.* Since 1855 there have been a few verbal changes and the usual changes in punctuation.

It is probable that *Master Hugues* is one of the "lyrics with more music and painting than before" which Browning mentions in a letter to Milsand on February 24, 1853 (see my general discussion of *Men and Women,* above).

Master Hugues is an imaginary composer. The duchy of Saxe-Gotha, in central Germany, was the birth-place of Bach, who first developed the fugue as a great composition. Browning denied, however, that Master Hugues was meant for "the glorious Bach," but said

---

[60] See *Letters of E.B.B.,* ed. Kenyon, I, 383–406.

that he was intended for one of the dry-as-dust imitators.[61] The purpose of the poem is to catch in verse the atmosphere and temper of a fugue, which Grove defines in his *Dictionary of Music* as a "musical movement in which a definite number of parts or voices combine in stating and developing a single theme, the interest being cumulative." Browning had early become acquainted with learned German music, for his master John Relfe, a follower in the school of the Abbé Vogler, had taught him "not only Thorough-Bass, but the whole arcana of the science, so as completely to analyze any regular composition." [62] Browning all his life delighted in abstruse music and the study of music.

Bishop Blougram's Apology

Bishop Blougram's Apology was first published in *Men and Women*. It consisted of 1013 lines of blank verse, divided into thirty-eight sections. Throughout all distributions *Bishop Blougram* remained one of *Men and Women*. Since 1855 the text has suffered a moderate number of verbal changes, and the usual changes in punctuation. One new line (l. 979) has been added, "Long crumpled, till creased consciousness lay smooth."

The date of the composition of *Bishop Blougram's Apology* may be fixed conjecturally by several allusions in the poem. It is, as the reference to Strauss (l. 577) shows, a by-product of Browning's work upon *Christmas-Eve and Easter-Day,* and was probably written after that long poem, which was finished early—probably in February—in 1850. The reference to Blougram's title (ll. 972–4),

> . . . styled *in partibus*
> *Episcopus, nec non*—(the deuce knows what
> It's changed to by our novel hierarchy),

is obviously a reference to the change in Cardinal Wiseman's title, in October of 1850; for Cardinal Wiseman (1802–65) is avowedly the figure which served somewhat as a model for Blougram. Wiseman had been consecrated bishop in 1840 and sent to England as Vicar Apostolic of the Central District; his title from this date was "Melipotamus *in partibus infidelium.*" By a papal bull in October, 1850, England was divided into districts and Wiseman became Archbishop

[61] See Herbert E. Greene, "Browning's Knowledge of Music," in *PMLA* 62:1098 (1947).
[62] See DeVane, *Browning's Parleyings,* pp. 254–6.

of Westminster and head of the Catholic Church in England. On the other side, as Sir Frederic Kenyon noticed,[63] Blougram speaks of Pugin, the ecclesiastical architect with whom Wiseman disagreed, and of D'Orsay, as still living. Both of these men died in 1852. And again, the war mentioned in line 938 must have been the Crimean War which began in March, 1854. I think, therefore, that the poem was probably written during the winter of 1850 and the spring of 1851, at Florence, and was probably given its final form when Browning was setting his poetical house in order in June, 1854. The next summer Browning was in London with his fifty *Men and Women* completed.

It has been said above that *Bishop Blougram's Apology* is a by-product of Browning's cogitations for *Christmas-Eve and Easter-Day*, concerning the nature of modern Christian faith. One may conjecture that the idea of *Bishop Blougram* may have come to Browning in his many conversations with Father Prout, the ex-Jesuit and brilliant *littérateur* who had written for *Fraser's Magazine*, and who had come to Italy as correspondent for the *Daily News* in 1846 when Dickens was editor. Father Prout, whose true name was F. S. Mahony, visited the Brownings nightly in Florence in the autumn of 1848, and was described by Mrs. Browning as kind-hearted and clever, but skeptical and even cynical, and lacking somewhat in tact.[64] The Brownings tired of him after a short time, and I suspect him of being the model for "Gigadibs, the literary man," though not, of course, exactly copied. I think that it was from this source that Browning learned all he wished to know of Wiseman's character and career—such points, for instance, as the Cardinal's influence in the literary world, "whether here, in Dublin or New York" (ll. 957–69). Wiseman had founded the *Dublin Review* in 1836. When Browning was accused by his old friend John Forster and by Sir Charles Gavan Duffy, shortly after the publication of the poem, of enmity towards the Roman Catholic faith, he was surprised; and though he admitted that Cardinal Wiseman had served as model, he added that he did not consider it a satire, and that there was nothing ungenerous about it.[65] Wiseman's biographer repudiates the portrait, and says that it is "quite unlike all that Wiseman's letters and the recollections of

[63] *Centenary Edition,* IV, xx.

[64] *E.B.B., Letters to her Sister,* pp. 92–4. See also Cyril Clemons, "Father Prout and the Brownings," in *Dalhousie Review* 17:163–7 (1937).

[65] Gavan Duffy, *My Life in Two Hemispheres,* London, 1898, II, 258.

his friends show him to have been. Subtle and true as the sketch is in itself, it really depicts some one else." [66] The portrait, I think, is a composite one; there is something of Newman in the reference to a belief in miracles (ll. 374–8, 740–4). [67]

The word "Apology" in the title of the poem must be taken in the original sense of "argument" and not in the sense of a plea for leniency on the bishop's part. Browning's real purpose was to comment on the problem of faith in a skeptical world. [68] In an extremely able article, which informs much of my comment here, F. E. L. Priestly analyzes the whole poem. [69] The course of the argument is dictated by Gigadibs, a third-rate journalist, in his own estimation clever, rational, and a man of integrity, who thinks intelligence and faith incompatible and Blougram either a knave or a fool. The bishop, far cleverer than Gigadibs, understands the situation and elects to argue on Gigadibs' own ground. He anticipates Gigadibs' arguments as he drives the journalist from point to point. On Gigadibs' level, he proves that faith, unprovable by reason, is best for this world and the next. With amusement and irony he attacks Gigadibs' assumptions and defends his own way of life. He becomes sincere and eloquent when he affirms his own faith and the power of faith (ll. 182–97; 560–3; 621–5; 647–61; 693–7; 845–51). The crowning irony occurs when the bishop at the end challenges Gigadibs to publish what he has learned. The bishop is more successful than he knows, for Gigadibs the unbeliever, we learn at the end of the poem, has renounced his ambitions and proposes to follow a different ideal in Australia, seeking what he formerly despised, in a study of the Gospels. [70]

[66] W. Ward, *The Life and Times of Cardinal Wiseman*, London, 1897, II, 157.

[67] Wiseman had, however, written in 1851 *The Real Presence of the Body and Blood of our Lord Jesus Christ in the Blessed Eucharist, proved from Scripture in Eight Lectures.* Yet Browning's phrases point rather to Newman in this respect. See also *New Letters*, ed. DeVane and Knickerbocker, pp. 87–8, where a part of Wiseman's review of *Men and Women* is quoted.

[68] See C. R. Tracy, "Bishop Blougram," in *Modern Language Review* 34:422–5 (1939) for an acute comment. For the background to the poem as well as an able analysis of it see W. O. Raymond, *The Infinite Moment*, Ch. 8, "Browning's Casuists," esp. pp. 135–41. See also the *Times Literary Supplement* of January 24 and March 21, 1935, for the source of Browning's remarks on sexual morality.

[69] "Blougram's Apologetics," in *University of Toronto Quarterly* 15:139–47 (1945–6). My comment does not do justice to this closely reasoned analysis.

[70] But see H. N. Fairchild's objection to Browning's "give-away" in *Blougram*, which he characterizes as an awkward attempt to extract the simple truth from subtleties too ambiguous for his audience, in "Browning the Simple-hearted Casuist," in *University of Toronto Quarterly* 18:234–40 (1949).

The monologue is one of Browning's subtlest, and was not understood even by Cardinal Wiseman, or his defenders. Understanding was not helped by the fact that Blougram used many of Browning's characteristic arguments, especially the poet's belief that faith is an act of the will and is not susceptible of intellectual proof.

Once published, the poem had a strange adventure. It was reviewed in *The Rambler*, a Roman Catholic review, in January, 1856 (5:54–71), and Cardinal Wiseman himself was the reviewer. Browning wrote to Furnivall on August 29, 1881, "The most curious notice I ever had was from Cardinal Wiseman on *Blougram*—i.e. himself. It was in the *Rambler*, a Catholic Journal of those days, and certified to be his by Father Prout, who said nobody else would have dared put it in." [71] The review in *The Rambler* ran in part:

"Bishop Blougram's Apology," though utterly mistaken in the very groundwork of religion, though starting from the most unworthy notions of the work of a Catholic bishop, and defending a self-indulgence which every honest man must feel to be disgraceful, is yet in its way triumphant. . . .

The reviewer did not see that the victory was entirely Blougram's, and after praising the poem for its "fertility of illustration" and "felicity of argument," he concluded,

Though much of the matter is extremely offensive to Catholics, yet beneath the surface there is an undercurrent of thought that is by no means inconsistent with our religion; and if Mr. Browning is a man of will and action, and not a mere dreamer and talker, *we should never feel surprise at his conversion.*

Bishop Blougram has always been accounted one of the cleverest of Browning's poems, and is much quoted. A good earlier commentary upon the poem is to be seen in E. M. Naish's *Browning and Dogma*, London, 1906, pp. 63–91.

Memorabilia

Memorabilia was the last poem in the first volume of *Men and Women*. It contained four stanzas of four lines each, each line of four feet. In 1863 the poem was grouped with the *Dramatic Lyrics*. Since 1855 the second and third stanzas especially have been altered somewhat, to improve the meter, but the sense remains the same; and there have been the usual changes in punctuation.

[71] *Letters*, ed. Hood, p. 195.

Memorabilia is an offshoot, I think, of Browning's labors upon the *Introductory Essay* for the twenty-five letters of Shelley, printed by Moxon, which turned out to be spurious. This essay was completed about December 1, 1851. Browning later told his friend W. G. Kingsland of an event which I believe took place in the fall of 1851, which was probably the inception of the poem. Kingsland had quoted two stanzas of *Memorabilia,* whereupon Browning

. . . outbroke with characteristic vehemence: "I was one day in the shop of Hodgson, the well-known London bookseller, when a stranger came in, who, in the course of conversation with the bookseller, spoke of something that Shelley had once said to him. Suddenly the stranger paused, and burst into laughter as he observed me staring at him with blanched face; and," the poet continued, "I still vividly remember how strangely the presence of a man who had seen and spoken with Shelley affected me." [72]

This scene in the bookshop must have taken place before Browning wrote his essay upon Shelley, for Browning was still full of admiration for the older poet at that time, and if we may trust his memory he had only Shelley's works to go by and had no knowledge of his life when he wrote the essay. [73] Some time afterwards, Browning made the acquaintance of Thomas Hookham, Jr., Shelley's publisher and book dealer, and learned from him the truth of the Shelley-Westbrook affair. [74] The disclosure was a great shock to Browning. *Memorabilia* was written, I believe, in the fall of 1851.

MEN AND WOMEN—VOL. II

Andrea del Sarto

Andrea del Sarto (*Called "The Faultless Painter"*) had the honor of being the first poem of the second volume of *Men and Women.* It consisted of 266 lines of blank verse. The poem has remained one

[72] "Some Browning Memories," in the *Contemporary Review* 102:206–7 (1912).

[73] See W. G. Kingsland, "Robert Browning, Some Personal Reminiscences," in *Baylor University Browning Interests,* Second Series, 1931, p. 33.

[74] See Miller, *Robert Browning,* pp. 168–70. Mrs. Miller, relying upon W. M. Rossetti's report of a conversation with Browning, believes Browning learned the facts of Shelley's desertion of Harriet Westbrook Shelley while he was preparing his essay; that is, in 1851. This contradicts Browning's statement to Kingsland. We learn from a letter to Miss Blagden dated November 19, 1862, that Browning has only fairly recently become unsettled about Shelley. It was probably in 1858 that he saw Hookham's material. See *Dearest Isa,* ed. McAleer, pp. 137 and 140.

of *Men and Women* throughout its history. Since 1855 a few verbal changes have been made in the poem, and of course the usual changes in punctuation; and the line which is now line 96 has been added.

Andrea del Sarto grew out of Browning's attempt to describe the painter's portrait of himself and his wife, which hung in the Pitti Palace at Florence, to John Kenyon, the friend and benefactor of both the Brownings. Kenyon desired a photograph of the picture, and when one was not available, Browning wrote the poem and sent it instead.[1] It is possible that *Andrea* may have been among those poems upon art and music which Browning describes himself as engaged upon, in his letter to Milsand on February 24, 1853.[2] From a letter of Mrs. Browning's dated April 13, 1853, we know that Browning was deep in his study of Vasari at this time.[3]

The account of Andrea del Sarto's life as given by Vasari is the true background of the poem, and Browning makes steady and confident use of it. He also verified Vasari's account by that in Filippo Baldinucci's *Notizie*,[4] as he had done in *Fra Lippo Lippi*. Baldinucci gives an emphasis to Andrea's story which tempers somewhat Browning's original conception of Andrea, and it is possible that Baldinucci directed Browning's attention to the account of Andrea del Sarto in the first edition of Vasari's *Le Vite de' Pittori*, where the character of Lucrezia del Fede, the painter's wife, is much more darkly painted than in later editions. Vasari was Andrea's pupil in painting and his words therefore have double weight.

Browning imagines Andrea on the evening when he conceived the picture of himself and his wife which hangs in the Sala di Giove of the Pitti Palace. It is indeed the autumn of Andrea's life. The account from Vasari is too long to quote, but in all essentials the facts are as Browning gives them. Andrea was the son of a Florentine tailor, and from this fact took the name of "del Sarto." His true name was Andrea d'Agnolo di Francesca di Luca. He was born in 1486. In time he was apprenticed to a goldsmith, and afterwards to several painters. He first won fame and the title of "Il Pittore senza Errori" by his

[1] See Mrs. Andrew Crosse's article, "John Kenyon and his Friends," in *Temple Bar* 88:477–96; esp. p. 489. Browning's letter to Kenyon, which seems to have been written between November 23, 1852, and March, 1853, is in the Library of Wellesley College.

[2] See Griffin and Minchin, *Life*, p. 189.

[3] Miller, *Robert Browning*, p. 187.

[4] *Notizie de' Professori del Disegno* . . . , IV, 185–97. See also DeVane, *Browning's Parleyings*, pp. 173–6.

work in the Church of the Santissima Annunziata. In 1513 he married Lucrezia, widow of a hat-maker, who served as model for many of his pictures, notably for his *Madonna del Sacco*. Yet from the day of his marriage Andrea's fortunes were doomed. In 1518 Andrea went by invitation to the court of Francis I, King of France, and encouraged and rewarded he there did some of his best work. Lucrezia, however, lured him home; and on his arrival in Florence he was persuaded to spend the money with which King Francis had commissioned him to buy paintings, upon a house for himself on the Via Gino Capponi. Deserted by his wife and servants during his last illness, he died of the plague on January 22, 1531. Most of his excellent works are in the galleries of Florence.

The opening words of Vasari's life of Andrea del Sarto are a description of the painter's character and work:

At length then we have come, after having written the lives of many artists who have been distinguished, some for colouring, some for design, and some for invention; we have come, I say, to that truly excellent Andrea del Sarto, in whom art and nature combined to show all that may be done in painting, when design, colouring and invention unite in one and the same person. Had this master possessed a somewhat bolder and more elevated mind; had he been as much distinguished for higher qualifications as he was for genius and depth of judgment in the art he practiced, he would beyond all doubt, have been without an equal. But there was a certain timidity of mind, a sort of diffidence and want of force in his nature, which rendered it impossible that those evidences of ardour and animation, which are proper to the more exalted character, should ever appear in him; nor did he at any time display one particle of that elevation which, could it have been added to the advantages wherewith he was endowed, would have rendered him a truly divine painter: wherefore the works of Andrea are wanting in those ornaments of grandeur, richness, and force, which appear so conspicuously in those of many other masters. His figures are nevertheless well drawn, they are entirely free from errors, and perfect in their proportions, and are for the most part simple and chaste; the expression of his heads is natural and graceful in women and children, while in youths and old men it is full of life and animation. The draperies of this master are beautiful to a marvel, and the nude figures are admirably executed, the drawing is simple, the colouring is most exquisite, nay, it is truly divine.[5]

Concerning Andrea, Michael Angelo said to Raphael, "There is a little man in Florence, who if he were employed upon such great works as have been given to you, would make you sweat." [6] Brown-

[5] *Lives of Seventy of the Most Eminent Painters, Sculptors and Architects* by Giorgio Vasari, ed. and tr. by Blashfield and Hopkins, N. Y., 1896, III, 234–5.
[6] *Idem,* III, 296.

ing uses these words in a slightly different way in the poem. Vasari was first introduced to Andrea by Michael Angelo, and throughout Vasari's account of Andrea there is a running comparison of Andrea with the greater artists, Leonardo, Michael Angelo, and Raphael.

Vasari's observation of Andrea's wife, Lucrezia, as it appears in the first edition of his work, is obviously drawn from personal knowledge:

At that time there was a most beautiful girl in the Via di San Gallo, who was married to a cap-maker, and who, though born of a poor and vicious father, carried about her as much pride and haughtiness as beauty and fascination. She delighted in trapping the hearts of men, and among others ensnared the unlucky Andrea, whose immoderate love for her soon caused him to neglect the studies demanded by his art, and in great measure to discontinue the assistance which he had given to his parents.

Now it chanced that a sudden and grievous illness seized the husband of this woman, who rose no more from his bed, but died thereof. Without taking counsel of his friends therefore; without regard to the dignity of his art or the consideration due to his genius, and to the eminence he had attained with so much labour; without a word, in short, to any of his kindred, Andrea took this Lucrezia di Baccio del Fede, such was the name of the woman, to be his wife; her beauty appearing to him to merit thus much at his hands, and his love for her having more influence over him than the glory and honour towards which he had begun to make such hopeful advances. But when this news became known in Florence, the respect and affection which his friends had previously borne to Andrea changed to contempt and disgust, since it appeared to them that the darkness of this disgrace had obscured for a time all the glory and renown attained by his talents.

But he destroyed his own peace as well as estranged his friends by this act, seeing that he soon became jealous, and found that he had besides fallen into the hands of an artful woman, who made him do as she pleased in all things. He abandoned his own poor father and mother, for example, and adopted the father and sisters of his wife in their stead; insomuch that all who knew the facts, mourned over him, and he soon began to be as much avoided as he had been previously sought after. His disciples still remained with him, it is true, in the hope of learning something useful, yet there was not one of them, great or small, who was not maltreated by his wife, both by evil words and despiteful actions; none could escape her blows, but although Andrea lived in the midst of all that torment, he yet accounted it a high pleasure.[7]

A spirited defence of Andrea's character and art has been made by modern scholars. It has been doubted on good grounds that Andrea stole the French king's money, and it has been suggested that An-

[7] *Idem*, III, 251–2.

drea was merely conveying money for the king to some great citizens of Florence whom he wished to influence. In art, though not denying that Andrea falls short of the very greatest artists, the scholars see in him a very great draughtsman, a skilful harmonizer of color, a most charming and pleasing painter.[8] There is a suspicion that the picture of Andrea and his wife in the Pitti Palace is not a single composition, but, rather, parts of two separate pictures which have been joined together. But Vasari supplied the materials from which Browning made his poem.

In her recent portrait of the poet Mrs. Miller reads a great deal of biography into the poem and finds a similarity between Browning and Andrea in temperament and situation; that is, they are both timid and both inhibited by their wives from exercising their deepest creative forces.[9] This seems to me a perversion of interpretation.

Browning knew early that *Andrea del Sarto* was one of his finest poems: he singles it out for mention in *One Word More*. In later years he read it occasionally when he was asked for a reading. Posterity has confirmed his judgment that it is perhaps the greatest monologue he ever wrote.

Before—After

Before and *After*, companion poems, were published in *Men and Women*. *Before* was composed of ten stanzas of four six-measure trochaic lines each. *After* was made up of eighteen lines rhyming in couplets. The poems were classed as *Dramatic Lyrics* in 1863. They have always been printed as separate poems. *Before* has suffered a few verbal changes in text, and the usual changes in punctuation since 1855; *After*, only the changes in punctuation.

There is no indication of the exact date, between the years 1846 and 1855, upon which the poems were written. On April 8, 1846, in a letter to Elizabeth Barrett, Browning had expressed his opinion on the ethics of duelling, and discussed at some length the reasons why society has tolerated it. Miss Barrett was shocked at Browning's somewhat bloodthirsty championship of the practice. The poem *After* shows that he has moved nearer to her position. As a consequence of a famous duel of 1843, in which Lieutenant Monro had reluctantly shot his brother-in-law Colonel Fawcett, a law had been

[8] *Idem*, III, 267, note 54; 299, note 105.
[9] Miller, *Robert Browning*, p. 187. See also p. 21.

passed in 1844 compelling duellists to stand trial by court martial.
The Prince Consort was keenly interested in this successful attempt
to suppress duelling in England. By 1855 duelling had fairly gone
out as a practice.

In *Before* the speaker is a second for one of the duellists. He seems
somewhat to share the medieval chivalric notion that "God will have
a stroke in every battle." The speaker in *After* is the victor in the duel.
Perhaps the last line of this poem is an unconscious echo of the famous line in Webster's *Duchess of Malfi* (IV, ii),

> Cover her face; mine eyes dazzle; she died young . . . ,

or of the words in *King Lear* (V, iii, 243),

> Even so.—Cover their faces.

But the phrase is natural and common enough.

In Three Days

In Three Days was published, with its companion-piece *In a Year*,
in *Men and Women*. *In Three Days* consisted of thirty-eight four-
measure iambic lines, divided into four sections. In 1863 it was
grouped with the *Dramatic Lyrics*. A few changes in words and the
usual changes in punctuation have been made since 1855.

This poem, like its companion-piece *In a Year*, and like *Love in a
Life* and *Life in a Love*, owes its being to the married life of the
Brownings in Italy. As far as I know, no particular experience called
it forth, and no specific date of composition may be ascribed to it.
The speaker is a man, and the language he uses is suggestive of the
language that Browning in his own person uses in *One Word More*,
which served as epilogue to *Men and Women*. Mrs. Miller suggests
that the poem may have been written in July, 1852, when Browning
went to Paris with his self-exiled father. It was the only occasion in
their married life when husband and wife were separated for so
long a time.[10]

In a Year

The history of *In a Year* is the same as that of its companion-piece
In Three Days, except that *In a Year* consisted of ten stanzas of eight
trochaic lines each. *In a Year* probably grew out of *In Three Days*.

[10] *Idem*, p. 181.

The speaker of *In a Year* is a woman, and it is evident that Browning is attempting a favorite theme of his, the difference of love in men and in women. *In a Year,* therefore, should be read with *Another Way of Love, A Woman's Last Word* and *Any Wife to Any Husband.* The manner of the treatment of this theme in *In a Year* foreshadows *James Lee's Wife* (1864). In all these poems women are the speakers observing the decay of love. Browning suggested the final four lines of the last stanza to Felix Moscheles in 1867 as suitable for an inscription to the artist's picture.[11]

Old Pictures in Florence

Old Pictures in Florence was published in *Men and Women.* It consisted of thirty-six stanzas of eight lines each, the lines being four-measure iambs and anapaests. In 1863 the poem was allotted to the *Lyrics* and in 1868 to the *Dramatic Lyrics.* In the first edition the printers mishandled this difficult poem considerably. The corrections that Browning intimated, in a letter to Rossetti,[12] should have been made were later made in the edition of 1863, and a number of other changes were introduced for the sake of the meter. The poem has been frequently altered in wording and punctuation, but the sense has not been affected.

Old Pictures in Florence, as the title and the poem itself suggest, is a product of Florence. The Brownings had begun to read Vasari's *Le Vite de' Pittori* earlier in Pisa, but the copy Browning owned was the edition published in Florence in 1846–57. Writing to Mrs. Jameson on May 4, 1850, Mrs. Browning reports,

Robert has been picking up pictures at a few pauls each, 'hole and corner' pictures which the 'dealers' had not found out; and the other day he covered himself with glory by discovering and seizing on (in a corn shop a mile from Florence) five pictures among heaps of trash; and one of the best judges in Florence (Mr. Kirkup) throws out such names for them as Cimabue, Ghirlandajo, Giottino, a crucifixion painted on a banner, Giottesque, if not Giotto, but *unique,* or nearly so. . . .[13]

It was obviously in honor of this event that *Old Pictures in Florence* was written. But certainly not all of the poem, if indeed any of it, was written in 1850, for as Sir Frederic Kenyon has pointed out,[14] stanza

11 *New Letters,* ed. DeVane and Knickerbocker, p. 178.
12 *Letters,* ed. Hood, pp. 41–2.
13 *Letters of E.B.B.,* ed. Kenyon, I, 448.
14 *Centenary Edition,* III, xix.

33 refers to Mrs. Browning's poem *Casa Guidi* as an event already past, and her poem was not published until midsummer, 1851. At any rate, *Old Pictures* is most certainly one of the poems on music and painting which Browning, in a letter of February 24, 1853, told Milsand he was writing; and the mention of March in the first stanza, as the month in which the poem was imagined, is probably to be taken as fact. The Mr. Kirkup mentioned was Seymour Kirkup, who discovered the Bargello portrait of Dante.

The poem is the product of Browning's assiduous study of painting and painters as he found them in the city of Florence and in Vasari's great biographical work, *Vite de' piu eccellenti Pittori, Sculptori ed Architetti* (1550–68), with which he occupied his mind in the spring of 1853. The first half of Browning's poem is a sermon upon the great nineteenth-century doctrine, the "philosophy of the imperfect," which John Ruskin had made famous in his chapter *On the Nature of Gothic.*[15] The unfinished campanile by Giotto was what gave rise in Browning's mind to this disquisition which is so characteristic of his thinking. The second half of the poem is a search for the reasons for Florence's neglect of the old masters: this he finds to be due to her enslavement to Austria. Radetzsky, the conqueror of Italian hopes at Novara, and military governor of northern Italy, is mentioned in stanza 32. At the close Browning unites the two halves of the poem by a prophecy—that some day Italy will be free, art will flourish again, and the fifty *bracci* which Giotto did not live to see added to his bell-tower will be added at last. Throughout the poem the speaker is obviously Browning, and the ideas are those which appear in *Fra Lippo Lippi, Andrea del Sarto,* and finally with great explicitness in the *Parleying With Gerard de Lairesse.*[16] He characteristically prefers Christian to Greek art because of its realism and its emphasis upon the personality of the individual artist.

The reader may find Browning's many references to painting and painters in any handbook of painting; or better, in any of the standard translations of Vasari's *Lives.* Here the biographies most significant for an understanding of the poem are those of Giotto and Cimabue. Giotto di Bondone (1276–1337) was a pupil of Cimabue and a friend of Dante. He is commonly thought to be the greatest of the early Italian painters. His Bargello portrait of Dante has already been mentioned. His greatest work is the unfinished campanile

[15] In *Stones of Venice,* II, Ch. VI.
[16] See DeVane, *Browning's Parleyings,* pp. 227–9.

of the Duomo at Florence; it is a structure of exquisite proportion and color. Milton was fond of it, and Browning is not unmindful of Milton in *Old Pictures,* echoing as he does Milton's reference to Chaucer,

> . . . him who left half told
> The story of Cambuscan bold.

Giovanni Cimabue (1240–1302) is especially significant for us because he initiated the long succession of Renaissance artists, and probably gave Browning his idea of the progress of modern artists beyond the perfection of Greece. It is possibly enough to add that "Bigordi," "Sandro," and "Lippino," of stanza 26, are Ghirlandaio, Botticelli, and Filippino Lippi.

The poem is one of the best of Browning's pieces in playful and grotesque rhyme.

In a Balcony

In a Balcony was first published in *Men and Women.* It consisted of 919 lines, and was divided into three parts: the second part began with the entrance of the Queen, and the third part with the re-entrance of Norbert. In 1863 *In a Balcony* was separated from *Men and Women* and placed among *Tragedies and Other Plays.* In 1868 it was removed from this category and given an independent position as a link-piece between *Men and Women* and *Dramatis Personae.* Since 1855 the text has undergone a few changes in word and punctuation, but the number of lines has remained the same. In 1863 the division into parts was dropped, and while the text stood as it does now, it was called *In a Balcony—A Scene.*

The tradition is that the poem was written at Bagni di Lucca in the three months—July to October—which the Brownings spent there in 1853; and in the edition of 1868 the poem is dated 1853, from that place. It probably received the final touches in Florence in June of the next year, when Browning began to set his poetical house in order. It was possibly the revival of *Colombe's Birthday* by Helena Faucit in the spring of 1853 which revived Browning's interest in the drama and stimulated him to write *In a Balcony.* As in *Colombe,* we have three persons in a political situation, but again it is of little importance that one is a queen and another a prime minister. The matter is all of love, and the world is forgotten.

In a Balcony is, I think, a product of Browning's imagination, and has no source in the usual sense of the word. But the subject of the difference of love in man and in woman, and the difference in love between wisdom of the heart and wisdom of the intellect, which concerns him in many of the poems in this volume, is here shown in another aspect. One can never read the first part of the little play without being reminded of the argument between Browning and Elizabeth Barrett in 1846, when Browning thought that the only thing to do was to go to Mr. Barrett to ask for his daughter's hand, and Miss Barrett was sure that that was the one thing that ought not to be done. In the incident from life Miss Barrett was undoubtedly right and Browning wrong. In the incident from *In a Balcony* Browning shows Constance to have been wrong in prohibiting Norbert from early informing the Queen of his love for Constance. The difference is in the characters of Mr. Barrett and the Queen.

That the poem was a favorite with the poet from the beginning is evident from his mention of Norbert in *One Word More*. Many controversies have arisen as to the conclusion of *In a Balcony*, but perhaps the poet's own words should have most weight. Mrs. Bronson, a friend of Browning's later years, reports that after the piece had been read to his friends

. . . one who sat near him said it was a natural sequence that the step of the guard should be heard coming to take Norbert to his doom, as, with a nature like the queen's, who had known only one hour of joy in her sterile life, vengeance swift and terrible would follow on the sudden destruction of her happiness. "Now, I don't quite think that," answered Browning, as if he were following out the play as a spectator: "The queen had a large and passionate temperament, which had only once been touched and brought into intense life. She would have died, as by a knife in her heart. The guard would have come to carry away her dead body." [17]

The dénouement proposed by Browning in this passage is characteristic of his dramas, but has failed to satisfy his critics. A very considerable disagreement has also risen among the commentators concerning the character of Constance, upon which the drama turns. The disagreement is admirably summarized and adjudicated by Elmer E. Stoll in his volume, *From Shakespeare to Joyce*, Ch. 17. He describes the dramatic convention by which a great tragic situation is necessarily set up in a very brief time, sometimes at the cost of probability, as it is in *In a Balcony*. In spite of the improba-

[17] Katherine deKay Bronson, "Browning in Venice," in the *Century Magazine* 63:578 (1902).

bility of the beginning situation, he finds such a tragic moment at the end of the drama. But the final word of the play is disappointing, lacking in fullness and tragic depth of tone.

Though it is certain that Browning never meant the playlet for the stage, it was nevertheless presented under the auspices of the Browning Society in London on November 28, 1884, with Miss Alma Murray in the part of Constance. Accounts of this performance may be seen in the *Academy* for December 6, 1884, the *Pall Mall Gazette* for December 1, and in *Browning Society's Papers*, II, 5*–7*. The character of Constance is well analyzed in Ethel C. Mayne's *Browning's Heroines* (London, 1913). Besides the performances in Browning's life-time, *In a Balcony* has been played since in London in 1912, and several times in America, but it is rather closet than stage drama.

Saul

The first nine sections of *Saul*—102 lines—were published in *Dramatic Romances* on November 6, 1845. Miss Barrett had suggested, probably in August, 1845, a considerable number of verbal changes, most of which were adopted for the first edition. The poem was printed in short half-lines; this was, I think, owing to the fact that the economical manner of printing the poems in *Bells and Pomegranates* (*q.v.*), with double columns of fine type, did not permit the long line of *Saul* as we know it now. These first nine sections were reprinted under *Dramatic Romances and Lyrics* in the collected edition of 1849: some revision had taken place. The poem was again printed in half-lines for economy's sake.

The entire poem first appeared, however, in *Men and Women* where ten new sections (10–19), consisting of 239 lines, were added. The ninth section had suffered considerable alteration, partly for the improvement of the meter, and partly to make the transition to the new sections more natural.[18] In the distribution of 1863 *Saul* became one of the *Dramatic Lyrics*, which it has since remained. Since 1855 the text, except for occasional verbal changes and the usual ones in punctuation, has been little altered.

Saul owes its first conception and composition, I think, to January,

[18] See *Macmillan Edition*, pp. 1345–6. See also C. Willard Smith, *Browning's Star-Imagery*, pp. 174–5.

1845. When Browning returned from his second Italian tour in mid-December, 1844, he attempted to catch up in his reading on books which had appeared during his absence. One of these was *Chambers' Cyclopaedia*, wherein was printed Christopher Smart's *Song to David*. Browning had known the *Song to David* as early as 1827 and it had profoundly affected his poetry. Years later in describing his view of Smart's *Song* early in 1845, he said, "I think it was the reprint in Chambers that I saw—not in Chalmers; indeed I am sure of it, although I discovered it there on an occasion that would excuse much mistiness in my memory." [19] The occasion was probably his first acquaintance with Miss Barrett. At any rate, Browning relates in his *Parleying With Christopher Smart* how he went from the *Song to David* to the rest of Smart's work. Smart's preface to his *Ode to Musick on Saint Cecilia's Day* gave Browning the idea for *Saul:*

> It would not be right to conclude, without taking notice of a fine subject for an Ode on S. Cecilia's Day, which was suggested to the Author by his friend the learned and ingenious Mr. Comber, late of Jesus College in this University [Cambridge]; that is David's playing to King Saul when he was troubled with the evil spirit. He was much pleased with the hint at first, but at length was deterred from improving it by the greatness of the subject, and he thinks not without reason. The chusing of too high subjects has been the ruin of many a tolerable Genius. [20]

Browning was never deterred by the difficulty of any subject, and so began the writing of *Saul*.[21]

On May 3, 1845, Browning wrote to Miss Barrett that he had a poem called *Saul* that he would show her some day. In the busy days that follow we hear nothing of the poem until August 27, when we learn that Miss Barrett has read it. She urges that he go forward with

[19] *Letters*, ed. Hood, p. 262.

[20] See DeVane, *Browning's Parleyings*, pp. 113–20; esp. pp. 116–7.

[21] W. L. Phelps in an article in *MLN* 24:162 (June, 1909), entitled "Dr. John Brown, *The Cure for Saul*," suggests that Browning may have known Brown's *Cure for Saul* (1763), a dramatic piece, "Set to select airs, Duets, and Choirs from Handel, Marcello, Purcel and other Eminent Composers." This suggestion is interesting but lacking in proof that Browning knew Brown's work. The same difficulty is encountered in G. S. Wyckoff's contention that Browning was influenced by Charles Mackay's *Saul and David*, published in 1840 in *The Hope of the World, and Other Poems;* see "A Possible Source of Browning's *Saul*," in *Philological Quarterly* 7:311–4. See also H. W. Yocum, "Some Additional Sources of Browning's *Saul*," in *Notes and Queries* for July 26, 1941, pp. 44–6. This article proves how familiar the story of Saul was to the nineteenth century, but does not show that Browning knew any of the sources cited.

the poem, but he expresses his dissatisfaction with the result. On September 9, Miss Barrett suggested that the poem be printed as a fragment in the forthcoming *Dramatic Romances,* and this course was adopted. The second part of *Saul* was probably written during the winter of 1852–3 when Browning began to think of a new volume of poems. It owes its matter and substance to the influence of his wife upon his religious thinking, as we have seen in *Christmas-Eve and Easter-Day,* and to Sir Thomas Wyatt's *Seven Penitential Psalms,* as we shall see below.

Now though Christopher Smart suggested the subject to Browning, the true source of the first *Saul* is to be found in *I Samuel* 16:14–23, and the context. But Smart supplied more than the hint. The *Song to David,* from which Browning had taken a suggestion for *Home-Thoughts, from Abroad,* which was written early in 1845, contains these lines:

> Blest was the tenderness he felt
> When to his graceful harp he knelt,
>   And did for audience call;
> When Satan with his hand he quell'd
> And in serene suspence he held,
>   The frantic throes of Saul.

And in another of Smart's poems, *On the Goodness of the Supreme Being,* the poet addressed David at great length, and ended thus:

> . . . for thy tuneful touch
> Drove trembling Satan from the heart of Saul,
> And quell'd the evil Angel.

But when Browning had concluded the first nine sections of *Saul* in 1845, he was dissatisfied; his poem had arrived at no conclusion, and he did not see how he was to end it. The first nine sections are a mere catalogue, in the manner of Smart, of the good things of the earth, with memories and traditions of Jewish history, hymns of festive or solemn occasions and ritual celebrations, activities and great deeds idealizing the King—the things that Saul should have praised Heaven for. It has been argued that Smart supplied Browning with a method of poetry in the *Saul* of 1845, and that Browning could not go on with the poem because he had exhausted the matter and the manner of his model. Browning found his way to complete *Saul,* probably in 1852–3, by pushing his own religious development forward. The writing of *Christmas-Eve and Easter-Day* (1850) pressed him to solve the religious questions which troubled him, and gave him his clue to the conclusion of *Saul*.[22] James A. S. McPeek has recently shown [23] that Browning used Sir Thomas Wyatt's *Seven Penitential Psalms* for the framework of the completed *Saul*, following Wyatt in structure, images, phrases, and words. At the end of the original nine sections David's medical task is done, but Saul is not yet healed. When the poem is resumed in the tenth section it has become a religious poem. David sees that Saul needs spiritual conviction. So he sings of great deeds and how they go on working in the world, and live in the memory of man. But that is as far as pagan consolation can go. Only the perpetuity of personal consciousness is satisfactory. Then David is suddenly transported by a revelation. He sees that he by his own love for Saul would give the King eternal life if it were in his power to do so, and it dawns upon him that if man would do so much out of love, God the all-powerful and all-intelligent will do much more. He rises to the point of prophecy: God will become incarnate to show his love—"See the Christ stand!" [24]

In all this Browning closely parallels Wyatt, and the question arises, why was he not able to complete his poem in 1845? The answer is, I think, that he was not spiritually ready to affirm his faith in the earlier year, but needed the influence of his wife and the conviction which he exhibits in *Christmas-Eve and Easter-Day* to do so. *Saul* therefore serves as a means of measuring the development of Browning's religious ideas as well as a means of measuring his theory of poetry. The second half of *Saul* is naturally less gorgeous, but certainly stronger and surer, than the first half. The poem should be read in conjunction with *Karshish* and *Cleon*.

The poem has appeared again and again in selections from Browning's poetry, and possibly is more esteemed than any other. When Sir Edmund Gosse asked Browning to name four poems of moderate length which would represent him fairly, the poet selected *Saul* or *Abt Vogler* as his choice for the lyric.[25]

[22] See DeVane, *Browning's Parleyings*, pp. 116–8, and A. W. Crawford's article, "Browning's *Saul*," in *Queen's Quarterly* 34:448–54, where the same conclusion is independently reached. A similar resolution of the poet's religious difficulties provides the informing idea of *Karshish* and *Cleon*, in *Men and Women*.

[23] "The Shaping of *Saul*," in *Journal of English and Germanic Philology* 44: 360–6 (1945). *The Poetical Works* of Sir Thomas Wyatt published by Pickering in 1831 belonged to Mrs. Browning and was in the library at Casa Guidi. This last fact is my addition.

[24] See the excellent interpretation of *Saul* in H. B. Charlton, "Browning as Poet of Religion," in *Bulletin of the John Rylands Library* 27:291–8 (1942–3).

[25] See *Letters*, ed. Hood, p. 235.

"De Gustibus—"

"De Gustibus—" was first published in *Men and Women*. It consisted of two sections, the first of thirteen lines descriptive of an English scene, the second of thirty-three lines descriptive of an Italian one.
In 1863 the poem was grouped with the *Dramatic Lyrics*. It has
always stood, since the distribution of the poems in 1863, just before
Home-Thoughts, from Abroad. The text has been altered a little for
the sake of smoothness, since 1855; but there is one change that in
the light of Browning's departure from Italy may be significant. The
last line, in 1855, read, "So it always was, so it still shall be!" and in
1863 and thereafter, "So it always was, so shall ever be!"

It is not possible to say precisely when the poem was written. As
Sir Frederic Kenyon observed, the scenery of the second part of the
poem is the landscape of the region of Naples, and the king "touched
in the liver-wing" is obviously Ferdinand II, a Bourbon, oppressor of
the Two Sicilies, who acquired in 1849 the name of "King Bomba." [26]
But Browning had not been to Naples since 1844. It is my conjecture
that the poem was composed at Bagni di Lucca in the summer of
1849. The nostalgia for England which informs the first section of the
piece came upon him when the first dread of seeing his home after his
mother's death had subsided. She had died in March, 1849, and in
that month the Austrians triumphed over hopes of Italian freedom at
Novara. It should be said, however, that almost as good a case can be
made for dating the poem from Siena in the summer of 1850; *"De
Gustibus—"* bears a resemblance to *Up at a Villa—Down in the City*,
which might safely, I think, be ascribed to Siena. But these conjectures must necessarily be uncertain; and Browning wrote to his friend
Miss Blagden many years later, "Tell me all the news about Rome
and Naples—I am always thereabouts in spirit." [27]

The allusion to Queen Mary by which Browning illustrates his
love for Italy he probably remembered from Wanley's *Wonders of
the Little World*, which was one of the favorite books of his youth.

Whether indeed there is no accounting for tastes—*"De gustibus
non est disputandum"*—it is a point of interest that in this poem
alone in *Men and Women* does there occur a glimpse of genuine
English landscape. And here that landscape is dismissed brusquely,
but perhaps too brusquely to convince the careful reader that the

[26] *Centenary Edition*, III, xx.
[27] *Dearest Isa*, ed. McAleer, p. 354.

cool moonlit English countryside is not dear to the poet's heart. "*De Gustibus—*" has always had the suffrage of the discerning as one of the truest products of Browning's lyrical genius.

Women and Roses

Women and Roses was first published in *Men and Women*. It consisted of eight stanzas, forty-eight lines in all. In 1863 the poem was grouped with the *Dramatic Lyrics*. It has undergone one or two changes in phrase since 1855, for the sake of better meter.

Women and Roses is one of several poems which were written, one a day, in fulfilment of a New Year's vow. It was written on January 1, 1852, when the Brownings were in Paris. *Childe Roland* was written on the 2nd, and *Love Among the Ruins* on the 3rd. *Women and Roses* is the record of a vivid dream, occasioned by some magnificent roses which someone had sent Mrs. Browning.[28] The poem is not at all in Browning's usual manner, and stands by itself in his verse.

Protus

Protus first appeared in *Men and Women* and consisted of fifty-seven iambic pentameter lines, rhyming in couplets save for one triplet. In 1863 it became one of the *Dramatic Romances*. Since 1855 the text has remained practically the same; the only changes are in punctuation.

So far as we know, there is no specific historical source for *Protus;* there is no prototype for Protus, nor for John, the usurper. The poem expresses Browning's feelings upon seeing the many busts of the half-emperors and quarter-emperors of the late Roman Empire in the East, and upon reading in history-books the rapid successions to power in those chaotic days. Perhaps there is something of the republican's commentary upon the fortune of kings in the career of Protus. At any rate, the poem, I think, owes its existence to the residence of the Brownings in Rome from December, 1853, until May, 1854. Whether the poem was written in Rome or later in Florence, where the poet went to get *Men and Women* ready for

---

[28] See the conversation of Browning upon these poems, reported in Miss Lilian Whiting's *The Brownings*, Boston, 1917, p. 261. See also Orr, *Life,* p. 362. But it should be added that Mr. Johnstone Parr has challenged the dating of these poems; see above, Vol. I. of *Men and Women*, n. 12.

the press, is not known. It is worthy of note that the name Protus is used in *Cleon* to designate the tyrant and patron to whom Cleon's letter is addressed. John, the usurper in *Protus*, came from Pannonia, a country north and west of Greece, and reaching to the Danube. It was famous for its breed of hunting-dogs, and it was perhaps there that the imaginary Protus found refuge.

Holy-Cross Day

Holy-Cross Day. (On which the Jews were Forced to Attend an Annual Christian Sermon in Rome) was first published in *Men and Women*. It consisted of a prose prologue—an imaginary entry in the "Diary of the Bishop's Secretary, 1600," fifteen lines long—two lines of prose commentary by the poet, and twenty stanzas of six four-measure lines each, rhyming in couplets. The poem was followed by the note,

[The present Pope abolished this bad business of the sermon.—R. B.]

In 1863 the poem was classed with the *Dramatic Romances*. Since 1855 the text has suffered a very few verbal changes, both in the prose preface and in the poetry. The concluding note by Browning was changed in the interest of accuracy to read "Pope Gregory XVI," instead of "The present Pope." The papal bull abolishing this practice was issued by the predecessor of Pius IX in 1846, a short time before the Brownings came to Italy.

Browning was in Rome from December, 1853, until May, 1854, and since Holy-Cross Day is September 14, he had probably never viewed the spectacle he describes. But that the papal bull did not entirely abolish the custom we know from an account called *Six Months in Italy* by a friend of Browning's, G. S. Hillard:

By a bull of Gregory XIII. in the year 1584, all Jews above the age of twelve years were compelled to listen every week to a sermon from a Christian priest, usually an exposition of some passage from the Old Testament, and especially those relating to the Messiah, from the Christian point of view. This burden is not yet wholly removed from them; and to this day, several times in the course of a year, a Jewish congregation is gathered in the church of S. Angelo in Pescheria, and constrained to listen to a homily from a Dominican friar, to whom, unless his zeal have eaten up his good feelings and his good taste, the ceremony must be as painful as to his hearers.[29]

[29] New York, 1853, II, 51. The Brownings are described in Hillard's book, a copy of which was probably sent to them.

A more vivid account, which Browning probably knew, is given in Evelyn's diary for January 7, 1645, when he was in Rome:

> A sermon was preached to the Jews, at Ponte Sisto, who are constrained to sit till the hour is done; but it is with so much malice in their countenances, spitting, humming, coughing, and motion, that it is almost impossible they should hear a word from the preacher. A conversion is very rare.[30]

Browning's poem is probably based on the tradition, of which he could have heard a great deal in Rome. The festival itself commemorates the dedication, in the year 335, of the churches built near Jerusalem on the sites of the Crucifixion and the Holy Sepulcher. *Holy-Cross Day* was probably written in Rome in the spring of 1854, or in Florence in the summer, when the poet was getting *Men and Women* ready.

Holy-Cross Day resembles *The Heretic's Tragedy,* also of *Men and Women,* in tone, though the concluding stanzas founded upon Rabbi Ben Ezra's *Song of Death* rise to a magnificent pronouncement of faith not reached in *The Heretic's Tragedy.* Concerning the proper interpretation of the passage, Browning wrote to Furnivall on February 17, 1888, that

> . . . in *Holy-Cross Day*, Ben Ezra is not supposed to acknowledge Christ as the Messiah because he resorts to the obvious argument "even on your own showing, and accepting for the moment the authority of your accepted Lawgiver, you are condemned by His precepts—let alone ours." [31]

Browning probably read Rabbi Ben Ezra (1092–1167) in Rome, where much of his work is preserved in the Vatican Library. *Holy-Cross Day* is the first indication of Browning's interest in Rabbi Ben Ezra, which led to his poem upon the sage in 1864.

The Guardian Angel

The Guardian-Angel: A Picture at Fano first appeared in *Men and Women.* It consisted of eight stanzas of seven iambic pentameter lines each. The stanza is a modified rime royal stanza. In 1863 the poem was classed with the *Dramatic Lyrics.*

The poem is a "fragmentary autobiography." The Brownings left Florence on the evening of July 17, 1848, to travel by coach to Fano, where they hoped to spend the summer. It was probably the 20th

---

[30] *The Diary of John Evelyn,* ed. A. Dobson, 1906, I, 203.
[31] *Letters,* ed. Hood, pp. 287–8.

when they arrived. They found Fano hot and unbearable, "yet the churches are beautiful, and a divine picture of Guercino's is worth going all that way to see." [32] They fled to Ancona after three days, and remained there, living upon fish and cold water. And here, during the last week of July, according to Browning's statement in the poem itself, *The Guardian-Angel* was written.

The picture which inspired the poem is called *L'Angelo Custode*, and it is in the Church of San Agostino at Fano. It was painted by Giovanni Francesco Barbieri (1590–1666), called Guercino, or "the squinter." The enjoyment of the picture at Fano was partly the pleasure of recognition, for Browning had seen pictures by Guercino in one of the favorite haunts of his youth, the Dulwich Gallery near his home. [33] At Fano he visited the picture on three successive days. The poem gives an excellent description of the picture, and shows, besides, several old and new influences at work. The address in the sixth stanza, to "Alfred, dear friend," and the question which concludes the poem, are directed towards Browning's friend Alfred Domett, whom the memory of Dulwich Gallery probably called to mind. (See my discussion of *Waring*, above). The earnest and religious nature of the thought in *The Guardian-Angel* forecasts *Christmas-Eve and Easter-Day*. Of course "my angel" of the seventh stanza is Mrs. Browning, who is largely responsible for the religious temper of the poem. In her portrait of the poet Mrs. Miller [34] sees Browning in this poem in a mood of lassitude and frustration. He was recovering from an attack of influenza, and his old headaches had recurred. But there is in the poem, as she asserts, a dependence and a need for moral support in the poet, beyond any physical weakness. Mrs. Miller is of the opinion that this dependence is an essential part of Browning's character.

In a letter from Mrs. Browning to Mrs. Jameson on April 2, 1850, both of the Brownings object vigorously to some derogatory remarks on Guercino in Mrs. Jameson's book, *Sacred and Legendary Art* (I, 82). But their travels in northern Italy during the next year enlightened them, and in a letter to Kenyon, dated July 7, 1851, Mrs. Browning admitted that she had given up Guercino after seeing other painters, notably Correggio. [35] I think the Brownings' more

[32] *Letters of E.B.B.*, ed. Kenyon, I, 380–1.
[33] See Griffin and Minchin, *Life*, pp. 14, 165.
[34] *Robert Browning*, pp. 154–7.
[35] *Letters of E.B.B.*, ed. Kenyon, I, 441; II, 9.

considered opinion may be reflected in the first lines of the eighth stanza,

> And since he did not work so earnestly
> At all times, and has else endured some wrong,—
> I took one thought his picture struck from me,
> And spread it out, translating it to song.

If this is so, these lines were probably substituted later, for the original ones.

In January, 1883, the Browning Society had a print from Guercino's picture at Fano reproduced and distributed among its members. In Browning's letter of thanks to Furnivall for a copy of the picture, there is perhaps a hint of disappointment in it:

I have been overwhelmed with your kindness in these last weeks: the papers, the illustrations—and now comes this really charming print. I probably saw the original picture in a favourable *darkness;* it was blackened by tapersmoke, and one fancied the angel all but surrounded with cloud—only a light on the face.[36]

The Guardian Angel has enjoyed a wide popularity; it is, perhaps, the tenderest of Browning's poems.

Cleon

Cleon first appeared in *Men and Women* on November 17, 1855.[37] The title was followed by the words "As certain also of your own poets have said " and the poem consisted of 353 lines of blank verse, divided into ten unequal sections. It has always remained one of *Men and Women*. Since 1855 the text has been changed only in a word or two, and has suffered a few changes in punctuation.

Cleon is a complementary poem to *Karshish,* and seems to have been written after it. For this reason, and others given below, it seems probable that *Cleon* was not written until the Brownings settled in Florence in June, 1854, after spending a comparatively idle winter in Rome.

It was most natural for Browning, after he had clarified his own religious faith in the writing of *Christmas-Eve and Easter-Day* and *Saul,*

---

[36] *Letters,* ed. Hood, p. 213.

[37] The pamphlet which purported to be an earlier edition of *Cleon,* supposedly printed for copyright purposes by Moxon in the fall of 1855, has been condemned as a forgery. See John Carter and Graham Pollard, *An Enquiry into the Nature of Certain Nineteenth Century Pamphlets,* London, 1934, pp. 177–8.

to imagine how Christianity in its infancy would appear to a detached, scientific Arab physician like Karshish. From that point it is a short step of the imagination to wonder how a cultured and philosophical Greek would feel about the advent of Christianity. The quotation which heads the poem is taken from *Acts* 17:28, and is a part of the address of Paul of Tarsus to the Greeks from the Areopagus in Athens. The poem purports to be a letter—as did *Karshish*—from Cleon in the Sporades to Protus the Prince, from the thinker and artist to the man of action.

In a suggestive article [38] A. W. Crawford has shown that the occasion of Browning's *Cleon* was Matthew Arnold's *Empedocles on Etna*, first published in 1852. In the edition of 1853 Arnold omitted *Empedocles* because he felt that the poem was ineffective, inasmuch as the suffering of Empedocles found no vent and the whole poem delineated a condition of utter despair. Browning thought of Empedocles' condition as illustrating the logical result of Greek paganism, and created Cleon as a later philosopher and poet who represented the final product of Greek culture, and who in the blindness of his pride rejected the Christianity which fulfilled every one of the needs already recognized by his own superb mind. *Cleon* is therefore a complementary poem to *Empedocles* as well as to *Karshish*. One may see Browning working out similar ideas in *Karshish, Saul, Fra Lippo Lippi,* and in *Old Pictures in Florence;* his final comment upon the failure of Hellenism may be seen in his *Parleying With Gerard de Lairesse.*

In 1867 Arnold reinstated *Empedocles* in his *New Poems,* and we learn from his letter to his brother in July of that year, that it was at the insistence of Browning:

I shall be interested in hearing what you think of the poems; some of them, I feel sure, will interest you. There are two or three bad faults of punctuation which you will observe and correct. "Empedocles" takes up much room, but Browning's desire that I should reprint "Empedocles" was really the cause of the volume appearing at all.[39]

The figure of Cleon in Browning's poem symbolizes the triumph of the Greek mind.[40] As philosopher and poet he is at the top in the Hellenic hierarchy. He is higher than Protus, the king and man of

[38] See "Browning's *Cleon,*" in *Journal of English and Germanic Philology* 26: 485 ff. (October, 1927.)

[39] *Letters of Matthew Arnold,* ed. G. W. E. Russell, London, 1895, I, 371.

[40] See the excellent interpretation of *Cleon* in H. B. Charlton, "Browning as Poet of Religion," in *Bulletin of the John Rylands Library* 27:282–90 (1942–3).

action who has appealed to him for help. He has earned his place by his achievements, and defends his comprehensiveness of attainment as the inevitable law of progress. And yet he is desperately unhappy, even more so than Protus because of his richer nature and higher development. His thought and imagination have driven him to the edge of the Christian doctrine of a God of love and immortality for the individual, but Greek thought could go no further. In his intellectual pride he casually dismisses Paul and Christus, who offer everything he yearns for, since "Their doctrine could be held by no sane man." The use of the word "sane" is significant. In this way Browning attempts to correct the suffering of Arnold's Empedocles; in place of a barren intellectual despair he offers faith in the Christian beliefs in a God of love and in individual immortality.

Cleon strikes so deeply into Browning's fundamental convictions that one can detect its kinship with a great many other poems. Its commentary upon Hellenism has already been considered. One ought to notice also the comment upon "life's mechanics" (ll. 187–220)—the biological aspect of nature—which is reminiscent of *Paracelsus*, V, 655–94, and which leads Browning as near to Darwinism as he ever comes.[41]

It is my opinion that *Cleon* was written in the summer of 1854, after Browning had written *Karshish* and had meditated upon Arnold's *Empedocles* of 1852, and its omission from Arnold's volume of 1853. That Browning thought well of *Cleon* may be guessed from his mention of it in *One Word More;* and the world has agreed with his judgment.

The Twins

The Twins with the motto, "*Give* and *It-shall-be-given-unto-you*," was first published in a pamphlet of sixteen pages entitled *Two Poems, by Elizabeth Barrett and Robert Browning*. It was printed by Chapman and Hall for Miss Arabel Barrett, sister to Mrs. Browning, to be sold for sixpence at a bazaar to aid a "Refuge for young destitute girls" which she was establishing. This pamphlet appeared in April or May, 1854. Mrs. Browning's poem was called *A Plea for the Ragged Schools of London. The Twins* was included in *Men*

[41] For an account of the place of *Cleon* among Browning's poems, see E. M. Naish, *Browning and Dogma*, London, 1906, pp. 29–59. See also my article "Browning and the Spirit of Greece," in *Nineteenth Century Studies* (Cornell), 1940, pp. 179–98.

and Women when that work appeared on November 17, 1855. It consisted of seven stanzas of four lines each. In 1863 the poem was grouped with the *Dramatic Romances*. The text has suffered only a few changes in punctuation since its appearance in 1855. The original autograph manuscript of *Two Poems*, with a letter to Chapman dated March 30, 1854, is in the Morgan Library in New York.

Mrs. Browning wrote to her sister from Rome on March 4, 1854, that she and her husband were going to send some verses for the bazaar. It is probable, therefore, that Browning's poem was finished at that time or shortly after. Sir Frederic Kenyon has pointed out [42] that the story told in the poem is older than Luther, for it appears in Odo of Cheriton and other medieval collections of moral tales. But it is evident that Browning read the tale in Luther's *Table-Talk*. William Hazlitt, in his translation, numbers the parable 316, and it occurs in the part called *Of Justification:*

> Give and it shall be given unto you; this is a fine maxim, and makes people poor and rich. . . . There is in Austria a monastery which, in former times, was very rich, and remained rich so long as it was charitable to the poor; but when it ceased to give, then it became indigent, and is so to this day. Not long since, a poor man went there and solicited alms, which was denied him; he demanded the cause why they refused to give for God's sake? The porter of the monastery answered: We are become poor; whereupon the mendicant said: The cause of your poverty is this: ye had formerly in this monastery two brethren, the one named *Date* (give), and the other *Dabitur* (it shall be given you). The former ye thrust out; and the other went away of himself. . . . Beloved, he that desires to have anything must also give; a liberal hand was never in want or empty.[43]

Only a few copies of the pamphlet were sold at the bazaar, and it became such a rarity that the price rose to three guineas. In 1887 a bundle of copies came to light, and sold rapidly at two shillings each. The pamphlet has again become something of a rarity.

Popularity

Popularity was first published in *Men and Women*. It consisted of thirteen stanzas of five lines each. In 1863 it was classed with the

---

[42] *Centenary Edition*, III, xxxvii.

[43] *The Table-Talk or Familiar Discourse of Martin Luther*, tr. Hazlitt, London, 1848, pp. 151–2.

Dramatic Lyrics. Since 1855 the text has been altered only in punctuation.

It is not possible to say when *Popularity* was written. It may have been inspired by the publication of Richard Monckton Milnes' (Lord Houghton) *Life and Works of John Keats* in 1848; it may have come from Browning's desire to memorialize Keats as he had done Shelley earlier in *Memorabilia;* or it may have arisen from recollections of Keats in Rome, where the Brownings stayed from December, 1853, to the end of May, 1854. This last conjecture seems to me most likely. Keats, almost as soon as Shelley, had become a great delight to Browning. It was probably in Shelley's *Adonais,* the elegy for the younger poet, that Browning first became acquainted with Keats, and C. Willard Smith in his book, *Browning's Star-Imagery,*[44] makes the suggestion that the "one man" of stanza 1 who saw Keats was Shelley. Several friends of Browning's young manhood had known Keats, notably Leigh Hunt and R. H. Horne; and later, in Italy, Browning made the acquaintance of Joseph Severn, who spoke of Keats:

One day Severn found Keats, who was studying Italian, deep in Ariosto. "Fine, isn't it?" he said. "Yes," answered Keats, sadly; then, tapping his own forehead, "but there's something here that could equal it, if they would give me but a chance." Domett, to whom Browning repeated this incident, believed that he would have made good the assertion, had he lived. "I believe it too," said Browning; and then expressed a very high opinion of his extraordinary powers of imagination and of the beauty of his diction.[45]

The poem is a commentary upon the neglect accorded Keats when he was living, and the admiration accorded many of his imitators during the thirty years after his death. Perhaps Keats's sonnet beginning, "Blue! 'T is the life of heaven . . ." gave Browning the figure of the murex and the royal dye that he develops through the poem. Thomas Hood, Tennyson, and later the PreRaphaelite poets, D. G. Rossetti and Morris, were among those who owed a great deal to Keats. But Browning was probably thinking of the hosts of Keats's lesser followers, at mid-century.

[44] See pp. 154–6. Mr. Smith connects the star-imagery of the first three stanzas, referring as he believes to Shelley, with the star-imagery which Browning had used for Shelley in *Pauline.*
[45] Griffin and Minchin, *Life,* pp. 262–3.

The Heretic's Tragedy

The Heretic's Tragedy. A Middle-Age Interlude was first published in *Men and Women*. It consisted of ten stanzas, each of nine four-measure lines save the fifth stanza, which had in place of the ninth line the words "Here one crosseth himself." There were two prose forewords, one in Latin and one in English, with the signature "R. B." appended to the latter. In 1863 the poem became one of the *Dramatic Romances*. The text has not been altered since 1855.

The poem is described in the second paragraph of the forewords: "It would seem to be a glimpse from the burning of Jacques du Bourg-Molay, at Paris, A.D. 1314: as distorted by the refraction from Flemish brain to brain, during the course of a couple of centuries." The poem purports to be "a conceit of Master Gysbrecht, canon-regular of Saint Jodocus-by-the-Bar, Ypres City." The scene of the burning was Paris, and I conjecture that the poem was inspired by some relic of Jacques du Bourg-Molay, or the Templars, which Browning may have seen in Paris during the several months he spent there between October, 1851, and July, 1852. It probably was written during the spring of 1852.

Jacques du Bourg-Molay, called "John" in the poem, was the last Grand Master of the Knights Templars, an order which had been immensely popular and powerful during the crusades. They had fought in the Holy Lands, governed Jerusalem, and had exercised much influence in the West as well; but when the ardor for the crusades had died away, they were envied for their great wealth, especially by Philip IV of France and Pope Clement V. The order was repressed, its property confiscated, and after many years in prison Molay was burnt in March, 1314. At the stake he repudiated his confession of simony, wrung from him by torture. He was hurried back to prison, but upon the same day was burnt to death by the order of Philip. It is possible that in Paris Browning resorted to his favorite *Biographie universelle* for information upon Jacques du Bourg-Molay.

The poem is a companion-piece to *Holy-Cross Day,* also of *Men and Women,* and resembles it somewhat in grotesqueness and grim humor. The grotesque quality and the horror of *The Heretic's Tragedy* remind the reader of *Childe Roland,* which was also written in Paris in 1852.

Two in the Campagna

Two in the Campagna was first published in *Men and Women*. It consisted of twelve stanzas, each of five lines. In 1863 it was grouped with the *Dramatic Lyrics*. Since 1855 the text has not been altered.

The poem owes its existence to the Campagna, and it has been truly observed that in the poem "the vague sense of the Roman Campagna is distilled into words." The May of the poem signifies May of 1854, when the Brownings were in Rome. On May 10, Mrs. Browning wrote,

The pleasantest days in Rome we have spent with the Kembles—the two sisters—who are charming and excellent, both of them, in different ways; and certainly they have given us some exquisite hours on the Campagna, upon picnic excursions, they and certain of their friends. . . .[46]

The poem, I think, was written either in Rome in May or in Florence where the Brownings went at the end of May.

There has been some controversy concerning the poem. Sharp, in his *Life of Robert Browning*,[47] suggested a personal application; Mrs. Orr denies the personal application altogether.[48] Mrs. Miller sees in the poem evidence of a growing gulf between Browning and Mrs. Browning, caused by their disagreements upon the manner of bringing up their son, upon Louis Napoleon, and spiritualism.[49] The poem is, I think, the dramatic embodiment of a mood which all men have. The perfect antidote to *Two in the Campagna* is *By the Fire-Side*, where love achieves perfect understanding. The mood of *Two in the Campagna* is the same as that of Matthew Arnold's poem, *Isolation,* in which he says, "We mortal millions live *alone.*" Because Browning's poem expresses so perfectly a universal experience, it has always been counted one of the most successful of his lyrics.

A Grammarian's Funeral

A Grammarian's Funeral [*Time—Shortly after the revival of learning in Europe.*] was first published in *Men and Women*. It con-

46 *Letters of E.B.B.*, ed. Kenyon, II, 165. See also Browning's letter of April 2, 1854, to Forster in *New Letters*, ed. DeVane and Knickerbocker, pp. 72–6.
47 London, 1890, p. 159.
48 *Life*, pp. 198–200.
49 *Robert Browning*, pp. 194–6.

sisted of 148 lines, alternating five-measure iambic and two-measure dactylic. It was divided into four unequal parts. In 1863 the poem was placed with the *Dramatic Romances*. Since 1855 it has suffered only a very few changes in punctuation.

It is not possible to say precisely when the poem was written; but it is certainly related to other poems which presumably owe their inspiration to Browning's residence in Rome from December, 1853, until May, 1854. The poem was probably written after Browning's return to Florence from Rome, for as we know, he then set himself steadily to work to get ready the *Men and Women* volumes.

The poem is a most successful attempt to catch the spirit of the scholars who hungered and thirsted after knowledge in the early Renaissance. It has been suggested that the hint for the poem may have come to Browning from Nathaniel Wanley's *Wonders of the Little World,* where in a chapter entitled *Of the exceeding intentness of some men upon their Meditations and Studies* the studious career and eventual death of Jacobus Milichius, a German physician, is given. Sir Frederic Kenyon, however, justly rejects this idea upon the grounds that the likeness is no more than general, that the date is not satisfactory, and that the poem was most probably written in Italy when Wanley's work was not available to Browning.[50] Other scholars have been suggested as models for the Grammarian. Gertrude Reese proposed Isaac Casaubon,[51] who had the proper thirst for learning, deplored the waste of time spent away from his grammatical studies, suffered from the cough and the calculus, and contemplated new projects while he was dying. Browning owned a copy of Aristotle, edited by Casaubon. But Casaubon's claim has been denied [52] and Linacre has been nominated in his place. He, too, had all the requisite attributes, and Erasmus said of him that he "only hoped he might live long enough to distinguish rightly the eight parts of speech." The probability is that Browning had several scholars of the early Renaissance in mind, and drew a composite figure. The Grammarian is one of the fundamental scholars who by their devotion to drudgery made the later Renaissance possible. His disciples recognize the boldness of his career. The likelihood is that the scene of the poem was meant to be Italy, and not Germany as has been suggested.

[50] *Centenary Edition,* III, xlii.
[51] *Notes and Queries* 192:470–2 (November 1, 1947).
[52] *Idem,* 194:284 (June 25, 1949).

The philosophy of *A Grammarian's Funeral* is the "philosophy of the imperfect," an idea which appears many times elsewhere in *Men and Women*, notably in *Old Pictures in Florence, Fra Lippo Lippi*, and in its reverse application is used in *Andrea del Sarto*. This philosophy found its classic expression in John Ruskin's essay *On the Nature of Gothic*, in his monumental *Stones of Venice*, the second and third volumes of which were published in 1853 and which we know the Brownings were reading in the early summer of 1854.[53] The idea, of course, is as truly the expression of Browning's personality as it is of Ruskin's. But it is essentially a medieval philosophy, and fits a little strangely into this poem which obviously has as its inspiration the early Renaissance.

The corollary idea of spending youth lavishly for a deferred goal, which is prominent in *A Grammarian's Funeral*, calls to mind *Rabbi Ben Ezra* of 1864; and it may be of significance that Browning used Ben Ezra's *Song of Death*, which is said to be in the Vatican Library in Rome, in *Holy-Cross Day* in *Men and Women*. I think it possible that the career of the Jewish rabbi (1092–1167), who was a scholar and wrote treatises on the Talmud, on Hebrew grammar, and a commentary on *Isaiah*, may also have been in Browning's mind when he was writing *A Grammarian's Funeral*. But the scholar of the poem is not Rabbi Ben Ezra, for the dates do not suit, and the Grammarian is a Greek scholar. "Hoti" is the Greek particle meaning "that"; "Oun" is the particle meaning "then," and "the enclitic De" is a Greek particle meaning "towards," so unemphatic as to be pronounced as part of the preceding word. The "calculus" which racks the poor scholar is the stone; the "tussis" which attacks him is a cough; "hydroptic" is used here in the sense of thirst.

The learning Browning displayed in the poem did not escape challenge. On November 21, 1874, he replied to the editor of the *Daily News*:

Sir,—In a clever article this morning [November 20] you speak of 'the doctrine of the enclitic *De*'—'which, with all deference to Mr. Browning, in point of fact does not exist.' No, not to Mr. Browning: but pray defer to Herr Buttman, whose fifth list ends also with 'De (meaning *"towards,"* and as a demonstrative appendage).' That this is not to be confounded with the accentuated '*De* meaning *but*,' was the 'doctrine' which the Grammarian bequeathed to those capable of receiving it.—I am, Sir, yours obediently,

R. B.

[53] *Letters of E.B.B.*, ed. Kenyon, II, 169–70.

A Grammarian's Funeral, in which Browning uses the grotesque in the service of grandeur, has always been accounted in meter and in manner one of his most successful poems.

One Way of Love

One Way of Love appeared first in *Men and Women.* It consisted of three stanzas of six four-measure iambic lines each, rhymed in couplets. In 1863 it was put, with its companion-poem *Another Way of Love,* among the *Dramatic Lyrics.* Since 1855 the text has not been altered.

In feeling, the poem is like *A Serenade at the Villa,* which probably owes its existence to Bagni di Lucca. The Brownings were there in the summers of 1849 and 1853. It is to be noticed that in the final distribution of the poems *One Way of Love* followed immediately upon *A Serenade at the Villa.* Here the lover, a man, resembles the lover in *A Serenade at the Villa* and the lover in *The Last Ride Together.* The poem is one of the clearest and simplest of Browning's lyrics.

Another Way of Love

Another Way of Love is the companion-piece to *One Way of Love,* and it also appeared in *Men and Women.* It consisted of three stanzas of eleven lines each. In 1863 it was grouped with the *Dramatic Lyrics.* Since 1855 the poem has undergone several changes in phrase and punctuation, possibly in an effort to make the meaning clearer.

Another Way of Love may have been written at the same time as its companion, though the poems are assuredly different. This poem, though hardly biographical, is more definitely than *One Way of Love* the product of Browning's married life in Italy. The speaker here is a woman; and the poems, taken together, are further analyses of the way of love with men and with women. The suggestion for *Another Way of Love* may have come from Mrs. Browning's repeated comment that her necessarily quiet way of life must be dull for her husband, a person of an altogether different temperament. Mrs. Browning had, occasionally, to force Browning to go out in the evening. But beyond the suggestion of the different temperaments in man and woman, the poem is a thing of Browning's imagination. *Another Way of Love,* though very melodious, has always suffered from being obscure. The wife, who is symbolized as June, speaks. Her husband has grown tired of the serene deadness of love, and the lady gives him leave to depart, hinting that one who appreciates her may come, or that now with her hard-won knowledge of men she may scorn them all, and by her lightning (scorn) rid herself of the insects (men).

"Transcendentalism: A Poem in Twelve Books"

"Transcendentalism:" A Poem in Twelve Books was first published in Men and Women. It consisted of fifty-one lines of blank verse, divided into four unequal sections. The poem, probably because it was neither a lyric nor a romance, has always remained one of Men and Women. In the final distribution this poem begins the section called Men and Women. Since 1855 the text has been altered in one detail. In 1866 Edward Dowden called Browning's attention to his mistake in calling Jacob Boehme, the German, "Swedish Boehme." Browning answered Dowden:

> The first blunder you point out is enormous—only explicable to myself —and hardly that—from the circumstances under which I well remember having written the poem, Transcendentalism. I was three parts thro' it, when called to assist a servant to whom a strange accident, partly serious, partly ludicrous, had suddenly happened; and after a quarter of an hour's agitation, of a varied kind, I went back to my room and finished what I had begun. I have never touched the piece since, and really suppose that the putting "Swedish" for "German" or "Goerlitzist" is attributable just to that—for I knew something of Boehme, and his autobiography, and how he lived mainly, and died in the Goerlitz where he was born.[54]

The text was corrected to "German" in the collected edition of 1868.

It is not possible to say when the poem was written. It is my opinion that Browning read Boehme in the spring of 1853 when Mrs. Browning and a great company of their friends—Frederick Tennyson, Powers the sculptor, and others—became interested in Swedenborgianism; for Swedenborg was a follower of Boehme. I should therefore ascribe the poem to the spring of 1853, a time when we know that Browning was busy writing. Jacob Boehme (1575–1624) was, however, a follower at a distance of Paracelsus, and it is possible that Browning's acquaintance with the German shoe-maker and mystic dated from 1834. It is impossible to say in what form Browning read Boehme's life and works; most of our information upon the

[54] Letters, ed. Hood, pp. 103–4.

mystic may be traced back to his own oral account to Frankenburg, and I suppose this is what Browning meant by saying that he was acquainted with Boehme's autobiography. The incident of Boehme's hearing the plants and flowers speak is thus transcribed, as an incident of the year 1600, by Bishop H. L. Martensen, in his book *Jacob Boehme: His Life and Teaching:*

Sitting one day in his room, his eye fell upon a burnished pewter dish, which reflected the sunshine with such marvellous splendour that he fell into an inward ecstacy, and it seemed to him as if he could now look into the principles and deepest foundations of things. He believed that it was only a fancy, and in order to banish it from his mind he went out upon the green. But here he remarked that he gazed into the very heart of things, the very herbs and grass, and that actual nature harmonized with what he had inwardly seen.[55]

It is probable that Browning knew the three-volume edition of *The Works of Jacob Behmen. . . . To which is Prefixed, The Life of the Author,* translated by William Law in 1764. Here he would have encountered the story of Boehme's communion with "the Herbs and Grass of the field," when "in his inward Light he saw into their Essences, Use and Properties . . . ," and here would have read of Boehme's settled conviction that "if God did but *once* put away that Duskiness, which moves about the Light, and that thy Eyes were opened, then in *that* very Place where thou standest, sittest, or liest, thou shouldst see *the glorious Countenance or Face of God and the whole heavenly Gate.*"[56]

The magician who serves as a contrast to Boehme was Johannes Teutonicus, a canon of Halberstadt, who in the poem becomes the John of Halberstadt who made roses spring up on every side. It is probable that Browning first became acquainted with this magician through Nathaniel Wanley's *Wonders of the Little World;*[57] but Wanley only says that John,

. . . after he had performed a number of prestigious feats almost incredible, was transformed by the devil into the likeness of a black horse; and was both seen and heard upon one and the same Christmas-day to say Mass in Halberstadt, in Mentz, and in Cologne.

[55] Tr. from the Danish by T. Rhys Evans, London, 1885, p. 7.
[56] See I, xiii, and I, 90. The latter is from Boehme's *The Aurora.*
[57] See Griffin and Minchin, *Life,* p. 23. Sir Frederic Kenyon advances the objections which I use here; see *Centenary Edition,* IV, xii. See also Wanley, 1806, II, 270.

It seems to me most likely that Browning called upon his recollection and ascribed to John of Halberstadt a conventional piece of medieval magic.

It is not known that Browning had any particular poet in mind as the author of the imaginary "*Transcendentalism.*" Perhaps the whole poem is a reply to Carlyle's reiterated advice to poets, that if they had anything to say they should say it in prose. Carlyle was, of course, a great transcendentalist. It is worth observing that Browning himself in his later days fell too often into the kind of verse which he here condemns.

Misconceptions

Misconceptions first appeared in *Men and Women.* It consisted of two stanzas of seven four-measure lines each. In 1863 the poem was grouped with the *Dramatic Lyrics.* The text has remained unaltered.

The date of composition is not known. The likelihood is that the poem was written early in Browning's stay in Italy, for the theme is similar to that of several earlier poems, notably *Cristina, Colombe's Birthday,* and the page's song in the second episode of *Pippa Passes.* The lyric is exquisite, and has been set to music by E. C. Gregory, and by Georgina Schuyler. It is also the subject of a painting by Byram Shaw.

One Word More

One Word More. To E. B. B. served as an epilogue and a dedication for the fifty poems of *Men and Women* when the volume was published. The original manuscript, signed and dated "London, September 22, 1855, R. B." is in the Morgan Library in New York. In the manuscript the poem was called "A Last Word: to E. B. B." The poem consists of 203 lines in trochaic pentameter, unrhymed. This measure, as Browning says in the poem, he wrote here for the first and the last time, in the hope that it would make "a strange art of an art familiar"; if he cannot turn to another medium to praise his beloved, as Raphael to poetry or Dante to painting, he can at least make his own art peculiarly distinctive upon this one occasion. In the edition of 1855 the poem was divided into twenty unequal sections. In the distribution of the poems in 1863 and in 1868 *One Word More* held its place in *Men and Women,* and concluded that category of Browning's poems. Since 1855 the poem has undergone certain changes. As it now stands it has only nineteen sections. No lines have been lost, but the one line, "What of Rafael's sonnets, Dante's picture?" which stood as the whole of section 8 in the original poem, has been incorporated into the following section, which now becomes section 8. There have also been one or two verbal changes; the most notable of these is the substitution of "Karshish" for "Karshook." Browning had, in April of 1854, written a poem entitled *Ben Karshook's Wisdom* (*q.v.*), and had given it to *The Keepsake,* an annual, for publication. It had not yet appeared, and Browning probably did not feel free to use the poem; later he did not care for it. The writing of "Karshook" in *One Word More* was a mere slip of the pen, and was later corrected. The usual changes in punctuation have been made in the text, and since the first edition the initials "R. B." have been added at the close of the poem.

Browning had long desired to dedicate a volume of his poems to his wife, and one may guess that he was especially eager after the publication of the *Sonnets from the Portuguese* in 1850. In *Men and Women* he found his first opportunity. The Brownings arrived in London on July 12, 1855, with the express purpose of delivering Browning's poems to the publisher. The fifty *Men and Women* were finished, the manuscript was shortly sent to the printer, and on August 17, 1855, Mrs. Browning wrote to her sister Henrietta that "Robert's book is partly printed." [58] It was probably in September, at 13 Dorset Street, that the poem was written; for in the manuscript Browning wrote the date, "London, September 22, 1855"; and Mrs. Browning wrote to her sister on October 3 that the volume was to be dedicated to her in a poem at the close.[59] It was therefore after the rest of the volume had gone to press that the poem was written. Though the poet had probably been contemplating the idea for some time, the actual writing came last of *Men and Women,* and evidently the theme came when he was trying to devise a suitable dedication to his wife.

In thinking how other artists had striven to give their work and lives to their loved ones, Browning despairs of emulating Raphael and Dante, who crossed from their chosen arts to others in which they

[58] *E.B.B., Letters to her Sister,* p. 219.
[59] *Idem,* p. 230.

were comparatively unskilled, in order to express their love. Browning had undoubtedly seen most of the madonnas by Raphael which he mentions here—the *Madonna di Foligno* at the Vatican, *Madonna del Granduca* in the Pitti Gallery at Florence, *La Belle Jardinière* at the Louvre, and many of the fifty others besides. The *Madonna di San Sisto* he probably had not seen. Browning almost certainly accepted the tradition—begun by Vasari's statement that Raphael loved a young girl, and remained devotedly attached to her all his life—that Raphael's lady was Margherita, sometimes known as La Fornarina, that she served often as a model for his madonnas, and that the painter addressed to her a century of sonnets.[60] There are two portraits of Raphael's lady, one in the Barberini Palace in Rome, and the other in the Pitti Palace in Florence; and both of these Browning probably saw. Three full sonnets and part of a fourth written upon the backs of some studies for the wall-painting of the *Disputa*, are the only sonnets of Raphael now known; they are at once passionate and highly finished.

In his reference to Dante, Browning is upon firmer ground. Boccaccio asserts that Dante had taken lessons in drawing from Cimabue, and that he was the intimate friend of Giotto. Browning's reference is to Dante's *Vita Nuova*, the thirty-fifth chapter of which memorializes the first anniversary of the death of Beatrice; that is, June 9, 1291. Concerning the picture of Beatrice which he was attempting to draw, Dante said,

> On the day upon which the year was complete since this lady was made one of the inhabitants of the eternal life, I was seated in a place where, having her in mind, I was drawing an angel upon my tablets. And while I was drawing, I turned my eyes and saw at my side certain people of importance. They were looking on what I did, and as I heard afterwards, they had been there some time before I was aware of it. When I saw them, I arose, and greeting them, said, "Another was with me just now, and because of that I was abstracted." And when they had gone away, I returned to my work, that is, that of drawing figures of angels; and while I was busy about this the idea came to me of putting words in rhyme, to be an anniversary poem for her, and of addressing those persons who had come to me.

[60] There is evidence that the sonnets did exist, though they are now lost. See "Browning Vindicated" in the *Times Literary Supplement* for May 25, 1940; Frederick Page cites Baldinucci's *Notizie*, IV, 26 to show that Guido Reni (1575–1642) had the book in which Raphael wrote his century of sonnets. Reni left the book to Signorini.

Browning loved this passage, and from it he drew the title for his volume of 1887, *Parleyings With Certain People of Importance in their Day*. Browning imagines Dante's pen to be corroded by the fierce writing of the *Inferno* of the *Divina Commedia;* but there is no support in the *Vita Nuova* for Browning's assumption that the "certain people of importance" were there to do injury to Dante, or that they were people of Florence who later found themselves in Dante's *Inferno*. Dante may have been composing the *Divina Commedia* in 1291, but the date he gives us for it is roughly 1300.[61]

The incident of Moses striking the rock, used in *One Word More*, Browning drew from *Exodus* 17, and *Numbers* 20.[62] Jethro's daughter, "white and wifely," was Moses' wife Zipporah, to be met in *Exodus* 2, 3, and 4. The moon-symbolism, which Browning uses in *One Word More* to express the completeness of his knowledge and love, was used by him several times in his later poems—always, I think, in speaking of his wife.[63] Mrs. Miller makes telling use of this fact in her analysis of Browning's late poem *Numpholeptus* (*q.v.*), where the poet sees himself as stained by life, in the presence of the pure white nymph of the moon.[64] To admirers of the Brownings *One Word More* is one of the most valued of all Browning's poems.

DRAMATIS PERSONAE

PUBLICATION

The volume which goes under the name of *Dramatis Personae* was published on May 28, 1864. The title-page read: "Dramatis Personae. By Robert Browning. London: Chapman and Hall, 193 Piccadilly. 1864." The volume was a crown octavo, consisting of vi pages—half-title, title-page, the printer's imprint, a table of contents—and 250 pages of text. There were eighteen poems in the volume, each preceded by a fly-leaf. The page-headings throughout the volume name particular poems. The first edition was bound in

[61] W. M. Rossetti noted the errors which Browning had made concerning Dante in *One Word More*. His comment is quoted in an article, "Browning and Dante," by Esther P. Defries, in the *Academy* for January 10, 1891.

[62] See W. H. French's note upon Browning's erudition in "The Sinai-Forehead's cloven brilliance" in *MLN* 62:188. The Hebrew verb for "shine" means "bright" and is derived from "horn." Medieval art showed Moses with horns.

[63] See DeVane, *Browning's Parleyings, With Daniel Bartoli*, pp. 79, 89–91.

[64] *Robert Browning*, pp. 278–80.

cloth boards of a dull red color. The price of the volume was Seven Shillings, a price a little higher than most volumes of poetry commanded.

TEXT

The table of contents of the first edition named the following poems:

James Lee
Gold Hair: A Legend of Pornic
The Worst of It
Dis aliter Visum; or, Le Byron de
   nos Jours
Too Late
Abt Vogler
Rabbi Ben Ezra
A Death in the Desert
Caliban upon Setebos: or, Natural
   Theology in the Island

Confessions
May and Death
Prospice
Youth and Art
A Face
A Likeness
Mr. Sludge, "The Medium"
Apparent Failure
Epilogue

Of these poems, several had appeared in print before their inclusion in *Dramatis Personae*. Stanzas 1–6 of section VI of *James Lee* had been printed in the *Monthly Repository* for May, 1836; the whole of section VI, called *Under the Cliff*, appeared in America in May, 1864, in the June number of the *Atlantic Monthly*, before *Dramatis Personae* was published in London. *Prospice* had likewise been published in the same number of the magazine; *Gold Hair* had been printed in the preceding number, for May, 1864.[1] *May and Death* had appeared in *The Keepsake*, a literary annual, for 1857.

The second edition was published in the same year as the first, and was made up of the same poems; but the changes in the text, notably the addition to *Gold Hair* of three new stanzas, at the instigation of George Eliot, make the second edition interesting. In the collected edition of Browning's poems in 1868 *Dramatis Personae* was included. Further changes were made in the text of the poems, and many new lines were added to part VIII of *James Lee's Wife* (*q.v.*). Two new poems were added to *Dramatis Personae* in 1868, both appropriate in character: *Deaf and Dumb; A Group by Woolner* was inserted between *May and Death* and *Prospice;* and *Eurydice*

[1] The pamphlet which contains *Gold Hair* and purports to have been privately printed by W. Clowes and Sons in 1864, before the appearance of *Dramatis Personae,* is condemned as a forgery by John Carter and Graham Pollard in their *Enquiry into the Nature of Certain Nineteenth Century Pamphlets,* 1934, pp. 181–2.

to Orpheus: A Picture by Leighton was inserted between *Prospice* and *Youth and Art. Dramatis Personae* has been included in every complete edition of Browning's works. George Eliot's copy of the first edition with Browning's corrections is in the Harvard Library.

GENESIS AND COMPOSITION; SOURCES AND INFLUENCES

In a sense *Dramatis Personae* carries on Browning's conception of the short dramatic poem—"utterances of so many imaginary persons, not mine"—and in part, but with some important differences, the volume is a continuation of *Dramatic Lyrics, Dramatic Romances* and *Men and Women.* The most significant differences between *Dramatis Personae* and *Men and Women,* which preceded it, seem to me to be these: in *Dramatis Personae* Browning speaks more often than before in his own proper person, and even when there is a character between us and Browning the dramatic disguise has worn thin; in *Dramatis Personae,* moreover, it is generally true that Browning is much more interested in voicing his opinion upon some topic of vital contemporary interest than he is in exquisite melody or in the nice delineation of character. The "persons of the drama" have become, in larger measure, exponents of contemporary ideas. The poet's powers of ratiocination have increased; but his creative impulses have slackened. The poetry, consequently, has become more argumentative and craggier.

Though the question of the date of composition of the poems will be discussed separately for each poem, some statement for the whole volume should be made here. Browning was not encouraged to go on in poetry by the reception which *Men and Women* received in 1855; but in the spring of 1856 he set himself to the task of revising *Sordello,* with no great results, and for recreation began to draw.[2] The next few years, mainly spent in Florence, were not fruitful for Browning's poetry. In 1858–60 he probably wrote some of *Mr. Sludge, "The Medium,"* some of the poem that was to be *Hohenstiel-Schwangau, Saviour of Society* (*q.v.*), and a few lyrics. The troubled state of affairs in Italy and Mrs. Browning's bad health probably did not often permit Browning's mind to be free for poetry in these years. Nevertheless, on May 18, 1860, Mrs. Browning wrote from Rome that "Robert deserves no reproaches, for he has been writing a good deal this winter—working at a long poem which I have not seen a line of, and producing short lyrics which

[2] *Letters of E.B.B.,* ed. Kenyon, II, 228–30.

I *have* seen, and may declare worthy of him." [3] The long poem I have named above; the short ones may have been such pieces as *Confessions, Youth and Art, Too Late, A Likeness* and *The Worst of It*. But in reckoning results in March, 1861, Mrs. Browning wrote her disappointment to the poet's sister, Sarianna Browning:

I wanted his poems done this winter very much—and here was a bright room with three windows consecrated to use. But he had a room all last summer, and did nothing. Then, he worked himself out by riding for three or four hours together—there has been little poetry done since last winter, when he did much. He was not inclined to write this winter. [4]

Browning had taken up modelling and sculpture instead of poetry; but later in the letter there is expressed the hope for better things: "He has the material for a volume, and will work at it this summer, he says." But on June 29, 1861, the greatest catastrophe of Browning's life occurred. Mrs. Browning died, and literary matters were forgotten.

Browning returned to England and made his home in London, save for the summers, which he now began to spend on the French coast in Brittany. To forget himself he plunged into the vigorous life of England. It had been difficult in Italy to get new books, and sometimes newspapers, but now they were at Browning's hand. In the years immediately preceding the publication of *Dramatis Personae* we find him reading such books as *Essays and Reviews,* Darwin's *Origin of Species,* Colenso's *Pentateuch,* Strauss's *Das Leben Jesu,* and Renan's *La Vie de Jésus*.[5] This contact with English affairs was to give a new touch to *Dramatis Personae* when it at last appeared.

Many of the poems of the volume owe their setting to the French coast near Pornic, Brittany, where Browning spent the summers of 1862 and 1863. Among these certainly are *James Lee, Gold Hair,* and *Dîs aliter Visum;* and Browning must certainly have written others as well during these summers. Meanwhile he was extremely busy looking after the education of his son, Pen; he saw Mrs. Browning's *Last Poems* through the press in 1862 and collected her prose essays under the title *The Greek Christian Poets and the English*

---

[3] *Idem,* II, 388. See also *Dearest Isa,* ed. McAleer, p. 212. *May and Death* was possibly written as early as 1853, and *Eurydice to Orpheus* in 1856.
[4] *Letters of E.B.B.,* ed. Kenyon, II, 435.
[5] See W. O. Raymond's excellent chapter, "Browning and Higher Criticism," in *The Infinite Moment,* Toronto, 1950; also C. R. Tracy, "Browning's Heresies," in *Studies in Philology* 33:610–25 (1936).

Poets, in 1863; besides completely rearranging and editing a three-volume edition of his own works during the same year.

It had been Browning's plan at first, as he wrote Miss Blagden on October 18, 1862, "to print a new book of 'Men and Women' (or under some such name) in April or May . . ."; [6] but *Dramatis Personae* did not appear in the spring of 1863 because the publishers, Chapman and Hall, thought it wise to make the most of the surprising sale which the three-volume set of his complete works was enjoying. Had the volume been published at that early date a number of the poems of *Dramatis Personae* as we now know it would have been missing. Indeed, some of the poems were written in the summer of 1863.

Written over a period of eight years, in such different places and changing circumstances, it is not surprising that the poems in the volume are so disparate in tone. A number of lyrics express the mood of lost love. But the chief characteristic of *Dramatis Personae* is this: that in an age when the poets were mainly interested in escaping to the past—Tennyson to Arthur's medieval kingdom, Arnold to Greece, Rossetti and Morris to the Middle Ages, the young Swinburne to Greece and Elizabethan England—Browning almost alone wrote of contemporary ideas and contemporary life, often in colloquial language and contemporary phrase. The true topics of *Dramatis Personae* are such live and pressing problems as science, higher criticism of the Scriptures, recent tendencies in the religious life of England, spiritualism, social conditions in the 1860's, and modern love. After Mrs. Browning's death in June, 1861, Browning purposely plunged himself into English life "with all its noises and hoarse disputes"—and there never had been a more troubled time. *Dramatis Personae* is the poet's straightforward answer to the perplexing questions of 1864. Besides the poems on controversial subjects, *Dramatis Personae* includes a surprising number of purely occasional pieces, such as *May and Death,* for example; and everywhere that it is possible to do so Browning has drawn his illustration and language from contemporary life. The seamy side of life is more observable in *Dramatis Personae* than in *Men and Women;* and yet, probably because of what he had suffered in the loss of his wife, the poet's spiritual fervor rose, perhaps even to its greatest height, in such poems as *Prospice, Abt Vogler, Rabbi Ben Ezra* and the *Epilogue.*

[6] *Dearest Isa,* ed. McAleer, p. 128.

Finally, on May 28, 1864, *Dramatis Personae* was published. The manuscript, presented to Frederic Chapman on June 20, 1864, by the poet, is now in the Morgan Library in New York.

AFTER-HISTORY

In spite of the comparatively high price of Seven Shillings, *Dramatis Personae* sold well, and a second edition was called for during the same year. It was Browning's first genuine second edition; and perhaps the most cheering fact for him was that most of the orders for the book came from young men at Oxford and Cambridge.[7] It is an interesting study to observe the difference between the critical reception of *Men and Women* in 1855 and this next volume nine years later. From the almost unmitigated censure of 1855, of which the *Athenaeum* criticism—with its description of *Men and Women* as "energy wasted and powers misspent"—is the worst representative, the tone had become almost entirely cordial.[8] In the nine years of silence *Men and Women* had been slowly making an impression upon the British public: the good sale of the collected edition of 1863 is a sign of the change, and the volume of selections from Browning's poetry by his friends John Forster and Barry Cornwall in 1863 had helped to exhibit the poet at his best. He had at last begun to be recognized for the force he was, and he was received with applause everywhere in England. In 1867 Oxford awarded him an honorary Master's degree, and similar honors were offered by St. Andrews. Even at the end of 1864 Browning could look with some pleasure upon the world, with only the grief that his wife had not lived to see his reward, to mar his enjoyment of his popularity. On December 19, 1864, he wrote to Miss Blagden:

I feel such comfort and delight in doing the best I can with my own object of life, poetry, which, I think, I never *could* have seen the good of before, that it shows me I have taken the root I *did* take, *well*. I hope to do much more yet: and that the flower of it will be put into Her hand somehow.[9]

[7] For an account of Browning's rising fame in the years preceding *Dramatis Personae* see Maurice B. Cramer, "Browning's Literary Reputation at Oxford, 1855–1859," in *PMLA* 57:232–40 (1942). See also *Dearest Isa*, ed. McAleer, p. 220, and *New Letters*, ed. DeVane and Knickerbocker, pp. 171 and 399.
[8] See, for example, the *Saturday Review* 17:753–4 (June 18, 1864).
[9] *Dearest Isa*, ed. McAleer, p. 201.

James Lee's Wife

James Lee—the title was changed to *James Lee's Wife* in the collected edition of 1868—was the first poem in the *Dramatis Personae* volume of 1864. It was a lyrical poem in nine sections, comprising 311 lines. Stanzas 1–6 of section VI were first published in the *Monthly Repository* for May, 1836 (N.S. 10:270–1), and were there signed "Z," the signature which Browning had used in the same periodical for *Porphyria, Johannes Agricola,* and "A king lived long ago." The whole of section VI, under the title *Under the Cliff,* was pirated in the *Atlantic Monthly* for June, 1864. The six stanzas which were published in 1836 had undergone a few changes in word and punctuation upon their publication in 1864. There are two significant periods of change in the text of *James Lee:* the first is between the first and second editions of *Dramatis Personae,* both published in 1864; the second is between 1864 and the collected edition of 1868, when as *James Lee's Wife* it had attained substantially its present form.

In the first edition the caption of the first section was merely *At the Window;* in the second edition this read *James Lee's Wife Speaks at the Window.* This new title to the first part made clear what was not so clear before, that the subject of *James Lee* was really James Lee's wife. The caption of the sixth part was altered in the second edition from *Under the Cliff* to *Reading a Book, Under the Cliff.*

The changes between 1864 and 1868 were even more significant. The title of the whole was altered in the collected edition to read *James Lee's Wife,* making the poem definitely a study in feminine psychology. And in the eighth section, called *Beside the Drawing Board,* twenty-two new lines were inserted to make up the second stanza of that section, and thirty-nine new lines were prefixed to the two lines,

> Go, little girl with the poor coarse hand!
> I have my lesson, shall understand . . . ,

which had made up the second stanza in 1864, to make up the third stanza of the eighth section as the poem now stands. After 1868 the changes in the text are unimportant.

It is clear that *James Lee's Wife,* to call it by its final and more accurate title, was composed upon the coast of France, and the scenery of Brittany is everywhere in the poem. Some of the poems may have been composed at an earlier time, as we know the stanzas, "Still ailing, Wind?" were, but the poem as a whole indubitably owes its being to the French coast. In a letter to Isa Blagden, from Ste. Marie, Pornic, Loire Inférieure, August 18, 1862, Browning wrote:

If I could, I would stay just as I am for many a day. I feel out of the very earth sometimes, as I sit here, at the window—with the little church, a field, a few houses, and the sea. . . . Such a soft sea and such a mournful wind! I wrote a poem yesterday of 120 lines and mean to keep writing, whether I like it or no.[10]

Earlier in the letter he had described Ste. Marie as

. . . a wild little place in Brittany something like that village where we stayed last year—close to the sea—a hamlet of a dozen houses, perfectly lonely—one may walk on the edge of the low rocks by the sea for miles —or go into the country at the back. . . . The place is much to my mind; I have brought books and write.

The sea, the fig-tree and the field of *In the Doorway* were seen from Browning's window. It is possible that Browning's poem of 120 lines was a part of *James Lee:* the conditions, however, fit better with *Gold Hair*. But the mood of Browning at this time, as may be seen in his letters, is the mood of James Lee's wife. Her problem, as Herford says, was like Browning's own—"how to live when answering love was gone." [11] One wonders if among the books which Browning took to France in the summer of 1862 was Meredith's *Modern Love*, which had been published on April 28. We know that Browning spoke of Meredith's poem with a "fervour of admiration." [12] The book was presented to Browning early in June, 1862. It is now in the Altschul Collection in the Yale Library. In the poem he might have seen Meredith attempting, with a difference, to depict intimately the same kind of tragic event which *he* had tried to draw in *James Lee's Wife*. Browning, answering a criticism by Miss Wedgwood in December, 1864, said, "You are quite right in your criticism—since I misled you into thinking the couple were "proletaire"—but I meant them for just the opposite—people newly-married, trying to realize a dream of being sufficient to each other, in a foreign land (where you can try such an experiment) and finding

[10] *Idem*, p. 119.

[11] C. H. Herford, *Robert Browning*, N. Y., 1905, p. 154.

[12] *Works and Days, From the Journal of Michael Field*, ed. T. and D. C. Sturge Moore, London, 1933, pp. 72–3. See also Miller, *Robert Browning*, p. 240.

it break up,—the man being *tired* first,—and tired precisely of the love. . . ."[13] Browning's poem, like Tennyson's *Maud,* is a lyrical monodrama, the moods taking the places of characters. *James Lee's Wife* is parodied in Swinburne's *Heptalogia* (1880), under the title of *James Lee and John Jones.*

Gold Hair

Gold Hair: A Legend of Pornic was the second poem in *Dramatis Personae* of 1864. It consisted of twenty-seven stanzas of five lines each. The poem had been printed before its inclusion in the volume, in America in the *Atlantic Monthly* for May, 1864 (13:596–9). The copyright pamphlet, purporting to be privately printed by W. Clowes and Sons in London, is almost certainly a forgery.[14]

The differences between the texts of the poem in the *Atlantic Monthly* and *Dramatis Personae* are negligible: the American spelling "armor" becomes "armour," and in the *Atlantic Monthly* the stanzas were not numbered. The text of the poem in the pamphlet agrees in all respects with that of the text in the first edition of *Dramatis Personae.* But between the first and second editions of *Dramatis Personae* Browning made important changes. George Eliot, the novelist, remarked to Browning one Sunday in 1864 when he called at the Priory that the motive of the girl's actions in hoarding the gold was not made sufficiently clear. Browning took George Eliot's copy of *Dramatis Personae* away with him, and returned it with three new stanzas interpolated after stanza 20. These are 21, 22, and 23 in the final arrangement, beginning, "Hid there? . . . ," "Truth is truth . . . ," and "Talk not of God. . . ."[15] Since the second edition of *Dramatis Personae* only a few negligible changes in word and punctuation have been made in the text of the poem.

Gold Hair was probably written during the summer of 1862. It may be the poem of 120 lines mentioned by Browning in his letter to Miss Blagden.[16] The mention of *Essays and Reviews* and Bishop

---

[13] *Robert Browning and Julia Wedgwood,* ed. Curle, p. 109.

[14] The gravest suspicion is cast upon this pamphlet by John Carter and Graham Pollard, *An Enquiry into the Nature of Certain Nineteenth Century Pamphlets,* London, 1934, pp. 181–2.

[15] Nicoll and Wise, *Literary Anecdotes of the Nineteenth Century,* 1895, I, 377–8. George Eliot's copy of *Dramatis Personae* passed into the possession of George Henry Lewes.

[16] *Dearest Isa,* ed. McAleer, p. 119, quoted above; see n. 10.

Colenso in the poem, together with Browning's presence in the region in this summer, make this date probable.

Browning found his story in Carou's *Histoire de Pornic,* and he has not diverged in any particular from the tale as he read it there. The church celebrated in the poem was dedicated to St. Gilles, and here in 1762 the gold was found. The church was destroyed in 1865, to Browning's disgust, to make way for a new one.[17]

But in *Gold Hair* Browning merely uses the old story to illustrate controversial subjects in the England of his own day. The *Essays and Reviews,* the publication of which was then called the most important single event in the history of the Church of England during the last two hundred years, appeared in 1860, and was a declaration by the Broad Church party of their right to free inquiry into the history of the Scriptures, of the Church, and of nature. The papers in *Essays and Reviews* were by several hands, among them Benjamin Jowett, Henry Bristowe Williams, and Rowland Wilson, the latter two of whom were tried for heresy and suspended from their livings. The sentences were reversed by the Privy Council.[18] The *Essays and Reviews* caused great excitement in England. Bishop Wilberforce especially was the great opponent of the *Essays* and edited a direct counter-attack, written by seven hands, called *Replies to Essays and Reviews* (1861). In 1861 John William Colenso, Bishop of Natal, wrote a *Commentary on the Epistles to the Romans,* and in 1862 he published his *Critical Examination of the Pentateuch.* As a free historical critic of the Scriptures he became a subject of great controversy. He was deposed from his bishopric in 1863 and was later excommunicated, but a judgment of the Privy Council re-established him in his place and rights.

In Italy in 1861 the Brownings had heard of *Essays and Reviews,* and Mrs. Browning was fearful of the effect the book would have upon Christian faith.[19] The object of Browning's poem, as he saw the trend of affairs in 1862, was to put in a word to show the efficacy of Christianity as a philosophy vital in the affairs of men. When Moncure Conway accused the poet of defending the doctrine of original sin in *Gold Hair,* Browning said Conway had missed his meaning; but the poem seems out of line with the usual direction

---

[17] *Dearest Isa,* ed. McAleer, pp. 219, 223.
[18] See A. W. Benn, *The History of Rationalism in the Nineteenth Century,* 1906, II, 114–33.
[19] *Letters of E.B.B.,* ed. Kenyon, II, 425–6.

of the poet's views in this respect.[20] The poem has not proved a general favorite; and some critics, because of the unpleasantness of the subject, the perverse moral, and such cryptic utterances as those in stanza 28, have found it, in Browning's own words, truly "horrible verse."

The Worst of It

The Worst of It appeared first in Dramatis Personae in 1864. It consisted of nineteen stanzas of six lines each. The poem, except for a few changes in punctuation, has remained unaltered. It bears some resemblance to the lyrics upon love in all its phases which so occupied the mind of Browning in Men and Women, and the poem may therefore be one of those which Mrs. Browning had seen in Italy in March, 1861. In The Worst of It the speaker is a man, addressing his unfaithful wife. The Worst of It should be grouped with four other poems in Dramatis Personae—Dîs aliter Visum, Too Late, Youth and Art, and Confessions, all of which take their start from one common theme, the worth of love. In all of these, save perhaps Confessions, Browning has dealt with the disappointed or even the tragic aspect of love, as he has also done in James Lee's Wife. This theme he had exploited in The Statue and the Bust, in Men and Women.

Dîs aliter Visum

Dîs aliter Visum; or, Le Byron de nos Jours first appeared in Dramatis Personae in 1864. It consisted of thirty stanzas of five lines each. Since 1864 the text has been altered in only a few minor points of punctuation. The scene of the poem is the French coast; and the poem may have been composed during Browning's sojourn near Pornic during the summers of 1862 and 1863. Yet it is possible that the poem was the product of Browning's summer of 1858, spent at Le Havre with his wife and his father. Dîs aliter Visum, the title of which came from Virgil's Aeneid (II, 428)—"To the gods it seemed otherwise"—is of a piece with several other poems in Dramatis Personae in presenting the ruin instead of the triumph of love. This poem is especially close in meaning to Youth and Art, the theme in each being the failure of lovers to grasp love when it is offered to them,

[20] See C. R. Tracy, "Browning's Heresies," in Studies in Philology 33:623–4 (1936).

and their subsequent regret for their ruined lives. In *Dîs aliter Visum* the woman has the last word and in a fit of scorn and chagrin informs her former lover that had he known a little faith with all his wisdom, he would have saved four lives from ruin; for both the woman who is the speaker in the poem and her former lover have been unfortunate in their subsequent marriages. Cynical disbelief in human goodness, or perhaps too subtle a wisdom of the brain, has been the tragic flaw of the man. Perhaps it was to catch this tone of cynical defiance which is the key-note of the poem that Browning reduced the verse to something like a jingle; for certainly that is often the effect attained by the internal rhyme in the second line of each stanza.

Schumann, "our music-maker now," died in 1856; Heine in 1856; Jean Auguste Ingres, "the modern man that paints," died in 1867 at the age of 88. The man of *Dîs aliter Visum,* an author "sure of the Fortieth spare Arm-chair"—that is, of election to the French Academy, whose membership was limited to forty—married Stephanic, a dancer, and the speaker had married a confirmed whist-player, to the detriment of at least two, and possibly four, lives.

The sub-title, *Le Byron de nos Jours,* has puzzled many commentators. Possibly the title is ironic, and Browning means to point the difference between the dashing Byron who never failed to assert his love when he felt it, and the over-cautious lover of this poem. Possibly Browning has in mind Byron's poem, *The Dream,* where he protests to Mary Chaworth that his life and hers would not have been ruined if she had accepted his love when he had offered it years before.

Too Late

Too Late followed *Dîs aliter Visum* in the *Dramatis Personae* volume of 1864. It consisted of twelve stanzas of twelve lines each. Save for one or two minor verbal changes for the sake of smoothness in the meter, the poem has been reprinted in all succeeding editions as it appeared in the first. There is nothing to indicate when the poem was written, except that it has the same theme of thwarted love which Browning had dealt with notably in *The Statue and the Bust* (1855), and was now treating again in the *Dramatis Personae* volume in *James Lee's Wife, The Worst of It,* and *Dîs aliter Visum.* Perhaps it is one of the poems which Mrs. Browning saw and spoke of in March, 1861. If so, it may be assigned to Florence in the later years of Browning's married life. As in the other poems named above, Browning in *Too Late* is attempting to comment upon modern love in modern terms. Here is another pair of lovers who have missed love, through a failure to grasp love when it came to them. The man did not speak his love when he should have done so, and now that Edith has died, after six years of married life with his rival, a poet, the lover ruminates upon his loss. Mrs. Miller calls attention to the similarity in appearance between Edith as she is described in stanza 11 and Julia Wedgwood with whom Browning was somewhat emotionally involved in 1864.[21]

Abt Vogler

Abt Vogler appeared first in *Dramatis Personae* in 1864. It consisted of twelve stanzas of eight alexandrine lines each. Little change has been made in the text of the poem since the first edition: a few alterations in punctuation have been made, and in line 2 of stanza 10 the word "likeness" was changed in the second edition of 1864 to "semblance" and has so remained.

There is nothing to set precisely the date of the composition of *Abt Vogler*, though we know that Browning sought consolation in music upon his return to England after his wife's death in 1861. The spiritual fervor of the poem, and its profound seriousness and beauty, leads one to think that it was written after Mrs. Browning's death.

The question has often been asked why Browning chose Abbé Georg Joseph Vogler (1749–1814) as the subject of his poem. The reasons are probably several: he needed a notable extemporizer; he needed a musician with a tradition of devoutness; and he always delighted in honoring little-known artists. In thinking of a musician who would meet these requirements Browning naturally came to Abt Vogler because he himself, as is not generally known, was schooled in the musical system which Vogler had invented. Vogler had been master to Weber, Meyerbeer, and Gänsbacher, and among others to the Englishman, John Relfe, who in time became musician-in-ordinary to George III of England and musical instructor to Robert Browning. Relfe's system of music was built upon Vogler's.[22] There

---

[21] *Robert Browning*, pp. 241–2.

[22] See DeVane, *Browning's Parleyings*, pp. 254–6. See also Herbert E. Greene, "Browning's Knowledge of Music," in *PMLA* 62:1095–9 (1947). The conclusion

can be little doubt that Browning first heard of Vogler from Relfe.

As an extemporizer in music, Vogler was famous. His pupil, Carl Maria von Weber, says, "Never did Vogler in his extemporization drink more deeply at the source of all beauty than when, before his three dear boys, as he liked to call us [Weber, Meyerbeer, and Gänsbacher], he drew from the organ angelic voices and words of thunder. . . ." [23] In 1803, Vogler and Beethoven at a musical soirée extemporized alternately, each giving the other a theme. In Gänsbacher's opinion—though he was not impartial—Beethoven's extraordinary powers as a pianist "could not raise me to the pitch of enthusiasm with which Vogler's masterly playing, unequalled as it was in harmonic and contrapuntal resources, inspired me." Browning's poem has given such an emphasis to Vogler's powers of extemporization that the fact that a good deal of Vogler's work is still extant has generally escaped notice.

As for Vogler's devoutness, there was indeed some question. After passing through the Jesuit Gymnasium and Lyceum in Würzburg, the place of his birth, Vogler was ordained a priest in Rome in 1773. The title "Abt" or "Abbé" was purely honorary. All his life he was devoted to music, and at different periods of his life was Kapellmeister at Mannheim, Stockholm, and Darmstadt. He looked upon himself as a missionary in some of the countries he visited. He travelled to all the great cities of Europe and was generally received with great enthusiasm. He was often accused by his enemies of being a charlatan and mountebank, but the charges were not proved. Perhaps Browning imagines Vogler as more spiritual than he really was, for he seems now more inventive than pious, more active in founding schools of music and in perfecting systems, than meditative. At any rate, the judgment of Griffin and Minchin was acute: "Vogler's countenance, if Zeller's portrait at Darmstadt does it justice, is expressive of shrewdness and good humour rather than of any marked spirituality." [24]

Vogler best exhibited his remarkable technique upon the organ, and he became notable as a master in the art of constructing organs,

of experts is that Browning was an intelligent lover of music rather than a musician, and that "Sliding by semitones, till I sink to the minor" is the "refuge of the destitute amateur-improviser."

[23] Helen J. Ormerod, "Abt Vogler, the Man," in *Browning Society's Papers*, II, 221–36. See also Grove, *Dictionary of Music and Musicians*. I have used these articles on Vogler throughout my discussion.

[24] *Life*, p. 231.

He also invented an instrument for measuring musical intervals with mathematical exactitude, and he devised a new system of fingering which was anathema to Mozart and has never been generally accepted. The "instrument of his own invention" was a small portable organ, about three feet square, called an orchestrion. It contained about nine hundred pipes, and was made in Stockholm in 1788. The organs which Vogler built seemed excellent when he played upon them himself, but other performers found difficulty in using them.

Abt Vogler is Browning's greatest poem upon music, and it exhibits all of the poet's characteristic conceptions of the function and effect of music, and its place among the other arts.[25] It should be compared with Browning's dicta upon music in *Pauline, Paracelsus, A Toccata of Galuppi's, Master Hugues of Saxe-Gotha, Fifine at the Fair* (ll. 1588–1611), and especially with the *Parleying With Charles Avison*.[26] Perhaps the philosophy of the poem may be said to be Christian-Platonic; nowhere else in his poetry does Browning come so near Plato in conception as in the concluding lines of the ninth stanza. This is allied, of course, to the nineteenth-century doctrine, "the philosophy of the imperfect."

The poem has always been included in volumes of selections from Browning, however few the poems chosen. It is possibly the poet's highest achievement in metaphysical verse; happy in beauty and in its love of music, as well as in its conveyance of profound thinking and feeling, it has received the suffrage of the English-speaking world. When asked by Gosse to select four poems of moderate length, which should represent their writer fairly, Browning chose *Abt Vogler* or *Saul* in the lyrical category.[27]

Rabbi Ben Ezra

Rabbi Ben Ezra was first published in *Dramatis Personae* in 1864. It consisted of thirty-two stanzas of six lines each. Beyond the usual

[25] See the excellent discussion of *Abt Vogler* in C. Willard Smith, *Browning's Star-Imagery*, pp. 183–7. Mr. Smith says, "Browning's selection, here, of the experience of improvisation as the clearest pattern of the process of artistic creation is a stroke of genius." *Abt Vogler* is a lyric, a dramatic monologue, and an argumentative poem, dealing with artistic, philosophical and religious themes, drawing a great deal of Browning into a compact poem, as Mr. Smith says. It may be, however, that the fervor of the poem declines somewhat when Vogler ceases to improvise, and begins to philosophize (stanza VIII).

[26] See DeVane, *Browning's Parleyings*, Ch. 7, where I attempt to show the derivation of many of Browning's characteristic ideas about music.

[27] *Letters*, ed. Hood, p. 235.

minor changes in punctuation to which all of Browning's poems were subjected, the text has remained unaltered in later editions.

It is not possible to say exactly when *Rabbi Ben Ezra* was written, though the probability is that it was not complete before 1862. It seems likely that the spark which caused Browning to write the poem was unconsciously supplied by Edward FitzGerald. FitzGerald had printed his pamphlet, *The Rubáiyát of Omar Khayyám*, in 1859, and though the pamphlet had no sale to speak of, we know that Dante Gabriel Rossetti and A. C. Swinburne picked up a dozen copies of the *Omar* at the shop of Bernard Quaritch, where FitzGerald had left them. Browning knew Rossetti, of course, and called upon him in 1862, and probably at that time Rossetti, as was his habit with all his vistors, made Browning acquainted with FitzGerald's transla-tion. Whether it happened in this way or not, Browning's philosophy of life, which he puts into the mouth of the Rabbi, meets squarely the way of life which is laid down by the Persian tent-maker. Espe-cially is this so in Browning's poem in the figure of the potter's wheel, stanzas 26–32. Here Browning definitely, I think, meets FitzGerald's wonderful but perversive poem.[28]

It is difficult to say how much Browning knew of Rabbi Ben Ezra's, or Ibn Ezra's, work, or where he found it. He knew Ben Ezra's magnificent *Song of Death*, which he probably saw in the Vatican Library, for he translated it nobly in Rome in 1854 and used his translation as the nine concluding stanzas of *Holy-Cross Day* in *Men and Women* in 1855. The figure of the potter's wheel, indeed, which Browning uses to answer FitzGerald, Browning knew in *Isaiah*, 64:8. Jeremiah also uses the figure of the potter (18:2–6), and the figure may be found again in *Romans* 9:21, where St. Paul says, "Hath not the potter power over the clay, of the same lump to make one vessel unto honour, and another unto dishonour?" [29] It seems probable that when Browning read of the potter and the pots in the *Rubáiyát* he thought at once of Isaiah's words, "But now, O Lord, thou art our father; we are the clay, and thou our potter; and we all are the work of thy hand"—and that he thought too of Rabbi Ben

[28] The likeness was observed and denied by E. L. Cary, *Browning* (1899), p. 129; W. L. Phelps noted the fact in *Browning, How to Know Him*, p. 342, but did not develop the comparison. In 1919 F. L. Sargent published *Omar and the Rabbi*, in which he arranged the words of FitzGerald and Browning dramatically, as if they were in debate.

[29] This passage had been called to Browning's attention by a letter of Owen Meredith (Lytton) of January 5, 1862. See *Letters from Owen Meredith to Rob-ert and Elizabeth Barrett Browning*, ed. A. R. and J. L. Harlan, Jr., 1936, p. 196.

Ezra's commentary on *Isaiah*. He then, remembering the fine robust spirit of Ben Ezra, used the general ideas of the Jewish philosopher to combat FitzGerald and Omar. Browning's knowledge of Ben Ezra's works, I imagine, did not extend far beyond a general idea of the temper and doctrine of that philosopher's opinions, though Browning was fond of rabbinical lore. The poem is chiefly valuable as an expression of Browning's own faith.

The figure of the potter's wheel and the clay, however dramatically appropriate for the Rabbi, gets Browning into some difficulties, for the metaphor seems to make man a creature without creative power himself, and that is contrary to Browning's usual creed. He therefore gives the clay an incongruous knowledge and a capacity to participate in its own making, and has to make the figure of clay give way to the figure of flesh.[30] The structure of the poem is not logical, but is a series of affirmations culled from experience and thought.

Abraham Ibn Ezra (or Abenezra) was born at Toledo, Spain, in 1092. His family was poor, and his early life was very hard. He showed great aptitude for learning but little for the practical business of making a living. Towards middle life the condition of his race drove him out of Spain, and Ibn Ezra spent the rest of his life a sojourner in foreign lands. He visited Egypt, Arabia, and Palestine; he lived for some years in Rome (where some of his manuscripts now are); he travelled in France and England, and lived for some years in London. His travels had the effect of increasing his interest in theology, science, and linguistics, and the latter half of his life, as Browning implies, was much more fruitful and satisfactory than the earlier half. Ibn Ezra was a strong believer in the immortality of the soul. He became renowned as an astronomer, physician, mathematician, teacher, philosopher, poet, and theologian. He made his greatest impression upon the world by his scholarly commentaries upon the books of the Old Testament. He died in Rome in 1167. The best account in English of Ibn Ezra's work is to be found in M. Friedländer's *Essays on the Writings of Ibn Ezra*, London, 1877.

Rabbi Ben Ezra has, of course, become one of the most famous and most popular of Browning's poems, perhaps because it expresses better than any other poem the peculiar quality of robust hope and cheerfulness which is Browning's contribution to the spirit of Eng-

[30] See H. B. Charlton, "Browning's Ethical Poetry," in *Bulletin of the John Rylands Library* 27:57–63 (1942–3).

lish literature. If it answers FitzGerald's *Omar*, as I think, it is possibly answered itself by Matthew Arnold's poem, *Growing Old*, published in 1867.

A Death in the Desert

A Death in the Desert was first published in *Dramatis Personae* in 1864. It consisted of proem, the body of the poem, and epilogue, 688 lines of blank verse in all. In the second edition of *Dramatis Personae*, also of 1864, the poem was reprinted as in the first edition, but in the collected edition of 1868 it is shorter by one line: line 23 in the first edition, "Closed with and cast and conquered, crucified," has been deleted. There were also in the edition of 1868 a few verbal changes, made generally in the interest of smoothness, and a number of changes in punctuation. Since 1868 no changes, I think, have been made.

It is not possible to state the precise date of the composition of *A Death in the Desert*. The poem is in the tradition of *Cleon* and *Karshish*, which were published in *Men and Women* in 1855, and may well have been written before Mrs. Browning's death in June, 1861.[31] As in *Cleon* and *Karshish*, Browning is here concerned with what he considered the first great crisis of history, the coming of Christ to the earth, and its effect upon the near contemporaries of that event. The attack upon the personality of the disciple and upon the authenticity of the *Gospel of St. John*, which was the spark which set Browning to writing the poem, had been going on for a number of years. Nevertheless, because Renan published *La Vie de Jésus* in June, 1863, and that book made a great sensation, many people supposed that Browning was answering Renan in *Dramatis Personae* in June, 1864. *A Death in the Desert* was written,[32] I think, at least in part, before Browning had read Renan in November, 1863, or Strauss's *New Life of Jesus*, published in January, 1864. I think that he probably added to his poem between January and June, 1864, when *Dramatis Personae* appeared. *A Death in the Desert* was probably written in the main either at Florence about 1860 or in Brittany during the summers of 1862 and 1863. In this early work it is probable

---

[31] See W. O. Raymond's chapter "Browning and Higher Criticism," in *The Infinite Moment*. Mr. Raymond pays special attention to *A Death in the Desert*, pp. 32–43.

[32] See *Browning Society's Papers*, II, Part III; The Abstract of the 48th Meeting.

that Browning was answering Strauss's earlier *Das Leben Jesu* (in George Eliot's translation) which had supplied him with material for *Christmas-Eve and Easter-Day*.

That Browning read Renan's *La Vie de Jésus* we know, for he wrote to Miss Blagden on November 19, 1863, these words:

I have just read Renan's book, and find it weaker and less honest than I was led to expect. I am glad it is written: if he thinks he can prove what he says, he has fewer doubts on the subject than I—but mine are none of his. As to the Strauss school, I don't understand their complacency about the book—he admits many points they have thought it essential to dispute —and substitutes his explanation, which I think impossible. The want of candour is remarkable: you could no more deduce the character of his text from the substance of his notes, than rewrite a novel from simply reading the mottoes at the head of each chapter: they often mean quite another thing. . . . His admissions and criticisms on St. John are curious. I make no doubt he imagines *himself* stating a fact, with the inevitable license—so must John have done.[33]

Here following, then, are the words which Renan had used in his attack upon the authenticity of the fourth gospel:

Is it indeed John, the son of Zebedee, the brother of James, (of whom no single mention is made in the fourth gospel), who was able to write in Greek these lessons of abstract metaphysics to which neither the synoptics nor the Talmud present any analogy? All this is weighty, and for my part, I dare not be certain that the fourth gospel was written entirely by the pen of an ex-fisherman of Galilee. But that in substance this gospel issued towards the end of the first century, from the great school of Asia Minor, which held to John, . . . is demonstrated, both by external evidence and by the examination of the document itself, in a manner that leaves nothing to be desired. A circumstance, moreover, which fully proves that the discourses reported by the fourth gospel are not historic, but compositions intended to cover with the authority of Jesus, certain doctrines dear to the compiler, is their perfect harmony with the intellectual state of Asia Minor, at the time they were written, Asia Minor was then the theatre of a singular movement of syncretic philosophy; all the germs of gnosticism were already in existence.[34]

Browning knew Strauss's early *Leben Jesu*, as one may see in *Christmas-Eve and Easter-Day;* it is almost equally certain that when Strauss's *New Life of Jesus* was published in January, 1864, he read Strauss's summary of the position of the *Gospel of St. John* in the judgment of the critics. To Strauss it seemed that Baur, the great Ger-

[33] *Dearest Isa*, ed. McAleer, p. 180.
[34] Ernest Renan, *The Life of Jesus*, tr. by C. E. Wilbour, N. Y., 1866, pp. 25 and 29. Browning read it in the edition of 1863.

man critic, had once and for all divorced St. John, the beloved disciple, from the John who wrote the Gospel towards the year 100 A.D. Strauss says:

The whole indivisible Gospel, advancing in all its strongly marked peculiarity, challenged criticism to an attack as decided, to a battle for life and death. In presence of this Gospel, it was incumbent upon criticism either to break in pieces all her weapons, and lay them at the feet of her antagonist, or force it to disavow all claim to historical validity. It was incumbent upon her to make it as possible to conceive this record to be a post-apostolic product, as it had been hitherto impossible to conceive it to be an apostolical work. It is the imperishable glory of the immortal Dr. Baur to have taken up this combat, and fought it out in a way which critical combats have been rarely fought before. . . . In his opinion this Gospel was a religious fiction freely drawn, and he recognized its fundamental idea to be the attempt to contrast the Jewish unbelief as the opposing principle of darkness, with the divine principle of light and life, as it appeared in Jesus, and to bring out into full relief the combat between the two principles, as an historical process, advancing forwards from step to step. . . .[35]

Browning was unable to meet Strauss and Renan upon their own ground of scholarship, but he determined to strike a blow for the personality of the beloved disciple, and for the authenticity of the Gospel, through his own weapon of art. As in *Gold Hair* Browning appealed from the rationalistic criticism of the Scriptures to their human truth, and as in *Cleon* and *Karshish* to our human need for Christianity. Browning gave Mrs. Orr in 1869 his reasons for thinking that humanity required Christ:

The evidence of divine power is everywhere about us; not so the evidence of divine love. That love could only reveal itself to the human heart by some supreme act of *human* tenderness and devotion; the fact, or fancy, of Christ's cross and passion could alone supply such a revelation.[36]

Browning accordingly dismissed one tradition which said that John, the son of Zebedee, was killed by the Jews about the year 70, and therefore could not have written the Gospel ascribed to him; and chose the older orthodox tradition that was begun by Polycrates, Bishop of Ephesus, who stated in the year 196 that John, the writer of the Gospel, lived until the time of Trajan (90–117) in extreme old age, and that he "who lay on the bosom of the Lord rests at Ephesus."

[35] D. F. Strauss, *A New Life of Jesus,* authorized translation, London, 1865, I, 141–3.
[36] "The Religious Opinions of Robert Browning," in *Contemporary Review,* December, 1891, p. 879.

The circumstances of St. John's death in the desert near Ephesus are imaginary, and so are all the characters of the poem, save the apostle and Cerinthus. Browning makes the apostle wonderfully prophetic, and makes him predict a time when men will doubt if such a person as John ever lived—an event which, in Renan and Strauss and many others, had come to pass at the time Browning was writing the poem.[37] The poet did Cerinthus, who flourished about 100 A.D., some injury. Cerinthus was a blend of Judaizing Christian and Gnostic. The only New Testament writing which he accepted was a mutilated Gospel of Matthew. Cerinthus believed that Jesus was the natural off-spring of Joseph and Mary, and that on him at the baptism descended the Christ, the divine power, revealing the unknown Father, and endowing him with miraculous power. This Christ left Jesus before the Passion and the Resurrection. In the postscript to *A Death in the Desert,* Browning seems to be striking through Cerinthus at the opin-ions of Renan and Strauss, as he comprehended them.

It is impossible not to see in *A Death in the Desert* a great number of Browning's most characteristic religious ideas. It has been called his most closely reasoned *apologia* for Christianity, with the possible exception of *The Pope* in *The Ring and the Book.* It should be com-pared with the poem *Development* in *Asolando,* as well as with *Christmas-Eve, Karshish, Cleon,* the *Epilogue* to *Dramatis Personae,* and other metaphysical poems. It has been well said that Browning attempted by these poems to turn the flank of the rationalistic critics of the Scriptures. *A Death in the Desert* is a sign of the falling off of the poet's creative faculty and the growth of his argumentative habit.

A number of critics at the time noticed that Browning was attempt-ing to reply to Strauss and Renan in this poem, notably the critic in the *Eclectic Review* (N. S. 7:68). Perhaps C. H. Herford has given the best judgment upon the poem:

A Death in the Desert, though a poem of great beauty, must be set, in intrinsic value, below these two [*Rabbi Ben Ezra* and *Abt Vogler*]. To at-tack Strauss through the mouth of the dying apostle was a smart pam-phleteering device; but it gave his otherwise noble verse a disagreeable twang of theological disputation, and did no manner of harm to Strauss, who had to be met on other ground and with other weapons,—the weapons of history and comparative religion—in which Browning's skill was only that of a brilliant amateur.[38]

[37] See Hoxie N. Fairchild, "Browning the Simple-hearted Casuist," in *Uni-versity of Toronto Quarterly* 18:236 (1949) for Browning's habit of using the "give-away" in his dramatic monologues.

[38] *Robert Browning,* p. 160.

Caliban upon Setebos

Caliban upon Setebos; or, Natural Theology in the Island was first published in *Dramatis Personae* in 1864. The title was followed by the motto: "Thou thoughtest that I was altogether such an one as thyself." The poem consisted of 295 lines, all blank verse save the two and one-half lines which constitute Caliban's song. The second edition of *Dramatis Personae* reprinted *Caliban* from the first edition, but in the collected edition of 1868 the motto from the fiftieth *Psalm* (verse 21) which heads the poem was left out. When Browning's attention was called to it by Mr. T. J. Wise, he said that it was a mistake and in the edition of 1889 restored the motto, which helps to a comprehension of the poem. Since 1864 the text of the poem has remained unaltered except for a few changes in punctuation.

Caliban was probably written in the latter part of the winter of 1859–60, although it may have been written in 1863–64. C. R. Tracy is inclined towards the earlier date because in December, 1859, the Brownings met Theodore Parker in Florence and were deeply impressed by him.[39] Parker, the American Unitarian, was reading Darwin's *Origin of Species* which had been published on November 24, 1859, and Browning's poem could not have been composed before Darwin's book appeared. Parker strongly believed that at every stage of human development man has produced a theology to express the highest reaches of his spiritual life; and he saw the need for humanizing the deity to suit the mind of men, that is, he saw the necessity for anthropomorphism in religion. His ideas were close to Browning's. Professor Tracy is persuasive, but does not rule out the possibility that *Caliban* was written in Brittany in 1863.

In any event the starting point of *Caliban* was Darwin's *Origin of Species,* which set Browning thinking of primitive man, perhaps of the "missing link," a popular phrase of the 1860's. The great debate between Samuel Wilberforce, Bishop of Oxford, and Thomas Huxley at the meeting of the British Association for the Advancement of Science on June 28, 1860, during which Wilberforce asked Huxley upon which side of his family he was descended from an ape, and Huxley answered appropriately, shows the state of popular excitement about the theory of evolution in the early Sixties. Fired by the conception of half-man, half-beast, Browning's mind leapt to the

[39] See C. R. Tracy's excellent study, *"Caliban upon Setebos,"* in *Studies in Philology* 35:487–99 (1938).

literary anticipation of such a creature—the figure of Caliban in Shakespeare's late play, *The Tempest*. Being Browning, he gave Caliban an interest in theology, which Shakespeare's monster certainly did not have to any notable degree; and again, being Browning, he made the poem a timely satire upon all those people who, having no revelation of God save that afforded by reason, insist upon creating Him in their own human image without admitting the limitations of their conception. But one must be careful in ascribing satire of such anthropomorphism to Browning, since he saw the human need for such thinking. It is Mr. Tracy's opinion that, allowing for the differences in evolution, Caliban's pair of deities represents a dual notion of divinity similar to Browning's. "Setebos," he writes, "was conceived empirically to explain hard facts in Caliban's everyday experience: the Quiet, on the other hand, is an intuitive answer to the deeper needs of his soul." [40] For Browning God the Father was never anthropomorphic; but Jesus was so, and felt our human emotions of love, anger, joy, and sorrow, and it was necessary for humanity to believe that the Unknowable had once taken on the form of the Knowable. It was the only way that God could make Himself available to our human minds. According to Mr. Tracy, Caliban is dimly beginning to see the ruling principle of the universe, but has not yet grasped the relationship between Setebos and the Quiet, and still believes in two gods who are opposed to each other.

Browning was convinced that he had merely developed hints from Shakespeare's Caliban. He wrote Furnivall:

Then, as to the divergence from Shakespeare's Caliban—is it so decided? There is no "forgetfulness of his love for music," since he makes a song and sings it; nor of his "visions of Heaven," for he speculates on what goes on there; nor of his resolve to "learn wisdom and such grace," seeing that he falls flat and loveth Setebos, and was a fool to gibe at a Power he had miscalculated. True, "he was a very different being at the end of the Play from what he was at the beginning" but my Caliban indulges his fancies long before even that beginning.[41]

The commentators upon *Caliban* have usually said that his use of the third person shows a primitive being. But in a close analysis of the poem E. K. Brown showed brilliantly that Caliban's shifts from the third to the first person and back again reveal his momentary

40 *Idem,* p. 491.
41 *Letters,* ed. Hood, p. 228.

mood and the tension he is under.[42] For example, at line 56 Caliban's use of the first person plural indicates impudent resentment; at line 68 he imagines himself as dealing with his inferiors—he is excited and pleased and feels like a god and talks like one; and then at the end where he is fearful that Setebos has overheard his angry tirades he drops back to the third person. But these are merely examples drawn from an extremely well-reasoned study. Caliban is a primitive being in whom there is a sharp conflict between fear and guile on the one hand and impudence and self-love on the other. The shifts in person in his speech reflect his mood.

Setebos figures in *The Tempest* (I, ii, 373) as the god of Caliban's dam, Sycorax. Shakespeare probably derived the notion that the Patagonians worshipped Setebos, "that is to say, the great devil," from Richard Eden's translation of Pigafetta's account of Magellan's voyage, in Eden's *History of Travaile*, 1577. The Quiet, as the over-god of all, seems to be Browning's own conception, derived, Mr. Tracy thinks, from the Unitarian idea of God.

Natural theology, or the art of reading the character of God from the evidence provided by nature, is, of course, an ancient study. It received new impetus in the nineteenth century with the rise of science. The famous *Bridgewater Treatises*, "On the Power, Wisdom, and Goodness of God, as manifested in the Creation," were published between 1833 and 1840, and had a great effect upon the popular imagination. Browning makes Sludge mention the *Bridgewater Treatises* in *Mr. Sludge, "The Medium"* (l. 1140). Nor were there lacking natural theologians who divined the features of the deity in the later readings of nature which were furnished by *The Origin of Species*. in 1859, and Lyell's *Geological Evidence of the Antiquity of Man*, which appeared in 1863. At any rate, Browning's *Caliban* was most timely, and satirized all those who fancied they had discovered the ultimate nature of God.

Many critics in 1864 recognized the aim of Browning in satirizing anthropomorphic theology, notably the reviewer in the *Eclectic Review* (N. S. 8:70). Others have seen the poem as a bitter attack upon Calvinism with its doctrines of predestination and eternal punishment. Perhaps the best critique in Browning's own day upon *Caliban* is that by J. Cotter Morison in *Browning Society's Papers*.[43] The poem

---

[42] "The First Person in *Caliban upon Setebos*," in *MLN* 66:392–5 (1951).
[43] I, 489–98.

has been recognized as a masterpiece in the grotesque, and Browning himself chose it in 1885 as perhaps one of his most successful attempts at dramatic poetry.[44]

Confessions

Confessions was first published in *Dramatis Personae* in 1864. The poem consisted of nine stanzas of four lines each. The text of the poem was unaltered in succeeding editions.

The poem was composed in Italy, perhaps in 1859, and was probably one of the shorter lyrics which Mrs. Browning had seen, for on February 22, 1860, she used the phrase, "Say it's mad, and bad, and sad," [45] which she took, I think, from the concluding stanza of *Confessions*. The poem, too, has a common theme with many poems in *Men and Women* (1855) in its insistence on the worth of love at any price. It should be grouped with *Too Late, The Worst of It, Dîs aliter Visum,* and *Youth and Art* from *Dramatis Personae*. As in most of these poems the commonness of environment and the meanness of the verse is according to Browning's design, and in *Confessions* it is his delight to pluck romance from such surroundings.

Augustine Birrell thought the poem "audacious in its familiar realism, in its total disregard of poetical environment, in its rugged abruptness: but supremely successful, and alive with emotion." [46]

May and Death

May and Death was first published in a literary annual, called *The Keepsake,* in 1857 (p. 164). Browning told Miss Blagden, in a letter dated August 1, 1857, that he had sent the poem to Miss Power, editor of the annual, "this very day." [47] It was included in *Dramatis Personae* in 1864, with the text altered in several words in the interest of melody. For instance, "Moon's birth" in *The Keepsake* became "moon-births" in 1864, and "prove May still May" became "be May still May."

The poem commemorates the death of James Silverthorne, Browning's cousin, in May, 1852,[48] and one may suppose from the phrase,

[44] *Letters,* ed. Hood, p. 235.
[45] *Letters of E.B.B.,* ed. Kenyon, II, 361.
[46] *Obiter Dicta,* First Series, 1897, p. 81.
[47] *Dearest Isa,* ed. McAleer, pp. 3 and 5, n. 13.
[48] See Griffin and Minchin, *Life,* pp. 54–5.

"when you died last May," that the poem was written some time later in the same year, or perhaps in May, 1853. It was too occasional and personal, probably, to find a place in the *Men and Women* volumes of 1855, and because *Dramatis Personae* was at once more occasional and personal than *Men and Women*, Browning included the poem in 1864.

James, John, and George Silverthorne were the children of Browning's mother's sister. She was the lady who paid for the publication of *Pauline*. In the Twenties and Thirties the Silverthorne boys, who have been described as "wild youths" and who were fond of music and the theater, were often the companions of Browning, and in the earlier days the boys often played together in Dulwich Wood—the wood referred to in the poem. James, the eldest boy, whose name becomes Charles in the poem, was Browning's favorite, and the poem probably records a tender memory. When Browning was married in Marylebone Church in 1846, James Silverthorne was one of the two witnesses.

The plant alluded to in the poem is the spotted persicaria which grew in Dulwich Wood. This flower becomes to Browning the symbol of the companionship between himself and his cousin. Because of its leaves, spotted with purple, the legend is that the plant grew beneath the Cross and received its coloration from the blood of Christ. It was a trick of Browning's memory that he always associated flowers with places he knew (see above, my discussion of *The Flower's Name*). An association of flowers and grief, similar to that in *May and Death*, may be seen in D. G. Rossetti's *The Woodspurge*.

Prospice

Prospice was first published in the *Atlantic Monthly* for June, 1864 (18:694). It was contrary to Browning's practice to publish in periodicals; he probably departed from his custom on this occasion as an act of friendship for James Russell Lowell, who had been editor, or for J. T. Fields, who was editor in 1864. Perhaps Browning did it to show his appreciation of the reception which his poems had been given in America. The poem was included in *Dramatis Personae*, which was published in London about the same time. The text of *Prospice* was established in the *Atlantic Monthly* and in the first edition of *Dramatis Personae*, and has not been altered since.

The poem was probably written in the fall of 1861. It is autobiographical in character—the poet speaks in the first person—and was written shortly after the death of Mrs. Browning. In his wife's Testa· ment after her death Browning wrote a translation of Dante's words concerning Beatrice (*Convito*, II, 9): "Thus I believe, thus I affirm, thus I am certain it is, that from this life I shall pass to another, there, where that lady lives of whom my soul was enamoured." [49] In writing the poem, also, Browning must have remembered the words of John Donne, for whom he had a great admiration: "I would not that death should take me asleep. I would not have him meerly seise me, and only declare me to be dead, but win me, and overcome me." [50] Donne is probably one of the "peers" that Browning had in mind in line 17. Beside being perhaps the most direct affirmation of Browning's belief in the immortality of the soul, the poem is a notable expression of courage, and phrases like "Yet the strong man must go," and "fare like my peers The heroes of old," seem to be drawn from words of a Norse or an ancient Saxon warrior. Perhaps this primitive love of battle conflicts a little with the Christian spirit of the ending of the poem.[51] *Prospice*, like Tennyson's *Ulysses*, written under a similar feeling of great loss, is a notable expression of courage. It has been generally accepted as one of the greatest of Browning's poems.

Youth and Art

Youth and Art was first published in *Dramatis Personae* in 1864 where it consisted of seventeen stanzas of four lines each. The text has remained unaltered in succeeding editions.

The poem was probably written in Browning's last years in Italy before the death of his wife, and is probably one of the shorter lyrics which she saw in March, 1861. The Bohemian atmosphere of the poem is that of the artistic colony in Rome, where John Gibson (1790–1866), the sculptor mentioned in the poem, had his studio.[52] The

---

[49] *Idem*, p. 297. See *La Saisiaz*, ll. 213–6.

[50] In a letter to Sir Henry Goodyer, dated September, 1608. See C. M. Coffin, *The Complete and Selected Prose of John Donne*, 1952, p. 375. I am grateful to Professor A. M. Witherspoon for pointing out this passage to me. That Browning proselytized in behalf of Donne's works may be seen in a letter from his friend Lytton in 1858. See *Letters from Owen Meredith*, ed. A. B. and J. L. Harlan, Jr., 1936, pp. 144–5. See also *Robert Browning and Julia Wedgwood*, ed. Curle, p. 86.

[51] For two attempts to analyze *Prospice* see the *Explicator* II, Item 53 (May, 1944) by the Editors; and III, Item 2 (October, 1944) by Harry M. Campbell.

[52] Mrs. Miller (*Robert Browning*, p. 225) attributes *Youth and Art* to Browning's friendship in Rome in 1859–60 with Val Prinsep and a French artist who introduced the poet to the more unconventional aspects of Rome's artistic colony.

prince mentioned in stanza 15 was probably Prince Albert, who died in 1861. Browning had known Gibson well in the Fifties in Italy, when he was reckoned England's greatest sculptor. He achieved even more fame with his *Tinted Venus,* which he exhibited at the International Exhibition in London in 1862. Giulia Grisi (1811–69) was, of course, the great operatic soprano. She was at the height of her fame in the Fifties and early Sixties.

The theme of *Youth and Art* is one which Browning had developed in *The Statue and the Bust* in *Men and Women,* where the lives of the lovers are ruined because of their failure to follow the prompting of their hearts. The same theme, with variations, is used in *Dramatis Personae* in *Dîs aliter Visum, The Worst of It,* and *Too Late. Youth and Art* shares with these three poems the poet's purpose to comment upon modern love in modern terms, and as in them the style is designedly familiar and colloquial. The embittered, rueful utterance of the speaker here should be contrasted with the scornful and cynical tone of the lady who speaks in *Dîs aliter Visum.*

A Face

A Face was published first in *Dramatis Personae* in 1864. It consisted of twenty-two lines. In subsequent editions the text remained unaltered, save that in the edition of 1889 lines 18–21 were indented.

This brief poem was written on October 11, 1852, in the album of Mrs. Coventry Patmore, whose grave and pure beauty is the subject of the poem. She was Emily Andrews Patmore, Patmore's first wife and the heroine of his poems, *The Angel in the House* (1854), *The Espousals* (1856), *Faithful for Ever* (1860), and *The Victories of Love* (1862). Her portrait was painted by John Everett Millais in 1851; a medallion of her was made by Thomas Woolner, the Pre-Raphaelite sculptor, at about the same time; and here Browning sets her beauty in verse.[53] It was commonly agreed that Mrs. Patmore lost her beauty when she laughed. She was admired by Carlyle, Tennyson, Ruskin, the PreRaphaelite Brotherhood, and many others. Mrs. Carlyle accused her of trying to look like Woolner's medallion of her.

But the situation in the poem, the two characters, and the artists mentioned are conventional enough. One hardly needs to go beyond the studios of Story and Gibson for the atmosphere.

[53] See Edmund Gosse, *Coventry Patmore,* 1905, p. 35. In the *Memoirs and Correspondence of Coventry Patmore,* by Basil Champneys, 1900, a copy of the portrait by Millais faces p. 116, and the medallion by Woolner, p. 118. Browning's poem is given on pp. 149–50.

A Face, like *May and Death,* was perhaps too personal to be included in *Men and Women* in 1855, but the occasional nature of *Dramatis Personae* permitted its publication there. Again, as in *May and Death,* the publication of the poem was commemorative of an old affection, for Mrs. Patmore had died in 1862.

A Likeness

A Likeness was first published in *Dramatis Personae* in 1864. It consisted of sixty-nine lines, divided into five unequal sections. Subsequently the text was unaltered, save for very minor changes in punctuation and in the indentation of several lines.

The poem gives evidence of having been written during the late Fifties, and was probably seen by Mrs. Browning. In a letter to Chapman, dated July 13, 1858, Browning requested that the publisher send him J. S. Rarey's *Art of Taming Horses* (1858).[54] Tom Sayers, "our champion," gained the championship in 1857, and retired from the prize-ring after his famous fight to a draw with the American, Heenan, "the Benicia Boy," on April 17, 1860.

The theme of the poem, the peculiar value which pictures may have for their owners and for few others, is reminiscent of *Men and Women,* but the familiar verse and the contemporary illustration make the poem more at home in *Dramatis Personae.* The poet has drawn upon his own recollections for the miscellaneous treasures of the sporting bachelor in the second section of the poem. Browning himself in his earlier days had ridden, danced, fenced, and boxed. In a letter to Miss Barrett in 1845, moreover, Browning complained amusingly of the way his own father kept prints, "fifty in one portfolio," and put treasures in helter-skelter among ordinary prints.

There is no difficulty in the interpretation of the first two incidents of the poem. The picture John prizes, his relatives call a daub; the portrait which the youth values above all else, his friend thinks a bad likeness of a girl they had danced with at Vichy. It is not entirely clear in the third incident what the emotion of the owner of the mezzotint would be if his etching were valued by his friend as much as he values it. Possibly in delight at seeing the picture appreciated he would give it to his friend at once; possibly he would give it away because the picture, when another admires it, has lost its peculiar value for him.

[54] *New Letters,* ed. DeVane and Knickerbocker, p. 107.

Mr. Sludge, "The Medium"

Mr. Sludge, "The Medium," was first published in *Dramatis Personae* in 1864. It consisted of 1525 lines of blank verse. The text has undergone only minor changes in word and punctuation in subsequent editions.

Most of the evidence indicates that the poem was written in Florence about the years 1859–60. As we shall see, the poem could not have been written before the summer of 1855 when Browning was present at a séance with Home, the model for Mr. Sludge; and the probability is that Browning would not have written this poem soon after his wife's death in 1861, so that presumably it was done before. *Sludge* was probably the long poem, "which I have not seen a line of," recorded by Mrs. Browning on May 18, 1860.[55] The illustrative material used by Sludge in his arguments fits the years 1859–60. Hawthorne, for example, who is mentioned in line 1441, visited the Brownings on June 9, 1858; the talk on that occasion turned to spiritualism. The Benicia Boy, the person Sludge sometimes imagines he would like to be (l. 1269), was Heenan, an American prize-fighter, who on April 17, 1860, fought a famous battle to a draw with Tom Sayers, the English champion. Though the poem was probably in almost final form by 1861, it was probably retouched in 1863 when Home was much in Browning's mind. It is not at all certain that Browning showed it to his wife.[56] She was a great believer in spiritualism for many years, and the poem would have given her pain, even though she had probably lost faith in spiritualism before her death.

For the prototype of Sludge Browning had in mind D. D. Home— or Hume—the American medium. Home himself was forced to recognize the fact, and he called the fourth chapter of his *Incidents in My Life,* Second Series (New York, 1872), "Sludge, the Medium.—Mr. Robert Browning.—Fancy Portraits," protesting meanwhile that "there is indeed nothing whatever to connect his portrait of Sludge with myself. . . ." Daniel Dunglass Home was born in Edinburgh in 1833.[57] He came to America when he was nine years old and lived at Troy, New York, and later at Norwich, Connecticut. His mother was gifted with second sight, and Home soon began to have visions him-

---

[55] *Letters of E.B.B.,* ed. Kenyon, II, 388.

[56] For a full background to *Sludge,* seen from the point of view of Mrs. Browning, see Miller, *Robert Browning,* pp. 191–9.

[57] This account is drawn from Home's *Incidents in My Life,* [First Series] *With an Introduction By Judge Edmonds,* New York, 1863.

self. At eighteen he began his mediumship, and the power continued upon him, save for periods of short duration when it was lost to him. IIe was in great demand during 1852 in New York and Springfield, Massachusetts, giving séances almost daily. Boston knew him in 1854. In 1855 he went to England, whither the great interest in spiritualism had preceded him, and received more engagements than he could fill. It was at the house of Mr. Rymer at Ealing on July 23, 1855, that Browning and Mrs. Browning attended a séance held by Home, which will be described in detail presently. In the autumn of that year Home went to Italy, and held a number of séances at Florence, among other places. On the day he consented to go to Rome, by his own account, the spirits told him he would lose his power for a year. At Rome he was confirmed in the Catholic Church and the rumor, which he later denied, was that he had promised the Pope to give up spiritualism. February of 1857 found Home in Paris being presented to their Majesties at the Tuileries, "where manifestations of an extraordinary nature occurred." IIe held séances every day in Paris during the spring of this year. He returned for a short time to America, but the "Press-gang," as he called the newspapermen, hastened his return to Europe. He met the Queen of Holland, revisited Rome, and in 1858 married the sister of the Countess de Koucheleff in St. Petersburg, Alexandre Dumas serving as "godfather" at the ceremony. Home held a séance for the Czar while he was in St. Petersburg. He and his wife returned to England, where the manifestations continued steadily. Mrs. Home died in 1862, and some time afterwards Home married another Russian lady of quality.

Only one or two incidents from Home's later life are of concern to us. In 1863, he published the first series of *Incidents in My Life*. In January, 1864, he was expelled from Rome as a sorcerer.[58] In 1867 Mrs. Jane Lyon, a wealthy widow, brought suit against Home for the recovery of an estate of £60,000 which the spirits had directed her to settle upon the medium when she adopted him as her son. Home continued to act as medium throughout his life. It is enough to say that though he was often accused of being a fraud the charge was never proved.

The meeting between Browning and Home which gave rise to *Mr. Sludge, "The Medium"* took place at the home of mutual friends, the Rymers, in Ealing, in the summer of 1855, when the Brownings had come to England to see *Men and Women* through the press. Home

[58] See *Incidents in My Life,* Second Series, New York, 1872, pp. 70–94.

did not mention Browning in his first series of *Incidents in My Life* (1863), but in the second series (1872), after *Mr. Sludge* had been published, Home gave a long account of the séance (pp. 105–6):

I have never seen Mr. Browning but twice. The first time was at the house of Mr. Rymer, at Ealing, at a *séance* there. Mr. Browning was then married to Mrs. Barrett Browning, whom I had known by repute, and through intimate mutual friends, for several years, and I thus became aware of her deep interest and belief in spiritualism, which continued up to the time of her death. Mr. and Mrs. Rymer and their family were present at the *séance,* which began by several of the ordinary manifestations. Mr. Browning was requested to investigate everything as it occurred, and he availed himself freely of the invitation. Several times during the evening he voluntarily and earnestly declared that anything like imposture was out of the question. Previously to the arrival of Mr. and Mrs. Browning some of the children had been gathering flowers in the garden, and Miss Rymer and I had made a wreath of clematis. This wreath was lying on a table, at a little distance from that at which we were sitting. The wreath was afterwards put on the table at which we were sitting, but whether naturally or by spirit hands I do not remember. During the *séance* this wreath was raised from the table by supernatural power in the presence of us all, and whilst we were watching it, Mr. Browning, who was seated at the opposite side of the table, left his place and came and stood behind his wife, towards whom the wreath was being slowly carried, and upon whose head it was placed, in full sight of us all, and whilst he was standing close behind her. He expressed no disbelief; as indeed, it was impossible for any one to have any of what was passing under his eyes, whilst Mrs. Browning was much moved, and she not only then but ever since expressed her entire belief and pleasure in what then occurred. It was the remark of all the Rymer family, that Mr. Browning seemed much disappointed that the wreath was not put upon his own head instead of his wife's, and that his placing himself in the way of where it was being carried, was for the purpose of giving it an opportunity of being placed upon his own brow.

The last sentence of Home's statement was a shrewd but, as we know, an unfair blow. His account of what happened is not altogether accurate. Browning denied leaving his place to stand behind his wife's chair as the wreath approached her; [59] he was suspicious of the phenomena, there is no doubt, and his suspicions were not allayed when he and all the others save Mr. Rymer were requested to leave the room when the manifestations were over. Not long afterwards he wrote to Miss de Gaudrion a curiously formal statement of his opinions of the séance:

[59] See the excellent article by W. L. Phelps, "Robert Browning on Spiritualism," in the *Yale Review*, N. S. 23:125–38, quoting new letters of Browning.

Mr. Browning presents his compliments to Miss de Gaudrion, and feels it his duty to say a word for himself in reply to her note—though he has to overcome a real repugnance at recurring to the subject.

Mr. Browning did, in company with his wife, witness Mr. Hume's performances at —— on the night Miss de Gaudrion alludes to —— and he is hardly able to account for the fact that there can be another opinion than his own on the matter—that being that the whole display of "hands," "spirit utterances," etc., were a cheat and imposture. Mr. Browning believes in the sincerity and good faith of the —— family. . . . Mr. Browning has, however, abundant experience that the best and rarest of nature may begin by the proper mistrust of the more ordinary results of reasoning when employed in such investigations as these; go on to an abnegation of the regular tests of truth and rationality in favour of those particular experiments—and end in a voluntary prostration of the whole intelligence before what is assumed to transcend all intelligence. Once arrived at this point, no trick is too gross; absurdities are referred to "low spirits," falsehoods to "personating spirits"—and the One, terribly apparent spirit—the father of lies—has it all his own way. Mr. Browning had some difficulty in keeping from an offensive expression of his feeling at Mr. ——'s —he has since seen Mr. Hume and relieved himself.[60]

Two days after the séance Browning had attempted to make another appointment with Home at the Rymers' and he proposed to bring with him his friend, the actress, Miss Helen Faucit. His request was refused. The relief of his feelings, which Browning comments upon in his statement above, is probably a reference to his second meeting with the medium, when Home came to call at the Brownings' apartment a few days later. Home records the incident thus:

We were shown into the drawing-room, and he, advancing to meet us, shook hands with Mrs. Rymer; then, passing by me shook hands with her son. As he was repassing me I held out my hand, when, with a tragic air, he threw his hand on his left shoulder, and stalked away. My attention was now drawn to Mrs. Browning, who was standing nearly in the centre of the room, and looked very pale and agitated. I approached and she placed both her hands in mine, and said, in a voice of emotion, "Oh, dear Mr. Home, do not, do not blame me. I am so sorry, but I am not to blame. . . ." For a moment all was confusion, but at last we were seated, I scarce know how, when Mr. Browning began in an excited manner, saying, "Mrs. Rymer, I beg to inform you that I was exceedingly dissatisfied with everything I saw at your house the other night, and I should like to know why you refused to receive me again with my friend." I replied to this, "Mr. Browning, that was the time and place for you to have made objections regarding the manifestations, and not now. I gave you every possible opportunity, and you availed yourself of it, and expressed yourself satisfied."

[60] *Elizabeth Barrett Browning in her Letters,* ed. Percy Lubbock, 1906, pp. 355–6. See also the letters referred to above, n. 59.

He said, "I am not addressing myself to you, sir." I said, "No; but it is of me you are speaking, and it would only be fair and gentleman-like to allow me to reply." Mrs. Rymer said, "Mr. Home is quite right, and as regards not being able to receive you and your friend, we could not do so on account of our engagements." Mr. Browning's face was pallid with rage, and his movements, as he swayed backwards and forwards on his chair, were like those of a maniac. At this moment I rose to leave the room, and, passing him, shook hands with Mrs. Browning, who was nearly ready to faint. As she shook hands with me she said, "Dear Mr. Home, I am not to blame. Oh, dear! oh, dear!" [61]

One other encounter between Browning and Home seems to have had a part in the poet's conception of Mr. Sludge. On April 19, 1863, Browning wrote to Miss Blagden:

I never read Hume's book [*Incidents* . . . (First Series)],—avoid looking at an extract from it. Did I tell you that, just before I went to Paris, I went to a party at Lady Salisbury's and came right upon *him*, though I could not believe my eyes: presently the Marchioness' sister asked me, "what I thought of him?"—I said my say, as briefly as possible—"Why, he's gone!" said she—and so he had,—I can't help flattering myself, that the announcement of my name did him no good.[62]

Since Browning did not read Home's book in 1863, it would be interesting to know where he learned the many facts about Home's early life that he uses in Sludge's account of his youth. For Home, like Sludge, was led on to become a medium by eager demands for more manifestations. And Home did sail for England from Boston, where Browning places the scene of the poem, though of course Home admits to no such forced departure as Sludge suffers from Hiram H. Horsefall, his American patron. Browning does, indeed, make for a time a very sympathetic case for Sludge, and his censure falls even more heavily upon those who encourage Sludge to become the liar he is. In the end of the poem, of course, Sludge is seen to be despicable. In vanity, candor, and subtle knavery, the figure is reminiscent of Chaucer's Pardoner.

Recent commentators have observed Browning's strong animus against Sludge, "the meanest and most contemptible of his casuists"; [63] and also have remarked upon the quantity of Browning's doctrine and diction which Sludge is permitted to use. They also see that society is guilty in encouraging Sludge to trifle with spiritual im-

[61] *Incidents in My Life*, Second Series, 1872, pp. 107–8.
[62] *Dearest Isa*, ed. McAleer, p. 160.
[63] See W. O. Raymond, "Browning's Casuists," in *The Infinite Moment*, and D. A. Smalley, *Browning's Essay on Chatterton*, pp. 64–76.

pulses as he does. H. N. Fairchild sees in the exposure of Sludge's true character at the end of the poem a prime example of Browning's habit of appending a "give-away" to the monologues of his specious characters. Having had his fun, Browning does his duty.[64]

As for the curious Americanisms which Sludge uses in his speech, it is to be hoped that they never existed outside the poet's imagination. It must be admitted, however, that Browning had ample opportunity to observe Americans of many sorts in Italy.

The subject of spiritualism is one of the few upon which Browning and Mrs. Browning disagreed. It is worth notice that, according to her son Robert Wiedemann Browning, and contrary to Home's assertion, Mrs. Browning changed her opinion of spiritualism somewhat:

What, however, I am more desirous of stating is that towards the end of her life my mother's views on "spiritual manifestations" were much modified. The change was brought about, in a great measure, by the discovery that she had been duped by a friend in whom she had blind faith. The pain of the disillusion was very great, but her eyes were opened and she saw clearly.[65]

Browning continued to despise Home and to disbelieve in spiritualism. He believed fundamentally that God did not grant, nor mankind need, miracles in these late ages, as he shows in *A Death in the Desert, Development,* and elsewhere.

Apparent Failure

Apparent Failure was first published in *Dramatis Personae* in 1864. It consisted of seven stanzas of nine lines each. In succeeding editions the text has remained unaltered.

The poem was probably written in Pornic on the coast of Brittany, in the summer of 1863. It is here that Browning probably saw the *"Paris Newspaper,"* a quotation from which headed the poem: "We shall soon lose a celebrated building." The phrase "seven years since" of the first line indicates 1863, for Prince Louis Napoleon, the only son of Napoleon III, was baptized in June, 1856, and Browning was a spectator of that event. The Imperial Congress to end the Crimean War met in Paris early in 1856. The Brownings were in Paris from October, 1855, until June, 1856, and were, of course, immensely in-

---

[64] "Browning the Simple-hearted Casuist," in *University of Toronto Quarterly* 18:235 (1949).
[65] *Times Literary Supplement* for December 5, 1902.

terested in Count Cavour's successful attempt to get Piedmont recognized as one of the great powers of Europe, as a reward for the troops which Piedmont had sent to the aid of France and England in the Crimean Peninsula. Prince Alexander Gortschakoff (1798–1883) was the Russian statesman present at the Congress in Paris. He later became Minister for Foreign Affairs in St. Petersburg. Count von Buol-Schauenstein (1797–1865) represented Austria.

Browning's comment upon the three specimens of the débris of nineteenth-century life which have at last come to the morgue to be claimed—the youth mad with ambition, the old red socialist, the man mad with lust—has not always been understood, and the poet has been called heartless for preaching so trite a moral over the three corpses. It is my opinion that the moral—the first three lines of the last stanza—is meant ironically as the kind of moral which the self-righteous might preach. The six concluding lines of the last stanza are Browning's faith, sincerely expressed. At least, Browning saw the evil and suffering of the world face to face here, and the poem should go some way towards answering the criticism that his optimism was easily won. Browning told his friend, Alfred Domett, that *Apparent Failure* was a favorite poem of Tennyson's.[66] The "Doric little Morgue," threatened in 1803, still stands.

Epilogue

The *Epilogue* was the concluding poem in *Dramatis Personae*. It consisted of 101 lines in all, divided in this manner: First Speaker, *as David*—21 lines in four stanzas; Second Speaker, *as Renan*—44 lines; Third Speaker—36 lines in twelve stanzas of three lines each. Save for very minor changes in punctuation, the text has been reprinted unaltered in subsequent editions.

There is little doubt, I think, that the *Epilogue* was conceived and written when all the other poems in the volume were in hand. The fact that Renan is made a speaker in the poem seems to indicate that the *Epilogue* was written after November 19, 1863, when Browning, in writing to Miss Blagden that he had just finished reading Renan's *La Vie de Jésus*, criticized it sharply. The poem was probably written soon after that date.

The *Epilogue* is intimately related to a group of poems in *Dramatis Personae* which makes up the bulk of the volume: *Gold Hair, A*

[66] Griffin and Minchin, *Life*, p. 208.

Death in the Desert, Caliban upon Setebos, and *Mr. Sludge, "The Medium."* All these poems, as well as others in the volume, have to do with the state of religion in the sixth and seventh decades of the nineteenth century. The *Epilogue* is a survey of the two major tendencies which Browning observed in contemporary religious thought, and a final statement of his own position.[67] The dramatic disguise of the poet, kept almost continuously throughout the volume, is dropped in the speech of the Third Speaker of the *Epilogue.* He is Browning.

The three aspects of modern Christianity which the poet observes in the *Epilogue* are, with small changes, the three aspects of the same problem which he had delineated in *Christmas-Eve* in 1850. In that poem he had considered the sacerdotal, ritualistic, Catholic position in his description of the mass at St. Peter's in Rome. Since 1850 the movement towards ritualism had progressed; the Oxford Movement had not only sent numbers to Rome, but had influenced the Anglican Church immensely in the direction of the High Church; and in 1860 the Tractarians who had stayed in the Anglican Church formed the English Church Union. In the *Epilogue,* the First Speaker, *as David,* is made to speak for this ritualistic point of view, honoring the House of the Lord, the Church, as the residing-place of God.

The second aspect of religious thought which Browning deals with in the *Epilogue* is that of the higher criticism of the Scriptures. In *Christmas-Eve* Browning had depicted the German professor rationalizing Christianity away in his lecture-room at Göttingen. There Browning was obviously aiming at Strauss and the Tübingen school of critics, for he had recently read Strauss's *Leben Jesu* in translation. In 1864 the spokesman of higher criticism is Renan, whose book *La Vie de Jésus* Browning had just read, as he tells in a letter to Miss Blagden dated November 19, 1863. He found Renan's book "weaker and less honest than I was led to expect." And he adds, "I am glad it is written; if he thinks he can prove what he says, he has fewer doubts on the subject than I, but mine are none of his." [68] The Second Speaker, *as Renan,* is represented in the *Epilogue* as voicing the sorrowful conclusions of a skepticism to which he has been driven by the great increase in historical knowledge. In grief, he sees the historical reality of Christ fade from him. Browning hardly does justice

---

[67] See the excellent paper by Watson Kirkconnell, "The Epilogue to *Dramatis Personae,*" in *MLN* 41:213–9. See also the very helpful comments by W. O. Raymond in *The Infinite Moment,* pp. 49–50.

[68] *Dearest Isa,* ed. McAleer, p. 180. See also above, *A Death in the Desert.*

to Renan's position, for the personality of Christ is very precious to the French critic, and his attempt is to make "the face" more vivid, rather than less.

These two representative aspects of contemporary Christianity are answered by Browning as the Third Speaker; "Friends, I have seen through your eyes, now use mine." Browning's position is very much the same as it had been in *Christmas-Eve*—or rather very much the same as the position held by Elizabeth Barrett, and assented to by himself, in 1846.[69] In *Christmas-Eve* Browning had agreed with Miss Barrett in "liking beyond comparison best, the simplicity of the dissenters," though he agreed with her that he "could worship anywhere and with all sorts of worshippers." In the third part of the *Epilogue* Browning answers the ritualistic Churchman by declaring that God is everywhere in the universe,

> Why, where's the need of Temple, when the walls
> O' the world are that? What use of swells and falls
> From Levites' choir, Priests' cries, and trumpet-calls?

God is not limited to buildings of stone and brick.

To the higher critics Browning's answer is that the face of Christ, instead of fading as we inspect the facts of the world, grows more complete and vivid to us,

> That one Face, far from vanish, rather grows
> Or decomposes but to recompose,
> Becomes my universe that feels and knows!

Here Browning has appealed from historical criticism to intimate personal feeling, to the need for Christ in life and the human heart. This is the position he had taken in *Saul, Karshish, Cleon,* and *A Death in the Desert,* and the position he was to hold to the end of his days. When Browning once read the *Epilogue* to Mrs. Orr, he said to her, "That Face, is the face of Christ. That is how I feel him." [70]

Deaf and Dumb

Deaf and Dumb; A Group by Woolner was first published in the collected edition of 1868. It was there placed among the poems which made up *Dramatis Personae*. This was most appropriate for, like

[69] See the discussion of *Christmas-Eve* in this volume, where both Miss Barrett and Browning are quoted; or *Letters of R.B. and E.B.B.*, II, 429–37.

[70] Mrs. Sutherland Orr, "The Religious Opinions of Robert Browning," in the *Contemporary Review*, December, 1891, p. 880.

Eurydice to Orpheus, the poem was occasional, in a sense, and thus came easily within the scope of *Dramatis Personae.* The poem in 1868 consisted of eight lines, and the text has not been altered since. It followed *May and Death.*

The poem was written in 1862 to accompany Thomas Woolner's group of sculpture of Arthur and Constance, the deaf and dumb children of Sir Thomas Fairbairn. On April 24, Woolner recorded in his Diary, "Robert Browning called to leave stanza for group." [71] Woolner's sculpture was exhibited in the International Exhibition of 1862, but the lines did not appear in the Exhibition catalogue. It is possible that Browning met Woolner, the PreRaphaelite sculptor, at the studio of D. G. Rossetti, which Browning visited twice in January, 1862, though it is probable that Browning had already met Woolner at Coventry Patmore's home early in 1852. (See *A Face.*)

Eurydice to Orpheus

Eurydice to Orpheus; A Picture by Leighton was first printed in the Royal Academy Exhibition catalogue for 1864 (p. 13), where it served as a descriptive piece for a picture by Frederick Leighton, called *Orpheus and Eurydice.* It was printed as prose in the catalogue, which somewhat spoiled its effect, and was signed "Robert Browning, *A Fragment.*" A manuscript of the poem exists with the date April 5, 1864. The poem was not included in the first or second editions of *Dramatis Personae.* It was included in a volume of selections from Browning's works in 1865 under the title *Orpheus and Eurydice,* and in 1868 the poem, under the title *Eurydice to Orpheus: A Picture by Leighton,* was placed with the poems of *Dramatis Personae.* Because of the kinship of association the poem was fittingly placed after *Prospice,* in which Browning addressed his own dead wife. Since its first appearance the poem has suffered only a few alterations in punctuation. It consists of eight lines.

The subject must have been peculiarly poignant to Browning in 1864. The face of Eurydice in Leighton's picture, according to Mrs. Orr, the painter's sister, "wears an intensity of longing which seems to challenge the forbidden look, and make her responsible for it. The poem thus interprets the expression, and translates it into words." [72]

[71] *Thomas Woolner, R. A., Sculptor and Poet: His Life and Letters,* by Amy Woolner, N. Y., 1917, p. 216.
[72] Orr, *Handbook,* p. 248.

Leighton had been a friend of the Brownings in Italy; in Rome he had made a pencil drawing of Browning which the poet had inscribed with the date, March 28, 1859; and, after Mrs. Browning's death, it was Leighton to whom the designing of Mrs. Browning's monument in Florence was entrusted. In *Balaustion's Adventure* (ll. 2671–4), Leighton is the great Kaunian painter who "has made a picture of it all."

The poem as it appeared in the catalogue of the Royal Academy was ridiculed by *Punch* on May 28, 1864.

☙ V ❧

THE RING AND THE BOOK

The Ring and the Book was published in four separate volumes, the first appearing on November 21, 1868, the second on December 26, the third on January 30, 1869, and the fourth on February 27. The volumes were post octavo, bound in dark green cloth boards, and sold for Seven Shillings Sixpence each. Because of a fire on the premises of the binder, the two middle volumes sometimes lack the Roman numerals II and III on their spines, but in spite of the fire the publication of the work proceeded on schedule. In the first volume the title-page read as follows: "The Ring and the Book. By Robert Browning, M.A., Honorary Fellow of Balliol College, Oxford. In Four Volumes. Vol. I. Smith, Elder and Co., London. 1868." All the other volumes bore the same title-page, save for the necessary substitution of the different volume number and the different year in the last two volumes. Smith, Elder and Co. were new publishers for Browning; they had taken over the poet's works from Chapman and Hall [1] in 1867, and it was probably in appreciation of the work of the company that Browning gave the manuscript of *The Ring and the Book* to Mr. George Murray Smith, the senior member of the firm. The manuscript is now in the British Museum.

TEXT

According to the irregular system of numbering half-lines as whole lines in the first edition there are 21,116 lines of blank verse in the poem. The whole work was proportioned as follows:

[1] See *New Letters,* ed. DeVane and Knickerbocker, *Appendix C.* Smith offered handsome terms for *The Ring and the Book;* see *Dearest Isa,* ed. McAleer, p. 197, n. 10.

Vol. I.   I. The Ring and the Book, 1416 lines.
             II. Half-Rome, 1547 lines.
            III. The Other Half-Rome, 1694 lines.
Vol. II.   IV. Tertium Quid, 1640 lines.
              V. Count Guido Franceschini, 2058 lines.
             VI. Giuseppe Caponsacchi, 2105 lines.
Vol. III.   VII. Pompilia, 1845 lines.
           VIII. Dominus Hyacinthus de Archangelis, Pauperum Procura-
                  'tor, 1805 lines.
             IX. Juris Doctor Johannes-Baptista Bottinius, Fisci et Rev.
                  Cam. Apostol. Advocatus, 1577 lines.
Vol. IV.   X. The Pope, 2134 lines.
             XI. Guido, 2425 lines.
            XII. The Book and the Ring, 870 lines.

In the final text of *The Ring and the Book*, prepared for the collected edition of 1888–9, we find that Browning has given the whole poem his usual care in revision. Most of the changes in the text were made for the second edition, in 1872. Yet the surprising fact is that so few changes were made in the vast bulk of the work. In Books I through VII the revision of word and punctuation, which went on in Browning's usual way, left the total number of lines at the same number as in the first edition. Books VIII through XII suffered more extensive changes during the revision, and by addition and rearrangement of paragraphs, seventeen new lines are made. Nine of the new lines appear in Book VIII, scattered between lines 1200 and 1400, and most of the additions are made for the sake of clarity. But throughout one gets the impression that the text of the poem was settled in 1868–9, and that Browning was generally content to let it stand as it was.[2]

GENESIS AND COMPOSITION

It was about noon of a June day in 1860 that Browning found the Old Yellow Book which is the main source of *The Ring and the Book*, upon a book-stall in the square of San Lorenzo in Florence. He called "Stall" and gave his lira—"eightpence English just"—and the vellum-covered volume of some 250 pages, nine-tenths in type, the rest in manuscript, was his own. With what avidity Browning read the book,

[2] For a detailed account of the changes after the first edition, see A. K. Cook, *A Commentary upon Browning's "The Ring and the Book,"* 1920, *Appendix XI.* This book is indispensable for a study of Browning's poem. C. W. Smith in *Browning's Star-Imagery*, pp. 219–21, calls attention to the changes made in Fra Celestino's sermon in Book XII, a passage that Browning thought especially important.

and how that sultry night his imagination reconstructed the whole tragedy, as he leaned on his balcony at Casa Guidi and looked over the festive lights of the Church of San Felice, he has told vividly in the first part of the poem (I, 38–119, 469–77). But from the history of the composition of *The Ring and the Book* as we know it, it would be a mistake to think that the whole conception of the gigantic poem came to him in that moment. Browning's moral judgments upon the characters and their actions were probably made as soon as he read the Old Yellow Book, but his method of telling his story and his detailed plan were probably not arrived at until 1864, when the actual writing began. The numerous points of similarity between his own murder story and the materials which Shelley had used for *The Cenci*—points of similarity observed by Mrs. Miller—must have occurred to Browning very early.[3]

In the meantime, Browning asserts that he took the book with him to Rome (I, 423–7) with an idea of investigating further the matter therein. He and Mrs. Browning spent the winter of 1860–1 there, and were still there in May. Browning, moreover, pushed his inquiries in Arezzo (XII, 782) in the spring of 1861. During that winter he offered the Old Yellow Book to one of his friends, Miss Ogle, the novelist, as a subject to her hand, and he also offered it to W. C. Cartwright, with the suggestion that he should write an account of the affair. Nothing is heard of the Old Yellow Book thereafter for a year. Mrs. Browning's health grew worse, and she died at Florence on June 29, 1861, and Browning and his son left Italy soon afterwards; and after spending the summer on the coast of France at St. Enogat they settled in London. There Browning had his hands full of work. He had to see through the press Mrs. Browning's *Last Poems* and her essays, *The Greek Christian Poets and the English Poets*, as well as his own three-volume collection, the *Poetical Works* of 1863, containing many changes and corrections, and he had to finish his volume, the *Dramatis Personae* of 1864. At the same time Browning was attempting to educate his son.

The first notice we have of Browning's growing interest in the Old Yellow Book appears in a letter to Isa Blagden from Ste. Marie on September 19, 1862. In this letter Browning asked her to obtain for him from Mrs. Baker, a mutual friend, "a M.S account of the trial of Count Francesco Guidi for the murder of his wife,—which I am anxious to collate with my own collection of papers on the

[3] *Robert Browning*, pp. 246–8.

subject." [4] When Browning next writes to Miss Blagden from London on October 18, 1862, he has received Mrs. Baker's manuscript, which as we shall see is probably the so-called "Secondary Source," and he comments as follows:

. . . pray thank Mrs. Baker for her kindness, and say it will be particularly useful to me: it would be of little use to anybody without my documents, nor is it correct in several respects, but it contains a few notices of the execution etc. subsequent to my account that I can turn to good: I am going to make a regular poem of it . . . which shall be a strong thing, if I can manage it.[5]

On November 19, 1862, the poet gives Miss Blagden a glimpse of his plans, "Early in Spring, I print new poems, a number: then, a new edition of all my old things, corrected: then begin on my murder-case." [6] But as we know, the edition of old poems came first, in 1863, and actually, by its success, delayed the publication of the new poems, *Dramatis Personae*. It was probably not until this last volume was published on May 28, 1864, that Browning felt free to address himself to the task which his Roman murder-case presented.

From the statements in Browning's letters given above, it is clear that the Roman murder-case was continuously in his mind from 1860 on, and that by October, 1862, he had resolved to write a poem about it. Concerning the date and place at which his plan crystallized in the form familiar to us in the finished poem our evidence is less certain. The commonly accepted account has been that drawn from the diary of William Michael Rossetti, which connects the plan with the Pass of Roland. But Professor Cundiff (see note 4) inclines toward a contradictory account based on Browning's statement to Rudolf Lehmann, as given in his book *An Artist's Reminiscences*, published in 1894. It is not clear when Browning gave Lehmann his information. I deal with both of these accounts below, first with Rossetti and then with Lehmann.

[4] *Dearest Isa*, ed. McAleer, p. 124. The chaos into which Browning scholarship was thrown by Mrs. Orr's mistake in dating this letter as of 1864 has been admirably set in order by W. O. Raymond's chapter, "New Light on the Genesis of *The Ring and the Book*" in *The Infinite Moment*. See also A. K. Cook, *Commentary, Appendix I*, and Professor Paul A. Cundiff's paper, "The Dating of Browning's Conception of the Plan of *The Ring and the Book*," in *Studies in Philology* 38:543–51 (1941). I have drawn upon these studies for the present account of the genesis and composition of the poem.

[5] *Dearest Isa*, ed. McAleer, p. 128.

[6] *Idem*, p. 134.

In the summer of 1864 Browning pushed further to the south along the French coast than he had in the three preceding years, hoping to find a pleasant place at St. Jean-de-Luz. No accommodations were to be had there, "So here we are at Cambo, a village in the Pyrenees fifteen or sixteen miles from Bayonne. . . . The country is exceedingly beautiful, the mountains just like the Tuscan ranges, with plenty of oak and chestnut woods, and everywhere the greenest of meadows." [7] Browning spent a great part of August and two weeks in September in Cambo. The feature in the neighborhood which most impressed the poet was the *pas de Roland,* which he visited and mentioned in no less than four letters written at about this time. The Pass of Roland may well have been vivid in his consciousness, for there on August 20 the great conception of *The Ring and the Book* seems finally to have sprung into Browning's mind. This we know from the record in the diary of William Michael Rossetti for March 15, 1868, when he had just seen Browning:

Browning's forthcoming poem exceeds 20,000 lines: it may probably be out in July, but he would defer it if he finds that more conducive to the satisfactory completion of the work. He began it in October '64. Was staying at Bayonne, and walked out to a mountain-gorge traditionally said to have been cut or kicked out by Roland, and there laid out the full plan of his twelve cantos, accurately carried out in the execution. [8]

In Lehmann's volume, *An Artist's Reminiscences* (p. 224), however, Browning is quoted as follows: "When I first read the book [the Old Yellow Book], my plan was at once settled. I went for a walk, gathered twelve pebbles from the road, and put them at equal distances on the parapet that bordered it. These represented the twelve chapters into which the poem is divided and I adhered to that arrangement to the last." This account implies that Browning's plan for the poem was settled in Florence, and probably as early as 1860. In the light of the evidence we have, such a conclusion seems extremely unlikely. As Mr. Cundiff says, W. M. Rossetti is characteristically inaccurate; but so was Browning's memory, and if he gave Lehmann the account quoted above a decade or more after 1864, as seems likely, his account recorded by Rossetti is nearer the date of the event. Perhaps it is possible to reconcile the two ac-

---

[7] Henry James, *William Wetmore Story and his Friends,* 1903, II, 154.

[8] *Rossetti Papers,* 1903, p. 302. C. H. Herford observed the association between the plan of *The Ring and the Book* and the Pass of Roland (*Browning,* 1905, p. 171), but W. O. Raymond first put all the pieces of the puzzle together. See his "New Light on the Genesis of *The Ring and the Book,*" as above, n. 4.

counts: the vivid event of the pebbles placed upon the parapet to crystallize the plan of the poem could not have been easily forgotten, but the event may have happened at the Pass of Roland in August, 1864, when Browning was at last free to turn his mind fully to his next poem.

In any case Browning, writing from Biarritz to Miss Blagden on September 19, 1864, reported his condition:

For me, I have got on by having a great read at Euripides—the one book I brought with me, besides attending to my own matters, my new poem that is about to be; and of which the whole is pretty well in my head,— the Roman murder story you know.[9]

Once back in London in October Browning began to work at his great poem. He laid out the program, which he seems to have followed intermittently for the next four years, of writing at least three hours a morning upon his poem. He told William Rossetti that *The Ring and the Book* was written consecutively from start to finish. He read the material of the Old Yellow Book over eight times during the years he worked upon it. On October 17, 1864, he wrote to ask his friend Leighton to verify a description which he needed for Book II of *The Ring and the Book:*

A favour, if you have time for it. Go into the church St. Lorenzo in Lucina in the Corso—and look attentively at it—so as to describe it to me on your return. The general arrangement of the building, if with a nave—pillars or not—the number of altars, and any particularity there may be—over the High Altar is a famous Crucifixion by Guido. It will be of great use to me. I don't care about the *outside.*[10]

This was the church in which Pompilia was married and where the bodies of the Comparini were later exhibited.

We catch glimpses of *The Ring and the Book,* when it is thoroughly under way, in Browning's letters to his friends. On October 3, 1864, he told Miss Wedgwood that he would write the twelve books in six months; on the 19th of the same month he informed Miss Blagden that he expected to have his long poem ready by the following summer; on November 1, 1865, in speaking to Allingham, he estimated that his poem had reached 15,000 lines. The great bulk of the poem was written then in the year from October, 1864, to November, 1865. Mr. Cundiff has charted Browning's further prog-

[9] Orr, *Life,* p. 250.
[10] *Idem,* p. 273.

ress.[11] From November 1, 1865, to April 23, 1867, he added 1000 lines; from April 23, 1867, to October 10, 1868, about 5000 lines were produced. The year 1866 was a lean one, but there was a spurt of writing in April and May, 1867, when the poem reached 18,000 lines. As he approached the end of his task in the fall of 1867 he was eager to finish, but determined not to let his poem appear until he had brought it satisfactorily to an end, even if it took another two or three years. On July 30, 1868, Browning still had not arrived at his final title for the poem, but late that summer he corrected the proofs at Audierne, Brittany. We learn on September 2, 1868, that the plan of publication in four monthly volumes has been adopted, and on November 21, 1868, the first volume was ready for the public.

In an elaborate and skilful study, "The Narrative Structure of Browning's *The Ring and the Book*," [12] R. B. McElderry, Jr. shows with what great care and organizing power Browning avoided repetition in his poem, and he thinks the poet must have worked from sketches and plans. For example, the various books of the poem are analyzed and charted to show how the emphasis falls upon one major episode or another of the story, such as the marriage, the flight, the murder, and the trial, etc., appropriate to the time of the monologue and the character of the speaker. Professor McElderry concludes that *The Ring and the Book* has psychological and organic rather than rational unity and is a gigantic series of insights and intuitions, with, however, great ingenuity in the structure.

In the midst of his writing, of course, Browning was deeply occupied with personal affairs. On June 14, 1866, his father died in Paris at the age of eighty-four. That summer also Browning was desperately instructing his son in Greek and Latin for a hoped-for entrance into Balliol College. The next year was a very busy one for him socially, for he was in great demand. He was honored by Oxford in the spring by being given by diploma the degree of Master of Arts, a fact which he gratefully records on the title-page of his great work. He was also made an honorary fellow of Balliol College. He spent the summer of this year at Croisic again, and on September 30 he wrote *Hervé Riel;* he possibly wrote also some of *The Two Poets of Croisic* during the summer. In June of 1868 Miss Arabel Barrett, Mrs. Browning's sister and a constant companion to the poet, died. It must have seemed to Browning that a large portion of

[11] See above, n. 4.
[12] In *Research Studies, State College of Washington* 11:193–233 (1943).

his life had gone into making the poem. It was almost nine years since the day in June, 1860, when he had found the Old Yellow Book. Meanwhile, he had lost his wife, his father, and his wife's sister; and his boy had become a young man.

The Ring and the Book, as we now can see, was the natural outgrowth of the method of the dramatic monologue which Browning had perfected in *Men and Women* and *Dramatis Personae.* Yet it is worth observing that Browning told William Allingham on May 26, 1868, that "I began it in rhymed couplets, . . . but thought by and by I might as well have my fling, and so turned to blank verse." [13] The idea of having many people view the same event differently is suggested in the index or table of contents of Browning's source, as we shall see, and probably was a part of the poet's original plan. His wife's simple gold ring possibly suggested the circle of monologues somewhere in the midst of which lay the central truth. The division of the poem into twelve parts, three for the hearsay of Rome, three for the law, four for the central characters, and two—first and last—for the poet, must also have been a fairly early conception. The great form of the poem, I think—the steady great rise to the height, culminating in Pompilia's speech (Book VII), and then the deliberate dropping into anticlimax in the speeches of the opposing lawyers, and then the sharp rise to the Pope's great utterance in the second peak of the poem—this conception of the form must have come as *The Ring and the Book* was being written. At any rate, the artistry is final and consummate.

In substance as well as in craftsmanship Browning intended *The Ring and the Book* to be his masterpiece. Here we may see the principal strands of his life-long intuitions and thoughts. The sordid murder story gave him a domestic tragedy in a religious context, and an opportunity to employ his intuitive psychology and all his moral and aesthetic philosophy. Though the subject of the poem was abhorrent to many people, including Mrs. Browning, it seemed to the poet a heaven-sent story for his peculiar talents and interests, and he determined to make the poem his reading of life.

SOURCES AND INFLUENCES

Of course, the primary source of Browning's poem was the Old Yellow Book, which now is in the possession of the Balliol College Library, as Browning desired it should be. In 1908 this work was

[13] Allingham, *Diary,* p. 181.

made available to the world by C. W. Hodell's magnificent volume, published by the Carnegie Institution of Washington, bearing the title *The Old Yellow Book, Source of Browning's "The Ring and the Book," In Complete Photo-Reproduction With Translation, Essay, and Notes.* In this book Professor Hodell undertook to lay before the reader the complete sources, in Latin and Italian, of Browning's story, in the form that Browning himself had known it, and also to supply an English translation.[14] The title given to the Old Yellow Book by Cencini, the lawyer of Florence to whom the documents and letters had probably been sent in 1698, and who had had them bound into the book as Browning found it, was translated thus by Hodell: "A Setting-forth of the entire Criminal Cause against *Guido Franceschini*, Nobleman of Arezzo, and his Bravoes, who were put to death in Rome, February 22, 1698. The first by beheading, the other four by the gallows. Roman Murder-Case. In which it is disputed whether and when a Husband may kill his Adulterous Wife without incurring the ordinary penalty." This title-page was followed by an *Indice* or table of contents, probably also compiled by Cencini. It is translated by Hodell thus:

1) Sentence of the Criminal Court of Florence in the criminal case against Gregorio Guillicini, Francesca Pompilia Comparini, wife of Guido Franceschini, etc. December, 1697.
2) Argument in defense of the said Franceschini, of the Honorable Signor Giacinto Arcangeli, Procurator of the Poor in Rome, made before the Congregation of Monsignor the Governor.
3) Argument of the Honorable Signor Advocate Desiderio Spreti, Advocate of the Poor, in defense of said Franceschini and his associates.
4) Argument of the abovesaid Signor Arcangeli in defense of Biagio Agostinelli and his companions in crime.
5) Summary of fact made in behalf of the Fisc.
6) Argument of Signor Francesco Gambi, Procurator of the Fisc and of the Reverend Apostolic Chamber, against the abovesaid Franceschini and his companions in crime.
7) Argument of Signor Giovanni Battista Bottini, Advocate of the Fisc and of the Reverend Apostolic Chamber, against the abovesaid.
8) Summary of fact in behalf of Franceschini and his associates in crime.
9) Another argument of the abovesaid Signor Arcangeli in favor and defense of the abovesaid.
10) Another argument of Signor Advocate Spreti in favor of the above.
11) An account of the facts and grounds, made and given by an Anonymous Author.

[14] Hodell's translation, *The Old Yellow Book*, with an *Introduction* was made generally accessible in 1911 by its appearance in Everyman's Library.

12) Another summary made on behalf of the Fisc.

13) Argument of Signor Gambi, Procurator of the Fisc, against the abovesaid Franceschini and his companions.

14) Another argument of the Signor Giovanni Battista Bottini, Advocate of the Fisc.

15) Another argument of the abovesaid against the said defendants.

16) A response to the abovesaid account of fact as given by the Anonymous Author.

17) The sentence of Signor Maria Antonio Venturini, Judge in criminal causes, which declares that the adultery was not proved, and which restores to her original fame the memory of Francesca Pompilia Comparini, wife of Guido Franceschini.

18) Argument of Signor Antonio Lamparelli, Procurator of the Poor in the said case.

19) Letter written by the Honorable Signor Giacinto Arcangeli, Procurator of the Poor, to Monsignore Francesco Cencini in Florence, in which he tells him that the sentence of death had been executed in Rome against the Guilty on February 22, 1698—that is, that Franceschini had been beheaded, and the other four hanged.

20) Two other letters, one written by Signor Gaspero del Torto and the other by Signor Carlo Antonio Ugolinucci to the aforesaid Monsignore Francesco Cencini.

21) Argument of Signor Advocate Spreti in favor of Franceschini, etc.

Besides these documents bound into the Old Yellow Book, Browning had another pamphlet which has become known as the Secondary Source. W. O. Raymond has succeeded in identifying this secondary source with the pamphlet which Browning, with the help of Miss Blagden, got from Mrs. Baker in October, 1862.[15] This pamphlet, used extensively in the early Books and again in Book XII of the poem, was also included in translation in Hodell's *The Old Yellow Book*. Its title there is as follows: "The Death of the Wife-Murderer Guido Franceschini, by Beheading." The pamphlet was a contemporary account of the whole affair, with particular attention to Guido's mutilation of the Comparini and his own execution.

In 1900, when Browning had been dead for eleven years, a third account of the Franceschini affair was discovered in the Royal Casanatense Library at Rome. The volume in which it was found had also an account of the trial of Beatrice Cenci. The Franceschini account was translated by W. Hall Griffin, in the *Monthly Review* for

[15] See "Browning's First Mention of the Documentary Sources of *The Ring and the Book*," in *MLN* 43:445–50 (November, 1928). By pushing Browning's use of this source forward two years, Professor Raymond has greatly clarified the whole problem of the genesis of *The Ring and the Book*. This article is now Ch. 5 in his book, *The Infinite Moment*.

November, 1900, and appears as *Appendix B* in his *Life of Browning.*
It is also translated in Hodell's *Old Yellow Book.* The title of the
pamphlet is "Trial and Death of Franceschini and his Companions,
for the Murder of Comparini, his Wife and Daughter, Which happened during the time of Innocent XII." Browning, as far as we
know, never saw this pamphlet, and its chief interest lies in the
fact that it parallels rather neatly Browning's view of the gossip
which went about Rome during the trial of Guido.[16] Other materials
upon the case which have come to light recently, and which Browning could not have known, are mentioned later in my discussion.

The story which was told in the Old Yellow Book and in Browning's Secondary Source was briefly this: In 1693 Guido Franceschini,
a nobleman of Arezzo of the second rank, poor and not too respectable, married Francesca Pompilia, who had been brought up in Rome
as the daughter of Pietro and Violante Comparini. Soon after the
marriage, Guido took his bride to Arezzo and for three years and
more they lived unhappily together. Guido had misrepresented his
condition to the Comparini, as they found to their grief when they
came to Arezzo to enjoy their relationship to the nobility. After a
stay of four months they returned to Rome, and presently brought
suit against Guido for the return of Pompilia's dowry. This move
was the result of Violante's late revelation to Pietro that she had
all these years represented Pompilia, really the daughter of a strum-
pet, as her own in order to gain an inheritance left to them on condition of their having a child. After this Guido, who had always been,
according to Pompilia's testimony, an impossible husband, became,
in his wounded vanity, vindictively cruel to her. On the other side,
Pompilia, according to Guido, was disobedient and unfaithful. She
attempted to escape from the house of her husband many times. On
April 28–9, 1697—Browning makes it April 23, St. George's day, to
symbolize the rescue—Pompilia fled from Arezzo towards Rome
under the care of Giuseppe Caponsacchi, a young canon, with the
intention, as she declared, of joining her supposed parents, the Comparini. Guido followed the flight of his wife and her protector, and
caught them at an inn in Castelnuovo, about fifteen miles from Rome.
Pompilia brandished a sword, but she was disarmed and arrested
with Caponsacchi upon a charge of adultery; the two were taken to

---

[16] T. L. Hood is of the opinion that Browning *did* know this pamphlet. See
his *Letters of Robert Browning,* pp. 85, 351. The case cannot be proved, but
seems plausible.

Rome and tried, and in September, 1697, a judgment was delivered. Caponsacchi was relegated to Civita Vecchia for three years "for complicity in the flight, and for the seduction of Francesca Comparini and for carnal knowledge of her"; and Pompilia was sent during further inquiry to the nunnery of the Scalette, a place for penitent women. Because of her pregnancy she was shortly sent under bond to the house of the Comparini in Rome. There on December 18, 1697, eight months after her flight from Arezzo, she gave birth to a boy who was named Gaetano. On January 2, 1698, Guido came with four of his henchmen, and gaining entrance by pretending to be the bearer of a message from Caponsacchi, he murdered and mutilated the Comparini, and left Pompilia for dead with twenty-two wounds in her body. She died four days later at the house of the Comparini in the Via Paulina.[17] Guido and his fellows made for Arezzo, but were easily captured, and were accused of murder before the tribunal of the governor. The fact that Guido had committed the deed was easily established, but more difficult questions arose, chief of which was the one appearing on the title-page of the Old Yellow Book, "whether and when a Husband may kill his adulterous Wife without incurring the ordinary penalty." This opened again the question which the courts had never considered settled, as to whether Pompilia had committed adultery with Caponsacchi. In short, the whole question of the past conduct and characters of the Comparini, Guido, Pompilia, and Caponsacchi was thrown open in order that the court might arrive at a decision as to whether Guido was justified in any way whatever in his triple murder. The pleadings of the lawyers for the prosecution and the defence make up the text, in large part, of the Old Yellow Book. On February 18, 1698, the court rendered judgment against Guido and condemned him to be beheaded and his fellows hanged, as befitted the difference in their ranks. Because Guido held a minor office in the Church, he appealed to Pope Innocent XII to set aside the judgment. The Pope refused the appeal and Guido and his companions were executed on Febuary 22, 1698. In September, the court gave verdict against the Monastery of the Convertites, the place where Browning mistakenly thought Pompilia had been incarcerated, which had claimed its traditional right to inherit the property of a debased woman. Pompilia's fame and reputation was restored by the

---

[17] For all questions of location in the poem consult the invaluable work by Sir Frederick Treves, *The Country of "The Ring and the Book,"* London, 1913. See especially pp. 101–3; and also Cook, *Commentary, Appendix II.*

court; she was declared innocent and Gaetano, her little son, was declared rightful heir to her property.

Such is the story in bare outline. It must be borne in mind that in the Old Yellow Book we do not hear the words of Guido, Pompilia, and Caponsacchi in the first person, but merely hear them quoted by lawyers, and we see the actions of the chief characters through descriptions by the lawyers and through the accounts of the Anonymous Authors. Thus while Browning found the method of using a series of accounts by different people inherent in his source, he was under the necessity of creating dramatic monologues from these formal records. The amount of his imaginative liberty may be seen, for example, when one observes that the records show no occasion for the speech of Caponsacchi. We do not know that he was even at the trial, and Browning was under the necessity of creating his occasion, which he did with great ingenuity.

It may be of use to the reader if he is given here in compact form the particular materials which Browning used for each of the Books of his poem, though it should not be forgotten that the poet ranged over the whole of the Old Yellow Book and the subsidiary material for the matter of each Book.

Book I. *The Ring and the Book.* Here Browning himself is the speaker. His chief purpose is to explain his title by the figure of the manufacture of the fine gold ring of Etruscan workmanship which Mrs. Browning had worn. He points the significance of his whole artistic procedure in the use of fact and imagination. Browning presses his figure too far. The fancy or imagination of the poet, which is the jeweller's alloy in shaping the ring, does not, happily, "fly off in fume" in the poem, but remains as the most essential part of the work.[18] In the course of this Book Browning manages to make us acquainted with the chief features of the story he is to deal with, and already directs our judgment as he would have it go. For the materials of Book I, Browning ranges over the whole of his available source material. The Book fittingly concludes with the poet's magnificent dedication of the whole work to his "Lyric Love," his wife. Though the poet told W. M. Rossetti that he wrote the poem consecutively, there can be little doubt, I think, that what was first written in the early fall of 1864 was considerably altered in 1868 when the whole poem was finished.

[18] See the defence of Browning's metaphor by A. G. Drachmann, "Alloy and Gold," in *Studies in Philology* 22:418–22, and the careful interpretation of it in Paul A. Cundiff's article, "The Clarity of Browning's Ring Metaphor," in *PMLA* 63:1276–82 (1948). Mr. Cundiff thinks that Browning knew that the squirt of acid merely removed the alloy from the face of the ring, and replaced it by a film of gold, while his fancy (alloy) still contributed to the structure of the interior to make it durable and shapely.

Book II. *Half-Rome.* The speaker in Book II is the first of the group of three anonymous commentators upon the crime which Guido has committed. He is of the street, a married man who is having difficulty with his wife, as he informs us in his concluding words; and this fact colors his narration and his sympathies. He sees the point of view of Guido, and he speaks without much genuine information upon the day after the murder, January 3, 1698, while the bodies of the Comparini lie on exhibition in the church of San Lorenzo, and Pompilia lies at the point of death from her wounds. This monologue, designed to give color, depth, and verisimilitude to his story, and to provide information (sometimes false) to the reader, is founded mainly on the eleventh of the pamphlets in the list I have given above, "An account of the facts and grounds, made and given by an Anonymous Author." This pamphlet, attempting to sway public opinion in behalf of Guido, was published in Italian at Rome while the case was in the courts. Browning drew from elsewhere in his sources, of course, for some of the matter of Book II, and especially from his Secondary Source, "The Death of the Wife-Murderer Guido Franceschini, by Beheading," for his description of the mutilated bodies of the Comparini. As we have seen, on October 17, 1864, Browning requested a description of the inside of the church of San Lorenzo from his friend Leighton, and he was probably engaged upon Book II soon after that date. If we accept the contention of Dean T. L. Hood that Browning also knew the manuscript in the Royal Casanatense Library at Rome, it is likely that Browning used this also for Book II, for his device of presenting several aspects of popular opinion in Rome is there neatly anticipated.

Book III. *The Other Half-Rome.* The speaker of this monologue is a bachelor of altogether nicer perception and better instincts than those of *Half-Rome.* The youth and hard fate of Pompilia rouse pity in him, and he is susceptible to her beauty. He speaks in the center of the Barberini Piazza, probably on January 4, two days after Guido's crime. He takes the side of Pompilia against Guido. The monologue of Book III is drawn chiefly from the second anonymous pamphlet, the sixteenth in the list I have given above, "A response to the abovesaid account of fact as given by the Anonymous Author." Beyond this pamphlet, it is evident that Browning had the deposition of Fra Celestino, who attended the dying Pompilia, in mind as he wrote (included in the sixth pamphlet in the list above), as well as the deposition of Pompilia herself (included in the eighth pamphlet in my list, the summary for the defence of Guido). The poet picked up hints also from the Secondary Source, such as Guido's failure to provide for his escape after the murder, and if Dean Hood's opinion that Browning knew the pamphlet in the Royal Casanatense Library is correct, he got some information upon the Abate Paolo from that source.

Book IV. *Tertium Quid.* The monologist here is a nobleman of a most judicious temper. He decides no questions, but he sums up, weighs, and arranges all the evidence of the two speakers who have gone before him, and of the whole case. In none of the records of the Roman murder case is there such a character, and for the matter of this Book the poet draws from the whole body of evidence. The Book is an extremely clever re-creation of the aristocratic Rome of 1698. This Book was probably written early in 1865.

Book V. *Count Guido Franceschini.* Browning represents Count Guido as making his speech to the judges a few days (possibly on January 6) after the crime "in a small chamber that adjoins the court" (I, 950). Guido is here represented as a man of 49 years (he was in reality only 40), just from the torture rack. He makes an amazingly clever defence of himself by detailing with transparent candor the course of his life, the hardships and humilities of the poorer nobility as they wait for help from great patrons, the treachery of the Comparini, and the faithlessness of his wife. So good a case does he make for himself that some have been willing to acquit him upon the spot, but for the poet's whole conception one must see Book XI. There the wolf sheds his sheep's clothing. In the records of the Roman murder case Guido does not speak, save through his lawyers, and it is upon the pamphlets of Arcangeli and Spreti in his defence that Browning has chiefly drawn. In the list above, the following pamphlets contributed most to Guido's first speech: 1, 2, 3, 4, 8, 9, 10, and 11. Perhaps of these the eighth, "Summary of fact in behalf of Franceschini and his associates in crime," is the most important, though the ninth and tenth are almost equally so.

Book VI. *Giuseppe Caponsacchi.* So far as we know Caponsacchi did not appear at the trial of Guido. He is represented in the Old Yellow Book only by his deposition upon his examination during the Process of Flight, the earlier trial of himself and Pompilia, which was admitted as evidence in the trial of Guido. His deposition appears in the eighth pamphlet in the list above, "Summary of fact in behalf of Franceschini and his associates in crime." It is possible, of course, that the judges may have summoned Caponsacchi from his relegation in Civita Vecchia to answer Guido's charges that he had often been seen in the neighborhood of Pompilia's home since his banishment. This possibility gives Browning his opportunity, and he makes the young priest address the judges about four days after Guido's crime, while he is still in the throes of his first mad grief at the slaughter of Pompilia. His speech is very poignant: love and pity for Pompilia fill his heart, hatred for Guido, and scorn for his judges. There is hardly a hint of this in the records. There Caponsacchi is a "gallant man," adventurous and light of heart, with no trace of genuine love for Pompilia. The growth of Caponsacchi under the influence of his love for Pompilia into the "soldier-saint," a St. George, a man of the greatest moral perceptions, is the creation of the poet's imagination. Mr. G. K. Chesterton was the first, I believe, to point out in detail (*Robert Browning,* pp. 107–10) the very close correspondence between Caponsacchi's flight with Pompilia and Browning's with Elizabeth Barrett in 1846. For its excellent judgment upon Caponsacchi, see Mr. A. K. Cook's *Commentary,* especially *Appendix V.*

Book VII. *Pompilia.* Though Browning draws upon the whole of the documentary evidence for the character and actions of Pompilia, and indeed his conception transcends altogether his sources, as we shall see, two passages from the Old Yellow Book provide the poet with most of his matter. These are (1) Pompilia's deposition upon the Process of Flight, made for her trial in May, 1697, and included in the eighth pamphlet in the list above, "Summary of fact in behalf of Franceschini and his associates in crime," and more importantly (2) the Attestation on January 19 of Fra Celestino, "the bare-footed Augustinian priest," who on January 6, 1698, received Pompilia's confession and attended her at her death. This is included in the fifth pamphlet in my list above, "Summary of fact made in behalf of the Fisc." Browning condenses all this into the dying speech of Pompilia. The poet believed implicitly that the Pompilia of his poem was the lady of the Old Yellow Book, and told his friend, the Rev. John W. Chadwick, as reported in the *Christian Register* for January 19, 1888, "I assure you I found her in the book just as she speaks and acts in my poem." An inspection of the documents does not at all bear out Browning's contention; there we see a pathetic, ignorant young girl, flirtatious perhaps, and at times desperate in her suffering, driven into lying to help her case, who yet makes a touching and rather noble death-scene. (See the excellent treatment of the real Pompilia as against the Pompilia of Browning's imagination in Mr. A. K. Cook's *Commentary,* pp. 139–45, and *Appendix V.*) But she is a long way from Browning's magnificent heroine, whose interest is in the protection of her new-born son, Gaetano, and in her desire to clear the "lustrous and pellucid soul" of her champion, Caponsacchi (VII, 930–41). Mrs. Orr is indubitably right in saying that Browning in dealing with the unusual subject (for him) of mother-love, and in the more usual subject of a woman's love for her rescuer, has his wife, Elizabeth Barrett Browning, constantly in mind. "I am convinced," says Mrs. Orr, "that it entered largely into the conception of *Pompilia,* and so far as this depended on it, the character of the whole work." (Orr, *Life,* pp. 270–2.) We can only conclude that Browning did his creative genius a great wrong in his insistence that his Pompilia was only a copy of the pathetic wife of Guido in the Old Yellow Book.

Book VIII. *Dominus Hyacinthus de Archangelis.* Browning's clever sketch—perhaps it is a caricature—of the jovial and garrulous defender of Guido and his fellows in crime is built upon his pamphlets in behalf of his client, but mainly upon the second in the list above, "Argument in defense of the said Franceschini, of the Honorable Signor Giacinto Arcangeli, Procurator of the Poor in Rome, made before the Congregation of Monsignor the Governor." The Argument was made in January, 1698, when the trial of Guido had just begun. Though many have objected to the presence of the lawyers in *The Ring and the Book,* we can see that their parts are necessary to provide relief and variety after the great monologues of Caponsacchi and Pompilia and before that of the Pope. But the wit and humor of Books VIII and IX need no apology, and the delightful relations between Arcangeli and his son—the poet's invention—well deserve the space given. It was probably Browning's treatment of the lawyers which first roused Judge Marshall Gest to challenge the poet's reading of history in this case (see below), and there is surely much in the Judge's contention that in reality Arcangeli and Bottini conducted their cases with learning, dignity and point. Arcangeli properly grounds his defence of Guido on *honoris causa*. It should be added that, for the lawyers, Browning uses the Italian names as well as the formal Latin equivalents.

Book IX. *Juris Doctor Johannes-Baptista Bottinius.* For the sake of variety Browning makes the Fisc, or as we should call him the Prosecuting Attorney, a very different person from his rival, Arcangeli. To avoid monotony Arcangeli is made by Browning to speak at the very beginning of the trial, while Bottini's argument is, in effect, a summing up. The matter of Bottini's monologue Browning drew from all the speeches made in the trial by the prosecutors, but he mainly used the pamphlet which is the fourteenth in the list above, "Another argument of the Signor Giovanni Battista Bottini, Advocate of the Fisc." The portrait of Bottini is even more of a caricature than that of Arcangeli, for the Fisc, as Judge Gest shows at length (see below), is a genuinely able lawyer, though occasionally absurd. Browning could not forgive Bottini, however, for his many admissions of Pompilia's possible wantonness—Bottini, primarily interested in convicting Guido, dared not stake too much of his case on Pompilia's purity. The thing that set Browning against the lawyer was Bottini's dreadful professional spirit, as may be seen in Book XII. This spirit made Bottini, when he found himself on the other side in the suit brought to regain Pompilia's property from the Convertites, more eager to defame her good name than he had formerly been to defend it.

Book X. *The Pope.* Pope Innocent XII, Antonio Pignatelli of Naples, is mentioned several times in the Old Yellow Book, generally in the way of formal compliment, but no word of his occurs there. Browning's authority for this monologue rests upon the fact that on February 21, 1698, the Pope refused to delay Guido's execution although the murderer had claimed clerical privilege. There is no verdict or judgment upon Guido included in the Yellow Book, but in the three letters written to Francesco Cencini in Florence (19 and 20 in the list of documents above) the fact of the Pope's refusal was reported. Arcangeli writes, "the Sanctity of Our Lord (the Pope) did not deem it wise to postpone the execution of the sentence already decreed, he has seen best by special writ to make denial of any clerical privilege." Gaspero del Torto wrote to Cencini, "the Pope yesterday issued his warrant, and ordered that it be carried out completely to-day." Carlo Antonio Ugolinucci wrote, "last evening at eight o'clock Monsignor signed of his own accord the warrant, in denial of the clergyship so far as it might be alleged."

It has become the common belief that the Pope in Book X is Browning speaking, and in many respects this is a correct view of the case. The judgments of the Pope upon the characters of the tragedy—Pompilia, Caponsacchi, and Guido—are very close indeed to the poet's own judgments of them, as one may see by comparing Book X with Books I and XII, where the poet speaks in his own name. The theology with which Browning endows Innocent XII is an anachronism and may be definitely ascribed to Browning. It is the theology that we have seen formulating itself in *Christmas-Eve and Easter-Day, Saul, Cleon, Karshish,* and *A Death in the Desert,* to mention only a few. It is a good theology, and one can hardly argue that theology is out of place in a pope's discourse, but the particular kind of theology which is offered is not papal, nor is it of the seventeenth century. A number of critics have objected to the theology in Book X, as indeed the Pope did himself as he paused before sending his judgment to the governor (X, 1252). If *The Ring and the Book* were history the objection would be well taken, but since the poem is, properly speaking, Browning's reading of life, one ought not to complain of this noble and masterful presentation of the poet's theological position. Nor ought one to deplore the fine analysis which the Pope makes of Euripides' theology (X, 1670–1790), for Browning had been reading Euripides ever since his wife's death, and his delight in the Greek dramatist was to bear fruit in *Balaustion's Adventure,* his next production.

It is a mistaken notion, however, to think that Browning invented his Pope without reference to history. Mr. A. K. Cook has brilliantly shown in *Appendix VII* of his *Commentary* that Browning consulted excellent authorities and took great pains to be accurate in his description of Innocent XII, who occupied the papal throne from 1691 to 1700. Among the documents which Browning consulted were two *Relazioni* of affairs in Rome at the time of Innocent, sent by the Venetian envoys to their government. These documents, used again by Browning in Book XII, are quoted and summarized in Ranke's *History of the Popes* (III, 462–3), where an excellent account of Innocent XII may be found. This Pope instituted many reforms; he abolished the sale of appointments, made himself accessible to the poor and lightened their burdens, lived abstemiously, and worked hard at his task. The only objections made against Innocent by historians are that he was sometimes irresolute and sometimes overswayed by foreign influence, such as that brought upon him by Louis XIV to condemn Fénelon's *Explication des maximes des saints sur la vie intérieure* as being Quietist in doctrine.[19] Browning makes both Guido in Book XI and the Venetian gentleman of Book XII gibe at the Pope for his subservience to France. No satisfactory identification has been suggested for Browning's Sagacious Swede, the contemporary expert upon the laws of probability. The most widely discussed work of the time in this field was by a Dutchman, John deWitt—*La Valeur des ventes viagères en raison des ventes libres ou rembousables,* La Haye, 1671.[20]

By a consensus of critical opinion *The Pope* has been declared one of the noblest utterances of Robert Browning.

Book XI. *Guido.* That Browning gave Guido a second monologue in *The Ring and the Book* must be set down to his delight in the creation and the analysis of slippery villains. Book XI has been attacked on the grounds that Guido did not deserve such space in the poem, but it has

[19] For an able comment upon Browning's use of Molinism, Quietism, and Jansenism in his poem, see William Coyle, "Molinos: 'The Subject of the Day' in *The Ring and the Book*," in *PMLA* 67:308–14 (1952). These movements were live issues in Rome in the last quarter of the seventeenth century, but were often confused in the popular mind. The Pope is gentle with Molinism, but Guido (XI) is quite wild in his references.

[20] I am indebted to Professor Oystein Ore, Sterling Professor of Mathematics at Yale, for this information.

been ably defended because of its intrinsic worth and interest.[21] There is little authority in the Yellow Book, or in the other documents, for Guido's full revelation of himself. The records provide Guido with a very edifying end, and according to them he died repentantly and gallantly. The Secondary Source, "The Death of the Wife-Murderer Guido Franceschini, by Beheading," gave Browning his occasion: "At the eighth hour [2 A. M.] Franceschini and his companions were informed of their death and were placed in the Consorteria. There they were assisted by Abate Panciatichi and Cardinal Acciajoli, nor did they delay in preparing themselves to die well. The condemned were made to go downstairs and were placed upon separate carts to be drawn to the place of execution. . . . When the last named [Franceschini] had mounted the platform, he asked pardon for his sins, and begged them to pray for his soul. . . . When he had made the confessor announce that he was reconciled, he adjusted his neck upon mannaia and, with the name of Jesus on his lips, he was beheaded."

The Guido of Book XI is, then, the poet's own amazing creation, made out of what the poet imagined his Guido would have said and done as his doom approached. As we read the Old Yellow Book we can see that Browning has taken a weak and rather stupid, though occasionally shrewd, specimen of a degenerate nobility and made a consummate and intellectualized villain of him, one who is not altogether unworthy of being placed beside Shakespeare's Iago. In Book XI the hypocritical Guido of Book V is unmasked. He shows his wolfish nature, and shows that he has all the time been motivated by sheer hatred of his superiors, his Church, and above all of Pompilia—a hatred as subtle and pervasive as Iago's hatred of the decent people about him. Guido's monologue rises, through vivid pictures of the Italy of his day and blinding flashes of revelation of his true nature, to the perfect crescendo of terror in the closing lines when the Company of Death approach his cell. It is dramatically superb, but some question has risen as to its precise meaning. Did Guido, as the Pope hoped might be the case, at the last moment in his appeal to Pompilia see her truth and save his soul? Or is this, as Mr. Cook believes (See his *Commentary, Appendix X*), the last and "startling revelation of the unspeakable meanness of a lost soul"? For my part, I am inclined to believe with Mr. Cook that no spark but abject terror disturbs the clod which is Guido.

Book XII. *The Book and the Ring.* In the last Book of the poem Browning himself is the speaker, but in the course of tying up the loose ends of his story he introduces several other speakers, some real and some imaginary. For his account of the death of Guido and his companions the poet drew primarily upon the Secondary Source, the pamphlet entitled, "The Death of the Wife-Murderer Guido Franceschini, by Beheading." Here

[21] In November, 1868, Julia Wedgwood began in her correspondence with him to attack Browning's "scientific interest in evil," and his preoccupation with it in *The Ring and the Book*. Her criticism evoked an interesting defence of his point of view from the poet, but she remained sentimentally convinced that Browning had "spent all these years on a mistake." See *Robert Browning and Julia Wedgwood,* ed. Curle, pp. 136–55, 172; also see W. O. Raymond on Miss Wedgwood's criticism, in *The Infinite Moment,* pp. 210–1.

we read: "On February 22 was seen in the Piazza del Popolo a great platform with mannaia, and two great gallows, which had been built for the execution of the criminals. Many stands were constructed for the accommodation of those curious to see such a terrible execution, and so great was the concourse of people that some windows brought as much as six dollars each. . . . The first to mount the cart was Agostinelli, the second Giambassini, the third Pasquin, the fourth Baldeschi, and the fifth Franceschini, who showed more intrepidity and composure than the others to the wonder of all." The general purport of the documents is that Guido died gallantly and piously.

The four reports which Browning gives us in Book XII are a mingling of real and imaginary documents. The first of these, the letter of the gay Venetian gentleman, visiting at Rome, written just after Guido's execution, is in the main imaginary, but it draws in part from the Secondary Source and upon Browning's historical reading for this period which is mentioned in my discussion of Book X.

The second report is the letter of Arcangeli to Cencini in Florence, the lawyer who bound the documents relating to the case into the Old Yellow Book. It is based upon the nineteenth document in the list I have given above, but when the official business is finished, Arcangeli adds a postscript which reveals his true opinion of the Pope and Bottini, and gives us further examples of the precocity of his son, whom we have already seen at length in Book VIII.

The third report purports to be a letter from Bottini, written two days after the execution, to an unnamed person, and gives us the professional callousness of the lawyer who is now prepared to turn against Pompilia (see my discussion of Book IX). This is an imaginary document.

The last report, likewise imaginary, is the sermon which Fra Celestino preached on Sunday, February 23, at the church of San Lorenzo concerning the Roman murder-case. It purports to have been sent as an enclosure in Bottini's letter. In the sermon of Fra Celestino,[22] to whom Browning was grateful for his Attestation of Pompilia's innocence and purity, the poet has a chance to bring his tragic story to a sober close, and to voice some of his conclusions concerning the whole case. Fra Celestino's expressive figure of the catacombs tells us that we are not to lay flattering unction to our souls that the case before us affords any cause for an easy belief that virtue is triumphant, that right has again been vindicated, and so will always be. How many Pompilias go down without their cries being

[22] Browning relied heavily upon Fra Celestino's affidavit for his interpretation of Pompilia's character. He was unjustified in doing so, as the Rev. Paul E. Beichner, C.S.C. has recently shown; "Fra Celestino's Affidavit and *The Ring and the Book*," in *MLN* 58:335–40 (May 1943). The affidavit was based on Pompilia's confession, and Celestino could not disclose any confession of guilt under the Seal of Confession, nor could he remain silent, lest such silence be construed as an admission of guilt. As evidence Celestino's statement carries no validity. The other affidavits in the case are similarly inadmissible for professional reasons, and all of them should have been stricken from the record. This is an important article because of Browning's great reliance upon Celestino's statement.

heard! How many Guidos stalk the world unpunished! How often has
God spoken no word, but kept up his terrible composure! We may take
these cogitations of the Augustinian brother to be Browning's own. This
is one of his most truthful and noble pronouncements.

The long work is concluded by a last reference by the poet to the ring
and his Book and to his wife, his "Lyric Love," whose verse linked England and Italy.

From this detailed analysis of Browning's indebtedness in each part
of his great poem, we rise to the larger question of the poet's fidelity
to the spirit of the Old Yellow Book. How far did he give truth and
truth only as he found it in his source? How far tenable is his own contention (I, 686–7) that he merely resuscitated, rather than created,
the personages of his drama? How far has his imagination, which he
calls Fancy, wrung the fact of the murder-case to fit a preconceived
view? How far has the alloy given form and color to the golden ring,
and how much alloy remains in the finished poem? This question in
its many ramifications has troubled scholars since the poem appeared,
and it is a question worthy of debate, since through it we attain a
knowledge of the essential Browning.

We have seen what infinite pains Browning took to arrive at the
truth. He read the Old Yellow Book eight times; he searched in Rome
for more materials; he travelled to Arezzo. All the knowledge of Italy
and of the Italian Renaissance, stored in him through many years of
unconscious preparation, rushed to his aid. How vast that learning
was one may see by consulting Mr. A. K. Cook's *Commentary upon
Browning's "The Ring and the Book."* What a tremendous effort the
poet made to transcribe the truth of small details from his sources can
only be appreciated by one who has read the Old Yellow Book almost as often as did Browning.

Yet Browning was an artist, a creator and an interpreter, and we
may say boldly that the events of the Franceschini affair in Rome in
1697–8 were never enacted by the characters which Browning gives
us. The question indeed need never have risen save that Browning became more and more convinced as the years went on that he had
merely read and reproduced the Old Yellow Book. Since his own statements, too, many enthusiasts have been so ill-advised as to push
Browning's claims as an historian at the expense of his rights as a creative poet. The evidence will make it clear, I think, that Browning was
great not as an historian of seventeenth-century Italy, but as a poet of
nineteenth-century England. Far from being imbued with a scientific spirit, as the earlier commentators suggest, Browning was gifted

with that peculiar strong-mindedness of the great figures of nineteenth-century literary men, which warped all history to their purposes. Macaulay wrung the history of England to prove a political
thesis; Carlyle bent French history to satisfy a personal philosophy;
Browning made a section of obscure Italian history into a reading of
life as he viewed it in his own day.

Professor Hodell attached to his translation of the Old Yellow Book
a splendid essay which he calls "The Making of a Great Poem. An
Essay on the Relationships of *The Ring and the Book* to the Old Yellow Book." Here he shows that the poet has lifted the whole action
of the major characters of the poem to a higher and more significant
level than the actions and personages of his source—just as the Greek
dramatists exalted human nature by magnifying it in tragedy. Guido
is a far more consummate villain in Browning's poem—the blackest
blot of blackness—than he was in life or in the Book. Caponsacchi, a
daredevil of gallantry in the Yellow Book, is given the subtle and
tender spirit of a soldier-saint—he becomes St. George, and the date
of his rescue of Pompilia is obligingly moved from April 29, when it
occurred in fact, to April 23, St. George's day. Pompilia in the poem,
with her love of God, of her child, Gaetano, and of Caponsacchi, is
glorified far beyond the patient, devout, outraged girl of the narra
tive in the Yellow Book. Having shown these things, Mr. Hodell
thus summarizes the significance of his source study, but it is an odd
fact that his thinking is always bolder than his conclusions:

To all this [the facts of the Old Yellow Book] Browning has brought the
wealth of a richly endowed personality. The deeper spiritual meaning of
the three major characters and of their play upon one another is purely a
part of the Poet's vision. They are hopelessly obscured to ordinary sight
in the Book. One phase after another of the Poet's deeper life breathes
forth in these monologues so that, in the end, we have in the Poem not
merely the story retold from the Book, but the wise, sane thought of
Browning's full maturity; and it is this, and not the rough ore of fact, that
has made the Poem what it is.[23]

This is, in general, wisely if not boldly said. But Hodell too often admitted Browning's contention that the characters of the Old Yellow
Book "were no mere fictitious creations which he might shape or
reject or amplify as he pleased." In a portion of his essay which he
calls "Browning's Fidelity to the Fact of his Source-Material," he
says:

[23] *The Old Yellow Book, Source of Browning's "The Ring and the Book,"*
. . . *with Translation, Essay and Notes,* 1908, p. 290.

The names and characters, the dates, the events, the situations, and motives, the very turns of expression in the Poem, are continually drawn from the matters of fact in the Book. Browning's debt in these respects can scarcely be overstated. On the other hand the passion of the story, as Browning has conceived it, the spiritual meaning of the tragedy—all the real poetry—are created by the Poet. They are created, however, in strict accordance with the detail fact in the Book. In few cases, indeed, does the Poet violate the ascertained fact of his sources, even in his freest range of creation.[24]

The first part of this statement is impeccable, but the latter part of his opinion here given has been strongly, and I think successfully, challenged. In 1920 Mr. A. K. Cook published his *Commentary upon Browning's "The Ring and the Book,"* and in a series of appendices and introductions to the several Books of the poem has examined most carefully the relation of the poem to the Old Yellow Book. In considering the differences between the words of Pompilia and Caponsacchi as we have them in the Old Yellow Book and in the poem, he greatly strengthens the conception of Browning's creativeness, and finds that the poet chose and altered his originals with consummate skill, made mere hints into superb passages of poetry; he concludes that "the charm and nobility of the finely contrasted characters of the hero and heroine were entirely his creation." [25] In inquiring further as to how far the facts of the Yellow Book supported the general conclusions at which the poet arrived, Mr. Cook says with the utmost justice,

He told W. M. Rossetti that the Book supplied a "mass of almost equally balanced evidence," but his reflections upon that evidence led him to an assured conviction that the charge of misconduct brought against Caponsacchi and Pompilia was a false charge, based on evidence which was for the most part a deliberately false concoction. In spite of the contradictions which I have noticed most readers of the Book will share that conviction. They will not, I think, discover a "true St. George" and an absolutely blameless heroine in the Caponsacchi and Pompilia who appear there. It is true that the Caponsacchi of the Book makes a favourable impression. He is humane, manly, resolute, adventurous; he speaks the truth, so far as we can judge, without reserve, and does not calculate the consequences too nicely. We do not, however, detect in him any spiritual exaltation and enthusiasm or any real qualifications for a hero of romance; for such a rôle he seems all too matter-of-fact.[26]

[24] *Idem*, pp. 255–9.
[25] *Commentary*, p. 293.
[26] *Idem*, pp. 292–3. See *Appendices IV* and *V*, and *VII* for a different case.

Such was Mr. Cook's well-taken position. In 1925 Judge John Marshall Gest pushed further the charges against the claim of Browning's perfect fidelity to the fact of the Old Yellow Book in his volume, *The Old Yellow Book, Source of Browning's "The Ring and the Book," A new Translation with Explanatory Notes and Critical Chapters upon the Poem and its Source.* Judge Gest brings a trained legal mind to bear upon the trial of Guido, and his words upon the law, the lawyers, the evidence, and the characters of the persons before the court have weight. He finds that Mr. Hodell's translation erred at a number of critical points in the law-case; he finds, as Mr. Cook found before him, that Browning's knowledge of the law was limited and faulty; he exonerates the two lawyers, Arcangeli and Bottini, from the poet's charge that they were professional sophists, dull and fatuous, heartless and insincere, and shows them to have been advocates of standing and ability who conducted their cases with dignity and a fair amount of astuteness. From the evidence Judge Gest concludes that Guido was rightfully executed, and indicates that he would probably rank Guido's crimes against the laws by which he was judged in this order: (1) the murder of Violante and Pietro Comparini in unwarranted revenge for the wrong they had done him; (2) the carrying of concealed weapons (a capital offence in Roman law at that time), and the conventicle of more than four armed men, which constituted rebellion; and (3) the killing of Pompilia in the cause of his honor.

But of more interest to our present question is Judge Gest's summary upon the three major characters:

Guido, Pompilia, and Caponsacchi and the others were real persons, of whose sayings and doings we have a real account. Guido was merely an avaricious man, vicious by force of circumstances as well as from inherent defects of character. Pompilia was an ordinary girl, deprived of advantages in childhood, with sufficient good looks to attract, and insufficient character to resist temptation, and with instincts stronger than her principles. The victim of an unhappy marriage, she is an object of compassion rather than of admiration. Caponsacchi was a frivolous young fellow, on the lookout for adventure, light in thought and unscrupulous in action.[27]

Judge Gest views the case as a lawyer, and is not conscious of the right of the poet exercised extensively by Shakespeare, for example, to transfigure his crude materials by means of his creative imagina-

[27] Judge J. M. Gest, *The Old Yellow Book* . . . Boston, 1925, p. 624.

tion. Possibly, too, he has some animus against the poet for his treatment of the lawyers.

A more violent but less judicious assault upon what Hodell called Browning's "fidelity to fact" was made in Frances Theresa Russell's *One Word More on Browning* in 1927.[28] In her chapter, "Gold and Alloy," Mrs. Russell's protest against the claims of historical accuracy is mainly concerned with an interpretation of the various major characters from the evidence of the Old Yellow Book. She is at some pains to show what the poet deleted from his account, as well as to show what he added. She writes,

Of the nine speakers of monologues in *The Ring and the Book* four are practically imaginary and one quite so, a proportion of more than half.[29]

She further charges that Browning grossly misrepresented Guido, Caponsacchi, Pompilia, and the two lawyers. Concerning the Pope, who only appears in the Yellow Book to deny Guido's appeal to clerical privilege, Mrs. Russell says:

Innocent XII was of course a verifiable personage, the only one of historical rank in the story, and described indeed as a man of fine, high character. But neither from *The Old Yellow Book* nor from ecclesiastical biography did the poet get his mellow sage, voicing a profound and emancipated philosophy; his interpretation being as ridiculous in fact as it is sublime in conception.[30]

One cannot but feel that, as right as Mrs. Russell is in some respects, she has definitely overshot her mark. This was the feeling of J. E. Shaw in his excellent article entitled "The 'Donna Angelicata' in *The Ring and the Book*." [31] He agrees essentially with Mrs. Russell that Browning's poem is a glorious misrepresentation of the matter

[28] Mrs. Russell published an earlier draft of her chapter "Gold and Alloy," in which she deals with Browning's historical accuracy, in *Studies in Philology* 21: 467–79 (July, 1924).

[29] *One Word More on Browning*, p. 115. Mrs. Russell evidently thinks of the speakers of *Half-Rome* and *The Other Half-Rome* as imaginary, as the speakers are, but their monologues are founded on the Anonymous Pamphlets, mainly.

[30] *Idem*, p. 116. Compare Cook, *Commentary*, Introduction to Book X.

[31] In *PMLA* 41:55–81 (March, 1926). More recently, H. B. Charlton in discussing the difference between historical and poetic truth comes to the conclusion that Browning is historically wrong in his judgment of Pompilia and Caponsacchi, that Pompilia is lying about her inability to read or write, and also about her arrival at the Inn in Castelnuovo. See "Poetry and Truth, an Aspect of Browning's *The Ring and the Book*," in *Bulletin of the John Rylands Library* 28:43–57 (1944). Charlton's contention, however, that Browning's misreading of history is of little importance, is angrily disputed in *Notes and Queries* for May 6, 1944.

of the Old Yellow Book. His interest is primarily in Pompilia, and he reaches the conclusion that the love-letters which were offered in evidence as from Pompilia to Caponsacchi, and which Browning thought it so essential to brand as forgeries by Guido—a part of his malicious plot to drive his wife from him and trap her in a compromising situation—are genuine. Professor Shaw says,

It is evident . . . that Browning's Pompilia is not the Francesca of the Old Yellow Book . . . but it is also evident that she is not merely a whitewashed Francesca, she is not a bad girl made into a good girl; the testimony of Fra Celestino Angelo, in the *Book,* represents her as innocent, modest, and forgiving, dying like a saint. The lies she seems to have told in self-defense aroused no condemnation in a country where literal truthtelling has never seemed as important as it does to puritanical peoples. As a victim of the sordid passions of her relatives she enlisted the sympathies of all charitable persons, and she had the charm of youth and no doubt of beauty. The difference is that in *The Ring and the Book* she has become transfigured with a holy light shed upon her by the poet, which clings to her.

Professor Shaw is chiefly interested in the more important question of how Browning in all sincerity could have so glorified Pompilia and yet have believed that she was the figure he had found in the Yellow Book. The answer strikes to the very root of the character of the poet. Professor Shaw's argument in brief, though brevity does it little justice, is that Browning had transformed Pompilia into the tender memory of his own wife who had died in Florence in 1861, and that the strong chivalric nature of Browning himself had acted the part of Caponsacchi in snatching Elizabeth Barrett away from Wimpole Street. It was Caponsacchi's chivalrous action that probably first struck Browning's imagination (I, 580), and this conception colored the poet's thinking all through the poem. The notion that the memory of Mrs. Browning had a large part in the character of Pompilia had been suggested by Mrs. Orr and others, but perhaps Professor C. H. Herford gave it its best expression:

The story of Pompilia . . . gathered a subtle hallowing association with what was most spiritual in that vanished past of which it was the last and most brilliant gift. The poem which enshrined Pompilia was thus instinct with reminiscence; it was, with all its astounding vitality, yet commemorative and memorial; and we understand how Browning, no friend of the conventions of poetic art, entered on and closed his giant task with an invocation to the "Lyric Love," as it were the Urania, or heavenly Muse, of a modern epic.[32]

[32] C. H. Herford, *Robert Browning,* 1905, pp. 170–1.

From Herford's position, Professor Shaw pushes his argument to show how the figure of Pompilia fused with that of Mrs. Browning, and how Mrs. Browning was indissolubly linked in the poet's mind with Dante's Beatrice, as we know from the poet's own words.[33] Thus as Beatrice was the "Donna Angelicata" of the great medieval poetic tradition, so Pompilia became of that tradition also.

In recent years,[34] two sets of material bearing on the Roman murder-case which Browning did not know have come to light. In 1938 W. O. Raymond discovered in the Baylor University collection a pamphlet, contemporary with the murder, which was longer, more detailed, and more vivid than Browning's Secondary Source.[35] This pamphlet, in addition to correcting a number of errors in Browning's sources, is especially full in its descriptions of the murder, the death of Pompilia, and the execution of Guido and his fellow criminals.

While Mr. Raymond was editing this document, Beatrice Corrigan discovered a considerably larger group of documents which she is in the process of preparing for the press. Her documents contain four versions or copies of pamphlets included in the Old Yellow Book, and an entire codex of 378 pages containing most of the material of the Old Yellow Book and the Secondary Source, and other material

[33] See Griffin and Minchin, *Life*, p. 297.

[34] For a summary of recent scholarship on *The Ring and the Book* see W. O. Raymond, *The Infinite Moment*, pp. 209–24. Some studies may be specifically mentioned here: E. D. H. Johnson in his *Alien Vision of Victorian Poetry* (pp. 120–30) emphasizes Browning's scorn for conventional social opinions and standard social attitudes in church and state; C. W. Smith in *Browning's Star-Imagery* (pp. 188–224) analyzes the poet's use of such symbols for Caponsacchi and the Pope, and shows how Browning consciously drew his images together in Book XII; Louise Snitslaar in *Sidelights on Robert Browning's "The Ring and the Book"* emphasizes the importance of the minor characters in the poem; D. A. Smalley in *Browning's Essay on Chatterton* (Ch. 2) draws the parallel between the early pleading of the early essay and the similar trait, deepened and more partial, in *The Ring and the Book;* C. M. Smith, in *PMLA* 56:219–29 (1941), analyzes Browning's use of "Proverb Lore in *The Ring and the Book*"; E. E. Stoll in his "Poetry and the Passions Again," in *Journal of English and German Philology* 40:509–25 (1941), stresses the improbability in character of Pompilia's act of seizing Guido's sword to defend Caponsacchi—"she is not the woman to do it" however morally and artistically admirable her action is; and H. B. Charlton in "Browning's Ethical Poetry," in *Bulletin of the John Rylands Library* 27:63–9, analyzes the poet's moral principles as they exhibit themselves in the conduct of the Pope, Pompilia, and Caponsacchi.

[35] *Browning's "Roman Murder Story" as Recorded in a hitherto unknown Italian Contemporary Manuscript*, Translated by E. H. Yarrill, With an Introduction by William O. Raymond, in *Baylor University's Browning Interests*, Series Eleven, December, 1939. See also *The Infinite Moment*, Ch. 6.

in addition. In an article in 1952 called "New Documents on Browning's Roman Murder-Case," [36] Miss Corrigan gives an account of what is in the documents. We learn, for example, a great deal about the marriage of Pompilia and Guido, the dower arrangements, the assets of Pietro, and Guido's poverty, the suits at law between Guido and Pietro, and Pietro's incredible folly in putting himself at Guido's mercy. More interestingly we learn that Pompilia was not illegitimate, but was the daughter of a poor widow, Corona Paperozzi, who was persuaded to aid Violante in her deception of Pietro. It was the opinion of the writer of the document that the Pope ordered the immediate execution of Guido because he was fearful that the great people of Rome would intercede for him. At his execution, Guido made a special plea for his brother, Paolo.[37]

But to return to the poem. To estimate the influences that worked upon Browning, we must keep in mind that his conception of life was essentially chivalric, ideal, and, in spite of his warning, in the main optimistic. In his youth he kept ever before him on his desk a copy of Caravaggio's picture, "My Polidoro's perfect Andromeda," and in *Pauline* he set that up as the symbol of his belief (ll. 656–65). He rested in the faith that "some god . . . would come in thunder from the stars" to save truth in the nick of time from the forces which beset her. In his life he performed the part of Perseus to Miss Barrett's Andromeda. He gave the idea expression in his poetry steadily. As I pointed out in an article called "The Virgin and the Dragon" in the *Yale Review* in 1947, Browning used the Perseus-Andromeda myth and its cognate legend of St. George slaying the dragon no less than thirty times in *The Ring and the Book*. Each speaker's version and interpretation of the myth is a touchstone of his character. In *The Ring and the Book* there are two great crises, both of the same sort: Pompilia is snatched from the beast Guido by Caponsacchi in the first; in the second the Pope, the other hero of the poem, saves truth just in time by his condemnation of the sophistries of evil.

The Ring and the Book was called in the nineteenth century the greatest spiritual treasure since Shakespeare. This praise has often

---

[36] *Studies in Philology* 49:520–33.

[37] In an amusing article Frederic E. Faverty traces the subsequent history of "The Absconded Abbott in *The Ring and the Book*," in *Studies in Philology* 36:88–104 (1939). Ten years after the trial Paolo is still pursuing his intricate ways and is suing for a pension from King Charles III of Spain. A bishopric was awarded him, but though he was delayed in getting it, he probably finally got it, "and lived to a villainous and prosperous old age."

seemed to me to be misguided, notably in this, that a much truer comparison may be drawn to *Paradise Lost*. For Browning's poem, like Milton's, is finally an attempt to justify the ways of God to man, to show that everywhere in the world God has set Himself to meet evil in mortal combat. Above all, Browning has given us, not history, but an idealized reading of life; and though he cautions us in the last Book against reading into his story too cheerful a confidence in the chances of virtue in this world, to view the chances hopefully was habitual with Browning throughout his life.

AFTER-HISTORY

The Ring and the Book, the apex of Browning's career as a poet, and the epitome of all his thought and artistic habits, was completely before the world in February, 1869. It was his *magnum opus*. The great reviews—the *Quarterly*, the *Edinburgh*, the *London Quarterly*, among others—gave the poet unstinted praise. The review by John Morley in the *Fortnightly Review* [38] for March 1, 1869, is generally reckoned as the most notable, in its expression, grasp, and judgment. Perhaps the *Athenaeum* for March 20, 1869, was the most fulsome in its praise, for the reviewer said there,

We must record at once our conviction, not merely that *The Ring and the Book* is beyond all parallel the supremest poetical achievement of our time, but that it is the most precious and profound spiritual treasure that England has produced since the days of Shakespeare.

Of course, the reviewers were not unanimous, and some, especially the critics of the earlier volumes, found the subject sordid and the treatment murky, and objected in general to Browning's method of dealing with his story. The *Dublin Review* (65:48–62) objected to the poet's attitude towards priests, and others had their special quarrels. Edward FitzGerald, who could never read Browning, could make nothing of *The Ring and the Book;* Tennyson thought the first parts of the poem "full of strange vigour and remarkable in many ways," but he was "doubtful whether it can ever be popular." Carlyle is said to have commented to Browning on the work, "It is a wonderful book, one of the most wonderful poems ever written. I re-read it all through—all made out of an Old Bailey story that might have been told in ten lines, and only wants forgetting." [39] On another occasion Carlyle praised *The Ring and the Book* to Allingham as being

[38] N. S. 5:331–43; later included in *Studies in Literature.*
[39] *Letters of D. G. Rossetti to W. Allingham*, ed. C. B. Hill, 1897, p. 284.

excellent in parts and better than "anything else of Browning," but he added, "But the whole is on a most absurd basis. The real story is plain enough on looking into it; the girl and the handsome young priest were lovers." [40] In a franker mood Carlyle said to Browning "that of all the strange books produced in this distracted earth, by any of the sons of Adam, this one was altogether the strangest and the most preposterous in its construction; and where, said I, do ye think to find the eternal harmonies in it?" And he commented, "Browning did not seem to be pleased with my speech, and he bade me good morning." [41]

In spite of its length the poem sold very well, and a second edition was called for in 1872. Since 1869 the poem has been considered the crown of Browning's work and a vast literature has gathered around it. There have been at least two notable parodies of *The Ring and the Book:* Calverley's "The Cock and the Bull," in *Fly-Leaves,* is one of the most skilful in literature, and Kipling wrote one called *The Flight of the Bucket.* Two other works taking their rise from the poem would, I am sure, have delighted Browning more. In August, 1912, Henry James published in *The Living Age* a most interesting paper called "The Novel in *The Ring and the Book,*" which he included in 1914 in his book, *Notes on Novelists,* and in 1926 Miss Rose A. Palmer and Mr. Arthur Goodrich introduced to the New York stage a play called *Caponsacchi,* which with Mr. Walter Hampden in the title-rôle had a considerable success during the fall and winter of 1926–7.

In Browning's day the poem made him a national figure; [42] it raised

---

[40] Allingham, *Diary,* p. 207.

[41] D. A. Wilson, *Carlyle,* VI, 176.

[42] I have allowed my comment here to stand as it appeared in 1935 (with the exception of an additional opinion of Carlyle's) because I think it is fundamentally correct. My comments have been challenged, however, by three papers which make some appropriate modifications. In 1936 Helen P. Pettigrew published her article "The Early Vogue of *The Ring and the Book*" in *Archiv* to show that the praise early accorded to Browning was mixed with disappointment, and that as the years went on there was more dislike expressed for the sordid subject matter of the poem, its confusing structure, abstruse and rough style and its inordinate length. Mrs. Pettigrew's industry is enormous, her judgment somewhat indiscriminate. In 1937 B. R. McElderry, Jr., published a paper, "Browning and the Victorian Public in 1868–69," in *Research Studies of the State College of Washington* 5:193–203, demonstrating a point already well known, that the tide had turned in Browning's favor with the publication of *Dramatis Personae* in 1864, and observing that the critics and the public were prepared in 1868–9 to give Browning all the advantages of their previous doubts. In 1939 Mr. McElderry published a second paper, "Victorian Evalua-

him in the popular imagination to a greatness, though not a popularity, equal to Tennyson's. In the memoirs and diaries which record English social life after 1869 we often hear of Browning reading aloud parts of *The Ring and the Book*. It is not surprising that he seems most often to have read *Pompilia*.

tion of *The Ring and the Book*," in *Research Studies of the State College of Washington* 7:75–89, elaborating his earlier thesis that the reviewers of 1868–9 strove to make amends to Browning for their long neglect of him. Both Mrs. Pettigrew and Mr. McElderry object to my comment that "In Browning's day the poem made him a national figure."

≋ VI ≋

THE
WORK OF THE SEVENTIES

BALAUSTION'S ADVENTURE

PUBLICATION AND TEXT

Balaustion's Adventure, Including a Transcript from Euripides was published on August 8, 1871, just as Browning set out for his holiday at Loch Tummel in Scotland. The book was post octavo, bound in reddish-brown cloth boards, and sold for Five Shillings the copy. It consisted of the title page: "Balaustion's Adventure: Including A Transcript from Euripides. By Robert Browning. London: Smith, Elder and Co., 15, Waterloo Place. 1871"; the dedication to the Countess Cowper; a quotation of four lines from Mrs. Browning's *Wine of Cyprus;* and the text, pp. 1–170. The text consisted of 2705 lines of blank verse. In succeeding editions Browning made his usual changes in punctuation and a few alterations in word and phrase, but in general the text of the final edition of 1888–9 corresponds closely to that of the first edition. The manuscript of the poem is in the Balliol College Library.

GENESIS AND COMPOSITION

In the graceful dedication of the poem to Katrine Cecilia, Countess Cowper, a lady of beauty, charm and learning, wife of the seventh Earl Cowper, Browning says:

If I mention the simple truth: that this poem absolutely owes its existence to you,—who not only suggested, but imposed on me as a task, what has proved the most delightful of May-month amusements—I shall seem honest, indeed, but hardly prudent; for, how good and beautiful ought such a poem to be!

Euripides might fear little; but I, also, have an interest in the performance; and what wonder if I beg you to suffer that it make, in another and far easier sense, its nearest possible approach to those Greek qualities of goodness and beauty, by laying itself gratefully at your feet?

This dedication to the first poem which Browning wrote after *The Ring and the Book* was dated July 23, 1871, when the poem must have been already in the press. The poem was written during the May of 1871, and it is probable that the finishing touches were put upon it in June. The manuscript has the words in Browning's handwriting, "Begun and ended in May, 1872," but this is an obvious error, for the poem was published in August, 1871. The date of composition has considerable significance when we remember that just ten years earlier, in June, 1861, Mrs. Browning had died, and that she "imposed" the task upon her husband quite as much as did the Countess Cowper. Upon the reverse of the page in which Browning dedicated the poem to the countess he printed a quatrain from Mrs. Browning's *Wine of Cyprus:*

> Our Euripides, the Human,
> > With his droppings of warm tears,
> And his touchings of things common
> > Till they rose to touch the spheres.

Moreover, it has been observed by many commentators that however different *Balaustion's Adventure* is from *The Ring and the Book* the characters of Pompilia and Balaustion have a great deal in common, and that the element common to them was supplied by the character of Mrs. Browning as the poet tenderly remembered it. Mrs. Browning, too, was as great an admirer of the works of Euripides as Balaustion was. Mrs. Miller in her portrait of the poet justly sees in the poem the first expression by Browning of his deep remorse for his "unfaithfulness" to his wife's memory in his proposal of marriage to Louisa, Lady Ashburton, in September, 1869.[1] This may be seen in Balaustion's interpolations, for which there are no counterparts in Euripides' play, of Admetus' recognition of his selfishness in accepting Alcestis' sacrifice, and in his reluctance to take a new wife.

Though the poem seems to have been composed with amazing swiftness, one should remember that it is really the product of a life-long interest in the Greek drama, and especially in Euripides. It was eminently fitting that Browning should have chosen Euripides from

[1] Miller, *Robert Browning*, p. 268–9.

among the Greek dramatists for his special admiration, for there was a genuine kinship of purpose between Euripides and himself. The new elements which Euripides brought to the Greek drama and which made him distasteful to the conservatives of his day are described by Professor Gilbert Murray in his introduction to his translation of the *Alcestis*. Euripides, he says, "has subjected the story and its characters to a keener study and a more sensitive psychological judgment than the simple things were originally meant to bear." [2] This is surely an excellent description of a great deal of Browning's poetry. His delight in Euripides had met great encouragement from Elizabeth Barrett. Before he had met her he had written *Artemis Prologizes* (1842) which was a fragment suggested by Euripides' *Hippolytus*, but correspondence with Miss Barrett concerning her version of Aeschylus' *Prometheus* had led the two poets to agree, in spite of their admiration for the Greeks, that, as she put it,

The old gods are dethroned. Why should we go back to the antique moulds? . . . Let us all aspire rather to *Life*, and let the dead bury their dead. If we have but courage to face these conventions, to touch this low ground, we shall take strength from it, instead of losing it; and of that I am intimately persuaded. For there is poetry *everywhere:* the 'treasure' . . . lies all over the field.[3]

It was probably his conviction of the deadness of the antique mould which led Browning to give us the transcript of Euripides' *Alcestis* in the modern framework of story, commentary, and interpretation by Balaustion and by Browning himself.

A delight in matters Hellenic, and especially in the dramas of Euripides, was one of the many ties in the friendship between Walter Savage Landor and Browning during the years the Brownings spent in Italy. Mrs. Browning's death in 1861 seems to have had the effect of sanctifying Euripides, and it was no doubt partly for remembrance of her that after that date Browning undertook the serious study of her favorite Greek dramatist. At any rate, in September of 1864 we find Browning in the Basque country in southern France "having a great read at Euripides—the one book I brought with me." [4] Between that reading of Euripides and the composition of *Balaustion* a number of things happened which influenced the poet in his con-

---

[2] *The Alcestis of Euripides, Translated into English Rhyming Verse* . . . London, 1915.

[3] *Letters of R.B. and E.B.B.*, I, 45–6.

[4] Orr, *Life*, p. 250; Mrs. Orr misdates the letter as of 1862. For W. O. Raymond's correction of the error, see above, *The Ring and the Book*, n. 15.

duct of the piece. There had been in the Sixties a distinct revival of interest in the Greek drama. The work of Matthew Arnold in favor of Sophocles had begun to tell on the reading public. As we know from a study of *Cleon,* Browning had been much interested in Arnold's *Empedocles* (1852) and had asked Arnold to reprint it in 1867. In 1858, in *Merope,* Arnold had rendered in a Sophoclean manner a subject suggested by the *Cresphontes,* a lost play of Euripides. In 1865, moreover, Swinburne had come into the field with his *Atalanta in Calydon,* which has been called an attack upon nineteenth-century Christianity in the guise of a drama imitated from the Greeks. Browning's opinion was not complimentary: he called Swinburne's play a "fuzz of words." Three years later William Morris had incorporated his version of the story of Euripides' *Alcestis,* which he called *The Love of Alcestis,* into the first volume of *The Earthly Paradise.* It is quite likely, as we shall see below, that Browning took a hint for his own version from Morris's treatment of the tale. Of course, Browning knew what his fellow poets were writing, but the spark which seems to have fired Browning to his ardent championship of Euripides was the attack made by several critics upon the Greek dramatist at about the same time. (See below, under *Aristophanes' Apology.*) For example, among the nine editions of Euripides' works in the Browning library upon its dispersal in 1913, there was a translation of the tragedies by T. A. Buckley, published in two volumes in 1868, at the end of the introduction to which, because of Buckley's lack of appreciation of Euripides, Browning expressed himself so violently in Greek that the matter is better not translated. *Balaustion's Adventure* therefore may be looked upon somewhat as a vindication of Euripides; the task of vindication was undertaken more systematically in *Aristophanes' Apology.* In the meantime Euripides' name had been appearing more frequently in Browning's other verse. Bishop Blougram had spoken appreciatively of the Greek poet, and the Pope in *The Ring and the Book* deals extensively and admiringly with him.

In *Balaustion's Adventure* Browning puts two delightful anachronisms into the mouth of his heroine, a girl of Rhodes in the fifth century B. C. She is made to say (ll. 2668–75):

> I know the poetess who graved in gold,
> Among her glories that shall never fade,
> This style and title for Euripides,
> *The Human with his droppings of warm tears.*

I know, too, a great Kaunian painter, strong
As Heracles, though rosy with a robe
Of grace that softens down the sinewy strength:
And he has made a picture of it all.

The poetess, of course, was Elizabeth Barrett Browning; the italicized words are from her poem, *Wine of Cyprus*. The painter was Frederick Leighton, the friend who had designed and superintended the erection of Mrs. Browning's tomb in Florence. In 1864 Browning had written verses to accompany Leighton's picture, *Eurydice and Orpheus* (see Browning's poem, *Eurydice to Orpheus*). In 1869 Browning had translated a passage from Pindar's *Seventh Olympian Ode* to accompany Leighton's *Helios and Rhodes*, a picture which the poet especially admired,[5] and in the spring of 1871 Leighton had exhibited at the Academy his most important picture of the period, *Hercules Wrestling with Death for the Body of Alcestis*. This is, of course, the picture referred to in Browning's poem. Both Leighton and Browning were passionate lovers of music, and in the spring of 1871 were enjoying Gluck's classical operas, among them the *Orpheo* and the *Alceste*. Browning was therefore thoroughly prepared to write this "little new Poem,—done in a month,—and I think a pretty thing in its way." [6]

The "brisk little somebody" of ll. 304–8 is Alfred Austin who succeeded Tennyson as poet laureate many years later. He had criticized Browning severely in *Temple Bar* (26:327) in 1869 and repeated his attack in his book *The Poetry of the Period* in 1871. It was not until the *Pacchiarotto* volume of 1876 that Browning retaliated in full force.

SOURCES

The source of the body of Browning's poem was, of course, Euripides' *Alcestis*, written about the year 438 B. C. As we shall see, the English poet made some significant changes in the meaning. The framework which Browning placed about the transcript, he took from Plutarch's *Life of Nicias* where there is a description of the suffering of the Athenians who were captured in the disastrous expedition against Syracuse in 413 B. C. The faltering thrust against Syracuse was

[5] See Martha Hale Shackford, *The Brownings and Leighton*, 1942, pp. 18–22. For F. T. Palgrave's criticism of Leighton's picture, see his letter to Browning on May 25, 1871, in *Intimate Glimpses from Browning's Letter File*, in *Baylor University's Browning Interests*, Series Eight (September, 1934), p. 52.
[6] *Dearest Isa*, ed. McAleer, p. 362.

made in the second half of the Peloponnesian War, when Sparta was gradually winning her military supremacy over all Greece. Many of the Athenian prisoners were treated cruelly: they were set to work and to starve in the stone-quarries near Syracuse, and were branded upon the forehead with the sign of the horse. This was not the fate of all, for, says Plutarch,

Some were saved for the sake of Euripides. For the Sicilians, it would seem, more than any other Hellenes outside the home land, had a yearning fondness for his poetry. They were forever learning by heart the little specimens and morsels of it which visitors brought them from time to time, and imparting them to one another with fond delight. In the present case, at any rate, they say that many Athenians who reached home in safety greeted Euripides with affectionate hearts, and recounted to him, some that they had been set free from slavery for rehearsing what they remembered of his works; and some that when they were roaming about after the final battle they had received food and drink for singing some of his choral hymns. Surely, then, one need not wonder at the story that the Caunians, when a vessel of theirs would have put in at the harbor of Syracuse to escape pursuit by pirates, were not admitted at first, but kept outside, until on being asked if they knew any songs of Euripides, they declared that they did indeed, and were for this reason suffered to bring their vessel safely in.[7]

This, then, was Browning's starting-point. Balaustion, the girl from Rhodes, whose name means "wild-pomegranate flower," was of course Browning's invention, and her choice of the *Alcestis* as the drama she wished to re-tell was a happy one because Heracles was a god especially honored in Syracuse. Murray describes Heracles in the *Alcestis* as "halfway on his road from the roaring reveller of the Satyr play to the suffering and erring deliverer of tragedy." That it was the story from all Greek legend most appropriate for Browning to use in honoring his wife, dead now for ten years, we have already seen.

The question of what Browning did with his chief source is both interesting and important. In his attempt to resuscitate the ancient drama Browning has given himself some aids. There is a play within a play within a play, for Browning himself speaks occasionally, as in the lines 343–7, " 'T is the poet speaks. . . ." Then Balaustion de-cribes the play—she does not merely translate it—working into her account the stage-directions, the scenery, and the expressions upon the faces of the actors—or the expressions that should have been

[7] *Nicias,* XXIX.

on their faces under the masks—as she had seen the play when it was presented in her village the year before. In this way Browning is able to avoid the bleakness of translation, as well as the cumbering artificial form of a mere classical imitation. He also has greater freedom to interpolate or omit as suits his purpose.

It was the opinion of J. P. Mahaffy in 1880 that "By far the best translation of the *Alcestis* is Mr. Browning's." [8] Yet it should be observed that in spite of Browning's close following of the text of the *Alcestis*—interspersed with Balaustion's commentary and interpretation—he has made some changes which perhaps Euripides would not sanction. Two speeches by the little boy of Alcestis, wailing for his dead mother, Browning has described very briefly (ll. 942–5), probably because he could not bear to translate them. But his most subtle alterations are wrought in the character of Admetus. Browning does not quite take at its face value the responsibility of Admetus to make Heracles, his guest, welcome at his home. Hospitality was a sacred law to the Greek. And again, it is Browning's purpose to portray a development in the character of Admetus which it is certain that Euripides did not intend to be quite so complete. Browning, therefore, makes Admetus before the death of Alcestis a spoiled, selfish, insensitive and perhaps unimaginative man, and only gradually is he brought to value his wife adequately—if ever—and only gradually does he shake off his selfishness to the point where he would not let Alcestis sacrifice herself for him if the choice were ever to be made again. This dramatic development is rather Browning's than Euripides', and is modern rather than Greek. Yet, as Mr. Gilbert Murray says in his introduction to *Alcestis*, Euripides was certainly out of sympathy with many of the social conventions of his own day and would not have thought Admetus' hospitable welcome to Heracles entirely natural or quite praiseworthy. Euripides surely must be suspected of some quiet irony in his presentation of Admetus as the conventional man. He intended, it is clear, some change to take place in the character of Admetus, but I think Browning has pushed the change further than Euripides would have wished.

Concerning Alcestis, it is impossible not to read personal elements into the character which Browning has given us—in his glorification of the self-sacrificing and entirely noble woman, dying with the knowledge that her children will not be left fatherless, and with the

[8] *History of Greek Literature*, I, 329.

promise from Admetus that he will not impose a step-mother upon them. Yet it ought to be said that Browning's Alcestis and the situations in which she is placed are very close indeed to Euripides.

Browning should have ended his story, perhaps, when Balaustion finished reciting *Alcestis* to the Syracusans. But having kept faith with Euripides throughout the play, Balaustion feels it is now her turn to speak, and she feels that in some respects she could better the play. Her position is, of course, that of a modern person—Browning —who reads the psychology of the characters in another way than the Greek. She does not see how Alcestis, when she is restored to life by Heracles, could ever live happily with Admetus—however changed he is—once he has shown his selfishness in his willingness to let her die for him. Therefore Balaustion proposes to change the character of Admetus. She would have it that when Apollo came to live as a subject of Admetus, before the play began, the nature of the god so affected Admetus that he became an ideal king, living for the good and honor of his people. When he is cut short in his good life, like Matthew Arnold's Mycerinus, he resents the injustice of the decree, but prepares calmly to die. Alcestis has been warned, however, and has secured Apollo's consent to let her die for her husband. But when the moment comes, Admetus will not accept her sacrifice. Alcestis tells him it is too late, and dies for him. Yet fate is cheated, for the nobility and love of the two will not let Alcestis die, and she is returned to life,

> And so, before the embrace relaxed a whit,
> The lost eyes opened, still beneath the look;
> And lo, Alcestis was alive again,
> And of Admetus' rapture who shall speak?

The most interesting thing about Balaustion's proposed improvements of Euripides' *Alcestis* is that the chief of them had been anticipated in William Morris's story, *The Love of Alcestis,* in *The Earthly Paradise,* three years before *Balaustion's Adventure* appeared. We know, too, from a letter to Miss Blagden that Browning had read *The Earthly Paradise* in 1870.[9] It seems probable, therefore, that though Browning did not approve of Morris's poetry in *The Earthly Paradise,* he was nevertheless not averse to using a suggestion which came from that source. In Morris's story Admetus was a simple and industrious king, kind and affectionate to his wife and family. He is not

⁹ *Letters,* ed. Hood, p. 134.

the central figure of Morris's poem, and when the time comes for the fulfilment of the decree of the Fates he calmly lies down to what he supposes will be his last sleep. When he wakes and sees the dead Alcestis by his side he realizes what she has done for love of him. Her fame spreads through all the world, but in Morris's tale no Heracles came and Alcestis was not brought back to life. Of all possible plots, Morris's simple one does the character of Alcestis, as well as that of Admetus, most honor.

AFTER-HISTORY

Balaustion's Adventure, a "May-month amusement," and considered by Browning to be a trifle, was one of the most popular of all his works. An edition of 2500 copies was sold in five months, and a new edition was issued in January, 1872. It was, as Browning said, "a good sale for the likes of me." *Balaustion* was helped by the fame which *The Ring and the Book* had brought him. As we can now see, *Balaustion* marks the close of Browning's best period, a period which had begun thirty years earlier in the writing of *Pippa Passes.* The numerous volumes of the next years add little to Browning's stature.

It has generally been recognized that Browning was one of the pioneers in the nineteenth century in rehabilitating the fame of Euripides in England. He began the work which was carried on by the Greek scholar Mahaffy—for whom he translated the lyric from Hippolytus, *O Love! Love* (*q.v.*)—and which culminated brilliantly in the scholarship of Gilbert Murray. One correction should be made. It is asserted by certain Browning enthusiasts that though the poet did not know it at the time in naming Balaustion "wild-pomegranate flower," he had hit upon the floral emblem of the isle of Rhodes. This is not true, for the emblem of Rhodes is the rose.

Probably at the beginning of his task the poet thought that the translation of Euripides' *Alcestis* was his chief aim. But his greatest triumph was in the creation of the character of Balaustion. She made such an impression upon his mind that in 1875 he wrote a sequel to her adventure and called it *Aristophanes' Apology.* In 1887 Browning prefixed a prologue to his volume of *Parleyings* which he called *Apollo and the Fates.* In this prologue Browning recounts the maneuvers of Apollo in winning consent from the Fates for the continuation of Admetus' life, provided he could find a substitute to die for him. This prologue to the *Parleyings* would have served admirably as a prologue to *Balaustion's Adventure.*

PRINCE HOHENSTIEL-SCHWANGAU

PUBLICATION AND TEXT

Prince Hohenstiel-Schwangau, Saviour of Society was published about December 16, 1871. The book was post octavo, bound in dark blue cloth boards, and sold for Five Shillings the copy. It consisted of the title-page: "Prince Hohenstiel-Schwangau, Saviour of Society. By Robert Browning. Smith, Elder and Co., London. 1871"; a fly-leaf, containing a motto in Greek from Euripides' *Heracles* (ll. 1275–80) and Browning's translation of it; and the text, pp. 1–148. There was no separate second edition. In the poem as published in 1871 there were 2146 lines of blank verse, but nine new lines (ll. 2135–44) were added in the final collected edition of 1888–9, the whole poem was repunctuated, and a few words were altered. The manuscript is now in the Balliol College Library at Oxford.

GENESIS AND COMPOSITION

We have comparatively full information as to the date of composition of *Hohenstiel-Schwangau*. In the manuscript which Browning gave to Balliol College he had written at the conclusion of the poem these words: "A few lines of the rough draft written at Rome, 1860. Resumed, in the middle of August, and finished at Milton House, Glen Fincastle, Perthsh[ire], Oct. 7. '71." In a letter to Edith Story, daughter of W. W. Story, the American sculptor, Browning is even more explicit concerning the beginning of *Hohenstiel-Schwangau.* The letter is dated January 1, 1872, and reads in part as follows:

I really wrote—that is, conceived the poem, twelve years ago in the Via del Tritone—in a little hand-breadth of prose,—now yellow with age and Italian ink,—which I breathed out into this full-blown bubble in a couple of months this autumn that is gone—thinking it fair to do so.[1]

It has been generally supposed that *Hohenstiel-Schwangau* was the long poem which Mrs. Browning in her letters from Rome early in 1860 mentions her husband as working upon. Possibly a letter in March, 1860, may refer to an early draft:

Robert and I began to write on the Italian question together, and our plan was (Robert's own suggestion!) to publish jointly. When I showed him my ode on Napoleon he observed that I was gentle to England in comparison to what he had been, but after Villafranca (the Palmerston

[1] *Letters,* ed. Hood, p. 152.

Ministry having come in) he destroyed his poem and left me alone, and I determined to stand alone.What Robert had written no longer suited the moment. . . .[2]

Mrs. Browning's ode was *Napoleon III in Italy* which appeared in her *Poems before Congress* in 1860. It was written in the light of the armistice of Villafranca, July 11, 1859, and it is evident that Browning's *Hohenstiel-Schwangau* got its first impetus from that event which showed Napoleon III so unreliable a friend of Italian freedom. *Hohenstiel-Schwangau* was taken in 1871 to be Browning's comment upon Napoleon's more recent catastrophe—the disaster of France in the Franco-Prussian War and the loss of the throne by Napoleon—and so in part it was, though to Browning it seemed that his prophecies were merely fulfilled. It is said that the name of the poem was suggested by Browning's friend, W. C. Cartwright.

At any rate, Browning laid the poem aside until 1871, when Napoleon had fallen and gone into exile at Chislehurst in England. Browning perhaps became interested once more in the interpretation of Napoleon's character by the publication in January, 1871, of a poem called *Napoleon Fallen,* by Robert Buchanan. Early in 1871 Browning wrote to Buchanan:

Why speak at all disparagingly of your poem, which I am sure is very admirable in every way, full of power and music, besides, I see my fancies or fears that you might treat in your undoubted right the main actor after a fashion repugnant to my feelings were vain enough. I think more savagely *now* of the man, and should say so if needed. I wrote, myself, a monologue in his name twelve years ago, and never could bring the printing to my mind as yet. One day, perhaps.[3]

As we can see from the letters which Browning wrote to Isa Blagden during the spring and early summer of 1871, the subject was much in his mind. When *Balaustion's Adventure* was published in August Browning, now at the home of his friends the Benzons, Milton House, Glen Fincastle, Perthshire, was ready to go forward with *Hohenstiel-Schwangau.* In mid-August he began to write. But if one may judge from the scratched condition of the manuscript and from utterances in his letters, the task was not easy. Nevertheless on October 1 the poet wrote to Miss Blagden,

I never at any time in my life turned a holiday into such an occasion of work: the quiet and seclusion were too tempting,—and, bringing with me

[2] *Letters of E.B.B.*, ed. Kenyon, II, 368–9.
[3] *Letters*, ed. Hood, p. 145.

a little sketch begun in *Rome in '60,* that I have occasionally fancied I should like to finish, or rather expand,—I have written about 1800 absolutely new lines or more, and shall have the whole thing out of hand by the early winter,—that *I* can't help thinking a sample of my very best work. . . .[4]

A guest of Benjamin Jowett's in the neighborhood at that time describes Browning as "perpetrating 'Hohenstiel Schwangau' at the rate of so many lines a day, neither more nor less."[5] It was a mode of composition that Browning had adopted for *The Ring and the Book.* One may conjecture that the new lines of the poem are those in which Browning interjects a sketch of an ideal career for Louis Napoleon if he had lived up to the ideal instead of following the expedient advice of Sagacity. The manuscript looks as if Browning thought he had finished the poem on September 30, 1871, for that date stands opposite what is now line 1908 of the poem. The date is cancelled, however, and the final date "Oct. 7, '71," when Browning was still in Perthshire, is appended at the end of the manuscript. On November 8 he gave the poem to his publishers.

SOURCES AND INFLUENCES

Speaking of *Hohenstiel-Schwangau* to Isa Blagden in a letter of December 29, 1871, Browning says,

By this time you have got my little book and seen for yourself whether I make the best or the worst of the case. I think in the main, he meant to do what I say, and, but for the weakness,—grown more apparent in these last years than formerly,—would have done what I say he did not. I thought badly of him at the beginning of his career, *et pour cause;* better afterward, on the strength of promises he made, and gave indications of intending to redeem,—I think him very weak in the last miserable year.[6]

In another letter to her on January 25, 1872, Browning gives, in little, the whole intention of his dramatic monologues, speaking specifically of *Hohenstiel-Schwangau* in its relation to Napoleon: ". . . it is just what I imagine the man might, if he pleased, say for himself."

The character of Napoleon III is one of several subjects, like spiritualism, upon which Robert Browning and his wife could not agree. The Brownings scarcely wrote a letter during the Fifties in which Louis Napoleon does not figure. To Mrs. Browning the man

---

[4] *Dearest Isa,* ed. McAleer, p. 367.
[5] Abbott and Campbell, *Life of Jowett,* II, 12–3.
[6] *Dearest Isa,* ed. McAleer, p. 371.

was justified in almost all his deeds, and she placed upon him all her hopes for the final freedom of Italy. To Browning he seemed a complete opportunist—radical and a member of the Carbonari in his youth, conservative and repressive when he had come into power. His liberal ideas, which were genuine, gave way before expediency and pressure. Browning's essential conception of the character was given to Miss Blagden in a letter dated January 23, 1871:

> I daresay we are altogether,—you and I,—in sympathy, about Paris: mine begins, however, at the point when Paris renounced the wretched impostor and all his works: we all, in our various degrees, took the man on trust, believed in his will far too long after the deed was miserably inadequate to what we supposed the will; but when the mask fell and we found a lazy old and worn-out voluptuary had neglected every duty, ignored every necessity, engaged in this awful war because his wife plagued him and *"something"* must be done to brighten matters at the end of his life,—just as when, at the Fair in my young days, Richardson the showman, at any crisis of his tragedy found the action halt, he set the blue fire burning and ended the scene with éclat.[7]

The Brownings seemed destined to be nearby when any great event took place in the life of Napoleon. They had been in Paris on December 2, 1851, when Napoleon carried out his *coup d'état:* indeed the Emperor rode under the Brownings' windows, and Mrs. Browning contended that "he rode there in the name of the people, after all." The Emperor's demand from the Assembly, a little earlier, for universal suffrage may now seem to us a political trick, but Mrs. Browning took it seriously, and Browning in *Hohenstiel-Schwangau* (ll. 932-5) has something to say on the matter. The Brownings were again in Paris early in 1856 when Napoleon won his diplomatic victory over the Russians to conclude the Crimean War; and as we know from the study of *Apparent Failure,* Browning witnessed the baptism of the young prince who was born on March 16, 1856. After Napoleon's victory over the Austrians at Magenta (June 4, 1859), in behalf of Italian freedom, Mrs. Browning hailed him, in her poem *Napoleon III in Italy,* as "Emperor evermore," and she continued to hope good things from him after the armistice of Villafranca (July 11, 1859) and the treaty of Turin (March 24, 1860), when Napoleon took Savoy and Nice for France in exchange for his consent to the association of the central Italian states with the northern ones.

We may be sure that Browning watched the faltering diplomacy of Napoleon in Italy, Germany, and Mexico during the Sixties with

[7] *Idem,* p. 356.

interest, and probably with growing contempt. The Emperor's support of the Pope by keeping troops at Rome, thereby delaying the ultimate unity of Italy, was especially abhorrent to Browning. During the summer of 1870, when the Franco-Prussian War was being fought, Browning was at St. Aubin in Normandy, and judiciously left the country when he was mistaken for a German spy. The opinions of Browning, written to Isa Blagden during the summer, are emphatic: "Not one human being could venture to approve the conduct of the Emperor—for what was ever more palpably indefensible?" And later,

. . . but with respect to Napoleon,—he should simply be blotted out of the world as the greatest failure on record. The "benefits of his reign" are just the extravagant interest which a knavish banker pays you for some time till he, one fine day, decamps with the principal, and then where are you? But there has been no knavery, only decline and fall of the faculties, corporeal and mental.[8]

On September 2, 1870, the Emperor surrendered at Sedan with 80,000 men, and on the 4th the Empire fell. The Assembly of Bordeaux on March 1, 1871, declared Napoleon "responsible for the ruin, invasion and dismemberment of France." When the war was concluded, he retired to Chislehurst, England, with his wife, the Empress Eugénie—who had been delighted at the prospect of a war with Prussia—and his son. He died on January 9, 1873.

Upon his long, but not intimate, observation of Napoleon's character, therefore, Browning built his poem. It is not safe to call *Hohenstiel-Schwangau* a satire upon the Emperor, for the poem is not consistently satirical in intention. Browning permits Hohenstiel-Schwangau to say some very just things in defence of his career and gives him some very sensible opinions upon almost every conceivable topic of interest in 1871. Browning's attitude towards the Emperor is best expressed in a letter to Edith Story on January 1, 1872:

. . . I don't think, when you have read more, you will find I have "taken the man for any Hero"—I rather made him confess he was the opposite, though I put forward what excuses I thought he was likely to make for himself, if inclined to try. I never at any time thought much better of him than now; and I don't think so much worse of the character as shown us in the last few years, because I suppose there to be a physical and intellectual decline of faculty, brought about by the man's own faults, no doubt—but I think he struggles against these; and when that is the case, depend on it, in a soliloquy, a man makes the most of his good in-

[8] *Letters,* ed. Hood, pp. 142, 143.

tentions and sees great excuse in them—far beyond what our optics discover." [9]

Browning's poem should more properly be called a satirical portrait: it is a portrait because Browning earnestly attempts to let Napoleon delineate himself through his opinions; it was a satire in effect because, as we now know, Browning did not believe that any justification of the Emperor's conduct was possible.

AFTER-HISTORY

In the letter of December 29, 1871, to Isa Blagden which is quoted in part above we learn that *Hohenstiel-Schwangau* sold well: "I am told my little thing is succeeding: sold 1400 in the first five days, and before any notice appeared." The reviewers could hardly have been of great assistance to the sale, for they seem to have been baffled by the poem. The *Edinburgh* called it a "eulogism on the Second Empire" and another review called it "a scandalous attack on the old constant friend of England." The difficulties of interpretation were probably owing to the conflict in Browning's own nature, between his genuine dislike of Napoleon and his desire to let the man say what good of himself he could. Thanks to the letters, we are in a better position than his contemporaries were to see what Browning really meant.

Hohenstiel-Schwangau is a poem of case-making, and it resembles other poems where Browning has imagined the defences which slippery characters would make for themselves.[10] The character is in the tradition of Chiappino of *A Soul's Tragedy*, of Blougram, Sludge—whom it resembles more definitely—Guido, Don Juan of *Fifine at the Fair*, and the Elder Man of *The Inn Album*. The philosophy of government as it is developed by Hohenstiel-Schwangau is remarkably like that described in the *Parleying With George Bubb Dodington*. Of late years the poem, being rather contemporaneous and topical in interest, no longer attracts many readers.

[9] *Idem*, p. 152.
[10] D. A. Smalley in *Browning's Essay on Chatterton*, Ch. 4, sees the poem as an example of Browning's formula of imposture in the main line from *The Return of the Druses* to the *Parleying With Dodington*. W. O. Raymond in *The Infinite Moment*, Ch. 8, "Browning's Casuists," analyzes the poem with his usual acumen and adds that in *Hohenstiel-Schwangau* the poet's "sinewy thought and psychological insight" have run amuck, and have become the masters rather than the servants of poetic inspiration.

FIFINE AT THE FAIR

PUBLICATION AND TEXT

Fifine at the Fair was published about June 4, 1872. The volume was post octavo, bound in dark brown cloth boards, and sold for Five Shillings the copy. It consisted of a half-title; the title-page: "Fifine at the Fair. By Robert Browning. London: Smith, Elder and Co., 15 Waterloo Place. 1872"; an excerpt from Molière's *Don Juan*, with Browning's translation of it, on the reverse; the *Prologue*, called *Amphibian*, pp. vii–xii; the text of *Fifine at the Fair*, pp. 1–168; and the *Epilogue*, called *The Householder*, pp. 169–71.

The text of the volume was made up as follows: the *Prologue* consisted of nineteen stanzas of four lines each; *Fifine* was composed of 2355 alexandrine lines, rhyming in couplets, and divided into 132 unequal sections; the *Epilogue* was made up of four stanzas of eight lines each. The volume did not attain a separate second edition, and when it was included in the complete edition of 1888–9, the text was republished with very few changes, those made being chiefly in punctuation. The manuscript of the volume is now in the Balliol College Library at Oxford.

GENESIS AND COMPOSITION

Fifine at the Fair owes its inception to Pornic, Brittany, probably in 1865, as line 10 of the main poem informs us. It was at the fair of St. Gilles that Browning saw the handsome gypsy rope-dancer who suggested the character of Fifine to him, and it is through Pornic in fair-time that the speaker of the poem, Don Juan, passes with his wife, Elvire. The poem was not written for some years after 1865, for the manuscript in the Balliol College Library records that it was begun in December, 1871, and finished on May 11, 1872. We are able to follow in some detail the course of *Fifine* as it was being written. *Hohenstiel-Schwangau* was published in December, 1871, yet on the 29th of the same month Browning wrote to Miss Blagden: "I am half-way thro' another poem, of quite another kind." On January 25 he reported to her that in "Spite of my ailments and bewailments I have just all but finished another poem of quite another kind, which shall amuse you in the Spring, I hope." Yet on March 30 *Fifine* seems to have taken a new lease on life: "I have been hard at work," writes Browning, "the poem *growing* under me, and seeming worth attending to: it is *almost* done." [1] In April, Browning told his friend Domett—"Waring," who had recently returned from New Zealand—that he had "just finished a poem, 'the most metaphysical and boldest he had written since *Sordello,* and was very doubtful as to its reception by the public.'" [2] The condition of the manuscript shows that Browning worked hard over it. He interpolated new sections after the poem seemed complete, the most interesting of which are the lines on Byron (section LXVII, ll. 1119–25). These lines were occasioned by Browning's quarrel with Alfred Austin, which was now in its early stages and which was to reach its full development in *Pacchiarotto* in 1876. Browning told Domett that he protested against Byron's glorification of the ocean, in the interest of Christianity. The manuscript shows, besides several additions, that the arrangement of the poem into sections was an afterthought. The poem was finished on May 11, and published early in June.

SOURCES AND INFLUENCES

It is probable that Browning made only a note of his subject in Pornic in 1865. He was at that time deep in *The Ring and the Book,* and when that great work was finished he took a well-earned rest; then in 1871 he wrote *Balaustion's Adventure* and *Prince Hohenstiel-Schwangau,* somewhat as occasional pieces, I think, developing ideas that had been in his mind for some time. One of the events which was in Browning's mind and was reflected in *Fifine* in December, 1871, and the first months of 1872, was, I think, the feud between Dante Gabriel Rossetti and Robert Buchanan which was the literary sensation of the winter 1871–2. [3] Browning was friend to both men, but in the quarrel he sided with Buchanan. After many years of preparation, Rossetti had published his *Poems* in 1870. In the *Contemporary Review* for October, 1871, Buchanan, under the pseudonym of Thomas Maitland, had attacked Rossetti in an article called *The Fleshly School of Poetry—Mr. D. G. Rossetti.* Rossetti vindicated himself in the *Athenaeum* for December, 1871, in an article called *The Stealthy School of Criticism.* The debate was personal and acrimonious. In May, 1872, Buchanan returned to the at-

---

[1] *Dearest Isa,* ed. McAleer, pp. 371, 376.

[2] Quoted in Griffin and Minchin, *Life,* pp. 248–9.

[3] See my article, "The Harlot and the Thoughtful Young Man: A Study of the Relation between Rossetti's *Jenny* and Browning's *Fifine at the Fair,*" in *Studies in Philology* 29:463–84 (July, 1932). There I have space to enter into the evidence for my belief.

tack with a pamphlet which was the earlier article in the *Contemporary Review* enlarged and envenomed, and it was this pamphlet, *The Fleshly School of Poetry and Other Phenomena of the Day*, which convinced Rossetti, his mind already fevered by a troubled conscience, chloral and whisky, that there was a conspiracy "to hound him from the society of honest men." When on June 4 Rossetti read the copy of *Fifine at the Fair* which Browning had sent him, some lines towards the end of the poem convinced him that Browning had joined the conspiracy against him, and he flung the book from him and broke off a friendship of twenty-five years' standing.[4]

Buchanan's chief charge against Rossetti was sensuality, and one of the crucial poems in the attack was Rossetti's *Jenny*. This poem, which Rossetti had written and rewritten between the years 1847 and 1870, and which he had put in the coffin of his wife in 1862 and had disinterred in 1869, was a monologue by a "young and thoughtful man of the world" concerning Jenny, a harlot of London. It was begun at the time when Rossetti looked upon Browning as the greatest living poet, and was written in the manner of Browning's dramatic monologues. The poem, Rossetti contended, was a sermon against the evils of prostitution. His speaker, the thoughtful young man, after spending an evening at a dance-hall with Jenny, takes her to her lodgings. There he spends the night musing while the weary Jenny sleeps, her head upon his knees. He leaves at daybreak, compassionate and innocent of heart, and as he goes he puts gold in Jenny's hair. In his attack Buchanan identified the monologist in *Jenny* with Rossetti himself, and in his defence of the poem, Rossetti gradually came to accept that identification.

Browning knew Rossetti's poems, but did not like them. In a letter to Miss Blagden on June 19, 1870, he wrote that he hated "the effeminacy" of Rossetti's school.[5] Moreover, Browning told Buchanan of his feelings and strengthened Buchanan's opinions. We know that Browning knew *Jenny*. He told Domett that he "did not much admire Rossetti's poetry, 'hated all affectation.' He laughed at the cant about 'delicate harmony' of his rhymes about the Haymarket [*i.e.*, in *Jenny*]. He quoted Buchanan's parody of them, adding a line or two of his own, similarly rhymed:

> 'But grog would be sweeter
> And stronger and warmer,' etc." [6]

---

[4] W. M. Rossetti, *Memoir of Dante Gabriel Rossetti*, London, 1895, p. 308.
[5] *Letters*, ed. Hood, pp. 137–8.
[6] Griffin and Minchin, *Life*, p. 257.

It is equally certain that Browning followed the quarrel between Buchanan and Rossetti with intense interest during the winter of 1871–2. This, as we have seen, was the time at which *Fifine at the Fair* was being written.

In writing *Fifine* Browning chose a situation closely similar to Rossetti's. He has his young and thoughtful man of the world in Don Juan, and his harlot in Fifine. Don Juan walks through the fair at Pornic with his wife Elvire, his pale "spiritual lady," beside him, and sees the gypsy-girl Fifine, who is the perfect representative of the flesh. Don Juan muses upon lust and love, much as Rossetti's young man does, only with more casuistry and sophistry than Rossetti was capable of, and he does not see why it is not possible to love Elvire in the spirit and Fifine in the flesh at the same time. At the end of Rossetti's poem the young man leaves Jenny's room in all innocence and compassion; in *Fifine* we discover that Don Juan has—inadvertently, he pretends—slipped gold instead of silver into Fifine's tambourine, and he finds a note from the gypsy-girl, making an assignation, slipped into his glove. He rushes away from Elvire to clear up the misunderstanding, as he says, but Browning hints that he will not return as soon as he says he will, and that when he comes home he will find that the "spiritual lady," his wife, has left him. It was the conclusion of Browning's poem, where Don Juan hurries off to Fifine, that probably led Rossetti to believe that Browning had joined Buchanan in a conspiracy against him.

The primary motive in the composition of *Fifine,* however, was a far more personal mood of Browning's spirit, as W. O. Raymond has brilliantly shown.[7] In September, 1869, Browning had proposed marriage to the rich and beautiful but somewhat overpowering widow, Louisa Lady Ashburton.[8] The proposal was put in such terms that it was impossible for the lady to accept, and much gossip and quarrelling ensued. After considerable entreaty on Lady Louisa's part, Browning visited her at her home Loch Luichart on October 2, 1871, but the effort at reconciliation failed. It was in a bitter mood of self-reproach for his "unfaithfulness" to his wife that Browning wrote *Fifine* in the winter of 1871 and the spring of 1872. It was a mood that recurred during the rest of his life, and was reflected frequently in his later poetry. One would not say that Browning felt

[7] See W. O. Raymond, "Browning's Dark Mood: A Study of *Fifine at the Fair,*" first published in 1934 in *Studies in Philology* 31:578–99, now Ch. 7 in *The Infinite Moment.* It is a model of insight and thoroughness.

[8] See Dean T. L. Hood's *Appendix* to his *Letters of Robert Browning,* 1933, entitled "Browning and Lady Ashburton."

towards Lady Ashburton as Don Juan feels towards Fifine; but just as the gypsy-girl came between Don Juan and his wife, Elvire, so did Lady Ashburton come between Browning and the spiritual presence of Elizabeth Barrett Browning. Browning bewailed his loss again later in *St. Martin's Summer* in 1876, in 1884 in the *Epilogue* to *Ferishtah's Fancies,* and in the *Parleying With Daniel Bartoli* in 1887. He found that "The Present intercepts the Past." In *Fifine at the Fair* Browning is caught in a web of sophistry in making a case for one who deserts his trust. And though Browning is no Don Juan and does not condone that character's actions, yet there is enough similarity between them to give the poet an understanding of his imaginary character. Like Don Juan, Browning was "Frenetic to be free" (VI, 43), and in his letter to Miss Blagden of October 1, 1871, he senses that desire in himself: "In all my journeyings in Italy, I could never venture to leave the straight line of obligation to get from such a place, in such a time, to another . . . Ba could not go, I could not leave her." [9] After Mrs. Browning's death the poet's obligation for the next decade was to his son.

There is much more in the poem than Don Juan's casuistical defence of his perfidy. Though Browning's speaker in the poem typifies inconstancy in marriage, the connection between *Fifine* and the Don Juan legend of Molière and Byron is only formal.

Don Juan is a modern man of the world, perhaps with a wicked heart, but certainly with a subtle and sensitive mind, and he speaks to his wife upon a wide range of contemporary topics. There are notable passages in the poem upon religion, music, science, and art. Especially noticeable is Don Juan's explanation of the attraction which Fifine has for him; he compares his wife, Elvire, to a picture by Raphael, a permanent and prized possession of which he tires sometimes in favor of Doré's latest picture book which represents Fifine.[10] Most of the consternation of Browning's readers in the years following 1872 was caused by the fact that the villain had most of the tastes, opinions, and feelings upon these matters which were generally accredited to Robert Browning. The effect was that of Satan quoting Scripture, and Satan seemed careful to change the word as little as possible.

Before and after this mass of very dubious sophistry which makes up the main poem, Browning has placed his *Prologue* and *Epilogue,*

---

[9] *Dearest Isa,* ed. McAleer, pp. 367–8.
[10] Sections XXXV–XXXVI. See also *Dearest Isa,* ed. McAleer, p. 315.

lyrics in which he is undoubtedly thinking of his wife, dead now eleven years. The exquisite little poem called *Amphibian,* which serves as prologue, is the product of Browning's late-found delight in swimming. The butterfly which flutters over the swimmer far from shore is obviously the "psyche," or soul, of Elizabeth Barrett Browning, and the cogitations of the swimmer show admirably Browning's mood in 1872 as we discover it in his letters. The *Epilogue,* called *The Householder,* is a dialogue, jocular and yet tender, between the householder and his dead wife who comes back to visit him; that is, between Browning and his wife. The genuine expressions of his old faithfulness and love for his wife long gone are meant, I think, to set off more vividly the sophistical and cynical faithlessness of Don Juan in the main poem. For Browning it is a scene of reconciliation between himself and his wife after the affair with Lady Ashburton has been put definitely behind him.[11] But, as we have seen, he could not so easily forget his inconstancy to the memory of his wife.

Browning was right in describing *Fifine* to Domett as "the most metaphysical and boldest he had written since *Sordello,*" and he was equally right in doubting its reception by the public. Perhaps Don Juan is, of all Browning's slippery characters, the most insidious in his reasoning. The poet made so good a case for Don Juan that he persuaded many readers that he was such a man as the hero. Of course, the end of the poem should have cleared all, for there Don Juan's actions show the true drift of his arguments, but the end of the poem, unfortunately, was not explicit enough; it was too hinted and suggestive to be understood. It is safe to say that Browning anticipated no misunderstanding of his own character when he was doubtful of the public reception of the poem. He was merely afraid that it would not be understood, and his fears were justified.

The poem was especially misunderstood by the critics, and Browning's reputation for perversity, which for a while had given indications of being lived down, grew again to great proportions. Perhaps the best review of *Fifine* was that in *Temple Bar* for February, 1875. One should read also Mrs. Orr's wise words [12] upon Browning's mood at the time *Fifine* was written.

But though the poem was generally condemned, and perhaps now

[11] See W. O. Raymond's chapter referred to above in note 7, for a full and excellent account of the relations between the *Prologue* and the *Epilogue* and the main text of *Fifine at the Fair.*

[12] *Life,* pp. 282–6.

only the most dauntless undertake it, there have always been those among Browning's readers who are especially fond of *Fifine* and who delight in its playful mastery of ideas. Browning wrote two passages in Greek upon the manuscript of *Fifine* before it was given to Balliol College. The first came from Aeschylus' *Choephoroe* (816–8); the second was from Aristophanes' *Thesmophoriazusae* (1128–31). They were both written, I think, several months after the publication of the poem. One may translate the first passage roughly thus:

And reading this doubtful word he has dark night before his eyes, and he is nothing clearer by day.

And then Browning adds in English,

—if any of my critics had Greek enough in him to make the application!

The second quotation is dated "Nov. 5, '72," and may be translated roughly thus:

To what words are you turned, for a barbarian nature would not receive them. For bearing new words to the Scaeans you would spend them in vain.

With these somewhat bitter words Browning quit the subject.

RED COTTON NIGHT-CAP COUNTRY

PUBLICATION

Red Cotton Night-Cap Country or Turf and Towers was published during the first week of May, 1873. The book was post octavo, bound in dark green cloth boards, and sold for the comparatively high price of Nine Shillings the copy. It consisted of the title-page: "Red Cotton Night-Cap Country or Turf and Towers by Robert Browning London: Smith, Elder & Co., 15 Waterloo Place 1873"; the dedication to Miss Thackeray; and the text, pp. 1–282, dated at the end "January 23, 1873." The manuscript is in the Balliol College Library.

TEXT

The text of the poem consisted of 4247 lines of blank verse, divided into four large parts. No second edition of the poem was called for, and in the final collected edition of 1889 the poem was reprinted with only a few changes in word and punctuation.

GENESIS AND COMPOSITION

Browning spent part of August and half of September, 1872, at St. Aubin, Calvados, on the coast of Normandy. In a simple cottage, barely furnished and with but one book, Browning lived with his sister. He had the companionship of his friend Milsand, who is described with all the poet's admiration in lines 2890–2946, and who first interested Browning in the story told in the poem. Five miles away, at Lion, called in the poem "Joyeux," or "Joyous-Gard," Anne Thackeray, daughter of the novelist and later Lady Ritchie, was spending the summer. She called the region "White Cotton Night-Cap Country" because of the headdress of the women and the general somnolence of the country. Browning took her phrase for his title, but changed the white to red because of the bloody nature of the tragedy which occurred there, and which he describes in the poem. The volume is dedicated to Anne Thackeray, and the poem is the story imagined as told to her by the poet, probably just as he had told it on one of her visits to St. Aubin. She has described the region and the Browning cottage in her book, *Records of Tennyson, Ruskin, and Browning* (1892).

Writing on May 16, 1889, to J. T. Nettleship, Browning explains the manner in which the subject came to him:

I heard, first of all, the merest sketch of the story on the spot. Milsand told me that the owner of the house had destroyed himself from remorse at having behaved unfilially to his mother. In a subsequent visit (I paid one every year while Milsand lived there) he told me some other particulars, and they at once struck me as likely to have been occasioned by religious considerations as well as passionate woman-love,—and I concluded there was no intention of committing suicide; and I said at once that I would myself treat the subject *just so*.

Afterward he procured me the legal documents. I collected the accounts current among the people of the neighbourhood, inspected the house and grounds, and convinced myself that I had guessed rightly enough in every respect. Indeed the facts are so exactly put down, that, in order to avoid the possibility of prosecution for Libel—that is, telling the exact truth— I changed all the names of persons and places, as they stood in the original "Proofs," and gave them as they are to be found in Mrs. Orr's Handbook.[1]

The material for the new poem was gathered on the spot, then, during August and September, 1872. On September 19, 1872, Browning wrote Miss Blagden from Fontainebleau delightedly, "I bring

[1] *Letters*, ed. Hood, p. 309.

back with me, for winter-work in London, a capital brand-new subject for my next poem. . . ." [2] Once in London, Browning told Domett, "I have got *such* a subject for a poem, if I can do justice to it." [3] The manuscript in the Balliol College Library shows that Browning began writing the poem on December 1, 1872, and finished it on January 23, 1873. The extreme rapidity of composition, which his friend Domett deplored and which is evident in the clear manuscript, may be partly the cause of the public's indifference to the poem. A better reason is the sordid nature of the subject.

The long delay between the conclusion of the composition and the publication of the poem is explained by the fact mentioned in Browning's letter above. When the poem was in its first proofs Mr. Smith, the publisher, held it back for fear of a libel suit from some of the participants in the tragedy which is the material of the narrative. [4] The contest over the will of Antoine Mellerio, the chief character of the poem, had just been decided in the courts at Caen. Browning appealed to two lawyers, the second of whom was Coleridge, the Attorney General, and when opinion was given that an action might be brought upon the grounds of libel, Browning changed the names of all the principal persons and places. I have listed below the principal real names of people and places to be found in the manuscript, with the corresponding fictitious names appearing in the published work, in the second column. A full list may be found in Mrs. Orr's *Handbook*.

In manuscript	As published
Mellerio Brothers	The Firm Miranda
Antoine Mellerio	Léonce Miranda
Anna de Beaupré	Clara de Millefleurs
St. Aubin	St. Rambert
Debacker	Muhlhausen
Lion *or* Lioness	Joyeux, Joyous-Gard
Caen	Vire
La Délivrande	La Ravissante
Tailleville	Clairvaux
Miromesnil Street	Coliseum Street

[2] *Dearest Isa*, ed. McAleer, p. 385.
[3] Griffin and Minchin, *Life*, p. 250.
[4] See Browning's letters to Smith upon this subject, in *New Letters*, ed. DeVane and Knickerbocker, pp. 211–2, 213–5, 216, 217.

The story which Browning used for *Red Cotton Night-Cap Country* was an ugly story of mental disturbance, culminating in suicide, which took place in Normandy in 1870. Antoine Mellerio, son of a wealthy jeweller of Paris and Madrid, had led a dissipated life with many women in the time he could spare from his work, until he met Anna de Beaupré, who was already married to a tailor named Debacker. The affair could not be legally approved, and Mellerio therefore retired into Normandy with the woman and spent several years in seeming happiness, making many architectural improvements and additions to his estate at Tailleville, among them a belvedere or tower, which will figure in the story later. Mellerio was summoned to Paris by his mother in order that she might expostulate with him concerning his extravagance. He was so affected by his mother's reproaches that he threw himself into the Seine. He was saved, and Anna, his mistress, nursed him back to health. He was again summoned to Paris soon afterwards and found his mother dead. Overwhelmed at his loss and believing himself to blame, he was about to will his property to his relatives, reserving only a little for himself and Anna, when instead, in a fit of self-accusation, he plunged his hands into a fire until they were burned away. When he recovered, after three months of nursing, he sold the jewelry business to his relatives, and came again to live at Tailleville with his mistress. During this time Mellerio made many gifts to the Church and to charity. In 1870 he made his third, this time successful, attempt at suicide when he plunged from the belvedere on his estate to the turf below. In his will it was found that he had given all his fortune to the Church, reserving a life interest for Anna. His relatives brought suit at Caen, questioning his sanity when the will was made. The trial was interrupted by the Franco-Prussian War, but in the summer of 1872 the Court upheld the sanity of Mellerio and approved the will. As we have seen, Browning was on the scene of the tragedy in 1872; he collected evidence from the stories of the natives as well as from local newspapers and legal documents, and according to Mrs. Orr's account, he saw Anna de Beaupré, the lady of the tragedy, herself.

Such were the facts of the case. Browning reserved the right of the artist to interpret the motives which lay behind the actions of the characters. It was a thing he had been doing since he rewrote

Leigh Hunt's story of *The Glove and the Lions* in 1845. In this case
Browning did not believe that the "hero," Mellerio—or as we shall
now call him, Miranda—had intended suicide when he leapt from
his belvedere. By his sub-title, *Turf and Towers,* the poet wished to
show the two forces which he thought were contending for the
mastery of the deranged man. The sub-title cut several ways. By
the "Turf" Browning meant the low-earthy life of Miranda—the
love, illicit as it was, but happy, which he had with Clara Muhlhausen
(Anna); by the "Towers" he meant Miranda's religious aspirations.
The tower of the poem is not only the belvedere which Miranda has
built at Clairvaux (Tailleville), but it means also the Virgin of the
Ravissante—or in real life, the tower of La Délivrande—with the
statue of the Virgin upon it. In a sense the struggle in the heart of
Miranda is between the earthy Clara and the heavenly Virgin. The
two forces of his nature could not be reconciled. Miranda, when he
leapt from his tower then, according to the poet, did not intend to
commit suicide, but rather, since he had given all to the Church
and had cast his faith utterly upon the Virgin, looked in his anguish
towards the Virgin and asked for a miracle—that his faith be vindicated to him and that he be borne up and not let fall. The turf at
the foot of his own tower was his death. It was the failure of the
mad Miranda that the two aspects of his nature were incompatible
and could never be harmonized. By nature Browning was tremendously interested in the soul of a man who expected God to show
himself in a miracle at this late day.

AFTER-HISTORY

Like *The Ring and the Book, Red Cotton Night-Cap Country* is
built upon an ugly and sordid piece of history. But in the latter no
great characters emerge, and we are left with the vulgar, contemporary story and the figures of a diseased man and a most ordinary
woman for hero and heroine. The poem loses in intensity because
it is narrative instead of dramatic monologue. In this respect, as in
its complete failure, it is comparable to *Sordello*. The poem was generally disliked.[5] Perhaps the *Daily News* for May 5, 1873, expressed
best the general opinion, that the theme and motive of the poem were
outside the sphere of true and healthy art. Hutton, the editor of the
Spectator, told Domett that he did not think there was a single line

[5] Miss Thackeray was made uncomfortable by the reviews of the poem. See
New Letters, ed. DeVane and Knickerbocker, p. 216.

of poetry in *Red Cotton Night-Cap Country*.[6] Readers of Browning's biography will cavil at this judgment in favor of the lines containing the noble expression of friendship for Milsand, the nearest of the poet's companions in later life, the friend to whom he went for help and judgment, and to whom he dedicated the revised *Sordello* and the *Parleyings With Certain People of Importance*.

One cannot resist recording that when Browning in 1882 was awarded the honorary degree of Doctor of Civil Laws at Oxford, an undergraduate wag let down from the ceiling a red cotton night-cap, and dangled it above the new doctor's head.[7] Under the date May 12, 1873, William Allingham records in his *Diary* that Carlyle had read *Red Cotton Night-Cap Country*, and "says there are 'ingenious remarks here and there; but nobody out of Bedlam ever before thought of choosing such a theme.'" On the next day Carlyle said, "Browning *will* very likely do the Claimant [the Tichborne Claimant; see *The Inn Album*] by and by . . . and call it *Gammon and Spinach*, perhaps."

ARISTOPHANES' APOLOGY

PUBLICATION AND TEXT

Aristophanes' Apology was published on April 15, 1875. The volume was post octavo, bound in dark green cloth boards, and sold for Ten Shillings Sixpence the copy. It consisted of a half-title: "The Last Adventure of Balaustion"; the title-page: "Aristophanes' Apology Including A Transcript from Euripides Being the Last Adventure of Balaustion By Robert Browning London Smith, Elder, & Co., 15 Waterloo Place 1875"; a motto in Greek from the *Fragmenta* of Aristophanes (693), with Browning's paraphrase beneath it; and the text, pp. 1–366. The manuscript of the poem is in the Balliol College Library.

In all, the poem was composed of 5705 lines, mainly in blank verse, though there are a number of incomplete lines, and the songs of the chorus in the transcription from Euripides, and the other songs, are in rhyme. No separate edition was called for, and it was not until Browning got the poem ready for the final collected edition of 1888–9 that it was revised. Besides the usual changes in word

---

[6] Griffin and Minchin, *Life*, p. 251.
[7] *Idem*, p. 271.

and punctuation, the poet added six lines, scattered throughout the text. *Aristophanes' Apology* has the distinction, after *The Ring and the Book* and *Sordello*, of being the longest of Browning's poems.

GENESIS AND COMPOSITION

Aristophanes' Apology, as its sub-title implies, is a sequel to *Balaustion's Adventure*, and it was probably because of the success which that poem enjoyed that Browning continued the story of the girl of Rhodes. Like *Balaustion's Adventure*, the later poem contains a transcript from Euripides, this time the *Herakles*—or as it is more generally known, *Hercules Furens*—set into its matter; but it is obvious that the *Herakles* holds no such central place in *Aristophanes' Apology* as the *Alcestis* holds in *Balaustion's Adventure*. The arguments of Balaustion and Aristophanes, in point of space, overwhelm the play by Euripides, though the personality of Euripides himself is the substance of the poem.

From the manuscript of *Aristophanes' Apology* in Balliol College it is evident that Browning wrote the poem in two parts. The transcript from Euripides, *Herakles*, is written upon the paper which Browning usually used for composition, and is dated at the end "June 17. '73." This part was obviously done at home in London. The surrounding matter which makes up the bulk of *Aristophanes' Apology* is begun and concluded on the usual paper, but the greater part of the poem is done on a different and inferior paper. The whole is signed in this way: "Begun about August 11—ended Saturday, Nov. 7. '74. Mers, Picardy." If Browning returned from his summer holiday in 1874 in October, as he usually did, I conclude that he had begun *Aristophanes' Apology* before he left London and finished it again in London, but that the bulk of the poem was done in Mers in August, September, and October, 1874. Browning's intensive study of Aristophanes seems to have been begun at St. Aubin in the summer of 1873.[1] The dates of composition fit well with the opinion of Frederick M. Tisdel that Browning got his erudition from a few books rather as a poet than as a scholar, and developed in his poem the difference of opinion upon the Greek dramatists which the critics found between Augustus Wilhelm Schlegel and John Addington Symonds.[2]

[1] See *Letters*, ed. Hood, p. 158.
[2] F. M. Tisdel, "Browning's *Aristophanes' Apology*," in *University of Missouri Studies*, 1927.

SOURCES AND INFLUENCES

Concerning the conception and the sources of *Aristophanes' Apology* a significant fact should be pointed out. Just as the poet had leapt to the defence of St. John in *A Death in the Desert* (*q.v.*) when the authenticity of the fourth Gospel was challenged by Strauss, Renan and other higher critics, he now in *Aristophanes' Apology* leapt to the defence of the Greek tragedian Euripides who had been attacked by the critics. Dean T. L. Hood [3] writes as follows concerning Browning's sources in this poem:

In connection with *Balaustion's Adventure* and *Aristophanes' Apology*, a sharp distinction is to be drawn between what comes from ancient sources directly and what comes primarily from Browning's immediate predecessors and contemporaries in classical interpretation. . . . [Schlegel's] *Lectures on Dramatic Art and Literature* determined many points and provided many details on which Browning focused attention in *Aristophanes' Apology;* indeed, in that poem it is Schlegel's criticism of Aristophanes that provides most of the ideas about Aristophanes' work, and his notorious antipathy to Euripides that Browning makes the chief object of attack. From Augustus Meineke's *Historia Critica Comicorum Graecorum* Browning drew in *Aristophanes' Apology* not only the critical judgments of the writers of the Old Comedy but particulars of the ancient laws and other checks restraining Comedy. *The Scholia in Aristophanem* contained the information which Meineke adduced regarding these laws and checks; Browning, it is clear, had also read the *Scholia;* but the use of this class of materials in *Aristophanes' Apology* is of such a nature as to indicate primary indebtedness to Meineke. John Addington Symonds's *Studies of the Greek Poets* (First Series) suggested not only many of the critical ideas in *Aristophanes' Apology* but something of its tone. The works of Landor exercised conspicuous influence. It is only in the light of such associations that Browning can be criticised as a Victorian Hellenist. But between such considerations and the task of identifying Browning's direct borrowings from ancient sources a sharp line should be drawn.

This is undoubtedly true; and A. W. von Schlegel's opinion that Euripides wrecked classical poetry in Greece, which Browning might have seen in the new edition of his *Lectures Upon Dramatic Art and Literature,* published in 1871, was the kind of challenge to set Browning in opposition. We have already seen in *Balaustion's Adventure* how an unappreciative introduction to T. A. Buckley's translation of Euripides' *Tragedies* (1868) caused a violent and vituperative comment to be made by Browning. To answer the attack upon his

[3] *Browning's Ancient Classical Sources,* in *Harvard Studies in Classical Philology* 33:79–80.

favorite Greek dramatist, who like himself was a thinker, a psychologist, and an innovator, Browning began to study the works of the great comic poet of the Greek drama who had attempted to laugh Euripides off the stage, and who was now in 1870 extravagantly praised by the critics, as Browning thought, for an essentially inferior art. And the monograph by Carl Newell Jackson entitled *Classical Elements in Browning's "Aristophanes' Apology"* [4] shows that Browning knew at first hand and intimately the plays of Aristophanes and Euripides, the *Scholia* upon their plays, and a tremendous amount of the tradition and legend which had grown up about the playwrights and their works.

For the form of the poem, the debate upon the merits of comedy and tragedy between Aristophanes and Balaustion, as well as for some of the substance of the debate, Browning is indebted to Plato's *Symposium*. But though Socrates and his friends debated upon the relative efficacy of comedy and tragedy as correctives of the ills of society, there is no evidence that Aristophanes ever made such an "apology" to Euripides as Browning here represents him as making. The situation of the poem—Balaustion on the journey home to Rhodes after the fall of Athens, dictating to her husband Euthukles an account of the visit which Aristophanes had made to them a year earlier—is of course imaginary. In order to make the death of Euripides the cause of the "apology" it is necessary for Browning to set the time of the fall of Athens and the flight of Balaustion in the year 406 B. C., when in truth Athens did not capitulate until April 25, 404 B. C. The fine description of the destruction of the long wall of Athens came to the poet from Plutarch's *Life of Lysander*, and Browning again used the *Lysander* ingeniously when he identified Plutarch's person—"Someone from Phokis," who by chanting a chorus from Euripides' *Electra* delayed the destruction of Athens—with Euthukles, the husband of Balaustion. It was a feat comparable to Balaustion's first adventure when she saved her company by the recitation of the *Alcestis*.

It has been justly said that while in *Aristophanes' Apology* Browning shows the great comic poet addressing Balaustion as the representative of the dead Euripides, he makes Aristophanes chiefly concerned with satisfying his own conscience about his conduct towards the tragic poet. For the arguments which Aristophanes brings forward to justify himself Browning literally ransacked the eleven

[4] *Harvard Studies in Classical Philology* 20:15–73 (1909).

extant plays of Aristophanes, together with the fragments which are left to us; and even created an imaginary play, called the *Grasshoppers*, which some Browning commentators have set down seriously as a play by Aristophanes. It is difficult to exaggerate Browning's knowledge and use of the plays for the development of the comic poet's "apology." Patches, sentences, lines, words, and references interlace the English poem. By their relation to Aristophanes' argument some plays are naturally more significant than others. The *Clouds* (423 B. C.) is laid under heavy tribute, for Aristophanes, a natural conservative who loved the old order and the old gods, thought the new philosophy as represented by Socrates, the friend of Euripides, an imposture and an impiety. It was at this play, according to Aelian,[5] that Socrates stood up so that all foreigners might know the object of Aristophanes' attack. And as Socrates was the philosopher of the new spirit of intellectual inquiry and culture in Athens which Aristophanes despised so heartily and satirized so brilliantly, so was Euripides the tragedian of that new spirit. Socrates cared little for most tragedy, but would go any distance to see a tragedy by Euripides. Besides the *Clouds*, Aristophanes directed his satire against Euripides in a series of brilliant plays. Browning drew heavily upon this group—the *Acharnians, Knights, Birds, Peace,* and the *Lysistrata*, which shocked Balaustion by its obscenity—but the occasion which Browning imagines to have brought forth the "apology" was the *Thesmophoriazusae*, a play which is largely made up of parodies of the works of Euripides. In this play, the title of which means "Priestesses of Demeter," or "Female Celebrators of the Feast," Euripides is accused and condemned at the female festival because he has shown women at a disadvantage. The women plot to murder Euripides, but their intention is discovered to Euripides by his hairy father-in-law, who has been sent disguised among them. This play was first produced in 411 B. C., but for his purposes Browning makes the first production of the *Thesmophoriazusae* occur in 407 B. C., when it failed to win a prize; and from fragments of a second play of the same name he imagines a second play which in 406 B. C. took, as Browning represents it, the prize for comedy. Indeed, it is upon the very night of Aristophanes' victory, when he is celebrating, that Browning represents Sophocles as coming solemnly in to the feast to announce the death of Euripides in Macedonia. Browning imagines this vivid scene from the known fact

---

[5] See *Letters of R.B. and E.B.B.*, I, 540.

that in his *Proagon* in March, 406 B. C., Sophocles brought his chorus on the stage without garlands, in mourning for his great rival who had died in 407 B. C. It is upon the evening of Aristophanes' triumph and the announcement of Euripides' death that the comic poet, half-drunk, is represented as breaking in upon Balaustion and Euthukles when they are about to read the *Herakles* as a commemorative act for Euripides.

Browning perpetrates a mild anachronism when he makes Aristophanes upon that evening in 406 B. C. speak of his play, the *Frogs,* which was not to appear until 405 B. C. In the *Frogs* Euripides is satirized again, and brilliantly. The plot of the play is as follows: In the troubled times of the Peloponnesian War, when the fate of Athens seems sealed, the city finds itself without poets, for Aeschylus and Euripides are now both dead. In this pass Dionysus descends to Hades in order to bring a poet back. In Hades Aeschylus and Euripides contend for the honor of being brought back to life: each poet speaks his weightiest line into a set of scales—though Aeschylus contends that the contest is not fair, for his poetry has not died with him, and therefore is not at hand to quote, whereas all of Euripides' poetry has come down to Hades with him. After a moment's pause Euripides' words prove light and the scales kick the beam against him! Aeschylus has the victory. Balaustion represents the *Frogs* as having already been played in 406 B. C. when she was sailing for Rhodes, which of course could not have been the fact.

But Browning not only knew intimately the plays and fragments of plays, but he knew the *Scholia,* or commentary, upon the plays of Aristophanes. Browning, indeed, told Dr. Furnivall that "the allusions require a knowledge of the *Scholia,* besides acquaintance with the 'Comicorum Graecorum Fragmenta'—Athenaeus, Alciphron, and so forth, not forgotten. But I wrote in France, at an out of the way place, with none of these books." [6] It is probable, as Mr. Hood suggests, that he knew the matter of the *Scholia* through Schlegel, Meineke, Symonds and others. At any rate, from these sources Browning drew that great knowledge of the Athenian theater which he exhibits in the poem; and ultimately from the *Vitae* of the *Scholia* and the *Prolegomena* he culled directly or indirectly descriptions and anecdotes concerning Aristophanes, and much information concerning the history of the old comedy upon the Athenian stage.

That Browning was as familiar with the plays of Euripides as

[6] *Letters,* ed. Hood, p. 208.

he was with those of Aristophanes goes without saying: the transcript of the *Alcestis* in *Balaustion's Adventure* and the translation of the *Herakles* here—"a fine play, finely translated"—amply prove it. But in *Aristophanes' Apology* Browning does not make so much of the plays of Euripides as he does of the *Scholia* upon the plays, and especially of the *Vitae* which are attached to the *Scholia*. Concerning the *Vitae* Mr. Jackson says, "This repository of idle gossip, circulated by detractors of the tragic poet's genius, furnished Browning with material the true value of which he was not slow to recognize. Almost every scrap of information contained within them he has utilized in one way or another."[7] This information comprises many things—Euripides' personal appearance, his solitary habits, his misanthropy, his love of books, his dislike of women, his sea-cave at Salamis, his voluntary exile in the court of Archelaus, where he proved himself statesman as well as poet and where, according to one rumor, he was torn to pieces by hounds. All of this information Browning used most ingeniously, putting the matter favorable to Euripides in the mouth of Balaustion, and the matter unfavorable to him in the mouths of the Athenian mob.

For the quarrel between Euripides and Aristophanes which Browning sets forth, it is enough to say that the comic poet was of the old conservative order, who idealized the old Athens of the time of the Persian Wars, as he shows us in the *Birds,* and who hated all "newfanglenesse"—new philosophy, new poetry, new demagoguery in politics. He saw Athenian life in process of disintegration and hoped by castigating vices and the proponents of those vices—notably Socrates and Euripides—to bring about a reformation. Euripides was a curious mixture of the old and the new. Of an old family proud of its place, Euripides observed most strictly the form of the ancient drama. Yet he was one of the *sophoi,* the new group, and a friend to Socrates. And though he observed the old forms, he filled his plays with the most daring of modernisms. He humanized the old legends upon which the Greek plays were founded; he denied that the gods were of the nature which was popularly ascribed to them; he introduced psychology of a new sort on the stage; he was at once a leader in the theater for the new realism and for romanticism.[8] He studied with Anaxagoras, one of the most advanced scientists

[7] *Classical Elements in Browning's "Aristophanes' Apology,"* p. 56; see n. 4, above.

[8] See Gilbert Murray, *Euripides and his Age,* 1914.

of the day. Coming at the time he did and representing men as he did, now realistically and again romantically, it is dubious, in spite of Balaustion's contention to the contrary, that Euripides was any more helpful to Athens than was Aristophanes, though his influence upon the times that followed was certainly more positive than that of the comic poet.

In 1940 D. A. Smalley published an informative article, "A Parleying with Aristophanes," showing what Browning himself added to the poem beyond his sources.[9] Perhaps the chief thing added was the strong bias in favor of Euripides and against Aristophanes. Closely connected with this, is the fact that Browning was conscious that his exposition of Euripides' poetic principles represented in good part a justification of his own poetic principles. Moreover, Browning was defending himself against a contemporary attack, for "Dogface Eruxis" of ll. 1671–6 was Alfred Austin, who was to be the victim of the poet's attack in *Pacchiarotto* (*q.v.*). Aristophanes' attacks upon Euripides in the poem resolve themselves into the charge that Euripides tried to poetize a system—a system very like Browning's (ll. 2176–7); and Euripides' defence was Browning's defence of his own realism, his psychology, his progressive ideas, and his conception of poetry and its function in moving men to noble action.

AFTER-HISTORY

When *Aristophanes' Apology* appeared in mid-April, 1875, it was generally received with bewilderment. There was more admiration for Browning's learning than liking for his poetry, and most of the critics were of the opinion which Domett expressed to the poet:

I remarked, however, upon the large demands Browning makes in this book on his readers' knowledge, and said that I believed no one would be able to understand all the allusions without referring over and over again to the Comedies: and that he thus wilfully restricted the number of his readers to comparatively few. He would not hear of explanatory notes; said it could not be helped, but that he was not likely to try anything of the kind again.[10]

The *Athenaeum*, in a generally appreciative review on April 17, 1875, thought the poem too much an essay in verse and too recondite for the general reader. The reviewer supposed, perhaps playfully, that

[9] In *PMLA* 52:823–38.
[10] Griffin and Minchin, *Life*, pp. 255–6.

the poem was the result of one of Browning's "Oxford Symposia with Jowett." This nettled the poet, and especially so when "half a dozen other critics reported the poem to be 'the transcript of the talk of the Master of Balliol.'" [11] This Browning indignantly denied. Most of the other reviews made less of the poem than did the *Athenaeum.*

Browning's ardent partisanship for Euripides as against Aristophanes did not escape without challenge. In the *Academy* for April 17, 1875, John Addington Symonds, upon whose studies in the *Greek Poets* [12] Browning is said to have drawn, spoke thus in an excellent summary of the contest between the comic and the tragic poets:

As a sophist and a rhetorician of poetry, Mr. Browning proves himself unrivalled, and takes rank with the best writers of historical romances. Yet students may fairly accuse him of some special pleading in favour of his friends and against his foes. It is true that Aristophanes did not bring back again the golden days of Greece; true that his comedy revealed a corruption latent in Athenian life. But neither was Euripides in any sense a savior. Impartiality regards them both as equally destructive,—Aristophanes, because he indulged animalism and praised ignorance in an age which ought to have outgrown both; Euripides, because he criticised the whole fabric of Greek thought in an age which had not yet distinguished between analysis and scepticism. . . .

What has just been said about Mr. Browning's special pleading indicates the chief fault to be found with his poem. The point of view is modern. The situation is strained. Aristophanes becomes the scapegoat of Athenian sins, while Euripides shines forth a saint as well as a sage. Balaustion, for her part, beautiful as her conception truly is, takes up a position which even Plato could not have assumed. Into her mouth Mr. Browning has put the views of the most searching and most sympathetic modern analyst. She judges Euripides, not as he appeared to his own Greeks, but as he strikes the warmest of admirers who compare his work with that of all the poets who have ever lived.

In 1881 Browning was impelled to defend his position in regard to Aristophanes to his fellow-poet, Swinburne:

Indeed, I am no enemy of that Aristophanes—all on fire with invention,—and such music! I am confident that Euripides bore his fun and parodying good humoredly enough—as even Cleon did: but a friend of Euripides,—above all, a woman friend,—feels no such need of magnanimity: when I had done with her, I had *all but* done with anything like enmity to him—the reservation being simply due to the circumstance that Euripides was not triumphantly happy like Sophocles. [13]

[11] *Letters,* ed. Hood, p. 171.
[12] First Series, 1873; Second Series, 1876. The chapters had appeared serially in the *Fortnightly* and other magazines before they were published in book form.
[13] *Letters,* ed. Hood, p. 193.

Though *Aristophanes' Apology* did not raise Browning's fame in his own day, the poem was not unappreciated. Carlyle liked it; and Mahaffy, the Greek scholar, was fond of the *Herakles*. The modern reader may find an intellectual pleasure in the poem, and many wonderful passages of poetry, such as the description of the fall of Athens, the festival where Aristophanes is celebrating his victory, the majestic entry of Sophocles, and above all the song, *Thamuris Marching*. This song Browning made from a hint in the life of Socrates, combined with other suggestions from Euripides' *Rhesus* and Homer's *Iliad* (II, 594). Browning was especially fond of reading aloud this splendid song in later years, and he read it with feeling and force.

THE INN ALBUM

PUBLICATION AND TEXT

The Inn Album was published towards the end of November, 1875. It was also published from advance sheets on three successive Sundays—November 14, 21, and 28—in the *New York Times*. The London book was post octavo, bound in dark green cloth boards, and sold for Seven Shillings. It consisted of a half-title; the title-page: "The Inn Album by Robert Browning London Smith, Elder, & Co., 15 Waterloo Place 1875"; and the text, pp. 1–211. In all, the poem consisted of 3078 lines of blank verse, divided into eight large parts. The manuscript is in the Balliol College Library.

Mrs. Orr remarks that when Browning was preparing the final edition of his poems for the press (1888–9) he gave *The Inn Album* his special attention.[1] But this shows in the final text only in changes of word and punctuation, made chiefly in the interest of clarity and smoothness. In the revision only one new line is added.

GENESIS AND COMPOSITION

The poem, according to the manuscript in the Balliol College Library, was written in two months. It was begun on June 1, 1875, and completed on August 1.[2] The manuscript shows that the poem was

---

[1] *Life*, p. 379.

[2] According to Elisabeth L. Cary, *Browning, Poet and Man*, pp. 204–5, *The Inn Album* was decided upon and the plot constructed in one day, and written at the rate of 20 to 30 lines a day, a rate which Browning considered good. This rate, however, would not have brought about the completion of the poem in two months. See also *New Letters*, ed. DeVane and Knickerbocker, p. 227.

written smoothly and easily, save for two places: first, there is considerable blotting, scratching, and rewriting towards the end of section VII; and second, the concluding lines of the poem seem to have cost the poet some labor. But in spite of all his pains, he has not made an understanding of the text easy for hasty readers. After the poem was finished, Browning went on his summer vacation to Villers-sur-Mer, on the coast of Normandy, and here he corrected the proofs.

It is interesting that Browning first thought of casting the story of *The Inn Album* in the form of a play. On December 9, 1875, he told his friend Domett that he "had intended originally to write a tragedy upon the subject, but hearing Tennyson was engaged upon one (*Queen Mary*) gave up the idea." [3] The marks of this first intention are still upon *The Inn Album,* not only in the concluding words "let the curtain fall!" but in the limited *dramatis personae,* the observance of the unities of time and place—all the action takes place within a few hours, and either at the parlor of the inn or nearby—and in the mixture of narrative verse and dramatic dialogue. Indeed, remote as *The Inn Album* and *Balaustion's Adventure* are from each other in subject and mood, the method—the poet acting as commentator upon a piece of dramatic action—is not fundamentally different. One may be sure that when Browning contemplated making a play of his materials the Greek form, with which he had been recently occupied, was not far from his mind.

SOURCES AND INFLUENCES

It was Carlyle's ironic expectation, after Browning had recounted a contemporary *cause célèbre* in *Red Cotton Night-Cap Country* (*q.v.*), that Browning would next take up another famous case in law, the case of the Tichborne Claimant—which held the attention of all England from 1867 to 1874—and call the poem "*Gammon and Spinach,* perhaps." He had observed well Browning's peculiar inclination, during the late Sixties and the Seventies, to take up cases of crime, preferably from actual life, and, in short, to make himself a kind of metrical Balzac. Nor was Carlyle much mistaken, for Browning was tremendously interested in the case of the Tichborne Claimant in 1874. He dined with the Chief Justice, Sir Alexander Cockburn, and was present in court for part of the long charge to the jury.[4] Of course the Tichborne case itself could not be put into a poem, chiefly be-

[3] Griffin and Minchin, *Life,* p. 257.
[4] *Idem,* p. 254.

cause of the danger of an action for libel as in *Red Cotton Night-Cap Country*, but, as we shall see, the Tichborne case actually influenced the writing of *The Inn Album*. It is enough at present to realize that this famous trial really was, as Carlyle had supposed, in the poet's mind in 1874 and 1875 when *The Inn Album* was being conceived.

At the time that Browning told Domett that he had at first planned to make a play of his material, his friend records that "He said the nucleus of the story was actual fact: he had heard it told thirty odd years ago of Lord de Ros." [5] Instead, then, of taking the immediately contemporary scandal, Browning went back for the subject of his poem to a story he had heard in his younger days; and the earlier story, like the later one, was a tale of seduction, proposed adultery, and gambling at cards in high society. Browning was reminded of the earlier scandal of Henry William, nineteenth Baron de Ros, by the publication of the famous *Greville Memoirs, A Journal of the Reigns of King George IV and King William IV by the late Charles C. F. Greville, Esq., Clerk of the Council to those Sovereigns*, in 1874. This work was published in three volumes, and because of its intimate revelations concerning the life of high society four decades earlier, was much discussed. The Queen disapproved heartily of the publication. In the *Memoirs* Browning found the name of de Ros, and was reminded of the story he had heard concerning the peer many years before. The story which Browning uses in *The Inn Album* does not appear in the *Memoirs*, but Lord de Ros's character as a *roué*, a man-about-town, extremely clever and extremely dissolute, a gambler who made his living by fleecing young and innocent fellows who desired to be hardened worldlings themselves, is clearly presented. Lord de Ros was for a while a very close friend to Greville, and Greville's admiration for his friend's abilities and his surprise that these abilities were never used to any honorable end, are very like the admiration and surprise of the "Younger Man" in *The Inn Album* for the "Elder Man."

Greville, because of his former friendship, could not bring himself to record the final disgrace of de Ros. In July, 1836, de Ros was charged with cheating at cards at Graham's Club, and the information got into the newspapers. Early in 1837 de Ros, who had fled to the continent, returned to England and brought action for libel against one of his accusers named Cumming. The hearing at the Court of King's Bench lasted for two days, February 10 and 11, and

[5] *Idem*, p. 257.

such a mass of evidence was brought against de Ros that the jury deliberated only fifteen minutes before rendering a verdict in favor of Cumming.[6] The shifty peer, de Ros, went into retirement and two years later died, not violently, as Browning pictures him dying in *The Inn Album*, at the hands of the outraged young man, but naturally, of a protracted illness.

The *Greville Memoirs* do not constitute the only possible reminder to Browning of the case of de Ros. As early as 1830 in *Paul Clifford* Bulwer-Lytton had depicted de Ros, hardened swindler and soldier of fortune and pleasure that he was even then, in the character of Henry Finish. We know that Browning had admired Bulwer-Lytton's plays and novels, and had been ever since on friendly terms with the family. But Browning was explicit to Domett: he had heard the story which he used for *The Inn Album*. It is probable, I think, that Browning heard the story at Macready's theater in 1838. In 1837 Fanny Kemble, the actress, wrote a play called *An English Tragedy*, founded upon the story of Lord de Ros, and naturally containing many of the features that *The Inn Album* later exhibited. On December 19, 1838, the play was sent to Macready. It made a tremendous impression upon him, for the next day he records in his *Diaries:* "Finished the reading of Mrs. Butler's [Fanny Kemble's] play, which is one of the most powerful of the modern plays I have seen—most painful, almost shocking, but full of power, poetry, and pathos." [7] But the very power of the play and the danger of legal difficulty frightened the actor-manager, and he canvassed his friends, Forster, Bulwer, Miss Martineau, who returned a similar adverse verdict. As we may see from Macready's *Diaries* Browning was steadily at the theater during the last days of 1838 and the first days of 1839, and it is likely that he heard the story of de Ros at that time. The poet and Fanny Kemble met in Rome in 1854, and it is possible that they talked the ancient scandal over again at that time. Miss Kemble's play was not acted until it was put upon the boards in New York in 1864. The play under the title of *An English Tragedy* was published in a volume of her *Plays* in 1863, and it is likely that Browning knew this book. But whether Browning knew Miss Kemble's story or not, he most certainly knew the scandal from current gossip as early as 1838, and when *The Inn*

[6] See the *London Times*, February 11 and 12, 1837, and also editorial of February 14.

[7] Macready, *Diaries*, ed. W. Toynbee; entries under December 19 and 20, 1838.

Album appeared there were many people still living who knew the tale. Four months after the appearance of Browning's poem Dr. F. J. Furnivall wrote in *Notes and Queries:*

It ought to be more widely known that the story told by Mr. Browning in this poem is, in its main outlines, a real one—that of Lord ——, once a friend of the great Duke of Wellington, and about whom there is much in the Greville *Memoirs.* The original story was, of course, too repulsive to be adhered to in all its details, of, first, the gambling lord producing the portrait of the lady he had seduced and abandoned, and offering his expected dupe, but real beater, an introduction to the lady, as a bribe to induce him to wait for payment of the money he had won; secondly, the eager acceptance of the bribe by the young gambler, and the suicide of the lady from horror of the base proposal of her old seducer. The story made a great sensation in London, over thirty years ago, and I get its details from one who well remembers it.[8]

Since there is no contemporary and explicit account of the actual happenings it is difficult to say how much Furnivall may have been influenced by reading Browning's poem, but the essential facts of the story are there, and we may see at a glance the major adaptations made by the poet. The most notable addition is Browning's creation of the young girl who not only adds a much-needed charm to *The Inn Album* but serves the useful purpose of being the cause of the assembly of the three major characters at the inn. The other great change which Browning makes in the story is in the character of the young man, for where Furnivall's account has the young man accept with delight de Ros's offer of his paramour to delay the payment of the debt, the "Younger Man" of *The Inn Album,* when he realizes what the "Elder Man" has done, flies at him and kills him. Browning has, therefore, invented the marriage of the ruined lady to the country parson, and it is by threats of exposing to her husband her former life that the "Elder Man" expects to compel her to comply in giving herself to the "Younger Man" as payment of the gambling debt. These changes seem to owe something to Miss Kemble's play, *An English Tragedy.*

Beyond these changes in plot, it is clear that Browning has created his characters out of mere hints in the story. The magnificent lady of the poem bears kinship in her ideas and nature to many other ladies created by Browning. The "Younger Man" has the air of being made up of Browning's observations of the young men of Oxford, where the poet had been a frequent visitor since 1867; still he is Browning's

[8] Fifth Series, 5:244 (March, 1876).

characteristic lover and possesses the superior insight into the heart of the lady which was the chief virtue of the young lover in *The Glove,* of Gismond, and of Caponsacchi. Yet here he has differences, for he is represented—before love makes him a man of action—as crude, immature, and bungling. As for Furnivall's remark that the original story was, of course, too repulsive to be adhered to in all its details, it ought to be noticed that Browning took away none of the crimes of the original story and added murder to the list; he does, however, give some of the characters a nobility that they do not seem to have had in real life. In speaking to Domett, Browning "maintained that there was sufficient motive for the young man killing the old one, who had attempted to make him the instrument of degrading the woman he was in love with under threat of ruining her." [9]

But beyond the story of de Ros Browning drew, one must think, upon certain details of the famous case of the "Tichborne Claimant." In 1854 Roger Charles Tichborne was lost at sea between Rio de Janeiro and London, and shortly thereafter he was declared dead, his affairs settled and his insurance paid. All save the mother, Lady Tichborne, gave the young man up for lost. She advertised widely until in 1865 a person resembling her son was found in Australia. In 1867 Lady Tichborne acknowledged the man as her son. In 1871 suit was brought by the Claimant for the ejection of the trustees of the estate of Roger Tichborne. This trial lasted a hundred days and upwards of a hundred people testified for the Claimant. The case was decided against him. In 1873 the Claimant was brought before the bar—a public subscription had been raised for his defence—and after a trial of a hundred and eighty-eight days, on February 28, 1874, the Claimant was declared guilty of perjury and other crimes and sentenced to fourteen years of penal servitude. In the course of the trial the early career of Roger Tichborne was given a thorough airing, not greatly to the young man's credit, and especially was Tichborne's youthful love affair with his cousin laid bare to the world. The situation exposed during the trial is remarkably like that of *The Inn Album* where the "Younger Man" is eager to marry his cousin but finds opposition in her family because of his dissipations. Then again, the indignant answers of Lady Radcliffe, Roger Tichborne's cousin, when she was under the necessity of refuting an ungrounded charge by the Claimant against her character,—*i. e.,* that he had seduced her years ago—seems to have suggested to Browning the righteous wrath

[9] Griffin and Minchin, *Life,* p. 257.

of his lady, in *The Inn Album,* who had been seduced by the "Elder Man." [10] As we have seen, Browning was present at a good deal of the trial.

Though *The Inn Album* was built mainly upon the forty-year-old scandal of Lord de Ros, Browning determined to make it a completely contemporary poem.[11] The text is filled with the names which were great in 1875, such as Bismarck, Disraeli, Gladstone, Carlyle, Tennyson, Dickens, Trollope, Ruskin, Salvini, Millais, Holman Hunt, Brahms, Sir Charles Barry; and in the manuscript Browning had put the name of Kenealy, the advocate for the Tichborne Claimant, but had later stricken it out. Perhaps the roll-call of Victorian greatness was nearly completed when the "Elder Man" remarked upon a poem in the album in the following words:

> That bard's a Browning; he neglects the form:
> But ah, the sense, ye gods, the weighty sense!

—an amusing jibe at a popular criticism of his own works.

AFTER-HISTORY

In the same entry from Domett's diary which I have quoted above (December 9, 1875) we learn several further facts concerning *The Inn Album.* Browning "seemed to have seen all the critiques on *The Inn Album,*" says his friend, "laughed at some abuse in the *Guardian* on the style, confessed to a slip in grammar noticed by the *Saturday Review* . . ."—though he confessed to it in 1875 he refused to alter it in 1889—"Smith and Elder told him that 1100 copies out of an edition of 2000 had already been sold." [12] The poet must have read with mixed feelings the praise of the volume in the *Athenaeum* for November 27, 1875, for the reviewer was inclined to rank *The Inn Album* higher than *The Ring and the Book* and to couple it with *Pippa Passes* as among the poet's best work. Swinburne's enthusiasm for Browning's "new sensation novel," publicly expressed in his essay on George Chapman, was both gratifying and baffling. In a private letter Swinburne said that the poem "is a fine study in the later manner of Balzac, and I always think the great English analyst great-

---

[10] A full account of the Tichborne Claimant may be found in J. Brown, *The Tichborne Case compared with previous Impostures,* 1874, and also in T. Morse, *Famous Trials,* 1874, pp. 5–234.

[11] For Browning's attack upon speculation in the poem, see J. T. Foster, in the *Explicator,* X, Item 18 (December, 1951).

[12] Quoted in Griffin and Minchin, *Life,* p. 257.

est as he comes nearest in matter and procedure to the still greater Frenchman." [13]

But such was not the general opinion, and the *Guardian,* the *Spectator,* and the *Academy* (J. A. Symonds) were rather hard upon the poem. The *Academy* objected to the poet's device of making the mask of each character "a mouthpiece for his casuistic and psychological expertness." Perhaps the most notable review was that by Mr. A. C. Bradley, who wrote in *Macmillan's Magazine* for February, 1876. He found the characters and the action imperfectly fused, and he had the impression "that the author is using his actors as vehicles for his own reflections." In short, he found the poem imperfect in material, treatment, and form. Browning was pleased that his old friend, John Forster, liked the poem.[14] In America the poem was reviewed unfavorably by Henry James in *The Nation* for January 20, 1876. He felt that the poet had been altogether too hasty in this work. It has been the opinion of later critics that the poem is strong, impressive, a remarkable *tour de force,* but that it is lacking in attractiveness and beauty. *The Inn Album* concludes a period in Browning's life which began with his studies for *The Ring and the Book.* That delight in criminal records, in making a case for a clever villain, in writing sordid matters out in long and difficult poems, comes to a close with *The Inn Album.*

PACCHIAROTTO AND HOW HE WORKED IN DISTEMPER: WITH OTHER POEMS

PUBLICATION AND TEXT

The collection of short poems, headed by the longer one *Of Pacchiarotto, and How He Worked in Distemper,* was published on July 18, 1876. The volume was post octavo, bound in slate-colored cloth boards, and consisted of a half-title; the title-page: "Pacchiarotto and How He Worked in Distemper: With Other Poems. By Robert Browning. London Smith, Elder, & Co. 15 Waterloo Place. 1876"; a list of contents; and the text, pp. 1–241. The published price was Seven Shillings Sixpence. The manuscript is in the Balliol College Library. The contents of the volume were as follows:

---

[13] *Letters of Algernon Charles Swinburne,* ed. E. Gosse and T. J. Wise, 1918, I, 246–7.

[14] See *New Letters,* ed. DeVane and Knickerbocker, pp. 229–31.

Prologue

Of Pacchiarotto, and How He
  Worked in Distemper

At the 'Mermaid'

House

Shop

Pisgah Sights. 1.

Pisgah Sights. 2.

Fears and Scruples

Natural Magic

Magical Nature

Bifurcation

Numpholeptos

Appearances

St. Martin's Summer

Hervé Riel

A Forgiveness

Cenciaja

Filippo Baldinucci on the
  Privilege of Burial

Epilogue

GENESIS AND COMPOSITION

It has been generally supposed, as this was the first volume of shorter poems since *Dramatis Personae* in 1864, that the book contained pieces written over that long interval of time. The supposition is not borne out by the manuscript. Save for three poems—*Natural Magic, Magical Nature,* and *Hervé Riel*—all the poems of this volume are dated between February 1, 1874, and May 19, 1876; upon the latter date the book was already at the press. *Natural Magic* and *Magical Nature* are undated in the manuscript, and one supposes they are left over from an earlier time, perhaps from Italian days. *Hervé Riel* was signed September 30, 1867. This last poem was written at Le Croisic, Brittany, but most of the poems which make up the volume were written, one judges by the dates attached, when Browning was in London.

SOURCES AND INFLUENCES

The *Pacchiarotto* volume must remain a book of great importance to the critic and biographer of Browning, for here the poet speaks, more directly than anywhere else in his poetry, concerning his own art and his feelings towards it. His usual conception of poetry as dramatic—"so many utterances of so many imaginary persons, not mine"—is almost completely thrown over. As one analyzes the volume the poems fall into several groups. *Of Pacchiarotto* stands by itself as a jocular-savage assault upon the critics of Browning's own day—notably Alfred Austin—who had, to use Browning's phrase, been "flea-biting" him for several years. A second group comprises *At the "Mermaid," House, Shop,* and the *Epilogue,* and here Browning is chiefly interested in commenting upon the poet and his art, upon his own place among the poets, and finally upon his rights to personal privacy, though a poet. Near this group surely should stand the *Prologue*, which does not insist upon personal privacy, but glories in it; and the *Cenciaja* is not far away from the art of poetry, for it is a footnote which Browning appends to Shelley's *Cenci*, and Shelley was once Browning's idol. The remaining poems, not so easily classified, are of several kinds: the philosophical and religious strain is present in *Pisgah-Sights* and *Fears and Scruples;* the analysis of the nature of love, trivial or profound, is the subject of such poems as *Natural Magic, Magical Nature, Numpholeptos, Appearances, St. Martin's Summer,* and *A Forgiveness;* in *Bifurcation* we are set a moral problem, as in *A Light Woman* years before; in *Hervé Riel* we touch the heroic-ballad style of *How They brought the Good News;* in *Filippo Baldinucci* we touch again, rather obliquely, Browning's old interest in painting.

There is little doubt that the main intention of the volume was to castigate the critics. Hence the points of emphasis in the book were given to *Pacchiarotto, At the "Mermaid," House,* and the *Epilogue.* When Browning's friend Domett objected to these lacerations of the critics in verse, the poet said, "I don't mind leaving on record that I had just that fancy about the people who 'forty years long in the wilderness' criticized my works." [1] As K. L. Knickerbocker has shown, Browning's wrath had been stored up for a long time, kept in abeyance for a while by the success of his wife's *Aurora Leigh* and his own rising fame in the Sixties, but revived by the reviews his poems had received in the Seventies. [2] It will be seen that Browning chooses Alfred Austin in *Pacchiarotto* and elsewhere in the book for the bad eminence of representing the critics. Perhaps the only thing that makes *Pacchiarotto* tolerable as a castigation was the intolerable provocation which Austin had given him. Even so, the tactics which Browning adopted were surely mistaken. Happily for himself Browning did not live long enough to see Alfred Austin succeed Tennyson in the laureateship.

AFTER-HISTORY

As one might have expected, the critical reception of *Pacchiarotto* was not enthusiastic. But it should be said for the critics in general that they took the volume with equanimity. Perhaps the most violent of the reviews was that in the *Saturday Review* for August 12, 1876. The *Standard,* the London newspaper in which Austin had "flea-

---

[1] Griffin and Minchin, *Life,* p. 260.
[2] "Browning and his Critics," in *Sewanee Review,* July, 1935, pp. 3–11.

bitten" Browning since 1869, charged Browning with meanness in its review of the volume. The book was reviewed by R. H. Hutton in the *Spectator* for August 26; and the poet James Thomson (B.V.) wrote the article in the *Secularist*. Perhaps the most able review of the book was that by Edward Dowden in the *Academy* for July 29, 1876. Dowden, one can see, was disappointed in the volume. Later critics have been more severe than were the contemporary critics of the *Pacchiarotto* volume. The best that most of them will do is to choose a poem or two in which they see the spirit of poetry still at work in Browning.

Prologue

The *Prologue* ("Oh, the old wall here!") to the *Pacchiarotto* volume in 1876 consisted of six stanzas of four lines each. As it appeared in the final edition of 1888–9 the poem was unaltered, save that the exclamation mark after "heart" in stanza five was changed to a period. The manuscript does not indicate when the poem was written.

Like many of Browning's prologues and epilogues after *The Ring and the Book,* the *Prologue* refers to the poet's old love and life with Elizabeth Barrett Browning. It is in the nature of a dedication; indeed Browning had first called it by that title, and had then stricken that out in the manuscript in favor of the present one. It is distinctly a personal utterance, and has no close relation to the rest of the volume, except perhaps to *Numpholeptos* and *St. Martin's Summer,* though the "storm-notes" of stanza five may refer to *Pacchiarotto,* which follows the *Prologue,* and stanza three makes the same sharp distinction between the public life and the private life of the poet which is so much Browning's concern in *House* and *Shop* later in the volume. In a volume of *Selections* in 1880 the poem was included under the title of *A Wall,* and was made the third of the *Pisgah-Sights,* but this arrangement did not continue.

Of Pacchiarotto, and How He Worked in Distemper

The poem, *Of Pacchiarotto, and How He Worked in Distemper,* was the long poem in Hudibrastic rhymes which gave title to Browning's volume of 1876. The poem consisted of 581 lines, and in the final edition was hardly changed at all save for the transposition of lines 49–50. *Of Pacchiarotto,* according to the manuscript, was begun on

April 15, 1876, and finished on May 1, 1876. We might guess this fact also from Browning's reference in the poem to May-day, when the chimney-sweeps—the critics—come to sweep out his chimney, and incidentally to trample his flower-garden; and also from his words "at week's end, dawns my birth-day" (May 7).

Browning was impelled to write this poem by a desire to castigate his critics. He had remained silent for forty-three years while, as he saw it, the critics had abused, misunderstood, and belabored him for his manner of writing. After the publication of *The Ring and the Book* Browning had reason to think that he had won his place among the poets of England, but the difficult and often unattractive volumes which he had published since 1868—notably *Hohenstiel-Schwangau, Fifine, Red Cotton Night-Cap Country, The Inn Album,* and *Aristophanes' Apology*—had given the critics ample opportunity to assault him. Hence in describing in *Pacchiarotto* the boys who come dressed fantastically for a May-day celebration in "the drabs, blues and yellows," Browning is indicating the colors of the great magazines in which his critics were accustomed to write. So the poem, *Of Pacchiarotto,* where the householder greets with the slops of the house the May-day celebrators who have come to jibe at him, embodies the wrath which Browning had stored up for over forty years. The poem begins in a mood of rollicking good humor, but the ending is savage.

From among his critics Browning selected one for special castigation. This was Alfred Austin (1835–1913), the five-foot poet and critic who in time succeeded Tennyson in the laureateship.[3] The description of Austin in the poem is quite explicit in lines 529–34 and the accompanying footnote, which, curiously enough, is not in the manuscript of the poem, but seems to have been added in the proof-sheets:

> While as for Quilp-Hop-o'-my-thumb there,
> Banjo-Byron that twangs the strum-strum there—
> He'll think, as the pickle he curses,
> I've discharged on his pate his own verses!
> "Dwarfs are saucy," says Dickens: so, sauced in
> Your own sauce, . . .*
>
>   * No, please! For
>   "Who would be satirical
>   On a thing so very small?"—Printer's Devil.

[3] See W. L. Phelps, "Robert Browning and Alfred Austin," in the *Yale Review,* N.S. 7:580–91 (1918). The story is told in great detail in T. L. Hood's notes to *Letters of Robert Browning,* pp. 358–63.

Austin's small size, the admiration for Byron which had led him to answer Harriet Beecher Stowe's *The True Story of Lady Byron's Life* with the *Vindication of Lord Byron* in 1869, and the wretchedness of Austin's poetic efforts, often imitated from Byron, are all catalogued. This was not the first time that Browning had attacked Austin; he had the small critic in mind as the "brisk little somebody" in *Balaustion's Adventure*, and again in describing Eruxis, the critic, now unknown, who had attacked Euripides in *Aristophanes' Apology* (ll. 1674–7; see also l. 130):

> 'Dogface Eruxis, the small satirist,—
> What better would the manikin desire
> Than to strut forth on tiptoe, notable
> As who, so far up, fouled me in the flank.'

Moreover, the somewhat unnatural gibes at Byron which had appeared in Browning's *Fifine at the Fair* (ll. 1104–28) in 1872, and from that time on in his poetry, were caused more by Austin, Byron's defender, than by Byron himself. It is not too fantastic to think that in *Pacchiarotto* Browning is attempting to match in grotesque and ingenious rhyme Byron's own masterpieces in that kind. Defending himself for his attack upon Austin in *Pacchiarotto*, Browning said,

He has been flea-biting me for many years past in whatever rag of a newspaper he could hop into—which I should never have turned on my side to escape; but there was talk of "administering castigation to poor Mr. Browning," which I have never brought myself to acquiesce in, even in metaphor. . . .[4]

Thus in *Pacchiarotto* Browning not only singled out Austin from the other critics for special abuse, but as we shall see rather made the whole story of Pacchiarotto, the mediocre artist and political reformer, apply to him.

The virulence and pertinacity of Austin as a critic of Browning is almost enough to justify Browning's counter-attack in the poem. The newspaper into which Austin most frequently hopped was the *Standard*,[5] to whose editorial board he was attached. His reviews of Browning's volumes as they were published may be traced in that newspaper, and there Browning's claim to be a poet is steadily ridiculed, often unfairly, as when Austin quotes a line for its bad meter and

---

[4] Griffin and Minchin, *Life*, p. 260.

[5] Austin printed "A Disclaimer," denying his authorship of most of the reviews, in the *Examiner* for June 10, 1876. See *Letters*, ed. Hood, pp. 359–60. His disclaimer was not generally believed.

leaves out a word. His great assault upon Browning had come in 1870, when in a volume called *The Poetry of the Period* he denied all of Browning's pretensions. The chapter allotted to Browning covers thirty-eight pages and some very sharp things are said therein. The claim of admirers, that Browning "is our great modern seer," is called by Austin "the most astounding and ludicrous pretension ever put forward in literature" (p. 42). At his most liberal Austin says, "Mr. Browning is not a poet at all—save in the sense that all cultivated men and women of sensitive feelings are poets—but a deep thinker, a profound philosopher, a keen analyser, and a biting wit" (p. 51). And finally in comparing Browning with English poets from Shakespeare to Byron, Austin concludes, "Poor Mr. Browning is both muddy and unmusical to the last degree. In fact, his style may fairly be described as the very incarnation of discordant obscurity" (p. 64).

The things which more immediately caused Browning's assault upon Austin, I think, were Austin's political activity during these years, and his satire, *The Golden Age* (1871), in which he held his own age up to scorn because it was dominated by the desire for gain. Austin was an ardent Tory: he stood for Parliament and was beaten; he published in 1876 two pamphlets, *Russia before Europe,* and *Tory Horrors or the Question of the Hour, A Letter to the Rt. Hon. W. E. Gladstone.* We see here, then, that Austin, like the painter Pacchiarotto, was a would-be reformer and a would-be politician—no more successful in either than was the Italian painter. That Browning drew Pacchiarotto, a very mediocre painter, as a parallel to Austin, a very mediocre poet, has generally escaped attention. The pun in the title has escaped detection almost as well.

In the process of making the parallel Browning was impelled to distort the career of the real Giacomo di Bartolommeo Pacchiarotto (1471–1540) to some degree. It is true that he was a mediocre Sienese painter contemporaneous with Pacchia, Beccafumi, and Bazzi, and that his disposition was turbulent. Browning took the story probably from the brief account given in the 1855 edition of Vasari's *Le Vite de' Pittori* as a footnote to the life of Sodoma; this he supplemented by the account in Baldinucci's *Notizie de' Professori del Disegno* (IV, 236), a work which he used for the next to the last poem in the volume as well. Pacchiarotto was of a revolutionary turn, a member of the Bardotti, a political club. In 1533 the Bardotti raised a civil tumult, and when the authorities put down the uprising, Pacchiarotto was forced to fly for safety to the vaults of the church of S. Giovanni

Battista della Morte, where he passed two days at close quarters with a recently buried corpse. He later had to seek out the monks at the Observanza. In 1539 Pacchiarotto was exiled from Siena because of his continued political activity, but he was permitted to return home and died in the next year.

The poem *Of Pacchiarotto, and How He Worked in Distemper* was the one which challenged the critics most directly, and was the one most commented on by the critics. (See above, on the *Pacchiarotto* volume.) Browning seemed to most readers to have broken a rule of good taste in thus assaulting his critics, though it is not quite clear why a poet should not defend himself with his best weapons. Perhaps Browning did not use his best weapons, and certainly he does not appear at his best. His rhymes in this poem have not the pungency of Butler's in *Hudibras,* nor the happy insolence of Byron's in *Don Juan, Beppo,* and the *Vision of Judgment.* At any rate, those who held the opinion that it was beneath the dignity of poetry to notice its critics were probably wise; but such was not Browning's way. We have seen him putting poetry to the uses of life constantly as we look into his literary career.

At the "Mermaid"

At the 'Mermaid' was the third poem in the *Pacchiarotto* volume of 1876. It consisted of eighteen stanzas of eight lines each, 144 lines in all. Save for the change to the present spelling of "orichalc," the poem was reprinted in the final edition as it stood. In the manuscript the poem bears the date "Jan. 15, 1876." Browning at this time was in London.

In the poem Browning is speaking behind the mask of Shakespeare, and the scene is supposedly laid at the old tavern in Bread Street, the Mermaid, renowned in song and story. The club which met at the Mermaid, tradition believes, was founded by Sir Walter Raleigh; Jonson, Beaumont, Fletcher, Carew, and Selden were members, and possibly Shakespeare. The same contemporary critical opinions which occasioned the poem *Of Pacchiarotto* seem to me to have given rise to *At the "Mermaid."* Alfred Austin especially concerned himself with the question of "Next Poet." In his volume *The Poetry of the Period* (1870) he dealt with Tennyson in his first chapter, and though he concluded that the Laureate was undoubtedly the best poet of the age, he was convinced that even Tennyson at best was only a third-

rate poet. In his chapter upon Browning he followed again the plan
of ranking the poets of the age (pp. 40–1):

The same coteries, and in many cases the very same people, who by dint
of persistence imposed upon the unreflecting crowd the exaggerated estimate of Mr. Tennyson against which I have protested, are now striving to
induce them to abandon their idol and set up another. Where they have
long put Mr. Tennyson, they now want to place Mr. Browning.

In *At the "Mermaid"* Browning disclaims any desire on the part of
Shakespeare, and inferentially on his own part, to be the "Next
Poet." Browning has chosen Shakespeare to speak the words in the
poem because to him Shakespeare is the completely dramatic poet,
never expressing his own ideas but always those of his characters.[6]
But in the poem *At the "Mermaid"* the voice is really the voice of
Browning, and his pretensions towards being completely "dramatic"
are absurd, for we do know very certainly what his opinions were,
and in many poems he has spoken very directly to us. Still Browning
has a right to warn us against the hasty identification of himself with
any character he has created—such unwise identification had taken
place in the character of Don Juan in *Fifine at the Fair*. At the *"Mermaid"* is a protest for personal privacy for the poet, and should be
read with *House, Shop,* and *Of Pacchiarotto* in the same volume.
But it must be insisted that Browning is not the completely dramatic
poet; he has enabled a great many people "to slip inside [his] breast";
indeed his poetry is a perpetual and increasing revelation of himself.

That Browning is the real speaker in the poem, and not Shakespeare, is borne out by the arguments adduced. In stanza 8 one suspects that he has Wordsworth in mind as the "last king" who bought
his laurels (see *The Lost Leader* and *House*); and it is fairly certain
that he had Byron in mind in stanzas 11 and 17 where remembering
Shelley's famous soubriquet for Byron he speaks of the "Pilgrim"—
of Byron's appeal to youth and the masses, and of Byron's *Welt-
schmerz*. I can find no Elizabethan parallels for these figures or opinions. Stanza 13 seems a clear reference to Austin and his fellow critics,
and stanza 12 is in the temper of Browning, not of Shakespeare. The
motto at the head of the poem was adapted from Ben Jonson's address *To the Reader* opposite the portrait of Shakespeare in the
great folio edition of Shakespeare's works in 1623.

---

[6] See Browning's words upon Shakespeare and Shelley as the "objective" and
"subjective" poets in his *Introductory Essay* for the letters of Shelley, 1852. See
also *House*.

Not a great deal of attention was paid to the poem in the reviews. In 1882 when Browning received the degree of Doctor of Civil Laws at Oxford, *Punch* published a pleasant parody of *At the "Mermaid"* in a "fancy portrait" by Sambourne called *Robert Browning, D. C. L., The Ring and Book-maker from Red Cotton Night-Cap Country.*

House

In the *Pacchiarotto* volume in 1876 the poem *House* followed immediately upon *At the "Mermaid."* It consisted of ten stanzas of four lines each, and in the final edition was reprinted without change. In the manuscript *House* follows *At the "Mermaid,"* and is dated February 1, 1874.

The informing idea in *House* is that of the whole *Pacchiarotto* volume—that every human being has a right to privacy in his life. Here, beneath the figure of the house destroyed by an earthquake, Browning is insisting upon literary privacy, that his own works are really dramatic—the "utterances of so many imaginary persons,—not mine." Browning's contention that his work is dramatic is very imperfectly true. In *House*, as in *At the "Mermaid,"* he sets up Shakespeare as the completely dramatic poet, and objects strongly to Wordsworth's dictum in "Scorn not the sonnet" that

> With this same key [the sonnet]
> Shakespeare unlocked his heart.

As early as 1852 in his essay upon Shelley Browning had extolled Shakespeare as the completely dramatic poet, and he refused to think of the *Sonnets* as autobiographical at all. It is needless to say that in general the world is of another opinion.

In my belief, something more immediate than Wordsworth's sonnet impelled Browning to write *House*. In 1870 Dante Gabriel Rossetti had published his *Poems* and had included in his volume his sonnet-sequence, *The House of Life*—a sequence dealing with married love, intimate and personal in tone, and written largely to his wife. I think it likely that Browning had Rossetti in mind when he speaks in the poem of the householder's odd furniture and his musty old books, his exotic and foreign habit of burning perfumes in his rooms. This idea is supported by the opinion which we know Browning had of Rossetti's poetry.[7] He probably felt that in *The House of*

[7] See my article, "The Harlot and the Thoughtful Young Man: A Study of the Relation between Rossetti's *Jenny* and Browning's *Fifine at the Fair,*" in *Studies in Philology* 29:463–84 (July, 1932).

Life Rossetti had betrayed the cause of personal privacy. Mrs. Miller in her study of the poet [8] uses *House* to illustrate his physical prudery and his dread of exposure. Browning's feeling was, from the point of view of the twentieth century, extravagant, but it was shared by many of his contemporaries. Because it is a downright pronouncement of Browning's feeling, the poem has been frequently commended; because it agrees so little with his practice, especially in his apprentice years and again in his decline, it has been even more frequently challenged.

Shop

The poem *Shop* followed immediately upon *House,* to which it is closely related, in the *Pacchiarotto* volume of 1876. In the manuscript the poem is dated "Feb. 11, 1874," showing that it was finished a few days after *House. Shop* consisted in the first edition of twenty-two stanzas of five lines each. In the final edition the poem was reprinted unchanged, save for the correction of one or two palpable misprints.

Like *Pacchiarotto, At the "Mermaid,"* and *House, Shop* is an insistence on Browning's part that every man, including the poet, has a right to a private existence behind his everyday appearance to the work-a-day world. The mood that produced the poem probably arose in Browning as a result of the many attempts that were made to obtain from him, after Mrs. Browning's death, biographical information concerning her, and concerning himself after the publication of *The Ring and the Book* had made him famous.

The poem is written in the familiar easy phrase of conversation, reminiscent of *Youth and Art, A Likeness, Apparent Failure* and others of his poems, and is full of contemporaneous allusion. One does not see until the concluding stanza that Browning has purposely courted doggerel, that the vulgar rhymes and phrases are a part of his plan to characterize the vulgar, everyday world of trade, and that he is to redeem all in the astonishing final stanza.

Pisgah-Sights

Pisgah-Sights, I and *II,* were first printed as companion poems in the *Pacchiarotto* volume in 1876. The first poem consisted of four stanzas of eight short lines each; the second, of six stanzas of eight short lines each. In the final edition they were reprinted without

[8] See *Robert Browning,* pp. 111–5.

change. In the *Selections* of 1880 the *Prologue* to *La Saisiaz* was added to the pair to make *Pisgah-Sights* 3, but this arrangement was discarded in the final edition. According to the manuscript the first poem was finished on December 28, 1875, and the second, probably done as a sequel, was finished on February 19, 1876. The poet was then in London.

Pisgah was, of course, the mountain from which Moses in his old age was permitted to see the Promised Land which he was not to enter (*Deuteronomy* 34:1–4). In the first poem Browning imagines how an old man at the point of death would look at the world and see the meaning of all things—good and evil, rough and smooth, the mixed existence of man. The vision is honey and gall, for now that he has learned to live he must die. In the second poem Browning imagines how a man with such knowledge would live his life, could he live again—wise, tolerant, content with his place in life, rather more of an observer than a doer. One is reminded of such earlier poems as *How it Strikes a Contemporary, Cleon,* and *Rabbi Ben Ezra.* Both poems show the reconciliation of old age with life, and are therefore a curious commentary upon some of the less genial poems of the *Pacchiarotto* volume.

Fears and Scruples

Fears and Scruples was first published in the *Pacchiarotto* volume in 1876. In the final edition of 1888–9 it was reprinted without change save for minor alterations in punctuation. In the manuscript the poem is dated February 26, 1876.

The poem has been called a parable, and so it is—all the more effective because the intention is concealed until the last word. The poem represents the state of Browning's mind upon matters of faith at this time, and foreshadows *La Saisiaz,* which was to appear two years later. The speaker of the poem is assailed by doubts. The "letters" which the speaker has received are meant to stand for the Scriptures, which the higher critics—Strauss, Renan and others— were now calling unauthentic in some cases (see *A Death in the Desert*); and the "actions" of the poem are now represented as being the acts of common humanity. The "actions" of stanza 2 were the miracles of former ages, once ascribed to God. In his plight the speaker still loves the unseen friend, and finds value in his love, though he wishes his friend would confirm his hopes, and though, too, he has to meet the objections raised by some that if his friend does not reveal his sympathy he is a monster. The speaker concludes with the line, "What if this friend happen to be—God?"

The poem has caused some difficulty in interpretation. In explaining its meaning to W. G. Kingsland, Browning said:

Where there is a genuine love of the letters and actions of the invisible friend, however these may be disadvantaged by an inability to meet the objections to their authenticity or historical value urged by experts who assume the privilege of learning over ignorance—it would indeed be a wrong to the wisdom and goodness of the friend if he were supposed capable of overlooking the actual love and only considering the ignorance which, failing to in any degree affect love, is really the highest evidence that love exists.[9]

Natural Magic—Magical Nature

Natural Magic and Magical Nature, companion poems, were first published in the Pacchiarotto volume in 1876. The first consisted of two stanzas of nine irregular lines each; the second consisted of two stanzas of four lines each. In the final collected edition both poems were reprinted without change. The two poems must have been written some time before Browning thought of this collection of shorter poems. In the manuscript the poems are undated and are pasted in, not written in, the manuscript book. Natural Magic acknowledges the power of love to make life bloom like spring, though it be December. Magical Nature is a love-poem, praising the lady for the beauty which time cannot deface, since it is of the soul. The freshness of these love-poems is remarkable in a poet who has passed his sixtieth birthday.

Bifurcation

Bifurcation was first printed in the Pacchiarotto volume in 1876. It consisted of forty-two lines. In the final collected edition it was reprinted without change. In the manuscript the poem is dated "Nov. 29 '75," as nearly as one can make it out, for Browning had been at some pains to cancel the date.

The title of the poem, Bifurcation—"divided two ways"—very aptly expresses the subject of the poem. It is a poem characteristic of

---

[9] "Robert Browning, Some Personal Reminiscences," in Baylor University Browning Interests, Second Series, 1931, p. 33.

Browning's earlier days in that it poses a nice question in conduct, comparable to that in *A Light Woman.* Yet there is an echo of personal experience; as in the *Prologue, St. Martin's Summer, Numpholeptos,* and elsewhere in this volume Browning seems to have in mind his proposal to Louisa Lady Ashburton in 1869. In *Bifurcation* the lives of the lovers are presented in two epitaphs; the woman chose the path of duty, the man was left in the path of love. Of the two, there seems to Browning no question but that the lot of the man was harder, and the poet's sympathy is altogether with him. There is a trace of biography in the description of the hard lot of the man, once "the star is gone Whereby he steps secure nor strays from love," though the lady of the poem in no sense represents his wife—nor indeed does the man, in the large, represent Browning. The poet here is again taking delight in challenging the conventional solution of such a moral problem, as he had challenged such solutions in *The Statue and the Bust.*

Numpholeptos

Numpholeptos first appeared in the *Pacchiarotto* volume in 1876. The poem was made up of 152 iambic lines, rhyming for the most part in couplets, but with five triplets, and one unrhymed line. In the final collected edition of 1888–9 the poem was unaltered save for the shifting of a few words for the sake of smoothness. In the manuscript the poem is dated April 25, 1876.

The title of the poem was first put in the manuscript in Greek and then changed to the English letters. A nympholept is one who is caught by a passion for a nymph, and a nymph was one of the inferior goddesses of Greek mythology, a feminine creature not human, who dominates her victim without suffering in her turn any kindred feelings. The temper of Browning's poem is in some respects comparable to Tennyson's *Tithonus,* for Tithonus, bewitched by Aurora, rebelled and submitted in a perpetual cycle, just as the nympholept does here. But it should be noticed that the prevailing colors of Tennyson's poem are the delicate tints, silver and rose, the proper colors of dawn, but the colors of *Numpholeptos* are crude and strong, such as red and yellow.

Though the poem is, like so much else in the *Pacchiarotto* volume, a veiled biographical one, the myth owes its origin to Browning's recent studies in Greek lore. T. L. Hood ascribes the conception to

Plutarch's description of the term "Nympholepti" and the tale of
Numa Pompilius, who after the death of his wife loved and conversed with the goddess Egeria.[10] Concerning the meaning of the
poem, Browning wrote to Furnivall to set right some of the wild
guesses of the Browning Society:

Is not the key to the meaning of the poem in its title—νυμφόληπτος [caught
or entranced by a nymph], not γυναικεραστής [a woman-lover]? An allegory, that is, of an impossible ideal object of love, accepted conventionally
as such by a man who, all the while, cannot quite blind himself to the
demonstrable fact that the possessor of knowledge and purity obtained
without the natural consequences of obtaining them by achievement—not
inheritance—such a being is imaginary, not real, a nymph and no woman;
and only such an one would be ignorant and surprised at the results of a
lover's endeavour to emulate the qualities which the beloved is entitled
to consider as pre-existent to earthly experience, and independent of its inevitable results.

I had no particular woman in my mind; certainly never intended to
personify wisdom, philosophy, or any other abstraction; and the orb, ray-
ing colour out of whiteness, was altogether a fancy of my own. The "seven
spirits" are in the Apocalypse, also in Coleridge and Byron: a common
image.[11]

Browning's explanation is perhaps not so clear as the poem itself.
There we see that the nymph, like white light in her purity and cold-
ness, demands that her human lover experience all the life which is
represented by the seven colors into which the white light resolves,
and likewise that he come from the experience unstained by the ray
of light he has traversed. The man fails again and again, and at last
rebels against the inhuman conditions. The difficulty which he has
in holding by such abstruse and ideal love reminds one of the hard
lot of the lover in *Bifurcation* (*q.v.*). The rebellion of the lover in
Numpholeptos is short-lived, for he sees again the sad cold smile of
the nymph, and begins again the quest for experience without stain.

Mrs. Miller in her study of the poet [12] is right, I think, in her interpretation of the poem as an allegory of Browning's mood in 1876, his
feeling that his lot is harder than that of his dead wife—since he has
to live through all the temptations of a passionate nature while she
is immune from such experience—his momentary rebellion against
his bondage to a memory, and his capitulation to his fate. Mrs.

[10] See T. L. Hood, *Browning's Ancient Classical Sources,* in *Harvard Studies in
Classical Philology* 33:170.
[11] *Browning Society's Papers,* II, 338*. See also pp. 345*–6*.
[12] *Robert Browning,* pp. 278–80.

Browning, of course, is not to be precisely identified with the cold nymph; it is the legend of the lover's faithfulness which has enslaved him. A comparable mood of Browning's may be observed in *Fifine at the Fair*.

The poem is known and appreciated by only a few, but by those it is held in high esteem for its lyrical intensity. To most readers it is an enigma, rather grotesque and crude. In 1894 Swinburne published a poem upon the same subject, called *A Nympholept*, in the volume *Astrophel and Other Poems*.

Appearances

Appearances was first published in the *Pacchiarotto* volume in 1876, and consisted of two stanzas of six lines each. In the final edition of Browning's works the poem was reprinted without change. The manuscript is dated April 6, 1876, though the poem resembles the shorter poems of *Men and Women* in its lyrical quality and its situation. It is one of the most popular poems of the *Pacchiarotto* volume.

St. Martin's Summer

St. Martin's Summer appeared first in the *Pacchiarotto* volume in 1876. It consisted of seventeen stanzas of six lines each. In the final collected edition the poem was reprinted without change. The poem is dated March 27, 1876, in the manuscript.

St. Martin's Summer is that period between October 9th and November 11th—what we in America call Indian Summer. The significance of the title of the poem is obvious; the subject is second love and how the ghost of first love intervenes. Then when the ghost is exorcised, the man, the speaker of the poem, finds that he has lost the beneficent memories of the old love, and that the new love is a mere husk. One may say that sharp memories are at work in this little poem, and though it is not quite biography in verse, for fact has suffered a few artistic changes, nevertheless the conclusion is not far from experience. Browning's memory of his wife had been definitely disturbed by his proposal of marriage to Louisa Lady Ashburton in 1869.[13] The disagreement between the characters of the poem con-

---

[13] See T. L. Hood's *Appendix*, "Browning and Lady Ashburton," in his *Letters of Robert Browning*, where the story is told at length. See also my own chapter

cerning the kind of house they shall build is a reflection of the disagreement between Browning and the lady concerning the nature of their prospective marriage. Browning's desire was for a marriage of convenience. That Browning later regretted the proposal bitterly may be seen in St. Martin's Summer and again in the Parleying With Daniel Bartoli.

Hervé Riel

Hervé Riel was first published in the Cornhill Magazine for March, 1871. It consisted of 140 lines, divided into eleven unequal sections. It was reprinted in the Pacchiarotto volume in 1876 at the request of Mr. George Smith of Smith, Elder, and Co., who was also the publisher of the Cornhill. Save for minor changes in punctuation the poem was unaltered in its text in the Pacchiarotto volume and in the final collected edition.

The poem was dated in the Cornhill from "Croisic, Sept. 30, 1867." It was therefore written during that summer which Browning spent on the coast of Brittany, near the mouth of the Loire. The poem was seen by several people before 1870. We learn from a letter written by Browning to Smith, his publisher, that Sir John Simeon had praised it, and that Smith himself had requested Browning to sell it to him for the Cornhill. R. H. Shepherd, we learn from Furnivall's Bibliography of Browning, possessed an earlier draft of the poem, which is probably the manuscript now in the Morgan Library in New York. Browning was averse to publishing his poems in magazines, and he refused Smith's offer. But in February, 1871, he wrote to Smith and offered him the poem for the Cornhill, the proceeds to go to the Parisians who were starving after the city fell before the assault of the Prussians. Smith sent Browning a check for one hundred guineas, and this was sent to the suffering French. In a letter to his publisher on this occasion Browning estimated very truly the worth of the poem: "I fancy this is a case in which one may handsomely puff one's own ware, and I venture to call my verses good for once." [14] The whole transaction was as generous on both sides as it was gracious.

It was probably in a Croisic guide-book, Notes sur le Croisic, par

on Daniel Bartoli in Browning's Parleyings; and for a full and skilful interpretation of the poem see K. L. Knickerbocker, "An Echo from Browning's Second Courtship," in Studies in Philology 32:102–4 (January, 1935).

[14] Orr, Life, p. 279.

Caillo jeune, that Browning read the story of the unhonored hero of the village. In the dispersal of the Browning library in 1913, after the death of R. W. B. Browning, there came to light some notes in the hand of Sarianna Browning, the poet's sister, a transcript of the story of Hervé Riel from this book of purely local interest. With these notes there was half a sheet of notes by the poet from another source which has not been identified.[15] But the hero of the village was unknown and unsung until Browning properly celebrated his story in this stirring ballad. In May, 1692, the French fleet, sent by Louis XIV to restore James II to the throne of England, met the combined English and Dutch fleets off Cap la Hogue. The French were outnumbered and after a gallant fight D'Amfreville, leading twenty of the French ships, fled towards St. Malo, and was piloted into harbor by the sailor from Croisic.

Towards the end of 1881 Dr. Furnivall began to look into the story of Browning's poem. At St. Malo Browning's facts were denied, but when the reports of the French Admiralty were looked into, it was seen that the poet's facts were substantially correct. In one respect, however, the poet misread the *Notes sur le Croisic:* Riel demanded his complete release from the French Navy as his reward: "ce brave homme ne demanda pour récompense d'un service aussi signalé, qu'un congé absolu pour rejoindre sa femme, qu'il nommait la Belle Aurore." In a letter to Furnivall on December 20, 1881, Browning admits his mistake: "You are undoubtedly right, and I have mistaken the meaning of the phrase . . . an absolute discharge seems to approach in importance a substantial reward." [16]

Since its publication this ballad has had a great popularity. Its reputation is comparable to the fame of Tennyson's ballad, *The Revenge,* a poem resembling *Hervé Riel* in several respects. On February 28, 1871, when the poem was first published in the *Cornhill Magazine,* the *Daily News* carried a very appreciative leader upon it. It has become one of the best known of Browning's poems.

A Forgiveness

A Forgiveness was first printed in the *Pacchiarotto* volume in 1876 and there consisted of 396 lines, rhyming in couplets. In the final collected edition the poem was reprinted as it stood, save for a few

---

[15] *The Browning Collections* (Sotheby Catalogue, 1913), item 198.
[16] *Letters,* ed. Hood, p. 207.

minor changes in punctuation. In the manuscript the poem is dated February 5, 1876.

In the manuscript the poem was entitled at first "Komm Spanisch," and a little to the right of the title there appeared the name "(Egmont)." Browning cancelled the first title in favor of A *Forgiveness*, but the title "Komm Spanisch" appeared again on the manuscript table of contents to the volume, and was probably altered in proof-sheets. The name Egmont, coupled with the Flemish title, leads one to suspect that the story of the poem was, perhaps, a traditional tale connected with the great family of Egmont of Flanders, supporters in the sixteenth century of Charles V and Philip II of Spain. The greatest of this family were Maximilien d'Egmont, leader of the armies of Charles V, faithful and magnanimous, who astonished men by predicting the time of his own death in 1548, and Lamoral Egmont (1522–68), Prince of Gaveren, greatly beloved by the people of Flanders, a great servant of the Spanish crown, who though innocent was finally beheaded for treason by the Duke of Alva. Goethe wrote a five-act tragedy upon Lamoral Egmont, and Beethoven turned Goethe's play into an opera.

A search for Browning's source for A *Forgiveness* in the annals of of the Egmont family, however, has not been successful. It is possible that he heard the story in Antwerp when he went there to visit his son, who had taken a studio in 1873 and was studying to be a painter and sculptor. It is possible, also, that Browning may have seen in Brussels the new statue of Lamoral Egmont that was made by Fraiken in 1865. But the words "Egmont" and "Komm Spanisch," however, are only suggestions which lead one to think that Flanders might be the scene of the poem. A *Forgiveness* itself in its final form is undeniably Spanish in scene and psychology. Browning is at pains to observe the scrupulous code of honor which a Spanish nobleman of the old régime must obey. The nice gradations in the hero's feelings, however, from love to contempt, and from contempt to hatred and vengeance and to love again, are undeniably Browning's. The splendid description of the "arms of Eastern workmanship" which are portrayed in A *Forgiveness* as "horror coquetting with voluptuousness" (ll. 247–77), was suggested by a collection of such weapons which Ernest Benzon, a friend, had bequeathed to the poet.

In 1885 the late Sir Edmund Gosse applied to Browning for his choice of "four poems, of moderate length, which represent their writer fairly." For one representative of his narrative poetry, Browning chose *A Forgiveness*.[17] It is easy to approve this choice, for the poem is concise, swift and exciting, with a characteristic Browning-esque twist at the end.

Cenciaja

Cenciaja was first published in the *Pacchiarotto* volume of 1876, and there consisted of 300 blank verse lines. In the final collected edition of 1888–9 a number of verbal changes were introduced, lines 229–30 were transposed, and a few changes in punctuation were made. In the manuscript the poem is dated as finished on April 28, 1876.

It had probably been Browning's intention since he had finished *The Ring and the Book* to write some day this foot-note to Shelley's tragedy, *The Cenci*. It must have been with pleasure that Browning encountered in the Old Yellow Book, which was his source for his great poem, the lawyer's citation of the Cenci case.[18] The title of Browning's poem is a play upon the word "Cenci": it refers to Shelley's play, of course, but the word "cenciaja" means a bundle of rags, a trifle, as Browning explained to Buxton Forman. He went on to say that the Italian proverb at the head of his poem "means 'every poor creature will be pressing into the company of his betters,' and I used it to deprecate the notion that I intended anything of the kind." [19] Writing a little later to Buxton Forman, who was interested in Browning's poem because of Shelley, Browning told of his source for *Cenciaja*:

I have no objection whatever to your making what use of my poem you please, if you really prefer "my own words" to a paraphrase. I got the facts from a contemporaneous account I found in a MS. volume containing the "Relation" of the Cenci affair—with other memorials of Italian crime—lent me by Sir J. Simeon, who published the Cenci Narrative, with notes, in the series of the Philobiblon Society. It was a better copy of the "Relation" than that used by Shelley, differing at least in a few particulars.[20]

This very misleading statement by Browning has caused a number of commentators to say that Browning's source for the *Cenciaja* is Sir John Simeon's pamphlet, *Contemporaneous Narrative of the*

---

[17] *Idem*, ed. Hood, p. 235.

[18] See Hodell, *The Old Yellow Book, Source of Browning's "The Ring and the Book,"* pp. ci–cii.

[19] *Letters*, ed. Hood, p. 174.

[20] *Idem*, p. 176.

Trial and Execution of the Cenci, which was published in the *Miscellanies of the Philobiblon Society* for 1857–8. There is, indeed, in the *Contemporaneous Narrative* (p. 48) a brief notice of the crime which makes up the story of *Cenciaja*—the murder of Castanza Santa Croce by her son, Paolo Santa Croce. The bearing of the Santa Croce case upon the Cenci case was this: because of this new crime, wherein another parent was murdered by a child, the Pope was impelled to deny clemency to Beatrice Cenci. But the *Contemporaneous Narrative* was not the source of the *Cenciaja*. Kenneth L. Knickerbocker has shown that the true source is probably an Italian manuscript in the British Museum entitled, *Giustizia fatta da Onofrio Santa Croce per aver acconsentio al Matricidio commesso da Paolo Suo Fratello in persona della Signora Costanza loro Madre.*[21] To this account Browning probably added notes which he had taken from Sir John Simeon's manuscript concerning the Santa Croce affair, to make his poem. He also rearranged the material to suit his purposes, and added incidents to put the motives of Cardinal Aldobrandini in the worst light. Since Sir John died in 1870, it is probable that Browning consulted his manuscript before that date. The concluding section of Browning's poem turns the chronicler's idea concerning "God's justice" against the Pope most ironically by pointing out that tardy justice has come at last, and King Victor rules in 1876 in Rome. This is Browning's comment upon the recent liberation of Rome from papal rule.

Cenciaja interested the Shelley Society during the decade after its publication, but otherwise the poem has made little impression upon the world. It was the opinion of Edward Dowden, the biographer of Shelley and of Browning, that *Cenciaja* would have been better as a foot-note in prose to Shelley's tragedy.

Filippo Baldinucci on the Privilege of Burial

Filippo Baldinucci on the Privilege of Burial (A Reminiscence of 1676 A. D.) was the penultimate poem in the *Pacchiarotto* volume in 1876. It consisted of fifty-eight stanzas of eight lines each, 464 lines in all. When the poem was reprinted in the final collected edition of 1888–9 Browning made a few verbal changes and corrected

---

[21] K. L. Knickerbocker, "Browning's *Cenciaja*," in *Philological Quarterly* 13: 390–400 (October, 1934). In this excellent article Browning's poem and his Italian source are given in parallel columns.

a good many errors, such as the completion of the rhyme in stanza 16, which had escaped him in his haste in the first edition. For the poem was the last of this volume to be written; it was composed, as Browning told Edmund Gosse, "while the earlier sheets were passing through the press." [22] This is borne out by the manuscript, where the poem does not appear in the table of contents. A note to the printer instructs him to print the poem "the last but one," and gives explicit instructions concerning the italics and the quotation marks which are to be used in the poem. The manuscript is dated May 19, 1876.

It was probably the date 1676, marking an incident of two hundred years earlier, that first caught Browning's attention as he read in Filippo Baldinucci's *Notizie de' Professori del Disegno,* published at Florence in twenty volumes between 1681 and 1728. Browning had used the *Notizie* to verify the more colorful accounts in Vasari's *Lives of the Painters* ever since he had encountered Baldinucci's work in Italy.[23] Baldinucci had provided information for *Andrea del Sarto, Fra Lippo Lippi, Old Pictures in Florence,* and *Pacchiarotto,* and was later to be used in the *Parleying With Francis Furini* and *Beatrice Signorini.* But though he used Baldinucci's information, Browning despised the man for his narrow and bigoted nature, and he neglects no opportunity to satirize the Tuscan whom he calls "blockhead," "mild moral-monger," "scruple-splitting, sickly-sensitive." In the *Parleying With Francis Furini* Browning makes a violent attack upon Baldinucci for his dislike of paintings in the nude, and in *Filippi Baldinucci on the Privilege of Burial* he satirizes Baldinucci for his anti-Semitic feelings.

For the present poem Browning draws upon Baldinucci's account of the life of the Florentine painter, Lodovici Buti, who flourished about the year 1600.[24] He allows Baldinucci, who is the speaker in the poem, to recount in his old age a story, which he had told in his life of Buti, that he thinks a good joke upon the unbelieving Jews. Browning follows fairly closely the story as Baldinucci gives it—heightening, of course, the unconscious satire upon the speaker, through the thirty-fifth stanza of the poem. At that point he makes Baldinucci say

---

[22] *Letters,* ed. Hood, p. 174.

[23] For a full account of Baldinucci's significance for Browning see my chapter, *The Parleying With Francis Furini,* in *Browning's Parleyings.*

[24] See the *Notizie de' Professori del Disegno,* X, 35–41.

> . . . plague o' me
> If I record it in my Book!

and the vengeance visited upon Buti and the farmer by the son of the rabbi is, of course, Browning's own invention.

Griffin and Minchin call *Filippo Baldinucci on the Privilege of Burial* "a masterpiece in its kind," and they add that Browning "always wrote admirably when he wrote of Jews." It was this fact, in part, which gave currency to the report in later years that he had Jewish blood in him. Perhaps the noblest expression of this sympathy was in *Holy-Cross Day* in 1855. In *Filippo Baldinucci* Browning had used the term "High Priest," and when he was taxed with ignorance he replied as follows:

This comes of forgetting that one writes dramatically. The speaker, Baldinucci, is a typically ignorant Tuscan, and makes the gross mistake already noted in Arbuthnot's *Martinus Scriblerus*—of whom it is said, at the very beginning, "Those who had never seen a Jesuit took him for one, while others thought him rather some High Priest of the Jews." Somebody objected to a Jewish burying-ground being in the neighbourhood of any habitation, but Baldinucci tells the story, and describes the locality as he knew it—and I follow him, of course.[25]

But Baldinucci in the *Notizie* calls the leading Jews on at least one occasion "Rabbini."

Epilogue

The *Epilogue* ("The poets pour us wine—") concluded the *Pacchiarotto* volume in 1876. It consisted of twenty-eight stanzas of eight lines each, 224 lines in all. In the final revision of the poem Browning made several verbal changes for the sake of euphony, but the sense of the text was not changed. In the manuscript the poem is dated April 24, 1876. The title of the poem there and in the manuscript table of contents was at first "Cowslip Wine," but it was altered probably before the volume went to press. The original title, as one can see throughout, and especially in stanzas 21 and 22, bore directly upon the matter of the poem. The motto in Greek at the head of the poem, from Aristophanes' *Plutus* (l. 807), may be translated thus: "and pitchers full of dark flower-flavored wine."

Browning took the conception of his poem from Mrs. Browning's *Wine of Cyprus* (1844), and he adapts her line, "And the poets

---

[25] *Letters*, ed. Hood, p. 287.

poured us wine" for his own first line. Mrs. Browning's poem was an appreciative survey of Greek literature; her husband deals with English poets, and comments upon Shakespeare, Milton, Pope, and Byron, severely on the last two (stanzas 20 and 23), and the use they are put to in his own day. The stroke at Byron was probably aimed at Alfred Austin, Byron's defender in the Seventies, whom he had already belabored in *Of Pacchiarotto*. The *Epilogue* is really a defence of Browning's own particular brew of wine, and the poem stands half-way between Browning's assault upon contemporary critics in *Of Pacchiarotto* and his estimate of his place among the great poets of England in *At the "Mermaid."* Like so much of the *Pacchiarotto* volume, the poem is a direct expression of opinion upon the poet's own art.

The conception of the poetry of the great poets as wine for humanity may be a happy one, but Browning cannot be said to have proved his contention that the wine may not be strong and sweet at once. It is easy enough to refute him from his own works. The nettle-broth which he promised to the public was forthcoming in *La Saisiaz, Ferishtah's Fancies,* and the *Parleyings* of his last years.

THE AGAMEMNON OF AESCHYLUS

PUBLICATION AND TEXT

The Agamemnon of Aeschylus was published on Monday, October 15, 1877. The book was post octavo, bound in dark green cloth boards, and sold for Five Shillings the copy. It consisted of a half-title; the title-page: "The Agamemnon of Aeschylus Transcribed by Robert Browning London Smith, Elder, & Co. 15 Waterloo Place 1877"; a preface, pp. v–xi; a list of "Persons of the Drama," p. 2; and the text, pp. 3–148. There were in the text 1734 lines of very varied meter, and in the collected edition of 1888–9 the translation was reprinted with very few changes of word and punctuation.

GENESIS AND COMPOSITION

The manuscript of this work in the Balliol College Library is dated at the end April 23, 1877, and the preface dated at London, May, 1877. We may suppose that Browning was engaged on his translation during March and April of that year. The volume did not appear during the summer, probably because of the lateness of the season, and the preface in the book was re-dated as of October 1, 1877.

SOURCES AND INFLUENCES

A number of considerations had apparently led Browning to this work. The *Agamemnon* of Aeschylus (525–456 B. C.) was the first play of the great trilogy which generally goes under the title of the *Oresteia*. It was acted in 458 B. C., two years before the death of Aeschylus, and is generally thought to represent the dramatist's powers at their zenith. Browning's attention was naturally drawn to Aeschylus during his Greek studies for *Balaustion's Adventure* and for *Aristophanes' Apology;* and it seems to me probable that the struggle for the crown of Greek tragic poetry, which Browning makes Aristophanes mention as the subject of his next play (the *Frogs*) in *Aristophanes' Apology,* was the genesis of Browning's purpose to translate a play by Aeschylus. In the *Frogs* Aristophanes makes Aeschylus and Euripides contend in Hades for the honor of being the weightier poet; and it may be a point of consequence that in the contest Aeschylus is made to paraphrase one of the most famous passages in the *Agamemnon*.[1]

It is certain, however, that other things led Browning in 1877 to the task of translation. Chief of these was probably Carlyle's approval of *Aristophanes' Apology* and his advice to the poet soon afterwards, "Ye won't mind me, though it's the last advice I may give ye; but ye ought to translate the whole of the Greek tragedians —that's your vocation." [2] That Browning did mind Carlyle is amply attested by the concluding words of the preface to the *Agamemnon,* where he mentions the "dear and noble name" of his great contemporary.

Matthew Arnold, too, had his influence on the piece, as Browning's quotation, in his preface, of a passage from Arnold's preface to his *Poems* of 1853 will attest. Browning says here that if he were attempting to acquaint himself with such a famous tragedy as this, he would require exact literalness of translation, and that he has tried in this performance as translator to do as he would be done by:

Fortunately the poorest translation, provided only it be faithful,—though it reproduce all the artistic confusion of tenses, moods, and persons, with which the original teems,—will not only suffice to display what an elo-

[1] See the *Frogs,* ll. 1431–3.
[2] Griffin and Minchin, *Life,* p. 256.

quent friend [Matthew Arnold] maintains to be the all-in-all of poetry—
"the action of the piece"—but may help to illustrate his assurance that
"the Greeks are the highest models of expression, the unapproached masters of the grand style: their expression is so excellent because it is so admirably kept in its right degree of prominence, because it is so simple and
so well subordinated, because it draws its force directly from the pregnancy
of the matter which it conveys . . . not a word wasted, not a sentiment
capriciously thrown in, stroke on stroke!" So may all happen!

Now the play itself is one of the most formidable of all Greek plays
to comprehend, and presented a difficult task. Browning felt himself
prepared for it, however, by his long and careful studies, and took
pride in it. According to Domett, Browning mentioned with some
pleasure that while he was engaged upon the *Agamemnon* "he met
one of the first Greek scholars in England, who asked him if it were
true that he was translating the *Agamemnon.* Browning answering
in the affirmative, the other said, 'And can you understand it? For
I have known it these twenty years, and I can't.' " [3] The aim of translating with absolute literalness—"literal at every cost save that of
absolute violence to our language," as Browning says in the preface—
is achieved so well that a number of commentators have suggested
that the rendering is useful for nothing save a "crib" to those students
who have to achieve a painful exactitude. Browning aimed also to
approximate the hexameters of the Greek original, in a peculiar
eleven-syllabled line which has met with general disapproval. His
desire to approximate the Greek sounds had led him, much earlier,
to adopt a peculiar spelling for the Greek proper names—Klutaim-
nestra for Clytemnestra, for example—which is really no nearer the
Greek than is our familiar Latinization; and this practice of his,
ever since *Balaustion's Adventure,* had elicited comment from the
critics.[4] In the preface Browning here defends his practice; but the
fad which he sincerely espoused has been abandoned in spite of him.

In speaking of the *Agamemnon* Mrs. Orr, the biographer of the
poet who knew him personally, has an illuminating word to say:

Mr. Browning's deep feeling for the humanities of Greek literature, and
his almost passionate love for the language, contrasted strongly with his
refusal to regard even the first of Greek writers as models of literary style.
The pretensions raised for them on this ground were inconceivable to him;
and his translation of the *Agamemnon,* published in 1877, was partly made,

---

[3] *Idem,* p. 263.

[4] See the letter which John S. Blackie wrote to Browning on October 31, 1877;
in *Intimate Glimpses from Browning's Letter File,* in *Baylor University's
Browning Interests,* Series Eight, 1934, pp. 73–4.

I am convinced, for the pleasure of exposing these claims, and of rebuking them. His preface to the transcript gives evidence of this. The glee with which he pointed to it when it first appeared was no less significant.[5]

This statement, taken in conjunction with the reference to Arnold's claims for the pre-eminence of the Greek drama, suggests a hidden purpose in the publication of the volume. It was to demonstrate that the Greeks were not to be regarded, as Arnold and others regarded them, as models of literary style. Elizabeth Barrett had stated her opinion in an early letter to Browning:

> I am inclined to think we want new *forms*, as well as thoughts. The old gods are dethroned. Why should we go back to the antique moulds, classical moulds, as they are so improperly called? If it is a necessity of Art to do so, why then those critics are right who hold that Art is exhausted and the world too worn out for poetry. I do not, for my part, believe this. . . . Let us all aspire rather to *Life*, and let the dead bury their dead. . . .[6]

Browning, holding it as part of his essential creed that the world must progress, agreed with her, and would use the old themes only when he re-vitalized them and re-interpreted them, as in *Balaustion's Adventure* and *Aristophanes' Apology*. Such was still his opinion when, towards the end of his life, he came to speak, in the *Parleying With Gerard de Lairesse* (*q.v.*), concerning the Greek poets in general, and concerning Arnold's attitude towards them in particular. And here in the translation of the *Agamemnon*, with its strange preface, it is as if he were saying to Arnold: "Very well, here is your answer. I will give you the Greek drama, translated as accurately as possible so that you may see it in its essentials; I will choose from the general favorite Aeschylus, the play generally asserted to be his best. And when you see it thus, without the play of the poetic imagination, drawing 'its force directly from the pregnancy of the matter it conveys . . . not a word wasted, not a sentiment capriciously thrown in'—will you still see it as great? So may all happen!" An ironic wish, to be sure!

Browning foresaw that the writing of such a work could only prove a "fruitless adventure." Whether his choice of the most difficult of Greek plays, and his aim of translating it literally into a poetic form, are defensible or not, is a question. Sir Frederic Kenyon [7] saw that Browning had an ulterior purpose but interpreted the riddle other-

[5] Orr, *Life*, p. 294.
[6] *Letters of R.B. and E.B.B.*, I, 45–6.
[7] *Centenary Edition*, VIII, x–xi.

wise; he shows that Browning did not deal in this manner with Euripides in the *Alcestis* or even in the *Heracles,* and adds, "If he wished to carry further the controversy as to the rival merits of Aeschylus and Euripides, it was hardly fair to weight the scales in this way."

AFTER-HISTORY

The *Agamemnon,* as has been indicated already, has seldom met the critics' approval. Most are inclined to call it, with Sir Frederic Kenyon, "a perverse *tour de force.*" Because of Browning's eminence it was generally reviewed. In the *Academy* for November 3, 1877, John Addington Symonds gave the volume its most able and most charitable review. A small controversy was conducted in the *Athenaeum* (November 4 and 11) concerning Browning's accuracy in translating one or two passages. As for Carlyle, for whom the task was supposedly undertaken, he pretended to make nothing of it, yet with acute penetration he observed that for some reason Browning had followed the letter rather than the spirit of his advice. Allingham reports Carlyle's words:

Oh yes, he called down some months ago to ask if he might dedicate it to me. I told him I should feel highly honoured. But— O bless me! *Can you understand it, at all?* I went carefully into some parts of it and for my soul's salvation (laughs) couldn't make out the meaning. If any one tells me this is because the thing is so remote from us—I say things far remoter from our minds and experiences have been well translated into English. The book of Job, for instance. . . . Yes, Browning says I ordered him to do this translation—he winds up his preface (highly to his own satisfaction, in a neat epigrammatic manner) by saying so,—summing it all up in a last word; and I did often enough tell him he might do a most excellent book, by far the best he had ever done, by translating the Greek Dramatists—but O dear! he's a very foolish fellow. He picks you out the English for the Greek word by word, and now and again sticks two or three words together with hyphens; then again he snips up the sense and jingles it into rhyme! I could have told him he would do no good whatever under such conditions.

And when Browning called on Carlyle on his eighty-third birthday, Carlyle repeated his early advice:

I told him frankly about the *Agamemnon,* after praising his fidelity, that I could make nothing of his translation—could not understand it—had to turn to the Jesuit's book. R. B. admitted that all said it was of no use. . . .

I still exhorted him to give us, as the best possible thing, a Greek Theatre, done like that from Euripides in *Balaustion*.[8]

Certainly Browning had not sincerely followed Carlyle's advice; apparently he had begun with sincere intention, but as he toiled over the translation, from the very corrupt text, he perhaps grew more and more critical of those who extolled the greatness of the Greek plays as models of form and style. Certainly, as the preface shows, he became more interested in providing an answer to Matthew Arnold than in anything else. The performance is part of a strange perversity that grew on Browning in his later years: he would argue his opinions, or demonstrate the absurdity of the beliefs of others, without a thought that he was harming his own poetic genius in the process.

LA SAISIAZ AND THE TWO POETS OF CROISIC

PUBLICATION AND TEXT

The volume containing *La Saisiaz* and *The Two Poets of Croisic* was published on May 15, 1878. It was post octavo, bound in bluish-green cloth boards, and sold for Seven Shillings the copy. It consisted of a half-title; the title-page: "La Saisiaz: The Two Poets of Croisic: By Robert Browning, London: Smith, Elder, & Co., 15 Waterloo Place. 1878"; the dedication to Mrs. Sutherland Orr; the list of contents; and the text, pp. 1–201. The contents were as follows:

Prologue   Prologue
La Saisiaz   The Two Poets of Croisic
                    Epilogue

The *Prologue*, "Good, to forgive!" was a poem of twenty-four short lines, divided into three stanzas, and served as an introduction to the matter of the main poem. *La Saisiaz* consisted of 618 long lines, rhyming in couplets. The measure is that of Tennyson's *Locksley Hall*. The short untitled poem which was the prologue to *The Two Poets of Croisic* was made up of three stanzas of four lines each. *The Two Poets of Croisic* was composed of 160 stanzas of eight lines each, 1280 lines in all. The untitled poem, "What a pretty tale you told me," which served as epilogue to *The Two Poets*, consisted

[8] Allingham, *Diary*, pp. 257–60.

of eighteen stanzas of six lines each, 108 lines in all. The manuscript of the volume is in the Balliol College Library.

AFTER-HISTORY

The genesis of these poems, the sources which Browning used and the influences which operated upon him while he wrote, will be dealt with below under the titles of the two chief poems of the volume, but since the book was reviewed as a whole, it may be well to comment here upon its reception and its after-history. It ought to be noticed at the beginning, however, that the thought of the volume progresses steadily; the prologue to *La Saisiaz* touches lightly upon the theme of death and immortality which is the subject of the main poem; *The Two Poets of Croisic* deals with the question of earthly immortality, the poet's fame, and illustrates its brevity; the epilogue touches lightly and tenderly upon the gratitude of the poet to love. The several poems of the volume are bound together by these common themes.

In general *La Saisiaz* and *The Two Poets* received more complimentary reviews than any volume of Browning since *Balaustion's Adventure*, or perhaps even since *The Ring and the Book*. The reasons for this were mainly two. The new volume had more of the lyrical element in it than usual, and the subject of the major poem, *La Saisiaz*, was the timely question of the immortality of the soul. For these reasons the volume was widely, and generally favorably, noticed. Nowhere, perhaps, was more careful consideration given than in the *Athenaeum* for May 25, 1876. This review was not only the leading article, but occupied ten columns in that issue of the magazine.

To Browning's own generation *La Saisiaz* "was a memorable and helpful utterance." Since his time the poem has not held its readers so well, partly because the later generations have to some extent lost interest in the question of immortality, partly because later analyses, such as Henry Jones's in *Browning as a Philosophical and Religious Teacher*, have found Browning's reasoning less valid than the poet's own generation supposed. The emotion and imagery of the poem still hold, and Sir Frederic Kenyon has justly said of it, "*La Saisiaz* is perhaps a poem to be read only when the mind is attuned to it. . . ." *The Two Poets* and the lyrics of the book have generally been treated as appendages to the major poem.

La Saisiaz

First published in May, 1878, the poem *La Saisiaz* was reprinted in the final collected edition with a very few changes in word and punctuation. The manuscript was dated "Nov. 9, 1877," as was also the printed poem. This means that *La Saisiaz* was written between September 14, the day of the death of Miss Anne Egerton Smith who is commemorated in the poem, and November 9, when it was completed. It was probably begun soon after Browning's return to London in late September. Miss Smith's death was not precisely the *raison d'être* of *La Saisiaz*, but it was the shock which set Browning to reasoning upon the hope of immortality in the manner which he exhibits in the poem. That Browning went alone up Mt. Salève five days after the death of Miss Smith, and there reasoned with himself in the terms of *La Saisiaz*, as the poem tells us, there is no reason at all to doubt.

For many years Miss Smith had been the constant companion of the poet at almost all of the musical events in London. A common delight in music was the basis of their friendship. She was, moreover, a link with Browning's youth, for she was a close friend to W. J. Fox and the Flower family. (See above, my discussion of *Pauline*.) In 1874 and thenceforward, Browning, his sister, and Miss Smith spent their summer holidays together. In 1877 they had taken the chalet "La Saisiaz" (the sun) under Mt. Salève, some five miles southwest of Geneva. An ascent of the mountain was planned for September 14, and the preceding evening Miss Smith seemed in the best of spirits. Miss Browning, the poet's sister, told Domett later of the tragic discovery next morning:

> Browning had been for his usual bathe in a pool among trees down the mountain-side, and on returning found Miss Smith had not made her appearance. 'All right,' he thought, 'she is saving herself for the journey.' Miss Browning going into her room to look for her, found the poor lady lying with her face downwards upon the floor. She put her arm around her, saying, 'Are you ill, dear?' then saw that she was insensible. It was three hours before a doctor could be procured, they having to send to Geneva for one.[1]

Miss Smith was dead, and two days later she was buried in the nearby village of Collonges. On the sixth day after her death Brown-

[1] Griffin and Minchin, *Life*, pp. 263–4.

ing and his sister left for England. The poet was profoundly shocked by the suddenness of the event, and he did not soon recover from it. It was this tragedy that led Browning to the consideration of the abode of his friend's soul, now that her body was buried in Collonges.

During the summer of 1877 Miss Smith and Browning had been following in the *Nineteenth Century* a series of articles called A *Modern Symposium,* upon *The Soul and Future Life.* Two articles by Frederic Harrison under the latter title had appeared in the magazine in June and July, and in September the *Symposium,* having the earnestness, but not quite the brilliance, of Plato's *Symposium,* was in full flower. Papers were contributed by R. H. Hutton, Thomas Huxley, Lord Blatchford, and the Hon. Roden Noel. In the October number the *Symposium* was concluded by papers from Lord Selborne, W. G. Ward, and others. *La Saisiaz* may be said to be Browning's contribution to this debate. His arguments, like those of most of the contributors to the *Symposium,* deliberately left on one side the question of the authority of the Christian revelation. And thus it is that Browning took his part in the

> . . . fence-play,—strife
> Sundry minds of mark engaged in "On the Soul and Future Life."
> (*La Saisiaz,* ll. 163–4)

He spoke, then, according to the rules of the *Symposium,* but his arguments were those he had been preparing since *Christmas-Eve and Easter-Day,* and his position is somewhat foreshadowed by his opinions in *Saul, Karshish,* and more especially in the major poems of *Dramatis Personae. La Saisiaz* has been said to be "instinct with Christian feeling," yet without dogma. The poet's fundamental position was one of belief in the future life, and he still endorsed Dante's words which he had written in his wife's Testament after her death in 1861: "Thus I believe, thus I affirm, thus I am certain it is, that from this life I shall pass to another better, there, where that lady lives of whom my soul was enamoured." [2] But partly because the conditions of the *Symposium* forbade Browning to draw comfort and faith from his strongest belief in the Christian revelation, and partly because he was profoundly shocked by the suddenness of his friend's death, Browning gave voice in *La Saisiaz* to some of the most pessimistic of his utterances. He is inclined to deny that this life, without a future life to correct its mistakes and sufferings, either

[2] Quoted from *Letters,* ed. Hood, p. 172. The words are put into verse in *La Saisiaz,* ll. 213–6.

for the race of men or for the individual man, is worth the pain. He says for himself,

> I must say—or choke in silence—"Howsoever came my fate,
> Sorrow did and joy did nowise,—life well weighed,—preponderate."
> (*La Saisiaz*, ll. 332–3)

And in his argument Browning develops, for the first time at length, the idea characteristic of his later thinking, that our human knowledge is of no use to us whatever in solving the riddle of our doubtful doom. In short, we cannot prove anything about God by our human intellects, and must resort to the intuitive knowledge of our hearts. This position Browning was to elaborate at length in the *Parleying With Francis Furini*. He invariably concluded that it was morally best for us to be left in uncertainty concerning God and the future life; but for his own part he was strongly reassured by his belief in the revelation of Christ.

The poem is more than "mere grey argument." It is partly autobiography, partly elegy, partly a fine, subtle, instinctive kind of reasoning, and partly description of a grand mountainous country. It is the country of Rousseau, Voltaire, Gibbon, Shelley, and Byron, and one may profitably compare Byron's comments upon the first three of these persons in the third canto of his *Childe Harold*, with Browning's remarks here. But the words, "ivy plucked for Byron's sake" (*La Saisiaz*, l. 556), show that Browning is in the mood to make amends for the assaults he had made upon Byron in *Fifine at the Fair* and elsewhere. The real object of his wrath had always been Alfred Austin.

Browning and his wife had once passed, on their way to Italy, not very far from the country of *La Saisiaz*, and in the poem Mrs. Browning and Miss Smith are linked together in the exquisite passage which Browning transcribes from Dante's *Vita Nuova* in lines 210–6 of his poem.

The critics were quick to notice that Browning had taken for his poem the measure which Tennyson had made famous in *Locksley Hall*. Others noticed also the likeness between the debate of Reason and Fancy in *La Saisiaz* and the similar one in Tennyson's *The Two Voices*. But when one looks beyond these superficial appearances, the thought and the music are peculiarly Browning's. The passage on fame, towards the end of *La Saisiaz*, binds the poem somewhat loosely to *The Two Poets of Croisic*.

The Two Poets of Croisic

The Two Poets of Croisic was the longer of the two major poems which made up the *La Saisiaz* volume, though it was by no means as important as *La Saisiaz*. It is written in a lighter mood and its tie with the first poem is the theme of the brevity of human fame. *The Two Poets* took its place with *La Saisiaz* in the final collected edition of 1888–9, and there the text of the poem suffered a few alterations in word and punctuation. In the manuscript the dates indicate that the poem was written immediately after *La Saisiaz;* it was begun on November 10, 1877, and completed on December 8 of the same year. The short lyric which serves as prologue to *The Two Poets*—"Such a starved bank of moss . . ."—was probably written about the same time, though it is undated in the manuscript; and probably, like most of such prologues, was written to Mrs. Browning.

For the genesis of *The Two Poets* we must look back some ten years in Browning's life. During the summers of 1866 and 1867 the poet had been at Croisic, the little Breton village just north of the mouth of the Loire. It was at Croisic that Browning wrote *Hervé Riel,* and that hero of the town is mentioned again in *The Two Poets* (l. 160). The nature of the country—the sea-coast, the salt-marshes, the medieval town of Guérande and "wild Batz" a few miles inland, the prehistoric menhir—interested Browning, as did also the natives of the region, supposed in those days to be Saxons, with their strange survivals of prehistoric religious ceremonies. But in *The Two Poets* he concerns himself with more recent history.

The first of the Croisickese poets, who rose to fame in one splendid prophetic burst of poetry like the spirt of flame from a burning log, and was as soon extinguished, was René Gentilhomme (born 1610), page and poet of Henry, Prince of Condé (1588–1646), whose chief fame now is that he was father of the great Condé. For a while it appeared that Louis XIII and his brother Gaston would die without heirs, and in that case the Prince of Condé would have become King of France. But in 1638 Louis XIV was born, as René Gentilhomme had prophesied the year before, and the hopes of the Prince of Condé were dashed. René's prophecy therefore must have been made in 1637; and he was, after the fulfilment, given the title of "Royal Poet" by Louis XIII.

So small was René Gentilhomme's fame that his name can now be found in no biographical dictionary, nor in the memoirs of the reigns of Louis XIII and XIV. His fame was limited to Croisic, and it was probably from local traditions that Browning took the facts of Gentilhomme's case. In the sale of the Browning library in 1913 there came to light some notes written by Sarianna Browning, the poet's sister, taken from Caillo jeune's *Notes sur le Croisic*,[3] upon the two poets which the town boasted, and it is thus evident that *The Two Poets* was suggested by the same little guide-book which had given Browning the story of *Hervé Riel*.

The second poet of Croisic has loomed somewhat larger in history than the first, but it is probable that Browning again followed local tradition and Caillo; for the account of Desforges-Maillard in the *Biographie universelle,* to which Browning may have resorted, would not have supplied him with all the facts he uses. Paul Desforges-Maillard was born in Croisic in 1699. He became a member of the academies at d'Angers, Rochelle, Caen, and Nancy. Today he is known for the stratagem which he practised upon the literary world of his country and time, by which even Voltaire was deceived. The story which Browning tells was used by Alexis Piron as the basis for his comedy *La Métromanie* which appeared in 1738, and it is quite likely that Browning knew that work. When Desforges-Maillard was told by De La Roque, editor of the *Mercure,* that none of his poetry would ever be printed in his paper, Desforges-Maillard's sister copied out some of his poems and sent them to the *Mercure* under the name of Mlle. Malcrais de la Vigne. De La Roque printed them, and others, and grew enthusiastic over the muse of Croisic. He wrote to Mlle. Malcrais, "Je vous aime, ma chère bretonne; pardonnez-moi cet aveu; mais le mot est lâche." Voltaire and Destouches, each jealous of the other, took up the praise of the lady. Voltaire sent her a copy of his *Histoire de Charles XII,* and with the book the verses which he was honest enough and amused enough to include in his works,

> Toi dont la voix brillante a volé sur nos rives;
> Toi qui tiens dans Paris nos muses attentives, . . .[4]

[3] *The Browning Collections* (Sotheby Catalogue, 1913), p. 45.
[4] See *Oeuvres complètes de Voltaire* (Kehl ed.) 1785, XIII, 64–7; *Epitre XXX, A une Dame ou soi-disant telle.* That Voltaire harbored no resentment for the trick played upon him may be seen from his later correspondence with Desforges-Maillard, LII, 255, 266.

In 1735, just before the stratagem was at length disclosed, there appeared *Poésies de Mlle. Malcrais de la Vigne,* and all the literary world of Paris was taken in. Then Desforges-Maillard disclosed the identity of the author of the poems, and the jest was his; but as an author he could never win renown in his own name. He returned to Brittany and died in 1772. In his life-time he published three other works: *Poésies francaises et latines sur la prise de Berg-op-Zoom,* 1748; *Arbres,* 1751; *Oeuvres en vers et en prose,* 1759, in two volumes.

Besides the stories of the two poets of Croisic who for a brief time enjoyed fame and then relapsed into obscurity, the poem contains many interesting ideas, which are the expressions of Browning's personal opinions. For example, at the close of the story of René Gentilhomme Browning pauses to marvel that once and once only was the poet touched by the spirit of prophecy and greatness, and this connects *The Two Poets* with the *Parleying With Christopher Smart,* for Smart, in Browning's opinion, suffered a comparable experience. Again, very happy is Browning's acknowledgment of John Donne, a poet to whom he owed much:

> Better and truer verse none ever wrote . . .
> Than thou, revered and magisterial Donne. (ll. 910–2)

And again, at the end of the poem, when Desforges-Maillard's story is told, Browning deduces some rather unexpected ideas from the examples he has given. Though in *La Saisiaz* he could state seriously, in the remembrance of the heavy blow he had just received, that sorrow rather than joy had been preponderant in his life, here in *The Two Poets* the mood is one of joy, not grief; and Browning is ready (stanza 155) to grant the honor of best poet to the one who has led the happiest life, who has best triumphed over suffering; and again (stanza 159), he seems to assert that it is the poet's duty to be radiant and cheerful, come what evils may.

Since Browning's day the poem has been held in esteem for the lightness, yet the firmness and pleasantness, of the treatment. The fact that the career of Paul Desforges-Maillard touched the lives of Voltaire and Piron has of course added to the interest in the poem.

Epilogue

The *Epilogue* ("What a pretty tale you told me . . .") to *The Two Poets of Croisic* bore no title in the published volume. It consisted of eighteen stanzas of six lines each, and was unchanged in the final collected edition. The manuscript shows that Browning first wrote "Eunomos of Locri" for the title, and then cancelled it. The poem was dated January 15, 1878, in the manuscript.

In this epilogue Browning has turned a poem by Paulus Silentarius in the Greek Anthology (VI, 54) into a poem with a pleasant contemporary setting.[5] In the story which Browning used the tale runs as follows in W. R. Paton's translation:

To Lycorean Apollo doth Locrian Eunomus dedicate the brazen cicada, in memory of his contest for the crown. The contest was in lyre-playing, and opposite him stood his competitor, Parthis. But when the Locrian shell rang to the stroke of the plectrum, the string cracked with a hoarse cry. But before the running melody could go lame, a cicada lighted on the lyre chirping tenderly and caught up the vanishing note of the chord, adapting to the fashion of our playing its wild music that used to echo in the woods. Therefore, divine Son of Leto, doth he honor thee with the gift of thy cicada, perching the brazen songster upon thy lyre.

It is probable that the girl of the poem is no real person. The application of the story (stanzas 14–5) to the poet who hopes for fame from his verses links the *Epilogue* to *La Saisiaz* and *The Two Poets*. The *Athenaeum* thought so well of the *Epilogue* that the poem was printed entire in the review of May 25, 1875. In the *Selections* of 1880, it appeared under the title of *A Tale*.

[5] See T. L. Hood, *Browning's Ancient Classical Sources*, in *Harvard Studies in Classical Philology* 33:96. The same story is told in the Greek Anthology IX, 584.

⚜ VII ⚜

THE LAST DECADE

DRAMATIC IDYLS [FIRST SERIES]

PUBLICATION AND TEXT

THE FIRST volume of *Dramatic Idyls* appeared on April 28, 1879. It was post octavo, bound in old-gold cloth boards, and sold for Five Shillings the copy. It consisted of the title-page: "Dramatic Idyls By Robert Browning London Smith, Elder, & Co., 15 Waterloo Place 1879"; a list of contents; and the text, pp. 3–143. Each poem in the volume is preceded by a fly-title. The list of contents was as follows:

Martin Relph	Ivàn Ivànovitch
Pheidippides	Tray
Halbert and Hob	Ned Bratts

GENESIS AND COMPOSITION; SOURCES AND INFLUENCES

The manuscript of this volume in the Balliol College Library unfortunately lacks the dates which Browning usually attached to his later poems. We can say with absolute definiteness only that *Ivàn Ivànovitch* and *Ned Bratts* were written at the Splügen Pass in the Alps in August or early September of 1878.[1] But it is very probable that the other poems, or most of them, were written about the same time, for they bear resemblance both in form and matter to those two poems; and we know that Miss Sarianna Browning, who accompanied him on his holiday, expostulated with her brother about the amount of work he was doing at the Splügen. The manuscript has the word "Postage" written upon it, and bears also the signs of some rough usage. It is possible that Browning mailed the poems

---

[1] *Letters*, ed. Hood, p. 209.

to Smith, Elder and Co. from Venice in November, 1878. But if this was the case it is not clear why the volume did not appear until April 28, 1879. Perhaps the package was mailed from somewhere in England during the first months of 1879. Perhaps the publishers, receiving the manuscript from Venice, thought that immediate publication of the volume would follow too closely upon *La Saisiaz,* which had appeared in May, 1878.

The title for this volume, *Dramatic Idyls,* is most interesting. The word "dramatic" was chosen of course to link this group of poems with Browning's other volumes of short poems, *Dramatic Lyrics, Dramatic Romances,* and *Dramatis Personae.* Here again Browning's peculiar use of the word is apt, for the stories are for the most part told by speakers who are presumed not to be the poet himself, and the poems are again the "utterances of so many imaginary persons, not mine." And here again, Browning is intensely interested in motive, psychology, and character. But the surprising thing in *Dramatic Idyls* is the amount of narrative poetry. The narrators here are not always busy delineating their own characters, but are often intent upon telling a story in brief compass. *Pheidippides* will illustrate the point. In the first part of the poem Pheidippides himself recounts his journey to Sparta, without informing us greatly about his own character; in the second part the poet narrates Pheidippides' race from Marathon to Athens. The dramatic monologue in this poem and in some others of this series is more than half abandoned.

The use of the word "idyls" is even more significant. At first glance it suggests Tennyson, and the Laureate's comment to William Allingham [2] is amusing: "I wish he hadn't taken my word Idyll." Of course, Browning had as much right as Tennyson to the term. The Greeks used it to include a great variety of short poems which were of a rural or pastoral nature, wherein the peculiar landscape of a district generally played a part. The Greek idyl was often homely in nature; the treatment of the matter follows the epic and dramatic rules of composition rather than the lyric. These are, of course, the qualities which Browning sought after in the two series of *Dramatic Idyls,* and achieved in large part, save perhaps in the poem *Tray.* That he knew precisely what he was about we may see from his own words, written shortly before the publication of the first series, in a letter to Wilfred Meynell which was published in an article, *The Detachment of Browning,* in the *Athenaeum* for January 4, 1890:

[2] *Diary,* p. 291.

An idyl, as you know, is a succinct little story complete in itself; not necessarily concerning pastoral matters, by any means, though from the prevalency of such topics in the idyls of Theocritus, such is the general notion. These of mine are called "Dramatic" because the story is told by some actor in it, not by the poet himself. The subjects are sombre enough, with the exception of the Greek one; and are all in rhymed verse; this last in a metre of my own.

But it goes without saying that Browning could not have used the word "idyls" to describe such poems as *Martin Relph, Halbert and Hob,* and *Ned Bratts*—to confine ourselves to the English scene —without thinking of the startling difference between these poems and Tennyson's *English Idylls,* which included such poems as *Enoch Arden, The Gardener's Daughter,* and *Dora.* He must have had in his mind some not too flattering comment upon the sentimentality, the smooth unreality, of Tennyson's poetry in this kind. Such a criticism he had indeed made upon the *Idylls of the King* in a letter to Isa Blagden on January 19, 1870:

Well, I go with you a good way in the feeling about Tennyson's new book: it is all out of my head already. We look at the object of art in poetry so differently! Here is an Idyll about a knight being untrue to his friend and yielding to the temptation of that friend's mistress after having engaged to assist him in his suit. I should judge the conflict in the knight's soul the proper subject to describe: Tennyson thinks he should describe the castle, and effect of the moon on its towers, and anything *but* the soul. The monotony, however, you must expect—if the new is to be of a piece with the old.[3]

Even more to the point is the criticism of *Enoch Arden* which Browning wrote to Miss Wedgwood on September 2, 1864, and his sketch of what he himself would have done with the story.[4] The Browning version would have featured the psychology of Enoch and have treated with irony the complacent respectability of Annie and the Miller when Enoch, who had never disclosed his identity, was borne on a cart to his pauper's grave.

The *Dramatic Idyls* have a unity in theme and form, save for the poem *Tray* which should hardly have been given place. In four of the poems—*Martin Relph, Halbert and Hob, Ned Bratts,* and *Iván Ivánovitch*—Browning's interest is in watching the consciences of his characters at work. Each is, in its kind, a study in remorse. In

---

[3] *Letters,* ed. Hood, p. 134.
[4] *Robert Browning and Julia Wedgwood,* ed. Curle, pp. 48, 56–9.

Martin Relph the crisis is long past; in the other three conscience leads to immediate action. In *Iṽàn Iṽànovitch* there is a double problem of conscience: the conscience of the mother of the children betrays her crime; Iṽàn's conscience does not trouble him at all for the terrible, but righteous, deed which he has done. *Pheidippides* and *Tray* are accounts of heroic actions, modestly performed.

In meter, the poems are alike—save *Tray*—in Browning's use of the long swinging lines. The Greek idyl was in hexameter, and the measure of the *Dramatic Idyls* is an English approximation of that measure. In *Iṽàn Iṽànovitch* and *Martin Relph*, and perhaps in *Pheidippides*, it is admitted that Browning has triumphed notably in versification.

The sources of the separate poems are specifically dealt with, but the general statement should be made here that to a considerable extent the stories are reminiscences of tales which had long been familiar to Browning. Once he had decided upon a book of idyls, stories illustrative of the atmosphere of a country and a time came to him from the great store of anecdotes with which his mind was stocked.

AFTER-HISTORY

Dramatic Idyls, as a volume, was well received and reviewed widely. After the succession of long poems from Browning's pen, broken only by the *Pacchiarotto* volume, the *Dramatic Idyls* were refreshing to his readers. Several of the reviewers recognized that the volume was something of a new departure for Browning, and they generally extolled his brevity, his narrative method, and his insight into character. One of the most penetrating reviews was that by Theodore Watts (later Watts-Dunton) in the *Athenaeum* for May 10, 1879; and Mrs. Orr reviewed the volume in the *Contemporary Review* for May, 1879, with keen appreciation. *Dramatic Idyls*, first series, went into a second edition in 1882. Browning was so pleased with his new manner that he followed the first with a second series of *Dramatic Idyls* in 1880. Since his death, the critics have come to think of the *Dramatic Idyls* as among the most interesting of Browning's later works.

Martin Relph

Martin Relph was the first poem in the volume of *Dramatic Idyls* in 1879; it consisted of 152 lines divided into thirty-eight unnumbered stanzas. In the second edition and in the final collected edition it was reprinted practically unchanged in text.

There is no indication in the manuscript as to the date of composition of the poem, but it is fairly sure that it was written during the fall of 1878, at the Splügen Pass or in Venice or London, for the poem is related in thought to the other poems in *Dramatic Idyls* which were done at this time. There is likewise nothing to indicate what caused Browning to deal with the subject, save Mrs. Orr's statement in her *Handbook* (pp. 309–10), for which she probably had Browning's sanction, that it "embodies a vague remembrance of something read by Mr. Browning when he was himself a boy." I have not been able to find the incident upon which the poem is founded. The story, as Browning imagines it, must have been an incident in the uprising in behalf of Charles Edward, the Young Pretender, "Bonny Prince Charlie," against George II in 1745-6. The young Prince, the subject of Sir Walter Scott's *Waverley*, landed in Scotland in July, 1745, pressed as far down into England as Derby in the hope of support from a popular uprising, and was finally disastrously defeated at Culloden on April 16, 1746. The reference in line 29 is probably to the rebellion. It may be that one of Scott's novels, which Browning read in his youth and remembered vaguely years later, suggested the poem, though the names of Parkes, Relph, and Rosamund Page do not occur in Scott, nor does any quite comparable situation.

Like several other poems in *Dramatic Idyls*, *Martin Relph* is a study in the working of conscience; but in this poem, unlike the others, the crisis is long past. The necessity upon Martin Relph to tell his tale on every May-day is like the compulsion of conscience upon Coleridge's Ancient Mariner, but the gradual betrayal by Relph of the true motive for his action—which reveals him a murderer rather than a coward—is peculiarly Browning's. It may be that Browning has joined here two stories; one of the death of a female spy whose lover was just too late to save her with a reprieve, the other of a conscience-stricken man who might, but for obscure motives of jealousy, have saved her. Records of spies executed in the troubled times of 1746 are numerous, but they were not often women.

The poem has often been praised for its force and simplicity, and Browning probably, in placing it first in the volume, was putting his best foot forward.

Pheidippides

Pheidippides was the second poem in the volume of *Dramatic Idyls*, 1879. In the first edition the poem consisted of 118 lines, divided into fifteen stanzas, each of eight lines except the eighth and eleventh, which were of seven lines each. In the second edition of 1882 one line was added, line 86, and several other changes were made in the eleventh stanza; and after Browning's death line 62 was inserted in the text according to his instructions, appearing first in the Cambridge edition of 1895, and making, in the final text, fifteen stanzas of eight lines each. The failure to make the stanzas 8 and 11 perfect was not the fault of the printer, but of Browning's inability to keep the complicated rhyme-scheme in mind as he wrote.[5] He changed the text verbally to a considerable extent for the final edition, especially in stanzas 10 and 11, without altering the meaning.

The poem was probably written during the early fall of 1878 at the Splügen Pass, or later in the same year at Venice or London. The manuscript in the Balliol College Library bears no date. The legend of the Greek runner, so much like Browning's poem, *How They brought the Good News,* probably had been known to Browning since his boyhood, though it had been recently suggested by his studies in Greek literature. As early as 1876 in the poem *Of Pacchiarotto* he had used the name "Pheidippides" as a rhyme for "Euripides," and possibly at that time he was led on to investigate the story of heroism. At any rate, *Pheidippides* is in the tradition of *How They brought the Good News* and *Childe Roland to the Dark Tower Came,* and perhaps even *Prospice,* where a hard journey is undertaken and successfully concluded. It is the pattern of Browning's conception of the heroic in life.

The poet has made a very skilful use of his sources in piecing together his legend of Pheidippides.[6] The first source upon which Browning drew was Herodotus, who described Pheidippides as a

---

[5] See *Letters,* ed. Hood, p. 189.

[6] For an excellent account of Browning's sources and his use of them see John W. Cunliffe, "Browning and the Marathon Race," in *PMLA* 24:154–63. See also T. L. Hood, *Browning's Ancient Classical Sources,* in *Harvard Studies in Classical Philology,* Vol. 33, entries for *Pheidippides.*

professional courier who made his living by running messages. The battle of Marathon took place in 490 B. C., and Herodotus in his *History* (VI, 105–6) writes thus concerning the preparations of the Athenians for war:

And first, before they left Athens, the generals sent off to Sparta a herald, one Pheidippides, who was by birth an Athenian, and by profession and practice a trained runner. This man, according to the account which he gave to the Athenians on his return, when he was near Mount Parthenium, above Tegea, fell in with the god Pan, who called him by his name, and bade him ask the Athenians "wherefore they neglected him so entirely, when he was kindly disposed towards them, and had often helped them in times past, and would do so again in times to come?" The Athenians, entirely believing in the truth of this report, as soon as their affairs were once more in good order, set up a temple to Pan under the Acropolis, and, in return for the message which I have recorded, established in his honor yearly sacrifices and a torch-race.

On the occasion of which we speak, when Pheidippides was sent by the Athenian generals, and, according to his own account saw Pan on his journey, he reached Sparta on the very next day after quitting the city of Athens. Upon his arrival he went before the rulers, and said to them:—

"Men of Lacedaemon, the Athenians beseech you to hasten to their aid, and not allow that state, which is the most ancient in all Greece, to be enslaved by the barbarians. Eretria, look you, is already carried away captive, and Greece weakened by the loss of no mean city."

Thus did Pheidippides deliver the message committed to him. And the Spartans wished to help the Athenians, but were unable to give them any present succor, as they did not like to break their established law. It was the ninth day of the first decade, and they could not march out of Sparta on the ninth, when the moon had not reached the full. So they waited for the full of the moon.

Pausanias, in his *Description of Greece* (I, 28, 4), tells the same story, but the details he gives are all to be found also in the *History* of Herodotus. The first part of Browning's poem, which with some reason he puts into the mouth of Pheidippides, is thus based on Herodotus. What additions and changes Browning made will be noted later.

Plutarch's *Bellone an pace clariores fuerint Athenienses,* an essay in which he discusses whether the Athenians won greater glory in war or in the arts of peace, seems to have suggested to Browning the idea for the end of *Pheidippides,* though it will be noticed that Plutarch (3) gives the credit to others than Pheidippides:

Thersippus of Eroeadoea brought the first news of the victory at Marathon, as Heraclides of Pontus relates. But most report that Eucles, running armed with his wounds reeking from the fight, and falling through the door into the first house he met, expired with only these words on his lips, "God save you, we are well." Now this man brought the news himself of a fight wherein he was present in person.

It was Lucian who provided Browning with the motto to *Pheidippides*, "Rejoice, we conquer," and the conclusion of his poem. In his *Apology for a Mistake in Salutation*, Lucian explains the use of the phrase of greeting:

> The point of time when the use of the formulary of *chaire* or *chairete* began to be more restricted, is marked by an anecdote of the runner Pheidippides, who announced the victory at Marathon to the assembled archons, who were under great apprehensions about the event of the fight, in these words: Rejoice! We are victorious! And no sooner had he uttered them than he fell down dead, and his last breath was spent in delivering these joyful tidings.[7]

Thus Browning was the first to combine Herodotus' account of Pheidippides' journey to Sparta before Marathon, with the later stories of the run after the battle as told by Plutarch and Lucian.

The additions and changes which Browning makes in the legend of Pheidippides have been described in the article by Professor Cunliffe which is referred to above. Browning makes Pan give the runner a sprig of fennel as a prophecy of where the Athenian victory is to be, for Marathon is the "fennel-field." The English poet adds very characteristically the love of Pheidippides for "a certain maid," and his hope for reward of a very different kind from that which paid couriers usually got. Characteristically, also, Browning's hero dies, overwrought by his own exertions and emotions, whereas in Plutarch's account he had been wounded. It is Professor Cunliffe's contention that Browning made a careless mistake in setting the vision of Pan on "Parnes' ridge," ten miles out of Pheidippides' way to Sparta, instead of on Mount Parthenium, near Tegea. Browning's choice of Parnes has been defended, however, on the ground that Parnes was an Attic hill, whereas Mount Parthenium was in Arcadia.[8] Browning prefers to read at their worst the motives of Sparta for not helping Athens; and it is quite possible that the feast and the state of the moon which delayed the Spartan aid were mere subterfuges. The Spartans finally sent 2000 men, but they were too late

[7] Lucian, *Works*, tr. by C. M. Wieland, ed. W. Tooke, London, 1820, II, 402.
[8] Pausanias (I, 32) may have given Browning some justification for this. See T. L. Hood, *Harvard Studies in Classical Philology*, 33:157.

to be of service. But Browning had little love for Sparta. In the point of time, Browning has not been quite accurate, either in the demand of Persia for tribute, or in the time it took Pheidippides to run to Sparta and return. Pheidippides is supposed by the Greeks to have covered the 130 miles from Athens to Sparta in one day, whereas Browning allows him two days and two nights. The effect of most of Browning's changes is to heighten the artistry and the emotional impression which he wishes the story to produce.

Pheidippides has always been reckoned one of the most successful of Browning's later narratives. The *Athenaeum* objected to the long lines and, with perhaps more justice, to the rhyme-scheme of the stanzas, which does tax one's recollection of the earlier rhyme. Nevertheless the critics generally have accounted the poem a triumph for Browning, and have found the verse admirably adapted to the subject-matter. It may be of interest that Browning suggested to his son the meeting of Pan and Pheidippides as a subject for a painting.[9]

Halbert and Hob

Halbert and Hob made its first appearance in *Dramatic Idyls*, 1879, and there consisted of sixty-six lines in all, divided into sixteen sections of unequal length, rhyming in couplets. When the poem was republished in the final collected edition of 1888–9, Browning had made several verbal changes. In the first edition he had, in sections 11 and 12, confused the two men, and had made the father call the son "Halbert." This error was amended, and a few other changes made.

It is probable that *Halbert and Hob* was written in the busy days which Browning spent in the Splügen Pass in August and September of 1878, though the reference to Christmas in the poem may point to December of the same year as the time of composition. It is akin in its theme, the working of conscience, to *Martin Relph* and *Ned Bratts*, which were written at about this time. The suggestion for the poem came to Browning from Aristotle's *Nicomachean Ethics* (VIII, vi, 2), where Aristotle argues that anger and bad temper are more natural than desire for excessive and unnecessary pleasures, and he deduces the example from which *Halbert and Hob* came:

[9] *The Browning Collections* (Sotheby Catalogue, 1913), p. 39.

Witness the man who was had up for beating his father and who said in his defence, "Well, my father used to beat his father, and he used to beat his, and (pointing to his little boy) so will my son here beat me when he grows up; it runs in our family"; and the man who, when his son was throwing him out of the house, used to beg him to stop when he got to the door, "because he only used to drag his father as far as that."

The story also occurs in many variations elsewhere. It is interesting that Aristotle has dealt with four generations of a family, whereas Browning has only two.

Browning is obviously most interested in the conduct of old Halbert and the way his conscience works, for he permits his son, Hob, to drag him unresisting just as far as he, on another occasion, had dragged his father. It is not easy to understand why Browning laid the scene of his poem in the north of England, though he may have meant the poem as an ironic contrast to the grace and beauty of the heroic action in ancient Greece which we have just encountered in *Pheidippides*. The subject is certainly not essentially Hellenic, and Browning needed a sparsely settled and backward country for his scene. It is possible that Browning had in mind Ruskin's curious comparison of the Greek of Homer's day to a north-country farmer in England, in his chapter on *Classical Landscape*, in *Modern Painters*. At any rate, *Halbert and Hob*, as an idyl of English country life, is a startling contrast to Tennyson's domestic idylls. In the conclusion of the poem Browning suggests a theme, running through all his poetry but finding its clearest expression in the *Parleying With George Bubb Dodington*, that it takes the supernatural to awe ordinary men into decent behavior. The line in *Halbert and Hob* which is paraphrased from *King Lear*, probably Browning's favorite play, is Lear's agonized question (III, vi, 81–2), after he has "tried" his daughters, Goneril and Regan, in the farmhouse, "Is there any cause in nature that make these hard hearts?"

Ivàn Ivànovitch

Ivàn Ivànovitch was the fourth poem in the volume of *Dramatic Idyls*, 1879. It consisted of 424 long lines rhyming in couplets. In the final collected edition of 1888–9 it was altered only by a very few verbal changes for the sake of smoothness.

It is probable that the snows upon the mountains and pine-trees of the Splügen Pass brought back to Browning memories of his journey through Russia to St. Petersburg and back in March and April of 1834. We know certainly from a letter of Browning to Furnivall on March 11, 1882, that *Iuàn Iuànovitch* was written at the Splügen at the same time as *Ned Bratts*.[10] Soon afterwards, in Venice, Browning consulted a Russian lady about the names he had used in the poem. By its manner of dramatic narrative as well as by its interest in motive and retribution, the poem connects itself with other poems in the volume, notably *Martin Relph* and *Ned Bratts*.

Browning thought the story which he used in *Iuàn Iuànovitch* was an old Russian folk-tale. This, however, has recently been shown to be not true.[11] The story is not a familiar one in Russian folk-lore, but it has appeared many times in the literatures of other countries concerning Russia. The story probably came to Browning from a book published anonymously in England in 1855, called *An Englishwoman in Russia* (pp. 174–5):

A dreadful anecdote was told me of a peasant woman and her children, who were crossing the forest that stretched for many miles between her isba and the neighboring village. They were in one of those small country sledges, in shape something like a boat, drawn by a single horse. Suddenly they heard a rustling sound among the trees; it was but faint at first, but it rapidly approached; the instinct of the affrighted steed told him that danger was near at hand; he rushed on with redoubled speed. Presently the short yelp of a wolf aroused the mother; she started up and gazed around; to her horror she beheld a mighty pack of wolves sweeping across the frozen snow, in full cry upon their traces. She seized the whip, and endeavored by repeated blows to urge on the fear-stricken horse to even greater swiftness. The poor animal needed no incentive to hasten his steps, but his force was well-nigh spent; his convulsive gasping showed how painfully his utmost energies were exerted. But courage! there is hope! the village is in sight! far off, it is true, but we shall gain it yet! So thought the unhappy mother, as she cast a look of horror on the hungry savage beasts that were following in the rear, and saw that they were rapidly gaining upon her. Now they are near enough for her to see their open mouths and hanging tongues, their fiery eyes and bristling hair, as they rush on with unrelenting speed, turning neither to the right nor to the left, but steadily pursuing their horrible chase. At last they came near enough for their eager breathing to be heard, and the foremost was within a few yards of the sledge; the overspent horse flagged in his speed; all

[10] *Letters,* ed. Hood, p. 209. See also Orr, *Life,* p. 312.
[11] See M. Alekseev, "Die Quellen zum Idyl *Ivan Ivanovitsch* von Robert Browning," in *Jahrbücher für Kultur und Geschichte der Slaven,* N. S. 5:417–27 (1930); and "Zur Entstehungs-geschichte der *Dramatic Idyls* von Browning," in *Englische Studien* 66:54–6 (1931).

hope seemed lost, when the wretched woman, frantic with despair, caught up one of her three children and threw him into the midst of the pack, trusting by this means to gain a little time by which the others might be saved. He was devoured in an instant; and the famished wolves, whose appetites it had only served to whet, again rushed after the retreating family. The second and third infant were sacrificed in the same dreadful manner; but now the village was gained. A peasant came out of an isba, at sight of whom the wolves fell back. The almost insensible woman threw herself out of the sledge, and, when she could find sufficient strength to speak, she related the fearful danger in which she had been, and the horrible means she had employed to escape from it. "And did you *throw them all* to the wolves, even the little baby you held in your arms?" exclaimed the horrorstricken peasant. "Yes, all!" was the reply. The words had scarcely escaped from the white lips of the miserable mother, when the man laid her dead at his feet with a single blow of the axe with which he was cleaving wood when she arrived. He was arrested for murder, and the case was decided by the Emperor, *who pardoned* him, wisely making allowance for his agitation and the sudden impulse with which horror and indignation at the unnatural act had inspired him.

It is easy to see what Browning has done with the story which was his source. He has, in the first place, made the tale dramatic and psychological, and has put into the mouth of the mother the account of the loss of the children. In doing so, he has created, for completeness' sake, the character of her husband, Dmitri, and given the story of the journey an artistic logic which it did not possess in the original. He has also to a large extent created the character of the "Pope" of the village, making him somewhat like the Pope in *The Ring and the Book,* and given him, in little, a comparable philosophy. Indeed, other versions of the story almost invariably carry before the Emperor the case of the peasant who struck the blow. Then, too, Browning's vivid recollection of the scenery and atmosphere of Russia seems to have stood him in good stead, especially in his description of the long straight road through the endless versts (a verst is two-thirds of a mile) of pine. Of course, he has given Ivàn himself a local habitation and a name and a nature, which are barely indicated in the action of the peasant who beheads the unnatural mother. Elsewhere, Browning has added details which give an air of verisimilitude, such as the Russian belief that wolves were reincarnations of the wicked witches of Satan. He has accented the Russian names and words to fit the measure of his English verses.

There has been general praise for Browning's skill in the verse, the narrative, and the vividness of *Ivàn Ivànovitch.* The long lines of the poem fit themselves admirably to the matter; especially is this so in the description of the approach of the wolves. But there has been no such general agreement upon the terrible blow which Ivàn took upon himself to strike. It has been the opinion of some that Ivàn's action differs not at all from the lynch-law; and that no man has the right to think that he represents divine retribution. Others have defended warmly Browning's view of the case. William Allingham has recorded Tennyson's opinion: "I think the woman was right. The wolves would have eaten them all. She might have saved part by what she did." [12]

Tray

Tray was the fifth poem in the *Dramatic Idyls,* 1879. There the poem consisted of forty-five lines, and in the final collected edition of 1888–9 it was reprinted practically without change. There is no indication in the manuscript or elsewhere as to the date of composition, but there are good reasons to connect the writing of the poem with the *Symposium* in the *Nineteenth Century* on the topic, *The Soul and Future Life,* which Browning had used in *La Saisiaz.* These reasons are given below. The poem was therefore probably written late in 1878.

The subject of vivisection was much debated in the last three decades of the nineteenth century, and also in the twentieth. The wide use of anaesthetics after 1860, and the rise of experimental surgery and medicine, taught science many things which could not be learned from cogitation. No doubt the vivisectionists were occasionally wanton in their use of the new method, and there arose a tremendous movement in England against the vivisection of lower animals, especially of dogs; an association of anti-vivisectionists was formed in the Seventies, and a law against the practice was framed in Parliament, but it was passed in 1876 only after many destructive amendments had been added.[13] Browning was Vice-President of the Victoria Street Society for the Protection of Animals, and wrote *Tray* for the cause in 1878, and *Arcades Ambo* in 1889. In these two poems his sentiments are quite clearly expressed. To Miss Frances Power Cobbe, one of the most militant anti-vivisectionists, he wrote in 1874: "You have heard, 'I take an equal interest with yourself in

---

[12] *Diary,* p. 314.
[13] See *Frances Power Cobbe, by Herself,* Boston, 1894, II, 591–6, 604, 611, for an account of the anti-vivisectionists at this time.

the effort to suppress vivisection.' I dare not so honour my mere wishes and prayers as to put them for a moment beside your noble acts; but this I know, I would rather submit to the worst of deaths, so far as pain goes, than have a single dog or cat tortured on the pretense of sparing me a twinge or two." [14] In 1883 he wrote to Miss Stackpoole as follows: ". . . whoever cares to know does by this time know how much I despise and abhor the pleas on behalf of that infamous practise—Vivisection." [15] Browning was, indeed, consistent in his opinion, and it should not be forgotten that he had been a vegetarian in his youth, when he was under the influence of Shelley.

In an article entitled "The Source and Meaning of Browning's *Tray*," [16] C. R. Tracy has shown that the poem is more than a sentimental outcry over cruelty to an heroic dog. In *A Modern Symposium, The Soul and Future Life* in the *Nineteenth Century*, which had been of service to Browning in *La Saisiaz* (*q.v.*), Frederic Harrison, leader of the English Positivists, had participated. In the course of his arguments against the biological materialists he asserted: "It is a corrupting doctrine to open a brain, and to tell us that devotion is a definite molecular change in this and that convolution of grey pulp, and that if man is the first of living animals, he passes away after a short space, like the beasts that perish." He denies that "victorious vivisection" will ever solve the moral and spiritual mysteries of man, and as an illustration cites the affection of a dog, which will also need explanation. Browning did not subscribe to Harrison's Positivism, but he welcomed the attack on materialism, and there can be no doubt that Harrison's argument and illustration were in the poet's mind.

The poem *Tray* is said by Mrs. Orr [17] to have been founded upon an actual incident which a friend of Browning's witnessed in Paris and reported to the poet. It is probable that Browning, and not his friend, supplied the comment or application. It is Browning's purpose in the poem to set up a genuinely modest and modern hero as a contrast to the conventional heroes of poetry—the knight of medieval times who figured so largely in the poetry of Tennyson, Rossetti and Morris, for example, or the hero of Byron's poetry with his "sin-scathed brow." The poet's sympathy for animals assuredly does his

---

[14] Quoted in E. Berdoe, *Browning's Message to his Times,* p. 173.
[15] Quoted in Griffin and Minchin, *Life,* p. 254.
[16] *PMLA* 55:615–7 (1940).
[17] *Handbook,* p. 313.

heart credit, but in the light of the history of modern medicine one must think that he had a short view of the matter. Browning inherited his love of animals from his mother; and if the poem *Development* is taken as strictly autobiographical, one of his own dogs was named Tray. It is odd to find a French dog of the same name; but the scene is probably laid in Paris because the heroic action took place there, and because vivisection flourished with less opposition among the French than among the animal-loving Britons.

Ned Bratts

Ned Bratts was the sixth and final poem in the first series of *Dramatic Idyls,* and there it consisted of 326 long lines, rhyming in couplets. In the final collected edition of 1888–9 two new lines were added (ll. 325–6) and a few verbal changes were made. The most notable was the substitution of the name "Christian," which appears several times, for the first-edition form, "Christmas," by which Browning meant to indicate Ned Bratts's ignorance of the name of Bunyan's character. A foot-note upon the word "outstreats" (l. 180) which referred the reader to Donne's use of the word in his *Progress of the Soul* (l. 344) is omitted from the final edition.

We know from a letter of Browning to Furnivall, on March 11, 1882, that he wrote *Ned Bratts* at the Splügen Pass in August or September, 1878, where two other poems similarly concerned with the workings of conscience and with the portrayal of the provincial English scene, *Martin Relph* and *Halbert and Hob,* were probably also written. *Iván Ivànovitch* we know to have been written at the same time and place.

The story which Browning told Furnivall he had used for *Ned Bratts* was the tale of "Old Tod" from Bunyan's *Life and Death of Mr. Badman.* It "was distinctly in my mind," said Browning, "when I wrote *Ned Bratts*—at the Splügen, without reference to what I had read when quite a boy." [18] When Browning returned home early in November, he consulted a copy of Bunyan's *Works* in his own library, and entered his name and the date, "Nov. 6, 1878," in the book.[19] At that time he probably added the matter relating to Bunyan's life which makes up a large part of the poem.

[18] *Letters,* ed. Hood, p. 209.
[19] This was the edition of 1771, folio, published at Edinburgh. See *The Browning Collections* (Sotheby Catalogue, 1913), p. 85.

Bunyan tells the tale in a conversation between Wiseman and Attentive:

The Story of Old Tod

* Young Thieves take notice

Old Tod began his way to the Gallows by robbing of Orchards and the like.

Wise. Since you are entred upon Storyes, I also will tell you one, the which, though I heard it not with mine own Ears, yet my Author I dare believe.* It is concerning one old *Tod,* that was hanged about Twenty years agoe, or more, at *Hartford,* for being a Thief. The Story is this:

At a Summer Assizes holden at *Hartfort,* while the Judge was sitting upon the Bench, comes this old Tod into the Court, cloathed in a green Suit, with his Leathern Girdle in his hand, his Bosom open, and all on a dung sweat, as if he had run for his Life; and being come in, he spake aloud as follows: *My Lord, said he, Here is the veryest Rogue that breaths upon the face of the earth. I have been a Thief from a Child: When I was but a little one, I gave myself to rob Orchards, and to do other such like wicked things, and I have continued a Thief ever since. My Lord, there has not been a Robbery committed thus many years, within so many miles of this place, but I have either been at it, or privy to it.*

The Judge thought the fellow was mad, but after some conference with some of the Justices, they agreed to Indict him; and so they did of several felonious Actions; to all which he heartily confessed Guilty, and so was hanged with his Wife at the same time.

Atten. This is a remarkable Story indeed, and you think it is a true one.

Wise. It is not only remarkable, but pat to our purpose. This Thief, like Mr. *Badman,* began his Trade betimes; he began too where Mr. *Badman* began, even at robbing of Orchards, and other such things, which brought him, as you may perceive, from sin to sin, till at last it brought him to the publick shame of sin, which is the Gallows.

As for the truth of this Story, the Relator told me that he was at the same time himself in the Court, and stood within less than two yards of old Tod, when he heard him aloud to utter the words.[20]

To give *Ned Bratts* more interest than that aroused by the mere repentance and confession of a terrible wrong-doer, Browning has transferred the court-room scene from Hertford to Bedford, in order to bring John Bunyan, who was imprisoned there between 1660 and 1672, into his story. Browning imagines the time of his poem as midsummer, 1672, but in that year Bunyan's blind daughter, who plays a part in *Ned Bratts,* was dead. Browning has by this device connected the repentance of Ned Bratts and his wife Tab with Bunyan and Bunyan's "Book." The poet gives us several facts about Bunyan, which he probably learned from Robert Southey's life of Bunyan, at-

[20] Bunyan, *The Life and Death of Mr. Badman,* ed. B. Dobrée, Oxford, 1929, pp. 39–40.

tached to an edition of *Pilgrim's Progress* in 1830. In Bedford Bunyan was forced to make lace in prison to sustain himself and his family, and he was deeply attached to his blind daughter who sold the lace. Browning has given us a very good portrait of the inspired preacher, but his part in the conversion of Ned (Old Tod) and his wife is, of course, the poet's invention. Bunyan was released from Bedford jail in 1672 by the Indulgence of Charles II. Browning refers to the "Book" which Bunyan gave to Ned and Tab Bratts as if it were *Pilgrim's Progress;* Ned, indeed, has taken Master Faithful as his model and gives us an outline of his own progress from the City of Destruction to Vanity Fair. In this Browning was misled by Southey and the early biographers. The "Book" Bunyan might have given to these sinners from his long incarceration in Bedford jail was *Grace Abounding to the Chief of Sinners,* being an account of his own religious experiences, published in 1666. It is now generally held that *Pilgrim's Progress* was written in Bunyan's short incarceration in Bedford jail in 1675; it was published in February, 1678. It is very probable that Browning had seen the statue of Bunyan to which he refers in the last line of the poem. This was a statue in bronze, executed by Boehm; it was given to the town by the Duke of Bedford in 1874.

Browning has dressed the poem in a language suitable to such a creature as Ned Bratts, and has told the tale in his usual dramatic fashion. Though the piece is not reckoned among Browning's great poems, it has attracted considerable interest because of its connection with Bunyan,[21] as well as by its own merits. Browning's brilliant and satirical description of the court in session at Bedford is another example of his opinion of the law and lawyers, whose professional spirit had been the object of his attack in Books VIII, IX, and XII of *The Ring and the Book.*

DRAMATIC IDYLS, SECOND SERIES

PUBLICATION AND TEXT

The Second Series of *Dramatic Idyls* appeared about June 15, 1880. The book was post octavo, bound in dark brown cloth boards, and sold for Five Shillings the copy. It consisted of a half-title; the title-

---

[21] See, for example, the letter of Browning to W. H. White (Mark Rutherford) in *New Letters,* ed. DeVane and Knickerbocker, pp. 251–2. White was a fellow-admirer of Bunyan, and in 1905 produced a study called *John Bunyan.*

page: "Dramatic Idyls Second Series By Robert Browning London Smith, Elder, & Co., 15 Waterloo Place 1880"; a list of contents; the prologue, "You are sick"; the text, pp. 3–147; and the epilogue, "Touch him ne'er so lightly." Neither the prologue nor the epilogue were properly included in the text; unnamed and printed on unnumbered pages, they appeared in fine type. The list of contents was as follows:

Echetlos	Pietro of Abano
Clive	Doctor ——
Muléykeh	Pan and Luna

GENESIS AND COMPOSITION; SOURCES AND INFLUENCES

The book was an attempt to provide a sequel to the successful volume of the year before. From the manuscript in the Balliol College Library one sees that the six major poems which make up the volume were all written between January and April of 1880, when Browning was in London; the first to be finished was *Pietro of Abano* on January 20th, and the last was *Pan and Luna* on April 9th. The manuscript was sent to press on April 20th. The prologue and epilogue are undated in the manuscript.

In general the poems in the Second Series follow the plan of the first. *Echetlos, Clive,* and *Muléykeh* may roughly be called idyls in the same sense that the poems of the first series are idyls. More properly they are, as in the first series, realistic short-stories in verse, and in *Clive* Browning's narrative methods are very happily used. *Echetlos* and *Muléykeh* are excellent narratives, and *Pan and Luna* is an exquisite pastoral idyl in the classical kind.

But it is hardly possible to find in the Second Series a central artistic conception such as was apparent in the earlier volume. Browning's old interest in paradox is excellently exhibited in *Muléykeh*, and his delight in psychology and the intricacies of character is fully exploited in *Clive*. His pleasure in the heroic shows itself in *Echetlos*. His penchant for the grotesque and the fantastic, both in rhyme and matter, finds ample expression in *Pietro of Abano* and *Doctor* ——. There is also Browning's delight in odd subjects, and in this volume he is carried into Hebrew and Arabian legend, regions which he is to exploit further in the following volumes, *Jocoseria* and *Ferishtah's Fancies*. It is probably just, however, to say with Mrs. Orr that the second group of *Dramatic Idyls* shows the slow subsidence of the inspiration which made the first series a new and striking volume.

The reviewers in general noticed this subsidence, though they did not often understand it. They also observed that Browning did not always wait for inspiration to fall from heaven upon him, but sought, in some very unlikely places often, for subject-matter for his poems. *Clive,* more than any other poem in the volume, engaged the interest of the reviewers and the reading public, and won most commendation; *Muléykeh,* likewise, won much favor. Theodore Watts (later Watts-Dunton) reviewed the volume in the *Athenaeum* for July 10, 1880, and gave what was perhaps the fairest judgment.

"You Are Sick . . ."

The little poem of eleven lines which serves as prologue to the Second Series of *Dramatic Idyls* was reprinted in the final collected edition without change. It is undated and untitled in the manuscript, and Browning's directions to the printer were to print the lines in smaller type than that used in the body of the volume.

The prologue in a general way indicates the contents of the volume, but perhaps more specifically it is a word as to what Browning believes to be the proper province of poetry—man's soul. We have seen Browning's insistence on the importance of this view when he discussed Tennyson's treatment of the idyll,[1] and have traced through the first series his interest in motive and deed and moral health—this indeed has been his special province in poetry—and we shall see it again in this volume. This interpretation is given support by the fact that the epilogue is a pronouncement upon poets and poetry. As he had said in the dedication of *Sordello* to his friend Milsand in 1863, "my stress lay on the incidents in the development of a soul: little else is worth study." In straining for the surprise ending, however, Browning has made the events in a number of the poems, such as *Clive* and *Muléykeh,* seem arbitrary to the point of improbability.

Echetlos

Echetlos was the first poem in the Second Series of *Dramatic Idyls,* published in June, 1880. It there consisted of ten stanzas of three lines

[1] See my general discussion of *Dramatic Idyls,* First Series.

each, triple-rhymed, and save for the substitution of "for" in place of "since" in the first stanza the poem was reprinted without change in the final collected edition of 1888–9. In the manuscript the poem is dated February 2, 1880.

Echetlos was written as a companion poem for *Pheidippides* of the earlier series, and Browning has drawn his humble hero from the same great event which led to Pheidippides' heroism, the battle of Marathon in 490 B. C. Echetlos, "the Holder of the Ploughshare," the otherwise nameless hero, was probably first encountered by Browning in his search through Pausanias and Herodotus for material upon Pheidippides. Pausanias provided the legend of Echetlos in his *Description of Greece* (I, 32), as he was describing the scene of Marathon:

The township of Marathon is about equally distant from Athens and Carystus in Euboea. It was upon this part of Attica that the Persians landed, and were defeated, and lost some of their ships as they were putting out to sea in retreat. And in the plain is the tomb of the Athenians, and on it are pillars with the names of the dead according to their tribes. And another for the Plataeans of Boeotia and their slaves; for this was the first engagement in which slaves fought. And there is apart a monument to Miltiades the son of Cimon, whose death occurred afterwards, when he failed to capture Paros, and was on that account put on his trial by the Athenians. . . . And it chanced, as they say, in the battle that a man of rustic appearance and dress appeared, who slew many of the Persians with a ploughshare, and vanished after the fight: and when the Athenians made inquiry of the oracle, the god gave no other answer, but bade them honor the hero Echetlus. And a trophy of white stone was erected there.

In describing, earlier in his work, the Poekilé, or Painted Colonnade, at Athens, Pausanias had described the famous wall-painting by Micon which depicted the battle of Marathon (I, 15, 4):

And of the combatants there stand out most plainly in the painting Callimachus, who was chosen by the Athenians as Polemarch, and Miltiades, one of the generals, and the hero who was called Echetlus. . . .

The material gained from Pausanias Browning blended into Herodotus' more general account of the battle of Marathon (*History*, VI, 109–14). The center of the Greek line was stretched very thin to match the length of the Persian line, and the Greeks concentrated their weight in each wing. The war-minister Callimachus commanded the right wing. The Plataeans were on the left. Miltiades controlled the battle. Says Herodotus (VI, 114):

The battle at Marathon lasted a long time; and in the middle of the line, where the Persians themselves and the Sacae were arrayed, the barbarians were victorious.

Callimachus was killed, "having proved himself a brave man." But the Persians could not withstand the charges of the Greek wings, and when the left and right wings of the Persian army were routed, the center was massacred. The Greeks "followed the Persians in their flight, cutting them to pieces, till, reaching the shore, they called for fire, and attacked the ships." The Persians lost 6400 men and some of their ships; the Athenians lost 182 men.

Herodotus also provided Browning with a more explicit account of the wretched end of Miltiades at Paros (*History*, VI, 132–6). When Miltiades, wounded in the thigh, withdrew from Paros without having taken the fortress, he was tried by the Athenians on a charge of having deceived them. Of this Herodotus says,

The people so far favoring him as to acquit him of the capital offense, and having fined him fifty talents for the injury he had done, Miltiades soon after ended his life by the putrefaction and mortification of his thigh.

Browning probably went to Plutarch's *Themistocles* (29, 6) for his suggestion of the honors heaped upon that Greek at the Persian court at Sardis. In pointing to the great names which pass while the nameless "Holder of the Ploughshare" keeps his fame untarnished, it does not seem quite just for Browning to link Miltiades with the more treacherous Themistocles.

As one may see at a glance, *Echetlos* bears a relationship to Browning's other poems in the heroic manner, notably to *Hervé Riel*. Both heroes act with becoming modesty in naming their rewards. As a companion-piece to *Pheidippides*, and in its own merit, *Echetlos* has held a high place among the later poems of Browning, and the poet himself was especially fond of it.

Clive

Clive was the second poem in the Second Series of *Dramatic Idyls*, 1880. It there consisted of 240 lines, and save for a few changes in word-order and spelling, it was reprinted in the final collected edition of 1888–9 as it stood. In the manuscript the poem is dated as finished on February 27, 1880. From the evidence of the manuscript *Clive* was written in five days.

We are fortunate to have Browning's own account of the origin of *Clive*. Domett wrote in his diary:

Referring to that most vivid and thoroughly realistic narrative of Lord Clive and his duel, Browning told me he heard it first from Mrs. Jameson, soon after his marriage. Mrs. Jameson said she had it from Lord Lansdowne, to whom it had been told by Macaulay. The idea of what Clive would have done [*viz.* blown his own brains out] had his antagonist (after Clive's pistol was accidentally discharged, leaving Clive at his mercy) generously given him his life, at the same time reiterating his innocence of the cheating Clive had charged him with, instead of throwing down his pistol and confessing it—all this, he said, was merely his own invention, which he had no authority for, or for attributing it to Clive himself. 'But what else,' said he, 'could such a man as Clive have done? He could not have reasserted the charge, unless as a calumniator, for no one would have believed a man so magnanimous could have been capable of cheating at cards.' He added that he had only very recently read Lord Macaulay's article on Clive, and had looked up other authorities, but had not found the duel anecdote recorded anywhere. One would like to know how Macaulay got hold of it.[2]

Besides some incidents of the central story, one observes that Browning has invented the framework in which he puts it—for Browning imagines Clive in his fiftieth year, just a week before his suicide in 1774, telling the tale of his youthful adventure. The old Clive, addicted to opium, broken and unhappy, bore little resemblance to the gallant soldier who had won India for England at the battle of Plassy in 1757. In India Clive had amassed a great fortune, not altogether legally, and in 1773 his conduct had been investigated by Parliament. He was acquitted, but not with great honor to himself.

The story of Clive's exploit, which Browning could not find in his search in the great soldier's biography, came to Macaulay through Sir John Malcolm's *Life of Robert, Lord Clive*, published at London in 1836. Macaulay's essay, *Lord Clive*, published in the January issue of the *Edinburgh Review* for 1840, was, at first appearance, a review of Malcolm's biography. The story has suffered some notable changes on its way from Malcolm to Browning. Malcolm gives the story as follows (I, 46–7):

Soon after his arrival at this place, he was engaged in a duel with an officer, to whom he had lost some money at cards, but who, with his companion, was clearly proved to have played unfairly. Clive was not the only loser; but the others were terrified into payment by the threats of those who had won their money. This example had no effect on him; he

[2] Griffin and Minchin, *Life*, p. 268.

persisted in refusing to pay, and was called out by one of them who deemed himself insulted by his conduct. They met without seconds: Clive fired, and missed his antagonist, who immediately came close up to him, and held the pistol to his head, desiring him to ask his life, with which he complied. The next demand was, to recant his assertions respecting unfair play. On compliance with this being refused, his opponent threatened to shoot him. "Fire, and be d———d," said the dauntless young man; "I said you cheated; I say so still, and I will never pay you." The astonished officer threw away his pistol, saying, Clive was mad. The latter received from his young companions many compliments for the spirit he had shown; but he not only declined coming forward against the officer with whom he had fought, but never afterwards spoke of his behaviour at the card-table. "He has given me my life," he said, "and though I am resolved on never paying money which was unfairly won, or again associating with him, I shall never do him an injury."

If it could be assumed that Browning heard the story as Malcolm gave it, which of course is not a safe assumption, it would be an interesting study to observe what Browning's mind retained accurately for thirty years, such as Clive's unwillingness to refer to the incident afterwards, and what Browning consciously or unconsciously changed— such as the confession of Clive's antagonist, to which Malcolm makes no reference. It is necessary to correct Browning's words to Domett in one respect: Macaulay did refer very briefly in his essay to Clive's duel with a military bully at Fort St. David, and had probably recounted the story in full to Lord Lansdowne, who in turn told it to Mrs. Jameson.

Clive, partly because of the national fame of its hero, and partly because of Browning's brilliant success in employing his narrative devices—a story within a situation, the dramatic manner in which the story is told, the superb characterization—has always been reckoned one of the most delightful of the later poems. To many critics it, with *Muléykeh,* redeems the second series of *Dramatic Idyls* from drabness, though it must be admitted that both of these poems are open to the charge of improbability in their psychology and in their endings. Browning himself was fond of *Clive.* On March 15, 1885, in answer to a request from Edmund Gosse for a list of "Four Poems, of moderate length, which represent their writer fairly," Browning chose *Clive* as the poem he preferred in the "Idyllic (in the Greek sense)." [3] For Tennyson's amusing misunderstanding of Browning's subtle psychology in *Clive,* see William Allingham's *Diary,* p. 291.

[3] *Letters,* ed. Hood, p. 235.

Muléykeh

Muléykeh was the third poem in the Second Series of *Dramatic Idyls,* 1880. It consisted of nineteen stanzas of six long lines each, 114 lines in all. The poem was reprinted without change in the final collected edition of 1888–9. In the manuscript the poem is dated as finished on February 22, 1880, five days before the completion of *Clive.*

The story which Browning uses in *Muléykeh* is an old Arabian tale, the first evidence of that interest in Eastern tales and wisdom which was to find its way into the *Jocoseria* volume and to culminate in *Ferishtah's Fancies* in 1884. It is not known where Browning read or heard this story. A version of it—with different names but essentially the same in point and moral—appeared in Rollo Springfield's book, *The Horse and his Rider; or Sketches and Anecdotes of the Noble Quadruped* (1847):

A Bedouin, named Jabal, possessed a mare of great celebrity. Hassad Pacha, the governor of Damascus, wished to buy the animal, and repeatedly made the owner the most liberal offers, which Jabal steadily refused. The pacha then had recourse to threats, but with no better success. At length one Jafar, a Bedouin of another tribe, presented himself to the pacha, and asked what he would give the man who would make him master of Jabal's mare. "I will fill his horse's nose-bag with gold," replied Hassad, whose pride and covetousness had been irritated to the highest degree by the obstinacy of the mare's owner. The result of this interview having gone abroad, Jabal became more watchful than ever; and always secured his mare at night with an iron chain, one end of which was fastened round her hind fetlock, whilst the other, after passing through the tent cloth, was attached to a picket driven into the ground under the felt that served himself and his wife for a bed. But one midnight Jafar crept into the tent, and insinuating his body between Jabal and his wife, he pressed gently now against the one, now against the other, so that the sleepers made room for him right and left, neither of them doubting that the pressure came from the other. This being done, Jafar slit the felt with a sharp knife, drew out the picket, loosed the mare, and sprang on her back. Just before starting off with his prize, he caught up Jabal's lance, and poking him with the butt end, cried out, "I am Jafar! I have stolen your noble mare, and I give you notice in time." This warning, be it observed, was in accordance with the usual practice of the Desert on such occasions; to rob a hostile tribe is considered an honorable exploit, and the man who accomplishes it is desirous of all the glory that may flow from the deed. Poor Jabal, when he heard the words, rushed out of the tent and gave the alarm; then mounting his brother's mare, and accompanied by some of his tribe, he pursued the robber for four hours. The brother's mare was of the same stock as Jabal's, but was not equal to her; nevertheless, she outstripped those of all the other pursuers, and was even on the point of overtaking the robber, when Jabal shouted to him, "Pinch her right ear, and give her a touch of the heel." Jafar did so, and away went the mare like lightning, speedily rendering all other pursuit hopeless. The *pinch in the ear* and the *touch with the heel* were the secret signs by which Jabal had been used to urge the mare to her utmost speed. Every Bedouin trains the animals he rides to obey some sign of this kind, to which he has recourse only on urgent occasions, and which he makes a close secret, not to be divulged even to his son. Jabal's comrades were amazed and indignant at this strange conduct; "O thou father of a jackass!" they cried, "thou hast helped the thief to rob thee of thy jewel!" But he silenced their upbraidings, by saying, "I would rather lose her than sully her reputation. Would you have me suffer it to be said among the tribes, that another mare had proved fleeter than mine? I have at least this comfort left me, that I can say she never met with her match." (pp. 199–201.)

There is no external evidence to indicate that Browning knew Springfield's version of the story, but the likeness is so great that one is inclined to think that he did. The Arabian names and details are chiefly fictitious and a number of them seem to be of Browning's coining; but they are included to give the poem the verisimilitude of an Arabian idyl. For example, the name "Muléykeh" Browning took to be Arabian for "pearl"; it properly is the diminutive for "queen." The name "Hóseyn" signifies "one who is constantly occupied with a horse." The poem has generally been considered an excellent piece of pure narrative.

Pietro of Abano

Pietro of Abano was the fourth poem in the Second Series of *Dramatic Idyls*, 1880. It consisted of 444 lines of verse and two of music, divided into fifty-five stanzas of eight lines each and one stanza of four lines, and the music. There was attached to the poem the note in which Browning referred to his old friend Father Prout (Francis Mahony), and quoted his translation of four lines from Pietro. In the final collected edition the poem was reprinted as it first appeared, save for a few verbal changes. The manuscript shows that *Pietro of Abano* was more worked over by Browning than any other idyl. It was dated January 20, 1880, and therefore was the first of the Second Series to be written.

The story of Pietro had long been familiar to Browning. In a letter to Elizabeth Barrett on February 9, 1846, he had said,

Poor dear wonderful persecuted Pietro d'Abano wrote this quatrain on the people's plaguing him about his mathematical studies and wanting to burn him—he helped to build Padua Cathedral, wrote a Treatise on Magic still extant, and passes for a conjuror in his country to this day—when there is a storm the mothers tell the children that he is in the air; his pact with the evil one obliged him to drink no *milk;* no natural human food!

Browning then gives Pietro's quatrain and his own translation of it. Elizabeth Barrett tried her hand at translation, and so did Father Prout when Browning showed the quatrain to him in 1848 in Florence.[4]

It is probable that Browning was again reminded of Pietro in his travels through northern Italy in 1878 and 1879. At Padua he would have seen the tablet commemorating the great physician and magician in the wall of the sacristy of the Church of the Eremitani; at Abano itself he would have seen the fountain into which Tiberius threw, at the advice of the Oracle of Geryon, the golden dice, as Suetonius relates in his *Lives of the Caesars* (*Tiberius,* XIV), a fact to which Browning refers at the end of his poem. Travelling the familiar country after many years of absence, and hearing again the folk-tales about the medieval scientist, Browning was inspired to write a poem about him. He had seen Pietro's great work, *Conciliator differentiarum quae inter philosophos et medicos versantur,* published in Venice in 1470 (see the poem, ll. 419–20), and had possibly seen Pietro's manuscripts preserved in the Library of St. Mark's in Venice.

But when he returned to London in the fall of 1879 he seems to have consulted the *Biographie universelle,* an old familiar sourcebook for him, for the facts of Pietro's life. All the variants of Pietro's name which Browning tried in his own manuscript of the poem before he selected the present one are suggested in the *Biographie,* and there is given the account of the life which Browning seems to have followed. The *Biographie* says that Pietro of Abano, or Petrus de Apono or Aponensis, was born in 1250 [really in 1246]. At an early age he went to Padua to study medicine, and later to Constantinople to study Greek, and later still, to Paris to study philosophy. He returned to Padua as professor of medicine, with a tremendous reputation as a magician as well. He was brought before the Inquisition in 1306; one of the charges against him was that he had power over gold. No person who was paid by Pietro could keep the money; however

---

[4] See *Letters,* ed. Hood, p. 201. See also F. S. Mahony, *The Reliques of Father Prout,* 1873, pp. iv–v.

safely it was guarded, it always flew back into the purse of the magician. As a physician he was noted also for the extremely high fees which he charged for his cures. In 1306 Pietro defended himself successfully from the Inquisition, but towards the end of his life he was apprehended again and condemned to be burnt. He died in 1316 [1320] before the sentence could be executed. One legend concerning the magician Browning makes good use of: that Pietro, probably because of his pact with the devil, fell into a fainting-fit at the sight of milk or cheese.

The legend of the Greek who came to Pietro to win from him the secret of getting forward in the world does not occur in the account of Pietro's life. To illustrate Pietro's character as a magician Browning has grafted upon the account of his life this entirely different legend, a medieval Spanish one told in the *Libro de Patronio* or *El Conde Lucanor* (1335) by Don Juan Manuel. It is retold in the English translation of Dr. James York, called *Count Lucanor, or The Fifty Pleasant Tales of Patronio*, and published in 1868. The twelfth tale is an account "Of that which happened to a Dean of Santiago, with Don Illan, the Magician, who lived at Toledo." The story is too long for quotation, but since it is probably Browning's source, I give a condensed account of it.

The Dean of Santiago calls on Don Illan, the magician, at his house in Toledo in the hope of learning magic from the master in order to improve his position in the world. It is just after mid-day, and Don Illan calls to his maid and tells her to procure some partridges for their dinner. Then the two men converse for a while, and gradually we see in a vision the career of the Dean as he is aided by the magic of Don Illan. The Dean rises to be a bishop, a cardinal, and finally Pope. At each stage Don Illan as a former benefactor of the great man appeals for some small favor, until the Pope finally threatens the magician with the papal prisons as a heretic and a sorcerer. The Dean's sweet dream of power is ended as Don Illan calls out to his housekeeper that he will eat the partridges himself and that his guest will not stay for dinner. The Dean awakes to find that he still has his way to make in the world without the aid of Don Illan's magic.

The story is also told in a letter of Connop Thirlwall to a friend on August 24, 1866.[5] Though the letter was not published until 1881, Browning was acquainted with Thirlwall, and may well have heard the story from him. In some respects Browning's version is nearer to Thirlwall's than it is to York's. In Browning's story, as in Thirlwall's,

---

[5] Connop Thirlwall, *Letters to a Friend*, ed. A. P. Stanley, 1881, pp. 77–9. This was first suggested as a source by Miss Charlotte Porter in *Poet Lore* 3:577.

the applicant to the magician is a young student, but in most respects the stories of York and Thirlwall agree. The power to see into the characters of the men who deal with them, and by means of a dream to see the probable behavior of those they have benefited, was supposed to be a common attribute of those who dealt with the devil. In Browning's poem Pietro sees projected the whole career of the young Greek, as he rises from obscurity to the papal throne, in the instant that it takes to pronounce the two parts of the word *"benedicite."*

Though it is obvious that Browning took considerable pleasure in writing *Pietro of Abano,* few critics have found as much delight in reading it. The observation of his biographers, Griffin and Minchin, is just: "He was not a good judge of his own work, and appeared to lose, at times, his sense of beauty. His very facility of rhyming, in which he took great delight, sometimes proved a pitfall, as (to take the very worst example) in *Pietro of Abano*." [6] It was the opinion of Dowden that neither "the jest [n]or the frankly cynical moral of *Pietro of Abano* compensates for the jolting in a springless waggon over a rough road and a long." [7] The music attached to the poem is probably Browning's own.

Doctor ——

Doctor —— was the fifth poem in the Second Series of *Dramatic Idyls* in 1880. It consisted of 259 lines, divided into eighty-six stanzas of *terza rima*. The stanzaic form is a regular three-line one until the last two, where a rearrangement is made for the sake of concluding. Save for a few changes made for the sake of meter and punctuation, the poem was reprinted as it stood, in the final collected edition of 1888–9. In the manuscript the poem is dated as finished on March 10, 1880.

A search has not revealed the source of the poem, and we must take for truth Browning's words, "the Rabbi told it me." [8] The story is probably founded on Jewish oral legend, invented as an embroidery

---

[6] *Life,* p. 303.

[7] *The Life of Robert Browning,* Everyman's Library, p. 350. For articles on the poem see Furnivall on the *Dramatic Idyls, Second Series,* in the *Browning Society's Papers,* I, 10* ff., and the paper by J. Sharpe read before the Browning Society on November 25, 1881 (I, 191–7). For a good account of Pietro, see A. H. Thorndike, *Pietro of Abano.*

[8] See Judith Berlin-Lieberman, *Robert Browning and Hebraism,* Jerusalem, 1934, pp. 81–2.

upon the text in *Ecclesiastes,* 7:26: "And I find more bitter than death the woman, whose heart is snares and nets, and her hands as bands: whoso pleaseth God shall escape from her; but the sinner shall be taken by her." The proverb made from this text, "A bad wife is stronger than death," is tested and found true in *Doctor* —— when Satan, or Death, deserts the sick-bed of the Emperor as his own wife enters.

The story as Browning tells it is a mere *jeu d'esprit;* the jest is too poor and the manner of treatment is not light enough for the poem to be thoroughly pleasurable. It has been justly said that only Chaucer could have made great literature of the story. The subject forecasts Browning's use of Hebraic lore in *Jocoseria,* his next volume. The idyllic element in the poem is negligible, except that the story seems to be Jewish folk-lore.

Pan and Luna

Pan and Luna was, save for the brief epilogue, the concluding poem of the Second Series of *Dramatic Idyls* in 1880. It consisted of thirteen stanzas of eight lines each, 104 lines in all. In the final collected edition of 1888–9 the poem was reprinted as it stood, except for the correction in the spelling of the word "valleys." The poem, considerably worked over, is dated as finished on April 9, 1880.

Several things led Browning to deal with this legend of Pan entrapping Luna, the moon-goddess, in the mountains of Arcadia, where Pan was chiefly worshipped. Browning's success in treating Pan in *Pheidippides*—a legend that he liked so well that he offered it to his son as a subject for a painting—was a major factor. Pan had been a figure of great interest to Mrs. Browning, and she had written some of her best lyrics upon him, such as *A Musical Instrument* and *The Dead Pan.* It may have been to honor Pan for her sake that the poem was written. Three lines from Virgil's *Georgics* (III, 391-3) gave Browning the hint for his poem, and other material from the third *Georgic* was used. In giving advice to farmers concerning sheep, Virgil said,

If wool be your care, first clear away the prickly growth of burs and caltrops; shun rich pastures, and from the first choose flocks with white, soft fleeces. But the ram, however white be his fleece, if he have but a black tongue under his moist palate, cast out, lest with dusky spots he tarnish the coats of the new-born lambs; and look about for another in your teem-

ing field. 'Twas with gift of such snowy wool, if we may trust the tale, that
Pan, Arcadia's god, charmed and beguiled thee, O Moon, calling thee to
the depths of the woods; nor didst thou scorn his call.
—*Georgics* III, 384–93 (Tr. Fairclough).

The concluding lines are those which gave Browning the suggestion
for his delicate and fanciful poem. To Virgil the legend was an attempt by men of olden times to explain the first eclipse of the moon.

As we may see in *One Word More*, the *Epilogue* to *Ferishtah's
Fancies*, the *Parleying With Daniel Bartoli* and elsewhere, the moon
to Browning was always, after 1855, a symbol for his wife, Elizabeth
Barrett Browning. It is possible that in *Pan and Luna* Browning
meant to hint biography—to recall for himself in this exquisite legend
the brief happiness he had enjoyed with his wife. As an expression of
Browning's feeling about Elizabeth Barrett Browning in 1880, *Pan
and Luna* should be compared with *Numpholeptos* of 1876 and the
Prologue to *Ferishtah's Fancies* of 1884.

The poem, though little known, is much appreciated by a few.
Dowden says concerning it,

Browning's development of the Vergilian myth—"si credere dignum est"
—of Pan and Luna astonishes by its vehement sensuousness and its frank
chastity; and while the beauty of the Girl-moon and the terror of her
betrayal are realized with the utmost energy of imagination, we are made
to feel that all which happens is the transaction of a significant dream or
legend.[9]

"Touch Him Ne'er So Lightly . . ."

The untitled epilogue to the Second Series of *Dramatic Idyls*, 1880,
consisted of ten lines, divided into two stanzas, and was reprinted
without change in the collected edition of 1888–9. In the manuscript
the lines are undated, but the probability is that they were composed
after the main part of the volume was written. In the manuscript
Browning gave directions to the printer to set these lines in smaller
type than that used for the preceding poems, and this was done.

Many conjectures were made as to what poets Browning had in
mind—both for the lyrical poet who broke into song at the slightest
provocation and for the more deliberate poet who became "a nation's heritage." Shelley, Swinburne, and others were mentioned as
candidates for the first position; Tennyson, Milton, and Browning

---

[9] *Life of Robert Browning*, Everyman's Library, p. 352.

were suggested for the second. Concerning the nomination of himself as the "prophet-poet" of his nation—some of the critics supposed he meant to praise himself—Browning had something to say. In Venice in October, 1880, the poet re-wrote the lines in the album of Miss Edith Longfellow, daughter of the American poet, and added ten new lines, beginning "Thus I wrote in London," disclaiming the honor and asserting that Dante was the poet he had in mind as "a nation's heritage." [10] These verses have not been included in the collected editions of the poet's work published in England, but they appear in several American editions.

Whatever poets Browning had in mind, the lines "Touch him ne'er so lightly" constitute one of the most important of his later utterances upon the function of the poet and of poetry. They show his later conception of the poet as "prophet" rather than as singer, a conception that was very acceptable to the Victorian age. The lines should be compared and contrasted with other utterances by Browning, notably *Transcendentalism* and *How it Strikes a Contemporary* of 1855, and with his later doctrines in the *Parleyings With Christopher Smart* and *With Charles Avison*. The present age prefers by far Browning's earlier practice and theory. It is ironic that the first line of these verses, which describes the lyric poet rejected by Browning, should have been declared one of the best lines in all his poetry.

JOCOSERIA

PUBLICATION AND TEXT

Jocoseria was published on March 9, 1883. It had been almost three years since a volume by Browning had appeared. The book was post octavo, bound in dark red cloth boards, and sold for Five Shillings the copy. It consisted of a half-title; the title-page: "Jocoseria By Robert Browning London Smith, Elder, & Co., 15 Waterloo Place 1883"; a list of the contents; and the text, pp. 1–143. There was a separate fly-title for each of the ten poems. The list of contents was as follows:

Wanting is—what?	Solomon and Balkis
Donald	Cristina and Monaldeschi

[10] Browning was chagrined and angry when Miss Longfellow published his new lines in the *Century Magazine* for November, 1882 (pp. 159–60). See below, my discussion of these lines under "Thus I wrote in London."

Mary Wollstonecraft and Fuseli	Jochanan Hakkadosh
Adam, Lilith, and Eve	Never the Time and the Place
Ixion	Pambo

The manuscript of the poem is in the Balliol College Library.

GENESIS AND COMPOSITION

Concerning the title of this little volume of miscellaneous poems Browning wrote on March 10, 1883, to a friend,

. . . you will have received to-day, I hope, the little book with the Dutch-Latin title—taken, by an odd coincidence, from a little old rare book which my Father gave me so long ago, and which, to my amazement, was noticed at length in the "Blackwood" of last month—some three days after my own title had been announced.[1]

The little book which Browning had in mind was Otto Melander's *Jocoseria*, 1597, a collection of jests and anecdotes to which Browning had referred somewhat scornfully in a note to *Paracelsus*, "such rubbish as Melander's 'Jocoseria.' " In another letter, written to Furnivall on January 9, 1883, Browning had explained more fully the nature of his forthcoming book:

I have given, this afternoon, Smith my new book to print. It is a collection of things grav*ish* and gay*ish*—hence the title *Jocoseria*—which is Batavian Latin, I think. There are some eleven of these pieces, little and big; the main of them being the Deer-stalking poem, you remember, *Donald—Solomon and Balkis—Christina and Monaldeschi—Ixion—Mary Wollstonecraft and Fuseli*—and a long *Hakkadosch Jochanan*, a Rabbinical story; eleven pieces in all. May some morsels of this Olla Podrida take your taste! [2]

Since there were only ten poems in the published volume, there has been a good deal of speculation about the eleventh poem. The manuscript in the Balliol College Library is not helpful here, for the table of contents which Browning usually put at the beginning of his volumes is missing for *Jocoseria* and the manuscript itself includes only ten poems. But the question has now been settled, for among the new poems published by Sir F. G. Kenyon in the *Cornhill* in 1914 the missing poem appeared. It was entitled *Gerousios Oinos* (*q.v.*), and had been left out of the *Jocoseria* volume by Browning because he thought it better not to include such a contemptuous utterance upon the poets

---

[1] *Letters*, ed. Hood, p. 214.
[2] *Idem*, p. 213.

of his own time. It would have given much offence to many men whom Browning counted as friends.

It is not possible to say precisely when the poems of *Jocoseria* were written. On November 24, 1881, Browning wrote to MacColl of the *Athenaeum*, "I have written a poem or two, certainly, which may or may not go into a new volume of Idyls,—but whenever a volume of any sort there *is*—ready for press—I shall send exclusively to the 'Athenaeum' the particulars. . . ." [3] But by this date *Jocoseria* was not at all in a forward state of preparation, for on December 12, 1881, Browning wrote, "I may print such few things as I have, along with others yet unwritten, in a new volume,—and probably shall do so— but there is nothing designed, much less accomplished." [4] In the manuscript only one poem is dated, *Jochanan Hakkadosh*, which was finished on December 22, 1882. Miss Frances Power Cobbe wrote Browning on October 21, 1882, that she was looking forward to his deer-stalking poem [*Donald*]. If Browning worked in his usual swift manner, most of the poems were the product of the late summer and fall of the year 1882, when the poet was at St. Pierre de Chartreuse, and later in London. It ought to be remembered, however, that he had published nothing for three years, and some of the poems are certainly of a slightly earlier date.

SOURCES AND INFLUENCES

There is little to say concerning the influences which affected Browning as he composed this small volume of miscellaneous poems. The subjects indicate the range and oddity of his erudition. Three of the ten are upon subjects drawn from rabbinical legend—*Solomon and Balkis, Adam, Lilith, and Eve*, and *Jochanan Hakkadosh*—and this of course indicates the direction of Browning's interest. His pleasure in Hebraic legend had first shown itself in *Holy-Cross Day* (1855) and had blossomed in *Abt Vogler* and *Rabbi Ben Ezra* (1864). In *Jocoseria* and perhaps, in a disguised form, in *Ferishtah's Fancies*, this interest of the poet's is most fully expressed. Two poems of *Jocoseria* are lyrics, *Wanting is—what?* and *Never the Time and the Place*. The other poems take the reader to the Greece of ancient legend, or modern Scotland, to France and England of the eighteenth century, and to Italy.

[3] *Idem*, p. 204.
[4] *Idem*, p. 206.

AFTER-HISTORY

To the surprise of Browning and his publisher the volume was very well received. On April 17, 1883, Browning wrote: "This little 'Jocoseria' (joking even in the title) has had the usual luck of the little-deserving,—got itself sold (as Carlyle would say) at the rate of 2000 very early, and is now reprinting." [5] The publisher, Smith, remarked to the poet, "Had you let me read 'Jocoseria' I would have printed 500 additional copies at once." [6] *Jocoseria* passed through two separate reprintings. The reviews of the volume, though generally appreciative, made strange havoc of *Jochanan Hakkadosh*. One old friend of the poet's was not delighted with *Jocoseria.* Domett wrote in his diary: "It is questionable whether the poet would not have gained more admiration as well as given more pleasure had he condescended to attract the vast numbers his obscurity repels, by 'completing his incompletion' and letting his meaning 'pant through' the beauty of his poem a little more decidedly and distinctly." [7]

Wanting Is—What?

This small untitled poem of fifteen lines served as prologue to the *Jocoseria* volume, 1883. In the final collected edition of 1888–9 it is reprinted without change, save that the word "spot" in line four was changed to "blot." There is no indication of the date of composition.

The poem expresses succinctly Browning's conception of the emptiness of the world without the presence of human love. It is an exquisite lyric, showing the delightful faculty that still existed in the old poet in spite of much "mere grey argument." It has been the subject of many parodies, notably one by Swinburne.[8] Lines from this poem were quoted under A. W. Hunt's picture, called "A North Country Stream," when it was exhibited by the Royal Academy in 1883.[9]

[5] *Idem,* p. 218.
[6] *Idem,* p. 226.
[7] Griffin and Minchin, *Life,* p. 273.
[8] See T. J. Wise, *A Browning Library,* 1930, p. 112.
[9] Graves, *The Royal Academy of Arts: A Complete Dictionary* . . . *1769–1904,* IV, 196.

Donald

Donald was the first long poem of the *Jocoseria* volume, 1883. It consisted of fifty-nine stanzas of four lines each, 236 lines in all. In the final collected edition of 1888–9, the poem was reprinted without change. Concerning *Donald*, Browning wrote to a friend describing what he calls

. . . an old peculiarity in my mental digestion—a long and obscure process. There comes up unexpectedly some subject for poetry, which has been dormant, and apparently dead, for perhaps dozens of years. A month since I wrote a poem of some two hundred lines about a story I heard more than forty years ago, and never dreamed of trying to repeat, wondering how it had so long escaped me; and so it has been with my best things.[10]

The phrase, "a month since," dates the poem as being written at St. Pierre in August, 1882, when possibly the mountainous paths called up a situation of a story he had heard long before. That Browning got no pleasure in destroying birds and animals is well known; he had expressed himself against vivisection in *Tray*. He had a penchant for making friends with animals. Writing to Isa Blagden from Scotland in 1871, he had expressed his disgust at hunters, and hardly cared for the sport even when his son took it up and shot his stag: "Pen has got what he wanted," he wrote from Rosshire in August, 1869, "shooting and deer-stalking: he began operations the day before yesterday and much to his credit as a hunter, shot a splendid stag—'royal': the head of which will glorify his rooms at Ch[rist] Ch[urch]." [11] It is probable that Browning witnessed in Scotland, when his son was one of the undergraduate sportsmen at the hunting-lodge, just such a scene as he describes at the beginning of *Donald*.

Mrs. Orr asserts that the story of the poem was told to Browning by one who had heard it from the hero.[12] It is likely that Browning authorized her assertion—at least he read it and did not correct it. But the story had been told in prose by Sir Walter Scott in *The Keepsake*, an annual, for 1832. Strangely enough, Scott tells the story as having been heard by himself in his boyhood from the hero of the tale. Scott's hero is named Duncan. Browning possibly read the story

---

[10] Quoted by Mrs. Katherine deKay Bronson, "Browning in Venice," in *Century Magazine* 63:574–5 (February, 1902).

[11] *Dearest Isa*, ed. McAleer, p. 322; see also pp. 363, 365, 367, 383, 385.

[12] Orr, *Handbook*, p. 322.

in *The Keepsake* and forgot where he had encountered it, or confused the circumstances with those of another story. It is certain that
he did not have Sir Walter's version by him when he wrote *Donald*.

The versions given by Scott and Browning, though alike in essentials, differ interestingly. Sir Walter has far more sympathy for the
mountaineer than does Browning, but he comes to a similar conclusion: "I could never approve Duncan's conduct towards the deer
in a moral point of view," he says; but he adds, "but the temptation
of a hart of grease, offering, as it were, his throat to the knife, would
have subdued the virtue of almost any deer-stalker." And earlier,
Scott gives details which make Duncan's action slightly less repre-
hensible. Duncan had gone across the mountain in search of lost
sheep, and the reason given for the man's failure to retreat was not
daring, but a knowledge that if he turned back the stag would be
upon him instantly. The deer was about to charge Duncan when he
thought of the expedient. The stag came, not trustingly as in Browning's poem, but with extreme caution, and Duncan, in Scott's version,
caught the deer by the horn as it approached and did not have the
opportunity to use his dirk, which he had drawn. Obviously, Browning has attempted to give greater moral point to his story.

Solomon and Balkis

Solomon and Balkis followed *Donald* as the third poem in *Jocoseria*, 1883. It consisted of fifteen stanzas of four lines each, sixty lines
in all, and in the final collected edition it was reprinted without
change. The poem is undated in the manuscript, but it was probably
written at St. Pierre de Chartreuse or in London in the summer or fall
of 1882.

The poem, like *Doctor* —— in *Dramatic Idyls*, Second Series, and
like *Jochanan Hakkadosh* in *Jocoseria*, is drawn from rabbinical lore.
The basis of the situation in *Solomon and Balkis* is the visit paid by
Balkis, Queen of Sheba, to King Solomon, as described in *I Kings*
10:2, and *II Chronicles* 9:1. About this visit many Jewish, Moham-
medan, and the Arabian legends arose.[13] These legends were full of
examples of Solomon's wit and wisdom in proving himself to be the
wisest man in the world: he guessed the sex of 500 youths and maid-
ens by observing how they washed their hands; he settled the ques-

[13] See Judith Berlin-Lieberman, *Robert Browning and Hebraism,* Jerusalem,
1934, pp. 77–80.

tion as to which of the flowers before him were artificial, which real, by opening the window to let the bees' instinct guide him; he answered all of the queen's riddles and propounded some which were beyond her ability to solve. In short he proved himself to be as wise as he had been reported.

It is impossible to say at present what Browning read in the Talmudic legends, but the conversation in the poem has some basis in legend, as also does the conclusion, however much it is in the mood of the poet in 1883: Solomon, for all his wisdom, forced by the Name upon the ring to speak truth, admits that vanity more than wisdom is his care; and Balkis under the same compulsion admits that for all her love of culture, she has come to the court to be loved by Solomon. Solomon's vanity and Balkis' amorousness are, however, from Hebrew legend. Indeed, the word Balkis, derived from an Arabic source, means concubine. The "Name" is the "ineffable Name" which Browning had used in association with Solomon in *Abt Vogler*. A similar humanizing of the motives of the two characters is seen in Edward Fitz-Gerald's poetic translation of the Persian Jami's *Salāman and Absal;* but while Balkis' motive is the same in both poets, in FitzGerald's treatment Solomon's motive is avarice rather than vanity. In his poem, *Adam, Lilith, and Eve,* Browning makes the lightning produce the same sort of truth-telling that the "Name" upon the ring does here.

Cristina and Monaldeschi

Cristina and Monaldeschi followed *Solomon and Balkis* in *Jocoseria,* 1883. It consisted of eighteen stanzas of eight lines each, 144 lines in all; and save for the change of "love" to "love's" in the last line of stanza 12, the poem was reprinted in the final collected edition without change. There is no indication in the manuscript as to its date of composition, but the poem was probably written during the late summer or fall of 1882. In going to St. Pierre de Chartreuse Browning necessarily passed through Paris, as he had done each year for a number of years, and it was his custom to stop in Paris for a week or more on his journey home. He knew the environs of the city well, and it is altogether probable that Browning heard or read there the story of the murder of Monaldeschi by Christina on November 10, 1657, at the palace of Fontainebleau, thirty-five miles southeast of Paris. There are other possibilities, however, as C. N. Wenger has shown.[14]

[14] C. N. Wenger, "Clio's Rights in Poetry: Browning's *Cristina and Monaldeschi,*" in *PMLA* 60:256–70 (1945).

Mrs. Anna Jameson, close friend of the Brownings, had dealt with the career of Christina in her *Memoirs of Celebrated Female Sovereigns* in 1832, and in 1880 the Lothian prize essay, won by Arthur Henry Harding of Balliol College, was on *Queen Christina of Sweden*. Browning as an Honorary Fellow of the College may have received the printed copy of this essay at the time. If so, he may have been reminded of a story he had heard or read some time earlier, concerning Christina. To Mrs. Jameson and Harding the Monaldeschi incident is a political one and not, as Browning treats it, a crime of passion.

The poem is founded upon the historical fact of Christina's execution of Monaldeschi. Christina—-Browning changed the spelling to Cristina—was born in 1626, the daughter of Gustavus Adolphus, King of Sweden. She succeeded her father to the royal power in 1644. In 1654 she abdicated in favor of her cousin, Charles Augustus, and spent the rest of her life in travelling about Europe and in living at Rome, where she joined the Roman Church. She died in 1689. She was learned, extravagant, and brilliant.

Upon her second visit to France in 1657, she was given apartments in the palace of Fontainebleau, built first by Louis VII in 1162 as a fortress, converted into a palace of great magnificence by Francis I, and added to by Henry IV, Napoleon I, and Louis XVIII. Here it was that Henry II had kept his favorite mistress, Diana of Poitiers, who according to rumor became the mistress of Francis I. Cristina in the beginning of the poem assumes the rumor to be true. The crescent moon was, of course, the emblem of Diana of Poitiers, and the salamander was the figure of Francis. In the poem Browning makes Cristina, speaking to her faithless lover Monaldeschi, refer ironically to the faithful love of Francis and Diana.

The Marquis Gian Rinaldi Monaldeschi was the Grand Equerry to Queen Christina and, according to the gossips of the time, her lover. The queen was suspicious of Monaldeschi before her arrival in Fontainebleau. She had him watched, intercepted his letters, and had good reason to believe that he had not only betrayed her interests, but that he planned to fasten his own guilt on another member of her court. She put the sealed packet of intercepted letters in the hands of Father le Bel, Prior of the Maturins, and swore him to secrecy. On November 10, she summoned Monaldeschi to the *Galerie des Cerfs* and there before Father le Bel and the three guardsmen she charged him with treason. When Monaldeschi protested that the letters were only copies made by the queen herself, she produced the originals and forced him to acknowledge them. His courage failed him and he begged for pardon and mercy. Christina listened to him for an hour, and then turned him over to Father le Bel to be shriven before the guards should kill him. At this point she left the gallery and remained in her room throughout the events which followed. Upon Monaldeschi's further pleas, the priest and the chief of the guards went to the queen to beg for clemency, but she refused to relent. When the guardsmen tried to kill him, they found that he was wearing a coat of mail, so they decapitated him. Christina told Father le Bel to dispose of the corpse and sent money to the Father's convent for prayers for Monaldeschi's soul. Monaldeschi was buried in the church at Avon, a village near the Park of Fontainebleau, and the coat of mail that he was wearing at the time of his execution was hung in the *Galerie des Cerfs*. There was official and public disapproval of Christina's action, but no action was taken against her, except that she was treated coldly by the court. After about three and a half months the queen went to Paris, and shortly thereafter to Rome.

A *Relation* of the execution of Monaldeschi was published by the court of Queen Christina.[15] Browning had probably read this account, or some of the many accounts derived from it, before he wrote his poem. Browning, however, follows rumor and makes the assassination of Monaldeschi a crime of passion on the part of the queen, in anger at the unfaithfulness of her lover. The *Relation* states that Monaldeschi came alone to the *Galerie des Cerfs*, and was already with the queen when the priests and guardsmen arrived. Browning's account of Christina leading her victim through Diane's gallery is poetic fiction, as is his account of her presence at the execution, among other details. The poet has dealt very freely indeed with history. The calmness of the queen after the murder is comparable to the calmness of Ivàn Ivànovitch in striking down the unnatural mother; in both instances the victims are executed summarily, without benefit of a genuine trial.

C. N. Wenger, in the article referred to above, raises the important question concerning the right of poets and their commentators to deal so freely with historical events. "Are authentic sources obligatory," he asks, "in the case of historically based poems? What are the limits of their license?" It is a pertinent question in Browning's case—and per-

---

[15] The *Relation* in justification of Christina's act may be seen in Arckenholtz, *Memoires concernant Christine, Reine de Suede*, Amsterdam, 1751, II, 3–4; see also 5–9.

haps also in Shakespeare's—two poets among others who dealt extensively with history. It is clearly the duty of the commentator, I think, to recognize the facts of the case in question, as well as the poet's handling of the facts.

Mary Wollstonecraft and Fuseli

Mary Wollstonecraft and Fuseli was the fifth poem in *Jocoseria*, 1883, where it consisted of three stanzas of ten lines each. The poem was reprinted, practically as it stood, in the final collected edition of 1888–9. There is no date for the poem in the manuscript. Probably Browning was reminded of Mary Wollstonecraft, the mother of Mary Godwin Shelley, by his stay in Venice in October, 1881; and further associations to prompt the writing of the poem were supplied in the summer and fall of 1882, by the country around St. Pierre de Chartreuse, where Shelley had been more than sixty years earlier.

The subject of Browning's poem is the unrequited passion of Mary Wollstonecraft (1759–97) for the artist and writer upon art, Henry Fuseli (1741–1825). In the Browning library there were copies of both Fuseli's books, *Lectures on Painting* and the *History of Arts*. Mary Wollstonecraft was a brilliant and attractive woman, author of *The Rights of Women*, a follower of Rousseau, and a holder of very unorthodox ideas upon marriage. She first lived with Gilbert Imlay in 1793, and later with William Godwin, whom she married in 1797. She did not long survive the birth of her daughter Mary, who was to be the second wife of Shelley and to be well known to all students of literature for her character and abilities.

Henry Fuseli (1741–1825) was born in Zurich, Switzerland, but left that country for England in 1763. He supported himself by writing but was persuaded by Sir Joshua Reynolds to devote himself to art. He was successful in that profession, especially as a painter of Shakespearean subjects, and was admitted to the Royal Academy in 1790. He became professor of painting at the Academy in 1799. He was famous for his biting wit, and his crushing retorts.[16]

In 1883 Browning's friend and admirer, Lytton (Owen Meredith) published *The Life, Letters and Literary Remains of Edward Bulwer, Lord Lytton, by his Son,* in which there were anecdotes about Fuseli. Possibly this work sent Browning to a book which was in his library,

---

[16] Mr. Curtis Dahl has permitted me to see his forthcoming article in *MLN*, in which he connects Fuseli with Browning's poem, *Ben Karshook's Wisdom* (*q.v.*).

John Knowles's *Life and Writings of Fuseli* which was Item 696 in the *Browning Collections*. In Knowles's *Life* Browning would have read of Mary Wollstonecraft's infatuation for Fuseli. Knowles represents her as being passionate and importunate in her love. He asserts that she went to Mrs. Fuseli and begged that she might become a member of the Fuseli family in order to be near the man who was the object of her passion. Mrs. Fuseli drove her from the house. In his *Memoirs* (1798) of his wife, Godwin admits her infatuation for Fuseli but describes it in much less passionate terms. Later biographers of Mary Wollstonecraft and Godwin have repudiated the story as false, and have reduced Mary's love for Fuseli to a warm friendship.[17] In the poem she is represented as the speaker.

Adam, Lilith, and Eve

Adam, Lilith, and Eve was the sixth poem in *Jocoseria*, 1883. It consisted of four stanzas of six lines each, and in the final collected edition of 1888–9 it was reprinted without change. There is nothing in the manuscript to indicate the date of composition, but it probably owes its existence to the summer or fall of 1882. It is in the mood of the other poems written at this time.

The poem is a brief study of a situation between two women and a man. One woman, Lilith, is the woman the man, Adam, might have married; the other woman, Eve, is the woman he did marry. Under the fear of the lightning they confess the true state of their emotions towards him years ago. The lightning has the same truth-compelling power as the seal upon Solomon's ring in *Solomon and Balkis*. Lilith would have succumbed to Adam's passion, had he pressed it; Eve would have fled from him at the altar if the man she loved had appeared. When the fear passes from them with the passing of the storm, they turn their confessions to jest.

The situation in the poem is a timeless one, and Browning meant it to appear so when he gave his characters general names. Only the name "Lilith," perhaps, suggests the direction of his recent interest in Hebrew legend, which showed itself also in *Jochanan Hakkadosh* and in *Solomon and Balkis*. Because one account of the creation, in *Genesis*, 2:21–4, asserted that man was created some time before

---

[17] See C. Kegan Paul, *Wm. Godwin, His Friends and Contemporaries,* London, 1876, I, 206–8.

woman, the Talmudic legend [18] explained that before Eve Adam had a wife who was shut out of Eden when she became wilful and proud. Lilith then became a demon and married the devil, by whom she had innumerable progeny. Only the names, however, are used by Browning in the poem.

Ixion

Ixion was the seventh poem in the *Jocoseria* volume, 1883. It consisted of 124 lines in an adaptation of the classical elegiac meter, unrhymed. Save for the change of "my kind" in line 97 to "mankind," the poem was reprinted in the final collected edition of 1888–9 without change. There is no indication of the date of composition in the manuscript, but the probability is that the poem was written during the late summer or early fall of 1882 at St. Pierre de Chartreuse.

The legend of Ixion is referred to in the *Odyssey* (XXI, 303) and again in Virgil's *Georgics* (III, 38; IV, 484). It is my opinion that Browning was led from the legend of Pan which he had used in *Pan and Luna* in the Second Series of *Dramatic Idyls*, to look further in the *Georgics*, where he hit upon the well-known tale of Ixion's crime and punishment. Browning did not use the complete story. According to the legend Ixion was the king of the Phlegyae, and married the daughter of Deianeus. When Deianeus demanded the wedding gifts which he had been promised, Ixion treacherously invited him to a banquet, and caused him to fall through a trap into a pit of fire. The gods were horrified at Ixion for this ghastly murder, and none would cleanse him of it until at last Zeus performed the rite. When Zeus invited Ixion to his table, the mortal made love to Heré, the Queen of Olympus. Zeus foiled Ixion by an apparition of Heré who bore a centaur instead of a child to him. For Ixion's want of gratitude he was chained hand and foot to a fiery wheel which rolled through the air of Hades. In addition to this punishment Ixion was scourged and made to repeat constantly, "Benefactors should be honored."

Browning has left out the earlier crime of Ixion and his purification by Zeus, and has begun where the mortal sat at the table of the gods —as an equal, says Browning. The poet has reduced the double treachery of Ixion to the mere human frailty of loving where he

[18] See Judith Berlin-Lieberman, *Robert Browning and Hebraism*, Jerusalem, 1934, pp. 83–4.

should not have dared to love. Browning's real object in *Ixion* is to set himself squarely, once and for all, against the belief in perpetual vindictive punishment by the gods.[19] The belief in Hell, which had subsided greatly in the eighteenth century, again became prevalent with the rise of the evangelical sects in the nineteenth century; and Browning, though an evangelical believer himself, could not tolerate the idea of eternal punishment. Therefore in *Ixion* Browning voices the revolt of an outraged humanity, in the manner of Shelley in *Prometheus Unbound*, against the heartless decree of the tyrant. It was a cause for which Browning was to speak again in *A Camel-Driver* (*Ferishtah's Fancies*, 1884), and for which he had already spoken indirectly in lines 1732-91 of *The Inn Album*, 1875. John Stuart Mill had been of the same opinion, and said that rather than obey an immoral supreme power "to Hell will I go." In this respect, as in others, Browning was not an orthodox evangelical Christian. Ixion, like Prometheus, predicts the downfall of such an immoral power, for righteousness is an eternal law, and stronger than vindictive Zeus.

The poem has been well elucidated by J. T. Nettleship in his *Essays and Thoughts*. Before its publication Browning read *Ixion* to Furnivall, and was profoundly affected as he read. It has been the general opinion of later critics that the poem is the greatest in the *Jocoseria* volume, and with the lyrics goes a considerable way towards redeeming the book from colorlessness and lightness.

Jochanan Hakkadosh

Jochanan Hakkadosh was the eighth and by far the longest poem in the *Jocoseria* volume, 1883. It consisted of 801 lines, divided into 267 stanzas in *terza rima;* the stanzas are linked together by rhyme. In the manuscript the poem proper is dated as finished on December 22, 1882. The note and the three appended sonnets follow below the date, and were probably written soon afterwards. In the manuscript Browning has directed the printer, "Print these sonnets in a smaller type, after the *Note*." The title of the poem in the manuscript was changed slightly and the words transposed on the advice of a Hebrew friend: in the manuscript it first read "Hagadosch Jochanan." In the subsequent reprint of *Jocoseria* the poem was unchanged, but Brown-

---

[19] See C. R. Tracy, "Browning's Heresies," in *Studies in Philology* 33:624 (1936).

ing made a few verbal changes for the final collected edition (ll. 339, 361, 427, 490, 704).

The poem shows strongly Browning's growing interest in rabbinical lore; the story is pieced together from many fragments,[20] but the controlling idea is his own. As early as the summer of 1864 Browning was reading the *Travels of Benjamin of Tudela* in a translation by the Rev. R. Gerrans (1784), for he recounts to Miss Wedgwood the story of Rabbi Perida which he uses in *Jochanan Hakkadosh*.[21] The story is laid at Schiphaz (Shearaz) in Persia. The word "Hakkadosh" means "holy," and was especially applied to Rabbi Jehudah I. Hannasi in recognition of his singularly moral life. The Rabbi of the poem bears a number of likenesses to him and his thoughts. Still Browning's Rabbi is a composite figure, made up from several Jochanans in Jewish history; probably Browning has chiefly in mind Jochanan ben Zakkai, the founder of Talmudic Judaism, a member of the Sanhedrin, who had a school in Jerusalem until the destruction of the city in 70 A. D. This Rabbi, according to Talmudic legend, lived to be 120 years old, with his career falling into three phases of forty years each. When he was about to die his life was prolonged by compassionate people who contributed periods of time to his life, for in him met all the Nine Points of Perfection. Writing to Furnivall on April 10, 1883, Browning says, "The whole story is a fiction of my own, with just this foundation, that the old Rabbins fancied that *earnest wishing* might add to a valued life." [22] Upon this conception Browning built his fancy that the beloved Rabbi Jochanan Hakkadosh, about to die at the age of seventy-nine, was granted an extension of fifteen months to his life by the gifts of life from five of his disciples, a lover, a warrior, a poet, a statesman, and an unnamed child. It is of course Browning's purpose to have the Rabbi conclude from each of the quarter-year extensions of his life that "ignorance confirmed by knowledge" is our proper state on earth, a favorite doctrine of Browning's in his later years.

It is the opinion of students of Hebrew that Browning's scholarly knowledge of Hebrew was small. "Hakkadosh," which means "the Holy," or "Saint," he put in the wrong position for idiomatic Hebrew in his first title. But his acquaintance with rabbinical lore was extensive if not profound, and throughout the poem he has interspersed

[20] See Judith Berlin-Lieberman, *Robert Browning and Hebraism,* Jerusalem, 1934, pp. 54–76. I am indebted to this study for much of the comment upon this poem.

[21] See *Robert Browning and Julia Wedgwood,* ed. Curle, pp. 41–2.

[22] *Letters,* ed. Hood, pp. 216–7.

Hebrew terms and facts from Jewish history—such as Mishna, "doctrine"; Halafta, the name taken by a number of expounders of the Talmud; and the ten martyrs under the emperor Hadrian, though as a result of his imperfect knowledge of Hebrew their names are not correctly given. Browning did all this, of course, to lend verisimilitude to an otherwise bald and unconvincing narrative, and for the same purpose he added the note at the end of the poem. The Hebrew treatise which there purports to be the poet's source has for its title, when it has been translated from its bad Hebrew, "A pack of many lies"; and the "pithy proverb" in the note which introduces the fantastic and ever-increasing wildness of the comparisons in the sonnets, has been rendered, "From Moses to Moses [*i.e.,* Moses Maimonides] arose none like Moses." The whole is, of course, pure mystification, though the legends of Og's bones and size are to be found in the Talmudic *Lügenmärchen* (*i.e.,* lying-tales). The legends concerning the giant Og rose from the reference to his iron bedstead in *Deuteronomy* 3:11.

The critics made very little of the poem upon its appearance. On April 10, 1883, Browning wrote to Furnivall:

I got an American paper, last night, wherein there is repeated that Jochanan revived by "a transfusion of blood." There is not a word about such a thing; on the contrary, the account in the poem makes it impossible. How could the "transfusion" bring experiences with it? or how could the boy's gift, "which he threw and it stuck," be taken in that manner? This comes of the critics reading attentively the criticisms of their brethren, and paying no attention at all to the text criticised. The writer of the article in *The Times* made the mistake first, and even the *Academy* article must needs follow him.[23]

It should be said for the critics that the poem is not one of the easiest to follow. Browning's main intention in the poem is to expound the favorite metaphysical doctrines of his old age—the superiority of the intuitive faculties over the intellectual ones in giving mankind a knowledge of God. Through the heart, rather than the head, man is able by a recognition of God's love to reconcile good and evil in life. In this respect *Jochanan Hakkadosh* takes its place with *La Saisiaz, Ferishtah's Fancies,* and the *Parleyings.* It has been the common opinion of later critics that while the poem expresses much of the matured wisdom of Browning the contents are insufficient to sustain the length.

[23] *Idem,* p. 216.

Never the Time and the Place

Never the Time and the Place, a lyric of twenty-two lines, was the ninth poem in *Jocoseria,* 1883. The text has remained unchanged in all later editions. In the manuscript the poem is not dated, but it was probably written in 1882, perhaps in May. The freshness and intensity of this charming lyric are reminiscent of Browning's love-poems of thirty to forty years earlier. The poem obviously refers with love and longing to the memory of Elizabeth Barrett Browning. The "enemy sly and serpentine" is time and change. In its form and success the poem allies itself with the other lyric in *Jocoseria, Wanting is—what? Never the Time and the Place* early gained recognition as one of the most exquisite of Browning's later lyrics. An admiring friend turned the poem into Latin hendecasyllabics, much to the poet's satisfaction.[24]

Pambo

Pambo, a poem of fifty-four lines in thirteen stanzas, served as epilogue to the *Jocoseria* volume, 1883. The text of the poem has been reprinted without change in succeeding editions. No date is appended to the manuscript, but presumably the poem was written between 1881 and 1883.

For the source of the little parable of Pambo, Browning went to a favorite book of his youth, Nathaniel Wanley's *Wonders of the Little World.* There in Book III, Ch. IV, under the heading, *Of the Veracity of Some Persons, and their great Love of Truth: and Hatred of Flattery and Falsehood,* he found this account of Pambo:

Pambo came to a learned man, and desired him to teach him some Psalm; he began to read to him the thirty-ninth, and the first verse, which is: 'I said, I will look to my ways, that I offend not with my tongue.' Pambo shut the book, and took his leave, saying, 'he would go learn that point.' And having absented himself for some months he was demanded by his teacher, 'when he would go forward?' He answered, 'That he had not yet learned his old lesson, to speak in such a manner as not to offend with his tongue.'

It is possible that Browning went on to the version of Pambo's story given by Socrates, the fifth-century historian of the church, in his *Ecclesiastical History,* Book IV, Ch. XXIII, to which Wanley referred

[24] *Idem,* p. 218.

the reader. In this version Pambo answers, when he is asked if he has mastered the verse of the psalm, "I have scarcely succeeded in accomplishing it during nineteen years." This is nearer Browning's phrase "Long years went by" than is Wanley's "some months," but Browning may well have made the period longer for the sake of the effect, without consulting Socrates' version.

Pambo has been called a brief and good-humored postscript to Browning's quarrel with his critics. The poem is in much better temper than those of the *Pacchiarotto* volume. Here Browning links himself with Pambo (*Arcades sumus ambo*); he has tried to look to his ways by the help of his critics, but like Pambo he has not yet learned the lesson of controlling his tongue. The reviewers of *Jocoseria* in general ignored Browning's "apology."

FERISHTAH'S FANCIES

Ferishtah's Fancies was published on November 21, 1884. The volume was post octavo, bound in olive-brown cloth boards, and sold for Five Shillings the copy. It consisted of a half-title, with mottoes from Jeremy Collier and Shakespeare's *King Lear* on the reverse; the title-page: "Ferishtah's Fancies By Robert Browning London Smith, Elder, & Co., 15 Waterloo Place 1884"; a list of the contents; and the text, pp. 1–143. The manuscript of the poem is in the Balliol College Library. The list of contents follows:

Prologue

Ferishtah's Fancies:

1. The Eagle	7. A Camel-Driver
2. The Melon-Seller	8. Two Camels
3. Shah Abbas	9. Cherries
4. The Family	10. Plot-Culture
5. The Sun	11. A Pillar at Sebzevah
6. Mihrab Shah	12. A Bean-Stripe: also Apple-Eating

Epilogue

The poem went through three editions; a second edition was called for in January of 1885, and another later in the same year; and it was of course included in the final collected edition of 1888–9. The text suffered a considerable number of changes in punctuation and word in succeeding editions; [1] the most notable was the addition of two lines to *The Melon-Seller*.

GENESIS AND COMPOSITION

The *Prologue* to *Ferishtah's Fancies* was dated from the Maison Delapierre, Gressoney St. Jean, Val d'Aosta, on September 12, 1883, and the *Epilogue* from the Palazzo Giustinian-Recanati, Venice, on December 1, 1883. It may be supposed that a good part of the volume was written during these two and one-half months; and this suspicion is partly confirmed by the manuscript, preserved in the Balliol College Library, in which *A Camel-Driver*, the seventh part of the poem, is dated September 23, 1883. But this was not entirely the case; the ninth part, now known as *Cherries*, was dated January 15, when Browning had probably returned to London, and the tenth, *Plot-Culture*, was dated January 17, 1884. We know also that the lyric which appears at the end of *Plot-Culture*, "Not with my Soul, Love!" was written late. It does not appear in the manuscript, but in its place is the poet's note, "(Leave room for a small poem's insertion here)." Furthermore, one may suspect the whole incident of *Apple-Eating* to be an addition to the twelfth part, made after Browning's return to London—partly from the numerous references therein to Persian matters and men which were probably not at hand to Browning in Italy, and partly from the state of the manuscript, where this incident (ll. 365–478) is inserted on pages numbered in a new series from 1 to 5, and at the end of page 5 appears Browning's instruction to the printer, "Go on to Epilogue p. 127." The lyric, "Why from the world," seems to be a late insertion between the text and the *Epilogue*. It is perhaps worthy of notice that in the course of writing the poem Browning changed his scheme of titles. He first had such titles for the various parts as *Belief, Incarnation, Pain, Gratitude;* the more whimsical titles of the printed volume came to him when he was three-quarters done.

With his sister Sarianna, Browning arrived at Gressoney, St. Jean, "a paradise of coolness and quiet" in the Italian Alps, in the latter part of August, 1883. It is possible that he had with him, already written, the first section of *Ferishtah*, called *The Eagle*. At any rate, at Gressoney there was little to do but walk, and it was here, I think, that the

---

[1] C. J. Lyall in a letter dated December 13, 1884, suggested a number of changes, chiefly in Persian names, for the second edition, most of which were adopted. See *Intimate Glimpses from Browning's Letter File*, in *Baylor University's Browning Interests*, Series Eight, 1934, pp. 100–1.

bulk of *Ferishtah* was written. By October 4 Browning was in Venice at the home of Mrs. Katherine Bronson. Mrs. Orr is authority for the statement [2] that the intercalary lyrics of *Ferishtah* were written on successive days, but this can hardly be true for all of them.

It was almost a year after the *Epilogue* was signed (December 1, 1883) that the volume was published. Probably this delay was advocated by the publishers to give the *Jocoseria* volume, published March 10, 1883, a chance to run its course, for it was doing well. The proofs were in Browning's hands early in September, 1884, and we hear again of *Ferishtah* in a letter from Browning to Furnivall on September 28, 1884. "I saw an advertisement, in last week's *Saturday Review,* of my new Poem—somewhat to my surprise, for there are reasons for keeping back the publication for at least a week or two. My part is done, however, and the last corrected 'proofs' are at the printers. I can't at all guess how people will like it, but I have managed to say a thing or two that I 'fancied' I should like to say." [3]

SOURCES AND INFLUENCES

According to Mrs. Orr the "idea of *Ferishtah's Fancies* grew out of a fable by Pilpay [Bidpai], which Mr. Browning read when a boy. He lately put this into verse; and it then occurred to him to make the poem the beginning of a series, in which a Dervish, who is first introduced as a learner, should reappear in the character of a teacher." [4] The edition of *The Fables of Pilpay* (Bidpai) which Browning read as a boy was probably the selection published anonymously in English in 1818. From Chapter II, Fable III of this book, "The Dervise, The Falcon, and the Raven," he took only his first part of *Ferishtah, The Eagle.* The other parables, homilies, or moral dialogues of *Ferishtah* are Browning's inventions. The stories and analogues are somewhat appropriate to Persia, where the scene is laid. For the Persian coloring of his poem Browning consulted, I think, not Firdusi's *Shah Nameh,* "The Book of Kings," for that poem was not available in its entirety in English, but instead Miss Helen Zimmern's *The Epic of Kings, Stories retold from Firdusi* (1882). Miss Zimmern was a friend of Browning's, and two other friends of the poet, Alma Tadema and Edmund Gosse, contributed to the volume. Browning received a copy of the book, in the preface of which Miss Zimmern had thanked him

---

[2] Orr, *Life,* p. 362.
[3] *Letters,* ed. Hood, p. 231.
[4] Orr, *Handbook,* p. 331.

(p. vii) for his encouragement and sympathy. Here are found the stories of the great heroes and the names of famous places which Browning uses in his poem. It is probable that Browning did not take the book to Gressoney with him. Most of his Persian references appear in the last 100 lines of *A Bean-Stripe: Also Apple-Eating*, which, as we have seen, he probably wrote in London with Miss Zimmern's book at hand, and inserted into the manuscript at a later time. Browning was perfectly aware of the thinness of the Persian disguise. "Do not suppose," he wrote a friend just before the publication of *Ferishtah*, "there is more than a thin disguise of a few Persian names and allusions. There was no such person as Ferishtah; and the stories are all inventions. The Hebrew quotations are put in for a purpose, as a direct acknowledgment that certain doctrines may be found in the Old Book which the Concocters of Novel Schemes of Morality put forth as discoveries of their own." [5] Ferishtah is hardly a disguise at all for Browning, and the whole is an ingenious device for giving the poet an opportunity once again to say his mind upon several moral and philosophical questions. In the opinion of C. R. Tracy, Browning is attacking some popular versions of Herbert Spencer's ideas upon historical Christianity.[6] Like the *Parleyings*, Browning's next volume, *Ferishtah* is a summary of his matured speculations. To each major part of *Ferishtah* there is attached a lyric expressing the idea of the section in terms of a love-lyric. Perhaps these are concessions which the philosopher in Browning makes to the poet.

AFTER-HISTORY

Ferishtah's Fancies was well received by the public and the reviews, considering the nature of the subject. On October 6, Browning had made arrangements to send to Barnett Smith, the critic of the *Times*, the final revises of the poem and an explanation of the Persian names.[7] Smith's review, a generally favorable one, appeared on November 18. Of all the reviews, that in the *Athenaeum* for December 6, 1884, was the fullest and most capable. A number of critics objected to the lack of dignity in the *Prologue*, and almost all complained that at times the preachment outweighed the poetry. Several noticed that Ferishtah occasionally forgets the land of his birth. The most serious charge against the volume was that Browning had attained too easily

[5] Nicoll and Wise, *Literary Anecdotes of the Nineteenth Century*, I, 470–1.
[6] "*Caliban upon Setebos*," in *Studies in Philology* 35:491–2 (July, 1938).
[7] See *New Letters*, ed. DeVane and Knickerbocker, pp. 309–10.

his optimistic philosophy; that he brushed away too easily the pain and misery of the world. Questions which had baffled man from the beginning of time were hardly to be solved in this categorical fashion. This aspect of the poem is best handled by the *Athenaeum,* whose critic said: "If the pessimism of the present day is to be confronted and answered, it is not by such an optimism as this." The most detailed, sympathetic, and yet judicious treatment of Browning's ideas upon philosophy and theology is to be found in Henry Jones's *Browning as a Philosophical and Religious Teacher* (1891 and 1902), in which, indeed, *Ferishtah* supplies much of the evidence.

Prologue

The *Prologue* to *Ferishtah,* dated September 12, 1883, at Gressoney, St. Jean, Val d'Aosta, consisted of forty lines, alternating long and short and rhyming alternately. The poem purports to celebrate one of the products of Gressoney which the poet enjoyed—ortolans, a kind of quail, cooked in Italian fashion; but in application the poem is a comment by Browning upon his own poetry in *Ferishtah,* hard on the outside, pungent next, but meaty at center. The *Prologue* is reminiscent of the *Epilogue* to the *Pachiarotto* volume, "The poets pour us wine"—where Browning describes his own brewage as strong and harsh.

1. The Eagle

The Eagle, a poem of thirty-five lines in blank verse, introduces Ferishtah, not yet a Dervish, nor a wise man, but a young man learning, from his observation of an eagle feeding some orphaned ravens, the lesson which becomes his stock in trade. He finally sees that God intends him to be as the eagle and to feed men weaker than himself. He quits the woods for the town, Ispahan, to set himself up as a teacher and sage. *The Eagle* was probably written in the spring or summer of 1883 before Browning left London, and from it developed the idea of the rest of the volume. Thereafter Ferishtah, as teacher, expounds Browning's favorite ideas.

The famous *Fables of Bidpai,* dating from India in the third century A. D., have been translated in one form or another into every language of Europe. The stories, like Aesop's, convey wisdom in the guise of beast-fables. Many translations were available for Browning's use, but the volume he read as a boy was probably the inferior collection called *Fables of Pilpay,* published anonymously in London in 1818. The book was probably bought by the elder Browning for his son soon after it appeared. There in Chapter II, Fable III (p. 53), "The Dervise, The Falcon, and the Raven," Browning found the story which he utilized in *The Eagle.* In the story from Pilpay there is only one raven to be fed, and the dead parent raven, found by Browning's Dervish at the foot of the tree, does not appear. The Dervise in Pilpay makes the same first misinterpretation of the feeding of the young raven as Ferishtah, and waits for heaven to feed him. But in a dream the Creator speaks to him: "If thou wouldst imitate any one of the birds thou hast seen to my glory, use the talents I have given thee, and imitate the Falcon that feeds the Raven, and not the Raven that lies a sluggard in his nest, and expects his food from another."

The lyric of twelve lines, in three stanzas, which concludes *The Eagle,* reinforces the lesson which Ferishtah has learned. In the first stanza Browning depicts the life of lovers in the solitude of nature; in the second he depicts the life of lovers in the solitude of a gorgeous palace. He rejects both lives for the busy life of mankind in the city, however squalid the vesture, harsh the voices, hateful the faces. Here is paralleled Ferishtah's resolve to go to Ispahan and mingle with his fellows. It is of course the choice which Browning has made throughout his life as poet. One may see this preference as early as *Sordello,* and one may see its brilliant application in the theories of painting expounded by Fra Lippo Lippi, in the function of the poet as seen in *How it Strikes a Contemporary,* and perhaps in the choice of the Italian person of quality in *Up at a Villa.* The title of one of his greatest volumes, *Men and Women,* is significant. This major characteristic of Browning's art is the more notable in a century so devoted to the appreciation of nature.

2. *The Melon-Seller*

The Melon-Seller appeared in the first edition of *Ferishtah's Fancies* as a poem of forty lines of blank verse. In the third edition, 1885, two new lines were appended, a translation of the Hebrew passage taken from *Job* 1:10, which originally closed the poem. The quotation is the text for the poem: "Shall we receive good at the hand of God And evil not receive?" This addition was kept in the collected edition of 1888–9.

It is not possible to say precisely when *The Melon-Seller* was written; the poem is not dated in the manuscript. But it follows naturally upon *The Eagle* and may be supposed to have been composed soon after the whole idea of *Ferishtah's Fancies* occurred to Browning, probably early in September, 1883. He carried the subject of *The Melon-Seller* in his memory for nearly forty years; he had read it, as we learn from his letter of August 6, 1846 (II, 405) to Miss Barrett, in a letter in the *Times*. This poem is a link between the derivative first part, *The Eagle*, and the others. Ferishtah is still a learner; he learns the proper attitude of man towards God from the melon-seller, once the Shah's prime minister. This truth too becomes a part of his stock in trade. Taking the melon-seller's advice he went to school; then at Nishapur he set up a school of his own.

In the phrase, "Some say a certain Jew adduced the word Out of their book," which Browning uses to introduce the sentence from *Job*, he is referring to a contemporary opinion that the *Book of Job* was derived from the Persian.

The lyric, two stanzas of three lines each, puts in terms of love the lesson which Ferishtah has learned. The lover invites the loved one to do injustice to him in order that his love may shine brighter when it is given where it is not deserved.

3. Shah Abbas

Shah Abbas, composed of 140 lines of blank verse, passed through all the editions of *Ferishtah* unaltered in text save for one minor change in punctuation (l. 36). The title of the poem in the manuscript is *Belief*, a more descriptive title than the final one. The manuscript gives no date of composition, but the poem was probably written at Gressoney in September, 1883. Ferishtah is now a full-fledged teacher, and the poem is a sample of his Socratic method with his pupils. Dialogue and analogy have begun to assume great place in the volume.

The problem posed by *Shah Abbas* is the question of belief. Ferishtah and his pupil Yakub argue the grounds of belief, Yakub asking for authoritative evidence, Ferishtah content to listen to the desires of his heart. The argument progresses by three analogies or fables: the feat of the great Shah Abbas, who ruled Persia from 1584 until his death in 1628, in catching a stag with one hand while he smote down a lion with the other, only to die from fear on seeing a spider in his wine-cup; the story of Thamasp who saw his love Zurah devoured by the nine-headed snake; and the story of the return of Ishak son of Absal, who returned home ten years after he was supposed to have been killed in the wars. All these incidents are apparently inventions by Browning; in all of them different kinds of faith are discussed. The feats and death of Shah Abbas are historical facts, says Ferishtah, well authenticated by documents and witnesses; the tale of Thamasp and Zurah illustrates the belief we lend to fiction—emotionally we are affected, intellectually we do not entirely concur. Easy acquiescence is not belief, nor is honest heart-searching disbelief. Ferishtah then illustrates the whole problem by the story of Ishak's return to his sons. One welcomes him, believing him to be Ishak; the other does not believe. The case is not simple; other motives enter, such as the inheritance which the sons must now forego if they believe. Ishak naturally prizes the son who believes in his return more than he does the son who will not believe it possible. It is evident that Browning prefers the will of the heart to believe, to the assent of the conviction of the head. Belief is an act of the heart and will. This is of course in line with the emphasis which Browning, in the later days of his career, put upon faith by intuition, rather than by intellectual proof. This position is delineated everywhere in his poetry after 1878, but especially in *La Saisiaz* and the *Parleyings*.

The lyric which concludes *Shah Abbas,* three stanzas of three lines each, expresses the idea that without love and trust we fail to understand the heart of another; with love and trust we see clearly and walk as in a lighted room.

4. The Family

The Family, consisting of seventy-four lines of blank verse, remained unaltered in later editions. In the manuscript the title of the poem was *The Father's Family;* the alteration to the present one probably was made in the proof-sheets. There is no indication of the date of composition, but the poem was probably written at Gressoney in September, 1883.

The theme of the poem is the efficacy of prayer, a much-mooted question during the Seventies. Tyndall, the scientist, proposed a statistical test: the patients on one side of a hospital ward were to be prayed for and those on the other were to be without the appeals of the pious; the rate of mortality in the ward would then tell the story.

The test was never tried, but London was much excited. With Browning the problem is this: If God is all-wise, all-good, all-mighty, is it not presumption in man to attempt interference by prayer against God's obvious decree? The husband and the three sons of the woman bitten by a serpent, each of whom feels differently about the physician's decree that the woman's leg should be amputated, represent different types of humanity. Ferishtah's conclusion is that since mere men cannot know the purposes of God it is well for us to express in prayer our human emotions of pity, sympathy, and fear, and leave the decision trustingly to God.

In the lyric, three stanzas of three lines each, the same idea is expressed in terms of love. The lover wishes to be a man, not an angel or anything else; the objects and emotions of the earth-dweller suffice for him. The little poem is possibly a protest on Browning's part against the extravagant adulation of Mrs. Bloomfield-Moore whose guest he was at St. Moritz in the summer of 1884.[8]

5. The Sun

The Sun, comprising 176 lines of blank verse, was the fifth part of *Ferishtah's Fancies.* In succeeding editions the text suffered few changes, one change in punctuation in line 87, and the substitution of the word "plainly" for "this wise" in line 149. In the manuscript (in Balliol College) there is no indication of the date of composition, but from internal evidence, since the poem seems to follow hard upon *The Family,* it is reasonable to suppose that it was composed at Gressoney in September, 1883. In the manuscript the title was *Incarnation;* the present title was probably substituted in the proof-sheets.

The Sun is Browning's most extended as well as his most successful use of sun-symbolism. In different ways he uses it in *La Saisiaz* and in the *Parleying With Bernard de Mandeville.* Since the scene of Ferishtah's teachings is Persia it is natural that he should use as illustrative matter the ancient religion of sun-worship, commonly associated with Zoroaster. The sun-symbolism Browning here turns to old and familiar uses. Ferishtah is confronted by a man who is angry because he had heard another say that "God once assumed on earth a human shape." By showing the naturalness of sun-worship in the ancient Persians, Ferishtah shows how men naturally took the next step and

[8] See Miller, *Robert Browning,* p. 287. See also below, "Not with my Soul, Love."

imagined that the sun was conscious of its beneficence to the earth, or that some power conscious of its life-giving potency ruled the sun. Thence man sees the need of some sign from that power that the power, or God, has the interests of man at heart. To answer that crying need, says Ferishtah, the legend arose that God once took human shape and came to man on earth. In answer to his angry disciple's demand for proof, or trace of proof, he says,

> What if such a tracing were?
> If some strange story stood,—whate'er its worth,—
> That the immensely yearned-for—once befell . . . ?

Then, concludes Ferishtah, instead of kicking and cuffing a man who is able to believe such a legend, we ought to praise, admire, and even envy him. This same conception, of course, had already informed some of Browning's most famous religious poems, such as *Saul, Cleon,* and *Karshish,* and reappears in *Bernard de Mandeville* and *Imperante Augusto Natus Est—.* Much discussion was aroused in the reviews and in the Browning Society by *The Sun.*

The lyric, "Fire is in the flint," a single stanza of six lines, compares the mystery of fire, struck from flint but forgetful of its birth, to the child in the cradle, come from heaven but now housed on earth. The idea is connected, of course, with that of the major poem. The comparison with Wordsworth's *Ode* on *Intimations of Immortality from Recollections of Early Childhood,* and the Platonic source of both poems, will of course occur to the reader.

6. Mihrab Shah

Mihrab Shah, consisting of 136 lines of blank verse, was unaltered in successive editions save for a very minor verbal change in the collected edition of 1888–9. No indication of the date is given in the manuscript, but in all likelihood it was written in the autumn of 1883. The original title of the poem in the manuscript was *Pain;* the change was probably made in the proof-sheets.

The theme of this "fancy" is the question, "If God is all-good and all-powerful, why is evil permitted in the earth?" To answer this question satisfactorily to himself had been the major effort of Browning since *Pippa Passes,* 1841. His peculiar solution of this problem is the central doctrine of his religious thought. It underlies, for example, his greatest single poem, *The Ring and the Book.* In *Mihrab Shah* he gives a somewhat different answer: Ferishtah cleverly traps his questioner into a sympathy for the Shah, whom the questioner would not admire for all his virtues, by telling him that the Shah has an internal ulcer. This then, says Ferishtah, is the use of pain and evil, that therefrom men learn pity, sympathy, and brotherhood. It likewise teaches them gratitude to God for the disasters they escape and the blessings they have received. Browning's justification here of the ways of God to man has not satisfied all his readers. To many it has seemed that the misery of the world was greatly out of proportion to the good achieved. They have found Browning's answer to the problem which has vexed man since he began to think, altogether too easy to be convincing.

The lyric, "So, the head aches," twenty lines in five stanzas, restates the idea, with a little difference, in the terms of a lover: "Closer we tread for a common tether."

7. A Camel-Driver

A Camel-Driver, comprising 111 lines of blank verse, suffered several verbal changes between the first edition and the final collected edition of 1888–9. The most interesting of these was the change of the name "Ruksh," into "Rakhsh" in the final edition. Rakhsh or Rakush was the intelligent horse owned by Rustem, the great hero of Firdusi's Shah Nameh. Browning probably wrote the first form of the name from his recollection of Matthew Arnold's Sohrab and Rustum, and changed it later when he was in London, to approximate more nearly the Persian form.[9] In the manuscript A Camel-Driver is dated as finished on September 23, 1883. Browning was then at Gressoney.

Here Ferishtah repudiates the idea of eternal punishment for sinners. Browning had dealt with this idea in The Inn Album (ll. 1732–86), and again notably in Ixion. In dialogue with one of his pupils Ferishtah shows by the camel-driver's treatment of a recalcitrant camel how men must punish the breakers of their codes to warn future offenders, but that such reasons need not apply to God at all. Before he is done, Browning repudiates also the idea that God would punish men because of their ignorance. Dante's conception that pagans, however virtuous, were condemned to the Inferno because of their misfortune in being born before Christ or in being

[9] See above, n. 1.

ignorant of Him, was unacceptable to Browning. The sins we commit in full knowledge inflict their own punishment. Browning treats this idea, with a difference, in *Development,* 1889.

In the lyric, "When I vexed you," three stanzas of four lines each, the lover chides the loved one for criticizing small faults too much, while the great faults which should have been crushed were overlooked.

8. Two Camels

Two Camels, consisting of 108 lines of blank verse, underwent several minor changes in punctuation, mainly in the interest of clarity, when it was printed in the collected edition of 1888–9. The manuscript does not indicate the date of composition, but it is reasonable to suppose that it was written late in September, 1883, in Gressoney, or in October in Venice.

In *Two Camels* Ferishtah—for Browning—expresses his disapproval of asceticism. It must be admitted that the opinion is much more suited to a Protestant occidental poet than to an oriental sage. Browning's dislike of asceticism is curiously like Tennyson's in *St. Simeon Stylites,* a poem which Browning admired. Both Tennyson and Browning preferred an active ideal of service (see Tennyson's *Galahad*) to the ideal of self-mortifying contemplation; both had been reared in the Protestant middle-class opinions of England. Browning had enunciated many times his opinion of the worth and dignity of the flesh, most notably in *Rabbi Ben Ezra,* 1864, and *Fra Lippo Lippi,* 1855.

In the *Two Camels* Ferishtah, taking the point of view that man's reason for existence is service to God, illustrates his point by the story of the hearty and the abstemious camels. The misguided abstemious camel broke down in the desert and lost his master's cargo; the camel who ate heartily and steadily pulled through. The Hebrew sentence in line 89 is translated in "Persian phrase" in the line below; the Hebrew word in line 95 is "Me Elohim," one of the names for God in *Genesis.*

The lyric which concludes the *Two Camels,* two stanzas of six lines each, illustrates what momentous consequences may come from minute actions; the first example is from science, the second from love.

9. Cherries

Cherries, 101 lines of blank verse, was unaltered in editions subsequent to the first, save the change of "eyes" to "eye" and one or two changes in punctuation for the sake of clarity. In the manuscript the poem was called *Gratitude;* the alteration of title was probably made in the proof-sheets. In the manuscript the poem was dated January 15, [1884]. This date was cancelled, perhaps because Browning added to the poem after that date. He was at that time in London.

The poem, by means of Ferishtah's parables, illustrates a belief which Browning had expressed as early as *Pippa Passes,* 1841, "All service ranks the same with God." The idea is also clearly expressed in *The Boy and the Angel* in 1845. As in the case of the "widow's mite," God looks upon the heart rather than the gift. "Mushtari" is the Persian name for the planet Jupiter.

The lyric, "Verse-making was least of my virtues," two stanzas of four lines each, is a personal utterance on Browning's part, I think. It refers to the subject of the main poem. His own service has been to make verse and to make love, and he has done both as best he could.

10. Plot-Culture

Plot-Culture, comprising sixty lines of blank verse, remained unaltered when it was reprinted in editions subsequent to the first. It was dated, in the manuscript, as finished on January 17, 1884; Browning was at this time in London.

The theme of the poem is that man owes his accounting directly to God. Man's morality is a question between himself and God only. When an impudent scholar, taking advantage of Ferishtah's tolerance, asks him what would happen if he made love to Ferishtah's daughter, Laila, the sage reminds the pupil that he must account to God for his little plot of earth, his life. The apparent permission for immoral acts—it is only apparent—is reminiscent of such poems as *The Statue and the Bust* and *Fifine at the Fair.*

The lyric, "Not with my Soul, Love!", two stanzas of eight lines each, expresses the desire of the speaker to love in such a fashion that finally sense would quench soul. This lyric was not included in the manuscript in the Balliol College Library. Instead, there were directions to the printer: "Leave room for a small poem's insertion here." The lyric, therefore, was written late, after the manuscript had gone to the printer. Mrs. Bloomfield-Moore, with whom Browning was staying in St. Moritz in September, 1884, records the genesis of the poem.[10] She was called to America and had to leave the poet and his sister suddenly; and as she departed she said to Browning, "Remember, I have loved you with the best and most enduring love—Soul-love." The poem is Browning's protest, as is the lyric attached to *The Family* in *Ferishtah*, against a Platonic infatuation. It is a surprisingly passionate utterance in a man of seventy-two. The "memories that intrude" were probably memories of Mrs. Browning. Mrs. Bloomfield-Moore adds, "Browning had more friends among noble-hearted women than fall to the share of many."

11. A Pillar at Sebzevah

A Pillar at Sebzevah, a poem of 150 lines of blank verse, suffered several changes of word and punctuation in the editions which followed the first. The changes are not of great consequence; they were made for the sake of clarity and smoothness. The poem is not dated in the manuscript; but internal evidence leads one to suppose that it was written in London during the latter half of January, 1884. The title in the manuscript read "A Pillar at Khorasan"; the change was probably made in the proof-sheets, and probably because Browning preferred using Sebzevah, which he had already used as a place-name, to introducing a new name unnecessarily.

In *A Pillar at Sebzevah* Ferishtah drops most of his earlier devices. The parable here is of the slightest sort, and dialogue plays small part; Ferishtah, or Browning, preaches unadorned doctrine. The theme of the sermon is the complete inefficacy of human knowledge. We should trust our hearts, our instincts, our intuitions, says Browning; for if we attempt to build on the products of our minds, our intellects, we shall find ourselves building houses on shifting sand. This aspect of Browning's philosophical thinking, easy to comprehend but not so easy to accept, is perhaps the most peculiar development of his thought in the last fifteen years of his life. Browning, it seems, began to distrust knowledge when the tide of historical

[10] See "Robert Browning" in *Lippincott's Magazine* 45:690. See also *New Letters*, ed. DeVane and Knickerbocker, pp. 307–8, n. 2, and Miller, *Robert Browning*, pp. 286–9.

and scientific fact went directly against most of the doctrines he held dear. He therefore repudiated the evidence of the intellect in a series of poems, from *La Saisiaz* to the end of his life, and correspondingly exalted the desires and intuitions of the heart. *A Pillar at Sebzevah* is perhaps the bluntest and clearest statement of this doctrine.

It should be said concerning the oriental names that "Hudhud" is Solomon's fabulous bird, according to Talmudic legend; "Sitara" is Persian for "star"; and that "Mushtari" is the Persian name for Jupiter.

The lyric, two stanzas of five lines each, honors the silent, intuitive, and the unspoken in love. The soul may speak more truly in a touch or a gaze than in the inadequate word.

12. A Bean-Stripe: Also Apple-Eating

A Bean-Stripe: Also Apple-Eating consists of 478 lines of blank verse. A few changes in word and punctuation, mainly in the interest of clarity, have been made in editions subsequent to the first. The most notable of these is the transfer of the speech in lines 329–33 from Ferishtah to the questioning scholar. No date for the completion of the poem is given in the manuscript, but the condition of the manuscript indicates that the poem was not easy of composition, and that it probably was done at more than one period of writing. The concluding section (ll. 365–478), *Apple-Eating*, was inserted into the manuscript after Browning had attached and dated the *Epilogue* to the volume. It is my opinion that the first part of the poem, to line 364, was composed in Venice, probably in November or December, 1883, and that the last lines (365–478) were written after Browning's return to London at the end of the year. It is worthy of notice that the Persian names occur mainly in the latter part. In the manuscript the title does not include *Also Apple-Eating;* this title was probably added when that parable was added to the poem in London.

In subject as in size *A Bean-Stripe: Also Apple-Eating* is the most formidable poem in the volume. The question under debate between Ferishtah and his stubborn scholar is the major question of Browning's later days: Does good or evil predominate in life? Browning had permitted himself some of his most pessimistic statements in debating this question in *La Saisiaz*. Through this "fancy" there runs the simile of the beans: are the beans white mainly, or black? To Ferishtah the general hue of life, though wonderfully mixed, is gray, whirling finally towards whiteness. To the questioner, the hue is nearer dun—even black when he contemplates the general miseries of men. His point of view here (ll. 137–47) and again in the passage (ll. 248–70) where Ferishtah comments upon "the sourly-Sage" makes one think that Browning had Thomas Carlyle in mind —as he assuredly did in the *Parleying With Bernard de Mandeville* —as the pessimist to whom life was all black, though he lived seventy years, laughed loud and enjoyed his dinner.

All Browning—or Ferishtah—can say to the general misery which seems to be in the world is that to him it has never seemed real; he knows only himself, knows that he suspects evil to be illusion, and that he never has seen evil that was irrevocably evil:

> Of absolute and irretrievable
> And all-subduing black,—black's soul of black
> Beyond white's power to disintensify,—
> Of that I saw no sample: such may wreck
> My life and ruin my philosophy
> Tomorrow, doubtless. . . .

Such was Browning's faith, and his poetic purpose from *Pippa Passes* to the end of his career was to make evil declare at the last moment the virtue that was in it. He had apparently recovered from the pessimistic mood of *La Saisiaz*. So Ferishtah, who trusts God and feels His goodness, but cannot know anything about Him, eats his apple, relishes what is ripe, admires it because half the crop is withered and the rest have maggots at their cores, and thanks God that his apple was good. Perhaps the doctrine is too narrow to be philosophical. Ferishtah is allowed the last word, but it is not clear that his scholar is beaten in argument.

The Persian names which appear here, Rustem, Gew, and Gudarz, are heroes in the *Shah Nameh,* which was also the ultimate source for Matthew Arnold's *Sohrab and Rustum.*

In the lyric, "Why from the world," two stanzas of seven lines each, Ferishtah, for Browning, disclaims any right on his part to expect from men love or generosity towards his poetry; he asks only justice. Content that he has done his duty, he refers his work to God. The lyric is important as Browning's statement of the purpose of poetry as he saw it; the ideas recall somewhat those in *How it Strikes a Contemporary.*

Epilogue

The *Epilogue* to *Ferishtah's Fancies,* seven stanzas of four lines each, was reprinted without change in all editions of the poem. In the manuscript the poem is dated as finished on December 1, 1883; the name of Mrs. Bronson's palace in Venice, where the poem was written, was probably added in the proofsheets.

The lyric is a personal utterance by Browning addressed, I believe, to his dead wife. The moon-symbolism used here is almost always reserved in Browning's poetry for references to her, his "moon of poets" (see *One Word More, Pan and Luna, Parleying With Daniel Bartoli,* etc.). The body of the poem deals with the subjects which had concerned Ferishtah, the evil and misery evident in the world. When the moon is free from cloud, and clearly seen, then the world is splendid and beautiful; the heroes of other years speak to Browning and give him courage; he fights with full faith in his leader, and his heart applauds perfection.

Then a sudden fear turns his blood to ice. What if his whole hopeful and happy view of the world be error? What if his philosophy be built on the accidental illumination cast upon an essentially dark world by a human love?

The expression of such sudden and paralyzing doubt is creditable both to Browning's poetry and to his integrity, and reminds one of his momentary pessimism in *La Saisiaz.* It is significant that this appalling doubt should be appended as an epilogue to the most dogmatic and blunt statement of Browning's cheerful creed. In phrase and imagery the lyric is akin to *Prospice* and the *Epilogue* to *Asolando,* both of which, however, express a resurgent courage which is lacking in this *Epilogue.* The comparison to Matthew Arnold's *Dover Beach* will occur to the reader.

PARLEYINGS WITH CERTAIN PEOPLE OF IMPORTANCE IN THEIR DAY

PUBLICATION AND TEXT

The volume of *Parleyings With Certain People of Importance in Their Day* was published on January 28, 1887. The book was post octavo, bound in reddish-brown cloth boards, and sold for Ten Shillings the copy. It consisted of a half-title; the title-page: "Parleyings With Certain People of Importance in Their Day: To wit: Bernard de Mandeville, Daniel Bartoli, Christopher Smart, George Bubb Dodington, Francis Furini, Gerard de Lairesse, and Charles Avison. Introduced by A Dialogue between Apollo and the Fates; Concluded by Another between John Fust and his Friends. By Robert Browning. London: Smith, Elder, & Co., 15 Waterloo Place. 1887."; a dedication, "In Memoriam J. Milsand obiit IV. Sept. MDLXXXVI. [sic] Absens absentem auditque videtque."; a list of contents; and the text, pp. 3–268. There was a separate fly-title for each division of the volume.

No separate second edition of the *Parleyings* was called for, and the volume was included in the final collected edition of 1888–9 with a very few small changes in the text of the poems. The manuscript of the work is now in the Balliol College Library at Oxford.

GENESIS AND COMPOSITION; SOURCES AND INFLUENCES

Ever since Browning's great fame had come to him with the publication of *The Ring and the Book*, and especially after the founding of the Browning Society in 1881, great pressure had been brought upon the poet to supply biographical details concerning his career. This Browning was most reluctant to do, being willing only to correct misstatements in the notices which were sent to him. In the last five years of his life the rumor was rife that the poet was writing his reminiscences, and this rumor persisted in spite of Browning's denial.[1] The dramatic mask from which Browning had voiced his opinions for many years was used less as the poet reached his last decade. Concerning *Ferishtah's Fancies*, he had written Furnivall in 1884, "I can't at all guess how people will like it, but I have managed to say a thing or two that I 'fancied' I should like to say." [2] In the *Parleyings* the disguise is dropped altogether; it is Browning who speaks, not Mandeville or Lairesse. The poems are not precisely "parleyings," but are monologues in which the poet addresses the mute spirits who are called up before him.

The men chosen as the subjects of the *Parleyings* were not taken at random, or for any reason of general interest. The *Parleyings* are notes for Browning's mental autobiography, and the seven men

---

[1] I have drawn steadily for this account of the *Parleyings* upon my work, *Browning's Parleyings, The Autobiography of a Mind*, New Haven, 1927. For the details see above, my *Introduction, passim*.

[2] *Letters*, ed. Hood, p. 231.

represent seven major interests of Browning's life—philosophy, history, poetry, politics, painting, the classics (Greek), and music. Moreover, the men chosen to be parleyed with had in some way been influential, usually in Browning's youth, in shaping his ideas upon their respective subjects; with one exception, the works of these men had been the boyhood books of the poet. Thus, though Browning disdained gossipy reminiscence and would not supply materials for the biographers to write up into accounts of him, he nevertheless in a very real sense contributed to our knowledge of his mind and his art.

Browning's plan in the *Parleyings*, however, grew to be more comprehensive than this. He planned to show not only the origins of his leading ideas, but to suggest his own growth in a particular subject, and finally to contrast his opinions in that subject with those of some outstanding contemporary in 1887. Thus in the *Parleying* with Dodington the subject is politics, and Browning shows how he drew certain characteristic ideas concerning statecraft from a reading of that statesman's *Diary* and a consideration of his character; he hints the growth of those ideas, and then applies them to the greatest politician of the nineteenth century, Benjamin Disraeli. In this way the *Parleyings* are intended to provide a comprehensive review of the poet's chief ideas from the beginning to the end of his life. In the review much light is cast upon his poetry.

The manuscript is lacking in the dates which Browning often appended to his poems, save for the *Parleying With Francis Furini* which is dated September 30, 1886, so that it is not possible to say precisely when, or in what order, the poems were written. The volume was begun in the summer of 1885, for on September 7 Browning wrote to Furnivall from Gressoney St. Jean, saying, "Yes, I am writing another poem," [3] and his words can only refer to the *Parleyings*. Much was written during the fall of 1885 at Gressoney and Venice, no doubt, and much in London in the spring of 1886. The unusual slowness with which Browning seems to have written the *Parleyings* is explained by his friend, Mrs. Orr:

. . . the revision of the work caused him considerable trouble. The subjects he had chosen strained his powers of exposition; and I think he often tried to remedy by mere verbal correction, what was a defect in the logical arrangement of his ideas. They would slide into each other where a visible dividing line was required.[4]

[3] *Idem,* p. 239. See also DeVane, *Browning's Parleyings,* p. xvi.
[4] Orr, *Life,* p. 347.

The summer of 1886 was spent in Wales, and from Llangollen on August 17 Browning promised to send one of his books to a friend: "I think the book shall be this one I am just engaged upon, which ought to be my best." [5] The *Parleyings* were turned into something of a memorial by the death of the poet's dearest friend, Joseph Milsand, on September 4, 1886, and it was probably at that time that Browning resolved upon the dedication and wrote the *Prologue, Apollo and the Fates*, which rises, I think, from his musings upon the death of his friend. The *Parleyings* were finished early in the fall of 1886, and appeared on January 28, 1887.

AFTER-HISTORY

Browning's plan for the *Parleyings* was a noble and ambitious one, but partly because of the crabbed manner in which the volume was written, partly because of the inattention of the reviewers, but primarily because the critics of 1887 did not possess the key which later students of Browning's life and poetry have provided us, the official reviewers regarded the volume as a perfect enigma. For example, Gerard de Lairesse, whom we now know to have been a major influence upon the poet in the matter of landscape and painting, was utterly unknown to the critics. Browning's publishers appreciated the difficulty of the *Parleyings*, and advance sheets were sent to Browning's friend, George Barnett Smith, who reviewed the work for the *Times* on January 28, 1887. How far he missed the purport of the *Parleyings* may be seen from his opening sentence: "The supposition that Mr. Browning's new work was to be of an autobiographical character," he wrote, "is entirely erroneous." General opinion was well represented by the criticism which appeared in the *Saturday Review* for February 26, 1887: "Mr. Browning, who often amuses himself by writing in a cipher to which he alone has the key, has seldom propounded to his disciples a more hopeless puzzle." The *Spectator* of February 5 was filled with commiseration for the future translator of the *Parleyings* into any foreign language, for such a person "will come upon difficulties to which even the difficulties of translators of a corrupt chorus of the Agamemnon will be trivial." In short, the reviewers read the volume with chagrin and bewilderment, the only notable exception being the critic in the *Academy* for February 12, who wrote briefly, but ably. Since that day students of Browning have come to see that the *Parleyings*,

[5] *Letters*, ed. Hood, p. 254.

though assuredly not one of the best of Browning's books, is one of the most illuminating as a history of his tastes and opinions.

Apollo and the Fates. A Prologue

Apollo and the Fates, consisting of fifty-three stanzas of five lines each, 265 lines in all, served as prologue to the *Parleyings.* The manuscript of the poem bears no date, but the poem was probably written soon after the death of Browning's friend Milsand on September 4, 1886. It was possibly this event that set the poet musing upon the destiny of man, his birth, life, and death, which makes up the matter of the poem. *Apollo and the Fates* is a weird and dark scene depicting the sun-god's intercession with the three dark sisters, the Fates, for the life of his friend Admetus when the time has come for that king to die. The scene would have served admirably as a prologue to *Balaustion's Adventure,* for Euripides' *Alcestis* which is transcribed in that poem begins as the Fates announce that it is time for Admetus to die. Before the play opens Apollo has tricked the Fates into an agreement that Admetus should live if someone could be found to die for him. It is this incident, Apollo in the act of tricking the Fates, which the poet deals with here.

Browning gives us, in a note at the head of his poem, references to the sources from which he derived his scene. From Aeschylus' *Eumenides* (ll. 726–7, 730–1) he made use of two addresses to Apollo:

Erin: Even such a part didst thou play in Pheres' [Admetus' father] house, persuading the Moirai to release a mortal from death!

and

Erin: Thou, thou it was, who abolishing old division didst deceive with wine those ancient powers.

From Euripides' *Alcestis* (ll. 11–4, 32–4) Browning took the boast of Apollo:

> The son of Pheres; him I snatched from death,
> Cozening the Fates: the Sisters promised me—
> "Admetus shall escape the imminent death
> If he for ransom gives another life,"

and the question to Apollo:

> Did this not suffice thee, to thwart that doom
> Of Admetus, when, all by thy cunning beguiled
> Were the Fates?

And finally from Homer's *Hymn to Mercury* (ll. 558–60) a description of the Fates:

From their home they fly now here, now there, feeding on honeycomb and bringing all things to pass. And when they are inspired through yellow honey, they are willing to speak truth.

From these hints Browning fashions his scene. In his poem Apollo surprises the Fates in their pit just as Atropos, the third sister, is about to shear the thread of Admetus' life. When he asks that Admetus' life be spared, the Fates show their cynical natures by doubting that it will be to Admetus' happiness to live longer. They see the life of man in its blackest colors, and think that only the glamor which Apollo gives to life makes it possible for man to live, and lures men on in a perpetual hope of better things. Apollo admits the truth of the charge, but believes that man has an independent virtue. As he speaks, he offers the Sisters drink from the bowl he has with him, and tells them the history of wine—how Bacchus, youngest of the gods, prompted men to invent wine as his gift to mankind. The Sisters drink, become intoxicated, dance, and under the influence of wine they begin to speak the truth and declare that man's life, properly seen, has magnificent potentialities and indeed may be a triumph. By wine, Browning means to symbolize the imagination, the latest gift of the gods to man. Imagination permits man to see life as a steady march of progress. An explosion from the center of the earth compels the Fates to return to their duties, but they grant, because they have seen what life may be, that Admetus may be saved if he can find someone to die for him. Apollo is pleased at his triumph, and thinks that all Admetus' subjects will rush to sacrifice themselves for their king, but he sees Admetus refusing their gift and dying nobly. The Fates, foreseeing the selfishness of all save Alcestis, laugh mockingly as the young and hopeful god ascends and the scene closes.

Apollo and the Fates strikes a number of chords which are heard again in the *Parleyings*. The Fates, when they view facts with imagination, see life as potentially good. In truth, good and evil are inextricably mingled in life, and in the stress of life good and evil are often indistinguishable, one from the other. Apollo, the god of poetry, gilds life with illusory hopes, and led by hope man struggles upward. These are the major ideas in the *Parleyings* which follow. Perhaps *Apollo and the Fates* was also put as prologue to this autobiographical volume to commemorate the poet's long love for Greek literature which was one of his earliest intellectual enthusiasms.

With Bernard de Mandeville

The *Parleying With Bernard de Mandeville* consisted of 321 iambic pentameter lines, rhyming irregularly but mainly in couplets, and divided into eleven unequal sections. The manuscript is not dated, but the probability is that the poem was written early among the *Parleyings,* perhaps in the fall of 1885.

The first of the *Parleyings* is devoted to the subject of philosophy, and in it Browning calls up Bernard de Mandeville (1670–1733), the author of *The Fable of the Bees,* to help him confute the gloomy view of life held by the poet's great contemporary, Thomas Carlyle. Browning's acquaintance with Mandeville dates from 1833 when on February 1, the centenary of the philosopher's death, the poet's father had given him a copy of the 1795 edition of the *Fable.*[6] The *Fable* was a notorious book in its day. In 1705 the Dutch physician, Mandeville, first published anonymously his rhymed fable as *The Grumbling Hive: Or, Knaves turn'd Honest.* Here is told the story of a hive of bees who conducted their affairs much as men do, and the swarm was busy and prosperous. But the bees often complained, in their zeal for reform, against the fraud and dishonesty in their society, until at last Jupiter in a rage swore that he would rid them of their sins. From that moment the hive became honest, all debts were paid, and the contentious spirit of the hive ceased. The business of the lawyers was thus destroyed. The business of the doctors was much lessened because no disease was complicated by the practice of quacks. The clergy had little to do; there was no self-seeking at court, and the business there could be done by a few honest bees. Trade languished because all vain desires had disappeared. The arts and crafts were neglected. Finally the bees left their hive as a last protest against extravagance and took up their residence in a hollow tree.

The implications of Mandeville's verse-fable were not appreciated, and in 1714 the philosopher incorporated the verses into a larger book called *The Fable of the Bees: or, Private Vices, Publick Benefits,* and made his meaning explicit by notes, and added an essay called *An Enquiry into the Origin of Moral Virtue.* In 1723 Mandeville's book was further enlarged by two additional chapters, *An Essay on Charity and Charity-Schools* and *A Search into the Nature of Society.* The book began to attract general attention and was

[6] See DeVane, *Browning's Parleyings,* Ch. 1.

condemned by the Grand Jury of Middlesex as having "a direct tendency to the subversion of all religion and civil government, our duty to the Almighty, our love to our country, and regard to our oaths." [7] In the edition of the *Fable* in 1724 Mandeville added a *Vindication* which Browning seems to have consulted especially for his *Parleying*. The *Fable* went through a number of editions in the eighteenth century; it was published in one volume in 1795.

In his *Vindication* Mandeville clearly stated his position:

After this, I flatter myself to have demonstrated, that neither the friendly qualities and kind affections that are natural to man, nor the real virtues he is capable of acquiring by reason and self-denial, are the foundation of society; but that what we call evil in this world, moral as well as natural, is the grand principle that makes us sociable creatures; the solid basis, the life and support of all trades and employments without exception: That there we must look for the true origin of all arts and sciences; and that the moment evil ceases, the society must be spoiled, if not totally dissolved. [8]

Mandeville achieves his brilliant and devastating paradox by the use of two different standards: private actions are judged by an ascetic standard of virtue, conduct being evaluated not by its consequences but by the motives that induced it; but the effects of the actions are judged by utilitarian standards, and thus anything productive of national happiness and prosperity becomes a benefit, and therefore "good." By his statement of this paradox Mandeville put his readers in a dilemma; they had either to renounce prosperity or to deny their Christian ascetic creed of virtue, and neither of these were they willing to forego. When he was pressed by his critics, Mandeville was careful to show that he had chosen virtue instead of greatness: "if I have shown the way to worldly greatness, I have always, without hesitation, preferred the road that leads to virtue." [9] But his choice of virtue was only formal and precautionary, and on every page of the *Fable* one may see that his whole sympathy was with the cause of worldly greatness, and that he was trying subtly to undermine the ascetic formula of virtue by showing its absurdity. The divines and philosophers of the eighteenth century felt this in Mandeville, and Hutchinson, Berkeley, and Law among others were ready to declare the Dutch physician "the sagacious sycophant of the baser instincts." S. T. Coleridge wrote in Southey's copy of the

[7] Quoted in *The Fable of the Bees,* 1795, p. 240.
[8] *The Fable of the Bees,* 1795, p. 251.
[9] *Idem,* pp. 254–5.

Fable, "Can anyone read Mandeville's fable of the Bees, and not see that it is a keen satire on the inconsistencies of Christianity, and so intended?"

How then could so keen a reader as Browning so mistake his man and call up Mandeville, a lover of the flesh and the world, to confute his brother-believer in the spirit and in the divinity of man, Thomas Carlyle? The situation is ironic. In the first place, Browning first read Mandeville at a critical moment between February and March, 1833, when he had just finished writing *Pauline,* and in his revolt from Shelley's atheism he was perhaps prepared to see "God and truth" everywhere, and with this preconception saw in Mandeville a stout defender of virtue. It was, nevertheless, an odd book for the elder Browning to give his son. But Mandeville's humor and daring and his love of clever paradoxes were ideally designed to catch the interest of the young Browning. It was these things that persuaded Browning of Mandeville's righteousness, as we may see from Mrs. Orr's report after speaking with the poet on the matter:

Mr. Browning fully accepts the vindication and even regards it as super-fluous. He sees nothing, either in the fable itself or the commentary first attached to it, which may not equally be covered by the Christian doctrine of original sin, or the philosophic acceptance of evil as a necessary con-comitant, or condition, of good: and finds fresh guarantees for a sound moral intention in the bright humour and sound practical sense in which the book abounds. This judgment was formed (as I have already implied) very early in Mr. Browning's life, even before the appearance of "Pauline," and supplies a curious comment on any impression of mental immaturity which his own work of that period may have produced.[10]

It seems all too clear that Browning did not re-read *The Fable of the Bees* with any thoroughness when he came to write his *Parleying.* He merely looked into Mandeville's *Preface* and the *Vindication,* and there he found a few passages which, though totally different in meaning when read in their proper context, seemed to chime with certain fixed ideas of his own in 1887. For example, Browning held that God used evil as a means of producing virtue in men's souls, but Mandeville means a very different kind of "good"—he means prosperity and physical well-being—in the following passage from the *Vindication:*

The short-sighted vulgar, in the chain of causes, seldom can see farther than one link; but those who can enlarge their view, and will give them-

[10] Orr, *Handbook,* p. 345.

selves leisure of gazing on the prospect of concatenated events, may, in a hundred places, see good spring up, and pullulate from evil, as naturally as chickens do from eggs.[11]

From such snatches as this Browning made himself, somewhat incongruously, an ally of Mandeville.

The antagonist to be confuted by Mandeville's help is unmistakable.[12] We would recognize Thomas Carlyle from his "bilious mood," the "groan" with "guffaw at the end, Disposing of mock-melancholy," even if Browning had not told Mrs. Orr that he was aiming at him who "yesterday was magisterial in antithesis." The astonishing thing in the *Parleying* is Browning's antagonism to a man with whom he had been friendly for more than forty years. The poet, seventeen years younger than Carlyle, had been an ardent admirer, and even a disciple, of the philosopher, and their relations had been cordial. But in the passage of years Browning had risen to a fame of his own and Carlyle had continued to treat him as a promising young man. Browning in his later days felt that Carlyle had not been altogether generous in according him public praise; Carlyle had sneered at Browning's poetry a number of times; and finally, in spite of his protestations, it is evident that the poet's opinion of Carlyle was shaken by the disclosures of Froude, Carlyle's biographer, after Carlyle's death in 1881. But in the *Parleying* Browning's attack is upon the pessimistic view of life which Carlyle held. Carlyle was well aware of the difference in their temperaments:

But there's a great contrast between him and me. He seems very content with life, and takes much satisfaction in the world. It's a very strange and curious spectacle to behold a man in these days so confidently cheerful.[13]

Yet the contrast was not so deep as either of them imagined. They were both products of the same age and were confronted by the same problems. The rationalists of the eighteenth century had put God, man, and nature into a system of checks and balances. Wordsworth and his contemporaries had broken the system and had found God in nature. Carlyle and Browning carried the revolt further and found God in man. But in the presence of the spirit in man, Carlyle looked about and saw the old faith lifeless. Browning, more affected

---

11 *The Fable of the Bees*, 1795, p. 252.
12 See *With Bernard de Mandeville*, ll. 39–43, 62–74, 173–6; see also DeVane, *Browning's Parleyings*, pp. 15–31.
13 Henry Jones, *Browning as a Philosophical and Religious Teacher*, 1902, p. 45.

by the evangelical creed, saw a new heaven and a new earth, and the old had passed away. He was younger than Carlyle and matured later. He seized intuitively upon the new science and the new spirit of hope abroad in the Thirties, and made from them a doctrine of moral progress. But to Carlyle—as to Matthew Arnold who matured still later than Browning when the first promise of science was seen to be a false dawn—the old faith was dead and the new as yet unborn. Thus Carlyle's pessimism rose from his conviction that while an absentee God laid the heavy burden of duty upon men, He offered no help, gave no sign of being interested or sympathetic in man's struggle. Browning believed, for his part, that he could see the tracing of God's design for man's destiny.

The bulk of the *Parleying* consists of Browning's delineation of his religious views. Here the poet speaks, without disguise, in his own voice and is consciously summing up his ideas. He is mainly concerned with the problem of the existence of evil in the world if we are to assume that God is all-wise, all-powerful, and all-loving. He concludes, in a manner that is by this time very familiar to us, that the evil of the world is illusory, put by God in the world to make man develop his moral nature. Happily, man can never be certain, and in the healthy atmosphere of doubt he strives and proves himself. When the evidence of our intellects as to the reality of evil becomes overwhelming, Browning casts doubt upon the efficacy of the intellect which is the creature of the senses, and prefers to trust the instincts of his heart, which in its desire for love and righteousness is a small reflection of the spirit of God. Thus Browning answers Carlyle's despair by setting up his own beliefs.

With Daniel Bartoli

The *Parleying With Daniel Bartoli* consisted of 342 iambic pentameter lines, rhyming irregularly but for the most part in couplets, and divided into eighteen unequal sections. The last section is in a regular seven-line stanza. There is nothing in the manuscript to indicate the date of composition, but the matter of the *Parleying* was in Browning's mind in June of 1886,[14] and we may well ascribe the composition to the early summer of that year. The *Parleying* is unique in that it is the only one that is not a disquisition; it is a swift narrative in Browning's best psychological manner. It is repre-

[14] See *Letters*, ed. Hood, pp. 249–50, 336.

sentative here of the poet's habit of grounding his stories upon a firm historical basis.

Browning first became acquainted with the works of Daniel Bartoli, the Jesuit historian of the seventeenth century, through the edition of Bartoli's *De' Simboli Trasportati al Morale* which Browning's tutor in Italian, Angelo Cerutti, published in London in 1830. The poet's name appeared in the list of subscribers to this book. Browning admired Bartoli's learning and ingenuity in this collection of miscellaneous essays, but he objected to the morals which Bartoli fitted to his anecdotes. It is quite evident that Browning read the *Simboli* as a model of Italian style, and for that reason carried it to Italy with him upon his journeys thither in 1838 and 1844; and thus he came to write in its covers *How They brought the Good News* and *Home-Thoughts, from the Sea*.[15] In the *Parleying*, however, Bartoli gets short shrift. Browning gives a brief sample (ll. 245–50) of the miraculous saints' legends which Bartoli is represented as telling, and then turns impatiently to a tale from real life better to his liking. Indeed, from the manuscript it is evident that the idea of addressing the *Parleying* to Bartoli is an afterthought, and that Browning went through the manuscript changing "Sir" to "Don" and "Doctor" to "Daniel." Was the *Parleying* first addressed to Nathaniel Wanley who had provided the poet with many a miraculous tale, though not with a saint's legend? But though Bartoli is unceremoniously passed over in the *Parleying* ostensibly devoted to him, he supplied the English poet with much out-of-the-way information.[16]

From the legendary and miraculous history of Bartoli Browning turns "to no legend but a chronicle," and begins the dramatic story of a druggist's daughter who refused to become a duchess because the act was seen to be detrimental to the welfare of the duke, her affianced husband. The poet tells of her subsequent marriage to a youth who saw her true worth, and of the later careers of the two men whose lives she had touched. Browning's choice of the story is dictated by his desire to exemplify one of the major tendencies of his own art, his delight in finding his poetic subjects in actual history; the poem is, moreover, an excellent example of his characteristic manner.

[15] Browning's copy of the *Simboli* is now in the Balliol College Library. For my materials in this study I have drawn chiefly from Ch. 2 of my *Browning's Parleyings*.

[16] See DeVane, *Browning's Parleyings*, pp. 56–9.

The story which Browning tells is drawn from the *Memoires* of the Marquis de Lassay, published at Lausanne in 1756.[17] Viola Cook has recently shown that Browning knew Sainte-Beuve's *Causerie* upon de Lassay, and drew a number of details from that source, such as the trade which Marianne's father followed and de Lassay's proper age at the time of the story.[18] Probably Browning was reminded of de Lassay by Sainte-Beuve's *Causerie*, but he seems to have used the *Memoires* for *The Glove* and other poems as early as 1845, whereas Sainte-Beuve's *Causeries du lundi* did not begin to be written until 1848.

The *Premier Partie* of the *Memoires* is the book of Marianne, and is called the "Recit de ce qui se passa dans le moment que M. le Duc *de Lorraine* alloit épouser Mlle. Marianne (*Marie-Anne Pajot*)." There are four figures in de Lassay's story: the garrulous lover, the Duke of Lorraine; Marianne Pajot, the heroine; M. le Tellier, the crafty minister of Louis XIV; and de Lassay himself. At the prenuptial banquet, just when all is prepared for the wedding of the duke to the poor but beautiful and good Marianne, the minister of the King enters and forbids Marianne, a subject of France, to marry unless the duke will assign his dukedoms to France after his death on terms already agreed upon. Marianne refuses to permit the duke to sign the agreement and the marriage is broken off; she pleads with the duke to tear up the King's paper in order to save his honor and her love for him; but though in high rage, the duke holds by his bargain with the King, and Marianne accompanies the minister to the court of Louis as a prisoner. This is the high scene of the *Parleying*, but in the sequel Browning gives us the future lives of Marianne and the duke. For her there was reward. A young man, de Lassay, several years her junior, admired her nobility of action and later married her. They fled the court and the camp and for a while lived happily in obscurity. Then she died, and de Lassay after a bitter period of grief took his old way in the world. Browning follows the duke, too, in his subsequent career. The necklace which Marianne had returned to him soon went to grace the throat of a dancer, and Browning imagines the duke's reveries at a later time:

[17] See the *Recueil de differentes choses* par M. de Lassay, I, 5–19. The story is reprinted in DeVane, *Browning's Parleyings*, pp. 64–7, 76–8.

[18] "Browning's *Parley* and DeLassay's *Memoire*," in *MLN* 59:553–6 (December, 1944). Miss Cook cites the *Causeries* 9:166 (1869).

> Fancy's flight
> Makes me a listener when, some sleepless night,
> The duke reviewed his memories, and aghast
> Found that the Present intercepts the Past
> With such effect as when a cloud enwraps
> The moon and, moon-suffused, plays moon perhaps
> To who walks under, till comes, late or soon,
> A stumble: up he looks, and lo, the moon
> Calm, clear, convincingly herself once more!
> How could he 'scape the cloud that thrust between
> Him and effulgence? Speak, fool—duke, I mean!
> (ll. 276–86)

And as the duke speaks there rises before us the Present which has intercepted the Past, the dark and fascinating figure of a woman who has subdued the duke to her will. The duke's strange address to the dark lady whom he loves and yet hates is set off in a verse-form of its own.

To even the casual reader the story of the *Parleying* is singularly like the story of *The Glove,* written and published in 1845, and the reason for the likeness is that de Lassay's *Memoires* gave Browning the story which he used to complete the earlier poem in his own fashion. In *The Glove* we have the young man who observes and admires the lady's action at the lion-pit, and who, when she is disgraced, follows her out and in time marries her; we have the poet Ronsard who in his understanding of the lady's action corresponds to the minister, le Tellier, in de Lassay's story; and we have De Lorge, the garrulous lover, who later marries a mistress of the King and lives to regret it. There are other likenesses in the two stories, but perhaps this indication is sufficient.

The Glove was written in 1845 when Browning was courting Miss Barrett, and that fact is reflected in the situation between the lady and her youthful lover. I believe that in the *Parleying With Daniel Bartoli* as well as in *The Glove* Browning had Elizabeth Barrett in mind as the model for his heroines.[19] In brief, through the story in the *Parleying* Browning is musing upon his own past life. He was himself the young man of *The Glove* and of the *Parleying* who understood the motives of the lady when she had retired from the world, who married her, and lived happily with her in obscurity until she died. The poem, like the other *Parleyings,* was autobio-

[19] I have demonstrated this point more fully in my book, *Browning's Parleyings,* pp. 83–8.

graphical. But more astonishing still, it has been shown that in the
projection of the career of the duke after Marianne has left him,
Browning was thinking of his own affair with Louisa Lady Ashburton in 1869–71.[20] She is the "bold she-shape," dark and overpowering, who was the Present intercepting the Past; or, to use
another phrase which Browning uses, she was the cloud which for
a while obscured the effulgence of the moon. The moon in Browning's poetry is always the symbol of his wife, who became in *One
Word More* "my moon of poets." We may see Browning on several
occasions, in the years after his proposal of marriage to Lady Ashburton, bitterly regretting his action. Here in the figures of the young
man and the duke Browning seems to be comparing his young and
his older self. In a volume as patently autobiographical as the
Parleyings it would be astonishing if Elizabeth Barrett Browning
did not appear. She does appear in the splendid figure of Marianne
Pajot.

With Christopher Smart

The *Parleying With Christopher Smart* consisted of 265 iambic
pentameter lines, rhyming irregularly but for the most part in
couplets, and divided into nine unequal sections. The manuscript
is not dated, but it is probable that the poem was written early
among the *Parleyings,* possibly late in the fall of 1885. The *Parleying* is devoted to the subject of poetry, and Browning tells us of his
early and lasting delight in Smart's magnificent *Song to David,* his
own progress in the theory and practice of poetry, and finally uses
Smart to help him comment upon a very different kind of poetry
—chiefly that of Swinburne—which was being written in the
Eighties.[21]

Christopher Smart (1722–71), the mad poet, had been the Sea-
tonian prize poet five times at Cambridge, writing on the various
attributes of the Supreme Being, and afterwards had done much
hack work in London. According to one curious tradition he had
sold his services to Gardner, a book-seller, for ninety-nine years.[22]

---

[20] T. L. Hood in his *Appendix* to *Letters of Robert Browning,* "Browning and
Lady Ashburton," has proved conclusively what I conjectured to be the case in my
book, *Browning's Parleyings,* pp. 89–91. For the fullest account of this affair
see W. O. Raymond, "Browning's Dark Mood," Ch. 7 in *The Infinite Moment.*

[21] See DeVane, *Browning's Parleyings,* Ch. 3.

[22] See Boswell, *Life of Johnson,* ed. Hill, II, 395.

Towards the end of a very unhappy life, in which he had been deeply religious and rarely sober, he had been driven mad by his cares and ill-health. Madness, in truth, had been very near to him since birth and had overwhelmed him on at least three occasions. On October 8, 1751, Thomas Gray wrote to Horace Walpole concerning Smart, "He is lousy, and he is mad: he sets out this week for Bedlam." [23] In 1756 he was again out of his mind, and in 1763 he was confined to a mad-house where he was visited by Dr. Johnson, who made the classic pronouncement on Smart's condition:

'Madness frequently discovers itself merely by unnecessary deviation from the usual modes of the world. My poor friend Smart shewed the disturbance of his mind, by falling upon his knees, and saying his prayers in the street, or in any other unusual place. Now although, rationally speaking, it is greater madness not to pray at all, than to pray as Smart did, I am afraid there are so many who do not pray, that their understanding is not called in question. . . . I did not think he ought to be shut up. His infirmities were not noxious to society. He insisted on people praying with him; and I'd as lief pray with Kit Smart as any one else. Another charge was, that he did not love clean linen; and I have no passion for it.' [24]

It is not certain, moreover, that Smart was sane when he died in King's Bench Prison on May 21, 1771.

According to tradition it was during Smart's confinement in a mad-house in 1763 that, in default of writing-materials which were not permitted to him, he indented at least a part of his *Song to David* on the wainscot with a key. In 1765 when he published *A Translation of the Psalms of David*, the *Song to David* fittingly concluded the work. But when his nephew, Hunter, collected Smart's poems in 1791 the *Song* which is now considered the crown and glory of the poet's work was not included because the editor saw in it "melancholy proofs of the recent derangement of his mind." [25] This was an astonishing judgment, for the *Song* is the one poem in the English language which catches the exaltation and the splendor of the *Psalms* of David without being a translation or a paraphrase. It is an amazing catalogue of the glories and beauties of the world which God has made:

> Glorious the sun in mid career;
> Glorious th' assembled fires appear;
> Glorious the comet's train:

[23] *The Works of Thomas Gray*, ed. Gosse 1895, II, 215.
[24] Boswell, *Life of Johnson*, ed. Hill, I, 459–60.
[25] *The Life of Christopher Smart* prefixed to *The Poems, of the late Christopher Smart*, ed. Hunter, Reading, 1791, I, xliii, note.

Glorious the trumpet and alarm;
Glorious th' almighty stretch'd-out arm;
    Glorious th' enraptured main:

Glorious the northern lights astream;
Glorious the song, when God's the theme;
    Glorious the thunder's roar:
Glorious hosanna from the den;
Glorious the catholic amen;
    Glorious the martyr's gore:

Glorious—more glorious is the crown
Of Him, that brought salvation down
    By meekness, call'd thy Son;
Thou at stupendous truth believ'd,
And now the matchless deed's achiev'd,
    DETERMIN'D, DAR'D, and DONE.

Smart did much else: he translated Horace in verse and prose; he wrote sonnets, odes, and fables in the approved manner of the eighteenth century. But only in the *Song* did he touch the top-most pinnacles of poetry.

Browning's father, an ardent book-collector, knew the story of Smart's life and possessed two of the poet's original manuscripts, a translation of *Psalm cxxxi* and a poem *On Gratitude, To the Memory of Mr. Seaton,* and these no doubt were shown to his son at an early date.[26] In 1824 Reuben Browning, an uncle, gave Browning Smart's translation of Horace, probably the poetic one of 1767. The collected edition of Smart's works was, as the *Parleying* implies, indubitably in the Browning library. Browning seems to have become first acquainted with the *Song* in a pamphlet edition of 1827, *A Song to David, By the late Christopher Smart, M. A. Fellow of Pembroke Hall, Cambridge; and Translator of Horace* . . . complete with an Advertisement, Extracts describing the writing of the *Song,* and notes.[27] This pamphlet supplied Browning with all the material he had need of for his *Parleying,* save for a general idea of Smart's other poetry. Browning read the *Song* again late in December, 1844, or early in January, 1845, in *Chambers' Cyclopaedia,* which had been published while he was in Italy. Years later he wrote to Furnivall concerning the *Song:* "I think it was the reprint in Chambers that I saw—not in Chalmers; indeed I am sure of it, although I discovered

[26] See *The Browning Collections* (Sotheby Catalogue, 1913), items 280 and 281. See also Griffin and Minchin, *Life,* p. 8.
[27] See DeVane, *Browning's Parleyings,* pp. 102–6.

it there on an occasion that would excuse much mistiness in my memory." [28] The event which would excuse much mistiness in his memory was undoubtedly the advent into his life of Elizabeth Barrett; and in his first letter to her on January 10, 1845, he uses the figure of the "Chapel-sight" concerning her which he uses extensively in the *Parleying*, to describe his feeling when he read again Smart's *Song*.[29] Browning, then, re-read Smart's complete works, looking in vain for another *Song to David*. It was probably at this time that he learned the *Song* by heart.

The influence of Smart on Browning's poetry was very considerable. The mystery of the production of the *Song*—that only in his madness did Smart produce poetry of amazing quality—indicated to Browning that the poet had suffered for once a divine revelation. This aspect of Smart's genius is mentioned specifically in *Paracelsus* (I, 770–4); it haunts all Browning's pronouncements on poetry in his middle years, shows itself plainly again in *The Two Poets of Croisic* in 1878, where a similar revelation is accorded to René Gentilhomme, and it is one of the main subjects of the *Parleying*. Smart also provided Browning with material for poetry. Perhaps the catalogue of the beauties of the earth in *Pauline* owes something to Smart; certainly the rich heaping of good things in such a lyric as "Heap cassia, sandal-buds and stripes" in *Paracelsus* (IV, 190 ff.) is in Smart's manner. Smart provided Browning with the subject of *Saul* in 1845, and Browning's manner of cataloging the delights of the earth for which Saul should have been thankful is precisely Smart's method. It is possible, too, that a stanza from the *Song to David* gave Browning his wise thrush in *Home-Thoughts, from Abroad*, written also in the spring of 1845, when Smart was much in Browning's mind. But perhaps above all Smart stood, to Browning, as a representative of a type of lyrical poetry—a poetry which poured out love and gratitude to God for the beauties and wonders of the good earth. It has been suggested that Smart was in Browning's mind when he was in the process of formulating his theory of poetry—that Smart contributed with Shelley to Browning's figures of the lyrical poets, Aprile and Eglamour in *Paracelsus* and *Sordello*, and perhaps to Pippa herself in her songs—in short, that Smart stood as representative of the poet of lyrical fervor while

[28] *Letters*, ed. Hood, p. 262.
[29] Compare *Letters of R.B. and E.B.B.*, I, 2, 6, and *With Christopher Smart*, ll. 26–63.

Browning was finding his own mature and intellectual manner.[30]

In the *Parleying* Smart is called in by Browning to help him confute the tenets of the Aesthetic Movement which was flourishing in the Eighties. Rossetti, Morris, and Swinburne, the chief poets of this school, saw the wonders and glories of the earth, but they did not, as did Smart and Browning, render fervent thanks to God for them. Rather, they were antagonistic to poetry with a moral or didactic purpose, and they were indifferent, at best, to religion. Browning has in mind especially, I think, Swinburne, for it was he who attempted with violence to free poetry from the shackles of morality; and his poetry was definitely pagan, and sometimes atheistic, in temper.[31] The closing thought of the *Parleying* is a warning against the atheistic tendencies of the verse of Browning's own late day.

With George Bubb Dodington

The *Parleying With George Bubb Dodington* consisted of 345 lines of iambic pentameter verse, rhyming irregularly but chiefly in couplets, and divided into seven unequal sections. The manuscript is not dated, but the poem was probably written during the spring of 1886. Of all the *Parleyings* this one was most evidently written for the sake of an attack on a contemporary; the simple and blundering methods of Dodington in politics are contrasted with the successful technique of Benjamin Disraeli. Since morals are out of court among such politicians as these, according to Browning, the poem is a discussion in sustained irony of the best manner of self-aggrandizement, and Disraeli becomes the hero of the piece.[32]

George Bubb Dodington, Lord Melcombe (1691–1762), was a politician who flourished in the reign of George II. He was a man of immense wealth, and controlled six seats in Parliament. He himself represented the borough of Bridgewater until he was beaten in 1754. He was of colossal size, of immense dignity, and of very considerable powers, but he was at the same time vain, impatient, fickle, and servile. Horace Walpole writes of him:

[30] The subject of Browning's indebtedness to Smart is treated at length in *Browning's Parleyings*, pp. 107–19.

[31] For a more detailed treatment of Browning's quarrel with these poets see *Browning's Parleyings*, pp. 120–5, 132–3. See also Kenneth L. Knickerbocker, *Browning and Swinburne*, in *MLN* 62:240–4 (April, 1947).

[32] See DeVane, *Browning's Parleyings*, Ch. 4.

This man, with great knowledge of business, much wit, and great parts, had, by mere absurdity of judgment, and a disposition to finesse, thrown himself out of all estimation, and out of all the great views which his large fortune and abilities could not have failed to promote, if he but preserved the least shadow of steadiness.[33]

He was commonly described by his contemporaries as a man of parts, but "unsteady, treacherous, vain," with no regard for truth when anything was to be gained by a lie. He betrayed one master after another, and thus ruined a promising career. Chesterfield attempted to give a final judgment on him:

With submission to my Lord Rochester, God made Dodington the coxcomb he is; mere human means could never have brought it about. He is a coxcomb superior to his parts, though his parts are superior to almost anybody's. He is thoroughly convinced of the beauty of his person, which cannot be worse than it is without deformity. His distinguished awkwardness he mistakes for a peculiar gracefulness. He thinks himself successful with women, though he has never been tolerated by any. . . . He talks of his ancestors, though no mortal knows that he even had a father. And what is difficult for him to do, he even overrates his own parts. Common coxcombs hope to impose on others, more than they impose upon themselves; Dodington is sincere, nay moderate; for he thinks still ten times better of himself than he owns. Blest coxcomb! [34]

Beyond his political career, Dodington was a literary patron and served as the model for the portrait of Bufo in Pope's *Epistle to Dr. Arbuthnot* (ll. 229–44). He gathered about him a number of literary men—Young, Thomson, Fielding, Whitehead, Glover, Welsted—a group not nearly so undistinguished as the satirist would have us believe.

The chief source of Browning's information upon Dodington was the *Diary* of that statesman published at Dublin in 1784 and edited by H. P. Wyndham. There were two copies of this book in the Browning library in 1913: the first had undoubtedly been the copy belonging to the poet's father, a keen student of history, and was probably read by Browning as a boy; the second was inscribed in the poet's hand "Jan. 20. '86," and was probably bought for use in writing his *Parleying* at that time.[35] The *Diary* does not give the reader a good objective picture of Dodington, but is rather a record of the hopes, fears, indignations, and satisfactions of the politician

[33] Walpole, *Memoirs of the Reign of George II*, 1846, pp. 87–8.
[34] *The Letters and Works of Lord Chesterfield*, ed. Mahon, 1853, V, 385.
[35] This copy is owned by Professor C. B. Tinker of Yale, who has graciously permitted me to use it.

between 1749 and 1761. It does give ample evidence of the perfidy and treachery of its author. From Wyndham's *Preface,* and from the extracts from Hawkins' *Life of Johnson,* Edgeworth's *On Education,* and Belsham's *George II* which had been inscribed by a former owner in the front of Browning's copy, the poet took in the main his conception of Dodington. One passage in Wyndham's *Preface* seems to have directed Browning's opinion:

However, I cannot patiently forgive the violent declamation of his Lordship [Dodington] against "the low and venal wretches of Bridgewater;" as if a bribe, taken by a miserable voter, and, possibly for the support of a numerous and indigent family, was more dishonourable, than a place or pension, enjoyed or coveted by the opulent, for the sole purposes, either of accumulating riches, or of extending the pomp of pride and power.[36]

This passage refers to Dodington's chagrin when he lost his seat in the election at Bridgewater in 1754. Another source supplied Browning with information. On December 22, 1880, Browning read *The Works of Sir Chas. Hanbury Williams,*[37] annotated by Horace Walpole and published in 1822; and in the first volume he found a number of satirical poetic assaults upon Dodington. Here, for example, is a stanza of *A Grub upon Bub,* "Written for the use of the Votesmen of Bridgewater, March, 1740–1," to the tune of "Packington's Pound":

> Good people draw near, and attend to my song,
>   And despise not my ballad for being a Grub;
> For if 'tis not a good one, at least 'tis not long,
>   And I'll tell you, in short, the fall of poor Bub:
>   How he lost his good place,
>   And is in disgrace,
>   And does not know where to show his flat face;
> For the Torys will never receive such a scrub,
> And no Whig at court will be civil to Bub.

From these sources it seems that Browning formed a somewhat erroneous impression of Dodington and his career. Dodington was abler than Browning imagined, and was not greatly dependent, as Browning implies, upon the support of the voters, but rather upon the favor of his masters, the King, Walpole, and Newcastle. Yet Browning's main interest was not in Dodington, but rather in Disraeli's method of managing the populace, and Browning therefore

[36] *Preface* to the *Diary,* p. ix.
[37] See *The Browning Collections* (Sotheby Catalogue, 1913), item 1212.

warped the conditions which Dodington met in the politics of the eighteenth century to conform with those which Disraeli met in the politics of the nineteenth.

Browning's portrait of Disraeli would be perfectly recognizable, even if Browning had not told Mrs. Orr that he intended it for the nineteenth-century statesman.[38] The portrait is the one usually painted by Disraeli's enemies, and in all probability Browning's is a first-hand impression. The poet was a Whig-Liberal in his politics and a friend of Gladstone, and to that party Disraeli, leader of the Tory-Conservative party, was a charlatan, the "Professor" of mystery, the Sorcerer, the outrageous liar, the "mysterious wire-puller." It is so that Browning portrays him in the *Parleying*, but with all emphasis upon Disraeli's amazing subtlety. The poet had disagreed with Disraeli on almost every major political issue from 1845 to 1887. As early as March 10, 1876, Browning described an encounter with Disraeli and told his friends of his intention of attacking the statesman in verse:

'What a humbug he is! Won't I give it him one of these days!' Royal Academy dinner. Dizzy's speech. 'What struck him most was "the *imagination* of the British School of Art, amid ugly streets and dull skies, etc. etc."'

Afterwards Disraeli came up to Browning and said, 'What do you think of this Exhibition?'

Browning wished to hear Disraeli's opinion. Disraeli said—'What strikes me is the utter and hopeless want of imagination' (as much as to say, you didn't think me such a fool as I seemed in my speech!)

Browning told this to Gladstone, who said pungently, 'It's hellish! He is like that in the house too—it's hellish!'

'And so it is,' added Browning.[39]

This was Browning's view of the statesman, and it was the view of half of England. The other half believed just as ardently in the greatness and righteousness of Disraeli.

In the *Parleying* Disraeli gives Dodington a lesson in the management of men because he knows the two great principles of the psychology of politics: the first of these is that man will not obey his like and equal; the second is the positive side of the first, that it is the supernatural only which awes man into obedience. These principles of political psychology had been long observed by Browning. In 1843

---

[38] *Handbook*, p. 351. The matter is treated in detail in my book, *Browning's Parleyings*, pp. 150–7, 164–5.

[39] Allingham, *Diary*, 1907, p. 246; see also pp. 250 and 268.

in *The Return of the Druses* the hero, Djabal, saw that he was power-less to help the Druses unless he proclaimed himself Hakem, or the incarnation of the Deity (IV, 125-7).[40] Bishop Blougram recognizes the value of the supernatural in ruling his "million imbeciles"; as long as Caliban can convince himself that Setebos is such another as him-self, he has no fear; Sludge, the medium, builds his villainy on the principle that "Man's nature owns a supernatural" (ll. 1165-7); upon the superstition of men Hohenstiel-Schwangau founded his empire. But of all of Browning's villains Disraeli is most master of these se-crets of political ruling, and his portrait is given the worst eminence in the poet's gallery of rogues. Because Dodington had not these se-crets he is merely a knave, and a fool into the bargain.

With Francis Furini

The *Parleying With Francis Furini* consisted of 616 lines of iambic pentameter verse, rhyming irregularly but chiefly in couplets, and divided into eleven unequal sections. The manuscript, much worked over, was dated as finished "Sept. 30, '86." The *Parleying* is some-thing of a catch-all, offering Browning an opportunity to say his mind on several subjects, and the result is a strange medley upon painting, theology, and science. Poetry and vituperation jostle each other. Since Furini was both a painter of the nude and a priest, Browning can retort upon the critics who had attacked his son, Robert W. B. Brown-ing, for his paintings in the nude, and at the same time can preach against the point of view of the Darwinian evolutionists.[41]

Francis Furini was born about the year 1600 at Florence; he was interested in painting at an early age, studied under Mateo Rosselli, and rapidly distinguished himself as a painter of frank feminine nudes. The subjects of a few of his paintings may be named: Cleo-patra, Lot and his daughters—a subject which he treated several times—Adam and Eve, Rachel, the Muses, the Bacchantes, and above all, Andromeda. Furini was much sought after by the nobles of Italy and France. He was easy with his money, used the most expensive colors, and paid high wages to his female models; he was generous to his family and friends, and was, not unnaturally, generally in debt. At the age of forty he repented his sinful life and became a priest of

[40] See D. A. Smalley, *Browning's Essay on Chatterton,* Ch. 3, "Fact and Formula: Three Studies in Imposture."

[41] See DeVane, *Browning's Parleyings,* Ch. 5.

S. Sano in Mugello, Tuscany. This office he administered with great care and generosity until his death in 1649. On his death-bed, the rumor went, he repented the lascivious pictures he had painted and begged his friends and relatives to collect them and burn them. As we shall see, Browning refused to believe this rumor.

Browning's acquaintance with the works of Furini seems not to have begun until in 1847 he and Mrs. Browning settled in Florence where most of Furini's paintings were. All Browning's information on the painter seems to have come from Filippo Baldinucci's life of Furini in his *Notizie de' Professori del Disegno*,[42] of which the account I have given above is an abstract. The *Parleying* is as much with Baldinucci as with Furini, for Browning rejects Baldinucci's interpretation of the painter's character. Browning had used the *Notizie* as early as 1847, for though Vasari's *Lives of the Painters* had been his chief source for *Fra Lippo Lippi, Andrea del Sarto,* and *Old Pictures in Florence,* Browning had corrected Vasari's facts by Baldinucci. In *Pacchiarotto*, in *Filippo Baldinucci on the Privilege of Burial* (1876), in the present *Parleying,* and in *Beatrice Signorini* (1889), the *Notizie* is the chief, if not the entire source.[43] But though he used his work, Browning did not like Baldinucci, and perhaps with cause, calling him on every occasion "blockhead," "mild moral-monger," "scruple-splitting, sickly-sensitive," and "a typically ignorant Tuscan." In the *Parleying,* as elsewhere, Baldinucci's offence is that he scolds Furini for painting the feminine nude and records with great moral unction the painter's last wish to have his paintings burnt. This brings upon his head an amazing vituperation from Browning (ll. 144–73)—amazing until we realize that Browning was striking through Baldinucci at John Callcot Horsley, a person very like Baldinucci in character and position, who had objected to the paintings of the feminine nude by Robert Wiedemann Browning, the poet's son, in 1885 and 1886.[44] Horsley was treasurer of the Royal Academy from 1882 to 1897, and its unofficial publicist; he was a patron of Burlington House, and himself a painter. Perfectly paralleled to Baldinucci in these respects, he shared the Florentine's aversion to the feminine nude. In 1884 he had refused to exhibit the younger Browning's statue of Dryope at Burlington House, and he

[42] First published at Florence, 1681–1728. I use the edition published at Florence in twenty volumes in 1767–74. Furini's life is given in XVI, 3–22.

[43] Browning's indebtedness to Baldinucci is treated at length in my *Browning's Parleyings,* pp. 167–81.

[44] See DeVane, *Browning's Parleyings,* pp. 180–4, 210–2.

led an attack upon the nude in art in the columns of the *Times* (May 20–5) in 1885. Browning refers to this in the *Parleying,* and because one of Horsley's letters was signed "A British Matron," the poet refers to him as "a satyr masked as matron" (l. 154). A list of the younger Browning's paintings during these years shows that he painted the feminine nude almost exclusively, but it was his picture of 1886, *Joan of Arc and the Kingfisher* (Joan about to bathe), exhibited in the Grosvenor Gallery, that brought the attack specifically upon him and caused the poet's counter-attack upon the critic in the *Parleying.* On May 12, 1886, Browning wrote to Furnivall:

> I am ashamed at the objection taken by some of the critics to the Eve-like simplicity of Pen's peasant-girl, who before going on to saintliness (which the Church still withholds from her) was satisfied with the proverbially next step to it—cleanliness. If they knew anything of Joan's habits even when advanced in her saintly career, they would remember she was no prude by any means. Her favored young cavalier, the Duc d'Alençon, mentions that he had frequently seen her undress, and that "aliquando videbat ejus mammas quae pulchrae erant"—in his very words.[45]

Browning had probably suggested the subject to his son, and he wrote seven lines of verse to accompany the picture when it was exhibited. These verses he included in the *Parleying* (ll. 601–7) as a description of a picture by Furini—a picture which Furini, of course, did not paint.

The second half of the *Parleying* rose from the fact that Furini was a priest as well as a painter. Browning was always ready in his later years to expound his religious views, and here he took up the argument where he had left off in the *Mandeville.* He commands Furini to preach, not as he would to his congregation in Mugello, but as he would to a congregation in London in 1887. The result is an expression of Browning's disagreement with the scientists of his day:

> Evolutionists!
> At truth I glimpse from depths, you glance from heights,
> Our stations for discovery opposites,—
> How should ensue agreement? (ll. 265–8)

Though Browning had as early as 1835 in *Paracelsus* (V, 685–710) in his own fashion partly anticipated the evolutionary conception of life, and had used the idea many times in his poetry,[46] he grew more

[45] *Letters,* ed. Hood, p. 247.
[46] See my extended treatment of this idea in *Browning's Parleyings,* pp. 193–9.

and more mistrustful of the doctrine, without understanding it well, as he grew older. His chief objection was that science seemed to "level downwards," to use a phrase of the day, to be interested in exposing the base origins of life, instead of pointing to man as the highest achievement of nature, reaching upwards towards God. To Browning, too, Huxley and Tyndall, the chief expositors of Darwinism, did not take into account sufficiently the Intelligence behind the operations of nature. They had no word for God.

The step from science to theology was an easy one for Browning, and it was made easier by the fact that Furini had painted a picture upon the subject of Andromeda. Here was another example of the feminine nude, but more importantly, here was the symbol of Browning's faith. One remembers from *Pauline* (ll. 656–67) the magnificent apostrophe to Andromeda "as she awaits the snake on the wet beach . . . quite naked and alone"; and the poet rested in the faith that "some god To save will come in thunder from the stars." He wrote all his first poems, as we know, with Polidoro di Carravaggio's *Andromeda*, "the perfect picture," before him. The idea became the major theme of Browning's poetry and life; it appears notably in *Count Gismond* and *The Ring and the Book*, and elsewhere; it led him to the rescue of Miss Barrett from Wimpole Street. In the *Parleying* the symbol is used in a different manner, for now Browning and his faith are in the position of Andromeda, and the waste waters of doubt and the blackness of ignorance shut them in on every side, and Browning awaits the deliverer. In this brilliant simile, then, does the poet once more assert his religious position in 1887. But before he leaves off he returns once more to the picture, *Joan of Arc and the King-fisher*, which his son had recently painted, and gives it his final tribute.

With Gerard de Lairesse

The *Parleying With Gerard de Lairesse* consisted of 434 lines, most of them iambic pentameter verses, rhyming irregularly but chiefly in couplets, and divided into sixteen unequal sections. The last section ends in an independent poem of nine lines, divided into three stanzas and rhyming in triplets. There is no date in the manuscript, but it is my impression that the poem was written early among the *Parleyings*, perhaps in the fall of 1885. The subject mainly dealt with is the question of the classical or Hellenistic tendency in modern painting and poetry, and Browning places himself on the modern side and disagrees with a number of contemporary practitioners, chief of whom is Matthew Arnold. [47]

Very early in his life Browning became acquainted with the work of the late seventeenth century Dutch painter who in his blindness became a writer on art. He not only saw Lairesse's paintings in the Dulwich Gallery, which he was accustomed to visit as a boy with his father, but he read in his father's library Lairesse's book, *The Art of Painting in All its Branches,* translated from the Dutch by John Frederick Fritsch in 1778. In the copy which Browning had read as a child, he wrote in 1874: "I read this book more often and with greater delight when I was a child than any other: and still remember the main of it most gratefully for the good I seem to have got from the prints and the wonderful text." [48] Inspired by the book, the young Browning went to the Dulwich Gallery to see Lairesse's pictures, *Pan and Syrinx in a Landscape, Apollo and Daphne in a Landscape,* and *Apollo flaying Marsyas.* The pseudo-classical pictures, full of flying shapes, centaurs, satyrs, and gods in the manner of Poussin, disappointed the youthful student of *The Art of Painting;* and in this Browning reflected the judgment of the world. For Lairesse, who was assured by the leading poets of his time of a glorious immortality, and who was mourned at his death as a "second Raphael," was soon forgotten as a painter, but his book kept his memory alive for more than a hundred years.

The most salient characteristic of Lairesse, both as a painter and an instructor, was his preference for the beauty and perfection of the classic antique as against the sordidness and "deformed ugliness" of the modern subject. In the midst of such stalwart Dutch realists as Teniers, Ostade, and Brouwer, Lairesse seldom condescends to treat a subject that is later than Ovid. He thus defends his position:

> But let us reflect on two arts, noble and ignoble or *antique* and *modern,* and see how much they differ both in objects and execution. *The antique is unlimited,* that is, it can handle *history,* sacred as well as profane, *fables and emblems* both moral and spiritual; under which three heads it comprehends, *all that ever was, is, and shall be; the past, present,* and *to come; and that, after an excellent manner, which never alters, but remains always the same: The modern, contrarily, is so far from being free, that it is limited within certain narrow bounds; and is of small power; for it may or can represent no more than what is present, and that too in a manner which is always changing: What is past and to come is without its power;*

[47] See DeVane, *Browning's Parleyings,* Ch. 6.
[48] Quoted in Griffin and Minchin, *Life,* pp. 9–10.

as also histories, fables and emblems, as well poetical and philosophic as moral. Hence we may judge what the *modern* art of painting is, and why it cannot be called *noble;* much less of any harmony with the *antique.*[49]

But as Browning in his youth turned from Lairesse's pictures, so in his age did he turn from Lairesse's theories.

Yet the English poet did not reject Lairesse entirely or all at once. The painter's conception of the beautiful in landscape, as well as of the horrible, made an immense impression upon the boy, and may be said to have shaped to a considerable extent the tastes of the man.[50] Lairesse's ideal landscape and his habit of suiting scenery and action to the light and the time of day seem to have directed Browning's description of the perfect land to which the lovers fly in *Pauline.* The same features may be seen in *Paracelsus, Sordello, Pippa Passes,* and indeed in most of the poems in which landscape is used on a large scale. Browning's conception of the horrible in landscape, as it may be seen at its extreme in *Childe Roland,* has been shown to have been derived almost directly, though unconsciously, from Lairesse's description of what he thought "unpainterlike" in nature.[51] In *The Art of Painting* (Book VI, Chs. XVI–XVII) Lairesse takes his pupils on an imaginary walk to show them the ideal and the horrible in landscape; and in the *Parleying* Browning attempts to match the painter's ideal scenes as he walks, with a series of his own. These are drawn, like Lairesse's, from classical legend, and so we have a grand vision of Prometheus at daybreak, a superb picture of the cold white Artemis in the dewy morning, a version of the story of the Satyr and Lyda in the deep forest at noon, the armies of King Darius III and Alexander the Great confronting each other at dusk, and at night the pallid ghost of the spirit of Greece, regretful for the past and hopeless of the future. In this series of pictures Browning is attempting to overmatch Lairesse, for the painter saw only the surface of his scenes, and Browning attempts to read more than the eye sees, through his deeper insight. In this he is notably successful, and he draws from this fact the idea that the world has progressed in insight and that we see more subtly than the men of the past.

In this *Parleying,* as in the others, the person of importance in old

---

[49] *The Art of Painting,* p. 99.
[50] This is exhibited at length in DeVane, *Browning's Parleyings,* pp. 221–6.
[51] See my article on "The Landscape of Browning's *Childe Roland*" in *PMLA* 40:426–32.

days is merely a stalking-horse for the expression of Browning's opinion upon contemporary men and tendencies. Lairesse preferred to find his subjects in the remote past and despised the vulgar present. Looking about him in 1887, the poet saw that he alone among the greater poets of his day had painted contemporary figures in the vulgar streets to any extent—that he alone had brought a realistic psychological insight to bear, in the manner of Fra Lippo Lippi in *his* day, upon the life about him. Tennyson's later fame rested on his medieval *Idylls,* Arnold had espoused Hellenism, Rossetti and Morris were confirmed medievalists, and Swinburne hardly touched earth at all. But Lairesse was an ardent lover of Rome and Greece, and therefore Matthew Arnold, the modern and the greatest champion of Hellenism, was singled out for refutation in the *Parleying.*[52] In his famous *Preface* to his *Poems* in 1853 Arnold had opposed the false contemporary view that poets must write upon "matters of present import," and he said in rebuttal:

A great human action of a thousand years ago is more interesting to it [our passions] than a smaller human action of to-day, even though upon the representation of this last the most consummate skill may have been expended, and though it has the advantage of appealing by its modern language, familiar manners, and contemporary allusions, to all our transient feelings and interests. . . .
Achilles, Prometheus, Clytemnestra, Dido—what modern poem presents personages as interesting, even to us moderns, as these personages of an "exhausted past"?

And Arnold practised what he preached; he wrote *Empedocles, Merope, Sohrab and Rustum* and a number of other poems which were modelled upon or drawn from the ancient classics. It is this view that Browning answers in the *Parleying* (ll. 381–94).

Browning and Arnold had shared an interest in the Greek drama, Arnold admiring Browning's *Artemis Prologizes,* and Browning insisting upon the republishing of *Empedocles* in 1867. But as early as 1845 Miss Barrett had expressed an opinion in which Browning had thoroughly concurred:

I am inclined to think that we want new *forms,* as well as thoughts. The old gods are dethroned. Why should we go back to the antique moulds, classical moulds, as they are so improperly called? If it is a necessity of Art to do so, why then those critics are right who hold that Art is exhausted and the world too worn out for poetry. I do not, for my part, believe this: and I believe the so-called necessity of Art to be the mere

[52] See *Browning's Parleyings,* pp. 234–40.

feebleness of the artist. Let us all aspire rather to *Life,* and let the dead bury their dead. If we have but courage to face these conventions, to touch this low ground, we shall take strength from it instead of losing it; and of that, I am intimately persuaded. For there is poetry *everywhere;* the 'treasure' . . . lies all over the field.[53]

We have seen that Browning meant his *Cleon* in 1855 to be an answer to the despair of Arnold's *Empedocles;* and in Browning's preface to his translation of Aeschylus' *Agamemnon,* where he quotes from Arnold's *Preface* of 1853, there is some reason to suspect the sincerity of Browning's approval of Arnold's position. In the *Parleying* there can be no doubt of his disapproval.

What, then, made Browning turn against the Greeks whom he so admired? The answer is given at the end of the *Parleying*—indeed, it was formulated in 1855 in *Old Pictures in Florence* and in *Cleon.* Browning's central belief was Christian and progressive, and his nature revolted when the Hellenists proclaimed the Greek civilization the greatest the world had seen.[54] To Browning the Greek ideal had reached earthly perfection in its kind, and had perished. In *Old Pictures in Florence* he had preferred the crudest of the early Christian painters to the most finished of the Greek artists, for the Christians were attempting to depict the soul. Again, the Greek philosophy had led men ultimately to despair; the Christian revelation had given men new hope. There is not a Greek, he says, not even Achilles, who would not slink back to life, if he could, on the meanest terms. The Christian has, what the Greek had not, a hope in immortality. The *Parleying* ends with an exquisite lyric, such as a modern poet might sing to spring; it probably commemorates the grave of Mrs. Browning. Under the title of *A Spring Song* the lines first appeared in *The New Amphion,* "The Book of the Edinburgh University Union Fancy Fair," in 1886.

With Charles Avison

The *Parleying With Charles Avison* consisted of 433 lines, most of them iambic pentameter, rhyming irregularly but chiefly in couplets. The last twelve lines make an independent song of three stanzas in honor of Pym and are set to the music of Avison's *Grand March.* The whole poem is divided into sixteen unequal sections. The manu-

[53] *Letters of R.B. and E.B.B.,* I, 45–6.
[54] See my article "Browning and the Spirit of Greece," in *Nineteenth-Century Studies* (Cornell), 1940, pp. 179–98.

script is not dated, but the poem itself leads one to believe (ll. 1–49) that it was written in March, 1886, or very soon afterwards. The *Parleying* is devoted to music, that life-long passion of the poet's, and with the aid of Avison's *Grand March,* Browning reviews his own experiences and ideas in music. This is the substance of the *Parleying,* but before he has done he more than hints that the great musicians of his own later day—Brahms, Wagner, Dvorak, and Liszt, who seem so thoroughly the last word in music in 1887—will in time be out-moded and all but forgotten, as are the great masters of the past.[55]

By a trick of association the name of the month, March, when the poet saw a black-cap struggling in the bleak weather for a scrap of cloth to make its nest, made Browning's memory fly back to his own childhood and pluck from his recollection a scrap of old music which his mother had played for him, Avison's *Grand March.* A manuscript copy of this piece of music by the eighteenth-century organist of Newcastle was in the possession of the poet's father,[56] and two copies of Avison's little book, the *Essay on Musical Expression,* 1752, were in the Browning library. Avison had taught the poet much concerning the history of music in the eighteenth century, and it is evident that in writing his *Parleying* Browning consulted the *Essay* again for the details he gives us concerning Handel, Buononcini, Geminiani, and others.

But Browning could not think of his early love for music without paying due homage to his music-master,

> Great John Relfe,
> Master of mine, learned, redoubtable. (ll. 81–2)

Relfe was musician-in-ordinary to George III, and one of the best teachers of pianoforte in London. His system of music was founded partly on that of the Abbé Vogler, and it was undoubtedly from him that Browning first heard of the German improvisator. From Relfe, indeed, Browning probably got the beginnings of his great knowledge of the history of music, as well as his knowledge of its technical aspects, for Relfe undertook to teach his pupils "not only Thorough Bass, but the whole arcana of the science, so as completely to analyze any regular composition." [57] It was his training under this rigorous

[55] See DeVane, *Browning's Parleyings,* Ch. 7.

[56] See *New Letters,* ed. DeVane and Knickerbocker, p. 341, and also Herbert E. Greene, "Browning's Knowledge of Music" in *PMLA* 62:1099 (1947).

[57] J. Relfe, *Remarks on the Present State of Musical Instruction with the Prospectus of an Improved Plan,* London, 1819, p. 31.

master that enabled Browning to set to music Donne's *Goe and Catch a Falling Star,* and other poems, and emboldened him to contemplate writing an opera before he was twenty-one.

The poet's mother, Avison, and Relfe gave Browning perhaps most of his characteristic ideas upon music, but in 1846 he encountered Ernest Bouton's *Esquisse biographique sur Claude Lejeune, natif de Valenciennes, surnommé le Phénix des musiciens* . . . , 1845, and that work seems to have crystallized a conception of the transiency of music for which he had been groping. On March 7, 1846, he wrote to Miss Barrett:

For music, I made myself melancholy just now with some 'Concertos for the Harpsichord by Mr. Handel'—brought home by my father the day before yesterday;—what were light, modern things once! Now I read not very long ago a French Memoir of 'Claude le Jeune' called in his time the Prince of Musicians,—no, 'Phoenix'—the unapproachable wonder to all time—that is, twenty years after his death about—and to this pamphlet was prefixed as motto this startling axiom—'In Music, the Beau Ideal changes every thirty years'—well, is that not *true?* The *Idea,* mind, changes —the general standard . . . so that it is no answer that a single air, such as many one knows, may strike as freshly as ever—they were *not* according to the Ideal of their own time—just now, they drop into the ready ear,—next hundred years, who will be the Rossini? Who is no longer the Rossini even I remember—his early overtures are as purely Rococo as Cimarosa's or more. The sounds remain, keep their character perhaps— the scale's proportioned notes affect the same, that is,—the major third. or minor seventh—but the arrangement of these, the sequence the law— for them, if it *should* change every thirty years!

Browning then proceeds to illustrate how the "unanswerable coda" of Corelli, Handel, or Rossini has become obsolete.

All Browning's characteristic ideas concerning music are summed up in the *Parleying With Charles Avison.* The comparison of the effectiveness of the several arts, which had been most notably expressed in *Abt Vogler,* here is presented again in a contest between poetry, painting, and music; and music is once again declared queen of the arts in poignancy and depth, though its effect is not as lasting as that of its rivals. Music is unrivalled in catching the "mysterious motions of the soul," "emotions not else to be revealed"; it casts its nets deeper into man's soul and brings up rarer prizes. But music is less capable than the other arts of fixing the transient emotions of men into a permanent form. The ideal changes, and what was once perfect becomes cold and lifeless. Hence comes that melancholy which always accompanies Browning's poems upon music, the nostalgia for a Venice "dead and done with" in *A Toccata of Galuppi's,* the "good tears" of Abt Vogler for the lost perfections of his improvisations. Then again, as Browning played music, invariably his mind peopled the past with human figures, suffering again their joys and sorrows—the young people taking their pleasure in Galuppi's or Schumann's Venice at carnival time, the saints who walk in the aisles of the church as the organist plays Master Hugues' fugue, the presences of the unborn or the "wonderful dead" in Abt Vogler's "house not built with hands." So too in the *Parleying* Browning peoples England with marchers in the stirring times of the rebellion against Charles I, as he plays over and over the simple music of Avison's *Grand March.*

One other characteristic feature of Browning's conception of music appears in the *Parleying.* In *Abt Vogler* we may see that he regarded music as a miracle. Poetry and painting were made of tangible earthly materials, and their creation was understandable; but music came to man intuitively, it was the voice of God speaking directly to man. This conception gives Browning another opportunity in the *Parleying* (ll. 339–60) to assert the characteristic doctrine of his later philosophy, to exalt the intuitive powers of man, the heart, at the expense of his intellectual faculties. And finally, though the fashion in music changes, music fundamentally is the most eternal of the arts, for it is grounded on the deepest emotions of man. Brahms, Wagner, Dvorak, Liszt, the most eminent composers of 1887, will have their day and pass, but new musicians will rise to put into sound the progress of the human spirit. Therefore, says Browning, let us honor Avison and his *Grand March* which in its day did its part to give courage and hope to men. He concludes the *Parleying* with a song which he has made in honor of Pym, who lived a hundred years before Avison, which he has set to Avison's *March.* In its hero, its musician, and its writer three generations of the English spirit are represented in the song.

Fust and his Friends. An Epilogue

Fust and his Friends, the *Epilogue* to the *Parleyings,* was a dramatic dialogue of 475 iambic pentameter lines, divided into ninety-five stanzas of five lines each. The manuscript is not dated, but the probability is that the poem was written after the *Parleyings,* perhaps in the early fall of 1886. In a volume as patently autobiographical

as the *Parleyings* it is fitting that Browning should pay tribute to the
art of printing; he does so here in an imaginary scene from the life
of Johann Fust. The scene is caught at the moment when the German
printer first makes known to his visitors the secret of printing. Without printing, the poet Browning would have been a very different
person, and he could not close his biographical account of himself
without acknowledgment of the medium through which he became
a voice to his age.

Johann Fust (?1400–66) was a banker of Mainz who had advanced
money to Gutenberg in order that the latter might experiment towards the invention of printing. In 1455 he brought suit successfully
against Gutenberg to recover his money, and it is generally supposed, though it cannot be proved, that Fust took Gutenberg's materials and tools to his own house and there soon afterwards began
to print with the help of his son-in-law, Peter Schoeffer of Gernsheim.
On August 14, 1457, he and Schoeffer published the *Psalter*, a remarkably beautiful work, the first printed book with a complete
date. It is at Fust's house on the evening of this day that Browning
places his scene. He gives all the honors for the discovery to Fust,
though history is inclined to award most of them to Gutenberg.

To the facts of history Browning has playfully added details from
the legend of Dr. Faust or Faustus, a very different person. The
friends of Fust who come to visit him are divines of Mainz and
they believe that Fust has sold his soul to the devil. They think that
Helen of Troy is his mistress. This notion is possibly remembered
from Marlowe's *Dr. Faustus*. Browning's description of the drinking-
bout which took place in Auerbach's cellar in Leipzig is taken, of
course, from Goethe's *Faust* (Part I, ll. 1720 ff.). But the greater
part of Browning's poem was suggested by the account of Dr. Faustus
given by Daniel Defoe, who seems to have been the first writer to
give currency in England to the idea that the printer Fust and Dr.
Faustus were the same person. Browning lays his scene in Mainz,
or Mayence, but it was suggested by Defoe's description of Dr.
Faustus in Paris:

Thus the famous doctors of the faculty at Paris, when John Faustus
brought the first printed books that had then been seen in the world, or
at least seen there, into the city and sold them for manuscripts: they were
surprised at the performance, and questioned Faustus about it; but he
affirming they were manuscripts, and that he kept a great many clerks employed to write them, they were satisfied for awhile. But looking farther
into the work, they observed the exact agreement of every book, one with

another, that every line stood in the same place, every page a like number of lines, every line a like number of words; if a word was mis-spelt in one, it was mis-spelt also in all, nay, that if there was a blot in one, it was alike in all: they began again to muse, how this should be; in a word, the learned divines not being able to comprehend the thing (and that was always sufficient), concluded it must be the Devil, that it was done by magic and witchcraft, and that in short, poor Faustus (who was indeed nothing but a mere printer), dealt with the Devil.[58]

The scene is achieved in Browning's poem when the divines who have come to exorcise the Devil in Fust forget their Latin; the printer steps into the next room and gets each of them a perfect copy of the psalm they are quarrelling about.

Fust and his Friends gives Browning an excellent opportunity to touch again upon certain major ideas of the *Parleyings*. Fust's dejection at the beginning of the poem is owing to his realization that in giving printing to the world he is providing a means for the spread of evil as well as good—they are inextricably interwoven in man's life—and Fust can only go forward with faith that God has his own purposes in the invention. It is a step in progress, which God approves. At the conclusion of the poem Browning makes Fust foresee such a man as Luther whose winged words will soon fly about the world by means of the new invention.

ASOLANDO: FANCIES AND FACTS

PUBLICATION AND TEXT

Asolando was published on December 12, 1889. That evening Robert Browning died in Venice at the house of his son. The volume was post octavo, bound in dark-red cloth boards, and sold for Five Shillings the copy. It consisted of a half-title; the title-page: "Asolando: Fancies and Facts. By Robert Browning. London: Smith, Elder, & Co., 15 Waterloo Place. 1890"; the dedication, to Mrs. Arthur Bronson; a list of contents; and the text, pp. 1–157. The volume was dated as of 1890 because the date 1889 upon its title-page would have made the book seem to be of last year very soon after its publication. The table of contents was as follows:

Prologue	Now
Rosny	Humility
Dubiety	Poetics

[58] Defoe, *Political and Modern History of the Devil*, Bohn ed., 1913, p. 559.

Summum Bonum
A Pearl, A Girl
Speculative
White Witchcraft
Bad Dreams   I
"   "   II
"   "   III
"   "   IV
Inapprehensiveness
Which?
The Cardinal and the Dog
The Pope and the Net
The Bean-Feast

Muckle-Mouth Meg
Arcades Ambo
The Lady and the Painter
Ponte dell' Angelo, Venice
Beatrice Signorini
Flute-Music, With an Accom-
    paniment
"Imperante Augusto Natus
    Est—"
Development
Rephan
Reverie
Epilogue

GENESIS AND COMPOSITION

It was Browning's purpose to give the manuscript of the *Asolando* volume to Balliol College, so that it would be with the manuscripts of all the poetry he had written since *The Ring and the Book*. He gave it to his son, who for some reason did not carry out his father's intention, and in the dispersal of the Browning library in 1913 the manuscript was sold to an American collector for the sum of £990. On December 25, 1924, the manuscript was given to the Morgan Library in New York by Mr. J. P. Morgan.

There is a general, though I think a mistaken, belief that the poems of the *Asolando* volume were written over many years of Browning's life, and that the collection included poems from all periods of the poet's career. It is certain that *The Cardinal and the Dog* was written in 1842, but in my opinion it is the only poem in *Asolando* which was not written during the last three years of Browning's life. The poems in the *Asolando* manuscript are generally not dated, but the few that are bear out my contention. A study of Browning's manuscripts shows that his usual practice was to publish his poems without hesitation at the first opportunity. Browning was not consciously making a last collection of his scattered poems in *Asolando,* and had not the activities of the Browning Society called his attention to *The Cardinal and the Dog* it would have remained uncollected and unimproved. A few of the poems, it is clear from the dedication, were written at Mrs. Bronson's villa, La Mura, in Asolo during September and October of 1889. All of them were revised there.[1] With some certainty we may ascribe several poems, such as *Development,*

[1] See Katherine C. Bronson, "Browning in Asolo," in *Century Magazine* 59: 920–31 (1900).

for example, to the last months of 1887. A good many of the poems were written during the first three months of 1888. In March of that year Browning began to prepare the text for what proved to be the final collected edition of his works, a labor which probably checked the composition of new poems. Some poems were written in the fall of 1888, and the book was well along in the summer of 1889. As late as July, 1889, he told friends that his new book was to be called *A New Series of Jocoseria.*[2] The final title—explained in the dedication as a form of Cardinal Bembo's fanciful verb, "Asolare," made as a play upon the name of Asolo, and meaning "to disport in the open air, amuse oneself at random"—was probably hit upon after Browning's arrival at La Mura, which was very near to Queen Catherine Cornaro's castle, where Bembo had served in the distinguished little court of the deposed Queen of Cyprus. A copy of Bembo's dialogues, *Degli Asolarii,* was in Browning's library. "This morning, I despatched to Smith the MS. of my new volume,— some thirty poems long and short,—some few written here, all re- vised and copied," [3] Browning wrote on October 15; and on the 20th he received news of its safe arrival. By the first of November Browning was at Palazzo Rezzonico, his son's house in Venice, and there he read the proof-sheets, sometimes aloud to his daughter-in- law and his sister. The volume was published on December 12, the day of his death; but before he died Browning was able to take pleasure in the news, sent by telegraph from London, of the very favorable reception of the volume by the critics and the public.

SOURCES AND INFLUENCES

It is difficult to analyze satisfactorily a volume as miscellaneous in its nature as *Asolando.* The poems fall roughly into three groups. 1) The love-lyrics are of two sorts. There are light, charming, in- genious lyrics, such as *Summum Bonum, Poetics,* and *Now,* which are surprising in a poet of seventy-seven, and which were possibly inspired by Browning's delight in his son's marriage to Miss Fannie Coddington on October 4, 1887, or by the presence of Edith Bronson, the daughter of his hostess at Asolo to whom the volume is dedicated. Then there are the more serious and moving love-lyrics, like *Dubiety* and *Speculative,* for the most part reminiscent of his happiness long

---

[2] *Works and Days, From the Journal of Michael Field,* ed. T. and D. C. Sturge Moore, 1933, p. 32.

[3] *New Letters,* ed. DeVane and Knickerbocker, p. 384.

ago with his wife; and others, such as *Bad Dreams,* referring to more recent events. 2) A second group may be called narrative poems; this group makes up the bulk of the volume and includes such poems as *Rosny, The Cardinal and the Dog, The Bean-Feast, Muckle-Mouth Meg, Ponte dell' Angelo,* and *Beatrice Signorini.* These stories are culled from Browning's wide reading in Italian, French, and English books of historical anecdote, or from his vivid recollection of incidents heard long ago. 3) A third group is made up of poems of more serious purpose, and includes such philosophical and personal utterances as *"Imperante Augusto Natus Est—," Development, Rephan, Reverie,* and the *Prologue* and *Epilogue.* These poems give the volume an air of finality, for they are largely restatements of opinions long held.

AFTER-HISTORY

Partly because of Browning's death on the day of publication, and partly because of the simplicity and brilliance of the poetry, *Asolando* had a great success. Nine reprints of the first edition were published within a short time. The first edition is said to have been exhausted in the first day. Naturally, there were no textual changes, so the text of the first edition stands as the final text. For the most part the reviews were inevitably half obituary-notices. The *Spectator* of January 25, 1890, spoke penetratingly of Browning's life-long eccentricity, and illustrated its point from *Asolando.* The *Athenaeum* of January 18, 1890, gave almost entirely a reminiscence and an appreciation of the poet. The *Academy* of January 11, 1890, gave what was perhaps the best review of the new volume. In general, the lighter love-lyrics won the favor of the critics; most of them had a good word for *Bad Dreams I;* very few neglected to quote the *Epilogue* in whole or in part, as a fitting conclusion to the great poet's work.

Prologue

The *Prologue* to *Asolando* consisted of nine stanzas of five lines each. In the manuscript, as in the printed text, the poem was dated from Asolo on September 6, 1889. It was evidently written within a very few days of his arrival in Asolo, at La Mura, the home of Mrs. Katherine Bronson, where Browning and his sister were visiting.

The *Prologue* suggests his arrival, for the subject is the impression which a place makes upon the mind at different periods in life. Browning had first visited Asolo shortly after June 1, 1838, on his first journey to Italy in search of material for *Sordello*. In what golden light he saw the country at that time may best be seen in *Pippa Passes,* and somewhat in *Sordello.* In the late September of 1878 he had returned to Asolo. His letters of that time hardly express disappointment, but the first delight of discovery had gone.[4] On Browning's last visit to Asolo in September and October of 1889, he found it pleasantly familiar. He wrote to his brother-in-law on October 22 that he had "been for six weeks or more in this little place which strikes me,—as it did fifty years ago, which is something to say, considering that, properly speaking, it was the first spot of Italian soil I ever set foot upon—having proceeded to Venice by sea—and thence here." [5] But Asolo was not altogether the same to him. In his mind the place had become a symbol of freshness and freedom in the long years of his absence. The first fine careless rapture was gone, and Browning's slight disappointment is recorded in the *Prologue.* In a letter written on June 10, 1889, he said, "I used to dream of seeing Asolo in the distance and making vain attempts to reach it— repeatedly dreamed this for many a year." And again on July 17, "I used to dream about [Asolo] so often in old days, till at last I saw it again, and the dreams stopped." [6] But characteristically Browning concludes in the poem that the fact of the present is better than the fancy of the past. The years have brought him "the philosophic mind." Browning could hardly have written these lines without remembering Wordsworth's *Tintern Abbey* and the *Ode* on *Intimations of Immortality.* Not only, then, does the poem concern itself with the main subject of the volume, but it illustrates also the subtitle, *Fancies and Facts.* The preference for facts is of course a part of Browning's poetic creed.

Rosny

Rosny, the first poem after the *Prologue* in the *Asolando* volume, consisted of four stanzas of seven lines each. *Rosny* was written, according to Mrs. Orr, late in December, 1887.[7] In the manuscript

---

[4] Orr, *Life,* pp. 309–10.
[5] *Idem,* p. 394.
[6] Lilian Whiting, *The Brownings,* Boston, 1917, pp. 282–3.
[7] *Life,* p. 379. Miss Whiting says in *The Brownings,* p. 267, that the poem was written in January, 1888.

the poem is not dated. In December Browning was at his home in London. In the poem, Clara muses upon the possible fate of her lover, Rosny, who has gone to battle, deciding that for honor's sake it would be better if he were slain. Rosny was the usual name of Maximilian de Béthune, Duke of Sully (1560–1641), a great Huguenot soldier, statesman, and economist; the name Rosny was taken from the chateau near Mantes where the duke was born. He was seriously wounded at the battle of Ivry in 1590, fighting under Henry of Navarre. Because of the ballad form of the poem and the old-fashioned conception of the struggle between love and honor, and Browning's strong predilection for historical facts, I think he may have had this event in the life of Sully in his mind when he wrote the poem, though search in the life of Sully has not revealed such a person as Clara. It may be pertinent that in 1592 Rosny snatched time from the campaign to marry his second wife, Rachel de Cochefilet (Chateaupers).

Dubiety

Dubiety, a poem of six stanzas of four lines each, seems to be in the mood of Browning in the autumn of 1889, and was probably one of the poems written at La Mura, Asolo, in September or early October. At rest and in reverie, the poet experiences what is not a dream or a vision, but a memory of what once befell him.[8] The memory, better than any fancy could be, was of an actual happening; the poem quite evidently refers to Elizabeth Barrett Browning, in this mood so appropriate to the autumn of Browning's life.

Now

Now, a poem of fourteen lines, introduces in Asolando a group of love-lyrics so vigorous and ardent as to be astonishing from a man of seventy-five or more. Except for the addition of an exclamation mark after the first line, the omission of which had been a printer's error, the text has undergone no change. A manuscript of the poem is extant bearing the date, January, 1888. Mrs. Miller conjectures that the poem should be laid to the credit of Mrs. Bloom-

---

[8] This memory of a special moment had long been with him. See, for example, Robert Browning and Julia Wedgwood, ed. Curle, p. 87.

field-Moore,[9] and if this is true it should be read with *Soul-Love* in *Ferishtah's Fancies*. The poem is an echo of many others of Browning's poems on the theme of catching and holding "the good minute." This was the mad hope of the lover in *Porphyria's Lover,* the failure of the lover in *Two in the Campagna,* the success of the lover in *By the Fire-Side*—to name only a few of the many.

Humility

Humility, two stanzas of six lines each, is another lyric of love, probably owing its origin to 1889. It is, perhaps, an old man's poem, and may, like the three poems which follow it, owe its existence to Edith Bronson, the daughter of Browning's hostess at La Mura. The poem is not dated in the manuscript in the Morgan Library.

Poetics

Poetics, two stanzas of four lines each, is a love-lyric, fit companion to *Now* and *Humility.* It, too, was probably written in 1889, though the manuscript is not dated. *Poetics* expresses in its own way the major theme of *Asolando,* that facts are superior to fancies, however lovely.

Summum Bonum

Summum Bonum, a single stanza of eight lines, belongs also to this group of love-lyrics, and is perhaps the best of them. It was probably written in 1889, though the manuscript is not dated. The poem is curiously reminiscent of the second stanza of Ben Jonson's lyric, "Have you seen but a bright lily grow," from *The Devil is an Ass* (II, vi).[10]

A Pearl, A Girl

A Pearl, A Girl, two stanzas of seven lines each, also probably owes its origin to 1889, though the manuscript is not dated. The ring mentioned in the first stanza may be the ring of Solomon, to which

[9] *Robert Browning,* p. 297.
[10] See H. F. Brown, "A Case of Poetic Affiliation: Ben Jonson and Robert Browning," in the *Spectator* for August 6, 1921.

Browning had referred in *Abt Vogler* and in *Solomon and Balkis.* The second stanza expresses an idea that was a favorite with Browning all his life—the conception of the transfiguring power of love, and its power to discover in the loved one another nature hidden from the world. This second aspect of the idea had received its most notable expression in *One Word More.*

Speculative

Speculative, two stanzas of five lines each, is more like *Dubiety* than its nearer neighbors, and has the appearance of a poignant personal expression. The poem refers, I think, to the poet's married life with Mrs. Browning, and his hope of seeing her again. For that reason, I am inclined to think it was written at La Mura, in Asolo, in September or early October, 1889. The poem is not dated in the manuscript.

White Witchcraft

White Witchcraft, three stanzas of three lines each, belongs as a love-lyric with *Poetics, Now,* and *Summum Bonum.* The poem was probably written at Primiero in the Dolomite Alps in September, 1888; the manuscript is not dated. Mrs. Orr says that "*White Witchcraft* had been suggested . . . by a letter from a friend in the Channel Islands which spoke of the number of toads to be seen there." [11] But it did not take shape until the early fall when Browning made the acquaintance of a young fox, "the most engaging of little vixens," kept by the innkeeper at Primiero. To Browning's delight the fox escaped, but came back to steal food and then vanished altogether. The poem suggests the life-long delight which Browning found in making friends with small animals. This trait he inherited from his mother; in her garden at Hatcham he had cultivated acquaintance with a toad which seemed to become very fond of him. By the term "white witchcraft" Browning refers to the witchcraft of love, the most benevolent of occult practices. It was a common medieval belief that there were good (white) witches as well as bad (black) ones. In the phrase "a pearl beneath his puckered brow" Browning refers to a widely accepted legend that the toad has a gem of magic properties concealed in its head. "Canidia" is the name which Horace

[11] *Life*, p. 379.

gives to a courtesan whom he calls a sorceress in his *Epodes V* and *XVII*. In *Epode V* the "gore of a loathsome toad" is one of the poisons used by Canidia. *Epode XVII* is a dialogue between Horace and Canidia, in which she refuses to use her magic except to increase his love. Horace says (ll. 21–6), "My youth is sped; departed is my rosy bloom; my bones are covered with a yellow skin; with thy essences my hair is white; night follows close on day, and day on night; nor is it possible to ease my straining breast by taking breath." In the reference to Canidia, Browning is glancing playfully at his own age and condition.

Bad Dreams

Four poems were associated under the head of *Bad Dreams*. There is no clear indication of the date of composition, but Mrs. Orr asserts that two or three of the *Bad Dreams* were written in London soon after the beginning of the year 1888.[12] Mrs. Miller cites a statement of Mrs. Bloomfield-Moore that *Bad Dreams* is a tribute to her which no one could understand as well as she.[13] It may be that Browning is recording a painful experience that he had at St. Moritz when he was a guest of Mrs. Bloomfield-Moore in the fall of 1888. The meaning of these poems is not of the clearest. The strain between a man and a woman has become severe, and in dreams, which they tell each other, the suspicions which they will hardly speak have found expression. The husband believes that his wife may be faithless, and is surely tired of her bond; she believes that he does not love her, but is her "life's cold critic bent on blame." The situation is not unlike the hard, bitter and intricate one delineated by George Meredith in *Modern Love,* though of course Browning does not develop *Bad Dreams* at length. It is something like *A Lovers' Quarrel* and *James Lee's Wife,* though developed in *Bad Dreams* from both sides.

In *Bad Dreams I,* two stanzas of four lines each, the dream seems to be that of the wife, though this is not clear. Though in the dream the husband declared "Faith gone, love estranged," her love has not altered.

In *Bad Dreams II,* twenty stanzas of five lines each, the dream related first is the husband's. In it he discloses his unconscious fears

[12] *Ibid.*
[13] *Robert Browning*, pp. 287, 297.

concerning his wife's faithfulness. He dreamed of a huge hall where people who hated each other danced together as if they were chained. He, coming into the hall, crept along its edge until he came to a chamber, or chapel, and there he saw his wife offering adoration to the dark spirit of the place. Yet here she is before him in the flesh, her usual self. He cannot reconcile these two aspects of his wife. She attempts to turn the subject by a whimsical account of a trivial and meaningless dream of her own.

In *Bad Dreams III*, three stanzas of twelve lines each, the dream is again the dream of the man. In the first part he sees a magnificent and primitive forest where some brute-type of man lives; in the second part he sees a great perfect city, empty save for himself; in the third part he sees the city in the midst of the forest, each destroying and ruining the other. Nature and art conflict inexorably. Perhaps the man means to say to the woman that love should be as free and wild as the forest, and that she has brought consciousness and intellect into their relationship.

In *Bad Dreams IV*, nine stanzas of five lines each, the dream is the woman's. She dreams that she is in her grave, and her marble slab is getting weather-stained and covered over. To her comes "that strong stern man my lover," her husband, and she shrinks, thinking that he comes to pry into her with his cold critic's eyes, as of yore. But he is weeping, and in a broken voice begs her back again. She cannot imagine what has so altered his stern bearing, until she follows his eyes to the tomb-stone and reads with him there the date when she died, long ago, of the stab of his scorn.

Inapprehensiveness

Inapprehensiveness, a poem of thirty-two lines in rhymed couplets, was written, as line 12 suggests, in September or early October, 1889, after Browning's arrival in Asolo. No date is appended to the manuscript of this poem. The tower upon which the wall-growths wave was probably the ruin of Queen Catherine Cornaro's castle which rose behind Mrs. Bronson's house. In a letter to a friend on October 8, 1889, Browning wrote, "I find the Turret rather the worse for weeding—the hawks which used to build there have been 'shot for food.' " [14]

In meaning, *Inapprehensiveness* suggests such an earlier poem as

[14] Orr, *Life*, p. 389.

Two in the Campagna; there, as here, the failure of the man and woman to pass the barriers of mutual comprehension is the subject. Mrs. Miller suggests that the poem reflects a moment at La Mura when Mrs. Bronson was gazing at the castle and its wall-growths, ignoring the "dormant passion" of the poet who is with her—a passion that would burst into immense life at a look.[15] The look was not given; Mrs. Bronson's was a calculated inapprehensiveness. She turns the crisis in a matter of fact way, and by his reply he accepts the situation upon her terms. "Vernon Lee" was the pseudonym of Violet Paget, who wrote many books on the *genius loci.* Browning knew her *Studies of the 18th Century in Italy,* 1880, and *Belarco: Being Essays on Sundry Aesthetical Questions,* 1882, and *Baldwin: being Dialogues on Views and Aspirations,* 1886.[16] Several of her books were in the Browning library upon its dispersal in 1913.

Which?

Which?, a poem of five stanzas of six lines each, concludes a group of lyrics on love which appear in the first part of *Asolando.* The temper of the poem indicates that it was probably written in 1888. The manuscript is not dated. The Abbé, judging the contest between the court ladies as to which was the best judge of love, overlooks the Duchesse who requires piety and loyalty in a man as well as love, the Marquise who requires purity and valor, and gives the decision for the Comtesse who asks only love.

The Cardinal and the Dog

The Cardinal and the Dog, fifteen lines in two parts, was the first of a series of stories in *Asolando.* The poem was written in May, 1842, for Willie Macready, the son of the actor, just before Browning wrote *The Pied Piper.* Writing to Furnivall on October 1, 1881, Browning said:

The "W. M. the younger" was poor William Macready's eldest boy—dead, a few years ago. He had a talent for drawing, and asked me to give him some little thing to illustrate; so, I made a bit of a poem out of an old account of the death of the Pope's legate at the Council of Trent—which he made such clever drawings for, that I tried at a more picturesque subject,

---

[15] *Robert Browning,* p. 297.

[16] *New Letters,* ed. DeVane and Knickerbocker, pp. 327–8. See also *Intimate Glimpses from Browning's Letter File,* p. 112.

the Piper. I still possess the half dozen of the designs he gave me. If you cared to have the Legend of the Legate I am sure you are welcome to it, when I can transcribe it from the page of the old book it remains upon. . . .[17]

In the London *Bookman* for May, 1912 there was printed a facsimile text of a version of the story of *The Cardinal and the Dog*, in the hand of Robert Browning, the poet's father.[18] There are some differences between this early text and the final text of the poem as we have it in *Asolando*, but in the main it is the same poem. One must conclude, I think, that the text printed in the *Bookman* was the elder Browning's copy of his son's poem. The difference between these two versions is interesting; the changes were probably made in 1888 when Browning, having decided to use the poem in his new volume, prepared it for the press. Besides a considerable number of verbal changes for the sake of smoothness, and a different arrangement of the lines—there were originally twenty-six short lines, instead of the thirteen long lines in *Asolando*—two new lines were added, the fifth and fifteenth. From the new fifth line one suspects that Browning consulted again in 1888 the source he had used in 1842. It is interesting that the version of 1842 had the date of the event celebrated in the poem in the right year, 1552; while the version in *Asolando* gives the date by mistake as 1522.

Browning's source was an old familiar book, Nathaniel Wanley's *Wonders of the Little World*, which also helped him to *The Pied Piper*. "I give mine Author's very words: he penned, I reindite," said Browning. In Wanley's book we find the story:

Crescentius the Pope's Legate at the Council of Trent, 1552, March 25, was busie writing of Letters to the Pope till it was far in the night, whence rising to refresh himself, he saw a black dog of a vast bigness, flaming eyes, ears that hung down almost to the ground enter the room, which came directly towards him, and laid himself down under the table. Frightened at the sight, he called his Servants in the Anti-chamber, commanded them to look for the Dog, but they could find none. The Cardinal fell melancholy, thence sick, and died at Verona: on his death-bed he cryed out to drive away the Dog that leaped upon his bed.[19]

The Cardinal Crescenzio was the legate of Pope Julius III and President of the Council of Trent, which met in 1551–2 to deal with the

---

[17] *Letters*, ed. Hood, p. 197.
[18] Vol. 42, p. 68. See also the letter by Mr. C. Elkin Mathews in the *Times Literary Supplement* for September 15, 1921.
[19] Ed. 1678, p. 611.

problem of the rise of Protestantism. Crescenzio was obnoxious to the Protestants because he would make no concessions.

The apparition of a black dog, especially when he is howling, has from time immemorial been considered a harbinger of death. The Cardinal died at Verona on June 1, 1552. The legend of the dog is said to have been told of him by his enemies.

The Pope and the Net

The Pope and the Net consisted of eight stanzas of three lines each. There is nothing to indicate the date of composition; the manuscript is not dated, but it was probably written in 1888. Had it been in existence very early it probably would have been included in such a volume as *Jocoseria*, 1883. It has greater point and maturity than *The Cardinal and the Dog*. Though Browning's poem is concerned with a pope whose father was a fisherman, none of the popes after St. Peter were fishermen or the sons of fishermen. The story here told is probably a fabrication of the poet's. There are innumerable tales of great prelates who have won to office by a false obsequiousness and have shown their true colors after their elevation. Of these, the most eminent was Sixtus V, Pope from 1585 to 1590. He was born of humble farming parents at Grottamara in Ancona in 1521, and was reared in extreme poverty. Through his great talents he rose to be a cardinal, and trod warily indeed until he was made Pope. According to Gregorio Leti's *Vita di Papa Sisto V*, Sixtus had represented himself as in bad health and in most humble mind when he was cardinal. But "when he perceived there was a sufficient number of Votes to secure his Election, he threw the Staff, with which he us'd to support himself, into the middle of the Chapel, stretch'd himself up, and appear'd taller, by almost a foot, than he had done for several years. . . ." [20] One of the cardinals, who was helping Sixtus put on his pontifical robes, was surprised at his vigor, and said to him, "I perceive, Holy Father, the Pontificate is a sovereign Panacea, since it can restore Youth to old, sick Cardinals." To this Sixtus replied in a grave and majestic manner, "So I find it." To another cardinal who remarked that he seemed quite a different man from the bent and stooped person of a few hours ago, Sixtus

[20] *The Life of Pope Sixtus the Fifth, Translated from the Italian of Gregorio Leti . . .* by Ellis Farneworth, London, 1754, p. 150. Leti is most untrustworthy, but may have been read by Browning for his many anecdotes.

replied, "Yes, I was then looking for the keys of Paradise, which oblig'd me to stoop a little; but now I have found them, it is time to look upwards, as I am arriv'd at the summit of all human Glory, and can climb no higher in this world." Gregory XIII, his predecessor, had left the country in a terrible condition, and Sixtus after his inauguration was compelled to be stern and ruthless in stamping out disorder and corruption. The seeming change in his character gave rise to innumerable stories of his wiliness, though the best judges are now convinced that he was one of the best of the popes. See *The Bean-Feast.*

The Bean-Feast

The Bean-Feast, a poem of forty-eight lines rhyming in couplets, is related in subject and manner to *The Pope and the Net* and was probably written at about the same time, that is, probably in London or Venice in 1888. The manuscript is not dated.

It is possible that Gregorio Leti's garrulous and inaccurate *Vita di Papa Sisto V,* from which Browning seems to have adapted *The Pope and the Net,* also supplied him with the story of Sixtus V which he here used. The wretched condition of Rome after the death of Gregory XIII forced Sixtus into many reforms, and it is evident that he had a care for the poor. There is no doubt that he employed many spies to see that his state was in order; and he was consequently greatly feared by the people. It is not recorded by Leti that Sixtus himself went incognito among the poor, but the act would have been in character. The incident which Browning seems to have adapted from Leti reads thus in the life:

Another time, as he pass'd through the city, seeing the gates of that Convent open, he suddenly got out of his chariot, and went into the Porter's lodge, where he found the Porter, who was a Lay-brother, eating a plate of beans with oil poured over them. As the meanness of the repast put him in mind of his former condition, he took a wooden spoon, and sitting down close to the porter, on a stair-case, first ate one platter full with him and then another, to the great surprise of those that were with him: After he had thank'd the Lay-brother for his entertainment, he turn'd to his attendants, and said, "We shall live two years longer for this; for we have eat with an appetite, and without fear or suspicion." And then, lifting up his eyes to Heaven, said, "The Lord be prais'd for permitting a Pope, once in his life, to make a meal in peace and quietness." [21]

[21] *Idem,* p. 299.

If this is, as seems likely, the story which suggested *The Bean-Feast* to Browning, his additions are characteristic. For a fuller account of Sixtus V see the discussion of *The Pope and the Net*.

Muckle-Mouth Meg

Muckle-Mouth Meg, a poem of ten stanzas of four lines each, bears resemblance to other stories in verse in *Asolando*, and in default of definite evidence as to the date of composition may, like them, be tentatively ascribed to 1888. The manuscript, which is in the Morgan Library, bears no date.

The incident recounted in the poem is a well-known story from the ancestry of Sir Walter Scott, and a picture of the event was kept at Abbotsford. Lockhart in his *Life of Sir Walter Scott* tells the story of Sir William Scott who was favored by James VI and in later years was fined by Cromwell. Sir Walter himself had told the story in more detail in his *Tales of a Grandfather*, though he does not mention the name of his ancestor.

A young gentleman, of a distinguished family belonging to one of these Border tribes, or clans, made, either from the desire of plunder, or from revenge, a raid, or incursion, upon the lands of Sir Gideon Murray of Elibank, afterwards deputy-treasurer of Scotland, and a great favourite of James VI. The laird of Elibank, having got his people under arms, engaged the invaders, and, encountering them when they were encumbered with spoil, defeated them, and made the leader of the band prisoner. He was brought to the castle of his conqueror, when the lady inquired of her victorious husband "what he intended to do with his captive?"—"I design," said the fierce baron, "to hang him instantly, dame, as a man taken red-hand in the act of robbery and violence."—"That is not like your wisdom, Sir Gideon," answered his more considerate lady. "If you put to death this young gentleman, you will enter into deadly feud with his numerous and powerful clan. You must therefore do a wiser thing, and, instead of hanging him, we will cause him to marry our youngest daughter, Meg with the meikle mouth, without any tocher" (that is, without any portion). The laird joyfully consented; for this Meg with the large mouth was so ugly, that there was very little chance of her getting a husband in any other circumstances; and, in fact, when the alternative of such a marriage, or death by the gallows, was proposed to the poor prisoner, he was for some time disposed to choose the latter; nor was it without difficulty that he could be persuaded to save his life at the expense of marrying Meg Murray. He did so at last, however; and it is said, that Meg, thus forced upon him, made an excellent and affectionate wife; but the unusual size of mouth was supposed to remain discernible in their descendants for several generations.[22]

Browning's ultimate source is probably Sir Walter Scott's story, but he told friends that his version came from Benjamin Jowett who had heard it from Lady Stewart, and that he had thought it was merely a legend and not a fact in Scottish history.[23] The manner in which Browning has dramatized the story is evident at a glance.

Arcades Ambo

Arcades Ambo, consisting of two stanzas of seven lines each, may have been composed upon August 27, 1889, for upon that date Browning wrote to Berdoe consenting to give his support to an anti-vivisectionist hospital.[24] The manuscript is not dated. The poem is a fitting companion to Tray in the first series of the Dramatic Idyls, which the reader should consult for Browning's interest in the anti-vivisectionest movement. Both poems express Browning's scorn for vivisectionists and, conversely, his great love for animals.

The Lady and the Painter

The Lady and the Painter is a dialogue of twenty-eight lines in rhyming verse. The poem was written at Asolo in September or early October, 1889. Mrs. Bronson records that one day as they returned from a drive to Bassano the poet fell strangely silent. Finally he announced that he had written a poem since they had left Bassano. When the ladies exclaimed, Browning said, "Oh, it's all in my head, but I shall write it out presently." Mrs. Bronson asked if he would not tell what had inspired the poem. Browning said, "Well, the birds twittering in the trees suggested it. You know I don't like women to wear those things in their bonnets." [25] The poem proved to be The Lady and the Painter.

[22] Ch. XXXVII. First published in 1828. The story had also been told in a poem called The Fray of Elibank in James Hogg's (the Ettrick Shepherd) The Mountain Bard.

[23] "Diary of Miss Evelyn Barclay," in Baylor University Browning Interests, Fifth Series, 1932, pp. 35–6.

[24] See E. Berdoe, Browning's Message to his Times, the chapter "Browning and Vivisection."

[25] Katherine C. Bronson, "Browning in Asolo," in the Century Magazine 59: 923 (1900).

The poem is propaganda against two things Browning did not care for. As a stroke against those who objected to painting the nude the poem is definitely milder than his savage attack in the *Parleying With Francis Furini*. As a plea against cruelty towards birds and animals it is a companion to *Tray* and *Arcades Ambo*.

Ponte dell' Angelo, Venice

Ponte dell' Angelo, Venice, consists of thirty-two stanzas of six lines each, 192 lines in all. The poem was probably conceived in November or December of 1888 when Browning was a guest of Mrs. Bronson in Venice. It was finished, according to the manuscript, on January 9, 1889. In her reminiscences of the poet Mrs. Bronson relates the following story:

A modern book was brought to his notice during his last sojourn (but one) in Venice. It is Tassini's "Curiosita Veneziane," which gives a history in brief of the old palaces, together with their divers legends; also the origin of the names of the streets and bridges. He was interested in this, and even mentions the book in a letter written after his return to London: "Tassini tempts me to dip into him whenever I pass the bookcase."

He was impressed by a story in this volume, which he afterwards told in verse. It is published in "Asolando," and is entitled "Ponte dell' Angelo." Not content with Tassini's version of the legend, the poet looked it up in the "Annals of the Cappucini" by Father Boverio. He said nothing of this to anyone until a certain day, when, to the question, "Where would you like to go?" he answered promptly: "To see the house of the Devil and the Advocate."

We rowed quickly to the place where three waterways meet, and where the Ponte dell' Angelo spans one of the narrow canals. Opposite stands the old Soranzo palace, with an angel carved in stone on the façade.

"Stop," he said to the gondolier, "the broad-backed Luigi," as he always called him. "Do you know the story of that angel?"

"Si, signore."

"Then relate it."

The boatman at once proceeded to repeat most volubly in the Venetian dialect the tale, familiar to him from childhood.

"Do you think it is true, Luigi?" said the poet.

"Yes, sir, it is really true; it has been printed." The man's faith in the veracity of print amused the poet immensely.[26]

From this it appears that Browning first found the story in Tassini's *Curiosità Veneziane* (1863), which was at Ca Alvisa, Mrs. Bronson's

[26] Katherine deKay Bronson, "Browning in Venice," in the *Century Magazine* 63:579 (February, 1902).

home, and tested the story by Father Boverio's *Annales . . . ordinio minorum S. Francisci qui capucini nuncipantur* (1632–9), to which he refers in the penultimate stanza of the poem; he then perhaps added color to his story from the oral version of the gondolier. The story of the famous bridge, as told by Tassini, may be translated as follows:

ANGELO (Street of the Bridge, Branch of that Street, Street and Bridge, Bridge, Ways along the canal, Street leading to the Ponte dell' Angelo) at St. Mark's. On the façade of a neighboring house may be seen a sort of little altar in marble, on which is carved the figure of an angel above two shields. The story which is said to have given rise to the sculpture is a curious one. We shall take it from Father Boverio's *Annals of the Capuchins,* and in part shall use his very words. The good friar narrates, then, that in the year 1552 the above-mentioned house was occupied by a lawyer of the ducal court, who, for all that he was a devout follower of the Blessed Virgin, had augmented his income with dishonest gains. He invited to dinner one day Father Matthew da Bascio, head of the Capuchins, and a man of exemplary life, and before taking their places at table, he told him that he had in the house a fine ape, so well trained that he attended to all his master's household duties. The good Father at once realized by divine grace that a demon was concealed beneath that disguise, and, having caused the ape, which had been hiding under a bed, to be brought before him, he said to it: "I command you in God's name to reveal to us who you are and why you have entered this house."

"I am the Devil, and have come here for no other purpose than to drag off with me the soul of this lawyer, which is owed to me on many counts."

"And why, then, if you are so greedy, have you not already killed him and taken him with you to Hell?"

"Only because before going to bed he has always commended himself to God and the Virgin; for had he neglected his accustomed prayer but once, I should have transported him without delay to the eternal torments."

Father Matthew, when he had heard this, made haste to order the Enemy of God to leave the house at once. But the Devil opposing him on the ground that he had been granted permission from above not to leave the house without doing some harm, "Very well," said the Father, "You shall indeed do some harm, but only what I shall command, and no more. As you go, you shall make a hole in this wall, and the opening you shall make shall serve as evidence of the occurrence."

The Devil obeyed, and the Father sitting down to dinner with the lawyer, reproved him with his past life, and at the end of his admonition, taking in his hands a corner of the tablecloth and twisting it, he caused blood miraculously to issue from it in great quantities, telling him that it was the blood of the poor which he had extracted with so many unjust extortions. The lawyer wept for his transgressions, and warmly thanked the Capuchin for the grace he had obtained; he expressed, however, his fear of the opening left by the Devil, and regarded himself as but poorly safe as long as the way remained open to so formidable an adversary. Father Matthew, however, reassured him, and enjoined him to have placed in the aperture the likeness of an angel, since the angels of Evil would flee at the sight of the good angels. This incident was of so public a nature, concludes Boverio, that a bridge near the house where the sculpture of the angel is seen is called to-day the Bridge of the Angel.[27]

The legend is one of the innumerable ones told of the power of the Virgin to protect those who pray to her. One may judge from Browning's treatment of lawyers in *The Ring and the Book* and elsewhere that he took some pleasure in depicting the profession in *Ponte dell' Angelo*.

Beatrice Signorini

Beatrice Signorini consists of 352 lines, rhyming in couplets. The poem was written, says Mrs. Orr,[28] just after *Rosny* in December, 1887. But the manuscript bears a cancelled date which seems to be April 23, 1889. At either time Browning was in London, and it was easy for him to put his hand upon Baldinucci's *Notizie de' Professori del Disegno,* a source book which had been of use to him for many years.[29] In Baldinucci's accounts of the lives of Artemisia Gentileschi (XIII, 3–13) and Francesco Romanelli (XVIII, 204–30) Browning found the story and the characters which he uses in *Beatrice Signorini.*

From the life of Romanelli Browning drew the facts of the painter's career and character which make up the background of the story. Romanelli (1617–62) was born at Viterbo; he studied under Cortona (*i.e.,* Pietro Berretini) and later under Barnini of Naples; he was patronized by many notable men in Italy and by Louis XIV of France. His marriage with the noble and beautiful lady, Beatrice Signorini, had the blessing of Cardinal Barberini. He painted in many towns in Italy, and made two sojourns in the French court. Baldinucci describes Romanelli as being witty and graceful and as having a noble appearance. He says,

His personal influence was such that every one with whom he came in contact was charmed and fascinated by him. During his sittings he always conversed with his subjects and thus kept them amused and interested by

---

[27] Tassini, *Curiosità Veneziane,* 1863, pp. 29–30.
[28] *Life,* p. 379.
[29] See DeVane, *Browning's Parleyings,* pp. 170–9.

his brilliant conversation and his lively descriptions. No obscene picture ever issued from his brush, which was ever inimical to a public display of the nude.[30]

The last sentence, a characteristic one for Baldinucci, was ideally calculated to anger Browning. He had already said his mind upon Baldinucci's prudery in the *Parleying With Francis Furini*. The reference in *Beatrice Signorini* to Ulysses, Penelope, and Calypso was brought to Browning's mind by the fact that Romanelli painted a picture called *Ulysses*.

For the main incident of *Beatrice Signorini* Browning went to Baldinucci's account of Artemisia Gentileschi (1597–1652?). Her father was Orazio Lomi, a painter of Pisa, who took the name of Gentileschi. She was a beautiful woman and a skilful painter. She studied under Guido Reni and painted in Rome, Florence, Naples, and in London. She had three specialties in painting—portraits, the nude, and fruit; she became renowned for her portaits. Her picture of herself is now in Hampton Court. She painted portraits of some members of the family of Charles I. Of the nude she made a number of striking pictures, *Aurora*, *The Rape of Proserpine*, and the *Desire* being the most famous. This last picture is mentioned by Browning in the poem. Artemisia had painted the subject for the younger Michael Angelo, in honor of the Buonarroti, but Baldinucci says:

. . . This figure [of the *Desire*] was completely nude, and so it had to be, according to the poetic conception of Buonarroti; but Lionardo, his nephew and heir, he, too, a gentleman of rare qualities, for the sake of the decorum and modesty with which he wished every part of his home to appear adorned to the chaste eyes of a handsome group of boys, his sons, and of Ginevra d'Esaù Martellini, his wife, desired that nakedness covered by Baldassarre Volterrano, at the request of him who writes these things [Baldinucci]; which Volterrano did to the point where he judged the pious sentiment of Lionardo could be satisfied without detracting in any way from the beauty of the painting.[31]

Artemisia's great fondness for and skill in painting fruit Browning changed, for artistic purposes, into a penchant for flowers. Browning had probably seen her most celebrated picture, *Judith and Holofernes*, in the Uffizi Gallery at Florence.

The story which makes up the body of the poem may be translated as follows from Baldinucci's account of Artemisia Gentileschi:

[30] Baldinucci, *Notizie de' Professori del Disegno* . . . , Florence, 1767–74, XVIII, 228.
[31] *Idem*, XIII, 10.

. . . She had another fine talent, which was to reproduce with marvelous naturalness every kind of fruit, and I do not wish to neglect to set forth here all the many trustworthy accounts which have come to me from the city of Rome to commemorate the good painter Giovanni Francesco Romanelli of Viterbo, disciple of Cortona. This artist was much made use of in that city at the time of Urban VIII, and was in great favor with the Casa Barberina; and because he was a lively youth and very fond of gallantry, having contracted an innocent friendship with the painter Artemisia, being often in her house for the pleasure he took in seeing her paint, and entertaining each other with agreeable discourses on Art, he desired to paint her portrait. It was at exactly that time in which she was giving great proof of her gifts in the very beautiful pictures of fruit which issued from her brush, whence Romanelli ordered her to make a picture all full of such paintings, leaving enough space in an opportune spot in which the portrait of the artist in the very act of painting should make a good appearance, this portrait to be done by his hand. Artemisia obeyed, and the painter in gentlest ways made the portrait, not for her but for himself, and so dearly did he hold it, that, returning to his own region he wished to carry it with him, on a par with every other and richer furnishing, of which he had acquired an abundance through different gifts received from prelates and princes. He showed it to his consort, and then gave it a well-chosen place among the other beautiful pictures with which he had adorned his house, and now and then, for a pleasantry, he would summon his wife and have her consider the portrait of Artemisia, and he would set about praising no less the artist's mother, who had made her so beautiful—which was as much as to admire the beauty of the young woman herself—than to praise the curious artistry with which in the picture she had counterfeited her fruits, enlarging, besides, on all that which the painting could not demonstrate, that is, the charm of her gentle manners, her graceful speech, her witticisms, and other similar qualities of hers. All this he did in order to enjoy the anger to which his wife, herself very beautiful, would give vent; she, often raging from excess of jealousy, finally one day flew into such a fit of rage that, seizing a time when her husband was not at home, and armed with a great pin or bodkin or awl, whichever it may have been, she began to surround with closely-spaced holes the face of that Artemisia so odious to her, and particularly those places where had their seat the qualities most lauded by her own husband, who when he perceived the clever revenge, and had taken it as an indication of the deeply rooted affection borne him by his dear wife, completely left off his praising that portrait, which, while I write these things, I hear is even now in the home of the same Romanelli's heirs.[32]

Browning told Miss Barclay (see note 23 above) that he thought *Beatrice Signorini* the best poem in *Asolando*.

[32] *Idem,* XIII, 11–3.

Flute-Music, With an Accompaniment

Flute-Music, With an Accompaniment, consisting of sixteen stanzas of twelve lines each, 192 lines in all, is a dialogue in verse. The poem, Mrs. Orr asserts, was written just after *Beatrice Signorini* in December, 1887, or January, 1888; [33] at this time Browning was at home in London. The date appended to the poem in the manuscript has been obliterated.

Flute-Music is a dialogue between lovers. *He* is delighted with the music he catches through the ash-tree tops; *She,* who has heard her neighbor playing this music on his flute many times, is not enchanted at all. *He,* as the dialogue progresses, is the champion of fancy; *She,* of reality. At the end of the poem *He* pleads for illusion in love: *He* would rather not know all, and escape knowing the worst.

"Imperante Augusto Natus Est—"

"*Imperante Augusto Natus Est—,*" consisting of 163 lines of blank verse, may, in the lack of definite evidence as to date of composition, be tentatively ascribed to 1888. The manuscript bears no date. It is likely that Browning would have published the poem earlier if he had had it in hand, for it is one of the most striking poems of his last volume.

Browning's chief purpose here is to catch vividly and concisely the pagan Roman world just at the advent of the new Christian era. How Christianity would strike a contemporary had been Browning's subject in two brilliant poems of *Men and Women—Cleon* and *Karshish.* In *Cleon* he undertook to delineate the Greek mind; in *Karshish* he set himself the task of picturing the world of that time and the mind of an Arabian scientist. In "*Imperante Augusto Natus Est—*" Browning attempts to depict the Roman world of 2 B. C. Ingeniously, he puts into the mouth of a senator the utterance of the Sibyl that in the reign of Augustus would be born a babe who would be master of the world. The Sibyl Browning has in mind is probably the Erythraean, whose utterances now make up the third book of the *Sibylline Oracles.* There (III, 55–60) we read the prophecy of Christ's coming, which was possibly an interpolation by later Christian propagandists: "But when Rome rules also after Egypt (having one end in view) then

---

[33] Orr, *Life,* p. 379.

shall appear the mighty kingdom of the immortal king, set over men. A holy king shall come wielding the sceptre over every land until all ages of advancing time." The mention of Egypt is a reference, of course, to Augustus' victory over Antony at Actium. The same prophecy of the coming of a Messiah is made in different phrase in the *Oracles* in Book VIII, in lines 211 ff. and elsewhere. It appears also notably in the tenth century in Suidas. In the eyes of medieval scholars Virgil had attained the rank of a prophet of the birth of Christ as early as the fourth century, because in his famous *Fourth Eclogue* (Pollio) he had sung the coming regeneration of the earth through the birth of a babe as the first-born of the new race.[34] The belief in Virgil's powers of prophecy continued very late. In 1712 Alexander Pope published his *Messiah,* in which the prophecies of Isaiah and Virgil are mingled, and Virgil is accorded equal honors. It was probably in Pope's poem that Browning first encountered this legend. It is now thought that Virgil's *Eclogue IV* may have been intended as a celebration of the peace of Brundisium (40 B. C.) between Octavianus and Antony. The child honored by Virgil was probably Pollio's son, Asinius Gallus, who played an important rôle in the reign of Tiberius.

For his brilliant portrait of Augustus, Browning has rifled Suetonius' account in *De Vita Caesarium,*[35] where one may find almost all the details which Browning puts into the mouth of the speaker at the bath, a Roman of senatorial rank. For example, Suetonius says (XXVIII) that Augustus "could justly boast that he had found it [Rome] built of brick and left it in marble." The buildings mentioned by Browning as built by Augustus—Thundering Jupiter, Avenging Mars, Apollo Palatine, the Forum, etc.—are mentioned by Suetonius (XXIX), as are also the improvements by Augustus in clearing the Tiber, straightening the Flaminian Way (XXX), and establishing the public games (XLIII). Suetonius also comments (XLVI) upon the twenty-eight colonies—Browning says thirty—which Augustus established in Italy. But the most interesting passage in common between Suetonius and Browning is the description of Augustus' appearance. Suetonius remarks (LXXIX) upon the "clear bright eyes,"

---

[34] See Domenico Comparetti's excellent book, *Vergil in the Middle Ages,* tr. Benecke, 1895, Ch. VII.

[35] Browning probably used Suetonius' *Lives of the First Twelve Caesars,* translated by A. Thomson, 1796, and also Suetonius: *Opera, Commentarius exhibente Jo. Schildio,* 1647. Both of these works were in *The Browning Collections* (Sotheby Catalogue, 1913), items 1121 and 1122.

the tawny hair, the eyebrows which meet over his eyes, and "his nose [which] projected a little at top and then bent slightly inward." How near this is to Browning's description one may readily see. In Suetonius (XCI) we likewise encounter a sentence which Browning made the most of. In speaking of Augustus' superstitious dread of evil he says, "It was likewise because of a dream that every year on an appointed day he begged alms of the people, holding out his open hand to have pennies dropped into it."

Besides his brilliant condensation of the career and personality of Augustus into a few lines, Browning has caught many other aspects of the life of Rome in the reign of the Emperor. The deification which Virgil, Horace, and Varius accorded the Emperor is true to history. We have ample record of it in the *Aeneid* (VI, 789–806) and the *Georgics* (IV), the *Odes* and *Epistles,* and similarly we may take Varius Rufus' panegyric for granted, though only two lines of it remain. But to bring these poets upon the scene was an anachronism, for Browning sets the time as during the thirteenth consulship of Augustus, which was in the year 2 B. C., and Virgil died in 19 B. C., Varius Rufus in 14 B. C. and Horace in 8 B. C.

All these elements—Suetonius' life of Augustus, the deification of Augustus by the Roman poets, the pagan conception of the revolutions in heaven which dethroned Chronos and Saturn and will in time dethrone Jupiter, the medieval tradition of Virgil's prophecy of the birth of Christ, which encouraged the Christian *Sibylline Oracles,* the condition of the times as they may be seen in Horace's *Satires—* all these elements Browning condenses into an effective poem. Browning's chief interest, it should be repeated, was to catch that pagan world at the advent of the Christian era. The likeness of the poem to *Cleon* and *Karshish* has already been suggested; in its condensation it resembles *The Bishop Orders his Tomb.* In *Asolando* it is the first of four serious poems which conclude the volume.

Development

Development is a poem of 115 lines of blank verse. There is nothing to indicate the date of composition, but it was probably written within the last two years of Browning's life. No date is appended to the manuscript. The tone of reminiscence, as well as Browning's activities, leads one to ascribe the poem to the fall of 1887 or the early part of 1888. The *Iliad,* which gives Browning his subject, was a life-long favorite with the poet. There were eight editions of Homer in the Browning library, and the work of Heyne and Wolf upon Homer were both represented there. But particularly in the last years of his life did the English poet resort to the *Iliad*. For example, he wrote to Furnivall from St. Moritz, Switzerland, on August 21, 1887, "To-day comes exactly such a snowstorm as I happened to read of this morning in the *Iliad*, the only book I brought with me." [36]

The poem is a delightful piece of biography, with yet a serious purpose behind the trivial events. The elder Browning had been something of a scholar and knew Greek, and there is nothing unlikely in the poet's account of his own first acquaintance with the story of Troy. Browning's first acquaintance with the *Iliad* at length was quite probably through Pope's famous translation, published 1715–20. The young scholar, when he came to Greek, would naturally have used one of the many editions, translated from the German, of Philipp Karl Buttmann's (1764–1829) excellent *Greek Grammar*. In consulting Heyne, Browning was in the orthodox highway of Homeric scholarship. Christian Gottlieb Heyne (1729–1812) labored for fifteen years over his edition of the *Iliad*, which finally appeared in 1802, and it was for many years a standard, though not the best, text. With Friedrich August Wolf (1759–1824) a new era in classical scholarship began. At Göttingen Wolf studied the *Iliad* under Heyne, but was disappointed by the master's lectures. He became a professor at Halle, and revolutionized the study of the classics and indeed of all the higher education in Germany. In 1795 Wolf published his famous *Prolegomena to Homer*. Here he contended that the Homeric poems were handed down by oral tradition, that they were not written down until about 550 B. C., that the text was deliberately improved by critics, that the artistic unity of the *Iliad* has been superinduced by later writers, and that the original poems which made up our *Iliad* and our *Odyssey* were not all by the same author. Wolf supposes an original Homer who wrote most of the matter we have, but he believes that many others helped to make the final poems as we have them. The *Prolegomena* caused a violent controversy among classical scholars, and instituted the higher criticism of Homer.

But of course, as Browning's contemporaries well understood, the higher criticism of Homer which practically wiped the bard out of existence was only a parallel to the higher criticism of the New Testament, and with that question Browning had been concerned

[36] *Letters*, ed. Hood, p. 268.

since *Christmas-Eve and Easter-Day. A Death in the Desert* had been written to restore the personality of John, the beloved disciple, after Strauss and Renan had done their worst.

But Browning clings to Homer, as he did to the Bible, and approves the pedagogical methods of his father in leading him gently into the world of morals and ethics as they appeared in action, before he plunged the boy into Aristotle's *Ethics,* the pure doctrine itself, which Browning even in old age finds it difficult to master. And behind this metaphor one sees Browning's love of the Bible as strong as ever. After all, was it not Aristotle himself who said that poetry was truer, in the higher sense, than history?

Rephan

Rephan, consisting of 108 lines, thirty-six stanzas of three lines each, offers no evidence to indicate the date of composition; but the mood of reminiscence in the poem and the teaching implied lead one to believe that it was composed within the last two years of Browning's life, probably in 1888. The manuscript is not dated.

The word "Rephan" occurs in the Roman Version of the New Testament in *Acts* 7:43. The English Authorized Version has "Remphan." The phrase in *Acts* was "Star of your God Rephan," and the writer was upbraiding the Hebrews for idol-worship. "Rephan" came from the Greek "Raiphan," which seems to be a mistake for the Hebrew "Kiyyùn," and the Babylonian "Kewan," the Babylonian name for the planet Saturn.

In a note to the poem Browning explains that the idea was suggested by his recollection of a prose story by Jane Taylor, "the noble woman and imaginative writer." Browning, probably thinking of William Taylor of Norwich, says Jane Taylor (1783–1824) was of Norwich. Jane Taylor really was of Ongar in Essex. She was a pious lady, and wrote, with her sister, many books of verse and prose for children. Her *Rhymes for the Nursery* (1806) contained her most famous poem, "Twinkle, twinkle, little star." Her *Hymns for Infant Minds* (1810) and her *Original Hymns for Sunday School* (1812) passed through many editions. It is likely, I think, that Browning's mother read to her children the stories which Jane Taylor contributed to the *Youth's Magazine* (1816–24), later collected under the signature of "Q. Q." The particular story in Browning's mind when he wrote *Rephan* was Jane Taylor's *How it Strikes a Stranger* published as Chapter XVI in *The Contributions of Q. Q. to a Periodical Work*, 1824. This title probably suggested to Browning the title of his poem in 1855, *How it Strikes a Contemporary*. Jane Taylor's story is too lengthy to quote in full, but it is necessary to recount the story, with some quotation, to show the reader how far Browning departed from the original suggestion.

In ancient times, a stranger of great intelligence and dignity was seen pacing the streets of an Eastern city. He was unacquainted with the language of the country but when he understood that the people wished to know from whence he came he pointed at the sky. When the people tried to worship him as a deity he rejected it with horror and fell upon his knees in prayer to show men that he too was a worshipper of the powers above. Under the protection of a nobleman, the stranger learned the language of the country, and upon request agreed to tell his protector of his home and state, after sunset. When it was dark the two went upon the balcony.

Then suddenly raising his eyes to the starry firmament he fixed them with an expressive gaze on the beautiful evening star which was just sinking behind a dark grove that surrounded one of the principal temples of the city. "Marvel not," said he to his host, "that I am wont to gaze with fond affection on yonder silvery star. That was my home; yes, I was lately an inhabitant of that tranquil planet; from whence a vain curiosity has tempted me to wander. Often had I beheld with wondering admiration, this brilliant world of yours, ever one of the brightest gems of our firmament: and the ardent desire I had long felt to know something of its condition, was at length unexpectedly gratified. I received permission and power from above to transverse the mighty void, and to direct my course to this distant sphere. To that permission, however, one condition was annexed, to which my eagerness for the enterprise induced me hastily to consent; namely that I must thenceforth remain an inhabitant of this strange earth, and undergo all the vicissitudes to which its natives are subject. Tell me, therefore, I pray you, what is the lot of man; and explain to me more fully than I yet understand, all that I hear and see around me."

The stranger was initiated into the pleasures of the world and soon set himself to the task of acquiring wealth. But one day he saw a cemetery, and heard for the first time about death. When he was told that all earth-dwellers must die he was in great perturbation. His friend referred him to the priests of the land.

The emotion which the stranger had betrayed when he received the first idea of death, was yet slight in comparison with that which he experienced as soon as he had gathered from the discourses of the priests, some notion of immortality; and of the alternative of happiness or misery in a future state. But this agony of mind was exchanged for transport when he learned, that by the performance of certain conditions before death, the state of happiness might be secured; his eagerness to learn the nature of these terms, excited the surprise and even the contempt of his sacred teachers. They advised him to remain satisfied for the present with the instructions he had received.

But the eager stranger would not be put off. He forgot his wealth and devoted himself utterly to the business of insuring his future existence. In being so earnest to gain heaven he excited the surprise and then the scorn of the world. For his part, he looked upon the in-difference of men to their eternal state with a naïve astonishment and compassion.

If ever he was tempted for a moment to violate any of the conditions of his future happiness, he bewailed his own madness with agonizing emo-tions: and to all the invitations he received from others to do any thing inconsistent with his real interests, he had but one answer,—"Oh," he would say, "I am to die!—I am to die!"

From Miss Taylor's story, it is easy to see what Browning used. She does not name the star from which the stranger came, and "Rephan," from *Acts* 7:43, is Browning's own addition. Nor does Miss Taylor describe, save by implication, the conditions of life upon the planet from which the stranger came. That is added by Browning for his own purposes. Miss Taylor was mainly interested in the peculiar na-ture of man and how he could ignore what should be the major con-cern of his existence. The behavior of her stranger upon earth is curiously like the behavior of the resurrected Lazarus in Browning's *Karshish* (1855).

The poem expresses a number of Browning's recurring ideas. The conception of "Other lives in other spheres, God willing" had been with him at least since 1845. The even level perfection of life on the planet Rephan is reminiscent of the even perfection of Greek art and the necessity for a new world and a fresh start, and a less perfect though a more aspiring aim, about which Browning had been think-ing in *Old Pictures in Florence, Fra Lippo Lippi, Andrea del Sarto* and elsewhere. The expression of Browning's conclusion,

> When the trouble grew in my pregnant breast
> A voice said "So wouldst strive, not rest?"

recalls George Herbert's poem *The Pulley*. Browning has changed Miss Taylor's story into a very different, but a very characteristic, piece of literature. The theme of translation to another planet is not without its modern religious parallels.

Reverie

Reverie consisted of 220 lines, divided into forty-four stanzas of five lines each. In the manuscript the poem bears a cancelled date which looks like October 14, 1889. In temper it follows naturally after *Development* and *Rephan*.

The reverie of the poet, now well along in the seventies, is another of his readings of earth. The old antithesis of power and love which he had first expounded in *Paracelsus* (1835) appears here again as the central problem. The world shows ample evidence of a Power, matched by an Intelligence as great. What is hard to see is a Love which equals the Power and the Intelligence. To find this Love and to reconcile it with the Power, was the life-long quest of Browning. This is the fundamental purpose of Browning's thought and art. It underlies *Christmas-Eve and Easter-Day*, *Saul*, *Karshish*, *A Death in the Desert*, to name only a few. It finds its most able and careful expression in the Pope's speech in *The Ring and the Book*. The whole question is restated in *Reverie*, in language which is reminiscent of *Rabbi Ben Ezra* and is worthy of the comparison. In the last two stanzas Browning announces again his faith: to him the Love is as evident as the Power, and if not here on earth "Then yonder, worlds away." The poem is one of the happiest expressions of Browning's metaphysics. In its imagery,[37] as well as its thoughts, it is a summary of his poetry.

Epilogue

The *Epilogue* to *Asolando* consists of twenty lines, four stanzas of five lines each. One wishes very much to know at what time these famous lines were written, but there is no evidence of the date of composition in the poem itself or in the manuscript. On April 19, 1863, Browning made a comment in prose to Isa Blagden similar to the second stanza of the *Epilogue*. He admits his mistakes of judgment in his relationship with his wife, but never a lessening of his love.[38] It is most likely, however, that the poem was written in 1888 or 1889, for the lines have evident signs of being a final utterance. They con-

[37] See C. Willard Smith, *Browning's Star-Imagery*, pp. 230–4.
[38] See *Dearest Isa*, ed. McAleer, p. 159.

clude Browning's life and poetry as appropriately as the lines, *Crossing the Bar,* conclude Tennyson's career.

An interesting story concerning the *Epilogue* is told in the *Pall Mall Gazette* for February 1, 1890: "One evening, just before his death-illness, the poet was reading this [the third stanza] from a proof to his daughter-in-law and sister. He said: 'It almost sounds like bragging to say this, and as if I ought to cancel it; but it's the simple truth; and as it's true, it shall stand.'"

It is well to have Browning's work conclude on such an inspiring note, for courage is the quality with which he best provides men, to meet the ills of this world. So Shackleton found at the South Pole when to keep his courage up he recited *Childe Roland to the Dark Tower Came;* so the soldiers of Britain found in the Boer War, when the *Epilogue* to *Asolando* was a great favorite. Browning's hope and courage are his permanent gifts to the world.

⚜ VIII ⚜

UNCOLLECTED WORKS

⚜⚜⚜⚜⚜⚜⚜⚜⚜⚜⚜⚜⚜⚜⚜⚜⚜⚜⚜⚜⚜⚜⚜⚜⚜

VERSE

The First-Born of Egypt

THE FIRST-BORN OF EGYPT, a poem of eighty-four lines in blank verse, is one of the two earliest poems extant from the pen of Robert Browning. It was a part of the volume which was named *Incondita*, which was in manuscript early in 1827 when Browning was fourteen years of age. The poem was probably written in 1826.

We owe our knowledge of *The First-Born of Egypt* to the ingenuity of Mr. Bertram Dobell, who first printed the poem in the *Cornhill Magazine* for January, 1914, in an article called "The Earliest Poems of Robert Browning." The poem had a strange history. Browning, it seems, was "mad to publish" his volume *Incondita* in 1827, and his parents attempted to find a publisher. Later in a fit of disgust and disappointment Browning destroyed his manuscript. But before the poems were destroyed a friend had shown them to Sarah Flower, who was later to become Mrs. Adams and to write *Nearer, My God, to Thee*. Miss Flower and her sister made a copy of *Incondita* for their album and to show their friend W. J. Fox. The album was probably destroyed; but in a letter dated May 31, 1827, Sarah Flower sent to Fox for his approval two of Browning's poems, *The First-Born of Egypt* and *The Dance of Death*, and this letter escaped destruction. When Mrs. Adams died in 1848 Browning was in Florence. Fearful lest his correspondence with the Flower sisters and his juvenile poems should fall into unscrupulous hands, he commissioned his friend R. H. Horne to recover them for him,[1] and thus the album copies were presumably destroyed. In 1871 after the death of Fox,

---

[1] *Letters*, ed. Hood, pp. 19–22.

Sarah Flower's letter containing the two poems seems to have been sent to Browning, and one must suppose that he either forgot to destroy the verses or found them not so unworthy as he had feared.

The biblical nature of *The First-Born of Egypt*, drawn from *Exodus* 11:4–10, and 12:1–33, and the persons who are involved in the history of the poem, show us an interesting fact concerning the social circle in which Browning's family moved. Benjamin Flower, the father of Sarah and Eliza, was a publisher of the Liberal and Non-Conformist *Cambridge Intelligencer*, where Coleridge had published some of his early poems. Flower spent six months in prison for the comments of his paper on Bishop Watson, who had taken up the cudgels against Thomas Paine. W. J. Fox was a Unitarian editor and preacher; he will be remembered for the enthusiastic reception he gave *Pauline* in 1833. The circle of Browning's earliest acquaintances is definitely Liberal in politics and Non-Conformist in religion.

Fox's opinion of the poems from *Incondita* was that they showed "too great splendour of language and too little wealth of thought"— a criticism somewhat ponderous for a lad's verses. But Browning's later confession that he wrote in his youth only musically is borne out somewhat by the smooth and easy road of his blank verse in this poem. Indeed, the verses are almost as skilful as those of Tennyson's earliest effort, *The Devil and the Lady*, recently published. Since the appearance of *The First-Born of Egypt* in the *Cornhill Magazine* the poem has been included in *New Poems of Robert Browning*, edited by F. G. Kenyon in 1914, and in the *Macmillan Edition*.

The Dance of Death

The Dance of Death is a poem of 103 lines, rhyming mainly in couplets. It is prefaced by two lines of verse translated from de Stael, and the body of the poem is divided into five sections—speeches by Fever, Pestilence, Ague, Madness, and Consumption. The poem shows an astonishing facility in a boy of fourteen. It reveals the influence of Coleridge's *Fire, Famine and Slaughter*, though it is by no means a slavish imitation. The history of the poem, its preservation and later publication, is identical with that of *The First-Born of Egypt*, just above.

Lines to the Memory of his Parents

This poem, inaccurately named, consisted of fourteen lines of blank verse as it was first printed in the *Cornhill Magazine* for February, 1914 (110:145), by F. G. Kenyon. The manuscript containing the lines, written in the hand of Miss Sarianna Browning, was sold at the sale of the Browning Collections in May, 1913. In *Notes and Queries* for June 12, 1948 (193:248–9), E. J. Bradford has shown that the poem with six additional lines first appeared in 1832 upon the gravestone in St. Mary's Church, Barnsley, Yorkshire, for James Dow, M.D., who died on October 9 of that year. Lines 9, 10, 14, 15, 16 are omitted from the manuscript from which the poem was printed, and lines 7 and 8 are compressed into one. The Dow family were friends of the Brownings, and lived near them in Camberwell in the 1830s.[2] In 1837 Browning became god-father to the son of his friend, William Alexander Dow, who was probably the son of James Dow for whom this poem was written. The lines from the manuscript may be read in F. G. Kenyon's *New Poems by Robert Browning*, 1914. The title should, I think, be "Lines to the Memory of James Dow."

"Eyes Calm Beside Thee"

The sonnet, beginning "Eyes calm beside thee (Lady, could'st thou know!)," was first published in *The Monthly Repository,* the magazine edited by W. J. Fox, for October, 1834. It was there signed "Z," Browning's usual signature in his early years, and bore the date August 17, 1834. It was in this magazine that Browning published *Porphyria, Johannes Agricola,* the lines "A king lived long ago" which were later incorporated into *Pippa Passes,* and the lines "Still ailing, wind" which were later used in *James Lee's Wife.* The sonnet was not collected by Browning. It was reprinted in *The Browning Society's Papers* (III, 36*–37*), in Gosse's *Robert Browning, Personalia,* 1890 (pp. 34–5), and in Nicoll and Wise's *Literary Anecdotes of the Nineteenth Century* (I, 470). It has since been included in all editions which aim at completeness.

There is no record of the occasion which called forth this poem. Griffin and Minchin suggest that it is possible that the sonnet was addressed to Eliza Flower.[3]

[2] See Orr, *Life,* p. 61; and also *A Forest Thought,* below.
[3] *Life,* p. 309.

A Forest Thought

A Forest Thought, a poem of fifty-two lines in four parts, was written by Browning on November 4, 1837. The occasion of the poem was the christening of the son of his friend William Alexander Dow. Browning was god-father to the boy and wrote the poem, the date, and these words for the family album: "Written and inscribed to W.A. and A.D. by their Sincere Friend, Robert Browning. 13 Nelson Sq."

The description of the "far Esthonian solitudes" which makes up the first half of the poem is a recollection of Browning's journey to Russia in March and April of 1834. The scenery is the same as that of *Ivàn Ivànovitch,* written forty years later. The poem first appeared in print in *Country Life* (London) for June 10, 1905; it was reprinted in F. G. Kenyon's *Robert Browning and Alfred Domett,* 1906 (p. xi), in Griffin and Minchin's *Life* (p. 305), and in the *Centenary Edition* of Browning's works.

The "Moses" of Michael Angelo

The sonnet, *The "Moses" of Michael Angelo,* was found in manuscript among the papers of George Smith, Browning's publisher and friend. The poem was first published in the *Cornhill Magazine* for September, 1914. To the poem Browning had attached the note, "From Zappi, R. B. (Given to Ba 'for love's sake,' Siena. Sept. 27, '50.)." The sonnet has since appeared in F. G. Kenyon's *New Poems of Robert Browning,* and in the *Macmillan Edition* of Browning's works.

The poem is a translation of Giambattista Felice Zappi's (1667–1719) sonnet *Sopra la statua di Mosè scolpita dal Buonaroti.* Zappi is accounted a poet on a small but perfect scale: some of the choicest examples of minor Italian poetry of the seventeenth and eighteenth centuries may be found in his *Rime,* edited by his wife, Faustina Martati Zappi.

Ben Karshook's Wisdom

Ben Karshook's Wisdom, a poem of five stanzas of four lines each, the whole divided into two main parts, was first printed in the annual, *The Keepsake,* for 1856. The annual was edited by Miss Power, a friend of Browning's. The lines were dated as of Rome, April 27, 1854. The poem was never included in any collection made by Browning. It was reprinted in the *Browning Society's Papers* (I, 56), and has since appeared in all editions of the poetical works which aim at completeness.

In *One Word More*, the poem in which Browning dedicated his volumes of *Men and Women* to Mrs. Browning in 1855, the poet originally wrote line 136 in this way: "Karshook, Cleon, Norbert and the fifty." The name "Karshook" was a slip of the pen for "Karshish," for *Ben Karshook's Wisdom* did not appear in *Men and Women*. The mistake remained in all later reprints of *One Word More* until Browning corrected it for the Tauchnitz Edition of 1872. On September 15, 1881, Browning wrote to Furnivall concerning the mistake: "*Karshish* is the proper word, referring as it does to him of the 'Epistle'—*Karshook* (*Heb:* a Thistle) just belongs to the snarling verses I remember to have written but forget for whom." [4] From this comment we may deduce that *Ben Karshook's Wisdom* became distasteful to Browning, and it was probably for that reason that he never collected the poem.

Judith Berlin-Lieberman has succeeded in identifying the Karshook of the poem with Rabbi Eliezer ben Hyrkanos, a famous teacher of the first and second centuries, A. D.[5] He was a severe and dominating individual. The first stanza of the poem is almost a direct translation from Eliezer's words. The second part of the poem seems to come from an anecdote which John Knowles in *The Life and Writings of Henry Fuseli* (I, 391) ascribes to the artist, Fuseli, who, like Eliezer, was a master of the crushing retort: "Fuseli was maintaining the immortality of the soul; a gentleman present said, 'I could make you or any man of sense disbelieve this in half an hour's conversation.' Fuseli immediately answered, 'That I am sure you could not, and I will take care you shan't.'" [6]

Though Browning had used the name "Karshook" in *The Return of the Druses*, *Ben Karshook's Wisdom* is one of the earliest of his poems to show signs of that interest in Hebraic lore which was to develop notably in his later years. The poem is probably a product of his Hebraic studies for *Holy-Cross Day* and the *Epistle . . . of*

---

[4] *Letters*, ed. Hood, p. 196.

[5] *Robert Browning and Hebraism*, Jerusalem, 1934, pp. 30–55.

[6] I am indebted to Professor Curtis Dahl for this suggestion. Browning had known Knowles's *Life . . . of Fuseli* since 1831, and used it for his poem, *Mary Wollstonecraft and Fuseli* (*q.v.*).

Karshish. Hiram, referred to in the last sentence of the poem, is the builder of the brass columns of Solomon's Temple (*I Kings* 7:13–22).

A Round Robin

A Round Robin, twenty-nine lines of playful verse probably all written by Browning, was first printed in Cornelia Carr's *Harriet Hosmer, Letters and Memories,* 1913 (pp. 275–6). The lines were addressed to Harriet, or Hatty, Hosmer, an American sculptress with whom the Brownings had been very friendly in Rome, by the members of a house-party at Loch Luichart, Dingwall, N.B. in Rosshire, Scotland, the estate of Lady Ashburton. The verses were signed by the eight members of the house-party and were dated September 5; 1869. The lines were reprinted in F. G. Kenyon's *New Poems of Robert Browning* in 1914, and again in the *Macmillan Edition* of Browning's works. More recently, the lines were reprinted by Dean T. L. Hood in his account of Browning's proposal of marriage to Lady Ashburton.[7] Browning's visit to Lake Luichart led to his proposal of marriage to that lady.

Helen's Tower

The sonnet, *Helen's Tower,* was dated in the manuscript as of April 26, 1870. It was written upon the invitation of the Marquis of Dufferin, who in that year built a tower at Clandeboye, Ireland, in honor of his mother, Helen, Lady Dufferin and Countess of Gifford. The poem was first published on December 28, 1883, when it appeared in the *Pall Mall Gazette.* In 1894 it was printed just after the title-page of the *Songs, Poems and Verses by Helen, Lady Dufferin,* collected by her son, the Marquis of Dufferin and Ava. Since that time it has appeared in *Sonnets of This Century* (ed. W. Sharp, 1886, p. 30); in Nicoll and Wise's *Literary Anecdotes of the Nineteenth Century,* 1895 (I, 476–7), and in every edition of the poems which aims at completeness.

Helen Selina Sheridan (1807–67) was the granddaughter of Richard Brinsley Sheridan. When she was seventeen she married the third son of Lord Dufferin and Clandeboye, who had at that time very little prospect of wealth or fame. On the death of the two older brothers the third son succeeded to the title, but did not live long

---

[7] See *Letters,* ed. Hood, pp. 331–2.

thereafter himself. His wife, Lady Dufferin, became a notable beauty of Victoria's time and was the center of a distinguished circle. She wrote poems and plays. Her son, the Marquis of Dufferin and Ava, later distinguished himself as an administrator of the Empire in Canada and in India.

It has been a cause of some wonder that Browning never included *Helen's Tower*, which is perhaps his most successful sonnet, in any of his volumes or collections. This was probably because of his extreme scrupulousness. The poem had been given to the Marquis of Dufferin and was therefore no longer the author's property. Tennyson wrote a poem for the same occasion which goes under the same name as Browning's sonnet. It was included in his volume *Tiresias and Other Poems* in 1885. Browning's happy figure of Helen at the Scaean gate, looking over the Greek host, is drawn from the famous passage in the *Iliad* (III, 121 ff.), which was a favorite with Browning.

To My Critics

To My Critics, seven stanzas of four lines each, with the additional words "Written Since my Late Publication," appeared above the signature "R—— B——," in the *Examiner* of August 5, 1876. Browning never collected the verses. They were reprinted in *The Browning Society's Papers* (I, 278) with a warning by Furnivall that the lines were not written by Browning. They are reprinted in Dean T. L. Hood's *Letters of Robert Browning* (p. 360) under the assumption that they were Browning's. Mr. Pearsall, in *Robert Browning: A Bibliography* (p. 13), states that "Browning was capable of such a poem . . . and since no word of disclaimer has come to us the poem should probably be retained in the canon." It is my opinion that the verses were composed by a clever wag who assumed Browning's manner and sentiments and sent the lines to the *Examiner*. An account of the verses is included here because it is one of the few doubtful ascriptions which have been made to Browning.

Whoever the author, the verses rose out of Browning's quarrel with Alfred Austin. In *Pacchiarotto* Browning had paid off Austin and the other critics for what he considered to be unfair abuse of him in newspaper and magazine. The *Pacchiarotto* volume was published in May, 1876. In the *Examiner* of June 10 Austin entered "A Disclaimer," asserting his innocence of most of the reviews of contemporary books with which he had been charged. The verses, *To My*

Critics, reply to the critics as if for Browning in the vein of *Pacchiarotto* and carry on the idea from that poem that Xantippe, the poet's housemaid, will empty a *skoramis* upon the critic's head if he comes near again. The verses are a parody, I think, of *Pacchiarotto.* On August 12, 1876, the editor of the *Examiner* sat as judge upon the quarrel and scolded both Austin and Browning.[8]

"Oh Love, Love"

The poem beginning "Oh Love, Love," two stanzas of nine lines each, is Browning's translation of a strophe of a chorus from Euripides' *Hippolytus* (ll. 525–44). The verses were translated at the request of J. P. Mahaffy, the Greek scholar, for his book, *Euripides,* in 1879. The poem appeared there on page 116, preceded by Mahaffy's note: "Mr. Browning has honored me with the following translation of these stanzas, so that the general reader may not miss the meaning or the spirit of the ode. The English metre, though not a strict reproduction, gives an excellent idea of the original." The note was dated December 18, 1878, and the translation was probably made shortly before that time. Mahaffy came to Browning because of the poet's intense delight in Euripides, but more especially perhaps because Browning had shown in *Artemis Prologizes* in 1842 how well he understood the spirit of the *Hippolytus.* The translation was afterwards printed in the *Browning Society's Papers* (I, 69), in Nicoll and Wise's *Literary Anecdotes of the Nineteenth Century* (I, 498), and in all editions of Browning's works which aim at completeness. Browning himself never collected the poem.

"The Blind Man to the Maiden Said"

The twenty lines, four stanzas of five lines each, which make up this lyric were first published in 1879 in a book by Clara Bell called *The Hour Will Come, A Tale of an Alpine Cloister.* Mrs. Bell's book was a translation of a novel by Wilhelmine von Hillern. The verses appeared in Volume I, page 174, without Browning's signature, but with the words, "The translator is indebted for these verses to the kindness of a friend." The poem was reprinted as Browning's in the

[8] A complete history of the quarrel between Browning and Austin may be found in *Letters,* ed. Hood, pp. 359–63. See also W. L. Phelps, "Robert Browning and Alfred Austin," in the *Yale Review,* N.S. 7:580–91 (1918).

Whitehall Review for March 1, 1883. In a letter to Furnivall on April 10, 1883, Browning owned the verses:

I did indeed translate that little song for Mrs. Bell, never dreaming anybody would suppose there was "another hand" in her work. See now! I should have thought it very mean had I told anybody "that's mine!", and she herself unnecessarily tells it—from sheer honesty, I have no doubt.[9]

The verses were subsequently printed in the *Browning Society's Papers* (I, 410), in Nicoll and Wise's *Literary Anecdotes of the Nineteenth Century* (I, 528), and in all editions of the poems which aim at completeness. Browning himself never collected it.

"Thus I Wrote in London, Musing on My Betters"

The ten lines of verse, "Thus I wrote in London," were written impromptu in Venice on October 14, 1880, as an appendage to the little poem, "Touch him ne'er so lightly," which concluded the Second Series of *Dramatic Idyls*. They are in the same measure and manner. The lines were written in the album of Miss Edith Longfellow, the daughter of the American poet, just beneath a transcript of "Touch him ne'er so lightly." In that poem Browning had preferred the poet as teacher and prophet, to the poet as the lyrical singer, and some critics chose to imagine that he was speaking in praise of himself. "Thus I wrote in London" is a disclaimer; Browning says that he had Dante in mind as the prophet-poet; this was a choice which Thomas Carlyle had made before him. Browning did not include the lines in any volume or collection of his poems, and he was chagrined and angry when Miss Longfellow published his impromptu lines in the *Century Magazine* (25:159–60) for November, 1882. The lines have subsequently appeared in the *Browning Society's Papers* (I, 48*), in Nicoll and Wise's *Literary Anecdotes of the Nineteenth Century* (I, 543–4), and in several American editions of the poet's works.

Translation from Pindar's Seventh Olympian, Epode III

The translation from Pindar's *Seventh Olympian, Epode III*, beginning, "And to these Rhodians she, the sharp-eyed one," consisted of twelve lines. The manuscript was discovered in the Brown-

---

[9] *Letters*, ed. Hood, p. 216.

ing papers when the library was dispersed in 1913.[10] With the manuscript there was a letter, dated from Warwick Crescent on January 14, 1883, addressed to the editor of the *Pall Mall Gazette*. Neither the letter nor the manuscript seems to have been sent.

The occasion of the poem was an incident in the famous trial, the Belt Case, a libel suit brought by Richard Claude Belt, a sculptor, against Sir Charles Bennet Lawes, a former pupil. Lawes had accused Belt in *Vanity Fair* and other periodicals of calling his own certain pieces of sculpture which had been done, or at least finished, by someone else. The case was famous in its day; it lasted from June 21 until December 28, 1882. Many noted artists were called into court as witnesses. Belt won the case and £5000 damages. The case was tried before Baron Huddleston, who quoted Aristotle and intimated that the Middlesex Jury were as competent judges of art as were Royal Academicians. Browning was, of course, delighted with such a trial and wrote as follows to the editor of the *Pall Mall Gazette:*

We have recently been favoured with a Greek quotation,—warranted however rather by the bench than the Book { case shelf } —on the subject of Art. Another one, as apposite, might be made from another old authority; and, curiously enough, it immediately precedes the passage which was illustrated, some years ago, by one of the finest pictures of the President [Lord Leighton]. For the general reader, I venture a rough version: the Middlesex Jury needs no reminding that the original occurs in Pindar's Seventh Olympian, Epode III.[11]

Browning's translation was first published in F. G. Kenyon's *New Poems by Robert Browning and Elizabeth Barrett Browning*, in 1914, and has since been included in the *Macmillan Edition*. A slightly different version of the poem was sent in a letter to his friend J. D. Williams of Cambridge, on March 10, 1883.[12]

Rawdon Brown

The sonnet to Rawdon Brown was first published in the *Century Magazine* for February, 1884 (27:640), "by Mr. Browning's permission, and that of the lady at whose request it was written." The lady was Mrs. Katherine Bronson, at whose home in Venice Browning visited several times in the last decade of his life. He dedicated *Aso-*

[10] *The Browning Collections* (Sotheby Catalogue, 1913), item 171.
[11] *Macmillan Edition*, p. 1335.
[12] *Letters*, ed. Hood, p. 214 .

lando to her, and she published her reminiscences of the poet in Venice in the *Cornhill Magazine* and the *Century* for February, 1902. The poem was dated November 28, 1883, and retold the exaggerated story of Brown's devotion to Venice, a devotion which Browning could well understand. Brown was learned in the ways of Venice and delighted in showing the place to visitors. The third and fourth lines of the sonnet, "*Anglus* Brown am I, Although my heart's Venetian," supplied the epitaph for his tomb. When the sonnet was printed the editor of the *Century* introduced it in this way:

> Mr. Rawdon Brown, an Englishman of culture well known to visitors in Venice, died in that city in the summer of 1883. He went to Venice for a short visit, with a definite object in view, and ended by staying forty years. An incident of his death is recorded in the following sonnet, which is here printed by Mr. Browning's permission, and that of the lady at whose request it was written.

The unfortunate phrasing of the introduction to the sonnet by the editor of the *Century*, "An incident of his death is recorded in the following sonnet," caused Brown's executor, Cavendish Bentinck, to take umbrage, and some discussion took place in the *Daily News* and the *Times*.[13]

The sonnet was never included by Browning in any collection. After the *Century Magazine* had published it, it appeared in the *Browning Society's Papers* (I, 132*), in the *Cambridge Edition*, in the *Florentine*, and in the *Macmillan Edition*. In this latter the Italian motto, signifying "Everybody follows his taste, and I follow mine," is omitted.

Goldoni

The sonnet *Goldoni* was first published in England in the *Pall Mall Gazette* for December 8, 1883. On December 3 of that year Browning wrote to Furnivall from Venice,

> They are going to unveil and display here a monument erected to Goldoni: and the Committee did me the honor to request a word or two for insertion in an Album to which the principal men of letters in Italy have contributed: I made a sonnet which they please to think so well of that they preface the book with it. I cannot stop for the ceremony,—but shall get—and let you have a Proof. . . .[14]

13 *Idem*, p. 227.
14 *Idem*, p. 225.

Mrs. Bronson says that the sonnet was written very rapidly, and that it was necessary to make only two or three trifling alterations in the original copy.[15] The sonnet was dated from Venice on November 27, 1883. Mrs. Orr gives the additional information that Browning wrote the sonnet while the messenger from the editor waited for it.[16]

Carlo Goldoni (1707–1793) was the most famous writer of comedy for the Italian stage. He was a great admirer of Molière, and attempted to do for Italy, and Venice especially, what Molière had done for France. With "wit, gaiety, elegance and simplicity" he caught the manners of his time. Some of his best plays are *Un Curiosa Accidente, Il Vero Amico, La Bottega del Caffè*, and *La Locandiera*. The qualities which Browning ascribes to Goldoni, "Dear king of Comedy," are oddly like those which Browning had ascribed to Baldassare Galuppi thirty years before. Mrs. Orr reports that during his visit to Venice in 1883, the year in which the sonnet on Goldoni was written, Browning had assisted at the unveiling of a commemorative tablet to Galuppi in his native island of Burano.[17]

Besides appearing in the *Pall Mall Gazette*, the sonnet was printed in the *Pall Mall Budget* for December 13, 1883; in the *Browning Society's Papers* (I, 98*); in Nicoll and Wise's *Literary Anecdotes of the Nineteenth Century* (I, 475); and in all editions of Browning's poetical works which aim at completeness. Browning himself never included the sonnet in any volume or collection of his works.

Gerousios Oinos

Gerousios Oinos, a poem of eight stanzas of six lines each, was first published in the *Cornhill* and the *Century Magazine* in April, 1914 (109:575–6). Galley-proofs of the poem had been found among the poet's papers when the Browning Collections were sold in May, 1913. Mr. Bertram Dobell was the purchaser of this poem. It seems clear that *Gerousios Oinos* was intended for the volume called *Jocoseria*, for at that time it was put into type. In a letter to Furnivall on January 9, 1883, Browning wrote, "I have given, this afternoon, Smith my new book to print. . . . There are some eleven of these pieces, little and big. . . ."[18] But when the volume appeared there were only ten

[15] See her article, "Browning in Venice," in the *Cornhill Magazine* and the *Century Magazine* for February, 1902.
[16] *Life*, p. 339.
[17] *Ibid.*
[18] *Letters*, ed. Hood, p. 213.

poems. One may conjecture that Browning withdrew the poem before *Jocoseria* was printed because his contemptuous remarks upon contemporary poetry were certain to give great offence to his brother-craftsmen. *Gerousios Oinos* had been removed from the manuscript of *Jocoseria* before it was sent to the Balliol College Library. It seems that Browning had intended the poem to come just before *Pambo,* for three pages—pages 74–7 in Browning's numbering—are missing from the manuscript at that point.

The title of the poem was taken from the *Iliad* (IV, 259), and may be translated as "Wine of the Elders." The title, of course, gives point to Browning's comment upon contemporary poetry, which seemed to him thoroughly watered and thin. The poem is in line with Browning's privately expressed opinions concerning the later Tennyson, Morris, Rossetti and Swinburne.[19]

Since its first appearance in the *Cornhill* and the *Century* in April, 1914, the poem has been published in *New Poems of Robert Browning,* and in the *Macmillan Edition* of the *Complete Poetical Works.*

The Founder of the Feast

(*To Arthur Chappell*)

The Founder of the Feast was written by Browning for the album which was presented to Arthur Chappell in recognition of his services in organizing the Popular Concerts at St. James's Hall. The poem was dated by the poet as of April 5, 1884. It was first printed in *The World* for April 16, 1884, and later in the *Browning Society's Papers* (II, 18*), and in Nicoll and Wise's *Literary Anecdotes of the Nineteenth Century* (I, 531–2), and elsewhere. In all these reprintings the poem is fifteen lines long. But there was found among the poet's papers when the Browning Collections were sold (item 191) a copy of the poem as it was printed in *The World* corrected to a sonnet, the ninth line of the original poem being omitted and the tenth changed slightly.

The poem shows Browning's extreme delight in music. He was a friend of Joachim and Clara Schumann, two of the performers mentioned here; and he attended the concerts regularly.

The poem is printed in its revised form in F. G. Kenyon's *New Poems of Robert Browning* (1914) and in the *Macmillan Edition.*

[19] *Idem,* pp. 134, 137–8.

The Names

(To Shakespeare)

At the request of Dr. Furnivall, eminent Shakespearean scholar and founder of the Browning Society of London, the sonnet, *The Names*, was contributed by Browning to the *Shakespearean Show-Book*, published in May, 1884, and was there printed on the first page. The Shakespearean Show was held on May 29–31, 1884, in the Albert Hall to aid the Hospital for Women in Fulham Road. The sonnet was dated March 12, 1884. It was reprinted in the *Pall Mall Gazette* for May 29, 1884, in the *Browning Society's Papers* (I, 105*), in Nicoll and Wise's *Literary Anecdotes of the Nineteenth Century* (I, 535–6), and in all the editions of Browning's works which aim at completeness. Browning himself never included it in any volume of his works.

Browning's praise of Shakespeare is very pleasant, and is in payment of an old and great debt. One is reminded by *The Names* of a story which Browning delighted to tell of Charles Lamb. Lamb, in gay fancy, was talking about how he should feel if the greatest of the dead were to appear in flesh and blood before him. When one suggested, "And if Christ entered this room?" Lamb "changed his manner at once, and stuttered out, as his manner was when moved, 'You see, if Shakespeare entered, we should all rise; if *He* appeared we must kneel.' " [20]

Why I am a Liberal

The sonnet, *Why I am a Liberal*, was first printed in a book called *Why I am a Liberal*, compiled by Andrew Reid and published in 1885. Browning's poem appears on page 11. The sonnet was reprinted in the *Browning Society's Papers* (II, 92*), in *Sonnets of This Century* (ed. W. Sharp, 1886, p. 31), and in Nicoll and Wise's *Literary Anecdotes of the Nineteenth Century* (I, 548). Though the poet himself never collected the sonnet, it has appeared in every edition of his works which aims at completeness.

The sonnet is interesting as one of the few direct expressions of Browning's politics in poetry. By the word "Liberal" he probably means more than the political party that uses that name. He is enunciating general principles, and has delineated successfully the tenets

[20] *Idem*, pp. 171–2.

of the old-fashioned Liberal of 1850. His doctrine is individualistic in the extreme. In general, Browning adhered strongly to the Liberal party in politics, admiring Gladstone and hating Disraeli, but Gladstone's adoption of the principle of Home Rule for Ireland in 1885–6 was hateful to the poet, and thereafter he avoided meeting the statesman. Browning's sonnet came at a time when the Liberal party had begun to split into many factions. Reid's book, in which Browning's sonnet was one of many statements of the Liberal position, was an attempt to clear the position of the party by many definitions. Not unnaturally, the book failed to avert the temporary disruption of the party.

Lines for the Tomb of Levi Lincoln Thaxter

The seven lines "Written to be inscribed on the gravestone of Levi Thaxter" were first published in Mrs. Orr's *Life and Letters of Robert Browning*, 1891 (p. 353). Thaxter had long been an admirer and a reciter of Browning's poetry, as Mrs. Thaxter wrote Browning from Newtonville, Mass., on March 14, 1880,[21] and when Thaxter died in May, 1884, his son asked the poet for some lines to put upon the tombstone. The lines are dated April 19, 1885. They are to be found in the *Cambridge Edition,* the *Florentine Edition,* and in the *Macmillan Edition.*

Epps

Epps, a poem of ten stanzas of six lines each, was first published in the *Cornhill Magazine* and in the New York *Outlook* for October, 1913. There the poem is printed as Browning left it, with alternate words in many lines. It is dated January 6, 1886. Epps was the maiden name of his friends, Mrs. Edmund Gosse and Lady Alma Tadema, and it was to honor playfully their Kentish ancestor, though they were not aware of the relationship, that Browning wrote this poem for them. Gosse supplied these facts to F. G. Kenyon,[22] and asserted that Browning showed the ladies the manuscript of the verses, "which he did not treat as a serious specimen of his poetic art." The manuscript was sold (item 196) in the sale of the Browning Collections in May, 1913.

[21] See Orr, *Life,* 1891, pp. 351–2.
[22] See *Macmillan Edition,* p. 1338.

As his authority for the story of Epps, Browning mentions (1. 57) "Donne and Dekker, brave poets and rare." In Grosart's edition of *The Complete Poems of John Donne*, which I use because it was dedicated to Browning and was in his library, there is a note to *Satire VI* (To Sir Nicholas Smyth) which gave Browning most of the matter for his poem. In lines 26–7 of the *Satire* Donne had made the comparison, ". . . like Epps it often wars And still is hurt." Grosart's note upon Epps, drawn from the longer panegyric upon Epps in Dekker's *Knight's Conjuring*, Chapter VIII (ed. Percy Society, pp. 57–9), is as follows:

> William Epps was a valiant but irascible Kentish man, killed at the siege of Ostend, 1601–4. He lost an eye on the walls; afterwards in battle he carried the colours, 'and the Regent that followed his ensigne (by being hardly set to) giving ground, and the enemies' ambition thirsting after his colours, threw at all in hope to winne them. But the destinies (who fought on their side) mistooke themselves, and insteede of striking the colours out of his hand, smote him: in so much that he was twice shot, and twice runne through the body, yet wold not surender his hold for all those breaches, but stripping the prize for which they strove off from the staffe that helde it up, and wrapping his dying bodie in it, drewe out his weapon, with which (before his collours could be called his winding sheete) he threw himselfe into the thickest of danger; whore after he had slaine a horseman and two others, most valiantlie, hee came off, halfe dead, halfe alive, bravelie delivering up his spirit in the armes of none but his friendes and fellow souldiers . . .'

Besides being published in the *Cornhill* and the *Outlook* the poem appeared in F. G. Kenyon's *New Poems of Robert Browning and Elizabeth Barrett Browning*, 1914, and in the *Macmillan Edition*.

Aeschylus' Soliloquy

The unfinished draft of the poem which has been called *Aeschylus' Soliloquy* was first published in the *Cornhill Magazine* and the *New York Independent* for November, 1913. In the *Cornhill* the poem is printed as it stands in the manuscript, with alternate words and queries. The manuscript, now in the British Museum, consists of 147 lines of blank verse, but there are places where some words are scarcely legible. The manuscript was offered for sale in May, 1913, when the Browning Collections were dispersed (item 188); and it was there supposed that Browning had intended to use the lines as a part of *Aristophanes' Apology*, but had not done so. This was mere conjecture on the part of the persons who prepared the catalogue for Sotheby, and it is difficult to see how the soliloquy of Aeschylus in Sicily, just before his death—described by tradition as caused by an eagle dropping a tortoise on his head—could have fitted into *Aristophanes' Apology*. It may be that *Aeschylus' Soliloquy* was written as a chip from the block of the longer poem, but the condition of the manuscript leads one to suspect that it was written earlier. The poem may have been composed in London in late February and early March, 1845, when Elizabeth Barrett and Browning were intensely interested in Aeschylus' *Prometheus*.[23] In the *Times Literary Supplement* for March 21, 1942, Martha Hale Shackford questions Browning's authorship of this poem on the grounds that Browning would hardly have written a poem on this subject after he heard of Miss Barrett's intention to write one on the same theme. She also adduces internal evidence to show that the lines were written by Miss Barrett, and thinks that the manuscript is possibly a copy which Browning made. Her arguments, however, are not convincing and she was effectively answered by G. D. Hobson on April 11, 1942, in the same journal. It is possible that the lines were written by Browning before he heard of Miss Barrett's plan, and were then withheld in order not to interfere with her work. Or the poem may have been composed in Florence under the inspiration of Landor, who was a great admirer of Aeschylus. The poem is thoroughly mature: the mood of Aeschylus is firmly delineated and the poetry is steadily excellent. The *Soliloquy* is unfinished, perhaps because of the difficulty of showing the catastrophe.

Browning seems to have drawn his legend of the death of Aeschylus from two sources, Plutarch's *Cimon* (VIII, 9–11), and the *Vita* of Aeschylus.[24] The *Vita* reads:

Some say that he went away to Hiero because he was unpopular at Athens, having been beaten by young Sophocles. . . . But some say that the bringing in of the chorus scattered about at the performance of the *Eumenides* so frightened the public that some were struck dumb, and some miscarried. Coming to Sicily . . . living three years more, being aged, he met his end thus. An eagle having seized a tortoise, not knowing how to get at his prey, went to drop it on the rocks to break the shell, but it being dropped on the poet, killed him. It had been prophesied, "A blow from heaven will kill you."

[23] *Letters of R.B. and E.B.B.*, I, 15, 31–8, 45, 61.
[24] See T. L. Hood, *Browning's Ancient Classical Sources*, entries under "Aeschylus," in *Harvard Studies in Classical Philology*, 1922.

Besides being printed in the *Cornhill* and the *Independent* the poem has appeared in F. G. Kenyon's *New Poems of Robert Browning and Elizabeth Barrett Browning*, 1914, and in the *Macmillan Edition*. The *Soliloquy* is one of the best of the poems which Browning left unpublished.

To Edward FitzGerald

The twelve lines, *To Edward FitzGerald*, were first published in the *Athenaeum* above Browning's signature on July 13, 1889. The poem was written and dated on July 8, 1889. Browning was at his club and opened the *New Letters of Edward FitzGerald*, edited by W. Aldis Wright, at the passage which FitzGerald had written on Mrs. Browning:

> Mrs. Browning's death is rather a relief to me, I must say: no more Aurora Leighs, thank God! A woman of real genius, I know; but what is the upshot of it all? She and her sex had better mind the kitchen and the children; and perhaps the poor. Except in such things as little novels, they only devote themselves to what men do much better, leaving that which men do worse or not at all.

Browning read this and was furious. He seems to have written his lines immediately, and to have sent them to the *Athenaeum* at once. Before the verses were printed Browning had a revulsion of feeling about publishing them. On July 9 Browning wrote a letter to MacColl, one of the editors, asking the return of the verses. He also sent a telegram to MacColl, asking him to withdraw the lines; but MacColl managed, by talking to a friend, to delay the opening of the telegram so that he could later tell Browning that the message had arrived too late to prevent the publication of the lines.[25]

On July 16 Wright, the editor of the FitzGerald letters, apologized for his gross neglect, and his letter was printed in the *Athenaeum* of July 20. Browning never withdrew his lines formally, but he did not include them in his collected works, or in any volume. They were reprinted in the *Browning Society's Papers* (II, 347*), and in Nicoll and Wise's *Literary Anecdotes of the Nineteenth Century* (I, 544), and in some later editions of Browning's works, such as the *Florentine*.

One can hardly fail to see in reading Browning's correspondence soon after July 8, 1889, that the unfortunate incident was a great

[25] See *Letters*, ed. Hood, pp. 311, 377–8, for an excellent account of this.

shock to him. It is not too much to say that the emotional crisis hastened his death. He did not break under the shock, but the brutal judgment of FitzGerald and his own rash action haunted and troubled him.

On Louvel's Reply

In an article in the *Times Literary Supplement* for October 6, 1945, entitled "The Young Browning," Frank Underhill suggests that this poem of twelve lines, rhyming in couplets, is by Browning. Lewis Peter Louvel assassinated the Duke de Berry at the door of the Opera House in Paris on Sunday night, February 13, 1820. When he was examined he asserted, "God is but a name, He never yet has been on earth," lines which appear in this poem. The poem itself is a reply to Louvel's words and is signed "Robt. Browning Junr." Mr. Underhill's grandfather worked in the Consol office of the Bank of England with Browning's father, and the poem came to him through his family. The difficulty of ascribing the poem to Robert Browning, the poet, lies in this: the lines were evidently written while Louvel awaited execution, and at that time the poet would have been about seven years of age. The poet's father sometimes signed himself "Robt. Browning Junr.," and it is possible that he may have written the lines.

Lines for Pictures, Jeux d'esprit, Versicles, Translations, Exercises

Latin Hexameters: Plane te valvam fas . . . , ten lines of Latin hexameters, was first published in the *Cornhill Magazine* for September, 1914, under the title, *On Being Defied to Express in a Hexameter: "You ought to Sit on the Safety-Valve."* The lines were dated February 22, 1866. The manuscript was discovered among the papers of George Smith, Browning's publisher and friend, upon that gentleman's death. It is not known who defied Browning to accomplish this feat. The lines were also published in F. G. Kenyon's *New Poems of Robert Browning and Elizabeth Barrett Browning*, 1914, and in the *Macmillan Edition.*

On Singers. The four lines, rhyming in couplets, beginning "All singers, trust me, have this common vice," are translated from Horace's First Book of *Satires*, III, 1–3, "Omnibus hoc vitium est cantoribus." Browning's lines appeared first in the *Pall Mall Gazette* for December 13, 1883, and in 1884 in the *Browning Society's Papers* (I, 99*), where they are said to have been written for Felix Mosche-les, the painter, to be placed on his piano. According to F. G. Kenyon the lines were written for a lady's album in which someone had written the lines from Horace. This seems the more likely explana-tion, and it is possible that Furnivall confused these lines with those on *The Isle's Enchantress* (*q.v.*). "All singers . . ." was reprinted in the *Macmillan Edition*.

Joan of Arc and the Kingfisher. These seven lines, beginning "Now, as she fain would bathe," were mistakenly given as hitherto un-published in F. G. Kenyon's *New Poems* and in the *Macmillan Edi-tion* of the *Complete Poetical Works*. The lines were used in Brown-ing's *Parleying With Francis Furini*, ll. 601–7. Browning first wrote the lines to accompany a picture of the same title, painted by his son R. W. B. Browning for exhibition at the Grosvenor Gallery in 1886. The manuscript of these lines was sold at the dispersal of the Browning Collections in 1913.

Scene in the Building of the Inquisitors at Antwerp. These five unrhymed lines were probably meant to accompany R. W. B. Brown-ing's picture of that title. The younger Browning studied painting under Jean-Arnold Heyermans of Antwerp for some time after 1874. The lines were first printed in F. G. Kenyon's *New Poems*, and in the *Macmillan Edition*. There is nothing to indicate the date of the composition of these lines.

"Yellow and pale as ripened corn." These four lines were ascribed to Browning by Ernest Rhys in his book, *Sir Frederick Leighton . . . An Illustrated Chronicle . . .* , published in London in 1895 (p. 51). The lines were written to accompany a picture by Leighton which has no title but is described as a "Picture of a little girl with golden hair and pale blue eyes." The picture seems to have been painted in 1887 but not exhibited. The lines have Browning's name under them. They have never been collected into any volume of Browning verse; they are quoted by T. L. Hood in *Letters of Robert Browning*, p. 368.

Jubilee Memorial Lines. These four lines beginning "Fifty years' flight!" were written shortly after December 17, 1887, for a window in St. Margaret's, Westminster, and were first published in the *Pall Mall Gazette*. On December 24, 1887, Browning wrote to his son,

Archdeacon Farrar applied to me, this day week, to write a "quatrain" for the Jubilee window about to be put up in his church—Tennyson, Lowell, and Whittier having done the same for three windows in honor of Caxton, Raleigh and Milton. I could not refuse, and it will be "cut in marble and inlaid with brass" forthwith—says the Archdeacon, who seems pleased with what I sent.[26]

The Jubilee, of course, was celebrated on the fiftieth anniversary of the beginning of the Queen's reign. The poem was reprinted in the *Browning Society's Papers* (II, 234*), where this description is given:

The window . . . contains a full length figure of the Queen, bearing the orb and sceptre, with scenes from the coronation and the jubilee service, the arms of the colonies, and other details.

The poem was also reprinted in Nicoll and Wise's *Literary Anecdotes of the Nineteenth Century* (I, 471). It was never collected into any volume by Browning, and has found its way only into the *Riverside Edition* (VI, 443) and the *Florentine* (XII, 281).

The Isle's Enchantress. The five lines which go under this title were composed by Browning, probably early in 1889, to accompany Felix Moscheles' picture of the same name. They were printed in the *Pall Mall Gazette* for March 26, 1889, and soon after in the *Star.* Writing to his son on March 30, 1889, Browning said,

Well,—did you hear of my wonderful stanza to illustrate Moscheles' really pretty and indeed imaginative picture? He urged me to give it a name and find a motto descriptive of it—and I threw off a line or two,—which so delighted him that, I cannot but think, he sent it to the "Pall Mall" and "Star"—which put it in with a flaming puff! I should say, the picture was refused, before I did this, by the "Grosvenor." [27]

In 1884 Moscheles had painted a portrait of Browning. The lines were also reprinted in F. G. Kenyon's *New Poems of Robert Browning* and in the *Macmillan Edition* of the works.

Reply to a Telegraphic Greeting. These four lines beginning "Bancroft, the message-bearing wire," were probably written some time

---

[26] *Letters*, ed. Hood, p. 280.
[27] *Idem*, p. 305.

after the installation of the telegraph in 1861. The lines are printed in F. G. Kenyon's *New Poems of Robert Browning* and in the *Macmillan Edition* of the works. M. A. DeWolfe Howe in his *Life and Letters of George Bancroft*, 1908 (II, 309) says that the quatrain was accompanied by a note from Browning: "I enclose a short metre with a view to saving your charges for the cable despatch!"

Replies to Challenges to Rhyme. These six exercises in ingenuity were published in F. G. Kenyon's *New Poems of Robert Browning,* and in the *Macmillan Edition.*

1) "If you ever meet a rhinoceros" (four lines)
2) "Hang your kickshaws and your made-dishes" (three lines)
3) "You may at Pekin as at Poggibonsi" (two lines)
4) "Ah, massa! such a fiery oss" (four lines)
5) "Venus, sea froth's child" (four lines)
6) "'Horns made the buck' cried rash Burdett" (four lines)

All of these *jeux d'esprit* were composed late in Browning's life, but only one, the fifth and the cleverest, can be dated with any degree of precision. The marriage of Miss Hannah de Rothschild to Lord Rosebery took place in 1887. Several of these pieces were sold at the sale of the Browning Collections in 1913 (items 177, 189).

Dialogue between Father and Daughter. These two lines, whose main purpose it is to rhyme "Mizpah" and "is, Pa!", were first printed in *New Poems of Robert Browning* by F. G. Kenyon, and later appeared in the *Macmillan Edition* of the *Complete Poetical Works.*

The Dogma Triumphant. "Epigram on the Voluntary Imprisonment of the Pope as proving his infallibility." These four lines, addressed to Herries, and signed "Italia," were sold in the sale of the Browning Collections in 1913 (item 178). They were probably written soon after the Vatican council, urged by Pius IX, proclaimed the infallibility of the Pope on July 18, 1870. In the next year the Pope went into "captivity" when the papal state was merged into the kingdom of Italy. The lines were printed in F. G. Kenyon's *New Poems of Robert Browning* and in the *Macmillan Edition* of the *Complete Poetical Works.*

PROSE

Except for his numerous letters, and prefaces to his own volumes of poetry and to his wife's works after her death, Browning wrote very little prose. It is possibly significant of his opinion of his formal prose works that he collected none of them. It was as a poet that he wished to be remembered. A full list of Browning's prose may be found in *Robert Browning: A Bibliography*, compiled by Broughton, Northup, and Pearsall (pp. 27–8). Two of Browning's prose writings, however, deserve to be noticed here,[28] partly because they were formal efforts on his part, but more importantly because they are concerned with poets and the art and theory of poetry, and cast a light upon Browning's principles and practice as a poet.

Essay on Tasso and Chatterton

This essay appeared first as an unsigned book review in July, 1842, in *The Foreign Quarterly Review*, whose editor was John Forster, a friend of Browning. It was Article VIII in that issue of the magazine and occupied pp. 465–83. It purported to be a review of Richard Henry Wilde's two-volume work, *Conjectures and Researches concerning the Love Madness and Imprisonment of Torquato Tasso*, published in New York early in 1842. The article, known to be Browning's by very few people, was discovered by Professor Donald A. Smalley and republished as *Browning's Essay on Chatterton*, Edited with Introductory Chapters and Notes, by Donald A. Smalley, at the Harvard University Press in 1948.

Though the article took its start from Wilde's work on Tasso, Browning, after a few paragraphs in praise of Wilde's methods of research, devoted almost the whole of his long review to defending Chatterton's character from his biographers, and especially from an anonymous work just published, C. B. Willcox's *The Poetical Works of Thomas Chatterton, with Notices of his Life*, Cambridge, 1842. Browning acknowledged his use of this book in a footnote.

---

[28] I do not include John Forster's *Thomas Wentworth, Earl of Strafford*, first published in London in 1836, but published for the London Browning Society in 1892 as *Robert Browning's Prose Life of Strafford*. Though Browning helped his friend Forster to complete the work, Dr. F. J. Furnivall's action in calling it Browning's goes much too far. See my comments upon this book under *Strafford*, above.

There was no occasion or reason for bringing Chatterton into a review of Wilde's work on Tasso, save that Tasso was also a poet, and suffered from mental disorders and the wilful conduct of his patrons, as Browning thought Chatterton had done. The essay owes its existence and nature to Browning's passionate love of Chatterton, and his eagerness to make a case against the poet's biographers. Mr. Smalley, indeed, sees Browning in the essay in the process of developing a pattern of imposture which was to serve him as a model for a number of the characters he was to produce, such as Djabal (in *The Return of the Druses*), Blougram, Sludge, Guido, Hohenstiel-Schwangau, Don Juan (of *Fifine at the Fair*), Dodington and Disraeli (in the *Parleying With George Bubb Dodington*). In Chatterton's case, however, Browning's sympathies are entirely on the side of the impostor, and the essay becomes what Mr. Smalley calls a laboratory model in special pleading. The habits of mind which we see at an early stage in Browning's development in the essay lead inevitably, in Mr. Smalley's view, to the larger and more serious misreading of history which we see in *The Ring and the Book*.

It is significant that the editor of *The Foreign Quarterly Review* in 1842 was Browning's friend, John Forster; the July issue of that year was the first to appear under his editorship. Forster had evidently called upon his friends to supply him with material, for Walter Savage Landor and Edward Bulwer also contributed to the issue. Browning probably "wrote the whole of the Essay within the five weeks preceding July 1, 1842, the day on which the July *Foreign Quarterly* was published. . . ." [29] Mr. Smalley is of the opinion that Willcox's biography of Chatterton was probably not available to Browning before May 27 of that year. Coming so early in Browning's poetic career, the essay is especially significant for the light it throws upon the poet's characteristic habits of mind, in the process of their formation.

Introductory Essay

The *Introductory Essay* to the *Letters of Percy Bysshe Shelley* was published early in 1852 by Edward Moxon, Browning's friend and the publisher of the *Bells and Pomegranates* series. The *Essay* occupied pp. 1–44 in the volume of *Letters* and was signed "R. B."

[29] *Browning's Essay on Chatterton,* ed. Smalley, p. 137.

Before the volume was distributed, however, the letters were found to be spurious and the book was withdrawn from publication. Browning never collected the *Essay,* but it was reprinted with his consent by F. J. Furnivall as the first of *The Browning Society's Papers* in 1881. Since that time it has been frequently reprinted and appears in many collections of the poet's works.

The *Essay* was written at Moxon's request in the fall of 1851. In a letter to Carlyle which Dean T. L. Hood dates as of October, 1851, but which I think should be dated almost two months later, Browning wrote from Paris,

I have just done the little thing I told you of—a mere Preface to some new letters of Shelley; not admitting of much workmanship of any kind, if I had it to give. . . . However it be done, it is what I was "up to" just now, and will soon be off my mind.[30]

The *Essay* was probably finished by December 1, when Mrs. Browning wrote that her husband was sending off his Shelley. On December 17 Browning acknowledged a liberal remittance from Moxon and promised to spare no pains with the proofs.[31] At the end of the *Essay* Browning appended "Paris, December 4th, 1851."

Browning was impelled to write the *Essay* by his love of Shelley, whose poetry had inspired his own *Pauline, Paracelsus,* and *Sordello.* He was to honor Shelley again in the poem *Memorabilia* in *Men and Women,* and to retain his reverence for the Sun-treader until he heard the facts of Shelley's treatment of Harriet Westbrook Shelley, possibly as late as 1858.[32] In the *Essay* Shelley represents the "subjective" poet, *par excellence,* as Shakespeare is the representative of the "objective" kind. The *Essay,* moreover, gave Browning an opportunity to express his poetic faith; and it is interesting to observe where his ideas come from. In the letter to Carlyle quoted from above Browning says,

But I have put down a few thoughts that presented themselves—one or two, in respect of opinions of your own (I mean that I was thinking of those opinions while I wrote).

Any debt to Carlyle in the *Essay* is general, however; Browning was probably thinking of the sage's lecture on "The Hero as Poet" in *Heroes and Hero-Worship,* part of which is devoted to a discussion

---

[30] *Letters,* ed. Hood, p. 36.

[31] *New Letters,* ed. DeVane and Knickerbocker, p. 53.

[32] Griffin and Minchin, *Life,* p. 185. Mrs. Miller, however, thinks that Browning's disillusionment occurred in 1851. See her *Robert Browning,* p. 169.

of Shakespeare. But as Griffin and Minchin show, Browning's debt to Joseph Milsand, the French critic 'and later Browning's most valued friend, was much more specific and greater.[33] In the August number of the *Revue des Deux Mondes* for 1851 Milsand published 28 pages on Browning's poetry as the second in his series, "La Poésie anglais depuis Byron." This article was at once searching and sympathetic, and Browning took pains to call it to the attention of Chapman, his publisher.[34] In his *Essay* Browning "apprehended, amplified and defined" [35] the theory of poetry put forward by Milsand. The French critic saw Browning as primarily an introspective poet, and secondarily as a "maker," and Milsand's analysis suggested Browning's contrast between the subjective and objective poets, Shelley and Shakespeare. Through Milsand's article Browning was able to see Shelley plain, and, more importantly, was able to formulate his own theory of poetry and see his own place as a poet, recognizing that in himself the subjective and objective elements were mixed.

Behind Browning's *Essay*, of course, there lay much reading and thinking. There is ample evidence in his next volume of poetry, *Men and Women*, 1855, that he steeped himself in Shakespeare's plays, especially in *King Lear*, his favorite; one has only to remember *Childe Roland* and *How it Strikes a Contemporary*. The profound Platonism which Mrs. Orr rightly saw in the *Essay* [36] partly came to him through Shelley, but Browning, of course, knew the original. The Platonic element in Browning's thought may be seen everywhere in the *Essay*, but nowhere better than when he is describing Shelley's "noblest and predominating characteristic,"

his simultaneous perception of Power and Love in the absolute, and of Beauty and Good in the concrete, while he throws, from the poet's station between both, swifter, subtler, and more numerous films for the connexion of each with each, than have been thrown by any modern artificer of whom I have knowledge.

Browning himself added to this Platonic view of the function of poetry his own strong religious bent.

Because Moxon withdrew the *Letters* when they proved to be spurious the volume was scarcely noticed in 1852. Browning him-

[33] *Life*, pp. 183–4.
[34] *New Letters*, ed. DeVane and Knickerbocker, pp. 53–4.
[35] Griffin and Minchin, *Life*, p. 184.
[36] Orr, *Life*, pp. 178–9.

self thought little of the *Essay* [37] soon after it was printed. Carlyle, however, "liked the Essay extremely well indeed," though he thought Shelley "an extremely weak creature . . . ; a poor, thin, spasmodic, hectic, shrill and pallid being. . . ." [38] It has remained for later times to see how clearly in the *Essay* Browning saw Shelley, and himself as a poet, as he began to prepare his greatest work, the volumes of *Men and Women* of 1855.

[37] *Letters of E.B.B.*, ed. Kenyon, II, 53.
[38] *Letters,* ed. Hood, pp. 367–8.

SELECTED BIBLIOGRAPHY

EDITIONS OF THE WORKS

In a study of Browning's literary career one must, of course, consult the first editions of his separate volumes, and the texts of the poems must be collated with the texts as they appear in the collected editions of 1849, 1863, and 1868, and especially with the final revised text of the author, in the collected edition of 1888–9 in seventeen volumes. All these collections were made by Browning himself. Critical editions which aim at completeness and which the student will find useful are:

The Complete Works of Robert Browning (Florentine Edition), 12 vols., edited with Introductions and Notes by Charlotte Porter and Helen A. Clarke, New York, 1910. Not altogether complete; profusely annotated and fully introduced. Referred to throughout as *"Florentine Edition."*

The Works of Robert Browning (Centenary Edition), 10 vols., edited with Introductions by F. G. Kenyon, London, 1912. The best text, with excellent introductory comment on the poems. Referred to throughout as *"Centenary Edition."*

New Poems by Robert Browning and Elizabeth Barrett Browning, edited by Sir Frederic G. Kenyon, London, 1914. Referred to as *"New Poems of Robert Browning."*

The Complete Poetical Works of Robert Browning, New Edition with Additional Poems First Published in 1914, 1 vol., edited by Augustine Birrell, New York, 1915. An excellent text, most nearly complete of all editions of the poet's works. This includes, in an appendix, the material first published in F. G. Kenyon's *New Poems of Robert Browning and Elizabeth Barrett Browning*, New York and London, 1914. Referred to throughout as *"Macmillan Edition."*

The Complete Poetic and Dramatic Works of Robert Browning, 1 vol., Boston, 1895. Not complete, but with some poems not printed elsewhere. Occasional annotation. Referred to throughout as *"Cambridge Edition."*

581

BIOGRAPHIES (ARRANGED CHRONOLOGICALLY)

Gosse, E. W., *Robert Browning, Personalia,* 1890. Vivid sketches of character; unreliable in detail.

Orr, Mrs. Sutherland, *Life and Letters of Robert Browning,* 1891. Revised edition by F. G. Kenyon, 1908. Much valuable information, especially of the personal sort; not always accurate in details. Unless otherwise noted, the Revised Edition is used throughout and is referred to as "Orr, *Life.*"

Chesterton, G. K., *Robert Browning* (English Men of Letters Series), 1903.

Dowden, E., *The Life of Robert Browning* (Everyman's Library), 1904. An excellent running commentary on the poems.

Herford, C. H., *Robert Browning,* 1905. Sound and penetrating comment.

Griffin, W. H., and Minchin, H. C., *The Life of Robert Browning, With Notices of his Writings, his Family and his Friends,* 1910. Revised in 1938, but with identical pagination almost throughout. The standard biography of the poet, accurate and thorough. The 1938 edition is used throughout and referred to as "Griffin and Minchin, *Life.*"

Lounsbury, T. R., *The Early Literary Career of Robert Browning,* 1911. The best account of the poet's reception by the reviewers through 1846. The opinions of Lounsbury, however, must be somewhat modified by the articles of Cramer and McElderry listed under General Studies below.

Berger, Pierre, *Robert Browning (Les grands écrivains étrangers),* 1912. A French view. Much insight; little new material.

Whiting, L., *The Brownings; Their Life and Art,* 1917. New material, especially on Browning's last years and his relations with America.

Browning, Fannie Barrett, *Some Memories of Robert Browning,* 1928. An intimate view of the poet's last days by his daughter-in-law.

Burdett, O., *The Brownings,* 1929.

Hovelaque, H.-L., *La Jeunesse de Robert Browning,* 1932.

Miller, Betty, *Robert Browning, A Portrait,* 1952. A study of the poet's personality and work from a twentieth-century psychological point of view. Much new material, freshly but not always judiciously interpreted. Referred to throughout as "Miller, *Robert Browning.*"

The following also provide useful biographical materials:

James, Henry, *William Wetmore Story and his Friends,* 2 vols., 1903.

William Allingham, A Diary, ed. H. Allingham and D. Radford, 1907. Referred to throughout as "Allingham, *Diary.*"

Garnett, R., *The Life of W. J. Fox,* 1910.

The Diaries of William Charles Macready 1833–1851, ed. William Toynbee, 2 vols., 1912. Referred to throughout as "Macready, *Diaries,* ed. W. Toynbee."

Renton, R., *John Forster and his Friendships,* 1912.

Minchin, H. C., *Walter Savage Landor, Last Days, Letters and Conversations,* 1934.

Marks, Jeanette, *The Family of the Barrett. A Colonial Romance*, 1938.
The Diary of Alfred Domett 1872–1885, ed. E. A. Horsman, 1953.

See also the articles by Baddeley, Clemens, Miller, and Reese under General Studies below.

LETTERS

The Letters of Robert Browning and Elizabeth Barrett Barrett, 1845–6, 2 vols., 1899. The most important collection of letters for a biographical and critical understanding of the poet. Referred to throughout as "*Letters of R.B. and E.B.B.*"

Robert Browning and Alfred Domett, ed. F. G. Kenyon, 1906. The letters are from the years 1840–6, and shed light on Browning's early career. Generous commentary by the editor.

Robert Browning and Julia Wedgwood. A Broken Friendship as Revealed by their Letters, ed. Richard Curle, 1937. Important biographically, and for Browning's opinions about poetry, his own and that of his contemporaries. Referred to throughout as "*Robert Browning and Julia Wedgwood*, ed. Curle."

Letters of Robert Browning, Collected by Thomas J. Wise, ed. with an Introduction, Notes, and Appendix by Thurman L. Hood, 1933. An especially important and comprehensive collection; well edited, and most useful. Referred to throughout as "*Letters*, ed. Hood."

New Letters of Robert Browning, ed. William Clyde DeVane and Kenneth Leslie Knickerbocker, 1950. Letters from the poet's entire career, especially important for his relations with publishers. Referred to throughout as "*New Letters*, ed. DeVane and Knickerbocker."

Dearest Isa. Robert Browning's Letters to Isabella Blagden, ed. with an introduction by Edward C. McAleer, 1951. These letters, important for Browning's poetry and biography, between 1861 and 1872, were first published by A. J. Armstrong in 1923 as *Letters of Robert Browning to Miss Isa Blagden;* are now supplemented and fully edited. Referred to throughout as "*Dearest Isa*, ed. McAleer."

One should see also the following collections of Mrs. Browning's letters:
The Letters of Elizabeth Barrett Browning, ed. with biographical additions by F. G. Kenyon, 2 vols., 1897. Referred to throughout as "*Letters of E.B.B.*, ed. Kenyon."

Elizabeth Barrett Browning: Letters to her Sister, 1846–59, ed. Leonard Huxley, 1929. Referred to throughout as "*E.B.B., Letters to her Sister.*"

Two volumes of letters to Browning are frequently useful:
Intimate Glimpses from Browning's Letter File. Assembled by A. J. Armstrong, 1934. Series Eight in *Baylor University's Browning Interests*.

Letters from Owen Meredith (Robert, First Earl of Lytton) to Robert and Elizabeth Barrett Browning, ed. Aurelia Brooks Harlan and J. Lee Harlan, Jr., 1936. Series Ten in *Baylor University's Browning Interests.*

BOOKS OF REFERENCE

Armstrong, A. J., *Baylor University's Browning Interests,* Series [One]–Fifteen, 1927–47. Miscellaneous materials, some of considerable value, published under the general editorship of Professor Armstrong. The volumes or articles most frequently used here are listed separately.

Berdoe, E., *The Browning Cyclopaedia,* 1902. Much information, not always accurate or pertinent.

Brooks, A. B., *Browningiana in Baylor University,* 1921. A catalogue of an important collection of Browning materials.

Broughton, L. N., Northup, C. S., and Pearsall, R., *Robert Browning: A Bibliography, 1830–1950,* Ithaca, 1953. A thorough and most useful work.

Broughton, L. N., and Stelter, B. F., *A Concordance to the Poems of Robert Browning.* Most useful.

The Browning Collections, 1913. The catalogue of Sotheby, Wilkinson, and Hodge, the auctioneers who dispersed the Browning library on the death of R. W. B. Browning. Very useful for a knowledge of the books in Browning's possession. Referred to throughout as *"The Browning Collections* (Sotheby Catalogue)."

The Browning Society's Papers (1881–1891). Contains F. J. Furnivall's useful materials for a bibliography, some good papers, and much scattered information.

Cook, A. K., *A Commentary upon Browning's "The Ring and the Book,"* 1920. An excellent and scholarly work.

Cooke, G. W., *A Guide-book to the Poetic and Dramatic Works of Robert Browning,* 1891. Not critical, but indiscriminately full. Referred to throughout as "Cooke, *Guide-book.*"

Corson, H., *An Introduction to the Study of Robert Browning's Poetry,* 1903.

De Reul, Paul, *L'Art et la pensée de Robert Browning,* 1929. A judicious and discriminating commentary; very suggestive.

Hood, T. L., *Browning's Ancient Classical Sources,* in *Harvard Studies in Classical Philology,* 1922. Most useful.

Machen, Mrs. M., *The Bible in Browning,* 1903.

Molineux, M. A., *A Phrase-Book from the Poetic and Dramatic Works of Robert Browning,* 1896. Useful.

Nicoll, Allardyce, *A History of Early Nineteenth Century Drama, 1800–1850.* 2 vols., 1930.

Nicoll, W. R., and Wise, T. J., *Materials for a Bibliography of the Writings of Robert Browning,* in *Literary Anecdotes of the Nineteenth Century,* Vol. I, 1895. Very helpful.

Orr, Mrs. Sutherland, *A Handbook to the Works of Robert Browning,*

1886, and with additions in successive issues. Chiefly interpretative, but important because Browning authorized and in a sense supervised the work. Referred to throughout as "Orr, *Handbook.*"

Symons, A., *An Introduction to the Study of Browning,* 1886.

Wise, T. J., *A Complete Bibliography of the Writings in Prose and Verse of Robert Browning,* 1897. The standard bibliography, in spite of the inclusion of forgeries. See Carter, John, and Pollard, Graham, *An Enquiry into the Nature of Certain Nineteenth Century Pamphlets,* London, 1934.

Wise, T. J., *A Browning Library,* 1931. The treasures of the collector are here described. Most useful, though some of the items have been condemned as forgeries.

GENERAL STUDIES

Articles and books dealing with specific poems or volumes of Browning are not included here unless their scope includes a general study of the poet's work. Specific studies are referred to under the discussion of the specific poem dealt with. The following list is by no means complete; it is made up of those items which seem to me to present an important or an interesting point of view upon Browning's work.

Armytage, W. H. G., "Some New Letters of Robert Browning, 1871–1889," in *Modern Language Notes* 12: 155–8 (1951).

——, "Robert Browning and Mrs. Pattison; Some Unpublished Browning Letters," in *University of Toronto Quarterly* 21:179–92 (1951–2).

Baddeley, Sir Vincent, K.C.B., "The Ancestry of Robert Browning, the Poet," in the *Genealogists Magazine* 8:1–6 (March, 1938).

Bagehot, W., "Wordsworth, Tennyson and Browning," in *Literary Studies,* 1895.

Barclay, Evelyn, "The Diary of Miss Evelyn Barclay," ed. A. J. Armstrong, 1932. Fifth Series in *Baylor University's Browning Interests.*

Berlin-Lieberman, Judith, *Robert Browning and Hebraism, A Study of the Poems which are based on Rabbinical Writings and other Sources in Jewish Literature,* 1934.

Birrell, A., "On the Alleged Obscurity of Mr. Browning's Poetry," in *Collected Essays and Addresses,* 1922.

Bonnell, J. K., "Touch Images in the Poetry of Robert Browning," in *Publications of the Modern Language Association* (September, 1922).

Brockington, A. A., *Browning and the Twentieth Century,* 1932.

Brooke, Stopford, *The Poetry of Robert Browning,* 1902. The orthodox Victorian criticism of the poet's works.

Charlton, H. B., A series of important articles, all in the *Bulletin of the John Rylands Library:* "Browning as Dramatist," 23:33–67 (1939); "Browning's Ethical Poetry," 27:36–69 (1942–3); "Browning as Poet of Religion," 27:271–307 (1942–3); and "Poetry and Truth. An Aspect of Browning's *The Ring and the Book,*" 28:43–57 (1944).

Clemens, Cyril, "Father Prout and the Brownings," in *Dalhousie Review* 17:163–7.

Cohen, J. M., "The Young Robert Browning," in *Cornhill Magazine* 163: 234–48.

Cramer, M. B., *The Foundations of Browning's Fame, 1833–1859.* A collection of offprints of three articles: "Browning's Friendships and Fame before Marriage (1833–1846)," from *Publications of the Modern Language Association* 55:207–30 (1940); "What Browning's Literary Reputation Owed to the Pre-Raphaelites, 1847–1856," from *Journal of English Literary History* 8:305–21 (1941); and "Browning's Literary Reputation at Oxford, 1855–1859," from *Publications of the Modern Language Association* 57:232–40 (1942).

Cunliffe, J. W., "Elizabeth Barrett Browning's Influence on Browning's Poetry," in *Publications of the Modern Language Association* 23:176 (1908).

DeVane, W. C., *Browning's Parleyings, The Autobiography of a Mind,* 1927.

———, "Browning and the Spirit of Greece," in *Nineteenth-Century Studies* (Cornell), 1940.

Dowden, E., "The Transcendental Movement in Literature," in *Studies in Literature,* 1882.

DuBois, A. E., "Robert Browning, Dramatist," in *Studies in Philology* 33:626–55 (1936).

Duckworth, F. G. R., *Browning: Background and Conflict,* 1931. Excellent comment, especially the last chapter.

Elliot, G. R., "Shakespeare's Significance for Browning," in *Anglia* (January-April, 1909). Full of matter.

———, "The Whitmanism of Browning," in *The Cycle of Modern Poetry,* 1929.

Elton, O., "The Brownings," in *Survey of English Literature, 1830–1880.* Judicious comment in small compass.

Fairchild, H. N., "Browning the Simple-hearted Casuist," in *University of Toronto Quarterly* 18:234–40 (April, 1949).

———, "Browning's Pomegranate Heart," in *Modern Language Notes* 66:265–6 (April, 1951).

Field, Michael (Pseud.), *Works and Days, From the Journal of Michael Field,* ed. T. and D. C. Sturge Moore, 1933.

Gingerich, S. F., *Wordsworth, Tennyson, and Browning,* 1911.

Greene, H. E., "Browning's Knowledge of Music," in *Publications of the Modern Language Association* 62:1095–9 (1947).

Greer, Louise, *Browning and America,* 1952.

Grierson, H. J. C., "Tennyson, Browning and Some Others," in *Lyrical Poetry of the Nineteenth Century,* 1929.

Groom, Bernard, *On the Diction of Tennyson, Browning and Arnold,* S.P.E. Tract No. 53, 1939.

Hatcher, H. H., *The Versification of Robert Browning,* 1928. The standard book upon Browning's meters.

Holmes, S. W., "Browning: Semantic Stutterer," in *Publications of the Modern Language Association* 60:231–55 (1945).

Horne, R. H., "Robert Browning," in *The New Spirit of the Age,* 1844.

Inge, W. R., "The Mysticism of Robert Browning," in *Studies of English Mystics*, 1906.
Jacobs, J., "Browning," in *Essays and Reviews from the "Athenaeum,"* 1891.
James, Henry, *Portraits of Places*, 1883.
———, "The Private Life," from *The Private Life*, 1893.
Johnson, E. D. H., *The Alien Vision of Victorian Poetry*, 1952.
Jones, Henry, *Browning as a Philosophical and Religious Teacher*, 1891. The most profound and excellent of books of this kind on Browning.
Ker, W. P., "Browning," in *Collected Essays*, 1925.
King, Roma A. Jr., *Robert Browning's Finances from his own Account Book*, 1947.
Knickerbocker, K. L., "Browning and Swinburne: An Episode," in *Modern Language Notes* 62:240–4 (April, 1947).
Lowe, R. L., "Browning and Donne," in *Notes and Queries* 198:491–2 (November, 1953).
Mayne, E. C., *Browning's Heroines*, 1913.
McElderry, B. R. Jr., "Browning and the Victorian Public, 1868–69," in *Research Studies of the State College of Washington* 5:193–203 (December, 1937).
Miller, Betty, "The Child of Casa Guidi," in *Cornhill Magazine* 163:415–28 (1948–9).
More, P. E., "Why is Browning Popular?" in *Shelburne Essays*, Third Series, 1905.
Palmer, G. H., "The Monologue of Browning," in *Harvard Theological Review* (April, 1918).
Parrott, T. M., "The Vitality of Browning," in *Studies of a Booklover*, 1904.
Pater, W., "Robert Browning," in *Essays from "The Guardian,"* 1901.
Phelps, W. L., *Robert Browning*, 1931. Excellent interpretation.
———, "Landor and Browning," in *Journal of English Literary History* 1:231–4 (December, 1943).
———, "A Conversation with Browning," in *Journal of English Literary History* 11:154–60 (June, 1944).
Pigou, A. C., *Robert Browning as a Religious Teacher*, 1901.
Pottle, F. A., *Shelley and Browning: A Myth and Some Facts*, 1923. The truth of Browning's first acquaintance with Shelley's poetry.
Raymond, W. O., *The Infinite Moment and Other Essays in Robert Browning*, 1950. A gathering of old and new papers upon the poet and his work by a judicious scholar. Most valuable.
Reese, Gertrude, "Robert Browning and his Son," in *Publications of the Modern Language Association* 61:784–803 (1946).
Russell, F. T., *One Word More on Browning*, 1927.
Saintsbury, G., "Browning," in *Corrected Impressions*, 1895.
Santayana, G., "The Poetry of Barbarism," in *Interpretations of Poetry and Religion*, 1900. The most devastating criticism which Browning has encountered.
Scott, Dixon, "The Homeliness of Browning," in *Men of Letters*, 1916. A brilliant and sympathetic essay.

Sessions, Ina Beth, "The Dramatic Monologue," in *Publications of the Modern Language Association* 62:503–16 (1947).

Shackford, M. H., *The Brownings and Leighton*, 1942.

Smalley, Donald, *Browning's Essay on Chatterton*, 1948. Browning's early prose essay in special pleading provides a pattern for his later treatment of his many impostors.

Smith, C. Willard, *Browning's Star-Imagery. The Study of a Detail in Poetic Design*, 1941.

Snyder, E. and Palmer, F. Jr., "New Light on the Brownings," in the *Quarterly Review* 269:48–63 (July, 1937).

Somervell, D. C., "The Reputation of Robert Browning," in *Essays and Studies by Members of The English Association*, XV, 1929. An excellent study.

Stephen, Leslie, "Browning's Casuistry," in *Living Age*, January 31, 1903.

Stevenson, Lionel, "Tennyson, Browning, and a Romantic Fallacy," in the *University of Toronto Quarterly* 13:175–95 (1943–4).

————, "The Pertinacious Victorian Poets," in the *University of Toronto Quarterly* 21:232–45 (1952).

Stoll, E. E., *From Shakespeare to Joyce*, 1944. A discussion of Browning's refinement of the dramatic monologue is included.

Thomson, James, "Notes on the Genius of Robert Browning," in *Biographical and Critical Studies*, 1896.

Tracy, C. R., "Browning's Heresies," in *Studies in Philology* 33:610–25 (1936).

Winchester, Caleb, "Browning," in *An Old Castle and Other Essays*, 1922.

Woodberry, G. E., "Late Victorian Verse: Browning, Swinburne, Tennyson," in *Studies of a Littérateur*, 1921.

❧ INDEX ❧

(Titles in capital letters indicate Browning's volumes of poetry: numerals in heavy type designate the main entry for each poem.)

Abt Vogler, 221, 238, 257, 279, 282, **290-2**, 298, 460, 464, 520, 521, 522, 531

Adam, Lilith, and Eve, 459, 460, 464, **468-9**

Aeschylus' Soliloquy, **569-71**

After, 206, **248-9**

THE AGAMEMNON OF AESCHY- LUS, 117, **414-8**, 519

Amphibian, 364, **368-9**

Andrea del Sarto, 155, 206, **244-8**, 251, 271, 412, 513, 551

Another Way of Love, 206, 250, 272, **272-0**

Any Wife to Any Husband, 205, **223,** 250

Apollo and the Fates, 357, 493, **494-5**

Apparent Failure, 279, **312-3**, 361, 401

Appearances, 392, 393, **406**

Arcades Ambo, 440, 525, **539**, 540

ARISTOPHANES' APOLOGY, 32, 117, 352, 357, **375-84**, 395, 396, 415, 417, 569, 570

Artemis Prologizes, 102, 103, **116-8,** 351, 518, 561

ASOLANDO, 36, 38, 236, 298, **524-53,** 563-4

At the Mermaid, 33, 392, 393, **398-400,** 400, 401, 414

Bad Dreams, 525, 527, **532-3**

BALAUSTION'S ADVENTURE, 31, 32, 117, 317, 335, **349-57**, 359, 365, 376, 377, 381, 385, 396, 415, 416, 417, 419, 420, 494

The Bean-Feast, 525, 527, 537, **537-8**

A Bean-Stripe: Also Apple-Eating, 474, 475, 477, **488-9**

Beatrice Signorini, 412, 513, 525, 527, **542-4**, 545

Beer; see *"Here's to Nelson's Memory"*

Before, 206, **248-9**

BELLS AND POMEGRANATES, 17, 70, **88-193,** 95, 97, 101, 102, 104, 135, 136, 137, 143, 145, 146, 150, 152, 172, 184, 189, 190, 191, 192, 193, 254, 577

Ben Karshook's Wisdom, 225, 276, 467, **557-9**

Bifurcation, 392, 393, **403-4,** 405

⚹Bishop Blougram's Apology, 206, 209, 240-3, 352, 363, 512, 577

⚹The Bishop Orders his Tomb at St. Praxed's Church, 19, 109, 113, 151, 152, **166-8,** 200, 547

"The blind man to the maiden said," **561-2**

A BLOT IN THE 'SCUTCHEON, 17, 88, 97, **136-45,** 146, 147

Boot and Saddle; see *Cavalier Tunes*

The Boy and the Angel, 151, **177-8,** 486

By the Fire-Side, 205, 209, **221-3,** 223, 226, 269, 530

⚹Caliban upon Setebos, 29, 279, **299- 302,** 314, 512

A Camel-Driver, 470, 474, 475, **484-5**

Camp (French); see *Incident of the French Camp*

The Cardinal and the Dog, 127, 128, 525, 527, **534-6,** 536

Cavalier Tunes, 70, 102, 103, 104, 105, **106-7**

Cenciaja, 392, 393, **410-1**

Cherries, 474, 475, **486**

589

Childe Roland to the Dark Tower Came, 24, 112, 154, 206, 207, 212, 228-32, 237, 268, 433, 517, 553, 579
CHRISTMAS-EVE AND EASTER-DAY, 23, 24, 194-205, 207, 223, 224, 240, 241, 256, 257, 262, 263, 296, 298, 314, 315, 334, 422, 549, 552
Claret and Tokay; see Nationality in Drinks
Cleon, 203, 206, 207, 209, 223, 225, 257, 260, 263-5, 295, 297, 298, 315, 334, 352, 402, 483, 519, 545, 547, 558
Clive, 445, 446, 448-50, 451
Cloister (Spanish); see Soliloquy of the Spanish Cloister
COLOMBE'S BIRTHDAY, 18, 71, 81, 88, 136, 145-50, 170, 175, 182, 252, 275
The Confessional, 151, 170, 171
Confessions, 279, 281, 288, 302
Count Gismond, 102, 103, 107, 110, 113, 389, 515
Cristina, 103, 120, 122-3, 214, 275
Cristina and Monaldeschi, 458, 459, 464-7

The Dance of Death, 7, 554, 555
De Gustibus—, 159, 163, 206, 208, 258-9
Deaf and Dumb, 279, 315-6
A Death in the Desert, 29, 203, 224, 279, 295-8, 312, 314, 315, 334, 377, 402, 549, 552
Development, 5, 298, 312, 442, 485, 525, 527, 547-9, 552
Dialogue between Father and Daughter, 575
Dîs aliter visum, 279, 281, 288, 288-9, 302, 305
Doctor ——, 445, 455-6, 463
The Dogma Triumphant, 575
Donald, 458, 459, 460, 462-3
DRAMATIC IDYLS (FIRST SERIES), 33, 35, 428-44, 446, 539
DRAMATIC IDYLS, SECOND SERIES, 33, 35, 431, 444-58, 463, 469, 562
DRAMATIC LYRICS, 14, 17, 88, 89, 101, 102-31, 151, 152, 159, 162, 163, 164, 165, 168, 169, 170, 171, 176, 177, 178, 179, 206, 207, 209, 212,

213, 214, 215, 216, 219, 221, 223, 226, 227, 228, 232, 235, 239, 243, 248, 249, 250, 254, 258, 261, 267, 269, 272, 275, 280, 429
DRAMATIC ROMANCES AND LYRICS, 14, 17, 88, 89, 103, 105, 107, 110, 111, 114, 116, 118, 120, 122, 123, 125, 126, 127, 150-84, 186, 206, 207, 209, 225, 227, 228, 233, 238, 239, 254, 256, 259, 260, 266, 268, 270, 280, 429
DRAMATIS PERSONAE, 28-9, 47, 209, 252, 278-317, 320, 321, 325, 347, 392, 422, 429
Dubiety, 35, 524, 526, 529, 531

The Eagle, 474, 475, 476, 478-9, 480
Earth's Immortalities, 151, 176-7
Echetlos, 445, 446-8
Edward FitzGerald; see To Edward FitzGerald
England in Italy; see The Englishman in Italy
The Englishman in Italy, 150, 157, 157-9, 163, 215
Epilogue to Asolando, 232, 490, 525, 527, 552-3
Epilogue to Dramatis Personae, 199, 279, 282, 298, 313-5
Epilogue to Ferishtah's Fancies, 35, 368, 457, 475, 476, 488, 490
Epilogue to Pacchiarotto, 392, 393, 413-4, 478
Epilogue to The Two Poets of Croisic, 419, 427
An Epistle . . . of Karshish, 203, 205-6, 209, 223-5, 257, 263, 264, 265, 276, 295, 297, 298, 315, 334, 422, 483, 545, 547, 551, 552, 558, 559
Epps, 568-9
Essay on Tasso and Chatterton, 18, 344, 576-7
Eurydice to Orpheus, 279-80, 281, 316, 316-7, 353
Evelyn Hope, 123, 205, 214-5
"Eyes calm beside thee," 556

A Face, 279, 305-6, 316
Fame; see Earth's Immortalities
The Family, 474, 481-2, 482, 487
Fears and Scruples, 392, 393, 402-3

FERISHTAH'S FANCIES, 35, 414, 445, 451, 460, 470, 472, 474-90, 491, 528, 530
FIFINE AT THE FAIR, 31, 32, 292, 363, 364-70, 399, 400, 406, 423, 486, 577
Filippo Baldinucci on the Privilege of Burial, 392, 393, 411-3, 513
The First-Born of Egypt, 7, 8, 554-5, 555
The Flight of the Duchess, 109, 141, 148, 149, 151, 171-6, 177, 181
The Flower's Name, 113, 151, 168-9, 169, 303
Flute-Music, With an Accompaniment, 221, 525, 545
A Forest Thought, 557
A Forgiveness, 392, 393, 408-10
The Founder of the Feast, 566
Fra Lippo Lippi, 25, 155, 205, 208, 216-9, 238, 245, 251, 264, 271, 412, 479, 485, 513, 518, 551
France; see Count Gismond
France; see The Laboratory

Garden Fancies, 18, 113, 151, 168-70, 169
Gerousios Oinos, 459-60, 565-6
Give a Rouse; see Cavalier Tunes
The Glove, 110, 148, 149, 151, 175, 181-4, 374, 389, 502, 503
Gold Hair, 279, 281, 285, 286-8, 297, 313
Goldoni, 220, 564-5
A Grammarian's Funeral, 206, 269-72
The Guardian Angel, 17, 119-20, 180, 197, 206, 207, 209, 261-3

Halbert and Hob, 428, 430, 436-7, 442
Helen's Tower, 559-60
"Here's to Nelson's memory," 162, 164, 165, 179
The Heretic's Tragedy, 206, 261, 268
Hervé Riel, 324, 392, 393, 407-8, 424, 425, 448
Holy-Cross Day, 206, 260-1, 268, 271, 293, 413, 460, 558
Home-Thoughts, from Abroad, 151, 162-4, 164, 165, 169, 176, 179, 256, 258, 507

Home-Thoughts, from the Sea, 154, 162, 163, 164-6, 164, 176, 501
House, 33, 392, 393, 394, 399, 400-1
The Householder, 364, 368-9
How it Strikes a Contemporary, 23-4, 206, 209, 236-8, 402, 458, 479, 489, 550, 579
How They brought the Good News from Ghent to Aix, 112, 127, 148, 150, 153-5, 165, 232, 393, 433, 501
Humility, 524, 530

Imperante Augusto Natus Est—, 224, 483, 525, 527, 545-7
In a Balcony, 206, 209, 233, 252-4, 558
In a Gondola, 102, 103, 105, 114-6, 221, 232
In a Year, 206, 249-50
In Three Days, 206, 249
Inapprehensiveness, 525, 533-4
Incident of the French Camp, 102, 103, 105, 111-2, 113
INCONDITA, 7, 8, 554, 555
THE INN ALBUM, 32, 363, 375, 384-91, 395, 470, 484
Instans Tyrannus, 206, 227
Introductory Essay (for the Shelley letters), 237, 244, 399, 400, 577-80
The Isle's Enchantress, 573, 574
The Italian in England, 150, 156-7, 158, 159, 171
Italy; see My Last Duchess
Italy in England; see The Italian in England
Ivàn Ivànovitch, 12, 428, 430, 431, 437-40, 442, 466, 557
Ixion, 459, 469-70, 484

James Lee's Wife, 250, 279, 281, 284-6, 288, 289, 532, 556
Joan of Arc and the Kingfisher, 514, 515, 573
Jochanan Hakkadosh, 459, 460, 461, 463, 468, 470-2
JOCOSERIA, 35, 445, 451, 456, 458-74, 476, 526, 536, 565, 566
Johannes Agricola in Meditation, 103, 104, 123-5, 134, 284, 556
Jubilee Memorial Lines, 573-4

Karshish; see *An Epistle . . . of Karshish*

"A king lived long ago," 90, 284

KING VICTOR AND KING CHARLES, 71, 75, 79, 81, 82, 88, 91, 92, **97-102**, 117, 132, 133, 135, 136, 137, 141, 149, 192

LA SAISIAZ AND THE TWO POETS OF CROISIC, **419-27**

La Saisiaz, 33, 203, 402, 414, 419, 420, **421-3**, 424, 426, 427, 429, 440, 441, 472, 481, 482, 488, 489, 490

The Laboratory, 151, 152, **170-1**, 171, 179

The Lady and the Painter, 525, **539-40**

The Last Ride Together, 206, 226, **238**, 272

Latin Hexameters: "Plane te valvam fas," **572**

Life in a Love, 206, **236**, 249

A Light Woman, 206, **233**, 393, 404

A Likeness, 279, 281, **306**, 401

Lines for the Tomb of Levi Lincoln Thaxter, **568**

Lines to the Memory of his Parents, **556**

Lines to the Memory of James Dow, see *Lines to the Memory of his Parents*

Lines for Pictures, etc. **572-5**

The Lost Leader, 37, 71, 81, 149, 151, 159, **159-62**, 192, 232

The Lost Mistress, 151, **162**

Love; see *Earth's Immortalities*

Love Among the Ruins, 24-5, 205, 207, 212-3, 229

Love in a Life, 206, **235-6**, 236, 249

A Lovers' Quarrel, 205, **213-4**, 225, 532

LURIA AND A SOUL'S TRAGEDY, 88, **184-5**

Luria, 88, **185-9**, 189, 190, 191, 192, 233

Madhouse Cells; see *Johannes Agricola in Meditation* and *Porphyria's Lover*

Magical Nature, 392, 393, **403**

Mansoor the Hierophant; see *The Return of the Druses*

Marching Along; see *Cavalier Tunes*

Martin Relph, 428, 430, 431, **432-3**, 436, 438, 442

Mary Wollstonecraft and Fuseli, 459, 467-8, 558

Master Hugues of Saxe-Gotha, 206, 219, 220-1, **239-40**, 292, 522

May and Death, 10, 279, 281, 282, **302-3**, 306, 316

Meeting at Night, 151, **178**

The Melon-Seller, 474, **479-80**

Memorabilia, 206, 238, **243-4**, 267, 578

MEN AND WOMEN, 14, 23, 24-6, 29, 48, 71, 103, 109, 116, 120, 123, 151, 152, 155, 162, 166, 181, **205-78**, 280, 282, 283, 288, 293, 295, 302, 303, 305, 306, 308, 325, 406, 479, 545, 558, 578, 579, 580

Mesmerism, 206, **225-6**, 227

Mihrab Shah, 474, **483-4**

Misconceptions, 206, **275**

Morning; see *Parting at Morning*

The Moses of Michael Angelo, **557**

Mr. Sludge, The Medium, 279, 280, 301, **307-12**, 314, 363, 512, 577

Muckle-Mouth Meg, 525, 527, **538-9**

Muléykeh, 445, 446, 450, **451-2**

My Last Duchess, 102, 103, 105, **107-9**, 110, 141, 149, 167, 175

My Star, 206, **226-7**

My Wife Gertrude; see *Cavalier Tunes*

The Names, **567**

Nationality in Drinks, 151, 152, 164, **179**

Natural Magic, 392, 393, **403**

Ned Bratts, 428, 430, 436, 438, **442-4**

Never the Time and the Place, 459, 460, **473**

Night; see *Meeting at Night*

Now, 524, 526, **529-30**, 530, 531

Numpholeptos, 278, 392, 393, 394, 404, **404-6**, 457

"Oh Love, Love," 357, **561**

Old Pictures in Florence, 155, 206, 218, **250-2**, 264, 271, 412, 513, 519, 551

On Louvel's Reply, **572**

On Singers, **572-3**

One Way of Love, 206, 226, **272**, 272

One Word More, 25, 206, 207, 208, 209, 222, 225, 227, 248, 249, 253, 265, **275-8**, 457, 490, 504, 531, 558

Orpheus and Eurydice, see *Eurydice to Orpheus*

PACCHIAROTTO: WITH OTHER POEMS, 353, 391-414, 393, 431, 474, 560, 561
Of Pacchiarotto, and How He Worked in Distemper, 32-3, 365, 382, 392, 393, 394, 394-8, 398, 399, 401, 412, 414, 433, 513, 560, 561
Pambo, 459, 473-4, 566
Pan and Luna, 445, 456-7, 469, 490
PARACELSUS, 7, 12, 13, 15, 16, 47, 48-58, 73-4, 75, 76, 77, 90, 102, 124, 131, 136, 145, 150, 161, 170, 195, 203, 265, 292, 459, 507, 514, 517, 552, 578
PARLEYINGS WITH CERTAIN PEOPLE OF IMPORTANCE: General; 31, 35-6, 74, 278, 414, 472, 477, 481, 490-524; Apollo and the Fates, 357, 494-5; Avison, 71, 107, 221, 238, 292, 458, 519-22; Bartoli, 31, 74, 148, 182, 278, 368, 407, 457, 490, 500-4; Dodington, 368, 437, 492, 508-12, 577; Furini, 155, 412, 423, 512-5, 540, 543, 573; Fust and his Friends, 522-4; Lairesse, 117, 213, 230-1, 251, 264, 417, 515-9; Mandeville, 482, 489, 496-500, 514; Smart, 236, 255, 426, 458, 504-8
Parting at Morning, 151, 178
The Patriot, 206, 238-9
PAULINE, 5, 6, 7, 8, 9, 10, 11, 12, 14, 16, 24, 39-48, 50, 57, 72, 73, 104, 110, 195, 196, 220, 267, 292, 303, 345, 421, 498, 507, 514, 517, 555, 578
A Pearl, A Girl, 525, 530-1
Pheidippides, 112, 154, 428, 429, 431, 433-6, 437, 447, 448, 456
Pictor Ignotus, 150, 155-6
The Pied Piper of Hamelin, 3, 103, 105, 127-31, 154, 534, 535
Pietro of Abano, 445, 452-5
A Pillar at Sebzevah, 474, 487-8
PIPPA PASSES, 14, 16, 17, 70, 71, 81, 82, 88, 90, 90-7, 98, 116, 117, 119, 133, 149, 176, 178, 180, 192, 275, 357, 390, 483, 486, 489, 507, 517, 528, 556
Pisgah-Sights, 392, 393, 394, 401-2

Plot-Culture, 474, 475, 486-7
Poetics, 524, 526, 530, 531
Ponte dell'Angelo, Venice, 525, 527, 540-2
The Pope and the Net, 525, 536-7, 537, 538
Popularity, 206, 238, 266-7
Porphyria's Lover, 103, 104, 105, 123, 124, 125-6, 284, 530, 556
A Pretty Woman, 206, 228
PRINCE HOHENSTIEL-SCHWANGAU, 32, 280, 358-63, 364, 365, 395, 512, 577
Prologue to Asolando, 35, 524, 527, 527-8
Prologue to Ferishtah's Fancies, 457, 474, 475, 477, 478
Prologue to La Saisiaz, 402, 419, 420
Prologue to Pacchiarotto, 392, 393, 394, 404
Prologue to The Two Poets of Croisic, 419, 424
Prospice, 232, 279, 280, 282, 303-4, 316, 433, 490
Protus, 206, 259-60

Queen-Worship; see *Rudel to the Lady of Tripoli* and *Cristina*

Rabbi Ben Ezra, 261, 271, 279, 282, 292-5, 298, 402, 460, 485, 552
Rawdon Brown, 563-4
RED COTTON NIGHT-CAP COUNTRY, 32, 370-5, 385, 386, 395
Rephan, 236, 525, 527, 549-52, 552
Replies to Challenges to Rhyme, 575
Reply to a Telegraphic Greeting, 574-5
Respectability, 116, 206, 232-3
THE RETURN OF THE DRUSES, 71, 79, 81, 82, 85, 88, 91, 92, 98, 131-6, 137, 149, 190, 192, 363, 512, 558, 577
Reverie, 525, 527, 552
THE RING AND THE BOOK, 4, 29-30, 31, 72, 110, 117, 203, 209, 298, 318-48, 350, 352, 357, 363, 365, 374, 376, 389, 390, 391, 394, 395, 401, 410, 420, 439, 444, 483, 491, 515, 525, 542, 552, 577
Rosny, 524, 527, 528-9, 542
A Round Robin, 559

Rudel to the Lady of Tripoli, 103, 105, 120-1, 122, 149

Saul, 151, 163, 177, 181, 203, 206, 207, 209, 224, 254-7, 263, 264, 315, 334, 422, 483, 507, 552
A Scene in the Building of the Inquisitors at Antwerp, 573
A Serenade at the Villa, 206, 226, 236, 272
Shah Abbas, 474, 480-1
Shop, 392, 394, 399, 401
Sibrandus Schafnaburgensis, 113, 151, 169-70
Soliloquy of the Spanish Cloister, 102, 103, 112-4, 168
Solomon and Balkis, 458, 459, 460, 463-4, 468, 531
Song: "Nay but you . . . ," 151, 177
SORDELLO, 4, 12, 14, 15, 16, 24, 32, 47, 59, 61, 71, 71-87, 88, 90, 91, 92, 93, 95, 98, 99, 100, 105, 107, 108, 110, 114, 120, 132, 133, 136, 149, 159, 167, 168, 188, 192, 195, 280, 365, 369, 374, 375, 376, 446, 479, 507, 517, 528, 578
A SOUL'S TRAGEDY, 70, 71, 81, 88, 89, 136, 149, 187, 189-93, 233, 363
Spain; see The Confessional
Speculative, 525, 526, 531
A Spring Song, 519
St. Martin's Summer, 368, 392, 393, 394, 404, 406-7, 407
The Statue and the Bust, 206, 207, 232, 233-5, 288, 289, 305, 404, 486
"Still ailing, Wind?", 285
STRAFFORD, 14, 15, 18, 24, 58-71, 76, 81, 89, 91, 98, 100, 105, 106, 107, 136, 141, 144, 149, 159, 161, 189, 192, 194, 576
Summum Bonum, 525, 526, 530, 531
The Sun, 474, 482-3

Through the Metidja to Abd-el-Kadr, 103, 105, 126-7, 154

"Thus I wrote in London," 458, 562
Time's Revenges, 17, 119, 151, 179-80
To Edward FitzGerald, 37, 571-2
To my Critics, 560-1
A Toccata of Galuppi's, 115, 205, 219-21, 292, 522, 565
The Tomb at St. Praxed's; see The Bishop Orders his Tomb
Too Late, 279, 281, 288, 289-90, 302, 305
"Touch him ne'er so lightly," 445, 457-8, 562
Transcendentalism: A Poem in Twelve Books, 206, 209, 238, 273-5, 458
Translation from Pindar's Seventh Olympian, Epode III, 353, 562-3
Tray, 428, 429,·430, 431, 440-2, 539, 540
The Twins, 206, 207, 265-6
Two Camels, 474, 485
Two in the Campagna, 206, 223, 236, 269, 530, 534
THE TWO POETS OF CROISIC, 324, 419, 420, 423, 424-6, 427, 507

Uncollected Works, 554-80
Up at a Villa—Down in the City, 159, 205, 208, 215, 258, 479

Wanting is—what?, 458, 460, 461, 473
Waring, 17, 102, 103, 118-20, 176, 180, 262
Which?, 525, 534
White Witchcraft, 525, 531-2
Why I am a Liberal, 37, 159, 567-8
A Woman's Last Word, 205, 216, 250
Women and Roses, 206, 207, 212, 229, 259
The Worst of It, 279, 281, 288, 289, 302, 305

"Yellow and pale as ripened corn," 573
"You are sick," 445, 446
Youth and Art, 279, 280, 281, 288, 302, 304-5, 401